D1356512

Divorce and Democracy

This book captures the Indian state's difficult dialogue with divorce, which was mediated largely through religion. By mapping the trajectories of marriage and divorce laws of Hindu, Muslim, and Christian communities in postcolonial India, it explores the dynamic interplay between law, religion, family, minority rights, and gender in Indian politics. It demonstrates that the binary frameworks of the private–public divide, individual versus group rights, and universal rights versus legal pluralism are insufficient in capturing the peculiarities of religious personal law in India.

The book historicizes the legislative and judicial response to decades of public debates and activism on the question of personal law and a uniform civil code in postcolonial India. It suggests that the sustained negotiations over family life within and across the legal landscape provoked a unique and deeply contextual evolution of both secularism and religion in India's constitutional order. Personal law, therefore, played a key role in defining the place of religion and determining the content of secularism in India's democracy.

Saumya Saxena is a British Academy Postdoctoral Fellow at the Faculty of History, University of Cambridge, and a Postdoctoral Associate at Jesus College, Cambridge. She is a legal historian interested in family law, religion, and gender politics in India. She writes on women's movements, secularism, and law in late-twentieth- and twenty-first-century South Asia.

Divorce and Democracy

A History of Personal Law in
Post-Independence India

Saumya Saxena

CAMBRIDGE
UNIVERSITY PRESS

University Printing House, Cambridge CB2 8BS, United Kingdom

One Liberty Plaza, 20th Floor, New York, NY 10006, USA

477 Williamstown Road, Port Melbourne, vic 3207, Australia

314 to 321, 3rd Floor, Plot No.3, Splendor Forum, Jasola District Centre,
New Delhi 110025, India

103 Penang Road, #05–06/07, Visioncrest Commercial, Singapore 238467

Cambridge University Press is part of the University of Cambridge.

It furthers the University's mission by disseminating knowledge in the pursuit of
education, learning and research at the highest international levels of excellence.

www.cambridge.org
Information on this title: www.cambridge.org/9781108498340

First published 2022

Printed in India by Avantika Printers Pvt. Ltd.

A catalogue record for this publication is available from the British Library

ISBN 978-1-108-49834-0 Hardback

To
Professor Sir Christopher Alan Bayly

To my grandfathers
Shyam Bihari Lal Saxena and Virendra Kumar Saxena

Contents

Figures

Acknowledgements

This book is drawn mostly from my doctoral thesis, completed over four years at the University of Cambridge. First and foremost, I thank my supervisor, Dr Shruti Kapila, without whose support this book would not have been possible. It is to her inexhaustible enthusiasm and keen insight into contemporary history and politics that I owe the development of some of my boldest ideas. I thank my PhD Adviser, late Professor Sir C. A. Bayly; he brightened up our lives, and to him I dedicate this book. I am extremely grateful also to Professor Tim Harper, my PhD examiner, and mentor during my postdoctoral fellowship. His continued support has been incredibly valuable.

I thank my external examiner Professor Thomas Blom Hansen whose scholarship has influenced me very significantly. Professor Faisal Devji, Professor Upendra Baxi, and Professor Marc Galanter have also had a profound impact on my research and I am indebted to them for their time and engagement with my research in personal conversations as well as in conferences and workshops.

I am indebted, in particular, to Dr Adeel Hussain, who has been repeatedly subjected to very rough drafts of my chapters; and also to Dr Leigh Denault and Dr Sunil Purushottam for their time, suggestions, and ideas. Their advice and insights were terrific. My work also benefitted from comments by and conversations with Dr Mitra Sharafi, Dr Iza Hussin, Dr Eleanor Newbigin, Professor Samita Sen, and Dr Jens Scherpe, whose expertise inspired me to explore the various alternative methodologies that could be deployed to respond to my research questions.

I am thankful to Professor Sujit Sivasundaram who has consistently supported early career researchers and I am grateful for the many opportunities he gave me to present my research. I must also acknowledge my immensely valuable conversations with Dr Shailaja Fennell.

My conversations/ramblings with Dr Alastair McClure, Dr Apurbo Podder, Dr Sagnik Dutta, Dr Aparna Chandra, Dr Parth Pratim Shil, and Dr Nicky Kindersley have had an undeniable impact on this book. I owe Barbara Row and Rachel Rowe for making my workplace, the Centre for South Asian Studies, Cambridge, lively, comforting, and inviting. I cannot thank Dr Kevin Greenbank enough for his unfailing support in all crises that I encountered in Cambridge, be it broken computers or broken confidence. Even as I slowly settle into my new office, I am reminded that no workspace can ever be closer to home than the green couches of the Centre on which I cradled countless cups of tea.

I shared findings of my research at various conferences and profited significantly from suggestions by Dr Tanja Herklotz, Siddharth D'Souza, Professor Srimati Basu, Dr Gopika Solanki, Dr Yuksel Sezgin, Dr Rohit De, Dr Kalyani Ramnath, Saptarshi Mandal, Jhuma Sen, Professor Mary Evans, and Dr Hilal Ahmed.

Many research institutions made this study possible. I am grateful to the British Academy, Corpus Christi College, Jesus College, and Faculty of History, Cambridge. I want to express my gratitude towards the staff of the Faculty of History and the Faculty of Law, Cambridge; Nehru Memorial Museum and Library, New Delhi; National Archives of India; Indian Law Institute, New Delhi; Dr Ambedkar Foundation, New Delhi; Uttar Pradesh Intelligence Bureau; Supreme Court of India; and Uttar Pradesh Legislative Library. Police records, from the Criminal Investigation Department, Uttar Pradesh, proved to be the most difficult to access but were truly worth the trouble. I thank Ms Tilotama Verma for making the access possible.

While the book draws mostly from all types of archives, I must also thank all the people who have become a part of this book through their insightful interviews which were, without doubt, my favourite part about doing contemporary, postcolonial history. I especially thank Mr Arif Mohammad Khan, Ms Reshma Arif, Mr Wajahat Habibullah, Mr Salman Khurshid, Mrs Sayeeda Hamid, Mr Gopal Subramanium, late Justice Leela Seth, Professor Tahir Mahmood, and Mr Shanti Bhushan who shared with me their experiences over numerous cups of tea. I realize the pressures on their time and therefore am extremely grateful to them for giving me so much of it, and for their interest in my work. I thank, in particular, late Justice J. S. Verma. These conversations encouraged an inquiry into the relationship between the lawmakers and the users of the law, and guided me to fresh sources.

I came across many inspiring women in the course of my research; I mention just a few here. I thank Shubhangi Singh, Zakia Soman, Hasina Khan, and Ruksana Lari for letting me have a window into their worlds; I will continue to admire them. My interviews in Lucknow would not have been possible without the wonderful Mr Mumtaz Ali Khan, Mrs Noor Khan, and Mr Tariq Khan. I thank Vaseem Akhtar from Action Aid and I am forever grateful to the ever-encouraging Talha Abdul Rehman. My special thanks also to Dr Atiyab Sultan for her unfailing support and friendship.

My little detour from academia into the policy world led me to work with the Law Commission of India from 2016 to 2018. I thank Justice B. S. Chauhan for his unwavering support and continued motivation towards fresh ideas on family law reform, despite pressures to the contrary. My research benefitted tremendously from the consultations held by the commission over two years.

I am very grateful to Qudsiya Ahmed for her support throughout the publication process and also for keeping me committed to deadlines. I thank the anonymous reviews of this book. I also thank Lucy Rhymer and Elizabeth Leake for their advice and support in this publication. I thank Ravi Atrolia for turning my multiple sketches into digitized images which eventually formed the cover of this book.

Finally, I acknowledge my family, my mother, father, and sister Dr Swati Saxena, for their love and support and, most importantly, for their patience. I thank in particular my brother-in-law, Dr Kaushal Vidyarthee, who had more faith in my research than I did. I thank my grandmother, Adarsh Saxena, who reminded me even in my most stressful stretches that there isn't anything that her mutton curry or *maal-pua* cannot fix. There are many others who supported my research by simple having faith in it, my parents-in-law, friends spread across continents, and my teachers particularly from my undergraduate years. Last but not the least I thank Sourav Roy for being an ardent supporter and friend; I can hardly articulate how meaningful his companionship has been.

Abbreviations

AALI	Association for Advocacy and Legal Initiatives
AICC	All India Congress Committee
AIMIM	All India Majlis-e-Ittehadul Muslimeen
AIMMM	All India Muslim Majlis-e-Mushawarat
AIMPLB	All India Muslim Personal Law Board
AIMWPLB	All India Muslim Women's Personal Law Board
AISPLB	All India Shia Personal Law Board
AIR	All India Reporter
AIWC	All India Women's Conference
AWAG	Ahmedabad Women's Action Group
AWAS	Association for Women's Assistance and Security
BJP	Bharatiya Janata Party
BMAC	Babri Masjid Action Committee
BMMA	Bharatiya Muslim Mahila Andolan
CAD	Constituent Assembly debates
CEDAW	Convention of Elimination of All Forms of Discrimination against Women
CPI	Communist Party of India
CPI(ML)	Communist Party of India (Marxist-Leninist)
CrPC	Criminal Procedures Code
DMK	Dravida Munnetra Kahzgam
FIR	First Information Report
HUF	Hindu Undivided Family
IIWA	Iqra International Women's Alliance
IPC	Indian Penal Code
ISIS	Islamic State of Iraq and Syria
IUML	Indian Union Muslim League
JIH	Jamaat-e-Islami Hind
LCI	Law Commission of India
LCR	Law Commission Report
MISA	Maintenance of Internal Security Act
MLA	Member of Legislative Assembly

MP	Member of Parliament
MWRN	Muslim Women's Rights Network
NAI	National Archives of India
NCW	National Commission for Women
NDA	National Democratic Alliance
NIA	National Investigation Agency
NGO	Non-Governmental Organization
NMML	Nehru Memorial Museum and Library
PIL	Public Interest Litigation
PLD	Partners for Law and Development
RSS	Rashtriya Swayamsevak Sangh
SAL	Social Action Litigation
SEWA	Self Employed Women's Association
SEBC	Socially and Educationally Backward Classes Commission
SCC	Supreme Court Cases
SCR	Supreme Court Reporter
UP	Uttar Pradesh
UPA	United Progressive Alliance
VHP	Vishwa Hindu Parishad
WRAG	Women's Research and Action Group
WLUML	Women Living under Muslim Laws

Introduction

I

Why do you get afraid the moment divorce is mentioned? Why do you think your women will leave their homes and run to courts?
        —Uma Nehru to N. C. Chatterjee and Nandlal Sharma
        Lok Sabha Debates on Hindu Marriage Bill, 2 May 1955.

Their 'fears', it appears, were somewhat realized as in the decades to come women not only took their husbands but also the very provisions of divorce under Hindu, Muslim, and Christian personal laws to courts, provoking polarizing political debate.

Rights of women, of minorities, questions of secularism, and constitutionalism dominated the political and judicial discourses in independent India. Assigning meanings to these terms produced contestations which were formative of India's democracy. Family law, arguably the most visible sphere of such contestation, emerged as a particularly hospitable arena for conversations between religious and legal regimes. As the Indian state attempted to confront its discomfort with divorce, it entered into intimate dialogue with citizens, which was largely mediated through religion. Personal law, therefore, played a key role in determining the legal place for religion and the content of secularism in India's democracy.

Religious personal laws refer to the corpus of family laws in India that ostensibly are religiously ordained and somewhat statutorily backed. The 'personal' in personal law could refer to the 'family'—to convey its status as a private realm beyond legal regulation. The term could also refer to religion, which as per certain idealized notions of secularism was deemed to be a private affair. The process of writing religion in statutory form, however, made both family and faith subject to public and parliamentary debates.

Personal law challenged the idea that separation between the church and the state was a precondition of democracy, as it made democracy contingent on the protection of religious freedom and diversity. This process had three significant consequences. First, it made religion more dynamic and capacious as it could be challenged by an ordinary citizen for violating or itself being violated by 'law'. Second, it made the law responsive to, as well as suspicious of, social and religious movements as religious reform began to be routed through institutions of the state. Lastly, it rendered the courts independent and powerful, equipped to interpret religious law, align it with constitutional law, or deem it to be invalid or inessential to religion. The institutions of the state leaned on religion and custom to legitimize governmental power in the domestic realm but as a corollary, the writing of religion into statutes also made religion 'amendable'. This development signalled a simultaneous expansion of the realm of law and religion in India, encouraging also a regime of regulation and litigiousness.

The book traces the response of the legislature, the courts, and civil society movements to the idea of 'divorce' that led invariably to questions of cultural rights and abstract citizenship. The book demonstrates that the controversy on personal law has contributed to a unique evolution of both the rule of law and the doctrine of secularism in twentieth-century India. The translation of marriage and divorce laws of Hindu, Muslim, and Christian communities into statutes introduced new questions on the tenuous links between the law and the sacred, as well as on the problematic rhetoric of the reformative potential of law. Personal law therefore directed political conflict towards the legal register. The centrality accorded to the 'law' in matters of faith, family, and freedom also led to contestations over the ownership of the constitution between citizens, movements, and even within institutions of the state—legislature, judiciary, police, administration.

Centrally, this book puts forth three arguments. First, that a continuing dialogue, refinement, and adaptation of personal law in independent India over time extended the reach and authority of the state into the intimate realm of the family. It was often through religion, opposition to it or support towards it, that the state, stakeholders, and movements entered into a dialogue with the family. Second, the very processes that were aimed at governmentalizing were undermined by the continuing demands for change by movements, civil society organizations, religious organizations, judicial activism, or political agendas driven by electoral calculation. This disallowed for the imputation of any will or directionality to the state as such. Third, Indian secularism was never a coherent philosophy but evolved as a set of pragmatic principles of regulation, and a systematic study of family law can tell us more about secularism and its various invocations in practice than abstract claims to unique Indian culture and historical legacies.

The Indian constitution promises to 'endeavour to secure' a Uniform Civil Code for all its citizens throughout the territory of India.[1] This clause is encased in Article 44 of the Indian constitution as one of the Directive Principles of State Policy that enshrine the aspirations of independent India. Directive Principles, although not enforceable by law, embody constitutional morality and guide the orientation of state policies. Article 44, the shortest directive that seeks a Uniform Civil Code, does not invoke personal or family laws in any explicit manner. Yet since its introduction to the constitution in 1948, it has been summoned for a range of arguments all of which relate to the management or replacement of religious personal family laws. The desirability of a Uniform Civil Code was argued for on the grounds of 'administrative convenience' in adjudicating matrimonial suits; 'national integration' apparently threatened by diverse religious laws; 'secularism' which was deemed to be inconsistent with religious laws; or 'equality' between sexes and 'women's rights', which has been particularly emphasized in the recent decades. Opposition to a Uniform Civil Code has been premised on arguments for 'legal pluralism', 'secularism', and 'freedom of religion', which includes freedom to be governed by one's religious laws albeit in the limited sphere of 'family laws'. It is also resisted to guard against threats of majoritarianism, and questioned over uniformity's uncertain impact on women's empowerment.

Personal law became one of the central themes around which constitutional and legal discourses were shaped, and party politics organized in the second half of the twentieth century. As the commitment to a Uniform Civil Code entered electoral agendas, identity politics and religious and social movements developed around the protection of legal difference. These political processes have transformed the very nature of statutory and constitutional law, as well as the relationship between citizens and their religion in contemporary India. What emerged as Hindu, Muslim, and Christian personal law codes continued to be challenged by citizens, political parties, and democratic movements simultaneously for the institutionalization of religious practices that contradicted the fundamental rights of some and for the tenuous and questionable link that the personal law codes shared with the sacred. Yet it was through a conversation on marriage and divorce that women also routed claims of equal citizenship. This is not, therefore, a book about the law itself but about the politics of law making.

---

[1] Article 44: 'The State shall endeavour to secure for the citizens a Uniform Civil Code throughout the territory of India.' Directive Principles of State Policy, Part IV of the Constitution of India.

II

Law as a Dialogue

Creative and parallel models of family law in India have attracted scholarship from various fields of gender studies, law, politics, and anthropology. This text historicizes the problem of personal law to uncover the constitutive context of the debates on uniformity and religion in post-independence India. The study hopes to contribute towards new understandings of law and its many lives, its creative use, the power dynamics it generates, and the performances it entails in the legal space and stage.

In South Asia, conventional tools to understand legal systems within democracy, through theories of social contract, or as emerging out of a 'general will', or as the command of the sovereign, collapse. One cannot completely gauge whether the power to exercise the law emanated solely from the 'state' in the form of juridical (legal-rational) authority, an elected but not necessarily representative parliament, or from a religious morality, custom, or tradition (invented or otherwise).[2] The understanding of law as an 'instrument of change' or an 'arena of conflict' also does not overcome the broad binary distinction between state and non-state, formal and informal law. Dewey's understanding of law as coercion[3] continues to find resonance as scholars fear the ever-accumulating carceral authority of the state hidden weakly behind arguments of securitization and 'enforcement' of rights.[4] However, the socio-legal anthropological studies have shown that in contemporary India, neither the sites of law nor the monopoly over violence and coercion are exclusive to the state. Even codified law is often authorized simultaneously by tradition[5] and its adjudication is chiefly shared between state and non-state forums.[6] Personal law, in particular, further pushed the definitions of law. What constitutes personal law could indeed be an 'eclectic collection of rules',[7] but these served to validate the regulatory authority of the state as well as absorb the democratic sentiment.

---

[2] Max Weber, 'The Three Types of Legitimate Rule', *Berkeley Publications in Society and Institutions* 4, no. 1 (1958): 1–11; Eric Hobsbawm and Terence Ranger, eds., *The Invention of Tradition* (Cambridge: Cambridge University Press, 2012); Christopher Alan Bayly, *Recovering Liberties: Indian Thought in the Age of Liberalism and Empire*, vol. 100 (Cambridge: Cambridge University Press, 2011).

[3] John Dewey, 'Force and Coercion', *The International Journal of Ethics* 26, no. 3 (1916): 359–67.

[4] Ratna Kapur, *Gender, Alterity and Human Rights: Freedom in a Fishbowl* (Cheltenham and Northampton: Edward Elgar Publishing, 2018).

[5] Werner Menski, *Modern Indian Family Law* (Richmond: Curzon Press, 2001).

[6] Gopika Solanki, *Adjudication in Religious Family Laws: Cultural Accommodation, Legal Pluralism, and Gender Equality in India* (Cambridge: Cambridge University Press, 2011).

[7] See the 'Introduction' in Archana Parashar and Amita Dhanda. *Redefining Family Law in India: Essays in Honour of B. Sivaramayya* (New Delhi: Routledge, 2008).

This text, while it concerns itself predominantly with the story of personal law after independence, advances two further ideas. First, it forwards the idea of 'law' as a language of democratic conversation between realms of the state, between and among movements, as well as among individual actors at various sites of authority. Second, following from the idea that sovereignty is not vested solely in the Indian state,[8] this analysis hopes to break down the 'state' by situating the politics of codification in individual actors to highlight the fragmented and incoherent nature of 'statutory' law which is as malleable or as rigid as customary, informal, or formal religious law.

The tools for the regulation and creation of law and order produced by the modern nation state are a heady mix of cultural beliefs and statutory procedures that have historically influenced, or indeed been translated, from one to the other. Basu, in her work on domestic violence and the workings of a family court, illustrated that courts and law enforcement venues only partially constitute 'law' in any given society.[9] Basu, De, Denault, and Newbigin, in colonial and postcolonial contexts, have focussed on the users of law who are often capable of ascribing new meanings and interpretations to the law, and show potential to generate new legal norms and strategies from social and cultural contexts.[10] On some occasions, legal norms are made to fit cultural needs, and on others, cultural norms are sought to be institutionalized which favour's a Hobbesian understanding of law, that is, that it generates disputes as much as it resolves them. Menski, Masaji, and Griffiths, through very distinct methodologies, also suggest that at no point are cultural and traditional beliefs replaced wholesale by statutes and codes,[11] and the two realms of official and unofficial law[12] may even maintain semi-autonomy of legal and normative orders.[13] Eckert argues precisely the opposite to show how state

---

[8] Thomas Blom Hansen and Finn Stepputat, 'Sovereignty Revisited', *Annual Review of Anthropology* 35 (2006): 295–315 and Shalini Randeria, 'The State of Globalization: Legal Plurality, Overlapping Sovereignties and Ambiguous Alliances between Civil Society and the Cunning State in India', *Theory, Culture and Society* 24, no. 1 (2007): 1–33.

[9] Srimati Basu, *The Trouble with Marriage: Feminists Confront Law and Violence in India*, vol. 1 (New Delhi: University of California Press, 2015); Srimati Basu, 'Playing Off Courts: The Negotiation of Divorce and Violence in Plural Legal Settings in Kolkata', *The Journal of Legal Pluralism and Unofficial Law* 38, no. 52 (2006): 41–75.

[10] Basu, *The Trouble with Marriage*; and Eleanor Newbigin, Leigh Denault, and Rohit De, 'Introduction: Personal Law, Identity Politics and Civil Society in Colonial South Asia', *The Indian Economic and Social History Review* 46, no. 1 (2009): 1–4.

[11] Menski, *Modern Indian Family Law*; Werner Menski, *Hindu Law: Beyond Tradition and Modernity* (New Delhi: Oxford University Press, 2008).

[12] Masaji Chiba, 'Legal Pluralism in Sri Lankan Society: Toward a General Theory of Non-Western Law', *The Journal of Legal Pluralism and Unofficial Law* 25, no. 33 (1993): 197–212.

[13] John Griffiths, 'What Is Legal Pluralism?', *The Journal of Legal Pluralism and Unofficial Law* 18, no. 24 (1986): 38.

norms 'adapt' to, and are shaped by, situational interpretations. Over a period, such laws have the potential to inform notions of 'common sense' in a society.[14] Both arguments nevertheless demonstrate the flow of ideas between official and non-official realms of law.

Others have understood the law as culture and power,[15] as a discursive idea which recognized that the law was capable of conferring permanence to power relations and contains within it the means for resisting and dismantling those very structures. These writings capture the negotiations of power while acknowledging the unequal terms of the debate—making law appear simultaneously empowering and coercive.[16] Such an analysis also presents a challenge to how subaltern histories have so far been written. It shows how marginal subjects rely on legal remedies that in many ways restate and reaffirm the 'hegemonic norm',[17] but phrasing demands in the requisite legal languages could also potentially allow for the satisfaction of personal notions of justice and retribution. In the case of personal law, the use of law by the state to create a space for religion, aimed ultimately at regulation, has a Foucauldian feel. Yet India is also often described as one of the least governmentalized societies, where the state does not have the monopoly over violence or religion.[18] The debate on personal law also allows citizens' groups and religious or issue-based collectives to extract and wield power, challenge dominant and majoritarian narratives, and to twist, use, subvert, influence, and strengthen the law. As Redding puts it, the law is more uncertain than fixed, clear, and predictable.[19]

Ethnographic studies suggest that laws are not simply established top-down but also bottom-up, and made a case for inter-legality[20]—interpenetration between different normative orders.[21] This inter-legality also meant that meanings and interpretations of religious texts as well as constitutional values such as secularism

---

[14] Julia Eckert, 'From Subjects to Citizens: Legalism from Below and the Homogenisation of the Legal Sphere', *The Journal of Legal Pluralism and Unofficial Law* 38, nos. 53–4 (2006): 45–75.

[15] See Geertz in Basu, 'Playing Off Courts'. Franz von Benda-Beckmann, 'Who's Afraid of Legal Pluralism?', *The Journal of Legal Pluralism and Unofficial Law* 34, no. 47 (2002): 37–82.

[16] Basu, 'Playing Off Courts'.

[17] Mindie Lazarus-Black and Susan F. Hirsch, eds., *Contested States: Law, Hegemony and Resistance* (London: Routledge, 2012).

[18] Hansen and Steppyat, 'Sovereignty Revisited'.

[19] Jeffery A. Redding, *A Secular Need: Islamic Law and State Governance in Contemporary India* (Seattle: University of Washington Press, 2020).

[20] Mengia Hong Tschalaer, *Muslim Women's Quest for Justice* (New Delhi: Cambridge University Press, 2017).

[21] Santos in Tschalaer, *Muslim Women's Quest for Justice*, 185. Katherine Lemons, *Divorcing Traditions: Islamic Marriage Law and the Making of Indian Secularism* (Ithaca, NY: Cornell University Press, 2019).

remained fluid and differed in meaning and import across adjudication forums. The ideas of rights, retribution, and justice are instead informed by the actors engaging the law.[22] The diversity of women's strategies in the face of changing political regimes, legal and non-state instruments has been exceptionally well documented in recent scholarship.[23] Solanki shows that the formal legal and non-state institutions often shared the adjudication of family law.[24] Tschalaer's study builds on this to illustrate that this inter-legality also emphasizes that the sites of law making and adjudication become not only spaces for meaning-making[25] but also enable translation of cultural struggles to legal ones, pushing legal disputes towards culturally acceptable solutions. Many of these writings provide 'thick descriptions' of how the law plays out and its usage, but this text focuses more on the ideas, processes, and events go into its making. This book's focus on the politics of codification is precisely to historicize the significant anthropological interventions in family law that highlight the interconnections between state and non-state legal sites.

The inter-legality visible in the domain of family law not only removes statutory law from its pedestal of being a 'means to an end' or holding immense 'reformative potential' but also counters the simplified criticism of law and legislation as solely carceral and regulatory that does not acknowledge the politics behind the codification. A dialogue on what should be codified is not limited to a conversation between state actors and institutions alone, but frequently utilized by individual women or women's organizations to negotiate and bargain within the family, with political parties, and with religious orthodoxy. How women engaged with the law—state, non-state, formal, or informal—fit no particular pattern and this has also encouraged a debate on religious and secular feminism. Neither modern secularism, religious movements nor forms of religious nationalism can solely determine the forms of politics and resistance the users of religious personal law may generate.

New postcolonial scholarship has countered elite histories by capturing the life of the law as experienced by its users; this study, however, shifts its focus back to the study

---

[22] Ajantha Subramanian, *Shorelines: Space and Rights in South India* (Stanford, California: Stanford University Press, 2009).

[23] Tschalaer, *Muslim Women's Quest for Justice*; Solanki, *Adjudication in Religious Family Laws*; Basu, *The Trouble with Marriage*; Lemons, *Divorcing Traditions*; Redding, *A Secular Need*; Sylvia Vatuk, *Marriage and Its Discontents: Women, Islam and the Law in India* (Women Unlimited, an associate of Kali for Women, 2017); Nida Kirmani, 'Claiming Their Space: Muslim Women-led Networks and the Women's Movement in India', *Journal of International Women's Studies* 11, no. 1 (2009):72–85; and others.

[24] Solanki, *Adjudication in Religious Family Laws*; Tschalaer, *Muslim Women's Quest for Justice*.

[25] Lila Abu-Lughod, 'The Romance of Resistance: Tracing Transformations of Power through Bedouin Women', *American Ethnologist* 17, no. 1 (1990): 41–55.

of state institutions and actors but views these as equally diverse, disaggregated entities. The uncertain state responds to the users of the law not in one voice but in multiple often contradictory ways and embodies and absorbs their biases and aspirations. This book explores the behaviour of state actors (often as individuals) to the pressures of religious movements, religious nationalism, or women's rights activism.

Gender remained the entry point for state intervention in personal law. There is a significant body of work that recognizes the reformative potential of law. How the potential of law is theorized is itself historically contingent. Scholarship in the 1970s was particularly hopeful of the law's emancipatory potential and the women's movement was also primarily led by academics who often interfaced with public policy. In some sense, the very turn to religious feminism in the past two decades, particularly for minority religions in India, can be mapped on to historical processes and events such as the rise of religious nationalism or judicial activism which impacted women's relationship with the law. This book builds on the rich and abundant scholarship on women's relationship with religion,[26] law,[27] and the state,[28] and also contextualizes some of these writings to demonstrate how the scholarship itself has moved from defending legal protections against religious practices to a firm critique of the law[29] over the last seven decades and is reflective of change in the political context in India.

Women and the Law

Personal laws have primarily attracted scholarship because a number of these laws, or the practices preserved as such, compromised women's rights as citizens.[30] An unequal share in the property or unequal rights to divorce were some of the axis on which women's fundamental or constitutional rights and religious laws emerged as irreconcilable in popular discourse.

Feminist writing of the 1950s identified how women remained beneficiaries rather than stakeholders in matters of policy. A study of five-year plans and

---

[26] Saba Mahmood, *Politics of Piety: The Islamic Revival and the Feminist Subject* (Princeton, NJ: Princeton University Press, 2011); Sylvia Vatuk, 'Islamic Feminism in India: Indian Muslim Women Activists and the Reform of Muslim Personal Law', *Modern Asian Studies* 42, nos. 2–3 (2008): 489–518.

[27] Ratna Kapur and Brenda Cossman, *Subversive Sites: Feminist Engagements with Law in India* (New Delhi: Sage Publications, 1996), 63–5.

[28] Zoya Hasan and Ritu Menon, *Unequal Citizens* (New Delhi: Oxford University Press, 2006).

[29] Flavia Agnes, 'Protecting Women against Violence? Review of a Decade of Legislation, 1980–89', *Economic and Political Weekly* 27, no. 17 (1992): WS19–WS33.

[30] Hasan and Menon, *Unequal Citizens*; Archana Parashar and Amita Dhanda, *Redefining Family Law in India: Essays in Honour of B. Sivaramayya* (New Delhi: Routledge, 2008); Flavia Agnes, *Family Law: Vol. 1. Family Laws and Constitutional Claims* (New Delhi: Oxford University Press, 2011).

labour archives reveals systemic barriers that precluded women from the public sphere and many policy initiatives identified the family as women's primary priority. In the 1970s, with the rise of autonomous women's movements, there was an enhanced focus on the reformative potential of the law to challenge social injustices. Women scholars and academics partook in policy debates and Vina Majumdar and Lotika Sarkar's contribution in shaping Law Commission reports is well acknowledged.[31] Lawyer-led activism and writing recognized the limits of the law but considered an engagement with the law as inevitable. While legal scholarship has relied on case law as their major archive, it has nonetheless successfully challenged the notion that personal laws were premised on the ostentatious divide between the public and the private spheres. Such a divide concealed the discrimination against women as private family matters.[32] Scholarship on women's rights called for the politicization of the personal sphere calling out hierarchies and discrimination within the family and, in particular, in marriage that prevailed under the garb of religion, culture, custom, or faith.[33]

Significantly, studies have also shown that religious practices that were accorded an 'inviolable' status in personal law codes contained 'eclectic rules'[34] or 'invented and tamed traditions',[35] rather than 'essential' practices of religion. The defence of personal laws as 'religious freedom' has mostly been dismissed in feminist scholarship as a form of cultural relativism,[36] but after the 1980s, many scholars have begun to treat separate law codes as a necessary recognition of religious differences. The acceptance of heterogeneity does not require women to choose between their religious identities

---

[31] Rukmini Sen and Saptarshi Mandal. 'Indian Feminisms, Law Reform and the Law Commission of India: Special Issue on Honour of Lotika Sarkar', *Journal of Indian Law and Society* 6, no. 2 (2014): XI.

[32] Ratna Kapur, ed., *Feminist Terrains in Legal Domains: Interdisciplinary Essays on Women and Law in India* (New Delhi: Kali for Women, 1996); Rajeshwari Sunder Rajan, *The Scandal of the State: Women, Law, and Citizenship in Postcolonial India* (Durham and London: Duke University Press, 2003).

[33] The early feminism of Wollstonecraft and the suffragette movement challenged the public–private divide but it was the second wave of feminism which introduced questions of equality-versus-difference feminism that challenged the unequal terms on which the women entered the public sphere. Radical feminism, Marxist and socialist, queer, and Third-World feminism also problematized the neat divisions between male and female. For an overview, see also A. M. Jaggar, *Feminist Politics and Human Nature* (Totowa: Rowman and Littlefield, 1983).

[34] Parashar and Dhanda, 'Introduction', in *Redefining Family Law in India*, xi.

[35] See chapter 3, 'Taming Custom', in Julia Stephens, *Governing Islam: Law, Empire, and Secularism in Modern South Asia* (Cambridge: Cambridge University Press, 2018).

[36] Zoya Hasan, *Forging Identities: Gender, Communities, and the State* (Oxford: South Asia Books, 1994).

and constitutional rights.[37] The unanimous and repeated rejection of a Uniform Civil Code by contemporary feminist scholarship is a recognition of the significance of religion to identity and selfhood. Global debates on Islamic feminism in particular have recognized important differences between women identifying as Islamic or Muslim feminists.[38] Mahmood's work also shows piety as potentially public and even political means to an end. Vatuk, among others in the Indian context, has also shown that women who often exercise agency in religious adjudication forums may not always self-identify as feminists. Kirmani, building on Spivak, suggests that women also apply 'strategic essentialism' to identify with their community as well as lean on state remedies in specific circumstances.[39]

The contemporary near-consensus within the Indian women's movement on preserving separate personal laws, particularly those of religious minorities, is also prompted by the rise of Hindu nationalist politics in the 1980s and 1990s, which usurped the agenda of bringing uniformity in personal laws. The impact of Hindu nationalism on the debates on Muslim personal law has been well documented in scholarship.[40] Whether at all a legal intervention would address problems generated

[37] Gopika Solanki, 'Beyond the Limitations of the Impasse: Feminism, Multiculturalism, and Legal Reforms in Religious Family Laws in India', *Politikon* 40, no. 1 (2013): 83–111; Nivedita Menon, 'State/Gender/Community: Citizenship in Contemporary India', *Economic and Political Weekly* 33, no. 5 (1998): PE3–PE10; Flavia Agnes, 'The Supreme Court, the Media, and the Uniform Civil Code Debate in India', in *The Crisis of Secularism in India*, ed. Anuradha Dingwaney Needham and Rajeswari Sunder Rajan (Ranikhet: Permanent Black, 2009), 294–315; Farrah Ahmed, *Religious Freedom under the Personal Law System* (New Delhi: Oxford University Press, 2016).

[38] Valentine M. Moghadam, 'Islamic Feminism and Its Discontents: Toward a Resolution of the Debate', *Signs: Journal of Women in Culture and Society* 27, no. 4 (2002): 1135–71.

[39] Kirmani, 'Claiming Their Space', 75.

[40] Menon, 'State/Gender/Community'; Siobhan Mullally, 'Feminism and Multicultural Dilemmas in India: Revisiting the Shah Bano Case', *Oxford Journal of Legal Studies* 24, no. 4 (2004): 671–92; Zoya Hasan, 'Gender Politics, Legal Reform, and the Muslim Community', in *Appropriating Gender: Women's Activism and Politicized Religion in South Asia*, ed. Patricia Jeffery and Amrita Basu (New York: Routledge, 1998), 71–88; Z. Pathak and R. S. Rajan, 'Shah-Bano', *Signs* 14, no. 3 (1989): 558–82; Thomas Blom Hansen, 'Globalisation and Nationalist Imaginations: Hindutva's Promise of Equality through Difference', *Economic and Political Weekly* 31, no. 10 (1996): 603–16; Sikata Banerjee, 'Armed Masculinity, Hindu Nationalism and Female Political Participation in India: Heroic Mothers, Chaste Wives and Celibate Warriors', *International Feminist Journal of Politics* 8, no. 1 (2006): 62–83; Arvind Rajagopal, *Politics after Television: Hindu Nationalism and the Reshaping of the Public in India* (Cambridge: Cambridge University Press, 2001); P. S. Ghosh, *BJP and the Evolution of Hindu Nationalism: From Periphery to Centre* (New Delhi: Manohar Publishers, 1999); Ashutosh Varshney, 'Contested Meanings: India's National Identity, Hindu Nationalism, and the Politics of Anxiety', *Daedalus* 122, no. 3 (1993): 227–61; David E. Ludden, ed., *Making India Hindu: Religion, Community, and the Politics of Democracy in India* (Oxford: Oxford University Press, 2005); Angana P. Chatterji, Thomas Blom Hansen, and Christophe Jaffrelot, eds., *Majoritarian State: How Hindu Nationalism Is Changing India* (London: Hurst & Co., 2020).

for women within a family, and whether all these issues were linked necessarily to religion or religious practice saw a significant feminist divide towards the turn of the twenty-first century. Regime change and the rise of religious nationalism provoked a distinct change in relationship between women's movements and the law. The supposed neutrality of legislative action came under doubt, leading also to a more activist role assumed by the courts. The balance of power between the legislature and the judiciary was tested on multiple occasions in the history of Indian democracy and personal law was a significant part of this story.

Civil society movements also found an ally in sporadic court rulings which offered either a univocal support for a Uniform Civil Code or occasionally produced newer interpretations of religious laws to safeguard the rights of women by aligning religious precepts with fundamental rights. Finding solace, however, in 'progressive interpretation' was only a stop-gap measure that momentarily obfuscated the glaring discrimination often written into the statutes. Overall, the relationship between the women's movement and the law remained an insufficient and uncomfortable one, as legislation as well as court judgments often perpetuated notions of a family that were informed by social stereotypes that glamorized an 'honourable' and a domesticated image of women litigants in both civil and criminal cases.[41]

Agnes' work points to the futility of state interventions on most occasions; Menon's writing also emphasizes the limits of the law. In her recent work, Kapur has taken a sterner stance against legal reform that is forwarded by the state on the pretext of enabling human rights. She describes this as attempts to enhance penitentiary powers of the state urging a distinction to be drawn between participatory aspects of law reforms and the potential homogenization of women's voices under a universal rights discourse that the law invariably leans towards.[42] Securitization produces a very specific impact on a society where religious minorities find themselves particularly vulnerable and a majoritarian state posits minority's freedoms in opposition to women's liberties and rights. This critique, however, also does not recommend a wholesale rejection of the law. A recent study of the impact of Law Commission on women's lives, quoted Mari Matsuda aptly:

---

[41] Agnes, 'Protecting Women against Violence?'; Kapur and Cossman, *Subversive Sites.* See also the discussion on the Mathura case (*Tuka Ram And Anr v. State of Maharashtra*, 1979 AIR 185) (Chapter 3) for an example of how the courts often produced conservative judgments unfavourable to women.

[42] Kapur, *Gender, Alterity and Human Rights.*

There are times to stand outside the courtroom door and say 'this procedure is a farce, the legal system is corrupt, justice will never prevail in this land as long as privilege rules in the courtroom'. There are times to stand inside the courtroom and say 'this is a nation of laws, laws recognizing fundamental values of rights, equality, and personhood'.[43]

This is particularly significant given the renewed will of religious feminist movements to seek statutory interventions in Muslim divorce law.[44] In practice, this demonstrated that women's strategies in negotiating divorces have varied substantially, and women have also accessed widely different legal sites. The broad umbrella of the women's movement acknowledges the differences in approaches and voices. Even the global categories of religious and secular feminism do not quite capture the particularities of Indian women's interface with the law. Women identifying as religious feminists in India, for instance, are relatively open to seeking state intervention in producing 'correct' interpretations of religious rights guaranteed through women by way of creating statutory law. Secular feminist organizations, on the other hand, have expressed reservations about state action that specifically prosecutes religious minority communities.

This book plots a longer trajectory of contestations within the Muslim women's movement to also show that it was not Hindu nationalism alone but a range of other factors that necessitated the broadening of the oversimplified notion that social justice was achievable through legal uniformity. This opposition to religious personal laws by a religious nationalist political party put the terminology of secularism in an extraordinary bind, where opposition to majoritarian nationalism entailed a defence of minority religion and, by extension, of religious minority's personal law. Thus, the third argument in this book leads the text to some of the contemporary debates on secularism, to explore whether religious personal laws were indeed the undoing of secularism or was secularism simply the language in which the state managed religion. Did secularism, indeed, make religion and law somewhat codependent? Secularism becomes relevant to this debate precisely because it is accused of generating permanent minorities who will perpetually occupy a position of ambiguity over their 'different' identity, which is bestowed by the state. And the state simultaneously grudges this difference as 'preservation of discrimination' and a 'compromise on secularism'.[45]

---

[43] Mari Matsuda, 'When the First Quail Calls: Multiple Consciousness as Jurisprudential Method', in Sen and Mandal, 'Indian Feminisms, Law Reform and the Law Commission of India'.

[44] Saumya Saxena, '*Nikah Halala:* The Petition, the Promise, and the Politics of Personal Law', in *Mutinies for Equality: Contemporary Developments in Law and Gender in India*, ed. Tanja Herklotz and Siddharth Peter De Souza (Cambridge: Cambridge University Press, 2021 forthcoming), 133–54.

[45] Talal Asad, *Formations of the Secular: Christianity, Islam, Modernity* (Stanford: Stanford University Press, 2003).

What of Secularism?

'Secularism is dead'. 'In its post-mortem we are hand-wringing over religion'. '[S]ecularism in India is still thriving'. '[S]ecularism gave up the language of religion'.[46] These are some of the headlines of August 2020, as public intellectuals weigh in on the fate of secularism in India. On 5 August 2020, Prime Minister Narendra Modi of the Hindu nationalist Bharatiya Janata Party (BJP) inaugurated the construction of a Hindu Ram Temple in the place of the Babri Mosque, demolished by Hindu extremists in December 1992. What secularism means for democracy has become a pivotal question in the present moment. Neither public nor academic debates, however, anguish necessarily over the lack of separation between the state and religion, but rather over the onslaught against religious minorities.

Historically, the dominant views have interpreted the presence of religion in state affairs as erroneous.[47] Contemporary and postcolonial scholarship, however, have challenged the Eurocentric model of the secular modern nation state to suggest that the modern state and democracy did not necessarily require a strict separation between the church and the state, or the privatization of religion.[48] Scholarship has problematized even the foundations of 'modern' European thought in pure or abstract reason and suggested that western notions of secularism were, in fact, also embroiled with Christian 'provincial' superstition.[49] In this vein, the contemporary 'religious' movements within Islam or even the nineteenth-century Hindu reform movements can be categorized as potentially secularizing trends.[50]

Indian secularism was premised on the ability of the state to engage with plurality. The experience of India did not follow a linear model of separation between the church and the state that modernity anticipates. The evolution of personal law in India is a history of entanglement between religion and the state. Unlike Europe, where the authority of the church plummeted with the rise of the modern state, in the Indian experience, religion was made dynamic by its

---

[46] 'In Post-Mortem of Secularism, We Are Hand Wringing over Religion, Missing the Real Crisis', *Indian Express*, 11 August 2020; 'Secularism Is Still Thriving', *Indian Express*, 21 August 2020; 'Secularism Gave Up Language of Religion. Ayodhya Bhoomi Pujan Is a Result of That', *The Print*, 5 August 2020.

[47] Max Weber, *The Protestant Ethic and the Spirit of Capitalism; with Other Writings on the Rise of the West*, 4th ed. (Oxford: Oxford University Press, 2002); D. E. Smith, *India as a Secular State* (Princeton, NJ: Princeton University Press, 1963).

[48] Asad, *Formations of the Secular*; Partha Chatterjee, *The Politics of the Governed: Reflections on Popular Politics in Most of the World* (New York: Columbia University Press, 2004).

[49] Dipesh Chakrabarty, *Provincialising Europe: Post-Colonial Thought and Colonial Difference* (Princeton, NJ: Princeton University Press, 2000).

[50] Humeira Iqtidar, *Secularizing Islamists?* (London: University of Chicago Press, 2011).

incorporation in the law of the state, especially as personal law. Scholars have labelled secularism in India as ameliorative,[51] equidistance,[52] contextual,[53] and minimal,[54] discarding the lens of the 'wall of separation' to understand its secular experience.

The writings of Madan, Chatterjee, and Nandy provided a severe critique of classical secularism as a western concept unsuitable for the Indian context and its heterogeneous society.[55] Their scholarship acknowledged the importance of religion in public life and borrowed in different measure from the Gandhian idea of religion as the provider of ethics, whether with respect to tolerance or non-violence. Nandy takes the argument further to suggest that it was the 'modern' commitment to secularism that aided the spread of communalism by replacing the idea of religion as a matter of faith to that of ideology.[56] It is worth noting, however, that many of these works produced a critique of secularism prior to the realization of the electoral and political potential of Hindu nationalism and its potential for violence.[57]

Bhargava's theorization of 'secularism' has proven to be quite resilient. He distinguishes between ethical and political secularism. The former was conduct derived from moralities rooted in human sources and non-religious ethics and values, while the latter, political secularism, was the 'accommodation' of opposing

[51] G. J. Jacobsohn, *Wheel of Law: India's Secularism in Comparative Constitutional Context* (Princeton, NJ: Princeton University Press, 2004).

[52] Varshney, 'Contested Meanings'.

[53] Rajeev Bhargava, 'The Distinctiveness of Indian Secularism', in *The Future of Secularism*, ed. T. N. Srinivasan (New Delhi: Oxford University Press, 2007), 20–53.

[54] Cecile Laborde, 'Minimal Secularism: Lessons for, and from, India', *American Political Science Review* 115, no. 1 (2020): 1–13.

[55] T. N. Madan, 'Secularism in Its Place', in *Secularism and Its Critics*, ed. Rajeev Bhargava (Delhi: Oxford University Press, 1998), ch. 9. Partha Chatterjee, 'Secularism and Toleration', *Economic and Political Weekly* 29, no. 28 (1994): 1768–77; and Ashis Nandy, 'The Politics of Secularism and the Recovery of Religious Tolerance', *Alternatives* 13, no. 2 (1988): 177.

[56] See chapter 4 titled 'Return of the Sacred: Politics of Religion in Post-Secular Age', in Ashis Nandy, *Regimes of Narcissism, Regimes of Despair* (New Delhi: Oxford University Press, 2013), 95–112.

[57] The Gujarat riots of 2002 resulted in the killing of more than 2,500 people, most of whom (more than 2,000) were Muslim. The Nanavati–Mehta Commission Report, 2014, on Gujarat riots indicated that the BJP-ruled state under the then chief minister Narendra Modi (current prime minister of India) deliberately delayed police action to prevent the violence. The special investigation team appointed by the Supreme Court, however, acquitted Modi in 2015. See also Steven I. Wilkinson, *Votes and Violence: Electoral Competition and Ethnic Riots in India* (Cambridge: Cambridge University Press, 2006). The text traces the links between electoral politics and ethnic violence.

or antagonistic religious communities that was attempted by political authority.[58] Bhargava asserts that Indian secularism was a robust doctrine since there was a degree of consensus on the desirability of 'political secularism', even if ethical secularism lacked appeal among the public. Political secularism was endorsed by traditional as well as modern elements in the Indian society although in very different ways. However, the insistence on making the doctrine of secularism as capacious as Bhargava claims raises the question of whether the idea of secularism has been reduced to a term that simply denotes any relationship between religion and the state which is identifiably not a theocracy.

The writings of Mahmood,[59] Agrama,[60] and Asad[61] offered a refreshing critique of secularism. Secularism's commitment to drawing a line between religion and politics, and its repeated failings in that sphere, provide the state with an opportunity for the expansion of regulation through the law.[62] Framing secularism as a potent idea or a state-led conspiracy, however, misses the fact that secularism has remained as contested as religion throughout history. The state's inability to capture both secularism and faith in statute is particularly evident in debates on family law. This text diverges from the scepticism over secularism because the state's deployment of secularism for the regulation of family life is so palpably poor and hindered that secularism appears capable of generating neither state regulation nor religious politics by itself. Secularism could well be generating the entanglement of religion and politics with the consequent production of the law. However, it also enabled feminist politics to utilize this entanglement to influence law and negotiate simultaneously with religious patriarchy and the regulatory state, rather than barter one for the other. Secularism's minimal impact and understanding but repeated deployment in political discourse tells us much more about Indian democracy than it does about the relationship between religion and the state.[63]

The question remains that whether in the absence of a modern secular state, is sexual behaviour, marriage, or family necessarily unregulated? Family and sexuality were

---

[58] Bhargava, *Secularism and Its Critics*. See also Bhargava, 'The Distinctiveness of Indian Secularism'.

[59] Saba Mahmood, *Religious Difference in a Secular Age: A Minority Report* (Princeton, NJ: Princeton University Press, 2015).

[60] Hussein Ali Agrama, *Questioning Secularism: Islam, Sovereignty, and the Rule of Law in Modern Egypt* (London: University of Chicago Press, 2012).

[61] Asad, *Formations of the Secular*.

[62] Hussein Ali Agrama, 'Secularism, Sovereignty, Indeterminacy: Is Egypt a Secular or a Religious State?', *Comparative Studies in Society and History* 52, no. 3 (2010): 495–523.

[63] Laborde, 'Minimal Secularism'.

historically regulated through religious as well as cultural practices;[64] adding state law and institutions to this mix of regulatory authorities could also produce new forms of agency rather than surveillance over family and sexual behaviour alone. It provided room to manoeuvre and destabilized power centres within groups as well as state agencies, through judgments countering legislation, and commissions rejecting electoral promises, all in defence of secularism. On the one hand, the state attempted to secure a monopoly over determining what constituted religion as well as the right to determine the validity and scope of religious practices. Paradoxically, on the other hand, statutes subjected to further legislative interventions, judicial interpretations, and challenges by social movements also made codified religion malleable and challengeable, thus undermining the state's authority to determine the content of religion.

In the Indian context, attempts to theorize the relationship between religion and the state in anthropological and historical studies in India have largely been made through an analysis of political actors working under the aegis of institutional interest, represented by the Hindu Mahasabha, Rashtriya Swayamsevak Sangh (RSS), the BJP,[65] and the like for Hindus, and organizations such as All India Muslim Personal Law Board (AIMPLB), Jamat-e-Ulema-e-Hind, Tablighi Jamaat, and others for Muslims, towards the achievement of certain political ends.[66] Such studies focus on the political impact of institutionalized religious interests. The study of religion, on the other hand, has either treated politicization as entirely exogenous[67] or focussed only on its political impact.[68] To view the relationship between the state and religion through the prism of interest politics obliterates the history of women's movements, religious movements, and of constitutional law over the longue durée. While interest politics may be an efficient way of understanding the dynamism of democratic regimes, it does not explain the more contemporary movements which have moved beyond influencing 'law reform' or 'electoral strategies' or ideas

[64] Kumkum Sangari and Sudesh Vaid, eds., *Recasting Women: Essays in Indian Colonial History* (New Brunswick, NJ: Rutgers University Press, 1990).

[65] S. Corbridge and J. Harriss, *Reinventing India: Liberalization, Hindu Nationalism and Popular Democracy* (New Delhi: Oxford University Press, 2013); Amrita Basu, 'The Dialectics of Hindu Nationalism', in *The Success of India's Democracy*, ed. Atul Kohli, J. Breman, and G. P. Hawthorn (Cambridge: Cambridge University Press, 2002), 163–190.

[66] Mushirul Hasan, *Legacy of a Divided Nation: India's Muslims since Independence* (London: Hurst & Co., 1997).

[67] Barbara D. Metcalf, 'Living Hadīth in the Tablīghī Jama'āt', *The Journal of Asian Studies* 52, no. 3 (1993): 584–608.

[68] Paul R. Brass, *Language, Religion and Politics in North India* (Cambridge: Cambridge University Press, 2005); Subrata Kumar Mitra, 'Desecularising the State: Religion and Politics in India after Independence', *Comparative Studies in Society and History* 33, no. 4 (1991): 755–777.

of community as an interest group. Instead, certain strands of social movements selectively allied with state institutions (police, judiciary, administration, and so on) to indeed strengthen their negotiating power within a community.

The works of Hansen and Jaffrelot have located the rise of religious nationalism in a broader framework beyond party political positions and electoral impact,[69] situating it in the broader realm of 'public culture'. Hansen's work reminds us that democracy often provoked and produced anti-democratic moral backlashes. The Hindu nationalist movement that began as a religiously informed endeavour eventually revised its language to demand 'true secularism'.[70] Such secularism was premised on an uncertain notion of absolute equality in which the recognition of separate personal law, or affirmative action policies, were posited as deviations from secularism and concessions to minorities. The replacement of separate religious personal laws with a Uniform Civil Code became one of the central preoccupations of the Sangh Parivar[71] and the Hindu nationalist movement, and also its central claim to secularism.[72]

This strange attempt to appropriate secularism by the Hindu nationalists also strengthened the counter-narrative that secularism was the sole force against the majoritarian intervention in minority law. Both the language of 'religion' and 'secularism' were selectively deployed by the institutions of the state to create usable legislation, and by religious organizations, women's organizations, and individual citizens to seek or stall statutory interventions. Religious movements have often moved the court to produce greater legitimacy of the sacred text, scripture, or practice. They demand that the courts embed religious justifications and 'true' or 'alternate' interpretations of religion into common familial disputes.

---

[69] Thomas Blom Hansen, *The Saffron Wave: Democracy and Hindu Nationalism in Modern India* (Princeton University Press, 1999); Christophe Jaffrelot, ed., *Hindu Nationalism: A Reader* (Princeton, NJ: Princeton University Press, 2009).

[70] Kaviraj talks about the importance of the shift in this vocabulary in his essay which highlights the capaciousness of the term 'secularism'. Sudipta Kaviraj, 'Languages of Secularity', *Economic and Political Weekly* 48, no. 50 (2013): 93–102.

[71] The Sangh Parivar connotes a group of organizations that share the ideology of Hindu nationalism; these include the RSS, Vishwa Hindu Parishad (World Hindu Forum), Bajrang Dal (organization inspired by the name of the Hindu God Hanuman, 'the strong one'), the BJP, and so on.

[72] Election manifestos of political parties make for an intriguing archive that records the orientation of political parties towards policies that could be compared against their actual performance. A study of manifestos suggests that personal law has been an important election issue particularly since the 1980s. Different manifestos defend the Uniform Civil Code as well as separate personal laws in the name of secularism, and secularism was emphasized by all political parties which proposed their own model and their own history of the doctrine of secularism.

This reveals an extremely complex system of law making which was, ironically, also a perversely democratic one as religious, cultural, regional, judicial, and legislative institutions negotiated and competed for exercising the authority over the family, but none could prevail in isolation. This book acknowledges the state's regulatory impulse to rely on religious categories for organizing social and domestic lives of citizens—but family law also represents the most phenomenal failure of the Indian state, an area of the law that proves to be ungovernable.

The emphasis on religious foundations for statutory laws in the realm of the family illustrates that secularism may never have been contingent on privatizing religion. The un-phasing need of finding a religious basis in ostensibly neutral legislation and judgments rendered personal law exceptionally public and debatable on religious and constitutional turfs. This study highlights that while secularism as a universalizing project is frequently deployed by the state to institute majoritarian uniformity,[73] it is also the language in which legal distinctiveness is demanded. Even as secularism made individual and group rights simultaneously relevant, but this can be taken a step forward to argue that it also became a strategy to exploit the instability of groups and generate conditions for permanent *resistance*. This makes the binary of individual and group rights somewhat untenable.

Individual and Groups Rights

The long history of India's democracy reveals that the state structures show a particular interest in the recognition of a 'community', whether religious, regional, caste, or cultural, in the form of maintenance of separate religious laws or caste-based reservations. A number of religious, federal, or caste distinctions qualify for legal exceptions. This complicates the idea of 'group rights' as the sheer diversity of recognized groups itself engenders a 'universal' agreement of the acceptance of a certain degree of 'difference'. This problematizes the idea of uniformity, as pluralism itself becomes the prerequisite for any universal rights discourse. Thus, works on minority rights[74] which overemphasize a group identity prove to be inadequate in explaining heterogeneity within the rights-bearing 'group'. The 'community' itself is based on an assumed degree of homogeneity that blurs internal differences, hierarchies, and discriminations.[75]

---

[73] Mahmood, *Religious Difference in a Secular Age*; Asad, *Formations of the Secular*.

[74] Rochana Bajpai, *Debating Difference: Group Rights and Liberal Democracy in India* (New Delhi: Oxford University Press, 2011).

[75] Ayelet Shachar, 'On Citizenship and Multicultural Vulnerability', *Political Theory* 28, no. 1 (2000): 64–89.

There is a significant body of work that locates the roots of India's democratic tradition neither in ideas nor in institutions, but in the political agency of marginal groups. For Chatterjee, democracy in South Asia is not a politics of civil society, or indeed of governmental institutions, but rather the 'politics of the governed' which resists elite civil society's liberal assumptions and draws its moral logic from the claims of the community.[76] However, feminist scholarship would argue that movements developing from claims of community often compromised women's access to the political or the public sphere.[77] 'Claims to community' were not always enabling spaces for women, and in bestowing identity these spaces could seek a 'moral solidarity' where women occupied a on of inferiority in perpetuity. The community could colonize a woman's life-world such that beyond it there could be a loss of identity.[78] Religion-based recognition of rights suffered from the problem of 'group essentialisms' that has imputed historically unchanging essences to particular groups which were granted a perpetual and seemingly permanent legal status. This propels us towards Benhabib's troubling question of whether democracy indeed rested on homogenizing models of identity or if the recognition of difference is meaningful only when the category or group that the recognition of 'difference' creates is also empowered and adequately represented in the state machinery.[79]

In Taylor's reading of recognition politics he fears forced exclusion of marginalized or minority groups as conflicting conceptions of selfhood invariably resulted in the suppression of difference in a society.[80] Habermas, on the other hand, prioritized 'individual will' and 'autonomy' above any specific cultural conceptions since he considered these conceptions as a form of delegation of consent to culture, which was subsumed under the will of the dominant persons within that culture or community.[81] However, Habermas's categorization of

---

[76] Chatterjee, *The Politics of the Governed*.

[77] Amrita Basu, 'Feminism Inverted: The Real Women and Gendered Imagery of Hindu Nationalism', *Bulletin of Concerned Asian Scholars* 25, no. 4 (1993): 25–36; Paula Bacchetta, 'All Our Goddesses Are Armed-Religion, Resistance, and Revenge in the Life of a Militant Hindu Nationalist Woman', *Bulletin of Concerned Asian Scholars* 25, no. 4 (1993): 38–51.

[78] Veena Das, *Critical Events* (Delhi: Oxford University Press, 1995). Tanika Sarkar, *Hindu Wife, Hindu Nation: Community, Religion, and Cultural Nationalism* (New Delhi: Permanent Black, 2001), 235.

[79] Seyla Benhabib, ed., *Democracy and Difference: Contesting the Boundaries of the Political*, vol. 31 (Princeton, NJ: Princeton University Press, 1996). Carol Gould, 'Diversity and Democracy: Representing Differences', in *Democracy and Difference*, 171–86. See also Akeel Bilgrami, 'What Is a Muslim? Fundamental Commitment and Cultural Identity', *Critical Inquiry* 18, no. 4 (1992): 821–42.

[80] Charles Taylor, *Multiculturalism* (Princeton, NJ: Princeton University Press, 1994); Jürgen Habermas, 'Religious Tolerance: The Pacemaker for Cultural Rights', *Philosophy* 79, no. 1 (2004): 5–18.

[81] Jürgen Habermas, 'Religion in the Public Sphere', *European Journal of Philosophy* 14, no. 1 (2006): 1–25.

individuals as 'secular' and 'religious' does not account for the spectrum of religiosities that exist in India ranging from religion-practising citizens, to atheists who continued to be governed by 'religious' personal law, to citizens who saw religion above the law or religious citizens who opted into non-religious statutory provisions. This spectrum of religiosity is particularly noticeable in parliamentary debates in India on Hindu, Muslim, and Christian marriages.

Thus, the 'reasonably expected disagreement' between the two or more sets of individuals that Habermas envisioned cannot explain the innovation within cultural groups[82] and their relationship with, and influence on, the state institutions. State law was itself invariably informed by cultural, colonial, and customary influences.[83] Given the importance of faith in determining family norms, religious reform movements often targeted the domestic sphere more successfully, albeit locally, than any introduction of 'secular' laws.

Further in the debate on personal law in the Indian context, the binary of individual and group rights does not always hold, since the rights-bearing entity has often been the 'family'. Both religious and statutory provisions competed to emerge as more reliable allies of the 'family' and of marriage.[84] The alliance betrayed the universal and profound discomfort with the idea of women being granted the right to divorce, which was shared across religious and state institutions.[85] As the following chapters will show, almost all debates on marriage and family overwhelmingly echo the sentiment that marriages (of a certain kind) should be made easy and divorce difficult. Repeated iteration of Allah finding divorce despicable, or that a Christian marriage is a union for life or a Hindu marriage being a union that extends beyond one's lifetime, marked these debates. It is in the constant reworking of tenets and statutes in state or non-state forums that one finds alternate interpretations of marriage and support for divorce. And fluidity between individual and group categories was important to enable such negotiations.

---

[82] Rodney Stark and William Sims Bainbridge, 'Of Churches, Sects, and Cults: Preliminary Concepts for a Theory of Religious Movements', *Journal for the Scientific Study of Religion* 18, no. 2 (1979): 117–33.

See also F. Kniss and G. Burns, 'Religious Movements', in *The Blackwell Companion to Social Movements*, ed. David A. Snow and Sarah A. Soule (Blackwell Publishing Ltd, 2004).

[83] Chiba, 'Legal Pluralism in Sri Lankan Society'.

[84] Basu, *The Trouble with Marriage*.

[85] Whether preventing divorce indeed protected the institution of the family, even against the wishes of the spouse/s, deserves a different inquiry; here, the focus was only on preserving the 'legal' unit of the family.

Democracy through Divorce

> The great essence of the Indian civilisation is in the purity of the family, the great ideal of chastity, the great ideal of Indian womanhood which has been our pride and our glory through the ages [...] Such a measure like divorce has never been put before an electorate ... isn't this type of a communal legislation repugnant to the spirit of the constitution?[86]

In one stroke, Chatterjee's speech ties honour to womanhood, womanhood to a glorious civilization, and the preservation of such glory to the law. Marriage in such a view is an institution that is not only meant to protect the family, children, and community but also promote women's safety, and is incentivized through tax or housing benefits and state support more generally. Social movements and feminist jurisprudence, on the other hand, highlight the *trouble with marriage*[87]—seeking new grounds for divorce, equal grounds for divorce, recognition of marital rape, and so forth. Political parties on occasions have opposed women's equal access to divorce and religious organizations on occasion have defended religious right to particular forms of divorce thus enabling tremendous scope for negotiation with the state on the dissolution of marriages. Thus, while a state may value a marriage, democracy has historically loved a divorce.

Scott famously compared divorce to democracy.[88] She argued, in the context of the French Revolution, that political democracy offered the weakest with an opportunity to rebel against the strongest, and similarly, in a family, divorce allowed the more vulnerable, that is, the wife, to rebel against male domination. In this sense, both democracy and divorce were tools for voicing dissent and protecting the weak. The repeated expression of fear in parliament on the introduction of a divorce clause during the debates on the Hindu Marriage Act in the 1950s, and the Christian marriage laws in the 2000s, and the state's disdain for simplified divorce under Muslim law as a threat to the structure of family, society, and the nation, strengthens Scott's thesis that patriarchy was instrumental to more than one discriminatory regime—the family, the community, and the state.

This work separates the process of codification from the law that is produced through it. For the creation of a law has historically followed the trajectory of initial fervour for reform, disappointment in legislation, occasionally a progressive

---

[86] N. C. Chatterjee, *Lok Sabha Debates*, 1955; *Lok Sabha Debates* on Hindu Marriage Bill, vol. V, part II, col. 6534–8.

[87] Basu, *The Trouble with Marriage*.

[88] Joan Walsh Scott, 'Gender: A Useful Category of Historical Analysis', *American Historical Review* 91, no. 5 (1986): 1053–75.

interpretation of the law by the courts, and eventually accounts of people's creative responses to formal and informal personal laws. Similarly, there is scholarship on good judgments reinventing bad legislation that show that statutory law is often problematic, certainly not 'neutral' nor divorced from tradition. Nonetheless, it can be deployed towards creating modularity and reinvented to meet multiple ends by the stakeholders. This book, therefore, is not an attempt to argue the dynamism or the breadth of difference the 'constitution' is capable of absorbing, but rather shows the diversity of laws—frequently sourced from texts outside the constitution—that democracy is capable of enabling.

This book leans towards Wolin's formulation that democracy is not a mode of governance alone, but a mode of being.[89] This allows for conversations around the creation and deliberation of inevitably imperfect laws which nonetheless have roots in democratic movements and are meaningful to the recognition of difference and identity. The aspiration of democracy has led to a quest for its 'ideal' models, its assessment as substantive or deliberative. The critique of democracy acknowledge that it is a system which is incomplete and contested, and yet meaningful.[90]

The politics of the codification of personal law and the chaos of its adjudication and mutuality of resistance and coercion indicate a fundamental and irresolvable conflict over constitutional and democratic values. It forces a periodic reinterpretation of all political ideas of liberty, secularism, and democracy. This book aims to illustrate the fractured power structures that lie behind 'statutory' law, and how the state institutions do not represent the collective will of 'the state' but political parties, judges, individuals, and organizations that are not merely managing protest but often succumbing to it. There are various ways in which people and institutions subvert, create, and reshape the law—formal, informal, statutory, and religious—in their everyday lives.

The analysis of the effects of legislation and judgments in legal scholarship blur out the politics that lies behind the codification which contains within itself moments relevant to a historian. For instance, the biases and deficiencies within Hindu law have been keenly debated, but a return to the legislative debates would also illustrate how the rhetoric in the legislative assembly was also that of the recovery of religion not merely its reform. Legislative conversations on Islamic law were often framed in the language of rejection or reform of a practise rather than recovery, thus forcing the conversation on the recovery of Islam to take place in judicial orders or altogether outside the realm of official law. De's detailed

---

[89] Sheldon S. Wolin, 'Fugitive Democracy', in *Democracy and Difference*, 31–45.
[90] Charles Taylor and Amy Guttman, *Multiculturalism and the Politics of Difference* (Princeton, NJ: Princeton University Press, 1992).

analysis of the ordinary citizen's relationship with the constitution also challenges the scholarship on law and legality that is unable to disengage from the law's identification with elite histories and linear narratives.[91] Eckert's writing similarly shows everyday resistance using tools provided by the law without a need to vernacularize or translate them.[92] Basu and Dave demonstrate that when a statute is translated, it is often converted into workable remedies rather than guarantees of constitutional rights.

Breaking down the state into institutions of the state and institutions into the persons who inhabited them allows for a closer understanding of the processes at work than a disembodied and abstract understanding of the law. 'Personal law', a sphere where alternate and multiple sovereignties have somewhat been acknowledged, provides a window into how it is not always the production of law for carcerality,[93] which ultimately empowers the state, but that citizens play a significant role in manipulating, stalling, and rendering a law dysfunctional. So diverse were the interpretations of personal law that legislation rarely managed to tighten the grip of the state on domestic lives. Thus, while myriad legal sites come with their own set of normative compulsions, it is only the demand for state intervention that triggers Foucauldian anxieties among scholars who tend to view the legal interventions as a surrender to the state's regulatory impulse. This is so, even as we witness the state's interventions in personal law being repeatedly and cyclically overturned, undermined, and remaining impermanent in nature.

This book will demonstrate that personal law has brought into conversation not merely citizens and the state but has also provoked contestations between provincial and central governments over the integration of regional customs into family law codes, as federalism took root in India in the 1960s. Further, it shows that personal law has also provoked contestations between institutions of the state, namely, the legislature and the judiciary, over the custody of the constitution. While the existing literature has linked judicial activism with the national Emergency of 1975 and political turmoil,[94] this book will illustrate how personal law was one of the primary issues which prompted the court into confrontational stances

---

[91] Rohit De, *A People's Constitution: The Everyday Life of Law in the Indian Republic* (Princeton, NJ: Princeton University Press, 2018), 21.

[92] Eckert, 'From Subjects to Citizens'.

[93] Kapur, *Gender, Alterity and Human Rights*.

[94] S. P. Sathe, *Judicial Activism in India* (New Delhi: Oxford University Press, 2002); Upendra Baxi, 'Taking Suffering Seriously: Social Action Litigation in the Supreme Court of India', *Third World Legal Studies* 4, no. 1 (1985): 107–32; and Pratap Bhanu Mehta, 'The Rise of Judicial Sovereignty', *Journal of Democracy* 18, no. 2 (2007): 70–83.

against parliament. By the 1970s, the autonomous women's movements lean on the law for social reform and confront religion through the law, making secularism ever more relevant to gender. In the 1980s, secularism became synonymous with the protection of minorities as religious nationalism was being reconfigured in electoral politics.

The 1990s and the 2000s are characterized by courts reclaiming the meanings of secularism which rendered them independent and powerful but also populist. The last decade, in some sense, shows the exhaustion of social movements with state structures where the fusion of forums for adjudication of personal law and community politics found fresh meaning and produced new power structures that shared a complex relationship with the state. This was an ever-evolving relationship affected by local, national, and international contexts. It is by tracing the parallel histories of law, religion, and democracy in India that this text chronologically guides the reader through one of the most intractable and yet significant debates in independent India.

III

Sources

This book has consulted a diverse range of sources aimed at bringing multiple archives into conversation. It analyses legislative debates, case law, political party manifestos, press reports, government documents, and personal interviews. A study of Constituent Assembly and parliamentary debates provides the foundation for unpacking controversial legislation and also offers an understanding of the stakeholders and the opponents in various bills relating to marriage and divorce.[95] Bajpai has convincingly shown that the principles professed by politicians contribute significantly to public reasoning and are critical for a gauge on policy and political outcomes.[96] These debates reveal not only public and political understandings of constitutional commitments to secularism, justice, rights of minorities, and so forth but also evidence dramatic performances playing to all sorts of galleries and audiences.

The collection of letters exchanged between India's first president, Rajendra Prasad, and Prime Minister Jawaharlal Nehru in the 1950s record

---

[95] The debates were available at the Nehru Memorial Museum and Library at Teen Murti, New Delhi, and at Vidhan Sabha, Uttar Pradesh Legislative Library, Lucknow.

[96] Bajpai, *Debating Difference*, 3.

their disagreement over the Hindu Code Bill. They reveal how each clause of personal law was laboured between the dual pulls of constitutional liberalism against democratic sanction.[97] The official correspondences between ministries and government departments provide an insight into the priorities of the state, and help understand why certain bills were enacted while others were dropped. Some of the official correspondences on legislative initiatives were also between governments and judicial committees and commissions and its outcomes surfaced in Law Commission reports. This study also consulted government reports, judicial commission reports, and enquiry commission reports. Election manifestos of political parties made for an intriguing archive and showed that personal law has been an important election issue particularly since the 1980s. Police records from the Criminal Investigation Department, post-1950s, remain inaccessible but records of the late 1940s offered interesting accounts of everyday protests around announcements of government's interventions in personal law.

The judgments tell us a story about the litigants' relationship with the law—their petitions reveal their hopes and expectations from the law. Legal spaces witness performances, politics, and outcomes that extend beyond the legal realm. Case law also illustrates the role of civil society in engaging the law towards specific ends. Cases concerning definitions of 'religion' or 'secularism' aid in tracing the development of judicial activism in India over personal law. Case law is supplemented by tracing how these cases were reported in the news.

Hindi, English, and Urdu dailies often reported events very differently. Their diverse focus is itself valuable for a historian as it allows for the identification of parallel narratives. A study of private papers and unofficial reports produced by influential members of the civil society, non-governmental organizations (NGOs), and also the pamphlets and publications of religious groups and non-statutory organizations, such as the AIMPLB or the Hindu Mahasabha, offered different and often conflicting narratives of the same events. Finally, the work also draws from interviews conducted with parliamentarians, heads of *dar-ul-qaza*s (Islamic courts), women's rights activists, politicians, lawyers, and academics.

Official correspondences were easier to access in the early decades after independence; this dwindled towards the later decades. Although a historical piece, this book borrows from anthropological writings in the final chapter to put some of the interviews in context, as they yielded similar findings. Since this book follows a broadly chronological arc, the nature of sources relied on also alter over the period considered. To an extent, this book focuses on one

---

[97] Granville Austin, *Working a Democratic Constitution: A History of the Indian Experience* (New Delhi: Oxford University Press, 2003).

major archive in each chapter. For instance, the first and fourth chapters draw chiefly from legislative debates, while the second chapter leans more on Law Commission reports and the consultations it entailed, and correspondences between state and central governments. Court decisions surface throughout the text but are more central to the analysis in Chapters 3 and 5 where judicial interventions were welded into political debates more firmly. Autonomous movements and critical figures leading social organizations see greater focus in Chapters 3 and 6 where the change in the movements' relationship with the state and the law is also palpable. Chapter 6 builds on interviews with some of the key people who remain active in the current debates on Muslim personal law, in particular, because Muslim divorce law was a central issue in public debates from 2015 to 2019. These interviews were conducted over a period of seven years from 2012 to 2019 in Lucknow and Delhi with the founders, members, or heads of non-state or semi-state institutions, the Firangi Mahal *dar-ul-qaza*, Lucknow, members of the AIMPLB and the All India Muslim Women's Personal Law Board, members of NGOs in Delhi and Lucknow, women running *sharia adalat*s (courts) and other counselling centres, and police-run cells. And some grew out of the consultations undertaken by the Law Commission of India between 2017 and 2018.

Recalling Harding's apt observation that there is no fixed feminist methodology,[98] this book attempts to tentatively engage with political theory and qualitative interviews, while relying predominantly on archival analysis. This book does, however, acknowledge the limits of the archival encounter as partial and structured by governmental power which at best can offer, as Ramnath notes, only fragments of a view into reality.[99] Chakrabarty's essay is also written out of a discomfort with the 'fixed and universal gaze of the law'.[100] Basu in her incredible study of family courts shows that the law requires litigants to fold their desires and experiences to inhabit legal categories to be legible to the state. But neither the 'law' nor 'rights' are static categories; people constantly infuse them with new meanings.[101] Redding demonstrates that the legal archive, therefore, is a 'construction' and, like the law itself, remains contestable—through which a vision of the law is sketched.[102]

---

[98] Sandra G. Harding, ed., *Feminism and Methodology: Social Science Issues* (Bloomington: Indiana University Press, 1987).

[99] American Society for Legal History Conference Panel, 'What is a Legal Archive', 20 November 2019.

[100] Dipesh Chakrabarty, 'The Subject of Law and the Subject of Narrative', in *Habitations of Modernity: Essays in the Wake of Subaltern Studies*, ed. D. Chakrabarty (Chicago: University of Chicago Press, 2002), 101–14, 105.

[101] Subramanian, *Shorelines*.

[102] Ibid.

Thus, the legal archive remains an 'optic' rather than the law's own gaze, where legal spaces merely provide multiple avenues of storytelling, some of which this book attempts to capture.

IV

Arc of the Book

This book has six chapters. Chapters follow a chronology, each identifying a distinct phase when the nature of the relationship between religion and the state, the demands of citizens' protests, or the stance of the Indian courts underwent some transformation.[103] This book broadly considers the commencement of the Constituent Assembly debates which revisited and reformulated personal law, secularism, and freedom and imbued these terms with new meanings as a significant moment of departure. The creation of a constitution that granted universal adult franchise and, more importantly, judicially enforceable rights enabled a transition from a colonial subject to a rights-bearing citizen.[104] This, however, did not mean that there were no obvious and intended continuities from the colonial debates on personal law.[105] The birth of the constitution, however, provided relevant vocabulary for the personal law debate and a new grammar for a conversation on the religion–state relationship.

The conversations on the codification of personal law were fairly ripe in the 1930s and 1940s, which the first chapter briefly traces. If the focus of the colonial state had been to manage the sphere of religion,[106] then independent India

---

[103] There remain some overlaps in these timelines.

[104] De, *A People's Constitution*; Madhav Khosla, *India's Founding Moment: The Constitution of a Most Surprising Democracy* (Cambridge, MA: Harvard University Press, 2020); and Gautam Bhatia, *The Transformative Constitution: A Radical Biography in Nine Acts* (New Delhi: Harper Collins, 2019).

[105] For an analysis of continuities and change from colonial to postcolonial law in the period of transition from colonial to the postcolonial state and its impact on personal law, see Eleanor Newbigin, *The Hindu Family and the Emergence of Modern India: Law, Citizenship and Community* (Cambridge: Cambridge University Press, 2013); Matreyee Sreenivas, 'Conjugality and Capital: Gender, Families, and Property under Colonial Law in India', *The Journal of Asian Studies* 63, no. 4 (2004): 937–60; Rochona Majumdar, 'Self-Sacrifice "versus" Self-Interest: A Non-Historicist Reading of the History of Women's Rights in India', *Comparative Studies of South Asia, Africa and the Middle East* 22, no. 1 (2002): 20–35; and Rohit De, 'The Republic of Writs: Litigious Citizens, Constitutional Law and Everyday Life in India (1947–1964)' (unpublished PhD thesis, Princeton University, 2013).

[106] David A. Washbrook, 'Law, State and Agrarian Society in Colonial India', *Modern Asian Studies* 15, no. 3 (1981): 649–721.

witnessed the legitimizing of religion through legislating new personal law codes. Codifying Hindu personal law became a means to salvage religion from the allegations of superstition and paganism that informed colonial codification and the nineteenth-century interventions banning sati (widow immolation) and regulating child marriage. On the other hand, with partition and the abolition of separate electorates, Muslim personal law remained the only available category of expressing the community's distinct identity through 'legal' difference. Non-religious grievances of Muslims on account of poverty, lack of education, or unemployment rarely provoked political debates until as late as early 2000s.[107] In the first decade after independence, religious law reform became the yardstick against which the success of a modern nation state was to be measured.[108] The codification of family law became a space for the articulation of a unique brand of liberalism where law was deployed to make religion appear 'rational' and religion to make the law appear democratic.

Religion became an instrument *of* control after independence, rather than a domain that needed to *be* controlled or contained.[109] While colonial categories remained salient, new democratic resources did impact them. Viewing personal law as predominantly a colonial inheritance undermines postcolonial politics on the subject. Religion was not only considered 'reformed' through codification but, with the creation of the constitution, it became challengeable by an ordinary citizen in court and amendable by popular or parliamentary consensus. The bill on Hindu marriages revealed the dual pulls of democratic sentiment and constitutional commitment to equality which was especially palpable in dealing with divorce and bigamy.

The second chapter explores the aftermath of the Hindu Marriage Act when the Act became an open and interpretable statute. The chapter argues that the state's consistent concern with codification of personal law showed its faith in the reformative potential of the law. Throughout the 1960s, government committees and commissions initiated bills to amend Christian and Muslim personal laws.[110]

---

[107] The Sachar Committee Report of 2004 focussed on Muslim welfare.

[108] *Lok Sabha Debates*, vol. IV, part II, Vidhan Sabha Collection, Lucknow, Uttar Pradesh (UP), on Hindu Marriage Act, 1955–56.

[109] T. R. Metcalf, *Ideologies of the Raj*, vol. 3 (Cambridge: Cambridge University Press, 1997); Radhika Singha, *A Despotism of Law* (Oxford: Oxford University Press, 1998). See Washbrook, 'Law, State and Agrarian Society in Colonial India', on rule of law in colonial India. Lauren Benton, *Law and Colonial Cultures: Legal Regimes in World History, 1400–1900* (Cambridge: Cambridge University Press, 2002). Washbrook and Benton disagree on whether there was actually 'non-interference' by the state in matters of personal law. See Chapter 1, section I.

[110] *Second Law Commission of India* (1958–61), Law Commission Reports 15th, 18th, and 22nd.

These committees functioned as the buffer zones for absorbing contestations and translating demands for social change into the legal language of the bills. Thus, while commissions were set up with the intention to incorporate social disquiet or even secessionist movements, its consequence, in effect, was the creation of modularity in family law codes that generated legal norms which resembled the Hindu Marriage Act, 1955. Such bills faced opposition from minority communities when put to the test in parliament. The reports of committees became the evidence of the limited success of the attempts at codification and betrayed the centralized nature of power that informed negotiations between the committees and the government in the 1960s.[111] The debates also reveal a cross-culturally shared anxiety about easing the process of divorce, particularly for wives, and accepting alternate imagination of marriage unions. This is precisely what renders commissions and committees as significant archives because regardless of their 'impact', they provided an archive of alternatives.[112]

The decade experienced a competitive codification drive as customary practices left unacknowledged by the Hindu code were given a fresh lease for debate as federalism flourished and provincial legislatures began to challenge the uniformity imposed by the Hindu Marriage Act.[113] Recognizing cultural differences was in the interest of the state so that citizens would surrender the defining or differentiating aspect of their cultural identity to the state in order to legitimize their right to that difference. In the process, the state tempered the demands for diversity and reiterated its monopoly in determining key practices of religion that deserved codification. It also laid the foundation for the modularity of any law to be challenged through the law itself.

In the 1970s, the unabsorbed potential of the reformist sentiment, which had been failed by the quasi-legal committees or commissions of the 1960s, took the form of activism, public protests, and agitations.[114] The debates on family law could not be contained within the institutional arena alone. The chapter documents the rise of civil society movements in the 1970s that focused on the question of Muslim personal law reform that precipitated a sharp reaction from the orthodoxy. Muslim conservatives hastened to consolidate the AIMPLB. The centralization of religious authority with a conservative and male-dominated

---

[111] Muslim Personal Law Committee 1961, File No. 53/17/CF-61 Cabinet Secretariat Cabinet Affairs, National Archives of India (hereafter NAI), New Delhi.

[112] Reg Graycar and Jenny Morgan, 'Law Reform: What's in It for Women?', *Windsor Yearbook on Access to Justice* 23, no. 2 (2005): 393–422.

[113] Hindu Marriage Act Madras Amendment, File No. 17/61/67 Judicial I, Ministry of Home Affairs, NAI, New Delhi.

[114] *Towards Equality Report* 1974, Committee on Status of Women. Ministry of Education and Social Welfare, Government of India.

body such as the AIMPLB, which had proximity to parliamentarians all through the 1970s, contributed significantly to the re-imagination and re-articulation of women's demands in alternate languages rather than through bills and amendments in the decades to come.

Therefore, the movement for the reform of the Muslim personal law predates the controversial *Shah Bano* case[115] and the Muslim Women (Protection of Rights on Divorce) Act of 1986. The growing movement for reform in the Indian state of Maharashtra in the 1970s and the Adoption Bill of 1972 triggered the first public confrontation between groups that desired legal reform and those that opposed any interference by the state in personal law. The chapter demonstrates the instrumentality of the law in initiating a conversation on religion as well as the family. While 'gender' or 'women's rights' was the banner behind which legal interventions were sought, it was ultimately 'religion' that formed the basis of granting of legal exceptions to communities.

The 1970s also highlight the manner in which apparently external and unconnected events influenced the debate on personal law. For instance, the hostility between the court and parliament that characterized Prime Minister Indira Gandhi's regime, the introduction of the word 'secularism' into the preamble of the constitution,[116] and the imposition of the Emergency in 1975, contextualized, influenced, and subdued the culture of activism in India respectively. The phase was marked by claims and contestations over the custody of the constitution between religious and social movements, as well as between the legislature and the judiciary. This was orchestrated through multiple amendments to the constitution which were repeatedly invalidated by the court's judgments. The ever-changing balance of power between the legislature and the judiciary also influenced the demands from religious and social movements in the decade which found allies in different elements of the state. Significantly, amidst the national Emergency, the 42nd amendment to the Indian constitution instituted the term secularism to the preamble. Secularism of the 1970s carried a specific meaning which was distinct from how the 'group versus community rights' debates in the 1980s invoked the term. Thus, the insertion of secularism in the Indian constitution, at the highpoint of anti-democracy, the Emergency, posed particularly potent questions about what indeed tied secularism to democracy.

---

[115] *Mohd. Ahmed Khan v. Shah Bano Begum*, 1985 AIR 945.

[116] *Lok Sabha Debates*, vol. 65, nos. 1–6, 5th Series, 18th session, Forty-Second Amendment Act, 1976.

The fourth chapter analyses the two landmark and controversial cases of Shah Bano's divorce and Roop Kanwar's sati to illustrate how religion shaped women's subjectivities in the late twentieth century. Departing from the reverence for the constitution that marked the 1970s, this period was characterized by the triumph of religion and customary law over constitutional morality. The 1980s witnessed a renewal of the public and political life of organized religion with the rise of Hindu nationalism and the controversy over Muslim personal law.

The Muslim Women (Protection of Rights on Divorce) Act of 1986 produced new operative understandings of secularism. While parliament claimed to produce 'religious legislation' which it saw as a secularizing process, the court embraced 'legal' secularism. Parliament pacified the conservative or the religious voices by promising exceptions to the fundamental right to equality for preserving religious laws, while the courts worked precisely to reinterpret religious law 'in the spirit of the constitution' to align it with fundamental rights. Both processes ultimately contributed to generating greater intimacy between the state and the citizen and the terminology of 'secularism' aided the state in accessing the domestic as well as the religious. Significantly, both processes also aided the proliferation of litigation and thereby the enlargement of the sphere of the law. Parliament codified religion and the court set legal precedents moving all religions towards uniform interpretations. Thus, despite disappointment with legislation, women's initiatives over time began to use legal spaces to produce a dialogue on progressive or even feminist interpretations of religion, challenging community hierarchies as well as state-produced law.

The political consolidation of Hindu nationalism undoubtedly had an impact on the framing of opposition to discriminatory practices within Muslim personal law. Committed simultaneously to the abolition of Muslim personal law and replacing a mosque with a temple in the disputed site of Ayodhya, the movement deployed religious terminology, rituals, speeches, and spectacles to portray Muslim men as the aggressors against women as well as Hindus. This concurrently also generated stereotypes of Hindu women as chaste, stoic, servile, and self-sacrificing, and shared the problematic imagery of women propagated by the locals defending sati in Deorala. Both the Hindu nationalist political front and those defending the practice of sati in the Roop Kanwar case also shared a will to find legitimacy in the 'legal' realm for their propaganda for the construction of the Ram Temple in Ayodhya and the sati temple in Deorala as their constitutional right to freedom of religion. The period was marked by a simultaneous crisis of feminism and secularism, which reached its zenith with the demolition of the Babri Mosque by Hindu extremists in 1992. In one sense, both the Hindu nationalist zeal for temple construction and the AIMPLB's insistence on creating a legal exception for Muslim women's right to maintenance upon divorce struggled to find an anchor in the law for their cause.

The fifth chapter focuses centrally on the Supreme Court's engagement with questions of secularism, religion, religious practices, and women's rights. This chapter argues that the 1990s and the 2000s were characterized by a contest for the custody of religion and its 'true' meaning and this contest was played out in courts. This was enabled by court's audacious interventions in the form of pronouncements over definitions of secularism, Hindutva, and Quranic texts through a range of judgments. Thus, contextualizing the rise of Hindu nationalism in the long history of the Indian democracy and the law, this enquiry seeks to extend beyond the electoral potential of 'Hindutva' but towards its legal definition that was established through a series of judgments. These rulings separated Hindutva— the Hindu nationalist ideology—from Hinduism, signalling that the court's enhanced authority to determine the limits of religion in public life as Hindu nationalism transitioned from being a movement to the government in the 1990s.

Cases analysed in this chapter demonstrate that the courts were instrumental in propelling debates on religion into the public discourse. These judgments decentralized the interpretations of personal law, and civil society organizations seized this opportunity to question the monopoly of parliament as well as orthodox religious organizations over the interpretation of religion. The chapter also brings out the intriguing arguments placed repeatedly before the court over the years particularly over the question of Muslim divorce. Arguments that centred on the Quran, gender equality, and 'good practices', 'essential practice' or arbitrariness of law. While important court decisions emerged across decades, some of the significant interventions by the courts made in the 2000s demonstrated how the courts were being accessed regardless of the impact of these judgments on personal law.

Although multiple forums for adjudication of family law were active throughout the history of independent India, in the last decade, personal law has dominated public debate with renewed fervour, captured in the final chapter. Article 44 that seeks a Uniform Civil Code found repeated mention in parliament, press, and even households. This chapter analyses the multiple forums of adjudication of family disputes to illustrate the very dynamic way in which ideas of law travel across sites of adjudication. It shows the increasing decentralization and diminishing authority over personal law by the state and the clergy. The chapter traces how sites of law making and adjudication demand not only different performances from its litigants and stakeholders but indeed provide multiple avenues of storytelling. It narrates experiences from across forums such as *dar-ul-qaza*s, family courts, *mahila adalat*s (women's courts), police helplines, and so forth. Many of these forums were capable of offering easier procedures to dissolve a marriage and simultaneous pressures to stay in one. Forums could emphasize 'saving a marriage' or provide women with easier exits from abusive relationships. But legal hybridity nonetheless allowed for cultural and religious identities of litigants to remain secure even as they made claims for constitutional guarantees.[117] It becomes apparent that each forum produced its own 'terms' on which the adjudication would take place—they could reinforce the supremacy of the constitution or that of the Quran. Negotiations for divorce across forums illustrated that religiosity and constitutional understandings of rights can be selectivity leaned on. For instance, a couple for whom the pronouncement of a third talaq by the husband remains a legal moment may never access the law to invalidate the divorce, but the wife may still negotiate maintenance with some reliance on legal instruments. People's idea of retribution, justice, or faith created a codependence between the law and religion. Who had the custody of authentic religious knowledge became deeply contested and decentralized.

Negotiations across forums use and conform to different sets of rules of acceptable behaviour, recognition of crime and of rights. Solutions they arrived at through negotiations could be tenuously linked to the divine, or invoke statutory law for justification or the constitution for borrowing the language of rights, or all of these. For instance, the *sharia adalat*s run by the Bharatiya Muslim Mahila Andolan (BMMA) frequently settled disputes and offered favourable decisions for women. The underlying principle was that the disputes were interpreted 'in light of the Quran' (*Quran ki roshni mein*).[118] Awaaz-e-Niswaan categorically rejected references to religious texts in deciding on matters.[119] In family courts, the protection of the family and emphasis on reconciliation and 'saving families' characterized the tone of the discussion.[120] Yet these multiple conversations across forums produced a new vocabulary of religion, new feminisms, and translated not just religious and statutory knowledge, but experiences and ideas.[121]

---

[117] Arzoo Osanloo, *The Politics of Women's Rights in Iran* (Princeton, NJ: Princeton University Press, 2009) discussed in Lemons, 'Introduction', *Divorcing Traditions*.

[118] Personal interview with Zakia Soman, founder of the BMMA, 14 March 2019, New Delhi.

[119] Vatuk, 'Islamic Feminism in India', 489–518.

[120] Basu, *The Trouble with Marriage*.

[121] Sally Engle Merry, 'Transnational Human Rights and Local Activism: Mapping the Middle', *American Anthropologist* 108, no. 1 (2006): 38–51.

This book, therefore, chronicles the negotiations not only between 'state and society' but within, between, and across state and non-state forums, actors, and movements. It presents the trajectories of Hindu, Muslim, and Christian family law codes to suggest that various academic constructions such as the public–private divide, individual versus group rights, and universal rights versus legal pluralism prove to be inadequate frameworks in addressing the peculiarities of the politics of personal law in India.

1

Personal Law and the Making of Modern Religion, 1946–56

The policy should be that marriage becomes easy and divorce difficult.
—H. V. Kamath, *Lok Sabha Debates*, Hindu Marriage Act, 1955

The vocabulary of 'personal law' may indeed have been a colonial creature, but after independence it was transformed into a tool for nation-building[1] that pieced together modern religion—through legislation. The very nomenclature of the 'Hindu' Code Bill or 'Muslim' personal law was at odds with modernity's alleged requirement of limiting the sphere of religion. Yet the 'modern' nation state and a 'secular' democracy of independent India prioritized the codification of religion as one of its foremost endeavours. In doing so, the state also acquired the power to regulate both public religion and the domestic sphere. It was only through the regulation of everyday religion that the modern nation state could expand its jurisdiction over the family in the early years of independence.

Globally, the period of the 1950s and 1960s was characterized by an engagement with family laws and personal status laws became contingent on various alliances between the new ruling classes and the religious elite.[2] There was, in some cases—such as Malaysia—a consistent marginalization of religious law over time, since when the colonial categories of personal law code had first emerged.[3] It was the marginalization of this legal domain of religion that began with colonialism and followed thereafter that produced the response in the form of codification of laws under civil, criminal, or religious-personal categories. This marginalization limited the domain of 'personal law' to merely 'family law' and caused representational claims and questions of 'personal status' to move further away from religious political thought, thus allowing for a permanent domination of the elite.[4]

---

[1] Narendra Subramanian, *Nation and Family: Personal Law, Cultural Pluralism, and Gendered Citizenship in India* (Stanford: Stanford University Press, 2014).

[2] Narendra Subramanian, 'Making Family and Nation: Hindu Marriage Law in Early Postcolonial India', *The Journal of Asian Studies* 69, no. 3 (2010): 771–98.

[3] Iza R. Hussin, *The Politics of Islamic Law: Local Elites, Colonial Authority and the Making of the Muslim State* (London: University of Washington, 2008).

[4] Ibid.

By contrast, in the Indian case, after independence, personal law became a cornerstone for Muslim politics, whereas for the Hindus, it became a tool to bring religious morality into universal statutes. The codification of religious personal law in the early years of independence acknowledged the centrality of religion in the lives of the citizens but tried to route their access to the avowedly divine laws, or essential practices of religion through institutions of the state.

Social legislation in colonial India, as in the case of the abolition of sati or child marriage, followed the logic of saving the subject from the tyranny of their own religion or custom.[5] The enactment of the Hindu codes, on the other hand, was an attempt to 'save religion', specifically Hinduism, from the clutter of customary law and, more importantly, to integrate it with certain constitutional provisions and visions of secularism. This was more than defining 'essential practices' of religion but codifying 'good practices' that were rarely contingent on any 'authentic interpretation' of religion. These were practices that could be generalized as 'universal' by appealing to majoritarian or the dominant elite's 'good sense', generalized as common sense. The potential to generalize Hindu law as universal laid the foundation for the vexed debate on the Uniform Civil Code.

While the zealous endeavour to codify Hindu law may indeed have dented or left structures of patriarchy and caste largely intact,[6] the idea of the Hindu Code Bill was also significant to the Indian state's own conception of modern or model 'citizenship'.[7] This chapter will demonstrate that the post-independence codification debates were centrally about acknowledging the place of religion in the personal, public, and political lives of the people.

While religious minorities used the category of religious *personal* law to negotiate the recognition of difference, women's groups used the category of *religious* personal law to make visible instances of discrimination against women within marriage and family that could be directly or tenuously related to religion or custom. The domain of personal law witnessed a conversation between nation, religion, and family which was formative to Indian secularism and democracy.

The chapter is divided into three sections. This first section focuses on the codification debate in the 1930s. The chapter does not labour over the question

---

[5] Lata Mani, *Contentious Traditions: The Debate on Sati in Colonial India* (Berkley: University of California Press, 1998).

[6] Archana Parashar, *Women and Family Law Reform in India: Uniform Civil Code and Gender Equality* (New Delhi: Sage Publications, 1992); Newbigin, *The Hindu Family*.

[7] Eleanor Newbigin, *The Hindu Family and the Emergence of Modern India: Law, Citizenship and Community* (Cambridge: Cambridge University Press, 2013); Flavia Agnes, 'Hindu Men, Monogamy and Uniform Civil Code', *Economic and Political Weekly* 30, no. 50 (1995): 3238–44.

of continuity or change before and after independence, which has been well addressed in the scholarship,[8] and this study encountered evidence of both. The section relies on secondary literature to contextualize the debates on the colonial distinctions of the public and private spheres, and between Indian and European, male and female subjects.[9] These distinctions were crystallized not only through legislative interventions but also the practice of law in the courts.[10] It shows that personal laws, on many occasions, were not derived from religion or custom but from judicial and legislative responses to familial and conjugal disputes to which religion was only incidental.

The Constituent Assembly debates analysed in the second section demonstrate that there was neither a consensus on secularism nor an understanding of what a Uniform Civil Code would entail, but an intervention in family law was seen by some as necessary for national integration, and simultaneously by others as a cause for disintegration. The question of women's empowerment or rights saw limited debate in the assembly in the discussion on a Uniform Civil Code. For a few in the assembly, a Uniform Civil Code represented the aspirations of a nation in the making, which would propel the independent nation towards becoming an ideal, sovereign, modern nation state. An idealist and an 'aesthetic' imagination of India marked these discussions, in which a Uniform Civil Code was posited as the final achievement of a democracy. This led some in the Constituent Assembly to reject the immediate revision of the Hindu law that was being contemplated by the Hindu Law Committee to prioritize the 'ultimate' establishment of a Uniform Civil Code. Simultaneously, the domination of the Hindu elite encouraged the containment of Muslim minority politics within the realm of personal law, as distinctions in language and

---

[8] Rohit De, *A People's Constitution: The Everyday Life of Law in the Indian Republic* (Princeton, NJ: Princeton University Press, 2018); Mitra Sharafi, *Law and Identity in Colonial South Asia: Parsi Legal Culture, 1772–1947* (Cambridge University Press, 2014); Newbigin, *The Hindu Family*.

[9] David A. Washbrook, 'Law, State and Agrarian Society in Colonial India', *Modern Asian Studies* 15, no. 3 (1981): 649–721; Thomas R. Metcalf, *Ideologies of the Raj*, vol. 3 (Cambridge: Cambridge University Press, 1997); Lauren Benton, *Law and Colonial Cultures: Legal Regimes in World History, 1400–1900* (Cambridge: Cambridge University Press, 2002); Tanika Sarkar, *Hindu Wife, Hindu Nation, Community, Religion, and Cultural Nationalism* (Bloomington: Indiana University Press, 2001); Rina Verma Williams, *Postcolonial Politics and Personal Laws: Colonial Legal Legacies and the Indian State* (Oxford: Oxford University Press, 2006).

[10] Elizabeth Kolsky, 'Codification and the Rule of Colonial Difference: Criminal Procedure in British India', *Law and History Review* 23, no. 3 (2005): 631–83; Mitra Sharafi, 'The Semi-Autonomous Judge in Colonial India Chivalric Imperialism Meets Anglo-Islamic Dower and Divorce Law', *Indian Economic and Social History Review* 46, no. 1 (2009): 57–81.

education were erased.[11] Muslims largely came to view a potential Uniform Civil Code as a tyrannous attempt to establish Hindu hegemony. Partition numerically weakened the Muslim community in India and the abolition of separate electorates had an impact on their representation within the machinery of the state.

There were contradictory pressures on the constitution of India for enabling democracy while guarding against populism. B. R. Ambedkar hoped to make the constitution 'ownerless'—a living document offering space for resistance to multiple stakeholders but to not be appropriated by any group. And on the other hand, it had to remain legitimate in the eyes of religious citizens and indigenous moral orders, a sentiment summarized well by parliamentarian Sucheta Kriplani's observation, 'what is a law if people don't believe in it'.[12] This chapter focuses on instances that show the centrality of religious (even caste and regional) identity in members' imagination of the nation.

While the Constituent Assembly (1946–49) permitted the continuation of personal laws, the new parliament (1952–57) restored certain religious practices as part of the process of decolonization, and weeded out others as a commitment to 'modernity'.[13] In its enactment of the Hindu codes, parliament was geared towards reforming Hindu law rather than addressing gender inequality. The final section of the chapter illustrates that the intention of the independent state was not merely to create a new modern Hindu legal subject through the Hindu Code Bill,[14] or to secure rights for women[15] but, above all, to find a legal space for religion so that conversations on religious reform could be routed through the state, and the regulation of the family would remain a state monopoly. Addressing women's rights was significant only to the extent that the Hindu Marriage Act was believed to be consistent with the imagination of a 'modern' nation state.[16] Religious reform was also significant to this project but was limited by the extent to which religious citizens continued to treat the Hindu Code Bill as an authoritative law. Recognizing the centrality of religion in the politics of codification allows newer

---

[11] For the emphasis on homogenization in the Constituent Assembly, see Chapter 1 discussion on minority report in Rochana Bajpai, *Debating Difference: Group Rights and Liberal Democracy in India* (New Delhi: Oxford University Press, 2011).

[12] *Lok Sabha Debates*, 2 May 1955, vol. IV, Part II, Vidhan Sabha Collection, Lucknow, UP, Sucheta Kriplani's speech col. 7274.

[13] Partha Chatterjee, *The Nation and Its Fragments: Colonial and Postcolonial Histories* (Princeton, NJ: Princeton University Press, 1993).

[14] Newbigin, *The Hindu Family*.

[15] Chitra Sinha, *Debating Patriarchy: The Hindu Code Bill Controversy in India (1941–1956)* (New Delhi: Oxford University Press, 2012).

[16] Reba Som, 'Jawaharlal Nehru and the Hindu Code: A Victory of Symbol over Substance?' *Modern Asian Studies* 28, no. 1 (1994): 165–94.

insights into the nature of Indian secularism, populist law making, and the framing of religious and social reform movements after independence.

There are broadly two narratives on the writing of Hindu law in independent India. One, that the law introduced a modern, radical, or progressive,[17] and therefore, a more just system of values centred on women's equality, and empowerment,[18] and, significantly, it made the law an important tool for resistance against patriarchy—governmental or familial. The second more critical reading suggests that the Hindu Family Law Acts addressed neither women's equality nor Brahminical domination.[19] Instead, codification may have given statutory force to discriminatory practices.[20] Both narratives ask similar questions about continuity and change from colonial law and offer either an endorsement or a critique of modernity and governmentality.

This chapter suggests that the codification of Hindu law cannot be reduced either to a reading of its 'achievements' or 'failures' with respect to women's rights or the 'modern' values it introduced to the institution of the family; or indeed the degree to which it granted the right to divorce or inherit property to women. These goals, to a varying extent, were somewhat realized. The Hindu Family Law Acts, however, more centrally, were attempts to rationalize and legalize certain aspects of religion, such that the state could legislate on the domestic sphere. The law had to lean substantially on religion, at least in name, to appear legitimate. This also made aspects of religion legally enforceable; but as a corollary, the act of placing religion in statutes also rendered the law sacred, and the sacred amendable. All that lay outside the scope of the law could be subject to criticism as superstition, customary practice, or myth while projecting the codified religion as 'liberal' or 'reformed'.[21] This conflict came to be written into the law in the form of religious family law codes and set the stage for the expanding and receding influence of religion in the decades to come.

---

[17]   Marc Galanter, 'The Displacement of Traditional Law in Modern India', *Journal of Social Issues* 24, no. 4 (1968): 65–90.

[18]   Sinha, *Debating Patriarchy*.

[19]   J. M. D. Derrett, *Introduction to Modern Hindu Law* (Bombay: Oxford University Press, 1963) and Newbigin, *The Hindu Family*.

[20]   Flavia Agnes, 'Law and Gender Inequality', in *Writing the Women's Movement: A Reader*, ed. Mala Khullar (New Delhi: Zubaan, 2005), 113; Rochana Majumdar, 'History of Women's Rights: A Non-Historicist Reading', *Economic and Political Weekly* 38, no. 22 (2003): 2130–34.

[21]   Rammohun Roy had held a similar position on reforming Hinduism. C. A. Bayly describes him as one of the first non-modern, nor secular 'liberal'. See discussion in chapter 1, 'The Social and Intellectual Contexts of Early Indian Liberalism, c.1780–1840', in *Recovering Liberties: Indian Thought in the Age of Liberalism and Empire*, vol. 100, edited by C. A. Bayly, 26–41 (Cambridge: Cambridge University Press, 2011).

I

The Codes of Convenience: Personal Law in the Late Colonial Period

Religious and customary practices varied significantly across regions, groups, and castes.[22] Colonial codification transformed custom and simultaneously strengthened the position of who it recognized as the 'competent subjects', that is, the pandits, *maulvi*s, and the local elite,[23] whose interpretations became the basis for district judges'[24] decisions. The very process of granting a custom the force of law transformed the custom into active law.[25] Sturman documents the colonial emphasis on the textual source and the fixity of written law[26] prior to which the *qazi* himself may not have been adhering to the *sharia* in absolute terms.[27] Or perhaps the *sharia* was not to be applied in such rigid and absolute terms as literatures on *ijtihad* tell us?[28] Significantly, Stephen's incisive inquiry also reveals that customs were frequently 'tamed' and the moral position or colonial morality of the executing officers and presiding judges deeply informed the way in which a custom was understood.[29]

There remained an inherent arbitrariness with respect to what warranted inclusion in the form of statutory religious law 'code' and what was left alone as custom, and which one of these customs were extended recognition by the courts. Thus, personal law in colonial India was premised on both questionable

---

[22] Geraldine Forbes, 'The Indian Women's Movement: A Struggle for Women's Rights or National Liberation?', in *The Extended Family: Women and Political Participation in India and Pakistan*, vols. 49–82, edited by Gail Minault (New Delhi: Chanakya Publications, 1981).

[23] Bina Agarwal, *A Field of One's Own: Gender and Land Rights in South Asia*, vol. 58 (Cambridge: Cambridge University Press, 1994).

[24] Rosane Rocher, 'The Creation of Anglo-Hindu Law', in *Hinduism and Law: An Introduction*, ed. T. Lubin, D. R. Davis Jr, and J. K. Krishnan, 78–88 (Cambridge: Cambridge University Press, 2010), 78.

[25] Ibid., 101.

[26] 'Usage once recorded upon the evidence given [...] immediately becomes written and fixed law [...] henceforth obeyed as a law administered by the British Court, and has really become a command of the sovereign.' Maine (1871: 72) quoted in R. Sturman, 'Marriage and Family in Colonial Hindu Law', in *Hinduism and Law: An Introduction*, 89–104, 94.

[27] Kugle, 'Framed, Blamed and Renamed'.

[28] Muhammad Qasim Zaman, *The Ulama in Contemporary Islam: Custodians of Change*, vol. 38 (London: Princeton University Press, 2010).

[29] Julia Stephen's, *Governing Islam: Law, Empire, and Secularism in Modern South Asia* (Cambridge: Cambridge University Press, 2018), see ch. 2, 'Taming Custom', 91.

generalizations of specific texts and creation of precedents out of custom.[30] It was driven by considerations of administrative ease, surveillance, and gaining the support of the local elite, among others. The strict distinction made between categories of law, whether civil, criminal, or personal, allowed the colonial administration to intervene selectively in 'criminal' religious practices through legislation, while maintaining a stance of non-interference in personal religious affairs.[31] Colonial laws, therefore, as Benton shows, did recognize group cultures with respect to family laws, but only sought to contain native specificity and difference in family law alone rather than acknowledge it in commerce and crime.[32] Even in the application of apparently neutral law, women were often more vulnerable to accusation and punishment. In the application of criminal law in cases of death of child brides, the conviction rates were very low.[33]

The translation of customs also overwhelmingly favoured Victorian notions of patriarchy, crystallized male privilege, and ushered in new familial hierarchies.[34] For instance, the high-handed approach towards abolishing the practice of widow immolation paid little attention to the voice of the victim as the debate focussed instead on whether or not Hinduism endorsed sati.[35] The banning of various 'barbaric' practices in India was part of a grander project of asserting the civilizational superiority of British modernity over native traditionalism.[36] For 'personal law' this meant, as Sturman aptly summarizes, 'We will rule you by your *own* laws, but the debased nature of your laws is precisely why we must rule you.'[37]

The surveillance of 'personal practices' was shared between the religious elite and the judiciary. In the absence of the rule of law and the separation of powers, the judiciary occasionally functioned as an extension to the legislature[38]

---

[30] Bayly, *Recovering Liberties*.

[31] Martha C. Nussbaum, *The Clash Within: Democracy, Religious Violence, and India's Future* (London: Harvard University Press, 2009).

[32] Benton, *Law and Colonial Cultures*.

[33] Tanika Sarkar, 'Rhetoric against Age of Consent: Resisting Colonial Reason and Death of a Child-Wife', *Economic and Political Weekly* 28, no. 36 (1993a): 1869–78. See also Padma Anagol, 'The Emergence of the Female Criminal in India: Infanticide and Survival under the Raj', *History Workshop Journal* 53, no. 1 (2002): 73–93.

[34] Stevens, *Governing Islam*.

[35] 'The Petition of the Orthodox Community Against the Suttee Regulation, Together with a Paper of Authorities, and the Reply of the Governor-General Thereto' (14 January 1830), in *Raja Rammohun Roy and Progressive Movements in India*, in Lata Mani, *Contentious Traditions*, 140.

[36] Ibid., 141.

[37] Sturman, 'Marriage and Family in Colonial Hindu Law', 101 (emphasis mine).

[38] Washbrook, 'Law, State and Agrarian Society in Colonial India'.

and occasionally as 'semi-autonomous'.[39] The project of 'uniform religious personal laws' thus also came to stand for facilitating control over the native people.[40] What constituted uniformity was, of course, historically contingent,[41] and therefore fluid. Hindus, Muslims, and Christians all had their unique encounters with codification. While for the Hindu and Muslim cases, the local elite and the pandits and *qazi*s moved from being socially dominant to becoming influencers of family law for their religious communities; for the Christians, the case was different. Even while Bishops maintained their influence and privilege, the colonial state appeared to consider itself far more entitled to legislate on laws relating to Christians than other religions.

Indian Christians occupied the peculiar category of people who had their personal laws codified under avowedly 'neutral' legislations such as the Indian Marriage Act of 1864, Indian Divorce Act of 1869, Native Convert's Marriage Dissolution Act of 1866, Indian Succession Act of 1925, and so on. While there were a number of Protestant and Catholic organizations that engaged with and voiced dissent against these Acts, these laws remained substantially borrowed from British legislation.[42] Chatterjee notes that these enactments saw only minor changes to suit the Indian context, and these were also made only to enable the spread of Christianity in India.[43] These concessions were visible in lowering the age of marriage from 21 in the British Act to 13 for women and 16 for men in the Indian version to suit the locally acceptable age for marriage. Further, recognizing conversion to Christianity necessitated that parental consent for marriage of converted minors had to be waived. Non-Christian parents were unlikely to give consent for their converted child's marriage to another Christian if the conversion was against their wishes to begin with. Thus, it is difficult to locate 'religion' as a *source* of law at the core of these conversations on personal laws, even while religion, here Christianity, as an end goal (its preservation, propagation, or reform) was apparent. A number of statutes and amendments to personal laws came simply to manage the complexities of conversion but were not guided by reformist or feminist agendas.[44]

---

[39] Sharafi, 'The Semi-Autonomous Judge in Colonial India'.

[40] Susanne Hoeber Rudolph and Lloyd I. Rudolph, 'Living with Difference in India', *The Political Quarterly* 71 (2000): 20–38.

[41] Nandini Chatterjee, *The Making of Indian Secularism: Empire, Law and Christianity, 1830–1960* (New York: Springer, 2011).

[42] Ibid.

[43] Ibid.

[44] Chatterjee shows that inclusion of the provision of restitution of conjugal rights in the Indian Divorce Act of 1869 which applied to Christians, among other reasons, can also be seen to be motivated by the problem of converted Christian men whose wives of other religions could denounce the marriage. For men, however, in the absence of a Christian law on divorce, they could not remarry while their former wives were alive.

Similarly in the Muslim case, in January 1931, Khan Bahadur Haji Wajihuddin moved a resolution in the Legislative Assembly for the appointment of a committee for the specific purpose of enacting a uniform law for 'all the Muslims in the Indian territory'.[45] The committee was aimed at addressing the questions of the dissolution of marriage and restoration of conjugal rights and divorce and these matters were to be determined by 'competent Mohammedans'.[46] This laid the foundation for the Shariat Application Act of 1937.

To make the new law palatable to the 'generality of Muslims', M. A. Jinnah, a lawyer, politician with the All India Muslim League, and later the founder of Pakistan, recommended that only particular sections of the Act should be made compulsory, whereas most provisions ought to remain voluntary.[47] Significantly, the legislation recognized women as absolute (although not equal) owners of property under Muslim personal law. This is popularly understood to be a legislation that saw relatively less opposition from within the Muslim community because it was a move professedly away from local custom towards a 'purer' form of religion. Some of the members of Anjuman-e-Khwatin-e-Islam, a Muslim women's organization that voiced women's right to property as one of its primary demands, also supported the Shariat Application Act of 1937.[48] However, colonial records miss out significant figures such as Ashraf Ali Thanvi, who were not only instrumental to the codification project but also distanced themselves from the shape that the Shariat Application Act, 1937, and the Dissolution of Muslim Marriages Act, 1939, ultimately took. Thus, the intent and consequences of the

---

[45] File No. 26/31 Home Department (Judicial) List no. 17-A, 26 January 1931, National Archive of India (hereafter NAI), New Delhi.

[46] Ibid.

[47] Partha Chatterjee, 'Secularism and Toleration', *Economic and Political Weekly* 29, no. 28 (1994): 1768–77. See also Faisal Devji, *Muslim Zion: Pakistan as a Political Idea* (London: Hurst & Co., 2013). Devji suggests that there were personal reasons as to why Jinnah did not insist on the uniform application of the Shariat Application Act of 1937.

In 2007, Jinnah's only daughter Dina Wadia filed a writ petition at the Bombay High Court, seeking the ownership of Jinnah's property. There were multiple claimants for this as per Muslim law, since Jinnah had died without leaving a will. However, his daughter's counsel, Fali Nariman, argued, ironically, that Jinnah being a Khoja-Shia did not follow the Muslim personal law and that his property was to be governed by the Hindu Succession Act. 'Muslim Law Doesn't Apply to Jinnah, Says Daughter', *Indian Express* (New Delhi), 13 October 2008.

[48] Gail Minault, 'Sisterhood or Separatism: The All India Muslim Ladies' Conference and the Nationalist Movement', in *The Extended Family: Women and Political Participation in India and Pakistan*, 83–108. See also Barbara D. Metcalf, 'Reading and Writing about Muslim Women in British India', in *Forging Identities: Gender, Communities, and the State*, ed. Zoya Hasan (New Delhi: Kali for Women, 1994), 6–14; Ayesha Jalal, 'The Convenience of Subservience: Women and the State of Pakistan', in *Women, Islam and the State*, ed. Deniz Kandiyoti (London: Palgrave Macmillan, 1991), 77–114.

new laws remained uncertain and its provisions voluntary. These laws did not quite unify Muslim personal law. Khojas, Kutchi Memons, among others, continued to follow Hindu laws of succession even as they identified as Muslim. Sharafi's work shows that even before the codification of Anglo-Mohammedan statutes, courts often recognized Muslim women's right to *talaq-e-tawfid* (delegated divorce) and even *khula* (unilateral divorce initiated by women) or upheld the inflation of dower amounts (*mahr*) in their readings of Islamic jurisprudence.[49] Therefore, the new law being an 'application act' impacted judicial discretion but also legally built in the *qazi*'s discretion into statutes. The 1930s, nevertheless, remained a significant decade for conversations on gender and religion and codification attempts across communities speeded up.[50] The interwar period saw the further dwindling of the authority of the central legislature that also paved the way for reformist agendas.[51] The codification of Hindu law, which is the focus of this chapter, also remained a persevering debate through the 1930s and 1940s and finally found statutory shape in 1950s as the foremost social legislation in independent India.

Codifying Hindu Law

The All India Women's Conference (AIWC), constituted in 1927, was extremely active, and circulated multiple drafts and produced frequent publications debating the various provisions of the potential Hindu Code Bill.[52] Other women's organizations such as the National Women's Agency (1917) and the National Council for Women (1925) evidence the growing strength of women's organization in the early twentieth century.

In 1935, a report on the 'Political and Economic Disabilities of Indian Women' engaged with questions of women's right to property under religious laws in remarkable detail. The 1935 report also reviewed Mohammedan law, Parsi law, and the Indian Christian Succession Act which applied to Indian Christians as well as to those who were married under the Special Marriage (Amendment) Act of 1923. The report recommended the recognition of women as absolute owners of property among other suggestions.[53] In 1939, another report titled 'Women's Role in Planned

---

49   Sharafi, 'The Semi-Autonomous Judge in Colonial India'.

50   For developments in Parsi personal law, see Sharafi, *Law and Identity in Colonial South Asia*.

51   Eleanor Newbigin, 'The Codification of Personal Law and Secular Citizenship: Revisiting the History of Law Reform in Late Colonial India', *Indian Economic and Social History Review* 46, no. 1 (2009): 83–104.

52   Draft bill to be introduced in the council of states F. No. Eco/81/38, 7, NAI, New Delhi. Interestingly, the bill also mentioned that its provisions would apply to a Hindu even after he has converted to another religion.

53   For an account of negotiations of property rights of women in the late colonial period, see M. Sreenivas, 'Conjugality and Capital: Gender, Families, and Property under Colonial Law in India', *The Journal of Asian Studies* 63, no. 4 (2004): 937–60.

Economy' was prepared for the Congress Party.[54] This was a radical document with its focus on the economic rights of women. With its focus on absolute ownership of property, recognition of independent income for women, and even the recognition of the economic value of household labour, this report in effect argued against making the 'family' an economic unit and instead recognized the 'worker' as an individual.

By 1938, soon after the Shariat Application Act recognized Muslim women as absolute owners of property, the Hindu Women's Right to Property Act of 1937 was also under review.[55] Even though there was a consensus on the convening of the creation of a committee, dissent arose when the presentation of the draft legislations commenced. The discussions also revealed that the traditional economic rights of women had been curtailed through judicial pronouncements against *stridhan* (women's wealth)[56] in attempts to achieve administrative clarity.[57] Two bills were floated in 1941 that dealt with interstate succession and laws on marriage. The B. N. Rau Committee, set up in 1944, considered these bills, but did not immediately include their recommendations. The all-male committee managed to offer hitherto unprecedented support to women's legal rights, particularly with regard to succession and inheritance. There was an attempt to unify two prevailing systems of inheritance among Hindus, the Mitakshara[58] and the Dayabhaga.[59] The former did not

---

[54] For an analysis of other provisions of the WRPE report, see Nirmala Banerjee, 'Whatever Happened to the Dreams of Modernity? The Nehruvian Era and Woman's Position', *Economic and Political Weekly* 33, no. 17 (1998): WS2–WS7.

[55] Eleanor Newbigin, 'The Hindu Code Bill and the Making of Modern Indian State' (Doctoral dissertation, University of Cambridge, 2008).

[56] *Stridhan* literally translates to woman's wealth, as per the discussion in the AIWC papers in the 1930s and 1940s. This may include (1) the gifts a woman receives from her husband, her husband's family, or her own family from affectionate kindred, and so on; (2) the property she gets through someone's will and given to her as an absolute gift; (3) property she holds by way of maintenance; (4) property she buys from her *stridhan*; (5) property she gets by adverse profession; (6) property acquired by skill or art or self-exertion. In case, however, of a married woman, she has no absolute ownership over property acquired by her own skill art or exertion and over property obtained as a gift from strangers during 'converture [*sic*]' and she cannot transfer such property without the consent of her husband; (7) property she inherits form her mother or a female relative and, in the Bombay presidency, also property inherited from father or brother. File No. 32–1048, AIWC Files, Nehru Memorial Museum and Library, New Delhi (NMML).

[57] Madhu Kishwar, 'Codified Hindu Law: Myth and Reality', *Economic and Political Weekly* 29, no. 33 (1994): 2145–61; *Bhagwan v. Warubai* (1908) 32 Bom 300; *Dattaray v. Gangabhai* (1922) 46 Bom 541.

[58] One of the systems of inheritance in Hindu law prevalent predominantly in northern India before the Hindu Succession Act, 1956, where the sons become joint owners of ancestral property at birth.

[59] System of inheritance in Hindu law prevalent in Bengal and parts of east India before the Hindu Succession Act, 1956.

grant women rights to inherit their husband's property, therefore, the latter, the
Dayabhaga system was given preference in the committee's considerations since
this protected the widow's right to property. Marriage and inheritance were closely
linked in these conversations in the 1940s, quite unlike the post-independence law
that followed in the 1950s. Two members of the Legislative Assembly, K. Radha
Bai Subbarayan and Prakash, had drafted a bill to restrict polygamous marriages
among Hindus.[60] A. de C. Williams, secretary to the Executive Council, circulated
the bill in the assembly in August 1938. The statement of objects and reasons of
the bill read:

> Although *enlightened Hindu opinion* does not approve of polygamy, Hindu Law as
> administered by the courts does not prohibit it, and there are numerous instances
> where a man who is already married to a loving and innocent wife has married a
> second wife without any reasonable justification, ill-treated his first wife, or
> otherwise caused her untold misery and unhappiness. It is necessary to put a restraint
> upon such polygamous marriages and hence this Bill.[61]

The bill allowed for bigamy in specific circumstances, such as if the wife was
suffering from an infectious and incurable disease. In such a case, the bill argued
for her *stridhan* to be restored to her, in addition to a third of the husband's share
of property, as a condition for obtaining the wife's permission to remarry. 'Loving
and innocent wives', therefore, could be recipients of good laws but if they were
not, that was sufficient justification of a second marriage. The drafters of the bill
thought that such a restraint on polygamy would perhaps be more acceptable 'to
the generality of Hindus' than necessitating 'divorce' to prevent bigamy.[62]

The codification of personal laws in colonial India were, therefore, hesitant
endeavours by the state, and even in its acceptance of different religious personal
laws, it admonished religion as barbaric and irrational therefore deserving of
exceptional status outside of 'rational' law making. It was through contrived
and laboured insistence upon difference between religious personal laws and
homogeneity within them that the colonial state claimed to have accommodated
parallel assimilative ideals of 'liberalism' on the one hand through uniformity
in codes of procedure, and 'difference' on the other, in personal law.[63]

---

[60] File No. Eco/81/38, The Hindu Polygamous Marriage Restraint Bill, 1938, Executive Council
Office, NAI, New Delhi.

[61] Ibid. (emphasis mine).

[62] Draft bill to be introduced in the council of states. File No. Eco/81/38, 7, NAI, New Delhi.
Interestingly, the bill also mentioned that its provisions would apply to a Hindu even after he
has converted to another religion.

[63] Metcalf, *Ideologies of the Raj*. See also Chatterjee, *The Nation and Its Fragments*, vol. 11.

This could then be used to justify difference between different subjects, British, European, and Indian. Religion, thus, was recognized as a legitimate category of 'difference' alongside race and caste.

Towards Independence

The Congress Party's launch of the Civil Disobedience movement in the 1940s drained some of the momentum from the women groups supporting the cause of family law reform.[64] Although the B. N. Rau Committee was not necessarily seen as a British creation, women were pressured to choose between a national cause and the cause of women's rights, particularly because the women leading the debate on the Hindu code were also largely identified as 'freedom fighters'.

With influential members like Hansa Mehta and Renuka Ray at its helm, the Hindu code gradually began to dominate the national press.[65] The AIWC zealously circulated questionnaires on age of consent, *stridhan*, and succession, and generally expressed faith in the committees for reform among Hindus.[66] There was substantial emphasis on the democratic consultation process of the committee. The AIWC pamphlet explained the notable provisions of the code, and there remained steady correspondence between the AIWC and the Hindu Law Committee.[67] The general male opinion, on the other hand, was largely consolidated against the bill. Agarwal's analysis of the proceedings on the Hindu Law Committee reveals that while 71 per cent women agreed on the curtailment of practices such as bigamy and on the introduction of divorce, only 35 per cent men supported the Hindu Code Bill.[68]

Nevertheless, Hindu law reform was an enduring debate through the process of decolonization, the Hindu Marriages Disability Removal Act, 1946, and the Hindu Marriage Validity Act, 1949, along with provincial legislations on divorce and prevention of bigamy in Bombay and Saurashtra, which had already been enacted before the central legislation. But the Hindu code debate received a firm Ambedkarite stamp in 1947. Bhimrao Ambedkar, the pivotal figure of Dalit politics, by this point also chaired the Drafting Committee for the Constitution of India and had become the symbol of religious reform in India.

---

[64] Agarwal, *A Field of One's Own.*

[65] Hansa Mehta Papers, Draft Bill, 27 September 1942, File No. 32, NMML. The draft code of 1942 recognized a wider variation in regional customary practices than the final version of the Hindu law codified in the 1950s.

[66] Hansa Mehta Papers 1928–42, notes and papers relating to the Age of Consent Bill, the Child Marriage Restraint Bill, the Hindu Code Bill, and so on, File No. 32, NMML.

[67] Ibid.

[68] Agarwal, *A Field of One's Own,* 209.

Ambedkar's Hindu Code Bill's jurisdiction was extended to 'all persons who were not Muslim, Parsi, Christian or Jew'. By naming who the bill excluded rather than who it included, Ambedkar generated a modularity around the code. It was the default family law, unless one was expressly exempted from it.

The bill pronounced on the entire gamut of personal law on marriage laws, solemnization of marriage and divorce, adoption, guardianship, joint family, and contained specific property laws related to succession, inheritance, and women's property, and maintenance.[69] The reform measures also illustrated an insistence on 'uniform Hinduism' (rather than women's rights) as the committee in its revised drafts recommended against even the matrilineal systems of inheritance such as Aliyasanthana[70] and Marumakkathayam.[71]

Ambedkar later clarified that certain customary practices could be preserved, but suggested that this ought to be yielded to on very few occasions.[72] For Ambedkar, only those customary practices which were more 'progressive' (or women-friendly) than the proposed code merited a discussion for inclusion in the bill and recognition. For instance, the Jatt Sikhs also argued forcefully for preserving the levirate (karewa) system as a sacramental form of marriage and even equated it with the 'progressive' ideas of widow remarriage. Ambedkar, however, dismissed the custom as yet another ploy to alienate women from the ownership of property that she stands to inherit as a widow, by forcing her to enter into a marriage with the deceased's brother.[73] Similarly, in the matter of divorce, while Ambedkar was insistent on the incorporation of judicial divorce, he warned that often customary divorce, however simple, was unfavourable to women and simply meant the repudiation of a marriage by the husband and therefore not progressive.[74]

While these initiatives for law reforms were guided by the 'progressives' within communities, this dynamic was transformed when progressive legislation required a democratic sanction after independence. Sezgin depicts India's transition from colonial to independent India's personal legal system as a normative unification

---

[69] See also the discussion on Hindu Women's Right to Property Act (Deshmukh Act), 1937, in Subrata K. Mitra and Alexander Fischer, 'Sacred Laws and the Secular State: An Analytical Narrative of the Controversy over Personal Laws in India', *India Review* 1, no. 3 (2002): 99–130.

[70] Matrilineal system of inheritance practised by the Billava, Bunts, and certain other communities in the coastal districts of Karnataka.

[71] A system of matrilineal inheritance prevalent in Kerala among the Nairs.

[72] Newbigin, *The Hindu Family*, 177–8.

[73] *Babasaheb Ambedkar Writings and Speeches*, vol. 14, Part 2 (New Delhi: Dr Ambedkar Foundation, 2013), 874

[74] Ibid., 269–70, 317. In the final version of the bill, customary divorce as well as levirate were preserved by silence on the subject.

through the constitution, since the institutional unification already existed in the form of unified courts.[75] The birth of the constitution meant that the multiple statutes on religious personal law, unlike customs, had to have some relationship with the constitution. These statutes could be challenged for not just injustice or inauthenticity but also for any incompatibility with the constitution. The debates on social legislations such as the Hindu Code Bill had to be reconciled with constitutional principles.

As the national movement became the national government, the codification of personal law which faced tremendous opposition from the people[76] was re-worded in the national press as a democratic pursuit. Nehru's and Ambedkar's stewardship translated to the support of the prime minister's and the law minister's office, despite substantial opposition even from within the Congress Party on intervention in Hindu law. The promise of modernity and of self-determination also served to co-opt women into state structures, through promises of five-year plans, universal adult franchise, and so on.[77] This phase witnessed the subsuming of the question of women's empowerment into the 'national growth' story, as the influence of the AIWC gradually diminished.[78]

Thus, the fact that the codification of the law was capable of yielding illiberal outcomes and undermined the flexibility of customary law has been well established in the works of Agarwal, Mani, Sharafi, among others, but it is the conundrums within the democratic state over establishing a place for religion in personal life which forms the central intrigue of this book. The reform movements and state-led reforms became far more enmeshed after independence. Democracy brought a constitution (or vice versa) through which the conversations between state institutions and citizens took the form of writs, petitions, and reports, and organizations dedicated to legal aid services multiplied over the years.[79] If the colonial state codified personal law for regulation and surveillance of the subject, post-colonial codification represented attempts to regulate and validate religion.

---

[75] Sezgin, *Human Rights under State-Enforced Religious Family Laws*, 7.

[76] Weekly Report of Political Activities (WRPA), Criminal Investigation Department (hereafter CID), vol. 1948–49, United Provinces, Sub Section 'Hindu Affairs', Police Record Room, Lucknow, UP. See also the Hindu Mahasabha publication the *Hindu Outlook* from 1941 to 1956. Managing editor Indra Prakash, editor V. G. Deshpande, 'Hindu Code Bill Disrupts Family System and Stable Society', 29 November 1948, 'Hindus "Distressed and Disappointed"', Mahasabha Gl. Secretary on PM's speech, 13 August 1951.

[77] Banerjee, 'Whatever Happened to the Dreams of Modernity?', WS2–WS7.

[78] See also Nirmala Buch, 'State Welfare Policy and Women, 1950–1975', *Economic and Political Weekly* 33, no. 17 (1998): WS18–WS20.

[79] De, *A People's Constitution*.

The constitution, however, also brought with it the directive principle of a Uniform Civil Code, or a common code for all family laws. What this meant for the Hindu Code Bill that was simultaneously being revised was unclear. Would a uniform code replace personal laws, or would they continue? What would prevail in case personal law contradicted provisions of the constitution? The vocabulary of secularism became particularly popular in the Constituent Assembly as it was deployed to argue for both the preservation of different personal laws as well as the abolition of personal law altogether. The overtones of Hindu supremacy and Muslim marginalization become apparent in discussions on the fundamental right to freedom of religion, the banning of cow slaughter, the minority report, reservation policies, and so on. This had potential to not just impact, but create new relationships between religious communities. Constituent Assembly debates provide a window into not just the contradictory pressures on the constitutions over family law but also what the terms of engagement were between religious communities at the founding moment of Indian democracy.

II

The Constituent Assembly and the Problem of Personal Law

There were two powerful and contradictory processes that informed the discussion on personal law in the Constituent Assembly. On the one hand, the assembly attempted to retrieve and redeem religion and religious knowledge—a counter-response to the colonial civilizing mission. On the other hand it was guided by the aspiration for a new, modern nation state, and a constitutional democracy. These two divergent themes were brought in conversation through the language of 'secularism'. A number of Muslim members sought recognition of 'difference' through separate personal law codes. This argument was premised on the idea that a 'secular' nation must accept diversity. Many Hindu members in the assembly equated the end of colonial rule with the triumph of indigenous values and sought the universalization of Hindu culture through uniformity in statute—the translation of religious morality to a Uniform Civil 'Code'—a 'law' was itself understood to be an act of secularism. For some, a unified common code was a means of creating conditions for national integration and the end of the rule of colonial difference. They saw that the directive of a 'secular-neutral' Uniform Civil Code as an aspiration for a mature democracy and hoped that universal adult franchise, the universal right to education, and fundamental rights would serve as a solution to all kinds of discrimination (Figure 1.1).

Figure 1.1 Jawaharlal Nehru addressing the House. Dr Sachchidananda Sinha, provisional chairman, in the presidential chair. On Jawaharlal Nehru's left is Mr H. V. R. Iyengar, secretary, Constituent Assembly Sectt. (13 December 1946)

Source: Nehru Memorial Museum and Library, Gallery.

As Pakistan moved towards a theocratic state, 'secular' India also sought a unitary identity.[80] In substantial extracts of the Constituent Assembly debates, the repeated invocation of Hindu religion or religious practices, as most 'liberal', 'sensible', and 'secular', remained notoriously consistent. The violence of the partition weighed heavily on the way a unitary Indian identity was to be imagined, and despite its allegiance to secularism, the Constituent Assembly had not quite worked out the relationship between religion and state. The eager and fervid rejection of Pakistan's theocracy in India allowed for Indian secularism to become anything that was not recognizably theocratic.

Hindu–Muslim riots in the major cities of UP in the same period compounded the sense of suspicion generated around Muslim personal law and that such 'fanaticism' must be contained rather than protected.[81] The vulnerability of Muslims is particularly palpable in Hussain Imam's hard-hitting articulation of the

---

[80] William Gould, *Hindu Nationalism and the Language of Politics in Late Colonial India* (Cambridge University Press, 2004).

[81] Julia Stephens, 'The Politics of Muslim Rage: Secular Law and Religious Sentiment in Late Colonial India', *History Workshop Journal* 77, no. 1 (2014): 45–64.

status of minorities, which reflected the insecurities that the partition generated and also betrayed the asymmetrical terms of engagement.

> It is very painful, Sir, to be reminded every day that we are responsible for bringing Pakistan into existence. In its creation the Congress was as much a party as anybody else. In that spirit I request that Muslims should not be regarded as hostages. They should be regarded as citizens of India with as much right to live and enjoy the amenities of India—the land of their birth—as anyone else.[82]

It was in this backdrop that the debate on a Uniform Civil Code unfolded, where the claims to the 'neutrality' of a potentially universal code were deeply suspect. The 'women's question' was only incidental to discussions on a Uniform Civil Code. Unless the discussion in the assembly was specifically on an issue such as the problem of women abducted in the partition violence, there was overall a poor representation of women as well as women's issues within the assembly. There were some references to religious practices, and the condemnation of purdah (the veil), articulated by the very few, but vocal women members of the Constituent Assembly.[83]

   The discriminatory tones against women's rights in the Constituent Assembly, however, remained apparent. One member, Rohini Kumar Chaudhary, in his concluding speech spoke of the 'fear' he experienced as a man by the 'threat' posed by women. He added a note of regret about the way in which women were 'elbowing out' men.[84] Likening women to the threat of 'stray cows', he stated that there was a need for a provision granting 'protection against women'.[85] This found support from Lokenath Misra who remained a prominent voice in the assembly, who further opined that if women were to compete with men, it would spell the 'end of the glorious Hindu civilization'.[86]

   Although significant women members of the Constituent Assembly such as Amrit Kaur and Hansa Mehta strongly advocated for a uniform family law as well as a Hindu Code Bill, the former remained a directive principle and not a fundamental right and the latter was deemed to be beyond the purview of a non-elected assembly. Personal law, therefore, predominantly became about negotiating the legal space for religion for the majority, and a cultural and political space for the religious minority, and remained irrelevant to any non-religious question.

---

[82] *Constituent Assembly Debates* (hereafter *CAD*); vol. VII, 8 November 1948, Hussain Imam's speech in context of status of Urdu, 304.

[83] See also Subramanian, 'Making Family and Nation', 771–98, for Minoo Masani and Hansa Mehta's speeches on family law in the Constituent Assembly debates. Women's speeches on personal law in this chapter are analysed in the next section on the Hindu Marriage Act.

[84] *CAD*, vol. XI, 1949, 22 November 1949, 791.

[85] Ibid.

[86] Ibid., 798.

Uniform Civil Code and the Muslim Question

It was B. Pocker Sahib Bahadur[87] who asked the crucial question, if the Constituent Assembly was not 'representative' enough to debate the Hindu Code Bill, could it legislate a Uniform Civil Code?[88] This raises other related questions: First, was democracy inherently incompatible with uniformity?[89] Why was the idea of a uniform family law more acceptable to the Hindu conservatives than the Hindu Code Bill? Did uniformity intrinsically privilege majoritarianism?[90] Or was the Hindu code perceived as an onslaught on Hindu culture but a Uniform Civil Code could be a uniform onslaught on all religions, specifically Muslims?[91] Did a Uniform Civil Code as a 'directive principle' and not a fundamental right, assuage these religious members?[92] Could a Uniform Civil Code and different personal laws coexist?[93] Were personal laws protected under the fundamental right to freedom of religion?[94] Most of these questions remained unanswered, but some of these speeches that raised them are considered below to demonstrate why and how personal law became crucial to Indian democracy. The only certain inference from the debates was that there was uncertainty over the understanding of what a potential Uniform Civil Code would entail.

A number of Muslim members in the assembly supported personal laws as a democratic expression of difference, that is, as a 'freedom' and, therefore, a fundamental right. The preservation of personal law here is worded as a compensation for the low representation and political marginalization of Muslims. Hussain Imam argued:

> The majority need not have the safeguard, because they are the majority, and nothing can be passed in the legislature without their full consent and concurrence, whereas,

---

[87] A representative from the Madras constituency, Indian Union Muslim League (IUML).

[88] *CAD*, vol. VII, Tuesday, 23 November 1948. B. Pocker Sahib: 'I know there are great differences in the law of inheritance and various other matters between the various sections of the Hindu community. Is this Assembly going to set aside all these differences and make them uniform?' (vol. VII, 23 November 1948, 545).

[89] Hussain Imam's speech, *CAD*, vol. VII, 546.

[90] Lokanath Misra's speech implied that India would have been 'perfectly secular' without Islam. *CAD*, vol. VII, 3 December 1948, 822.

[91] K. M. Munshi stated that 'it [Uniform Civil Code] is much more tyrannous to the majority'. *CAD*, vol. VII, 23 November 1948, 547.

[92] For an analysis of the relationship between directive principles and fundamental rights, see Gautam Bhatia, 'Directive Principles of State Policy: Theory and Practice', in *Oxford Handbook of Indian Constitution*, ed. S. Choudhry, P. B. Mehta, and M. Khosla (Oxford: Oxford University Press, 2016), 645–61.

[93] Ismail Sahib's speech, *CAD*, vol. VII, 540–41.

[94] Hussain Imam's speech, *CAD*, vol. VII, 546.

the minority have not got this privilege and therefore it is necessary that the personal law of the Muslims and other minorities who so desire should be preserved from interference by the legislature without the concurrence of a vast majority of the members thereof.[95]

Mohammad Ismail Sahib[96] suggested an amendment to the article, which read, 'the state shall endeavour to provide a Uniform Civil Code throughout the territory of India'. He proposed adding the proviso, 'provided that any group, section or community of people shall not be obliged to give up its own personal law in case it has such a law'.[97]

Hussain Imam's and Ismail Sahib's speeches also illustrate that they conceived of a Uniform Civil Code that existed parallelly with personal laws. It indicated that the Uniform Civil Code as an optional statutory alternative was conceivable so long as it did not affect Muslim personal law. Other members proposed similar changes to the clause on the Uniform Civil Code, then Article 35 of the Indian constitution. Naziruddin Ahmad[98] acknowledged that 'pernicious' practices may accompany practices based on religious belief systems. He argued for a positive right to be able to freely practice one's religion so long as there was no violation of the fundamental rights of the individual.[99] Both Ahmad and Pocker Sahib also referred to pamphlets they received from Hindu organizations which also described such 'interference' in personal law regimes as 'tyrannous'.[100]

Maulana Hasrat Mohani, a founding member of the Communist Party, emphasized that religion, culture, and language together constituted personal law, which was derived from the Quran and therefore inviolable:

If there is any one, who thinks that he can interfere in the personal law of the Muslims, then I would say to him that the result will be very harmful.... I say from the floor of this House that they will come to grief [sic]. Mussalmans will not submit to any interference in their personal law, and if anybody has got the courage to say so then I declare ... (interruptions) and they [opponents of Muslim personal law]

[95] CAD, vol. VII, Monday, 8 November 1948, 303.
[96] A Muslim member from Madras of the IUML.
[97] CAD, vol. VII, 23 November 1948, '... if people are allowed to follow their own personal law there will be no discontent or dissatisfaction. Every section of the people, being free to follow its own personal law will not really come in conflict with others' (540).
[98] A member from West Bengal.
[99] CAD, vol. VII, 542–43. Ahmad's Speech: 'Parliament may well decide to ascertain the consent of the community through their representatives, and this could be secured by the representatives by their election speeches and pledges. In fact, this may be made an article of faith in an election, and a vote on that could be regarded as consent' (542–43).
[100] CAD, vol. VII, 23 November 1948.

will have to face an iron wall of Muslim determination to oppose them in every way (Interruption).[101]

Mohani was a known Urdu poet, a self-proclaimed Sufi, a community-Muslim, and famously had deep appreciation for the Hindu god Krishna.[102] It is, therefore, difficult to work with categories of secular, religious, or even presume a right-leaning disposition for people who openly identified as religious. A religious person encouraging a faith other than their own in the assembly was identified as a liberal voice. A strict separation between religion and the state, as argued by member Tajamul Hussain,[103] was then considered a 'radical voice' in the assembly. He moved an amendment (to Article 19 on freedom of religion) towards a model of uniformity closer to one adopted by present-day France, suggesting that '[n]o person shall have any visible sign or mark or name, and no person shall wear any dress whereby his religion may be recognised'.[104] He claimed to be 'hundred years ahead of his time' when he asserted that one's 'name' as a marker of identity itself could lead to discrimination. He rejected the very terminology of 'minority' as a British creation. The defence of religion, culture, and language, and many other identifiers were strung into conversations about personal law indicating that the narrowing of personal law to 'family' may be a later development.

What started as an argument for cultural or religious freedom in the assembly soon began to include support for plurality in law. Exceptions had also been guaranteed to the North-Eastern states premised on the argument of a 'difference in the level of development';[105] reservations for seats or in services based on the recognition of caste difference and provisions for tribes[106] were all indicators of legal plurality based on a diverse understanding of the word 'community'. Thus, different legal realms had to be balanced in a plurality conscious way, which illustrate the inextricable links between religion and the state rather than its separation.

---

[101] *CAD*, vol. VII, Thursday, 2 December 1948, 759–60, Maulana Hasrat Mohani's speech in a discussion on Article 13, Fundamental Rights.

[102] Nafis Ahmad Siddiqui, *Hasrat Mohani aur Inqilab-i-Azadi* (Karachi: Oxford University Press, 2004).

[103] A Muslim member of the assembly from Bihar. *CAD*, vol. VII, 3 December 1948, 819.

[104] Ibid.

[105] *CAD*, vol. VII. Mr Hussain Imam (Bihar, Muslim): '... Look at the Assam tribes; what is their condition? Can you have the same kind of law for them as you have for the advanced people of Bombay?' (546).

[106] The Sixth Schedule of the constitution was added precisely to protect the customs and cultural practices of tribes that inhabited the north-eastern states—Assam, Tripura, Mizoram, Nagaland, Arunachal Pradesh, and Manipur.

While the assembly was amenable to granting exceptions to regions and tribes with respect to family law, local governance, and electoral practices, the articulation of Muslim distinctiveness increasingly became contained within their family law. The dominant Muslim opinion in the assembly remained decidedly in favour of preserving Muslim personal law. Much of the Muslim personal law had remained uncodified and some was contained in a few brief Anglo-Mohammedan statutes. Some of the property laws under Muslim personal law were made redundant as a consequence of the abolition of the *zamindari* system and other land reforms kept 'agricultural land' outside the purview of personal law. Further, tenure laws and revenue rules came about in various states and some central laws.[107] The banking and insurance policies and schemes also did not exclude Muslims despite the concept of 'interest' being *haram* (forbidden) in Islam. Yet the rhetoric in the assembly remained that Muslim exclusivity was the primary force that tripped the Uniform Civil Code and undermined India's secular commitments. The domestic then became the only space for articulation of Muslim politics where distinctiveness could be preserved as 'personal' law, as the mainstream discourses on language, nationalism, and patriotism became imbued with Hindu symbolism.[108] The speeches show that secularism and religion were essentially blurred, therefore the neutrality that secularism bestows on the law would reconcile with the dominant majority with greater ease.

The Questionable Neutrality of Uniformity

I hope our friends will not feel that this (Uniform Civil Code) is an attempt to exercise tyranny over a minority; it is much more tyrannous to the majority.[109]

K. M. Munshi, an influential voice in the assembly, argued that the right to freedom of religion did not necessarily restrict the state in legislating on matters that concerned religion, '[s]o far as it covers a secular activity or falls within the field of social reform or social welfare'.[110] He pointed that the 'hybrid communities'

---

[107] See chapter 5 in Agarwal, *A Field of One's Own.*

[108] For a study of how Hindu symbolism marked seemingly 'neutral' or 'secular' laws following independence, see Marc Galanter, 'Secularism, East and West', *Comparative Studies in Society and History* 7, no. 2 (1965): 133–59. See also Gyan Pandey, 'Can a Muslim Be an Indian?', *Comparative Studies in Society and History* 41, no. 4 (1999): 608–29.

[109] *CAD*, vol. VII, 23 November 1948, K. M. Munshi, member of the Indian National Congress, 547.

[110] Ibid. Munshi: 'Nothing in this article (19) shall affect the operation of any existing law or preclude the State from making any law (a) regulating or restricting ... or other secular activity which may be associated with religious practices; (b) for social welfare and reforms' (547–48).

such as the Khojas and Kutchi Memons followed Hindu customs for inheritance as well as Muslim personal law for other aspects of life, and were dissatisfied when the Shariat Application Act, 1937, was uniformly applied to them.[111] He asked, 'Where were the rights of minorities then?' Therefore, he imagined a Uniform Civil Code as an achievement of modernity, the 'greater good' for which he, as a self-professed liberal, was willing to pay the cost.

Munshi's allegiance to secularism as a 'rejection of religion', however, was suspect. His 'neutral' endorsements of uniformity have to be read alongside Munshi's early writings about Hindu supremacy.[112] While he rose in support of reducing the role of religion in public life, he was himself involved in movements for the rebuilding of the Somnath temple,[113] and had routinely opposed Gandhi's dependence on 'non-violence' as an effective tool against imperialism. In his earlier writings, he favoured the setting up of *akhadas* (an arena for wresting/physical training) for training Hindu men for 'self-defence' and supported movements that spoke directly to Hindu nationalism.[114] Jaffrelot distinguishes a figure like Munshi from Hindu nationalists, terming him a 'Hindu traditionalist', who at best indulged in Hindu 'chauvinism', representing a more benign subset of the Hindu nationalist ideology.[115] The traditionalists, Jaffrelot argues, were co-opted by the Congress as they served to mitigate and temper the demands of the Hindu nationalists and prevented the more extreme form of this ideology from gaining currency.[116] The Uniform Civil Code therefore had the support of many Hindus in the assembly who understood this to be the acceptance of the universality of Hinduism, or thought of neutrality as inherently compatible with Hinduism.[117]

---

[111] Ibid., Munshi, 548. However, as noted in the previous section, the Shariat Application Act of 1937 was not uniformly applied over all the sections of the population that were Muslim.

[112] Manu Bhagavan, 'The Hindutva Underground: Hindu Nationalism and the Indian National Congress in Late Colonial and Early Post-colonial India', *Economic and Political Weekly* 43, no. 37 (2008): 39–48.

[113] The Somnath Temple in the state of Gujarat, by most historical accounts, was plundered by the Turkish Muslims in 1024 or 1026. For the controversy around the temple, see Peter van der Veer, 'Ayodhya and Somnath: Eternal Shrines, Contested Histories', *Social Research* 59, no. 1 (1992): 85–109.

[114] van der Veer, 'Ayodhya and Somnath', 40.

[115] Christophe Jaffrelot, *The Hindu Nationalist Movement and Indian Politics: 1925 to the 1990s: Strategies of Identity-Building, Implantation and Mobilisation (With Special Reference to Central India)* (London: Hurst & Co., 1996), 96–160.

[116] Ibid.

[117] Parashar, *Women and Family Law Reform in India*. See also Ratna Kapur and Brenda Cossman, 'Communalising Gender/Engendering Community: Women, Legal Discourse and Saffron Agenda', *Economic and Political Weekly* 28, no. 17 (1993): WS35–WS44.

Thus, the support as well as opposition to religious personal law was so structured over religious identity that references to family law surfaced in sporadic unconnected speeches, with little discussion on what it was that a Uniform Civil Code would alter.

In a similar vein, the other prominent argument that surfaced was that uniformity was indeed a precursor for unity and integration as a marker of the 'oneness' of the country. Alladi Krishnaswamy Ayyengar[118] quoted the German and the French Constitutions to indicate that uniformity had an indirect link to the prosperity of these countries. He saw uniformity as the harbinger of modernity.

It was a sentiment of the triumph of indigenous or in particular that of Hindu culture,[119] and simultaneously an urge to make religion conform to somewhat secular moralities that enabled a contradictory opposition to the Hindu Code Bill and support for a Uniform Civil Code. For instance, in advocating for a Uniform Civil Code over a Hindu Code Bill, these members did not notice the contradiction between Hindu inheritance laws that did not allow women to be absolute owners of property and the fundamental right to equality (between sexes) enshrined in Article 14. They considered the social realm to be beyond the reach of the law and therefore saw the 'Hindu' Code Bill as the only visible statutory interference with religion, whereas a Uniform Civil Code was but a one-line directive, shrouded in mystery about what it would in fact entail. Uniformity, therefore, represented modernity, solidarity, and tyranny of the majority for different members of the assembly.

Ambedkar as the chairperson of the Drafting Committee, however, affirmed with some finality his refusal to add any additional waivers to the Uniform Civil Code provision:

It is perfectly possible that the future parliament may make a provision by way of making a beginning that the Code shall apply only to those who make a declaration that they are prepared to be bound by it, so that in the initial stage the application of

---

[118] A member from the Madras constituency, *CAD*, vol. VII, 23 November 1948, 549.

[119] In a personal interview with the politician Subramanian Swamy, he said,

See the thing is that the British made it an inferior thing to say that 'I am a Hindu' ... all bakwaas [rubbish] ... they made us feel inferior they were afraid that these *sadhoos sanyasis* [ascetics] might mobilise the public and therefore they tried to make one of them [seem] obscurantist ... and the Jawaharlal Nehru continued that, and it is only now with the rise of the Hindu, the Hindu as a political force. (8 July 2013, New Delhi)

the Code may be purely voluntary ... so that the fear which my friends have expressed here will be altogether nullified.[120]

Ambedkar introduced the element of choice in civil code, which still endures. Ambedkar's activism had historically been premised on the recognition of difference in his emphasis on establishing 'separateness' of the Dalit identity against Gandhi and Congress's attempts to subsume Dalit identity into the Hindu-fold as Harijans.[121] Ambedkar's eventual conversion to Buddhism can be read as a consequence of his exasperation with Gandhian politics and the Congress's attempts to obliterate 'difference' to keep Dalits within the Hindu fold.[122] Pandey observes that Ambedkar's own references to the *shastras* as 'your *shastras*' suggest that Dalits were caught in an extraordinary bind of not even having the separate legal status of a minority.[123] For Ambedkar, uniformity had not implied homogenization. He saw uniformity as a means to decentralize the custody of the constitution, wresting it away from Hindu upper-caste domination. By this point, he was already chairing the Hindu Law Committee, and saw the 'Hindu' Code Bill as inevitable which meant that a 'uniform' civil code would be deferred regardless of the Muslim opposition to it in the Constituent Assembly. Ambedkar had remained sceptical of the embodiment of popular sovereignty in any form and warned against the monopoly of any realm of the state over the determination of constitutional morality. He famously warned, 'Democracy in India is only a top-dressing on an Indian soil, which is essentially undemocratic.'[124]

---

[120] *CAD*, vol. VII, 23 November 1948, 551. Ambedkar:

> ... This is not a novel method. It was adopted in the Shariat Act of 1937 when it was applied to territories other than the North-West Frontier Province. The law said that here is a Shariat law which should be applied to Mussalmans who wanted that he should be bound by the Shariat Act should go to an officer of the state, make a declaration that he is willing to be bound by it, and after he has made that declaration the law will bind him and his successors.

> Ambedkar, however, also pointed out that before the 1937 Act, Muslims in many parts were governed by Hindu law and even Marumakkathayam system.

[121] On Ambedkar, see Shruti Kapila, 'Ambedkar's Agonism: Sovereign Violence and Pakistan as Peace', *Comparative Studies of South Asia, Africa and the Middle East* 39, no. 1 (2014): 184–95.

[122] B. R. Ambedkar, *What Congress and Gandhi Have Done to the Untouchables* (New Delhi: Gautam Book Centre, 1946).

[123] Gyan Pandey, *A History of Prejudice: Race, Caste, and Difference in India and the United States* (Cambridge: Cambridge University Press, 2013).

[124] *CAD*, vol. VII, Thursday, 4 November 1948. B. R. Ambedkar, 38.

Uniform Civil Code as a part of the directive principles for him, therefore, embodied the 'spirit of the Constitution' as justice and equality rather than for solidarity or secularism. Article 44 which read that the 'State shall endeavour to provide for its citizens a Uniform Civil Code throughout the territory of India' was not directly a comment on the relationship between the religion and the state. Nor was such a code specifically limited to family law. Whether or not it was to entail any legislation deserves a different exploration but the wording of Article 44 as an 'endeavour' towards a Uniform Civil Code conveyed a principle rather than practice.[125] The debate on personal law and Uniform Civil Code, however, was one among the many others on cow slaughter, reservation of seats in parliament, and the Minority Commission's Report, which informed the new republic's relationship with secularism and with religion.

'Minorities' and 'Caste': Difference and Constitutional Secularism

Unlike the discussion on Uniform Civil Code, the response of the Muslim representatives to the Minority Commission's Report was consolidated. While Ismail Sahib and Naziruddin Ahmad opposed the report vehemently, some members such as Lari and Begum Aizaz Rasul endorsed some aspects of it and agreed with the removal of reservations and separate electorates. Upon revision, the Minority Commission's Report presented in 1949 ruled out not just separate electorates for Muslims but also concluded against the reservation of seats in the legislature.[126] The assembly considered replacing the very terminology of 'minority' with 'special classes'.[127] While Ismail Sahib and Naziruddin Ahmad opposed the report vehemently, members such as Lari and Begum Aizaz Rasul[128] spoke in support of the removal of reservations and separate electorates.[129] The Minority Commission's Report did little to assuage Muslim vulnerability, even as it did not seek to relinquish personal law.

---

[125] Upendra Baxi, 'Sitting Secularism with Uniform Civil Code: A Riddle Wrapped in an Enigma', in *The Crisis of Secularism in India*, ed. A. D. Needham and R. S. Rajan (Ranikhet: Permanent Black, 2009), 267–93.

[126] *CAD*, Minorities Committee Report presented by V. B. Patel, vol. V, 27 August 1947, 197–251.

[127] Bajpai, *Debating Difference*, 53.

[128] Begum Aizaz Rasul was a member of the Muslim league but she later joined the Congress Party in 1952.

[129] *CAD*, vol. VIII, 282–98. Naziruddin Ahmad while opposing the reservation of seats explained, '... what is more important is that the Hindus have to seek Muslim votes.' 'They will flock to one candidate, or the other and this will lead to division among Muslims themselves on a false issue. I therefore submit that reservation for Muslims would be undesirable' (296).

Political scientists such as Bajpai suggest that while the partition contributed to the reduced bargaining power of the minorities, the dissolution of the Sikh Panthic Party and the disarray in the Muslim League were also factors that contributed to the silencing of dissent in the Constituent Assembly.[130] For Bajpai, Indian secularism entailed a degree of separation between the religion and the state, even while the degree of separation was not as high as that in western democracies. Others have argued that the decision against separate electorates was not rooted in notions of separating the state from religion but on highly contextual grounds that such a separation would sharpen and enhance communal differences and crystallize Hindu and Muslim distinctiveness.[131]

The most pronounced opposition to the question of reservation of seats for Muslims in the legislature, however, came from the Dalit member, Nagappa.[132] Nagappa's speech revealed that notwithstanding the tortuous relationship of Dalits with Hinduism, he identified as Hindu despite the disabilities that the Hindu caste system generated for the Dalits. Nagappa's speech was a scathing attack on Muslim leadership that sought reservation of seats in legislative bodies, which had been extended to the scheduled castes. He insisted that the Dalits or the Harijans truly were the 'sons of the soil' as opposed to being 'the migrants who came from elsewhere'.[133] He vociferously defended his extremely compromised terms of membership to the Hindu community. He said, 'We have been ill-treated for centuries and yet we have been sticking to our religion. There have been some scapegoats who have joined Sikhism and Christianity.'[134] He claimed his 'Hinduness' from having been at the forefront of clashes with Muslims.

---

[130] Bajpai, *Debating Difference*.
[131] Rajeev Bhargava, 'The Distinctiveness of Indian Secularism', in *The Future of Secularism*, ed. T. N. Srinivasan (Delhi: Oxford University Press, 2007), 20–53.
[132] S. Nagappa was a Congress member from the Madras constituency. *CAD*, vol. VIII, 25 May 1949, 291–95.
[133] Ibid. S Nagappa:

> We Scheduled Castes have not invaded this country from Arabia. We have not come here from outside and we do not have a separate state to go and live if we cannot absorb other people. We are not a separate nation; we are the blood and bone of the same religion, same culture, same custom; we are the true sons of the soil.... After all, you are the invaders, immigrants; you do not have as much interest as we have in this country and we are the people that produce the whole of the national wealth of country either by agricultural labour or by industrial labour. (292).

[134] *CAD*, vol. VIII. S. Nagappa, 292. Nagappa resigned from the Congress Party before the first general election in 1952 and joined the Kisan Mazdoor Praja Party (KMPP). He later joined the Congress again.

The speech extolled on the capaciousness of the Hindu religion and invoked Savarkar's ideas of shared soil and blood.[135]

Nagappa's insistence on maintaining his membership to Hinduism overpowered any desire for reservations (although he did argue for the transfer of wetlands to the Harijans),[136] or any recognition of 'otherness' unlike Ambedkar who formally converted to Buddhism in 1956 after his disappointment with the legal reform of Hinduism. Ambedkar's rejection of Hinduism was, therefore, not uniformly shared across Dalit consciousness and politics. Nagappa stated, 'If you are prepared to take to the Harijan community, you must be prepared to scavenge and sweep', conveying his acceptance of caste-determined employment.

The discussion on cow slaughter illustrated the centrality of religious beliefs, but more significantly of caste, in the negotiation of purportedly 'neutral laws' in the Constituent Assembly debates. Congress member Pandit Thakur Das Bhargava took up the issue of cow slaughter during the discussion of the then Article 38-A of the Indian constitution: 'The State shall endeavour to organise agriculture and animal husbandry on modern and scientific lines',[137] a clause purportedly unrelated to religion. Dr Raghu Vira, a member of the Hindu nationalist front, the Jana Sangh,[138] compared cow slaughter to the killing of a learned man, a Brahmin, stating, '*Brahma-Hatya* is equal to *Gau-Hatya*.'[139] He equated Dalits' beef-eating with the murder of an upper-caste Brahmin man. The speech implied beef-eating was, in fact, worse than the murder of a non-Brahmin. Such an argument effectively criminalized the cultural and dietary preferences of Dalits and Muslims. Although the Constituent Assembly eventually made cow slaughter a subject on which individual states (provinces) could legislate, the issue remained a source of tremendous controversy over the decades with potential to trigger riots and incite violence.[140]

---

[135] V. D. Savarkar was a prominent figure of the Hindu Mahasabha and spoke concepts of *punyabhumi* (holy land) and *pitrabhumi* (land of the forefathers), which implied that for Hindus, India was both *punya* and *pitrabhumi*, whereas for Muslims it was only the latter. V. D. Savarkar, *Hindutva: Who Is a Hindu?* (New Delhi: Hindi Sahitya Sadan, 2003). See also Dhananjaya Keer, *Dr. Ambedkar: Life and Mission* (Bombay: Popular Prakashan, 1995).

[136] *CAD*, vol. VIII, 291–95.

[137] *CAD*, vol. VII, Wednesday, 24 November 1948, Pandit Thakur Das Bhargava (east Punjab), 569–70.

[138] The Bharatiya Jana Sangh, or the Jana Sangh, was a nationalist political party formed in 1951 and was the political arm of Hindu nationalist organizations such as the RSS and the Hindu Mahasabha. It was reconstituted as the BJP in 1980.

[139] *CAD*, vol. VII, 575.

[140] A case of mob violence occurred in Dadri, UP, which resulted in the lynching and consequent death of a man, Mohammad Akhlaq, and the arrest of his family for allegedly consuming beef. 'Dadri Lynching: Court Orders FIR against Murdered Mohammad Akhlaq, His Kin', *Indian Express*, 8 June 2016.

Speeches made references to the holy cow Kamdhenu—as the fulfiller of all wants—and invoked the Hindu god Krishna's proximity to cows to argue for a ban on cow slaughter. Members reiterated the value that cows and other milch cattle held to the general way of life and economic wants of Indian people—'a form of Hindu-economics'.[141] Quoting Gandhi, Thakur Das Bhargava declared that 'cow-slaughter and manslaughter are, in my opinion, two sides of the same coin'.[142] Another member, Seth Govind Das, expressed disappointment over the fundamental rights being applicable only to human beings and not animals, since cow slaughter indicated the collapse of 'Dharma'.[143] In support of the ban on cow slaughter, he asserted that untouchability and cow slaughter must be declared an offence simultaneously, emphasizing again the link between Dalits and beef-eating. Not only did he insinuate that the practice of untouchability and cow slaughter were equivalent and comparable but also that only if cow slaughter was banned should untouchability be abolished for those who eat beef. In a certain sense, beef-eating was a marker of Dalit status, as Doniger observed, 'a Hindu is what a Hindu eats'.[144]

Thus, while both caste and religious identities disadvantaged some of the members in obvious ways, the consolidation of opinions over issues such as reservations and personal law aided the development of political communities for negotiation of rights. It prompted alliances with one's oppressors and negotiations between groups than within them. It made identities and groups relevant and therefore bestowed instrumental value to the ideologies of 'secularism' for negotiating freedom, difference, or assimilation.

Habermas in his influential study of religion in the public sphere argued that there is a binary of religious and secular citizens, where the obligation of balancing secular citizenship with religious faith is the responsibility of the citizens who may recognize themselves as 'religious'.[145] Such citizens could participate in public discourses and justify their convictions in religious languages if they could not find secular 'translations'.[146] Habermas's view appears to suggest that citizens who negotiate faith and secular citizenship are not the default citizens, as they attempt

---

[141] *CAD*, vol. VII, 569.

[142] Ibid., 570.

[143] *CAD*, vol. VII, Seth Govind Das, 571–72.

[144] Wendy Doniger, *The Hindus: An Alternative History* (Oxford: Penguin Press, 2009).

[145] Jürgen Habermas, 'Religion in the Public Sphere', *European Journal of Philosophy* 14, no. 1 (2006): 1–25. Habermas borrows the term 'theo-ethical equilibrium' from R. Audi, 'Moral Foundations of Liberal Democracy, Secular Reasons, and Liberal Neutrality Toward the Good', *Notre Dame Journal of Law, Ethics, and Public Policy* 19, no. 1 (2005): 197–218.

[146] Habermas, 'Religion in Public Sphere'.

to harmonize their own sense of religious piety with an outward acceptance of secular citizenship.[147] Habermas's categorization, however, does not necessarily capture the complexity of the *spectrum of religiosity* among citizens as he views the 'secular' and 'religious' as mutually exclusive categories. Moreover, if this categorization was to be applied to the Indian case, 'the default citizen' would, in fact, be the religious citizen who aspired for constitutional secularism in principle, but was unwilling to compromise on shrinking the sphere of religion in the private or public realm. Such a citizen would not achieve a 'theo-ethical'[148] equilibrium (or reconciliation of their religion with secular ethics) by aligning beliefs with secular citizenship. Instead, they would require that their secular citizenship should not disqualify their religious beliefs.

For instance, in Nagappa's case, a just face of Hinduism rather than 'secularism' was clearly more desirable than an absolute separation between religion and the state. Tradition and modernity or even secularism and religion were neither oppositional or doctrinal positions but positions with immense distance in their foundation that could still be convergent on practical conclusions.[149] Thus, 'languages' through which rationalist translations of religion are put forth simply bring religion 'at home with modernity'.[150] Invocations of secularism in political life with simultaneously an acceptance of the centrality of religion in citizens' lives led theorists to argue for multiple secularisms. Multiple secularisms explained the profuse use but uncertain import of the term in the Constituent Assembly debates. Seeking distance between religion and the state was recommended either by those in the Constituent Assembly who believed in a strict church–state separation as a commitment to or a condition for modernity, or those who feared proximity between religion and the state would demean the sacred.[151] Secularism also found an echo in the voice of those who espoused ideas of 'tolerance or mutual respect'; this strand eventually gave way to a broader understanding of religion as a 'way of life' rather than its narrow understanding as 'freedom to practice religion'.[152]

---

[147]   Ibid. See also Jürgen Habermas, 'Reconciliation through the Public Use of Reason: Remarks on John Rawls's Political Liberalism', *The Journal of Philosophy* 92, no. 3 (1995): 109–31.

[148]   Habermas, 'Religion in Public Sphere'.

[149]   Sudipta Kaviraj, 'Languages of Secularity', *Economic and Political Weekly* 48, no. 50 (2013): 93–102.

[150]   Ibid., 95.

[151]   'God is an impartial entity and should be allowed to remain so', Purnima Bannerji, *CAD*, vol. X, 438.

[152]   Shefali Jha, 'Secularism in the Constituent Assembly Debates, 1946–1950', *Economic and Political Weekly* 37, no. 30 (2002): 3175–80.

Bhargava suggests that India was committed to a 'contextual' doctrine of secularism, which advocated 'principled distance' from all religions and 'equal respect for all religions'. This was more than merely a doctrine of 'tolerance' but one that also permitted 'respectful' transformation of religions, even religious reform. Attempts to invoke the universality of Hindu religion in the Constituent Assembly debates, however, suggest that the distance between the state and religion was hardly principled. And the 'way of life' interpretation of religion was applied more favourably to Hindus than to minorities, as seen in the case of the ban on cow slaughter, discussion on religious symbols, and even fundamental rights. For instance, in the discussion on the clause allowing one to freely practice profess and propagate one's religion,[153] Lokenath Misra, a member from the Swatantra Party, attributed the partition of India squarely to the spread of Islam. He claimed, ironically, that had Islam not come to India, it would be 'perfectly secular'.[154] The Hindu nationalist or traditionalist support for a Uniform Civil Code also stemmed from this sentiment of universalizing the majority to eliminate Muslim personal law as 'that small difference that lay between majority and totality', where totality was understood as 'secular'.[155]

Mahmood's critique of secularism allows us to think about whether the insistence on the peculiarities of Indian secularism or identifying its varying degrees allowing the context to transform it essentially hollows out the idea of secularism to make it fit the Indian case.[156] This leads us to the question: was India indeed a secular state?[157] Agrama's critique of secularism also suggests that secularism, in practice, strengthens the state's regulatory capacity and reinforces its role as the adjudicator of religious conflict and simultaneously the protector of religious freedom.[158] Madan's critique of secularism comes close to Mahmood's as he questions whether it was the government alone that was required to keep India's secular institutions intact, or did the term have meaning in everyday lives.[159]

---

[153] *CAD*, vol. VII, 3 December 1948.

[154] *CAD*, vol. VII, Lokanath Misra, 3 December 1948, 822, in a discussion on freedom to propagate one's religion.

[155] Arjun Appadurai, *Fear of Small Numbers: An Essay on the Geography of Anger* (Durham, NC: Duke University Press, 2006), 11.

[156] Mahmood, *Religious Difference in a Secular Age*.

[157] Hussein Ali Agrama explores this question in the context of Egypt in H. A. Agrama, 'Secularism, Sovereignty, Indeterminacy: Is Egypt a Secular or a Religious State?', *Comparative Studies in Society and History* 52, no. 3 (2010): 495–523.

[158] Hussein Ali Agrama, *Questioning Secularism: Islam, Sovereignty, and the Rule of Law in Modern Egypt* (Chicago: University of Chicago Press, 2012).

[159] Triloki N. Madan, 'Secularism in Its Place', *The Journal of Asian Studies* 46, no. 4 (1987): 747–59.

This analysis made the hard-hitting claim that secularism was an elite or a western project, and could indeed be at odds with democracy itself.

Such a reading, however, presumes that secularism was a state-led strategy that undermined the relationship between a citizen and their secular or religious beliefs. In practice, a strict state and non-state binary does not always hold. This becomes even more apparent in the discussions on 'personal' law where state authority is contested and individuals and social movements pledge their commitment to religious or secular ideals, unmediated by the state as the rest of the book will demonstrate. It may instead be a more fruitful exercise to view these debates as the 'making of religion–state relationship' without ascribing any secularization theories to them. The years of the Constituent Assembly discussions (1946–49) saw the transfer of power, partition, and the making of a nation state. The Constituent Assembly's members' visions of secularism therefore were not informed merely by a regulatory impulse, but by events and processes—of the partition and independence. It grew out of concerns for the management of religious conflict and simultaneously of recognizing the democratic sentiment of the centrality of religion in determining public morality. Secularism did not find a mention in the final version of the constitution, but if the state was to be defined by what it opposed,[160] a secular status for India at the time of independence was the negation of theocracy, thus allowing the assembly to escape the need to define secularism or pluralism. Yet the diversity of critiques that the mere vocabulary of secularism enabled, and its sheer overuse, opens a window into its centrality in determining the law and stalling a theocracy.

Towards a Republic

The Constituent Assembly concluded on a congratulatory note, yet there was some regret expressed for the lack of a Hindu character for the new state.[161] Some asserted that the state being called a Hindu state would in no way have offended any one because 'there is no religion on earth which is more secular in character than Hinduism'[162]—a statement which received much applause from the members.[163] For other members, the fundamental right to freedom of religion was sufficient

---

[160] Veena Das, *Critical Events: An Anthropological Perspective on Contemporary India* (Delhi: Oxford University Press, 1995). Das writes that culture is defined by what it exterminates; Das, *Critical Events*, 55.

[161] Austin Granville, 'Settling into the Harness', in *Working a Democratic Constitution: The Indian Experience* (New Delhi: Oxford University Press, 1999), ch. 1, 13–38.

[162] *CAD*, vol. XI, P. D. Deshmukh, 22 November 1949, 776–77.

[163] Ibid., 'Hear! Hear!'

protection for minorities ('what more can the minorities ask for?').[164] Granting the continuation of personal law codes was largely seen as a favour to Muslims despite various such exceptions, such as the Sixth Schedule of the constitution that had been granted in acknowledgement of regional differences.

The Constituent Assembly members, however, found themselves in an entitled and entrusted position as the custodians of law and makers of the modern state. For some, obliterating differences through a Uniform Civil Code was a secular ideal; for others, the Uniform Civil Code was a fiction of a liberal fantasy which would indefinitely remain as a 'directive principle' of state policy than a policy itself. For yet others, who saw personal law as a matter of 'personal liberty' or freedom of religion, Article 44 spelt tyranny. Secularism remained the catch-all phrase that was invoked by the entire spectrum of religiosities (traditional, religious, liberal, or modern). The repeated invocation of a 'secular state' to dismiss or emphasize both the Hindu Code Bill and a Uniform Civil Code drew an exasperated response from Nehru:

> Another word is thrown up a good deal, this secular State business. May I beg with all humility those gentlemen who use this word often to consult some dictionary before they use it? It is brought in at every conceivable step and at every conceivable stage. I just do not understand it. It has a great deal of importance, no doubt. But, it is brought in in all contexts, as if by saying that we are a secular State we have done something amazingly generous.... We have only done something which every country does except a very few misguided and backward countries in the world. Let us not refer to that word in the sense that we have done something very mighty.[165]

Secularism, therefore, was a celebration of non-theocracy, but the place of religion in public life was not challenged by it. Despite the celebratory note on which the Constituent Assembly concluded its discussions, there were a number of unresolved questions with respect to the status of personal law. Now that a Uniform Civil Code was a mere directive, did that mean that uncodified religious practices and customs were uniformly protected under the 'fundamental right to freedom of religion'? If personal laws were protected under 'fundamental rights', how would the courts resolve a conflict between the fundamental right to equality (Article 14) or against discrimination (Article 15) and any religious practice under personal law? Did Article 13(1) of the Indian constitution, which read, 'All laws in force in the territory of India immediately before the commencement of this

---

[164] Ibid., Hansa Mehta, vol. XI, 796.
[165] *CAD*, vol. IX, 12 August 1949, 401.

Constitution, in so far as they are inconsistent with the provisions of this Part, shall, to the extent of such inconsistency, be void', include personal laws? Would personal laws be treated as 'laws in force'[166] or even 'laws'? Or did all 'customs and usage' that had the force of law constitute personal law?

Some of these questions were partly addressed soon after by the Bombay High Court in the now famous case of the *State of Bombay v. Narasu Appa Mali* in 1952.[167] Here, the petitioner challenged the Bombay Prevention of Hindu Bigamous Marriages Act, 1946, on the grounds that it violated the fundamental right to equality (Article 14) since it applied only to Hindus and not Muslims; as well as the prohibition of discrimination (discriminated against Hindus) (Article 15). He further argued that the Act violated freedom of conscience, and the free profession, practice, and propagation of religion (Article 25), as bigamy was consistent with the Hindu family's desire and need to produce a male progeny.

Making a sharp distinction between 'religious faith, and belief' and 'religious practices', the court concluded that the state protects only the former two. The judgment held that personal laws were not included under Article 13(1) and therefore could not be in violation of the fundamental rights. Further, the court observed that bigamy was not a practice 'essential' to Hinduism and therefore to Hindu personal law. Thus, in one stroke, the judgment not only granted perpetuity to the category of personal law but also provided a defence for the reformative codification by upholding the law against bigamy in Bombay. The court observed:

> Article 44 itself recognises separate and distinctive personal laws because it lays down as a directive to be achieved that within a measurable time India should enjoy the privilege of a common Uniform Civil Code applicable to all its citizens irrespective of race or religion. Therefore, what the Legislature has attempted to do by the Hindu Bigamous Marriages Act is to introduce social reform in respect of a particular community having its own personal law.[168]

What appeared to be a liberal judgment at the time has now become an albatross around the court's neck which prevents all personal laws from being tested against fundamental rights by deeming them not quite 'laws', and its legacy over the decades

---

[166] Article 13(b) defines laws in force: 'laws in force' includes laws passed or made by a Legislature or other competent authority in the territory of India before the commencement of this constitution and not previously repealed, notwithstanding that any such law or any part thereof may not be then in operation either at all or in particular areas.

[167] *State of Bombay v. Narasu Appa Mali* AIR 1952, Bom 84.

[168] Ibid., para 10.

is explored later in the book.[169] In many ways, such an observation encouraged the codification of personal law since it upheld the validity of the Bombay statute regardless of the fate of the Hindu Code Bill, which was then under consideration. But the case highlighted the resentment among Hindus towards the codification of Hindu law. It was in this context of disputed definitions of secularism, ambiguous status of personal law, and uncertain implications of a Uniform Civil Code that the Hindu Code Bill awaited enactment.

III

The Hindu Code Bill and the Making of Modern Secular-Hinduism

'GET OUT!'

There is much opposition to Dr. Ambedkar's Hindu Code Bill.

Figure 1.2 'There is much opposition to Dr Ambedkar's Hindu Code Bill' (26 February 1949)

Source: *National Herald*, 26 February 1949.

As the debate over the Hindu Code Bill gained momentum, socialist, reformist, and regional organizations (political or otherwise) collaborated and emerged both for

---

[169] *Shayara Bano v. Union of India* (2017) 9 SCC 1. In the recent judgment on *triple talaq*, the five-judge bench evaded the question of whether *State of Bombay v. Narasu Appa Mali* should be set aside. The 2017 judgment, in fact, skirted around the issue of Article 13(1), and instead ruled the practice of *triple talaq* to be invalid on the grounds that the practice was 'arbitrary' and did not find support in 'Islamic jurisprudence'. Discussed in Chapter 5.

and against the proposed bill.[170] Religious leaders like Swamy Karpatriji Maharaj, among others, with the support of the RSS[171] and the Hindu Mahasabha headed large-scale campaigns against the Hindu Code Bill.[172] In 1948, a new organization, the 'Dharma Sangathan', was formed in connection with the Jana Sangh, which had a single-issue agenda of opposing the Hindu Code Bill. Public meetings and rallies to oppose the bill became extremely frequent, and intensified towards the end of the 1950s (Figure 1.2).[173]

Until this point, the Jan Sangh and the Hindu Mahasabha held a mere six seats in the first parliament, and yet the Hindu Code Bill collapsed. The Hindu Mahasabha and local Congressmen, particularly in UP, were united in their opposition to the Hindu Code Bill and commitment to cow protection.[174] Members of the Congress such as Charan Singh and Purushottam Das Tandon, who were influential voices in UP, began to show antagonism and suspicion towards Muslims after the partition.[175] This resulted in the transfer of Muslim officials from their positions, and the recruitment of Muslims in the police force was also viewed with hostility. The bill brought Nehru in direct confrontation with many Congress members. The disagreement between Nehru and Rajendra Prasad, the first president of the country, over the Hindu Code Bill is well documented.[176] In 1951, Prasad voiced his disapproval of the bill in no uncertain terms, asserting that the move was forcing revolutionary changes upon Hindus, which the Muslims were spared.[177]

---

[170] Except for Bombay and Lahore, the earlier drafts of the Hindu Code Bill produced by the B. N. Rau Committee were largely met with condescension and greeted with black flags. 'Consideration of Hindu Code Bill Put Off: Decision in Union Parliament', *Times of India*, 1 September 1948; 'Marriage Bill for Public Opinion', *Times of India*, 21 December 1952.

[171] The RSS was banned in many parts of India, in the aftermath of Gandhi's death, during this period.

[172] Hindus 'Distressed and Disappointed', Mahasabha Gl. Secretary on PM's speech, 13 August 1951. The *Hindu Outlook*, a Hindu Mahasabha Affiliate. The journal's chief editor, V. G. Deshpande, was also a member of the Lok Sabha.

[173] 'Hindu Affairs', under Weekly Report of Political Activities, CID Files, United Provinces, vol. 1948–49, United Provinces, Police Record Room, Lucknow, UP.

[174] 'Problems Facing the Congress', *Times of India*, 23 July 1951.

[175] Paul R. Brass, *Factional Politics in an Indian State: The Congress Party in Uttar Pradesh* (Berkley: University of California Press, 1965).

[176] Rajendra Prasad to J. L. Nehru, 24 July 1948; Nehru to Prasad, 27 July 1948, *Indian Constitutional Documents*, vol. I, ed. K. M. Munshi (Cambridge: Centre for South Asian Studies, 1967).

[177] Letter dated 27 August 1950, Rajendra Prasad Collection, File 42, Prasad correspondence vol. 14, 104–6. NAI, New Delhi.

For Nehru, the Hindu Code Bill, however, remained a 'serious matter of grave constitutional importance'.[178]

In one way, the Hindu Code Bill was not a debate within a liberal-democracy but rather one of constitutional liberalism *against* democracy. Constitutional liberalism, therefore, bowed to the democratic principle of legitimation as the bill was successfully stalled in the unelected Constituent Assembly. The consistent rejection of the bill despite the concessions made by the Hindu Law Committee and, ultimately, the postponement of the bill by Nehru to the next parliamentary session provoked Ambedkar's resignation in September 1951.[179] The bill was reintroduced after the election in 1952, which was to act as an assurance of democracy but parliament had remained insufficiently representative, and continued to privilege north Indian Hindu upper-caste men.[180]

The effective campaign of Hindu nationalist organizations such as the Hindu Mahasabha,[181] accompanied by the support of influential members of the Congress,[182] necessitated successive revisions of the bill, which was increasingly watered down with each discussion, becoming softer on addressing male privilege. For instance, a clause was introduced to enable brothers to buy out their sister's property, and divorce was included on the condition that this would only be permitted three years after the marriage.[183] Other suggestions included reintroducing aspects of the Mitakshara system of inheritance, particularly those that compromised women's right to property.[184]

What would have been a consolidated corpus of rules on family law was broken down into four independent statutes: the Hindu Marriage Act, the Hindu Succession Act, the Hindu Minority and Guardianship Act, and the Hindu Adoptions and Maintenance Act. The whole had been undeniably greater than

---

[178] Nehru to Rajendra Prasad, 15 September 1951, *Indian Constitutional Documents*, vol. I.

[179] Letter to Ambedkar, 20 March 1949, *Selected Works of Jawaharlal Nehru* Series II, vol. 10 (Cambridge: Centre for South Asian Studies, 1984).

[180] Paul R. Brass, *The Politics of India since Independence*, vol. 1 (Cambridge: Cambridge University Press, 1994). See also Parashar, *Women and Family Law Reform in India*; Derrett, *Introduction to Modern Hindu Law*; and Flavia Agnes, 'Protecting Women against Violence? Review of a Decade of Legislation, 1980–89', *Economic and Political Weekly* 27, no. 17 (1992): WS19–WS33.

[181] 'Hindu Code Bill: Disrupts Family and Stable Society', *Hindu Outlook*, 29 November 1949. Hindu Mahasabha's Publication.

[182] This included not just President Rajendra Prasad, but also Sardar Patel, who implicitly supported Prasad's position but never explicitly confronted Nehru on the bill; J. B. Kriplani and Thakur Das Bhargava were among the other Congress members who opposed the Hindu Code Bill.

[183] File No. 1048, Draft Code, AIWC Papers, 1951, Nehru Memorial Museum and Library, New Delhi.

[184] Ibid.

the sum of its parts. Separating marriage from succession and succession from adoption weakened the collective force of the legislation. For instance, the bill did not make women coparceners in Hindu joint family property, citing that women will also have a share in matrimonial property, which in practice, was rarely ever accessible to women. Certain aspects of succession were linked closely to marriage and in many ways contributed directly to the unequal footing on which women entered marriages. Some members even offered common justifications for dowry, terming it 'women's share in the father's property' and this prevented its criminalization in the bill. After Ambedkar's resignation, much of the momentum and force of the legislation was lost.[185] The codification of Hindu law, however, continued to be largely credited to Ambedkar, who was hailed as the sole force championing Hindu women's rights in India (Figure 1.3).

Figure 1.3 Ambedkar pulling a Hindu woman out of the clutches of Brahminical patriarchy (1952)

Source: *The Tribune*, 1952.

---

[185] *Lok Sabha Debates*, 1954, vol. V, part II, (26 April–18 May), Sardar Hukum Singh's speech: 'This is not the original Bill.... That Hindu Code has practically been given up by the Government.' col. 7253–4.

While the code certainly crystallized privilege of the dominant, and of those who monopolized the authority to interpret religion and convert it to legislation, its more significant implication was that it rendered religion amendable, leaving the door open for challenges to the domination of the elite. The postcolonial state became not just the law giver but also the protector of faith, or rather the protector of state-approved practices of faiths.

Legitimizing the Law with Religion

Hindu law, and Hinduism more generally, which had suffered rejection and chastisement for its archaic 'anti-women' practices in colonial India, became a means for the independent Indian state to legitimize itself through the acceptance of Hinduism in the public domain.[186] Legislators repeatedly invoked the Vedic age, or 'Satya-yug', glorifying Hinduism as an ancient and egalitarian civilization that protected women's rights in a way that no new 'code' could. Such characterization of periods of history as 'dark' or 'glorious' which insisted on the replication of moral codes or political thought of a particular period suggested intellectual idolatry towards a Hindu past reminiscent of nineteenth-century revivalism.[187] Similar arguments had gained popularity too in the nineteenth century, in particular with the work of the historian Altekar who had alleged that the degradation of women was associated with Mughal and colonial rule.[188]

After independence, the state expanded its jurisdiction through consultations with religious texts and scriptures to discover the 'true' and progressive, modern, civilizationally superior face of religion. At the same time, religion was deployed to protect the domestic sphere from 'western influence' as long as citizens tolerated 'state influence'. Controlling personal law was instrumental not

---

[186] James Mill's *The History of British India* and, in particular, the long essay 'Of the Hindus' have received severe criticism for engendering hostility towards orientalism, India, and so forth. Countering this narrative, however, led to the creation of accounts that glorified Hindu tradition, which were then questioned in many feminist writings. See Uma Chakravarti, 'Whatever Happened to the Vedic Dasi? Orientalism, Nationalism and a Script for the Past', in *Recasting Women: Essays in Colonial History*, ed. Kumkum Sangari and Sudesh Vaid, 27–87 (New Delhi: Kali for Women, 1989).

[187] See also Amy Gutmann, 'The Challenge of Multiculturalism in Political Ethics', *Philosophy and Public Affairs* 22, no. 3 (1993): 171–206. Gutmann argues that similar universalistic claims that Aristotle's *Politics* and Plato's *Republic* were the foremost and only starting points for understanding politics or the organization of state amounted to 'intellectual intimidation leading to blind acceptance or unfamiliarity leading to blind rejection', both equally unfortunate.

[188] Uma Chakravarti, 'Beyond the Altekarian Paradigm: Towards a New Understanding of Gender Relations in Early Indian History', *Social Scientist* 16, no. 8 (1988): 44–52.

just to patriarchy but also to maintaining the rhetoric of the modern nation. The means of transitioning religious society into a modern nation state was to make religion consistent with the constitution. This attempted reconciliation made (Hindu) religion extremely capacious as it encroached upon the domain of law and statutes rather than be contained or constrained by them. The lawmakers preserved many aspects of religion, some codified, others deemed 'essential practices' of religion. Some prevailed as custom or personal law and personal law provisions could not be tested against fundamental rights violations after the precedent set in the case of *Narasu Appa Mali v. the State of Bombay*.[189] However, this was a two-way street, modernizing religion rather than separating it from the 'law' came at the cost severing certain religious customs and practices, which was lamented by many who formed the core opponents of the bill. For instance, one of the grounds on which some of the members raised objections to the bill was that the Hindu Marriage Bill interfered with ancient law or the *varna sanskar* and was also attempting to change the sacramental character of marriage by permitting divorce.[190] Members invoked legends of Hindu gods and goddesses, Ram,[191] and Sita[192] to paint a picture of domestic life and consulted texts of the *Manusmriti, srutis, smritis,* and the Vedas as sources of sacred law. The dual commitments of modernizing religion and glorifying tradition and myth produced a law with a wavering link to the divine.

H. V. Pataskar,[193] the law minister, began to tackle each of these objections by arguing that the application of the sources of Hindu law such as *Manusmriti* and Yagnavalakya's *Upanishad* was merely a temporal problem. He argued that the treatise had emerged 'in a particular context in the past' which was no longer relevant.[194] Despite repeatedly expressing his own indifference to the law's link to the sacred,[195] Pataskar could question merely the relevance of the law in a 'changed time and circumstance' rather than question the content of the law itself or how it innately disadvantaged women.[196]

---

189 *Narasu Appa Mali v. the State of Bombay* AIR 1952 Bom 84.

190 *Lok Sabha Debates*, col. 6482.

191 Ram is a Hindu god, the central protagonist of the epic *Ramayana*. He is considered to be the seventh incarnation of the Hindu god Vishnu.

192 Sita is the wife of Ram, who was also in her previous incarnations the wife of Vishnu, and is generally considered an epitome of female or spousal virtue.

193 Hari Vinayak Pataskar, a member of the Congress Party, took over as the law minister from C. C. Biswas in 1955, and presented the Hindu Marriage Act in parliament soon after he took office.

194 *Lok Sabha Debates*, 26 April 1955, col. 6476.

195 Ibid. After facing multiple objections, Pataskar asked: 'Why is it necessary to go at length to find out what the *smriti* may have said a thousand years ago?' (col. 6476).

196 Ibid., col. 6477–78.

On one instance, Pataskar, arguing in favour of reform, referred to a concept in ancient law when wives were 'bought and sold' to highlight the atrocity and redundancy of such practices. This prompted loud interruptions in the house. Upon insistence, Pataskar read from a Sanskrit couplet, which he translated as: 'neither by sale or desertion can a wife be released from her husband'.[197] Members raised sharp objections to such claims about Hindu law and the use of the word 'sale' and there was also a general disapproval for the term 'desertion'. The mention of the word 'released', however, which indicated the absence of the agency of the woman did not provoke any discomfort. Another couplet in Sanskrit which was cited as evidence of arguments against divorce translated as:

> ... once the partition of inheritance is made, once the damsel is given in marriage, and once does a man say 'I give'; these three are by good men done once for all and irrevocably. They have been interpreted as the authority for holding that marriage irrevocable and that it is thus, a sacrament [sic] ... [198]

The phrase 'I give', that commodified women, again passed without inviting any objection; but deviation from the 'indissoluble union' by introducing divorce was deemed disastrous to the 'spiritual heritage that elevates the Hindus from the rest of the peoples in the world'.[199]

On the other hand, the proponents of the bill attempted to justify codification of the law by insisting upon concessions and flexibility granted within the named and recognized religious texts. Borrowing from Rammohan Roy's brand of activism, they recommended reinterpretation rather than a rejection of religion.[200] For instance, B. C. Das suggested that the *shastras* themselves did not claim immutability.[201] The link between the law and the supremacy of the religious texts was not easy to establish but equally difficult to transcend or overlook given that the codification was taking place under the title of the 'Hindu' Marriage Act. In fact, the textual basis for the law was largely rejected rather than relied on, which may be consistent with Hinduism's lack of a central text, but in parliament, it also meant that anecdotal evidence and customary practices with a tenuous link to the divine were tamed, borrowed, and rephrased to argue for or against intervention. Das concluded by saying that those opposing divorce 'stood in the way of development of religion'.[202]

---

[197] Ibid., col. 6485.
[198] Ibid., col. 6492–94.
[199] Ibid., col. 6494.
[200] On liberalism and Rammohun Roy, see Bayly, *Recovering Liberties*, chs. 1–3, 20–84.
[201] *Lok Sabha Debates*, B. C. Das's speech on 2 May 1955, col. 7248.
[202] Ibid.

Another way in which 'the past' was discredited in parliamentary discussions on the Hindu Marriage Act was by arguing that religious law codified in British India was also far from authentic, and thus the current discussion represented an attempt to 'fix' the irregularities of colonial codification. V. Munniswami[203] alleged in his speech that many of the texts codified in British India were merely copied from each other. He claimed that Mulla, Maine, or Chandrasekhar Aiyyar's works, two of which continue to be used as reference texts in court, were potentially plagiarized.[204] Furthermore, these texts contained largely the colonial district court's rulings which were compiled to form the authority on religious law and gained authority and authenticity as the precedents aged. Few people like Munniswami asserted that if the will of the 'Gods' was to decide everything, the courts would be redundant. He concluded that it was 'high time we forget the Vedas'.[205] B. Rachiah too launched a scathing attack on *Manusmriti*, which led to such an uproar that his speech was expunged from the recorded minutes by the order of the chair.[206]

The debates indicated that there remained a deep-seated belief that a religious prefix granted a superior or an elevated status to the law, regardless of whether it was sourced from scripture or custom, and its source did not warrant critique so long as it did not claim immutability. J. B. Kriplani, a former member of the Congress, who later (in 1950) founded the Kisan Majdoor Praja Party, expressed his disapproval of the religion-neutral Special Marriage Act: 'They can have it [a wedding ceremony] without the blessings of a Brahmin [under the Special Marriage Act] but they want to enjoy the goodwill of that [Hindu] name.'[207] He raised questions about who was entitled to write Hindu law, and if it was the 'people of India' that the law minister represented, why did he not title the bill the *Indian* Marriage Act instead?[208] This again hinted at the contradictory idea of lending support to a neutral 'all India' framework of marriage while resisting any specific change to statutes claiming to constitute 'religious law'. For if indeed a priest-less, or civil, marriage was built into a uniform law, would members such as Kriplani endorse such a Uniform Civil Code?

N. V. Gadgil, a politician from Maharashtra who later held many cabinet positions, argued emphatically that he believed that the Hindu Code Bill was

---

203 Member of Tamil Nadu Toiler's Party from Tindivanam constituency in Tamil Nadu. Noticeably, the opposition to tradition often came from members who were neither north Indian nor Brahmin.

204 *Lok Sabha Debates*, col. 7344.

205 Ibid.

206 Ibid., col. 7647. Rachiah was a member of the Indian National Congress Party from the state of Mysore (later renamed Karnataka). Rachiah later joined the Janata Dal Party in 1977.

207 *Lok Sabha Debates*, Algu Rai Shastri, col. 6884.

208 *Lok Sabha Debates*, col. 6482–3.

indeed a step towards a Uniform Civil Code. Quoting Oppenheim, a renowned German jurist, he argued,

> Great are the advantages of codification, especially of codification that embraces a large part of the law.... Many controversies are done away with ... the science of law gets new stimulus. A more uniform spirit enters the country.... New conditions and circumstance become legally recognised. Mortifying principles and branches are cut off in one stroke.[209]

He reaffirmed that religion could be salvaged and its legitimacy maintained only through the sanction of the law, which would cut off its 'mortifying principles and practices', or whatever may appear mortifying to the popular morality at a specific time. J. M. D. Derrett has argued that discontinuities instituted through statutory changes remained superficial as modern legal concepts continued to be informed by the Hindu legal tradition.[210] The codification of Hindu law may be superficial, but it was a crucial modern legal device through which the Hindu legal tradition could be universalized after independence; not clandestinely, but openly and with a certain measure of pride. But while universalization was certainly the hope, the Act was a deeper entrenchment of religion into the family law debate, for from this point onwards, Hinduism could claim the reformed status while maintaining substantial distinctions and exceptions as customs, such as the Hindu undivided family as a taxable entity, and so on.

Religion and law were dependent on each other for legitimacy. Indian liberalism in the 1950s was also essentially not anti-religion. The debate on the Hindu Code Bill was not one between conservatives and liberals, or even Hindu nationalists or traditionalists and the Nehruvians, but rather about whether to source the codification of Hindu law in the sacred or in modern values. Its continuation was not in question. The dominant 'liberal' whose will ultimately prevailed was neither one who rejected religion nor one who valorized ancient tradition; it was one who desired religious reform. The opposition to Hindu orthodoxy in parliament came from the liberal intelligentsia which also attempted to recover upper-caste Hinduism rather than distancing the state from religion. Women's rights, therefore, had to be negotiated within the ambit of what was permitted by, or could be linked to, religion, or simply to popular consensus on a heteronormative family, a good Hindu household, which could always find root in some variation of Hinduism. Even in distancing themselves from religion, members of parliament reiterated the 'intrinsic goodness', 'modern scientific

---

[209] *Lok Sabha Debates*, col. 7291.
[210] Derrett, *Introduction to Modern Hindu Law*.

basis' of traditions, and 'authentic interpretations'. Such a link between religion with modernity allowed it to gain currency in conversations around development and policy.

Divorce as Destitution and Polygamy as Protection

V. G. Deshpande of the Akhil Bharatiya Hindu Mahasabha,[211] an influential voice in parliament, voiced his disapproval of divorce stating that it would spell desertion and destitution for women, as men would discard their wives at whim in order to remarry. He suggested that the solution for preventing the destitution of the wife was 'polygamy', which ensured that the first wife did not become 'disposable' when the man brought home a second wife.[212] He argued that polygamy ought to be permitted in specific circumstances such as if the wife was to become 'ill or impotent' in which case the husband would 'understandably' want to remarry and the Hindu Marriage Act would allow him to abandon the former wife.[213]

The discussion positioned polygamy and the inability to divorce as women-friendly provisions. Thus, 'protections' for women were often aimed at addressing the consequences of patriarchy such as desertion and neglect of the wife rather than patriarchy itself, which would address the question of *why* desertion or divorce disadvantaged women more than men? This invariably would lead to questions about inheritance, succession, and ownership of property. The Hindu Law Committee in 1941 had made this link explicit, '... if a widow is expected to be true to her deceased husband till death, she must be assured of the means of subsistence during her widowhood.' The AIWC in its correspondence observed, 'Succession bill is the magna carta of the Hindu Code Bill fiscal power, necessary for enjoyment of all other rights.'[214] Discussing the significant changes in the bill, the correspondence read:

> The widow of a man would get an equal share along with her children, that is, both with sons and daughters. As such the women who, out of a desire to preserve a larger fortune for their son, as a guarantee for their own future, were against giving a share to the daughter, need not continue to do so, as their own financial security would no

---

[211] He later joined the Bharatiya Jana Sangh and was one of the founding members of the Vishwa Hindu Parishad.

[212] *Lok Sabha Debates*, col. 6469–74.

[213] Deshpande proceeded to describe the three purposes of Hindu marriage, *arth*, *dharma*, and *kaam* (meaning, value, religion (way of life), and sex/procreation). Translation from Hindi: 'It is not only for sex, but also for dharma and for giving birth to sons (putr utpadan)', *Lok Sabha Debates*, col. 6508–11 (translation mine).

[214] Letter from Pushpa R. Mehta, general secretary, AIWC, File No. 209.

longer be dependent on their children in future.... The fear of a son in law a stranger being a disintegrating force is also removed [sic]. The married daughter will now be entitled to claim her share in family dwelling.[215]

The separation of the conversation between property and marriage disallowed an inquiry into the link between women's status in marriage and her compromised inheritance and vice versa, in the assembly. It was precisely this financial independence that would ensure that married daughters would inherit and the obsession with a male progeny could be disincentivized.[216] Yet even when women became absolute owners of property, in 1956, upon her death, a married woman's share devolved to her husband's parents rather than her own.[217] Ambedkar's disappointment with breaking the Hindu code into separate Acts was precisely over this uncoupling of marriage with succession.[218]

A number of amendments suggested that alimony ought to be contingent on the chastity of the woman, and others that listed the benefits of polygamy.[219] Polyandry, which was a prevalent customary practice in Himachal Pradesh, Haryana, and among other specific groups was largely not seen as a privilege, suggesting that if at all bigamy was to be maintained, it would be the exclusive privilege of men.[220] Polyandrous relationships in Haryana and the limited resistance to widow remarriage in these cultures was rooted in practices of levirate marriages to keep property within the family by marrying the deceased's wife to the deceased's (generally) younger brother, which women frequently did not consent to. *Draupadi vivah* (polyandrous marriages) and *maitri karar* (friendship deed or a casual marriage prevalent in Rajasthan) continue as customary practices and rarely ever found mention as problems of 'Hindu law', since the Hindu Marriage Act

---

[215] Ibid.

[216] For a discussion on the significance of gender roles and endogamy in a creating a 'legitimate marriage', see Samita Sen, Ranjita Biswas, and Nandita Dhawan, eds., *Intimate Others: Marriage and Sexualities in India* (Kolkata: Stree, 2011). For the Hindu Succession Act, 1956, see Srimati Basu, *She Comes to Take Her Rights: Indian Women, Property, and Propriety* (New York: SUNY Press, 1999).

[217] The consultation paper of the Law Commission of India published in August 2018 attempted to address this and suggested that the wife's property should also devolve to her parents, but it awaits implementation.

[218] The Hindu Succession Act, 1956, is beyond the scope of this book. For an analysis of property laws, see Bina Agarwal, 'Gender and Command over Property: A Critical Gap in Economic Analysis and Policy in South Asia', *World Development* 22, no. 10 (1994b): 1455–78; and Basu, *She Comes to Take Her Rights*.

[219] *Lok Sabha Debates*, col. 7557, 7830.

[220] For a discussion on polyandrous families in Haryana, see Prem Chowdhury, 'Customs in a Peasant Economy', in *Recasting Women: Essays in Indian Colonial History*, ed. Kumkum Sangari and Sudesh Vaid, (New Delhi: Kali for Women, 1989), 302–36. For a study on Himachal Pradesh, see Leela Seth, *On Balance, An Autobiography* (New Delhi: Penguin Books, 2003).

installed monogamy but conveniently preserved customs under section 29(2) of the Act which read:

> 29 (2) Nothing contained in this Act shall be deemed to affect any right recognised by custom or conferred by any special enactment to obtain the dissolution of a Hindu marriage, whether solemnized before or after the commencement of this Act. (Section 29 (2) of the Hindu Marriage Act)

Thus, the only way to achieve universality or modularity among Hindus, in family law, was ultimately to camouflage diversity as 'customs'. 'Hindu' laws, therefore, could be deemed as reformed, while the uncomfortable practices became the 'customary' exceptions. Similarly, another member, Venkataraman from Madras, argued that the provision of divorce already existed as a customary practice. He cited examples of communities where divorce could be symbolically pronounced merely by breaking a kitchen pot in public.[221] Bombay and Madras already had existing Divorce Acts, but the desirability of divorce remained deeply contested in parliament.[222] When Damodaran Menon,[223] from Kerala, argued in defence of preserving existing practices of divorce, his assertions were met with hostility. He argued:

> I value uniformity but for the sake of it, progress should not be ruined in the Hindu society [sic] ... Why should *marumakkathayam*[224] which is a superior system be brought to this level.... Where divorce can be granted unilaterally finalised in 6 months ... either of them [spouses] can petition the court and there is no trial whatsoever.[225]

> Jangade: (Translation): What does Mr. Damodaran mean by progressive? When he says that easier divorce is better.[226]

'Good practices' whether religious or modern were determined by the north Indian elite, often derived from upper-caste morality. N. C. Chatterjee insisted,

---

[221] *Lok Sabha Debates*, col. 7340.

[222] Ibid. Pandit D. N. Tewary (translation): 'Marriage itself was a progress from anarchy when men and women had unregulated relations. But then society evolved into community and marriage. And now in the name of progress you are again reverting to that system. Divorce is anti-progressive' (col. 7328).

[223] Parliamentarian from Kozhikode constituency in Kerala, from the Kisan Mazdoor Praja Party.

[224] Marumakkathayam literally meant inheritance by sister's children as opposed to sons and daughters. The word 'Marumakkal' in Malayalam means nephews and nieces.

[225] *Lok Sabha Debates*, Damodaran Menon's speech in col. 7930.

[226] Ibid., Jangade's speech (Original: *Pragati ki partibhasha kya hai?*), col. 7945.

'Do not make it [divorce] uniform. Let the backward castes evolve to higher more evolved standard of living, but not force upper caste to comply.'[227] Parliament characterized practices unfamiliar to the north Indian upper castes as immoral. This laid the ground for yet another civilizational battle which followed each clause that did not sit well with the dominant morality of the north Indian Hindu upper-caste male. In the end, neither Menon nor Jangade were pacified, as despite Menon's protest, Marumakkathayam was not retained and overlooking Jangade's objections among others divorce was incorporated.

Civilizational battles lines, therefore, were not always drawn on the modernity–tradition or secular–religious binaries but also along differences. Practices of intra-family marriage, bigamy, and procedure of marriage remained particularly contentious. Arguments commenced over which of these practices could be recognized as pure and codify-able religion and what would be deemed immoral customs. Battles over cultural superiority were enabled by the process of law making but not produced by it. Partha Chatterjee identifies these contradictory pulls within the new republic as critical in understanding the character of the nation. He argues that 'spiritual nationalism' of the colonial era provided a shape and foundation to the postcolonial 'material nation', whereby the spiritual and the material (the private and public spheres, communities and the state, and the subaltern and the elites) 'not only acted in opposition to and as a limit upon the other but, through this process of struggle, also shaped the emergent form of the other'.[228] There was no consensus on how modernity or progress could be translated to law without abandoning religion. This had two consequences. First, that both the proponents of religious law and of modern law claimed to be better protectors of women's rights. Second, both sides misunderstood uniformity as the religionists hoped to contain the 'modern' or the 'western' in the Special Marriage Act, such that Hindu morality could become uniform in other realms of family law. The modernists saw the Hindu Code Bill as a step towards a religion-neutral Uniform Civil Code.

The Bill and Its Beneficiaries: 'The Modern Honourable Hindu Woman'

Who do you think is going to benefit from the bill. Only those few butterflies who wear lipstick and face-powder and roam around here and there and start watching

---

[227] *Lok Sabha Debates*, N. C. Chatterjee, col. 7926.
[228] Chatterjee, *The Nation and Its Fragments*, vol. 4, 12.

films at an early age. Even if their marriages don't work there is no problem. What about those who have four kids and are ill?[229]

The overarching 'women's rights' agenda from which the bill drew its moral force was accessible exclusively to the 'honourable' Hindu female subject and not to women in general. The bill, in fact, served to contribute to the characterization of women as chaste, stoic subjects possessing tolerance and spirit of sacrifice. Even women's 'bravery' or 'courage' was measured by their ability to endure rather than resist.

The debate records instances where even the protection of practices such as sati was advocated for, in the interest of women.[230] N. C. Chatterjee intervened in praise of Indian civilization arguing that 'Indian womanhood is embodied in Sita, Savitri and Damyanti'.[231] Chatterjee's speech further elaborated how the abolition of sati was an imitation of the English, and the custom had been a great boon for women: 'This is what women want.'[232] He claimed: 'A *pativrata stri* (chaste wife) ... will be able to endure, like Sita.'[233] To this, Uma Nehru, a Congresswoman, responded: 'Then men should follow the ideal of Ram.... How do you expect us to be Sitas and Savitris when you are becoming Rakshasas.'[234] Shivrajvati Nehru, another woman member, also brought forth mythical tales of Tara, Ahalya, and Draupadi as models of women who were not conformist, but honourable. 'Honour' remained the underlying precondition for being considered worthy and

---

[229] *Lok Sabha Debates*, Nandalal Sharma, member of Ram Rajya Parishad, col. 7297. Nandalal Sharma was a member of the Akhil Bharatiya Ram Rajya Parishad, a political party founded by the Hindu religious leader Swamy Karpatri who was one of the most active and influential opponents of the Hindu Code Bill and regularly organized protests against the bill through the 1950s.

[230] *Lok Sabha Debates*, N. C. Chatterjee, col. 7698.

[231] Chatterjee further quotes Sister Nivedita:

> the so called tyrannised and tortured Hindu woman is as near perfection as any human can be. Once a wife, always a wife, even if the bond be shared with or remain only in name ... that other men should be only as shadows to her, that her feet should be ready at all times to go forth on any path, even that of death as the companion of her husband, ... Purity in every one of its forms in the central pursuit of Indian life. (*Lok Sabha Debates*, col. 6848)

[232] Ibid. Renu Charkravarty responded to Chatterjee, 'I have worked with women who want to start their lives again' (col. 7698–7711).

[233] Ibid., col. 7733. See also the Bombay High Court observation by P. B. Majumdar and Anoop Mohta, in 2012, where the bench suggested, 'Women should be like Goddess Sita' and follow their husbands.'

[234] Ibid., col. 7733 (*rakshasas*: monsters or demons, translation mine.)

deserving of rights. Women's politics remained firmly within what Forbes termed as the 'politics of respectability'.[235]

The speeches expressed disdain for the 'progressive woman', citing rather specific anecdotes of an actress in Bombay who married a Muslim, stayed with him a few months only to realize that her husband had given her unilateral talaq (divorce).[236] The speeches demonized the 'progressive woman', as a home-wrecker who is also vulnerable to exploitation by Muslims. In one stroke, this conveyed civilizational superiority and valorized a conformist imagination of a woman. Deshpande argued:

> A learned male gets married and then a few days later a learned woman comes along and destroys that household ... women should be punished for ruining married life of people, this bill is allowing them to do this.[237]

Many in parliament deemed equality of education between men and women as dangerous and undesirable for the institution of marriage. The significance of gender in shaping the notions of community and marriage has been explored extensively in scholarship.[238] Chakravarty's analyses of the scripture *Satpatha Brahmana* reveals a similar premise, as it warns men of women's adulterous tendencies and also prescribes punishments such as forcing unfaithful wives to eat pickled cow dung.[239] Echoing that sentiment, Deshpande, in his speech, also expressed 'concern' that women, who innately were distrustful beings, would now take advantage of the divorce clause in order to approach married men. Therefore, the possibility of men divorcing 'honourable and innocent' wives and educated women divorcing incompatible husbands generated substantial anxiety in parliament.

Women who spoke largely in support of the bill had their speeches frequently interrupted by verbal attacks, insults, mockery, and sarcasm.

---

[235] Geraldine Forbes, 'The Politics of Respectability: Indian Women and the Indian National Congress', in *The Indian National Congress: Centenary Hindsights*, ed. D. A. Low (New Delhi: Oxford University Press, 1988), 54–97.

[236] *Lok Sabha Debates*, col. 6525–6.

[237] *Lok Sabha Debates*, Deshpande, col. 6511.

[238] Rajeshwari Sunder Rajan, *The Scandal of the State: Women, Law, and Citizenship in Postcolonial India* (Durham, NC: Duke University Press, 2003); Kumkum Sangari, 'Politics of Diversity: Religious Communities and Multiple Patriarchies', *Economic and Political Weekly* 30, no. 51 (1995): 3287–310.

[239] Uma Chakravarti, 'Conceptualising Brahminical Patriarchy in Early India: Gender, Caste, Class and State', *Economic and Political Weekly* 28, no. 14 (1993): 579–85.

Subhadra Joshi retaliated with a sharp attack on Deshpande's speech, asserting that parliament should be 'ashamed of the state of educated women in the country'.[240] Joshi made bold assertions that women should rewrite the *shastras* and that the institution of marriage had become like that of prostitution because women had no agency to deny sex and no means to exit a troubled or even a violent marriage since they had no financial or social support outside of marriage. The most radical voice of a woman in parliament received the most brutal shunning. These observations resulted in an absolute disorder in the House, with members demanding that her speech be expunged from the official records.[241] Joshi raised many other issues about women's consent in marriage and choice of partner, but her speech was drowned in the commotion stemming from the 'prostitute comment'.

Sucheta Kriplani[242] of the Kisan Majdoor Praja Party, another important female voice in parliament, supported the bill as a necessary step towards a Uniform Civil Code, the absence of which she attributed to the 'minority problem'.[243] In arguing for economic independence for women, she alluded to the contribution of Rajput (upper-caste) women to the freedom struggle, and further condemned Joshi, who had compared a married woman to a prostitute. The beneficiary of the bill, therefore, remained a woman who was 'honourable' and not 'promiscuous film actresses' or 'prostitutes' or 'lipstick-wearing, movie-watching butterflies', since they were 'very different from the honourable girls in our households'.[244] The macro dynamic within a household and sexual division of labour remained intact, with the 'modern' woman viewed as a victim of inauthentic western values.[245] This is reflected in the general policy orientation of the state towards

---

[240] *Lok Sabha Debates*, col. 6526.

[241] Ibid.

> Thakur Das Bhargava: Maybe she means women are not treated properly. She did not mean it.
> Chairman: She did not mean it.
> Another member: This is vulgar language! (col. 6527–8)

[242] Sucheta Kriplani later joined the Congress and became the first woman to serve as the chief minister of UP from 1963 to 1967.

[243] *Lok Sabha Debates*, Sucheta Kripalani, col. 7274.

[244] Ibid.

[245] *Lok Sabha Debates*,

> Shivrajvati Nehru: Although we have been guaranteed equality in the Constitution but the society has a different perception of it which requires sacrifice, service and women-dharm and responsibilities are tied to a woman.
> R. K. Chaudhary: You are lamenting this? (col. 6897)

women which was limited to household- and motherhood-oriented welfare schemes. Their empowerment was not an end in itself but rather a contribution towards the making of a better nation, community, or society.[246]

The bill nonetheless targeted the exclusion of the institution of the family from the political, and somewhat successfully dented the shield of the 'personal' that preceded family law. For instance, Shivrajvati Nehru[247] recommended marriage registration to curtail dowry, which brought to light the burden of marriage expenses on the woman's family. Even practices such as bigamy, which had an implicit sanction on the pretext of preventing desertion, began to be questioned through examples and evidence of dissatisfied women produced before parliament.[248] B. C. Das questioned, 'Would a bigamous household where a concubine is installed be ideal for children or ensure the happiness of the first wife?'[249] Renu Chakravarti of the Communist Party pointed to the unequal right to inheritance for women and expressed her disapproval of the pamphlets circulated by the Hindu Mahasabha, announcing, 'We do not want to be Devis (Goddesses) we want to be human beings equally respectable as men.'[250] The success of the Hindu Code Bill debates lay in the fact that it called to question the privatization of discrimination within households, even if it did not successfully address this discrimination or its basis in religious morality.

Despite these attempts, however, the assembly did not concede to any change in the core patriarchal moral framework of marriage, which was reinforced by the fact that parliament ultimately preserved the restitution of conjugal rights, a colonial inheritance, with little discussion.[251] By contrast, there was unyielding opposition to the idea of cross-cousin marriages and uncle-niece marriages, which

---

[246] Banerjee, 'Whatever Happened to the Dreams of Modernity?' Banerjee discussed a speech by Nehru at a women's college in New Delhi in 1950 where he mentioned that women's education was important for making 'better homes, better family and better society'. Banerjee, therefore, argued that women's education was not an end in itself.

[247] Shivrajvati Nehru was the first women member of parliament from Lucknow, UP, and a distant kin of Jawaharlal Nehru.

[248] *Lok Sabha Debates*, Shivrajvati Nehru's speech, col. 6898.

[249] Ibid. B. C. Das, col. 7248.

[250] Ibid. Renu Chakravarti, col. 7250.

[251] The Indian physician Rukhmabai had famously refused to cohabit with her husband with whom she had married as a child. The case *Bhikaji v. Rukhmabai*, 1885, brought to light that Hindu women historically had the right to deny sexual intercourse to their husbands but under the British law of the 'restitution of conjugal rights', Rukhmabai's husband demanded her return to her matrimonial home. The public debate ultimately prompted the 'Age of Consent' Bill. Sudhir Chandra, 'Rukhmabai: Debate over Woman's Right to Her Person', *Economic and Political Weekly* 31, no. 44 (1996): 2937–47.

were common practices among Hindus in certain parts of southern India.[252] Arguably, intra-family marriages offered relatively better protection of property rights for women and in such cases brides would be better protected against exploitation as they were familiar with their matrimonial homes prior to the marriage.[253] Members such as Pandit Thakur Das Bhargava and U. M. Trevedi, both of whom represented constituencies in northern India, took firm positions against cross-cousin marriages within 'prohibited degrees of relationships' (*sapinda*)[254] referring to it as 'incest', and deeming such alliances to be 'unhygienic'.[255] Rama Rao of the Communist Party of India asked parliament to reconsider such a marriage under the Special Marriage Act.

> I want to appeal to our North Indian friends to not have a stone curtain before their eyes and look beyond the Vindhyas and understand the customs and laws of the South Indians.... Most of our thinking is conditioned by the things that we are used to.... Law minister with his prejudices even calls it 'promiscuous living together' I object vehemently to this.[256]

This plea was also rejected and Rama Rao was accused by fellow members for attempting to dilute the Special Marriage Act. All claims the participants made towards 'authentic' preservation of religion in law served only to create a limited legislation which, nonetheless, remained vulnerable to dissent given that codified religion was now also 'amendable'. Upon reconsideration, the exception for prohibited degrees of relationships was added as one of the last provisions to be included in the Act.[257]

---

[252] Cross-cousin marriages were also prevalent among Muslims and Christians in India.

[253] R. D. Baird, ed., *Religion and Law in Independent India* (New Delhi: Manohar Publishers & Distributors, 2005).

[254] Relative or kin connected by ties of consanguinity.

[255] *Lok Sabha Debates*, col. 7783, 7779, 7810.

[256] *Lok Sabha Debates*, Special Marriage Act, vol. 1954, col. 1214:

> Rama Rao: People in south India marry their maternal uncles' daughters. [*sic*] [marry their daughters to the maternal uncles of their daughters]. This is prohibited in the list and is very common in South India. Therefore, if you give people the permission to marry under one system of law why not allow people to marry under another system if they want to.

[257] Section 5 clause (iv): 'the parties are not within the degrees of prohibited relationship unless the custom or usage governing each of them permits of a marriage between the two'; and (v): 'the parties are not *sapinda*s of each other, unless the custom or usage governing each of them permits of a marriage between the two'.

While some such as Sardar Akarpuri lamented the application of the bill to communities such as the Sikhs without a consideration of their differences,[258] others such as Pandit Fotedar regretted that the Hindu Marriage Bill did not apply to the Hindus of Kashmir, a province that was granted exceptional status owing the territorial dispute with Pakistan. Nehru's speech conclusively changed the mood of parliament towards the bill. He made a case for the 'dynamic nature of law' condemning the moral high ground and cultural supremacy sought by religionists (*sanatanists*).[259]

The Hindu Marriage Act, 1955, once enacted applied to all marriages between persons of any region or religion, who were not Muslim, Christian, or Parsi. At this, Pataskar, the law minister, expressed his satisfaction claiming that the acceptance of the jurisdiction of this statute was achieved with less than minor opposition, which was dismissed as 'some indirect fling from quarters which was too feeble to even be noticed—unless one was careful enough to watch'.[260]

It can be concluded that although the dominant north Indian upper-caste male had indeed won the civilizational battle after independence, the Hindu personal law was prevented from becoming a site for Hindu nationalism owing to the tortuous link of the law to the divine, the insistence on presenting a 'modern' face of religion and, importantly, its Nehruvian stamp. Galanter argues that the link to the divine was so suspect that the enactment of the Hindu family law had practically 'displaced' indigenous law.[261] Menski, however, shows that the customary aspects of the Hindu law continued to dominate not just the lives of ordinary citizens but also their understanding of the law as rooted in Dharma, and dominant Hindu morality extended far beyond personal law, and the situation specificity of traditional law was never replaced by statutes and codes.[262] In stressing continuity, such an approach may miss the transformations, for it was not the case of the law replacing religion, but entering into a dialogue with it, and transforming

---

[258] *Lok Sabha Debates*, Sardar Akarpuri: 'If Muslims law is shown such deference, then why should Hindu personal law not be shown the same deference. If this is not done then please exclude the Sikhs from it. The house has no authority to pass this right [of divorce] it should be conferred on women only. Because man by nature is lustful' (col. 7466–71, translation mine).

[259] *Lok Sabha Debates*, J. L. Nehru, col. 7956–63.

[260] Ibid., Pataskar, col. 7428.

[261] Galanter, 'The Displacement of Traditional Law in Modern India', 65–90.

[262] Werner Menski, *Hindu Law: Beyond Tradition and Modernity* (New Delhi: Oxford University Press, 2003) and Werner Menski, 'From Dharma to Law and Back? Postmodern Hindu Law in a Global World', Working paper no. 20, Heidelberg Papers in South Asian and Comparative Politics, 2004.

the debates on religion in the years to come. The paradox of a modern, irreligious, and yet 'Hindu' law favoured a relationship between religion and the state where religious reform was firmly placed within the purview of the new nation state. The state incentivized religious reform in a way that religious leaders as well as reform movements would route their agendas through state legislatures for recognition and perpetuation.

The Special Marriage Act—A Footnote

> I do not understand these sanatanists who believe in castes and communities but are so insistent on a unified civil code.[263]

The simple answer to Dabhi's query in the discussions on the Hindu Marriage Act was that the potential of the Uniform Civil Code was grossly misunderstood at this point in history. The idea of 'uniformity' to some meant religious neutrality and to others meant Hindu universalism and yet others believed that the intervention would leave customs intact and the domestic space untouched. The Special Marriage Act, potentially a template for a Uniform Civil Code, which replaced the British Special Marriage Act of 1872, operated on premise that intercommunity marriages were rare, if not anomalous. Although enacted a year before the Hindu Marriage Act, a 'special marriage' became that residual category which included all those whom the 'default', intra-community, intra-caste partnerships could not accommodate. This was apparent in the continued insistence of many members of parliament on raising the age of consent for such a marriage in order to restrict the scope of the Act.[264] The Special Marriage Act was also made impervious to recognizing customary practices, in the name of neutrality,[265] fearing that 'there will be no end to concessions to all sorts of customary laws and the spirit of the bill will be lost';[266] the spirit of the bill being its lack of religiosity.

Members of the Hindu Mahasabha who indicated their disapproval of the Special Marriage Act such as V. G. Deshpande stated that '[t]he woman who uses this Act enters her matrimonial home with a red flag of revolution, revolting against

---

[263] T. F. Dabhi was a member of parliament as an independent candidate. He later joined the Swatantra Party. *Lok Sabha Debates*, col. 6882.

[264] *Lok Sabha Debates*, Special Marriage Act, 3 September 1954, col. 963–86.

[265] *Lok Sabha Debates*, Biswas: '... do not make a mockery of this Bill ... therefore in a scheme of this nature there can be no room for any customary variations so far as prohibited degrees of relationships are concerned' (col. 1219).

[266] *Lok Sabha Debates*, Dr Jaisoorya's speech, col. 1226. M. S. Gurupadaswamy: 'The purpose of a statutory enactment is to reduce the scope of customary law' (col. 1238).

Manu and Yagnavalakya, against the wishes of her father'.[267] N. C. Chatterjee further opined, 'The people in the villages, the rural population won't be touched by this Act.'[268]

For Hindus opting for the Special Marriage Act, the Act did not threaten their membership to the Hindu community. It was, after all, merely a list of practices that were 'frowned upon', and claimed no connection with the divine. Weeding out what parliament recognized as redundant customs from religion, therefore, not only transformed religion but also informed definitions of 'neutrality'. 'Immorality' could be tolerated under a different irreligious title and therefore even divorce provisions within the Act were deemed acceptable without much protest. Pandit K. C. Sharma, in his speech, offered a peculiar reasoning:

> The nature of marriages that will take place under the Special Marriage Act, the child [born to such a marriage] will prove to be a burden for both the partners and you can understand what the state of this child will be, who after being given birth to will be loved/wanted by neither this mother or father.[269]

The Special Marriage Act, 1954, enabled cross-community marriages or 'special'[270] marriages, which were not just rare but were treated as 'unworthy' of a religious law code as it entailed 'abductions and seductions'.[271] The recognition of women as absolute owners of property would have a bearing on their agency in choosing a partner. Therefore, fears about granting women property rights were also rooted in the threat of exogamy. Granting women a 'choice' in deciding their partners was presumed to be synonymous with irreligion, which conversely made the survival of religion contingent on denial of such a choice.

The Special Marriage Act, 1954, introduced an option to marry across communities without conversion of religion. The Special Marriage Act was, therefore, a crucial intervention that provided, however reluctantly, a 'legal' means to enter into exogamous relationships and to opt out of personal laws. Inter-community marriages became politically controversial in later decades when discouraging such marriages became a part of an open electoral agenda. The Hindu Mahasabha's propaganda against marriages of Hindu women to Muslim men was reworded as 'Love-Jihad' which alleged 'forced or fraud conversion' of

---

[267] Ibid., V. G. Deshpande, col. 1162 (translation mine).

[268] Ibid., col. 971.

[269] Ibid., col. 1137 (translation mine).

[270] Ibid., Pandit D. N. Tiwari (translation): 'Do not make the mistake of comparing this with religious marriages' (col. 1174).

[271] Ibid., V. G. Deshpande, col. 1163.

Hindu women through marriage.[272] The idea that a woman was presumed to have converted her religion upon marriage not only compromised women's position within marriage but also rendered her identity fluid, something that could be captured and changed. Marriage could, therefore, not only elevate or denigrate the class status of women but could bestow or deny her rights under the various personal laws.[273]

The call for compulsory registration of marriages has been made from even within feminist organizations and women's groups and echoed in Law Commission reports[274] and lower court orders;[275] however, the provision has remained contained within the Special Marriage Act alone. The suspicion around the Act led to provisions of surveillance such as the verification of the marriage after 30 days of registration which is frequently used by the families of eloping couples to harass and track them down.[276] In extreme cases, this has led to murders and honour killings. Yet the state remained suspicious of irreligious marriages and, procedurally, the Special Marriage Act continues to be tedious.

Conclusion

The colonial state's attempts to classify individuals into recognizable and manageable groups could be rooted in, at best, arguments of convenience and ease of governance and administration and, at worst, in arguments of civilizational superiority. Evolving from the civilizational battle between tradition and modernity in the colonial period, the Hindu Code Bill, once enacted, was an example of an upper-caste civilizational euphoria. Civilizational superiority did not completely wither away but began to operate alongside these new discourses. Competing moralities of different castes and regions were also played out as competing modernities rather than tradition versus modernity and also as tradition versus 'pure' tradition, textual tradition, and so on. And these had the potential of becoming resources

---

[272] See Chapter 5.

[273] See also B. R. Ambedkar, *Annihilation of Caste: An Undelivered Speech* (New Delhi: Arnold Publishers, 1990), paragraphs 16.8 and 16.9 where Ambedkar questions how the fourfold (*chaturvarna*) caste system understands the identity of women if their caste is deemed to be changed upon marriage.

[274] Law Commission Report 270 'Compulsory Registration of Marriages'.

[275] *Shashi v. PIO Sub-divisional Magistrate Civil Lines*, CIC/SA/A/2016/001556, in consultation with the organization, People for Law and Development. Similar concerns were voiced by a Lucknow-based organization's (Advocacy and Legal Initiative's) study in Jharkhand.

[276] Consultation with People for Law and Development (PLD), 5 July 2018.

for democratic discussion rather than simply as differences or the inconvenience of diversity that had to be overcome.[277] Democracy somewhat helped bridge the separation between socio-legal and political spheres that colonialism had maintained as separate.

The Constituent Assembly debates suggest that it was through discussions on personal law that the doctrine of secularism began to be reshaped in post-independence India. The question of personal law allowed for a public debate on religion in the legal universe. These debates also reveal that the assembly never laboured over the definition of a Uniform Civil Code and there was generally a sense of uncertainty that prevailed around Article 44. Ambedkar's defence of the clause was rooted in more normative objectives and the potentiality of the code,[278] rather than its interpretation in absolute and narrow terms of the imposition of uniformity. Influential scholarship on modern secularism emphasizes that the state's regulation of religion by deepening a public–private divide often produces a caricatured version of religion on statute. They show that religious personal law tries to be simultaneously old and authentic, as well as modern and progressive, causing a tension between popular democratic sentiment and the promise of reform. This, however, in the longer run makes religious family law an arena where the authority of the state can be contested, and alternative religious or non-state jurisdictions become powerful, ultimately undermining the very public–private divide the secular state purportedly hoped to create.

By addressing the role of religion in the domestic sphere through personal laws, the nascent state entered into an intimate relationship with the citizen. The Hindu Code Bill was the state's way of expanding its own authority by prefixing laws with religious nomenclatures. Religion was deployed to control the domestic and, subsequently, religion was protected by the state precisely to maintain control over the citizen's 'personal' life. State authority was legitimized by offering a law that did not overtly oppose religion. On the other hand, bills governing family law that did not seek religious prefixes, such as the Special Marriage Act, 1954, evoked little concern and were concluded in haste with the hope that these would govern a small category of non-religious citizens.

It has frequently been argued that reform measures in postcolonial societies were met with enthusiasm, but acquired new meanings only to reinforce existing

---

[277] Nivedita Menon, 'State/Gender/Community: Citizenship in Contemporary India', *Economic and Political Weekly* 33, no. 5 (1998): PE3–PE10.

[278] Peter Ronald D'Souza, 'Politics of the Uniform Civil Code in India', *Economic and Political Weekly* 50, no. 48 (2015): 50–7.

forms of domination.[279] While the debates on the Hindu Marriage Act endorsed a model of the family that left caste and gender hierarchies unchallenged, they also put in place the mechanism for further interventions which could be worded as amendments to a statute rather than challenges to Brahminical patriarchy alone. Once inequalities became legally enforceable, they also become visible and opposable through the instruments of the law and could be challenged in courts, in federal legislatures, and also individual clauses could become points of opposition around which social and religious protests could emerge as the next chapter will illustrate.

---

[279] Akhil Gupta, *Red Tape: Bureaucracy, Structural Violence, and Poverty in India* (Durham, NC: Duke University Press, 2012).

2

Committees, Codes, and Customs

Renegotiating Personal Law, 1957–69

Marriage is the basis of the family and family is the basic unit of a society. We should not by legislation do anything which may shake the foundations of our society to their very root. The path to promiscuity should not be opened out.
—Central government to Madras government, 1967[1]

Throughout its history, the pushback against the state's imagination of marriage (often shared with ways of the elite) has come from multiple stakeholders—individuals, activists, the women's movement, anti-caste movements, or even provincial/state governments. Yet the theorization of personal law regimes has tended to focus on particular legislations and cases such as the Hindu Code Bill debates in the 1950s or the *Shah Bano* case and the subsequent Muslim Women (Protection of Rights on Divorce) Act of 1986 as watershed moments.[2] The excessive focus on legislative changes or landmark judgments in personal law produces an incomplete narrative of debates on family law, as it ignores the various unsuccessful attempts towards creating new legislation, which nonetheless contributed significantly to the political and social discourse. This chapter explores the role of various state-led initiatives in recognizing, validating, reforming, or modifying customary law and ritual practices in Hindu, Muslim, and Christian family law in the 1960s, in the aftermath of the Hindu Family Law Acts.

---

[1] Central government to the Madras government on the Hindu Marriage (Madras Amendment) Act, 1967, File No. 17/61/67, Judicial I, Ministry of Home Affairs, National Archives of India (hereafter NAI), New Delhi, 13.

[2] Rochana Bajpai, *Debating Difference: Group Rights and Liberal Democracy in India* (New Delhi: Oxford University Press, 2011); Zoya Hasan, 'Gender Politics, Legal Reform, and the Muslim Community', in *Appropriating Gender: Women's Activism and Politicized Religion in South Asia*, ed. P. Jeffery and A. Basu (New York: Routledge, 1998), 71–88; Vrinda Narain, *Reclaiming the Nation: Muslim Women and the Law in India* (Toronto: University of Toronto Press, 2008); and Narendra Subramanian, *Nation and Family: Personal Law, Cultural Pluralism, and Gendered Citizenship in India* (Stanford: Stanford University Press, 2014). Subramanian's study traces some of the developments in minority personal laws since the 1970s, but largely views the 1960s as decades that were silent on personal laws of Muslims and Christians.

The various commissions, committees, and bills which attempted to amend Muslim and Christian family laws highlight the consistency of the state's concern and interest in codification. Law Commission reports on Christian marriage law and Muslim personal law illustrate also that these seemingly 'unsuccessful' attempts to spark legislative change were in fact transformative. The chapter probes the question, when and how is law reform deemed a success or a failure? The latter half of the chapter analyses how the state also confronted the diversity within Hinduism, as regional customs and practices were incorporated through amendments in different provinces. These parallel narratives of Christian, Muslim, and Hindu personal laws reveal the looming shadow of the Hindu Code Bill on family law debates.

As early as 1960–62, the Law Commission considered amendments to Christian marriage laws, and to the Indian Divorce Act of 1869.[3] Despite multiple attempts by the national government, the bill for amending Christian marriage laws lapsed by the third Lok Sabha (1962–67). It was not introduced by the subsequent government owing to objections raised by a number of Christian organizations, in particular the Catholic Church.[4] Consultations in committees and commissions, therefore, increasingly began to serve as the 'safety-valve' for absorbing civil society movements and any demands for change within religious communities. This chapter will reveal that these quasi-government bodies did not always lead to any concrete change in the law, and often succumbed to pressures of the more orthodox sections of religious communities. Yet they remained buffer zones for storing future legislations and became the paradigm for legal and democratic change.

In 1963, Nehru responded to the recommendations of another Law Commission report on the Convert's Marriage Dissolution Act, and instituted a committee for the specific purpose of bringing reforms in Muslim personal law.[5] While Nehru's support of the Hindu Code Bill has often been considered more symbolic than substantial,[6] his commitment towards the codification of personal laws can be seen to have extended well beyond Hindu law. Identical, however, to the fate of the Law Commission reports on Christian marriage law, the committee on Muslim personal law was also shelved before the introduction of a bill in parliament to effect any change. The committees provided a semblance

---

[3] 15th Report, 2nd Law Commission of India, 1960.
[4] 22nd Report, 2nd Law Commission of India, 1961.
[5] Committee for Reform of Muslim Personal Law of 1963, File No. 53/17/CF-61, Cabinet Secretariat, Cabinet Affairs – Addl. Secy, 4 January 1964, NAI, New Delhi.
[6] Reba Som, 'Jawaharlal Nehru and the Hindu Code: A Victory of Symbol over Substance?', *Modern Asian Studies* 28, no. 1 (1994): 165–94.

of negotiations between custom, religion, and statutory law, on the one hand, and between the judiciary, legislature, and the citizen, on the other. Both the potential bills, however, were centralized initiatives and their failure revealed the distance and dissonance between public and parliamentary opinion, reports and legislation, and paper and practice.

The government initiated these committees to streamline personal laws and also to respond to social, religious, and civil society movements by absorbing new contestations while these committees continued to emphasize the reformative potential of the law. The committees for reforms to personal laws hoped to keep alive the 'spirit' of the constitution and acted as the conscience keepers of the government. They served to safeguard the interests of groups by maintaining the separation of religious codes, on the one hand, and remained committed towards codification of customary practices, introducing greater regulation, on the other.

After the reorganization of states'[7] (provincial boundaries) in 1956, state legislatures enacted a number of laws extending and amending central enactments related to family law. Although the academic focus on this period has been on culture, language, and potential sub-national or secessionist movements,[8] an assertion of plurality in the law was, in fact, also a defining development in this period. The marking of a separate territory of land appeared to legitimize the existence of separate customs and practices as the new state legislatures began to extend, amend, or resist the application of prevailing family law codes.

In the 1960s, therefore, India witnessed a competitive codification drive between and within religious groups, a tendency to seek legal recognition of the group's 'right to be different or have different customs', and to belong to a separate, but statutory, category. All three cases of religious personal laws experience this tension in different ways. In the review of the Christian marriage law, the state attempted to incorporate customs that exhibited regional diversity but tried to omit those that compromised women's status to emphasize law's reformative potential. In the case of Muslim law, codification was part of a drive to de-emphasize differences within the community. This entailed the weeding out of customs from textual religion. It was also through the codification of personal law that a national Muslim identity was aspired for. And in the case of the Hindu Marriage (Madras Amendment) Act, the integration of customs into Hindu law contributed to affirming the territorial integrity of the nation and, in the process, it democratized Hindu law.

---

[7] The Reorganisation of States Act, 1956.
[8] Granville Austin, *Working a Democratic Constitution: A History of the Indian Experience* (New Delhi: Oxford University Press, 2003).

The state's selective patronage towards religious practices had favoured an upper-caste north Indian morality, and this was supported by the rhetoric that when transformed into a statute, religion only maintained its 'good' or 'liberal' aspects. This selective recognition of practices served to generate a hierarchy of customs, those which were worthy of codification and those which were not. Consequently, this also generated a hierarchy between groups that followed these customs and practices.

The Hindu Marriage (Madras Amendment) Act highlights how the recognition of customary law became crucial to the relationship between the central and state (provincial) governments. The state (here, Tamil Nadu) asserted its right to different customs but at the same time demanded that the custom should be incorporated within the 'religious' Hindu Marriage Act instead of the Special Marriage Act. Thus, following from the 1950s, religion continued to become more capacious and the state extended surveillance over a greater number of local religious or traditional customs.

All three cases of revision of Christian, Muslim, and Hindu religious personal laws took place in the larger context of India's gradually maturing federal design. Federalism, therefore, triggered two processes: First, it enabled the widening of the definition of religious categories so as to recognize customs and regional diversity *within* a religious community. Second, federalism allowed for a streamlining of regional identities by provincial legislatures. Collectively, these processes of accommodation and streamlining entailed exemptions, exceptions, or incorporation of religious practices. Religion and region became dialogic, producing both limited uniformity and pluralism.

Commissions and Committees: The Parking Lot for Social Reform

In the 1960s, the task of recommending legislative models of religious practices related to family law was assigned to judicial commissions, which mostly worded these potential bills as 'reform measures' rather than attempts to initiate a Uniform Civil Code. The Law Commission reports were treated as significant contributions that would inform law making and act as an interface of policy with society through committees.

Law Commissions were first instituted in India under the company rule in 1834 as executive bodies. Historically, these did not focus on any particular subject but followed the general logic of 'bettering the management' of the affairs of the people. Macaulay, who chaired the first Law Commission, produced a report that reviewed a range of enactments. The idea of 'law reform' was then premised on administrative efficiency rather than social uplift.[9] The content and not the consequence of the law on society lay at the heart of these revisions in colonial India. The subsequent Law Commission of 1860–61 made additions to the Indian Penal Code, the Criminal Procedures Code, and the Indian Evidence Act, and the gap between report and enactment of legislation ranged from over two years to two decades. In essence, the commissions were created to contribute directly to law making.

After independence, the role of the commission was reduced considerably with respect to effecting law making, but their scope expanded to cover a wider range of subjects.[10] The independent government established the first Law Commission in 1955. With the regularization of the frequency of the commissions to three years, its scope was expanded to review any and every law that prevailed in the country. One commission could produce several reports. The first Law Commission (1955–58)[11] produced 14 reports and the second (1958–61)[12] followed with seven more, and the eighteenth (2007–9)[13] produced as many as 32 reports.

The commissions were often constituted under the leadership of a retired judge and paved the way for the judiciary to advise the legislature directly on potential amendments, simplification of procedures, or reform of the official processes and policy. The reports by the commission provided parliament with a blueprint for social legislation. The nature of these interventions has been so dynamic that very often the agenda for a report was determined by an immediate event, incident, or a case.[14] These reports, therefore, increasingly became companions of the constitution and the 'conscience-keepers' of public sentiment without bearing the burden of representation. They were neither accountable to the public, nor constituted of, or by the people, but provided an efficient response

---

[9] See the Law Commission of India webpage, 'Early Beginnings', www.lawcommissionofindia. nic.in.

    For a critical study of Law Commissions in colonial India, see Ritu Birla, *Stages of Capital: Law, Culture, and Market Governance in Late Colonial India* (Durham: Duke University Press, 2008) and Ann Stoler, 'Colonial Archives and the Arts of Governance', *Archival Science* 2, nos. 1–2 (2002): 87–109. For a more specific text on colonial reforms of personal law, see Reena Verma Williams, *Postcolonial Politics and Personal Laws: Colonial Legal Legacies and the Indian State* (Oxford: Oxford University Press, 2006).

[10] Williams, *Postcolonial Politics and Personal Laws*. This text focuses on continuities from colonial India in personal law reform.

[11] 1st Law Commission of India, 1955–58.

[12] 2nd Law Commission of India, 1951–61.

[13] 18th Law Commission of India, 2007–09.

[14] For example, the 84th report in 1980 on 'Rape and Allied Offences-Some Questions of Substantive Law, Procedure and Evidence' was a direct consequence of the Mathura rape case of 1978, discussed in the next chapter.

to activism, converting social reform into a legal language of bills and proposals regardless of whether these became laws. The commission's non-permanent and non-statutory status made it ineffective but relatively independent. The reports offered generalized responses that could lack an informed sense of space, people, and customs.[15] Commissions sought to engage while standing at a considerable distance from subjects.[16] Consultations and surveys followed erratic and largely unknown methodologies. However, despite their scepticism for the effectiveness and potentiality of the commissions, feminist writing engaged substantially with the reports. Sarkar, for instance, described the law as a 'primary instrument for women's betterment'.[17] Commissions, therefore, could be seen as tentative precursors of limited reform.

Galanter's work on the aborted restoration of indigenous law explores the two-volume Law Commission report on 'Reforms of the Judicial Administration', 1958, which considered the question of integrating indigenous systems of law through delegation of some judicial powers to the local panchayats.[18] The reports concluded against such a devolution of judicial power and Galanter attributed this conclusion to the domination of the elite and, in particular, of lawyers trained in the West.[19] An enchantment with Nehruvian modernity and Ambedkarite disdain for local law as law that is steeped in caste consciousness loomed large over the republic in the 1960s. Galanter, however, also suggested that greater the attempts to obliterate indigenous law, the stronger the potential of indigenous systems to proliferate. He recalls the work of Paul Brass on the spread of modern medicine which was accompanied by a simultaneous 'revival' of indigenous medicine.[20] Brass terms it 'dual modernisation' whereby the introduction of modern systems encouraged the proliferation of indigenous customs or medicine

---

[15] For a critique of Law Commissions, see Upendra Baxi, *The Crisis of the Indian Legal System: Alternatives in Development: Law* (New Delhi: Vikas, 1982).

[16] Nidhin Donald, 'Gazing from a Distance: Spatial Reading of a Law Commission Report', *Journal of Indian Law and Society* 6, no. 2 (2014): 91.

[17] Lotika Sarkar, *National Specialised Agencies and Women's Equality: Law Commission of India* (New Delhi: Centre for Women's Development Studies, 1988). The critique of the law within the feminist movement became more pronounced in the late 1980s and 1990s, as is discussed later in the book in Chapters 5 and 6.

[18] Marc Galanter, 'The Aborted Restoration of "Indigenous" Law in India', *Comparative Studies in Society and History* 14, no. 1 (1972): 53–70.

[19] Ibid.

[20] Paul R. Brass, 'The Politics of Ayurvedic Education: A Case Study of Revivalism and Modernisation in India', in *Education and Politics in India: Studies in Organization, Society, and Policy*, ed. Susanne Hoeber Rudolph and Lloyd I. Rudolph (Cambridge, MA: Harvard University Press, 1972), 342–71.

in a new form. Modernization, therefore, provoked traditionalization, even as both transformations occur in a distinctly modern context.

Personal law, however, complicates this binary, as it constitutes that uncomfortable category which fits neither neatly in the category of indigenous law nor its modern counterpart. If one were to apply Brass and Galanter's analogies, then modernization would entail a church–state separation and 'indigenous' response would indeed be the assertion of religious/customary practices. While no model could be ascribed to Indian secularism, its discernible feature continues to be that it did not entail a strict separation between the realms of religion and the state as also illustrated by the previous chapter. Indian secularism was unique to Indian modernity.[21] The state's patronage to codification of personal law was one exhibit of Indian modernity, whereby not only did religion thrive in the public space as it had done historically but it was also subjected to a process of legitimation through the codification of personal law. To return to Galanter and Brass's argument, the transformation of personal law, therefore, occurred in a third way aside from traditionalization and modernization. Not only did personal law repackage the ancient as modern and progressive but it also simultaneously became a way to transform and resist the tradition and custom.

For instance, one type of transformation occurs when the state eliminates practices that were traditionally permissible (such as bigamy) for large sections of the population; but by sheer force or fear of the legislation, the elimination eventually begins to gain acceptability, that is, modernization. The second transformation—traditionalization—however, takes two forms. One, as Galanter predicted, the advocates of the indigenous law bargain for the practice of bigamy as one in the interest of women. They imitate and simulate the structure of modern law to find texts and scriptures in defence of the practice to serve as a parallel jurisdiction.

However, the second form of transformation through traditionalization entailed that legislation is co-opted into indigenous law and the eliminated practice is deemed as one that never had the support of authentic religion. This transforms religion as well as the law, as not only is religion reconciled with modern law, but modern law itself cannot generate a democratic consensus without leaning on tradition and occasionally accepting exceptions. The committees and commissions hoped to facilitate this third transformation and in doing so, it became a site for politics outside the legislative and electoral realm. These commissions evidenced histories of partial successes of social movements, potentially powerful bills, and moments of state–society engagement.

---

[21] Partha Chatterjee, 'Our Modernity', no. 1 (SEPHIS and CODESRIA, Rotterdam, 1997).

I

Law Commission on Christian Marriage Law: The Bill in Hibernation

The 15th Law Commission report, 1960,[22] considered laws relating to marriage and divorce among Christians in India. With the exception of minor changes contemplated at the time when the Special Marriage Act, 1954, and the Hindu Marriage Act, 1955, were under consideration, the subject had remained largely untouched since the Indian Divorce Act of 1869 and the Indian Christian Marriage Act of 1872.

The report recommended amendments to personal laws of the Christian community in India in an attempt to streamline the variations in laws of different regions, sects, and churches of the community. However, such was the centralized nature of these negotiations that out of the five members who gave their assent to the report, not one was Christian.[23] The report recognized differences within the community largely based on region noting that the Travancore-Cochin area (which had been merged along with some parts of Madras and reorganized to form Kerala in 1957) as well as Manipur had certain differences in the execution of customary law. Travancore and Cochin were first merged in 1949 which meant that the Indian Succession Act of 1925 would have governed Christians in these areas. However, in 1956, in *Kurian August v. Devassy Aley*,[24] the court had upheld the validity of the prevailing Travancore Act, 1916, and the Cochin Act, 1921, in deciding succession, clarifying that these enactments cannot be deemed as repealed. The Government of India also attempted to extend the Christian Marriage Act of 1872 across India in 1957. The Christian Civil Marriage Act was applicable in the Cochin state, but there was no such law in the Travancore state. The desirability of the Christian Civil Marriage Act, however, had not been ascertained in the newly consolidated state and, therefore, the state legislature stalled the extension of the bill to the new state of Kerala.

This report, in order to account for the distinctions specifically with respect to the solemnization of marriages, further acknowledged the Roman, Scottish, Indian, Burma, and Ceylon[25] churches. Despite noting these differences, the committee concluded that after its consultations with many delegations, the Christian community considered it desirable to bring the community under some

---

[22] 2nd Law Commission, 1958–61.
[23] The five-member team was constituted by T. L. Venkatrama Aiyar (chairman), L. S. Misra, G. R. Rajgopaul, N. A. Palkhiwala, and S. Chowdhary.
[24] *Kurian August v. Devassy Aley* AIR 1957 Travancore Cochin (1).
[25] The Anglican Church came to be known as the Church of India, Ceylon, and Burma.

sort of common law.[26] The recognition of these churches, which was initially placed within the purview of the provincial governments, was revised in 1961 in a follow-up report. The second report placed the recognition of churches within the powers of the central government under the revised draft of the Christian Marriage and Matrimonial Causes Bill, 1961.

The report had initially also suggested that a state authority ought to have a designated number of people officially recognized as ministers to solemnize marriages.[27] However, after the committee released the report for eliciting public opinion, the bill was amended to omit this requirement arguing that it would be impossible to monitor such a large number of ministers of the church.[28] In effect, the incorporation of various customs was often bartered for greater centralization and regulation by the state. By holding the power to recognize, the state also assumed the power to de-recognize. For customs and usages to be recognized, they had to be made legible and translated to a legal language. The presence of the state and its legal apparatus had the ability to transform communities and group identities as it demanded answers to questions like: Who is a Christian? What is a Church? Or for that matter, what is a custom?

The Hindu Marriage Act applied to all persons who were not Muslim, Christian, or Parsi, which had spared parliament from labouring over the definition of 'Hindu', but the named minorities then required more specific definitions. The report defined a Christian as 'a person practicing Christian religion'. Yet once the report was circulated for public opinion, other definitions emerged such as 'one who is baptised or a follower of the Church', or 'a member of a recognised Church', or 'a person who is an official member of any Christian Church in accordance of the rules and regulations of that particular Church'.[29] The 1872 Act had already settled this definition but after independence, the religious categorization was effected precisely through such commissions. This was different from the transformation that Kaviraj describes from fuzzy to enumerated communities engendered by the British census.[30] The re-negotiation of personal laws conveyed that this would in fact alter an individual's relationship with the state, as though the state was somehow restoring religious identity to people and, importantly, that the state was entitled to do so.

For instance, in the discussion on marriages between prohibited degrees of relationships, the recognition as well as the rejection of customary laws of

[26] 15th Report, Law Commission of India, 1960, 13–14.
[27] Ibid.
[28] 22nd Report, Law Commission of India, 1961.
[29] Ibid., 13, paras 13 and 14.
[30] Sudipta Kaviraj, 'Crisis of the Nation-state in India', *Political Studies* 42, no. s1 (1994): 115–29.

intra-family marriages became points of contestation. The discussion was rather brief and the committee readily accepted exceptions for customary practices of marriages between uncle and niece or across cousins. The report made a reference to the marriage between a girl and her mother's brother as a 'usual' custom, and also cited that the Pope can issue a 'papal dispensation' to allow for such marriages. Since there was no scheme for papal dispensation in the bill, the custom was allowed to prevail anyway. In the report, the uncle–niece matrimonial alliance was presented as a regional (North–South) divide,[31] rather than as something fundamentally opposed to Indian culture, as was claimed in the debates of the Hindu Marriage Act, 1955.[32]

Such benign treatment of what parliament had vociferously rejected as an objectionable alliance during the discussions of the Hindu Marriage Act suggests two possibilities. First, that the Law Commission reports were not representative of popular sentiment but a coterie of elite, handpicked members, even though the report claimed that it was a product of wide consultations and research.[33] Second, the issue had already been conceded to in the Hindu Marriage Act and it was, therefore, accepted without hesitation for the Christian minority. The former case appeared to be true since upon re-circulation, objections to permission of marriages between prohibited degrees of relationships resurfaced. The committee, however, was in a position to absorb and accept a controversial customary practice which the legislature was likely to oppose and stall. The committee in its follow-up report conclusively decided in favour of recognizing local custom over religious laws.

> Custom is a well-recognised source of law in the jurisprudence of this country as well as other countries. It has played an important part in shaping the societies. An exception has also been made in the Hindu Marriage Act, 1955. Now to prohibit custom will produce mischief and confusion in the law relating to family relations. We are therefore unable to agree that custom should be excluded.[34]

Thus, unlike Galanter's exploration of the restoration of panchayats, the writing of personal law, in fact, drew legitimacy from customary practice and religious texts selectively, depending on extent and the nature of resistance that emerged. Differentiating further between religion and custom, the report clarified:

[31] The Census of India reports that the distribution of the Christian population in India is dense in the North-Eastern states (Manipur, Arunachal Pradesh, Tripura, and Mizoram) and also concentrated in the southern states (Kerala, Tamil Nadu, and Goa).

[32] 15th Report, Law Commission of India, 1960.

[33] The first draft of the legislation was circulated in 1959. From April to November 1959, a number of associations had offered written and oral representations on the subject of the draft bill in New Delhi, Madras, and Bombay.

[34] 22nd Report, Law Commission of India, 1961, 10, para 13.

It is suggested [to the Committee] that custom must be one recognised by Church. But custom is according to its true concept, some rule in derogation of the general law, in vogue, [*sic*] in particular religion or community. There can be no such thing as customs of a Church. It can only mean 'rules of the Church'.[35]

Thus, the committee evolved its own distinctions between what was customary or religious. It is worth noting that customs were usually localized and given that the concentration of the population of Christians was geographically spread across the north-east (north-eastern states of Manipur, Arunachal Pradesh, Tripura, Nagaland, and Mizoram) and the southern states (Kerala, Tamil Nadu, Goa), they varied substantially. By being absorbed into the law, certain customary practices were normalized, others criminalized, and yet others valorized as not legally enforceable but as accepted and authoritative beliefs. The preservation of customs was also determined by potential threats to India's territorial integrity especially in the case of Nagaland, where the secessionist movement was strong.[36] In other states, such as Kerala and Tamil Nadu, the recognition of customs was not immune to party political considerations as Congress—the ruling party—struggled to find a foothold in these states and any threat to local customs or practices of the region could have had serious political repercussions.

Divorce and Its Discontents

The report exhibited a uniquely post-modern problem as it attempted to pander to customary and religious moralities and, at the same time, it upheld the rhetoric of 'reform' that the Law Commissions were designed to produce. On many occasions, these competing moralities were difficult to reconcile. One of the most controversial provisions of the Christian marriage law was the provision for paying 'damages' as compensation for adultery. The man involved in committing the adultery had to pay compensation to the husband of the woman he had committed adultery with. The very idea was premised on the treatment of women as chattel, or property of their husbands, such that the damage to property caused by adultery could be compensated for by the third party.[37] The 'damaged chastity'

---

[35] Ibid.

[36] Nagaland was given the status of an independent province within India in 1963, with the secessionist Naga leader P. Shilu Ao named as its chief minister. This mitigated the demand for a separate state. The agreement, the Naga Accord, guaranteed a 'total recognition of the genuine aspirations of the Naga people'. This was included in the 13th Constitutional Amendment to Article 371A in 1962.

[37] 15th Report, Law Commission of India. For a critical reading of the provisions for compensation in marriage, see also Flavia Agnes, *Family Law: Marriage, Divorce, and Matrimonial Litigation*, vol. I (New Delhi: Oxford University Press, 2011).

of the wife, as per this clause, could be compensated by fines from, or punishment to, her lover.

The committee dealt with this clause with extraordinary indifference to the fact that it dehumanized women and granted a husband exclusive right to his wife's sexuality.[38] In the 15th report, this clause suffered a mild critique and again the committee invoked the irrefutable 'custom' clause to suggest that while this practice may be considered to be against 'Indian sentiment' (or perhaps Hindu sentiment),[39] it was permitted nonetheless for Christians.[40] The report cited the Royal Commission on Marriage and Divorce, 1955, which stated that the provision in question had its origins in English common law and as a centuries-old Christian practice. This, however, had been amended in England.[41] Ironically, the Royal Commission on Marriage and Divorce had itself been very hesitant in simplifying the process of divorce in Britain and had instead extended grants to marriage guidance councils engaged in conciliation of marriages.[42] The Royal Commission had agreed to add three new grounds for divorce—wilful refusal to consummate a marriage, acceptance of artificial insemination without a husband's consent, and the fact that a partner to a marriage is a mentally defective person who by reason of dangerous or violent propensities has been detained in an institution for at least five years.[43] These, however, saw limited discussion in the 15th Law Commission report.

In the remainder of the 15th report, there were many provisions that were essentially attempts to bring the law in line with Hindu law. These provisions were met with objections to issues such as divorce, similar to objections encountered in the Hindu Marriage Act deliberations. Divorce, dissolution of marriages, and judicial separation remained topics that drew scepticism,[44]

---

[38] For a longer discussion on family laws that discriminate against women in India, see chapter 2, 'Women, Legal Regulation and Familial Ideology', in Ratna Kapur and Brenda Cossman, *Subversive Sites: Feminist Engagements with Law in India* (New Delhi: Sage Publications, 1996), 63–65.

[39] 'Indian sentiment' broadly implied that marriage was a divine sacrament and offences such as adultery could not be quantified.

[40] 15th Report, Law Commission of India, 1960.

[41] The primary grounds for divorce under the Matrimonial Clauses Act of 1857 were adultery by the wife or adultery with aggravating circumstances by the husband. If the husband committed adultery, then his wife could seek a divorce and alimony as a remedy upon divorce. If the wife 'misconducted herself', then her husband could seek a divorce and she would forfeit her right to alimony. Alimony remained a wife's remedy. Ibid., 29.

[42] Royal Commission, 'Marriage and Divorce: Report of the Royal Commission', *Probation* 8, no. 2 (1956): 27–30.

[43] Commission for Marriage and Divorce, Report 9678, I 1/6d.

[44] 15th Report, Law Commission of India,1960, 18, para 9.

particularly from Roman Catholics.[45] Divorce based on mutual consent, the centrepiece of female equality, was decidedly rejected by the commission[46] thus proving that the claim of protecting 'women's rights' through the codification of personal law was yet again not central to these revisions. However, the report did recognize that the law, as it stood, made an unfair distinction between husband and wife with respect to grounds for divorce (Section 10):[47]

> While adultery without more (another ground) is a ground for divorce, in a petition by the husband, in the case of the petition by the wife, there should, in addition, be some other element, such as that it should be incestuous adultery, or bigamy and adultery or adultery coupled with cruelty or desertion for two years. The criticism here is that is there no justification for maintaining this distinction between husband and wife. We agree with it.[48]

The report revealed a cross-culturally shared discomfort with granting women independent legal identity, even as committees attempted to balance demands for progressive civil society with conservative or populist sentiment. The committee selectively permitted customs to prevail over religious beliefs and occasionally let the modularity of the Hindu Marriage Act prevail over both custom and religious personal law of Christians. These quasi-legal committees served as buffer zones for absorbing tensions within a federalist state structure by acknowledging regional differences and addressing the north–south divide. In one sense, the committees tried to absorb the 'differences' to maintain the modularity of the Hindu codified law. Often it was this clandestine insistence on bringing other religions in line with Hindu law that caused these committee-recommended bills to fail in parliament.

The reports, therefore, became a parking lot for social change as they awaited enactment and constitutional recognition, and their recommendations resurfaced in parliamentary debates in the later decades. The work of the committee exemplified one of the many attempts at codification to co-opt religion into the state structure only to fortify the structure to manage conflicts between religion and the state or within religious groups. For instance, the demand of the ecclesiastical courts of the Roman Catholic Church for adjudicating matters

---

[45] Roman Catholics constituted the largest Christian church within India. 'Roman Catholics around the World', BBC Factfile, 14 March 2013.

[46] 15th Report, Law Commission of India, 1960, 'Introduction'.

[47] This was a significant observation which remained buried in the committee report until 2001, when the report resurfaced in parliament and Section 10 was amended. In 1983, the 10th Law Commission under K. M. Mathew had also recommended a revision of Section 10.

[48] 15th Report, Law Commission of India, 1960, 26–27.

was categorically denied in the report and it firmly pronounced on the illegality of religious courts.[49] The committee did, however, recommend a faster dispensation of cases by lower courts which did not require the validation of divorce by the high court. This model had already existed in the state of UP since 1957, but parliament had deferred an all-India legislation in a bid to build a federal consensus. Thus, again it was through the committee's report that the government sought to nationalize a provincial amendment, and incrementally moved towards uniform law.

The Indian Divorce UP (Amendment) Bill, 1957, was the first to abolish the requirement of a two-judge bench for confirming the decree of divorce. Justice K. N. Wanchoo recommended that the district courts and judges had sufficient powers to issue the final decree of divorce. UP Minister of Justice Syed Ali Zaheer headed the amendment in the state assembly on September 1957 and the bill received an immediate assent from the president with the following observation by the government:

> The present bill is an amendment of an all-India law, and therefore, for the sake of uniformity it would have been better if a parliamentary legislation for the whole country had been enacted. This matter could have been considered if the state government had consulted the government of India before promoting the present bill.[50]

The existence of a state-level model which altered Christian personal law paved the way for enabling an all-India legislation on the matter. The nationalization of this amendment was attempted immediately after, but it failed owing to resistance from some states and retired into the metaphorical waiting room of committee reports.

On 22 June 1963, parliament introduced an amendment based on the 1961 report despite substantial opposition by the Roman Catholic Church and some objections from the Protestant Churches.[51] The church, however, was not alone in its objections. Public opinion on divorce remained uncertain and even within parliament, members such as Mathew Maniyangadan objected to definitions of 'Christianity' proposed in the bill, and M. Ruthnaswamy observed that it was 'odd that a bill on marriage should provide also for divorce' and that '... it would offend a large body of Christians like the Roman Catholic who object consciously

---

[49]   15th Report, Law Commission of India, 'Decisions of Ecclesiastical Courts', 38, para 76.

[50]   No.17/135/57-Judl. (I) in File No. 17/135/57, Judicial II, Home Judicial, NAI, New Delhi. Consultations about this amendment to the Indian Divorce Act between the provincial and the national government dated back to 1950. Letter No. 5/142/49-Judicial, dated 5 May 1950, 27.

[51]   'Amendment Bill Introduced', *Times of India*, 22 June 1962.

to divorce and to combine marriage and divorce in the same Bill'.[52] One of the members of the Law Commission, P. Satyanarayan Rao, had also dissented from the majority opinion on the 15th Law Commission reports and urged for the application of the bill only to persons domiciled in India, arguing that personal law of parties domiciled outside India be allowed to prevail. He concluded that the bill, otherwise, would lead to a greater number of 'limping marriages'.[53]

The proposed bill surfaced several times in the press. Parliament appointed a joint committee to recommend further changes to the bill in 1962 to pacify the Catholic Church, but there was no consensus.[54] In 1962, the National Federation of Women also passed resolutions on reform of Christian and Muslim marriage laws and one of the prominent members of the federation, Renu Chakravarty, was the chairperson of the joint committee on the Christian Marriage and Matrimonial Clauses Bill. The bill continued to be pushed from one session of parliament to the next.[55] Newspapers reported on the benefits that could be engendered by the bill; others reported on the benefits of marriage counselling to avoid divorce.[56] In April 1969, the idea of a new Bharatiya Christian Democratic Party was mooted in Poona, Maharashtra. With Mr Vikram Kore as its chairperson, the party claimed to be committed to the purpose of codifying Christian marriage laws not derived solely from papal edicts.[57] They drafted fresh amendments which recommended simpler procedures of divorce and an emphasis on family planning to counter the fast-consolidating opposition to the bill by influential Christian organizations across the country.

Globally, the late 1960s witnessed a focus on family law reform.[58] In 1962, the United Nations organized a seminar in Tokyo on the 'Status of Women in

---

[52] 'Dissent' recorded in the Christian Marriage and Matrimonial Clauses Bill, 1962, Report of the Joint Committee. *Lok Sabha Secretariat*, Agrahayana, 1885 (Saka), New Delhi, 26 November 1963, xiv–xv.

[53] 15th Report, Law Commission of India, 156–58. P. Satyanarayan Rao in his statement also expressed objections on the bill's uncertainty on the question of domicile and its disregard for personal laws of foreign parties. Further the proposed bill leaned more on English law than other jurisdictions and was also not entirely consistent with English law.

[54] 'Christian Marriage', *Times of India*, 12 February 1966.

[55] 'Parliament Has to Tackle Several Bills, New and Old', *Times of India*, 22 October 1966.

[56] 'Divorce Indian Style', *Times of India*, 30 June 1968.

[57] 'Christian Marriage Law Reforms', *Times of India*, 23 April 1969.

[58] For a brief account on how the period of decolonization during the 1950s and the 1960s globally experienced debates on the retention or replacement of religious laws in Egypt, Malaysia, and Indonesia, see Narendra Subramanian, 'Making Family and Nation: Hindu Marriage Law in Early Postcolonial India', *The Journal of Asian Studies* 69, no. 3 (2010): 771–98. This was also an important decade for global feminism with Betty Friedan's *Feminine Mystique* published in 1963 and Kate Millet's *Sexual Politics* in 1970; both texts proved to be influential for women's movements across the world. See also Mary E. John, *Discrepant Dislocations: Feminism, Theory, and Postcolonial Histories* (Berkeley: University of California Press, 1996).

Family Law'.[59] In Canada, the 1968 Divorce Act[60] attempted to include 'formal equality' between spouses; the American senate popularized ideas of 'rehabilitative alimony' in the 1970s;[61] and in 1969, Britain enacted the Divorce Reform Bill. However, the hesitation on the subject of divorce was not exclusive to India. In Italy, the divorce law was passed in 1974, with a 59 per cent majority after a controversial and heated debate on the subject and strong objections from Vatican City. The discussion on the Divorce Reform Bill in the British Parliament also bore some uncanny similarities with the Indian debate and revealed a shared discomfort that the subject of divorce evoked.[62]

The British Parliament recognized 'irretrievable breakdown of marriage' to be a sufficient and exhaustive ground for divorce.[63] This was aimed at simplifying the judicial process and aided in curtailing the public nature of divorce trials in court. The Divorce Reform Bill, 1969, in Britain earned the title of a 'Casanova Charter'.[64] Alec Jones of the British Labour Party stated, 'All the world loves a wedding because it embodies the hopes and aspirations of all of us. But no one loves divorce. But if we want to discourage divorce, we cannot do it by law but by setting a far higher moral approach for others.'[65] H. V. Kamath in the discussions on the Hindu Marriage Act had echoed this: '[T]he policy should be that marriage becomes easy and divorce difficult.'[66] The criticisms of the English bill further included assertions claiming that simple divorce procedures encouraged 'trial marriages',[67] and 'We are trying to pledge this country to eternal promiscuity'.[68] The bill in Britain, however, was prioritized over 25 pending private member bills;[69] the British government's prioritization of this amendment was reminiscent of the passage of the Hindu Code Bill in India. The Indian government, however, did not show the same zeal for amendments to Christian law.

---

[59] Seminar on the Status of Women in Family Law: Tokyo, 8 to 21 May 1962, Document (United Nations) in File No. 53/17/CF-61- LEG II, Cabinet Secretariat Cabinet Affairs, NAI, New Delhi, 31–31C.

[60] Divorce Act, R.S.C. 1970, c. D-8.

[61] Mary F. Lyle and Jeffrey L. Levy, 'From Riches to Rags: Does Rehabilitative Alimony Need to Be Rehabilitated?', *Family Law Quarterly* 38, no. 1 (2005): 3–27.

[62] J. D. Singh, 'Divorce British Style', *Times of India*, 29 June 1969.

[63] Stephen Michael Cretney, *Family Law in the Twentieth Century: A History* (Oxford: Oxford University Press, 2003).

[64] Alec Jones, Labour Party, House of Commons Debate (HC Deb), 12 June 1969, vol. 784, c. 2028. *Hansard* (1803–2005).

[65] Ibid. c. 2023.

[66] H. V. Kamath's speech in Srimati Basu, *The Trouble with Marriage: Feminists Confront Law and Violence in India* (New Delhi: University of California Press, 2015), 44.

[67] Victor Goodhew, HC Deb, 12 June 1969, vol. 784, c. 2067.

[68] Peter Mahon, Labour Party, HC Deb, 12 June 1969, vol. 784, c. 2034.

[69] In India, the bill was taken up for consideration in 2001.

The Conversion Controversy

The resistance to the state's intervention in Christian personal law was consolidated also as a response to other occurrences—a major cause being the anti-conversion drives launched by some state governments that specifically targeted the work of Christian missionaries in India. In 1968, the Governments of Madhya Pradesh and Orissa enacted the Freedom of Religion Bill that regulated religious conversions.[70] These state legislatures believed that Christian missionaries had been taking unfair advantage of vulnerable sections of the society by 'luring' lower caste individuals, women, and tribal communities into Christianity by offers of medical and other benefits upon conversion.[71] The Freedom of Religion Bill, 1968, made such conversion from one religion to another by use of 'force' or 'allurement', a cognizable offence.[72] The proposal to elicit public opinion on the bill, however, was rejected by the state legislature. V. K. Saklecha,[73] the then deputy chief minister and a member of the Bharatiya Jana Sangh, piloted the bill and reiterated that the bill was not politically motivated but was introduced only because the missionaries were 'conspiring' to encourage disruptive and divisive forces in Nagaland, Mizoram, and the territory now recognized as Jharkhand. He assured that the new bill would counter this perceived danger to 'national unity'.[74]

The Freedom of Religion Bill endorsed the position of the controversial Niyogi Committee Report of 1956 on conversion and activities of Christian missionaries that '[a]s conversion muddles the convert's sense of unity and solidarity with his society, there is a danger of his loyalty to his country and State being undermined'.[75] The Christian Missionary Activities Enquiry Committee had been appointed by a resolution of the Government of Madhya Pradesh in April 1954.[76] However, subsequently the committee noted:

---

[70] In Madhya Pradesh, it was called the 'Dharma Swatantrya Vidheyak' or the Religious Freedom Bill.

[71] File No. 6/136/68, Home, NAI, New Delhi.

[72] This issue had also been contemplated by the Madhya Pradesh government in 1954 when it ordered an inquiry into the activities of the Christian missionaries by appointing the Niyogi Committee. The Niyogi Committee produced a controversial report in 1956 and indicted the missionaries for forced conversion. The report, however, did not propel any legislative action until it was reopened in 1968.

[73] V. K. Saklecha later joined the BJP and became the chief minister of Madhya Pradesh from 1978 to 1980.

[74] 'MP Bill Against Conversions', *Bhopal Patriot*, 20 September 1968.

[75] Niyogi Committee Report, 1956. M. Bhawani Shankar Niyogi, a retired chief justice of the Nagpur High Court was the chairperson of the Niyogi Committee that included five other members: M. B. Pathak, Ghanshyam Singh Gupta, S. K. George, Ratanlal Malaviya, and Bhanu Pratap Singh. https://archive.org/details/in.ernet.dli.2015.99238/page/n17, accessed on 4 June 2014.

[76] No. 318-716-V-Con., dated 14 April 1954.

[The committee] is not appointed under any enactment such as the Commission of Enquiry Act IX of 1952 but only under the inherent powers of the state Government. The Committee consequently functioned on a purely voluntary basis. It had neither the power to compel any one to attend before it, nor to make any statement, oral or written, nor to administer an oath. The Committee thus had no coercive power in any shape or form.[77]

These voluntary recommendations received official force in the 1968 Act. The Orissa government followed suit and also enacted a Freedom of Religion Act later the same year. This committee itself was a response to a protest movement by the Bharatiya Jana Sangh, which had organized a week-long protest against the foreign missionaries and against the work of the Christian missionaries in the newly integrated areas of Madhya Pradesh (from Bihar), Raigarh, Udaipur, Jashpur, and Surguja, which contained significant tribal and Adivasi populations.[78]

The Christian community unequivocally opposed both the laws on the grounds that the work of the missionaries was misconstrued as 'proselytization' particularly when the right to 'propagate' one's religion was a constitutional guarantee under the fundamental right to freedom of religion. The Archbishops of Visakhapatnam[79] and Bhopal wrote strongly worded letters to the president of India that these legislations targeted Christians and were against the spirit of the constitution, as they denied Christians their right to propagate religion freely. They expressed regret and disappointment that all social services offered by Christian missionaries were dubbed as attempts to convert, overlooking all their projects that were aimed at poverty alleviation and aid, which helped share the burden of the responsibilities of the state.[80]

A heated debate ensued within religious bodies over the bill. The controversy subsequently prompted responses from Islamic organizations such as

---

[77] Niyogi Committee Report, 1956, vol. 1, para 9.

[78] Ibid., vol. 1, ch. 2.

[79] Representing the Andhra Catholic Association (Diocesan unit).

[80] Letter dated 25 September 1968 from Dr E. D'Souza, the Archbishop of Bhopal, Madhya Pradesh. Addressed to chief minister of Madhya Pradesh, copied to the governor of Madhya Pradesh and the president of India.

> To quote the Naga rebellion, as some have mischievously tried to do, in favour of this legislation, it is to profess a complete ignorance of contemporary history. The myth that the Christians have been responsible for this situation has long since been exploded by several objective and top-level enquiries conducted by government of India. (File No. 6/136/68, Home, NAI, New Delhi)

Nizim Imarat Shariah,[81] in Bihar and Orissa, who also saw this Act as a violation of the right to preach and propagate religion.[82] The Shri Sanatan Dharma Sabha, a Hindu organization based in Hyderabad, emerged in support of the Act.[83] The Sabha made an appeal through letters to all chief ministers to follow suit, lauding the bill passed by the Government of Madhya Pradesh and demanded conversion to be included as an offence under a national law. The letter went as far as to allege that missionaries were aided by foreigners and, if unchecked, they would demand for a separate 'Christian-istan'.[84]

In October 1968, *The Herald* reported that a confrontation had ensued between the Madhya Pradesh government,[85] and the Church in the state. The archbishop stated that he will 'ask his flock to be ready to face any consequences ... even this means going to jail'.[86] On 28 November 1968, the Catholic Union of India filed a writ in the Supreme Court challenging the constitutionality of the Acts and issued a notice to the Ministry of Home Affairs and the Intelligence Bureau. The All India Prayer Fellowship Organisation appealed to Christians in the country to protest, and clashes resulted in the arrests of five pastors of the Baptist Church in Orissa.[87] However, without consultation with the Government of India, the bill became a law with a substantial majority in both provincial legislatures of Madhya Pradesh and Orissa. Its legality therefore could now only be challenged in the court of law.

The new law required all conversions to be reported to the district magistrate, and investigated by an officer of a rank not lesser than a police inspector, to assess the 'genuineness' of the conversion. This implied that the state was not satisfied with the knowledge of conversion for census purposes alone, but wanted to monitor whether the conversion was followed through, testing the religiosity of the converted individual. Thus, just as in the case of personal law, it was only through religion that the state could regulate the intimate lives of citizens. In the case of conversion once again, the state demanded a disclosure of not just religion but of lived religion, of the religiosity of an individual. In the absence of the suffix

---

[81] Imarat Shariah, in Bihar, Jharkhand, and Orissa, is a socio-religious organization of the Muslim ummah in the state of Bihar, Jharkhand, and Orissa. Established in 1921, it was formed to protect and propagate Islam and the *sharia*.

[82] Letter dated 13 October 1968 in File No. 6/136/68-FI, NAI, New Delhi.

[83] Letter dated 6 October 1968 in File No. 6/136/68-FI, NAI, New Delhi.

[84] Ibid.

[85] The government was headed by Chief Minister Govind Narain Singh who led a coalition government, the 'Samyukta Vidayak Dal'.

[86] 'Christian May Defy MP Conversion Bill: Archbishop Sends Notice to Chief Minister', *The Herald*, 25 October 1968.

[87] Letter dated 6 January 1969, Intelligence Bureau, File No. 6/136/68-FI, NAI, New Delhi.

of 'family' before the 'law' to provide the shield of the 'personal', the state's access to religion and to religiosity proved to be difficult to mitigate.

Both enactments on 'freedom of religion' were challenged in two famous cases[88] before the Supreme Court, and the court upheld the validity of these enactments. These state governments, therefore, successfully installed a mechanism for close regulation of conversion to Christianity. The attack on missionary activities further helped cement Christian opposition to any further changes in Christian personal law. The 15th Law Commission, therefore, failed to precipitate a change of law in parliament on Christian marriages and divorces, and after the election of 1967, the bill to amend Christian personal law lapsed. However, the issue was not entirely buried. Even though the all-India legislation had failed, the committee's bill became a point of reference from which state legislatures could borrow.

In 1969, the Maharashtra government reopened the question of amending the Indian Divorce Act, albeit focussed on a very specific clause of Section 17, which required that even after the divorce was confirmed by the district court, the decision had to be confirmed by a special bench of the high court.[89] The Legislative Assembly of Maharashtra pointed to the futility and the unnecessary delay in proceedings of dissolution for marriages.[90] In a letter to the Ministry of Home Affairs, the Government of Maharashtra communicated that the grounds for divorce under the National Act that governed Christian marriages were *even more antiquated* than the Hindu law of divorce.[91] Even when the Law Commission's report could not inspire an all-India amendment (until 2001), the Maharashtra legislature somewhat responded to the report and amended the law in line with the UP amendment of 1957.[92]

Thus, divorce was consistently and universally considered a controversial matter as far as the writing of law (whether religious or otherwise) in statutory form was concerned. Gradually, the Law Commissions and provincial legislatures began to question women's compromised rights to divorce, and the restricted

---

[88] *Reverend Stanislaus v. State of Madhya Pradesh*, 1977 SCR (2) 611; *Yulitha Hyde v. State of Orissa* (1977) I SCC 677.

[89] 'Amendment to Indian Divorce Act', Government of Maharashtra, File No. 17/99/69, NAI, New Delhi.

[90] This had been amended by the UP State Legislature in 1957. File No. 17/135/57, Judicial II, Home, NAI, New Delhi.

[91] File No. 17/135/57, Judicial II, Home, NAI, New Delhi (emphasis mine).

[92] The clause originally required that the decision of the district court on the decree of divorce be confirmed by a bench of not less than two judges of the high court and if any disagreements emerged, then the point of the disagreement needed to be stated before one or more judges of the high court, and the collective decision of all the judges included in the proceedings would confirm the decision of the district or a lower court. This was substituted in the Maharashtra Amendment with the amended UP that removed compulsory confirmation of the decree of divorce by a high court bench.

grounds for divorce in minor provincial revisions of family laws. Even though the Muslim Women (Protection of Rights on Divorce) Act was enacted only in 1986, the attempts to address Muslim women's limited rights in divorce were initiated as early as 1961. The 18th Law Commission report, 1961, dealt with Muslim women's inability to get a divorce even after conversion to another religion, whereas if a Muslim man converted out of Islam, the marriage was dissolved automatically. Although this report focussed essentially on the effects of the conversion of religion on marriage, it became the springboard for contemplating changes to the entirety of Muslim personal law relating to marriage and divorce in India.

The experience of the Muslim Law Committee, however, was decidedly different from the Christian Committee although the two met a similar fate in the end. The Muslim Law Committee was introduced in anticipation of reform and was endorsed by the highest echelons of power. The next section studies the intimate functioning of the government which provides an insight into the centralization of authority that characterized the Nehruvian years. The official correspondence with the Prime Minister's Office reveals that the negotiation over the formation of the committee on Muslim personal law was essentially a conversation between three men—Prime Minister Nehru, a barrister and activist, A. A. A. Fyzee, and the vice president of India, Zakir Hussain—and their pursuit to codify, reform, and preserve the Muslim personal law, respectively.

II

Muslim Personal Law: From Reports to Reforms[93]

In December 1961, the legislative department of the Government of India submitted a summary for the cabinet regarding the potential amendment of the Convert's Marriage Dissolution Act, 1866, based on the recommendation of the 18th Law Commission report. The report was concerned with the rights of spouses in a situation where one of the spouses converted from their religion, or the religion that they practised at the time of their marriage, to another. In most personal laws, there was in place an existing provision in the law for the spouse who had remained unconverted to exit or dissolve the marriage; thus, the report proposed a law aimed at addressing petitions specifically by the 'converted' spouse to dissolve a marriage.[94]

---

[93] A version of this section was published in Saumya Saxena, 'Commissions, Committees, and the Custodians of Muslim Personal Law in Post-independence India', *Comparative Studies of South Asia Africa and Middle East* 38, no. 3 (2018): 423–38.
[94] File No. 53/17/CF-1961, Cabinet Secretariat, Cabinet Affairs, NAI, New Delhi.

The Hindu Marriage Act, 1955, provided for a decree of divorce in favour of the petitioner on the ground that the other party had ceased to be Hindu.[95] The Law Commission on Christian Marriages (15th report) had also recommended that the proposed law relating to marriage and divorce among Christians should include a provision that a petitioner can move for divorce on the ground that the respondent had ceased to be a Christian.[96] The law under various family law provisions specified that conversion from one monogamous religion to another did not, *ipso facto*, put an end to the marriage but was a recognized ground for divorce for both partners. Therefore, unless a marriage was dissolved as provided by law, the converted party could not be permitted to remarry.[97] In case the conversion was from a monogamous religion to a polygamous religion such as Islam, the law also rather clearly laid out that the conversion itself did not always put an end to marriage.[98]

Under the Dissolution of Muslim Marriages Act, 1939, Section 4 also provided that the renunciation of Islam by a married Muslim woman, or her conversion to a faith other than Islam, did not imply that the marriage was automatically dissolved and nor was it a ground for divorce. The Act, therefore, did not allow the wife to seek divorce if she converted.[99] The converted woman had to obtain a decree of dissolution of her marriage on some other ground contained within the Dissolution of Muslim Marriages Act, 1939.[100] In the case of the conversion of the Muslim husband, on the other hand, the marriage would automatically dissolve.[101]

The Law Commission suggested a modification of the law to grant a Muslim woman the right to divorce a Muslim man if she converted to another religion without requiring any other compounding ground for divorce.[102] These discrepancies in religious laws were precisely what allowed gender to become the only point of entry for legal reform by the state through which an argument for uniformity could be advanced, and the modularity of Hindu law maintained.

---

[95] The Hindu Marriage Act, 1955, Section 13(1)(ii). Even under section 32(j) of the Parsi Marriage and Divorce Act, 1936, conversion was recognized as a ground for divorce; however, Parsi law is beyond the scope of this book.

[96] 15th Report, Law Commission of India, 1960.

[97] 18th Report, Law Commission of India, 1961.

[98] Ibid., 2.

[99] Dissolution of Muslim Marriages Act, 1939.

[100] For a fascinating account of how the enactment of the Dissolution of Muslim Marriages Act, 1939, complicated the question of conversion and apostasy as a ground for divorce in colonial India, see Rohit De, 'The Two Husbands of Vera Tiscenko: Apostasy, Conversion, and Divorce in Late Colonial India', *Law and History Review* 28, no. 4 (2010): 1011–41.

[101] Dissolution of Muslim Marriages Act, 1939.

[102] File No. 53/17/CF-61- LEG II, Cabinet Secretariat Cabinet Affairs, NAI, New Delhi, 31–31C.

The 18th report also presented a number of cases which listed scenarios where a man converted to Islam only with the object of acquiring a second wife. In various judgments, the courts had laid down that the mutual rights and obligations created by a monogamous marriage cannot be modified unilaterally by the conversion of either spouse.[103] In effect, the converted spouse could not claim the right to have more than one wife so long as the first marriage under a monogamous law existed.[104]

In 1961, in the *Itwari v. Smt. Asghari* case,[105] the Allahabad High Court had also taken a sympathetic approach towards the first wife in a case of bigamy even when no question of conversion was involved. In this case, the wife had filed a maintenance claim against her husband. After the marriage had gone sour, Asghari began to live with her parents and her husband married another woman. Responding to Asghari's maintenance claim, her husband filed a suit for restitution of conjugal rights. The court concluded that Asghari's husband had made no effort to reconcile with her. Moreover, the husband had filed a suit for restitution of conjugal rights only to defeat his wife's rightful claim of maintenance. Dismissing the appeal of the husband and reversing the order of the lower court, the high court concluded that it would indeed be 'inequitable to compel the first wife to live with such a husband'. This is when bigamy alone may not amount to cruelty in a Muslim marriage. Such cases suggest that the courts continued to give wider interpretations to concepts of 'cruelty' to uphold just maintenance claims, discourage bigamy, and grant divorces.[106] The 18th report concluded that 'it would, however, be advantageous to make the position clear by a statutory provision'.[107] The committees, thus, became effective mediators between the courts and the legislature as they aimed at converting judgments into active laws.

While the scope of the 18th report was limited to addressing the rights of a non-converted spouse, the discussion raised questions about the problems that were exclusive to polygamous religions that brought Muslim personal law to the centre stage of parliamentary discussions. Within nine days of the circulation of

---

[103] *Budansa Rowther And Anr. v. Fatma Bi and Ors.* (1914) 26 MLJ 260; *Robasa Khanum v. Khodadad Bomanji Irani* (1946) 48 BOMLR 864.

[104] File No. 53/17/CF-61, Cabinet Secretariat Cabinet Affairs, NAI, New Delhi, 6–14, correspondence dated 16 November 1961.

[105] AIR 1960 All 684.

[106] The court continued to condemn and grant relief to wives under cases of bigamy after conversion in cases such as *Vilayat Raj v. Sunila* AIR 1983 Delhi 351, in *re P. Nagesashayya*, 1988 Mat LR 123, and finally again in *Smt. Sarla Mudgal v. Union of India* (1995) 3 SCC 635, which prompted another Law Commission report (227th) on the subject.

[107] File No. 53/17/CF-61, Cabinet Secretariat Cabinet Affairs, NAI, New Delhi, 6–14, correspondence dated 16 November 1961.

the report, Nehru consulted A. A. A. Fyzee, a Cambridge-based lawyer and well-known barrister, on the issue of a convert's marriage under Muslim law. Nehru found a ready ally in Fyzee who was anxious to bring India in line with other Islamic countries that had codified the law differently with respect to marriage and divorce.[108]

Fyzee had written extensively on Muslim law and his most notable work—often cited in court judgments—was the *Outlines of Mohammedan Law* (1955) which covered most aspects of family law. The correspondence also revealed Nehru's consistent prioritization of, or perhaps apprehensions about, the continuation of personal law regimes in his vision of modern India. Nehru had sought Fyzee's expertise to contribute to the 'reform' of Mohammedan law dating back to 1938 as claimed by Fyzee himself in the course of his correspondence:[109]

> In all the humility, I had begged to be excused [in 1938], feeling that for a progressive community in the twentieth century, such as the Muslims should be, not reform but a root and branch change was necessary. The lapse of 25 years has made the author wiser, sadder, humbler. I shall be content with a modest but simple and well-considered enactment, dealing with the major needs of the community and leaving the main structure of the new law intact.[110]

From 1961 to 1964, there was regular correspondence between the Prime Minister's Office and Fyzee.[111] In the course of this correspondence, Fyzee proposed to set up a commission to review Muslim personal law.[112] While the committee was expected to have significant long-term consequences, an imminent United Nations conference on 'Status of Women in Family Law' scheduled to be held in Tokyo in May 1962 hastened the consultations.[113]

The debates that Fyzee's correspondence with Nehru brought to the fore in 1960s, in fact, anticipated several controversies on divorce procedure and provisions for alimony and maintenance that became relevant in the later decades with the infamous *Shah Bano* case. One of the foremost question that the discussions raised

---

[108] Nehru's minutes, 14 December 1961 in File No. 53/17/CF-61, Cabinet Secretariat, Cabinet Affairs, NAI, New Delhi.

[109] File No. 53/17/CF-61, Cabinet Secretariat, Cabinet Affairs, NAI, New Delhi (emphasis in original).

[110] Ibid., 4, para 26 (e).

[111] Ibid., copies of letters dated from 1962–64.

[112] File No. 53/17/CF-61 Cabinet Secretariat, Cabinet Affairs. NAI, New Delhi.

[113] Seminar on the Status of Women in Family Law: Tokyo, 8 to 21 May 1962, Document (United Nations) in File No. 53/17/CF-61- LEG II, Cabinet Secretariat, Cabinet Affairs, NAI, New Delhi, 31–31C.

was with respect to the definition of a 'Muslim' and to what degree the definition could accommodate the diversity of customs while remaining sufficiently Muslim.

Fyzee, in a long, detailed response, introduced the problem of 'religious-hybrid' communities in India. These included the Khojas, Ismailis, and Satpanths, who believed that Ali, the fourth caliph, was the reincarnation of Vishnu (a Hindu god).[114] The Meos were a tribe largely followed Islamic tenets but had Hindu names, performed Hindu ceremonies, and followed the Hindu law of inheritance, Aliyasanthana and Marumakkathayam. The Severas also selectively drew customs from more than one religion but identified themselves as Muslims. Fyzee emphasized that these communities whose legal status had never been determined could be termed religious 'hybrids' and 'amphibians'.[115] The diversity of customs within Islam raised the question: who really was the 'Muslim' that the Muslim personal law would govern? Fyzee recommended, 'Any person who formally professes Islam, that is, asserts that: "I am a Muslim. There is No Deity other than Allah; and Muhammad is the apostle of Allah"; is a Muslim for the purposes of the administration of law in India.'[116]

Thus, once the diversity of practices was acknowledged, practices of bigamy or a husband's unilateral right to divorce could also be challenged as 'customs' which were not uniformly observed and therefore neither inviolable nor central to Islam, or the *sharia*. Fyzee wrote that the practice of *mut'a*, or 'temporary marriage',[117] was permitted only among the Ithna Ashari Shia sect. Other sects such as the Fatimids and Zaydites rejected this as immoral, or *haram*.[118] Similarly, the practice of *talaq-e-bidat*, which was oral divorce by the utterance of the word *talaq* three times in succession, was 'unjust to the point of absurdity' and, more importantly, it was recognized only in Hanafi law, which was but one of the four schools of Muslim law.[119]

---

[114] A. A. A. Fyzee, *Outlines of Muhammadan Law* (Delhi: Oxford University Press, 1974).

[115] File No. 53/17/CF-61, Cabinet Secretariat, Cabinet Affairs, NAI, New Delhi.

[116] Letter Fyzee, 26(a)–26(f) in ibid.

[117] Temporary marriages contracted in certain sects under Shia law; children born to this marriage are legitimate, but there is no right of inheritance between the couple.

[118] Fyzee terms this a type of legalized prostitution. Letter from A. A. A Fyzee, titled 'Note on a Proposed Commission to Inquire into the Need for Reform in Muhammedan Law as Administered in India', 15 April 1962, Bombay, File No. 53/17/CF-61, Cabinet Secretariat, Cabinet Affairs, NAI, New Delhi. On the subject of inheritance, Fyzee mentions many anomalies in the way that the law is executed. He recommended a simpler system adopted by some countries which have replaced Imam Mohammad Ash-Shaybani's complicated rules by more straightforward translations offered by Abu Yusuf. The Pakistan Family Law Ordinance, 1961, as well as most countries of the Middle East have had used this translation as the basis for legislation.

[119] Letter Fyzee, 26(b)–26(c), in File No. 53/17/CF-61, Cabinet Secretariat, Cabinet Affairs, NAI, New Delhi.

The Committee That Wasn't

Nehru's correspondence with Fyzee laid the foundation for the committee on Muslim personal law. The committee was to be constituted by 'a few well-chosen men, not all of whom need be Muslims'.[120] The names of well-known jurists such as M. C. Setalvad, Vivian Bose, P. N. Sapru, M. C. Chagla, and Justice Wanchoo of the Supreme Court and high courts emerged with a further request from Fyzee to include 'one or two broad-minded Ulema'.[121] He also recommended Muslim lawyers who were well versed in Arabic, Persian, and Urdu and, interestingly, also sought the inclusion of someone familiar with comparative law and legal philosophy.[122] The recommended list, however, remained consistently and overwhelmingly male and contained a phenomenally elite coterie of individuals.

On 2 May 1962, Nehru formally conveyed to the Law Minister Ashoke Sen his desire to set up a committee for Muslim personal law reform in consultation with A. A. A. Fyzee, with the law minister himself as the chairman, just in time for the United Nations seminar on the 'Status of Women in Family Law'.[123] A meeting was convened for the purpose of deciding on the Indian delegation to the UN which was attended by Prime Minister Nehru, Finance Minister Morarji Desai, Minister of Transport and Communication Jagjivan Ram, Home Minister Lal Bahadur Shastri, along with other significant parliamentarians. The names and portfolios suggest that this was accorded utmost priority. At the end of the meeting, H. N. Sanyal, the additional solicitor general, and Shrimati Mithan J. Lam, the then president of the All India Women's Conference, were the two names chosen to represent India in the UN conference.[124]

Nehru's involvement in the UN seminar also illustrated the significance he attached to India's global image and the idea of family law reform as crucial to India's image as a secular, modern nation state. This was significant especially since the 18th Law Commission report had considered the international context of Islamic laws and highlighted that reforms relating to Muslim laws such as enforcement of monogamy by imposing restrictive conditions for polygamous arrangements had already been carried out in Morocco, Algeria, Tunisia, Libya, Egypt, Syria, Lebanon, and Pakistan.[125] The practice, however, prevailed in Saudi Arabia, Iran, Indonesia, and India.[126] Thus, as seen in the case of the Hindu Code

---

[120] Ibid.
[121] Ibid.
[122] He requested for the inclusion of people who are familiar with the philosophical works of C. S. Hurgronje, Bergstrasser Goldziher, and Schacht.
[123] File No. 53/17/CF-61, Cabinet Secretariat, Cabinet Affairs, NAI, New Delhi, 31.
[124] File No. 53/17/CF-61, Cabinet Secretariat, Cabinet Affairs, NAI, New Delhi.
[125] 18th Law Commission Report.
[126] Ibid.

Bill, Nehru's commitment towards setting up a committee for Muslim personal law timed to coincide with a UN seminar can also be viewed as the prioritization of symbol over substance, albeit a commitment that stretched across communities.[127]

The pace of the orders and approvals demonstrated a sense of urgency in commencing the committee. The committee was chaired by Basheer Ahmed, ex-judge, Madras High Court, and other prominent members included A. A. A Fyzee, Peerbhoy, the barrister from Bombay, among others.[128] Fyzee's original list of prominent judges and individuals well versed with works of Western philosophers had over time been replaced by prominent Muslim members.[129] Yet, until this point, all evidence indicated that the codification of Muslim personal law was imminent and Nehru at the helm of these consultations was attempting to repeat the history of the Hindu Family Acts.

Many members of the cabinet had suggested Vice President Zakir Hussain's candidacy for the chairmanship of the Muslim Law Committee.[130] Vice President Zakir Hussain was a Hyderabad-born educationist who had previously held the position of the vice chancellor of Aligarh Muslim University, and he later also became the president of India in 1967. Urdu newspapers like *Siasat* and the *Musalman* confirmed that if the committee that the government was contemplating was instituted, it would be chaired by the vice president himself.[131]

The opposition to the government's attempts to reform Muslim law came from influential educational institutions such as the Aligarh Muslim University, demonstrating that even the Muslim elite were divided on the issue. In Faruqi's biography of Zakir Hussain, Hussain's discomfort with the proposed amendments to Muslim personal law appears unambiguous.[132] In response to a letter from Maulana Abdul Majid Daryabadi,[133] who was an Urdu scholar at Aligarh Muslim University and an activist, Hussain vociferously refuted any claims of his proposed chairmanship: 'The news you have received about Muslim personal law is totally devoid of truth.'[134] He stated that he had, in fact, advised the government

---

[127] Som, 'Jawaharlal Nehru and the Hindu Code'.

[128] File No. 53/17/CF-61, Cabinet Secretariat, Cabinet Affairs, NAI, New Delhi.

[129] Ibid., correspondence dated 3 August 1963, 107–12.

[130] File No. 53/17/CF-61, Cabinet Secretariat, Cabinet Affairs, correspondence dated 3 August 1963, NAI, New Delhi, 97 (all correspondence was labelled 'Secret').

[131] *Siasat*, 30 June 1963.

[132] Z. H. Faruqui, *Dr. Zakir Hussain: Quest for Truth* (New Delhi: APH Publishing Corporation, 1999).

[133] Daryabadi was also member of the Royal Asiatic Society and had also been associated with the Khilafat movement.

[134] Faruqui, *Dr. Zakir Hussain*.

to drop the issue: 'The only thing resolved unanimously was that the government should not take up this issue.'[135]

On 20 August 1963, Atal Bihari Vajpayee,[136] a member of the Bharatiya Jana Sangh, and one of the few influential non-Congress parliamentarians at the time, raised a question in the Upper House of Rajya Sabha about the fate of the committee.[137] The cabinet note very succinctly summarized the decision to drop the committee for reform. 'The general feeling of the meeting was that in a matter which concerned the personal law of the Muslims, the initiative for any reform should come from the Muslims themselves ... [the committee] was not considered necessary for the present.'[138]

Law Minister A. K. Sen reiterated that the government could not be the 'initiator' of reforms but an 'enabler' of rights. In May 1964, with Nehru's death, the committee on Muslim personal law also appeared to have lived its day and there was no legislative initiative for codifying Muslim personal law for the following two decades. There were moments when aspects of Muslim law gained focus in the 1970s, but these were dealt with by a legislature by granting Muslims exemptions and exceptions rather than any proactive endeavours towards codification.

Personal law debates in parliament have witnessed high-profile resignations. Ambedkar had resigned over his disagreement with the Hindu Code Bill in 1951, as did Arif Mohammad Khan over the Muslim Women's Protection of Rights on Divorce Act in 1986. Strikingly, Zakir Hussain who was instrumental in derailing the committee on Muslim personal law in 1963, went on to occupy the highest office of the country as the president. This set the precedent that Muslim personal law could in fact be granted 'inviolable' status as it had the explicit sanction of the highest office of the country.

The elite within the community, who were co-opted by the government without a democratic consensus, reorganized themselves as activists in later decades to reclaim the reform agendas from the committees that never committed. This unabsorbed excess re-emerged in the form of organized civil society initiatives that are analysed in the next chapter. The centralized initiatives may have been postponed into hibernation until the fateful day of the *Shah Bano* judgment in 1985;

---

[135] Ibid., 320.
[136] Vajpayee later became the prime minister of India between 1996 and 1998, then in 1999–2004.
[137] File No. 53/17/CF-61, Cabinet Secretariat, Cabinet Affairs, NAI, New Delhi, 107–12.
[138] File No. 53/17/CF-61, Cabinet Secretariat, Cabinet Affairs–Addl. Secy, last correspondence dated 4 January 1964, 112.

the movement on the ground, however, began to develop from this failed initiative in the 1960s.[139]

The committees nonetheless influenced and even transformed prevailing practices. In the case of personal law, the process of codification transformed religious law by posing new questions about religious communities and how and with what traditions they chose to define themselves for the state as they transitioned into becoming 'legally homogenous communities' with codified personal laws. While these questions were raised in order to reinstate indigenous law, or in this case, religious law, the outcomes it produced in the forms of bills and statutes precipitated an equal urge to assert religious autonomy *from* the law, as both initiatives of Christian and Muslim personal law reform were shelved in the face of strong opposition.

The recent works on colonial law suggest that often it was only through court judgments that the arbitrariness, inconsistency, or fluidity of religious personal law came to the fore as an administrative inconvenience.[140] After independence, court rulings became significant for propelling amendments to law. The intent of the lawmakers and legislators in the 1960s was, therefore, a way of wresting personal law away from judicial discretion, which had historically monopolized the field of personal law, as its interpreters.[141] The underlying emphasis was that the problems that application and interpretation of the *sharia* encountered in India could be remedied only by legislation and 'not by the courts, under the fiction of exposition' as had been the case since the Anglo-Mohammedan codes emerged in the 1930s.[142]

---

[139] It is worth noting that Muslim personal law was actually not as untouched by the state as has often been claimed. The marriage or divorce law may have been left unamended but the Central Wakf Board Act was constantly subjected to changes following the abolition of the Zamindari Act in 1950. While the Hindu Succession Act substantially shielded the Hindu family properties under the banner of the Hindu undivided family, the ownership of *wakf* (charitable trust) boards and their management increasingly came under surveillance.

[140] Rohit De, 'Mumtaz Bibi's Broken Heart, the Many Lives of the Dissolution of Muslim Marriages Act', *Indian Economic and Social History Review* 46, no. 1 (2009): 105–30; Mitra Sharafi, 'The Semi-Autonomous Judge in Colonial India: Chivalric Imperialism Meets Anglo-Islamic Dower and Divorce Law', *Indian Economic and Social History Review* 46, no. 1 (2009): 57–81; Elizabeth Kolsky, 'Codification and the Rule of Colonial Difference: Criminal Procedure in British India', *Law and History Review* 23, no. 3 (2005): 631–83.

[141] Whether legislation indeed addressed the 'arbitrariness' of judicial interpretations is deeply contested. For an account on practices of family law in the informal setting of family courts after 1984, see Basu, *The Trouble with Marriage*. Judicial discretion in personal law matters after independence is explored in greater detail in Chapters 4 and 5.

[142] Letter from A. A. A. Fyzee titled 'Note on a Proposed Commission to Inquire into the Need for Reform in Muhammedan Law as Administered in India', 15 April 1962, Bombay, File No. 53/17/CF-61, Cabinet Secretariat, Cabinet Affairs, NAI, New Delhi, 26(d).

The 1960s were about legislative control over family laws—a spill over from the euphoria of the Hindu Code Bill.

The stories of two Law Commission reports provide two rather different narratives of how personal law became a significant public debate. Debates on personal law essentially became debates on religious reform to weed out redundant customs from what was otherwise deemed to be acceptable, legible religion. Commissions and committees worked towards streamlining the categories of personal law but the legality that this bestowed on 'custom' also encouraged groups to seek statutory backing for their own ways of life, thus creating an opposite effect of seeking statutory backing for customs and practices, and more plurality than less. One of the interesting examples of a group's insistence on statutory recognition of a local custom was the introduction of the Hindu Marriage (Madras Amendment) Act, in 1967.

III

Federalism and Statutorizing Local-law-ways: Amendments to Hindu Law

By the late 1960s, individual state legislatures began to rally for the recognition of the diversity of customs within religion. Such regional resistance to pan-Indian religious family law codes in the 1960s demonstrates that this was a period of the democratization of Hindu family law through the recognition of customary practices and of 'local-law-ways'.[143] With the redrawing of state boundaries after the reorganization of states in 1956, this phase experienced the widening as well as streamlining of religious law codes as they were challenged by regional forces. In the case of the Madras Amendment, the need for the recognition of diversity in customs aided the development of new political parties just as federalism also took root in India.

Correspondence between central and state government suggests that there were a series of amendments that different states initiated, sometimes without consultating the government of India, or even contradicting it. For instance, the UP government introduced changes to the grounds of divorce listed in the Hindu Marriage Act to include 'cruelty' as a ground for divorce in 1962, which was incorporated in the national Act only in 1976.[144] The Madras government

---

[143] The term 'local-law-ways' is borrowed from Bernard S. Cohn, 'Anthropological Notes on Disputes and Law in India', *American Anthropologist* 67, no. 6 (1965): 82–122.

[144] File No. 17/135/62, Judicial II, Ministry of Home Affairs, NAI, New Delhi.

desired the recognition of priest-less marriages under the Hindu Marriage Act, in 1967.[145] The Kerala government in 1962 moved to include 'hybrid communities'[146] under Muslim personal law and extended the application of the Shariat Application Act, 1937.[147]

Caste, region, and community were all identities deployed to challenge the modularity of the Hindu Marriage Act, 1955, and simultaneously the state governments also attempted the nationalization of minority personal laws through the extension of the Shariat Application Act. Thus, the creation of a basic structure of an internally homogenous religious-personal law became a precondition of the recognition of differences within that group, because it provided a statute that could be challenged.

The amendments to family law emerged as the modus operandi for provincial legislatures for asserting their exceptionality and difference in the cultural realm, sometimes at the cost of internal diversity within the newly consolidated territories. As a corollary, federalism posed challenges to any attempts by the central government towards cultural homogenization through pan-Indian family law codes. This section argues that the provincial urge to negotiate greater regional autonomy was sought through a broader interpretation of the constitutional right to freedom of religion to include customary practices within central laws. Edrisinha's work on federalism in Sri Lanka and Nepal addresses this tension between 'shared rule and self-rule' that ethnicity-based political parties inaugurated, as they desired to both affirm as well as transcend identity.[148] India's experience exhibited both demands for recognition of diversity under a national framework or a pan-Indian Hindu law as well as challenges to national identity, in this case exhibited through the resistance towards the central Hindu Marriage Act, illustrated through the Madras Amendment.

In 1961, Nehru inaugurated the National Integration Council and set up a Committee of National Integration and Regionalism. Following the report of the council, the Indian government enacted the 16th Amendment in interest of maintaining 'the integrity, and sovereignty of the Union', widely known as an

---

[145] File No. 17/61/67, Judicial I, Ministry of Home Affairs, NAI, New Delhi, and File No. 17/63/55, Judicial I, NAI, New Delhi. (Madras Amendment to Hindu Marriage Act, 1955.)

[146] Communities that identified with one religion socially or politically but followed the customary practices of another.

[147] File No. 17/171/62, Judicial, Ministry of Home Affairs, NAI, New Delhi (extension of the Shariat Application Act, 1937).

[148] Rohan Edrisinha, 'Debating Federalism in Sri Lanka and Nepal', in *Unstable Constitutionalism: Law and Politics in South Asia*, ed. M. Tushnet and M. Khosla (Cambridge: Cambridge University Press, 2015), 291–319.

Anti-Secession Amendment,[149] and ensuring the safeguarding of India's territorial integrity. In the same period in 1962–63, the social movement–turned–political party Dravida Munnetra Kahzgam (DMK) revised its demand to cede from India and form an independent state Dravidadesa or Dravida Nadu, and pledged their support to national solidarity against the Chinese aggression in 1962.[150] DMK had entered the electoral fray in 1953 but only formed the government in the 1967 election defeating the Congress in the state for the first time in independent India.[151] The very first initiative of the Government of Madras (renamed Tamil Nadu in 1969) was to raise concerns about validating a common customary practice of priest-less marriages.[152]

The validity of Suyamariathai form of priest-less marriages came under question in the landmark decision of the *Deivanai Achi v. Chidamberam Chettiar*, in 1954.[153] The Madras High Court held that the marriage was invalid on the grounds that it was not solemnized in accordance with the customary rites and ceremonies under the Hindu Marriage Act. The demand for the recognition of Suyamariathai or anti-purohit (anti-priest) marriages under the Hindu Marriage Act, 1955, was also asserted by the Madras government in the 1950s, but the Government of India did not heed to these demands on account of lack of clarity with regard to proof of marriage.[154] The national government had repeatedly asserted that such marriages did not follow any of the forms or procedures listed in the existing Anand Marriage Act of 1909 or even the Arya Marriage Act of 1937. Parliament had considered the Hindu Non-Conforming Marriages Bill in 1953, but it was deemed irrelevant after the enactment of the Special Marriage Act in 1954. The national government insisted that Suyamariathai marriages were 'new' and demanded a definition of such a form of marriage as well as the method of establishing proof of marriage. Validating customary forms of marriages fell

---

[149] The statement of objects and reasons of the Amendment Act stated:

> The Committee were further of the view that every candidate for the membership of a State Legislature or Parliament, and every aspirant to, and incumbent of, public office should pledge himself to uphold the Constitution and to preserve the integrity and sovereignty of the Union and that forms of oath in the Third Schedule to the Constitution should be suitably amended for the purpose.

[150] See also chapter 1, 'Settling into the Harness', in Austin, *Working a Democratic Constitution*.
[151] R. L. Hardgrave, 'The DMK and the Politics of Tamil Nationalism', *Pacific Affairs* 37, no. 4 (1964): 396–411. See also Christophe Jaffrelot and Sanjay Kumar, eds., *Rise of the Plebeians?* (New Delhi: Routledge, 2012), 451–86.
[152] File No. 17/61/67, Judicial I, Ministry of Home Affairs, NAI, New Delhi.
[153] *Deivanai Achi v. Chidamberam Chettiar* AIR 1954 Madras 657.
[154] Ibid.

in the 'concurrent list' (entry 5), which included a list on subjects on which both the central and the provincial governments could legislate. The provincial government's bills, however, required the assent of the president of India. This assent was denied to the Madras government in 1955.[155] This contentious issue of customary marriages had simmered since the enactment of the Hindu Marriage Act, 1955, but it was acted upon only in 1967.

Before delving into reasons for the delay of this legislation, it is worth exploring the history of Suyamariathai marriages which reveals a strong link between the recognition of such marriages and the political party in power in 1967 that finally enabled this amendment. In 1926, the social reformer E. V. Ramaswamy Naicker (Periyar) launched the Self- Respect movement, or the Suyamariathai Ikkayam, in Madras.[156] The movement was aimed at countering the evils of Brahminism and advocated a way of living that discouraged the observance of rites and rituals that were discriminatory to either sex, or redundant.[157] This was not only an ideological position but the movement also introduced practical strategies to transform 'ritual life' into 'revolutionary propaganda'.[158] E. V. R. Naicker's movement also prescribed dress codes, names, and home décor, besides marriage rituals as a part of the revolution. Initially a member of the Congress, Naicker quit the party in the mid-1920s deeming Gandhian and Congress politics to be incapable of challenging caste and gender hierarchies.[159]

The movement introduced the Suyamariathai form of marriage where the ceremony was not solemnized by a Brahmin priest. The marriage could be solemnized by a simple exchange of vows and garlands or rings, and required only two witnesses.[160] Thus, the couple was presumed to have entered into a bond of friendship, and were expected to treat each other as equals and comrades.[161] This form of marriage became the centrepiece of the Self-Respect movement. Hodges fittingly summarized that to write a social history of the Self-Respect

---

[155] File No. 17/63/55-Judicial (I), NAI, New Delhi.

[156] S. Anandhi, 'Women's Question in the Dravidian Movement c. 1925–1948', *Social Scientist* 19, no. 5/6 (1991): 24–41.

[157] Sarah Hodges, 'Revolutionary Family Life and the Self Respect Movement in Tamil South India, 1926–49', *Contributions to Indian Sociology* 39, no. 2 (2005): 251–77.

[158] Hodges, 'Revolutionary Family Life and the Self Respect Movement'.

[159] The South Indian People's Association in 1916 had also issued a 'Non-Brahmin Manifesto' to highlight the conditions of more than 95 per cent of the people who were disadvantaged relative to the Brahmin community. See Robert L. Hardgrave's *The Dravidian Movement* (Bombay: Popular Prakashan, 1965), for the beginnings of the movement.

[160] For an analysis of the critique of marriages and women's rights within the movement, see Anandhi, 'Women's Question in the Dravidian Movement c. 1925–1948'.

[161] Anandhi, 'Women's Question in the Dravidian Movement c. 1925–1948'.

movement is to write a history of its family life.[162] The movement rejected all rituals associated with high-caste marriages and it identified such family norms as a political project to retain Brahminical supremacy.

In 1937, Naicker joined the Justice Party. Alongside the causes of social uplift of the backward castes and fighting the practice of untouchability, anti-Hindi agitations and demands for a separate state also became central to the politics of the Justice Party. In 1944, the party was renamed Dravida Kahzgam, or Progress of Dravidians. In 1948, Naicker married Maniammai, who was 30 years younger to him in age, and soon after, he appointed Maniammai as his successor, elevating her position within the party organization. This caused a stir within the organization which resulted in a split initiated by C. N. Annadurai in 1949.[163] Under Annadurai's leadership, the split faction was renamed DMK and it gradually gained political momentum. It formed the government in 1967, and immediately called for the legal recognition of the Suyamariathai form of marriage as advocated by the Self-Respect movement. The recognition of Suyamariathai marriages became synonymous not just with Dravidian Progress but also with the recognition of the state's separate identity, even as the party conceded to remaining within the Union of India. With this, the state entered into a tension between 'self-rule' and 'shared rule'.[164]

'Wide Publicity Is the Hallmark of Hindu Marriage'[165]

The question of the recognition of such a marriage had come up again in 1966 in the case of *Rajathi v. Selliah*[166] before the Madras High Court and the Government of Madras subsequently drafted a new proposal for an amendment to Section 7 of the Hindu Marriage Act, which listed the ceremonies for a Hindu marriage. The Madras Amendment to the Hindu Marriage Act recommended giving a legal status to such priest-less marriages and rights of inheritance to the children born from such a marriage, upon the death of a parent or spouse.[167]

---

[162] Hodges, 'Revolutionary Family Life and the Self Respect Movement'. While the movement did include comprehensive policy objectives about the growth of education, textile, handloom sectors, and a focus on language as well as writings on the rights of workers, reservations for backward castes, and so on, the regulation of family life became one of the significant ways in which the other ends could also be achieved.

[163] See also Anandhi, 'Women's Question in the Dravidian Movement c. 1925–1948'.

[164] Edrisinha, *Debating Federalism in Sri Lanka and Nepal*, 291.

[165] File No. 17/61/67, Judicial I, Ministry of Home Affairs, NAI, New Delhi, 12.

[166] *Rajathi v. Selliah* (1966) II MLJ 40.

[167] The Anand Marriage Act, 1909, and the Arya Marriage Act, 1937, were also legislations that were aimed at regularizing customs by giving them statutory forms.

The Government of India responded by directing the Madras government not to pass the Hindu Marriage (Madras Amendment) Act of 1967 in the state legislature, and advised the president of India to withhold his assent to the bill.[168] The government objected to recognizing such a marriage on the grounds that it did not include any rituals, that is, *saptpadi*[169] (seven steps or circumambulations around the fire), garlanding, and so on, which were considered as crucial to a 'valid' marriage under the codified Hindu Marriage Act.[170] Thus, for all practical purposes, a marriage which was anti-Brahmin or against Brahminical rituals became 'de-religionized' in the process of codification as it was deemed insufficiently Hindu. The central government grouped non-Brahmin caste rituals under the *Special* Marriage Act while preserving the culture of the dominant through a religious prefix on the family laws of the Hindu community.

The central government raised several objections to the proposed bill, ranging from questions of the proof of marriage to the potential misuse of the new legislation since it regularized marriages retrospectively even when one of the partners was dead, allowing for potential conflicts over inheritance.[171] Parliament recommended to the Tamil Nadu government to accommodate its amendment on priest-less marriages within the framework of the Special Marriage Act. However, it clearly stated that even if it was recognized under the Special Marriage Act, the ex parte validation of a marriage after the death of one partner cannot be made permissible on 'moral' grounds. The government stated that this would be misused to validate an 'imaginary relationships' or 'an actual concubinage [*sic*]'.[172] The bone of contention for the central government was the lack of an elaborate ceremony in a Suyamariathai wedding which, the Government of India argued, would make the marriage 'extremely difficult to prove'.[173] Upper-caste rituals not only dominated codified laws on marriage but also became crucial to proving the validity of a marriage.

This was particularly problematic given that the Arya Marriage Validation Act, 1937, had also entailed a similar discussion on procedure and rituals in

---

168 File No. 17/61/67, Judicial I, Ministry of Home Affairs, NAI, New Delhi.
169 Ritual of taking seven steps around the sacred fire in a Hindu marriage
170 File No. 17/61/67, Judicial I, Ministry of Home Affairs, NAI, New Delhi, 5–6.
171 This chapter, however, is limited to exploring the way in which the provincial and national legislature articulated 'difference' and reconciled customary practices with personal law, especially since, as this discussion suggests, customary laws were often in contradiction of the codified national legislations.
172 'Amendment to Special Marriage Act', File No. 17/63/55, Judicial I, Ministry of Home Affairs, NAI, New Delhi.
173 File No. 17/61/67, Judicial I, Ministry of Home Affairs, NAI, New Delhi.

marriage and continued to remain in force even after the Hindu Marriage Act, 1955, was enacted. Arya Samaji weddings had simple procedures and a distinct system of certification of marriage, but no government, central or state, deemed it contradictory to Hindu law, which laid fresh procedures in 1955. However, in response to the demand for Suyamariathai marriages, the central government complained that 'a large function', the 'presence of a large number of men and women' at the scene of the wedding, and the observance of rites, with formalities spreading over a number of days, were necessary to ensure adequate publicity and sufficient proof of marriage of a 'permanent nature'.[174]

The Hindu Marriage (Madras Amendment) Act set up a confrontation between the provincial and central governments, as a few parliamentarians stated that such provisions were 'unheard of in a civilised society'.[175] The home ministry's correspondent cited the Supreme Court rulings,[176] arguing the word 'solemnised' referred to 'celebrated or performed with proper ceremonies and due form'.[177] The objection was premised on the assumption that 'wide publicity is a hallmark of Hindu Marriage' which, ironically, was precisely the practice the Self-Respect movement sought to end.[178]

Parliament also showed great reluctance in accepting the possibility of a simpler divorce available under the Suyamariathai marriages.

Marriage in one form or another is co-existent with the emergence of homo-sapiens on this Planet [sic]. In every *civilised society* marriage is either a sacrament or a contract. A Hindu marriage as always been regarded as a sacrament. Union of flesh and flesh, soul and soul and subsists even after death ... can be dissolved by a competent court.... Marriage is the basis of the family and family is the basic unit of a society. We should not by legislation do anything which may shake the foundations of our society to their very root. The path to promiscuity should not be opened out.[179]

The unease palpable in the central government's response to simpler ceremonies and the chastisement of any difference suggests that civilizational battles could be as easily framed within cultures and religions than between them.

---

[174] Ibid., 13.
[175] Ibid.
[176] *Bhaurao Lokhande v. State of Maharashtra* AIR 1965 SC 1564.
[177] File No. 17/61/67, Judicial I, Ministry of Home Affairs, NAI, New Delhi.
[178] 'Amendment to Special Marriage Act', File No. 17/63/55, Judicial I, Home, NAI, New Delhi, 12.
[179] File No. 17/63/55, Judicial I, Ministry of Home Affairs, NAI, New Delhi, 14–15 (emphasis mine).

Customs were placed into hierarchies of purity or righteousness that would qualify them as codification. For the Government of Madras, regularizing a form of marriage which was common and ubiquitous in the region was necessary for the purpose of protecting the rights of inheritance of surviving spouses and children born out of Suyamariathai marriages. The striking feature of the entire exchange, however, was the provincial government's refusal to opt out of the Hindu Marriage Act. Thus, the amendment served to widen the category of a Hindu, even when the custom of Suyamariathai marriages itself was borne out of a separatist movement that had aimed to distinguish itself from caste-based Hinduism.

The law ministry in its correspondence with the Government of Madras repeatedly invoked Article 44 (that recommended a Uniform Civil Code) to condemn the endeavour of the Madras government as a step away from uniformity rather than towards it. The central government also expressed its doubts on whether the Hindu Marriage Act could permit any and all customary practices as valid, and it perceived the Madras Amendment to be setting a wrong precedent.[180]

The central government defended a particular Hindu ritual as not only superior but further justified its modularity as a step towards 'secular' directive of a Uniform Civil Code. The Madras government, on its part, opposed the monopolization of Hinduism by the upper castes and unwilling to relinquish its link with religion, insisted on the inclusion of alternate rituals under 'Hindu' law and not any 'neutral' legislation. Both sides equally claimed that their enactments were 'secular' interventions, even as they battled over the religious prefix of 'Hindu' in their marriage Acts. These articulations again provide a window into a spectrum of religiosities within the state and its institutions which relied on languages of secularism as well as of religion which challenge the idea that modern secularism was a coherent regulatory strategy.

The central government expressed suspicion on the Suyamariathai form of marriage which had been introduced 'by the reformists' in the 1920s, and doubted whether it qualifies as a 'customary practice'.[181] They stated: 'It may be very hazardous to leave it to the whims and fancies of two witnesses who need not necessarily be Hindus or persons of the locality or even known to the parties.'[182] Thus, there was no consistent policy for the extent to which 'custom' could dictate the law and personal law remained a product of custom and usage capable even of inventing tradition.[183] The Hindu Code Bill had created a hierarchy between

---

[180] File No. 17/61/67, Judicial I, Ministry of Home Affairs, NAI, New Delhi.
[181] Ibid.
[182] Ibid.
[183] Terence Ranger and Eric J. Hobsbawm, eds., *The Invention of Tradition* (Cambridge: Cambridge University Press, 2012).

codified and un-codified tradition, and the Madras Amendment challenged precisely this hierarchy.

An attempt to define culture entails not just marking the aspects or practices it includes but also what it chooses to reject.[184] The codification of Hindu law was not only an exercise to legitimize culture but it was also an attempt to exterminate a number of practices from the purview of religion in order to present its pure form. The codification of Hindu law had rejected bigamy, cross-cousin marriages, Marumakkathayam and Aliyasanthana systems of inheritance, and priest-less or Suyamariathai marriages. The preserved practices were ones that the dominant Hindus believed to be 'good' practices to which religion could safely pledge allegiance to, and acquire the approval of the state for its preservation and perpetuation.

By the end of 1967, after extensive correspondence and debate, the central government revised its objections.[185] It reluctantly conceded to the Madras Amendment on the condition that the state legislature would introduce a provision for adequate proof of marriage in the bill. In the central government's interdepartment correspondence, it was suggested: 'Now at this stage to say "no" will create all sorts of difficulties.'[186] The very object of the Madras Amendment was to simplify procedures that necessitated the presence of a priest at the time of marriage, and the Government of Madras held its ground on seeking the elimination of the elaborate ceremonies that surrounded the event of the wedding while remaining under 'Hindu' law. The bill eventually became effective from 1968 and a clause 2(a) was added to the Hindu Marriage Act:

> Notwithstanding anything contained in section 7, but subject to the other provisions of this Act, all marriages to which the section applies solemnised after the commencement of the Hindu Marriage (Madras Amendment) Act, 1967, shall be good and valid in law.[187]

This amendment indicated that a variation within personal law could be better negotiated on the grounds of regional identities than on the grounds of gender or caste differences. This suggests that matters of family law very often were syncretized locally and did not possesses a uniform pan-Indian character drawn

---

[184] Veena Das, *Critical Events: An Anthropological Perspective on Contemporary India* (Delhi: Oxford University Press, 1995).

[185] Correspondence dated 21 September 1967; File No. 17/61/67, Judicial I, Ministry of Home Affairs, NAI, New Delhi.

[186] Ibid.

[187] The Hindu Marriage Act, 1955.

from universal notions of religion. Masaji Chiba's work on Sri Lanka suggests a tripartite model of law that provides a valuable insight to understanding the state's dilemma in the codification of customs.[188] In Chiba's model, 'official law' was not merely composed of law made by the state, but it included all law-like rules and precedents that find their basis in society or religion, which have been accepted by the state. Often the state features these rules as its own without acknowledgement or even awareness of their origins from religious or regional influences.[189] This helps explain the state's dilemma in accommodating customs. Whatever the state was unable to integrate in its indigenously, religiously or regionally informed laws was deemed a custom, that is, something 'in derogation of the general law'.[190] This argument also weaves in contributions of Derrett, Menski, and Subramanian who argue that there was an underlying Hindu morality informing India's legal tradition. The Madras Amendment was a challenge to Hindu universalism, while also ultimately making Hindu law more legally capacious. The case of Suyamariathai marriages highlighted the central problem that unity (of the federal state) was contrary to uniformity.[191] Further, a political party which had emerged from a movement that aimed to restructure family law had successfully challenged the Congress out of office, and promptly sought an amendment to the Hindu Marriage Act, thus reaffirming the centrality of family to state politics and law.

The significance of the codification of Hindu law was not the rights it claimed to grant women, but that through a process of continued amendments, it evolved as a model of personal law that was forced to accommodate diversity. Ironically, in theory, and principle, the Hindu code was executed for the purpose of achieving uniformity. The law in the decades subsequent to its passage gave legitimacy to various kinds of customary practices.[192] As Menski's writing demonstrates, law reforms create more legal pluralism, not greater national legal uniformity.[193]

The Madras Amendment demonstrated that the under-representation of the south Indian states in the making of Hindu law was reasserted through the structure of federalism. The 'Statement of objects and reasons' of the Amendment Bill

---

[188] Masaji Chiba, 'Legal Pluralism in Sri Lankan Society: Toward a General Theory of Non-Western Law', *The Journal of Legal Pluralism and Unofficial Law* 25, no. 33 (1993): 197–212.

[189] Chiba, 'Legal Pluralism in Sri Lankan Society'.

[190] 22nd Report, Law Commission of India, 1961, 6, para 13.

[191] Mark Tushnet and Madhav Khosla, eds., 'Introduction', in *Unstable Constitutionalism: Law and Politics in South Asia*.

[192] 'Diverse Justice: Flavia Agnes to Tanu Thomas K. on the Question of Uniform Civil Code', *Times of India*, 29 August 2003.

[193] Werner Menski, 'From Dharma to Law and Back? Postmodern Hindu Law in a Global World', working paper no. 20, Heidelberg papers in South Asian and Comparative Politics, 2004.

included a discussion on how 'Aryan' and 'Dravidian' practices blended together to form the Hindu community: 'The Dravidians have adopted the laws and usages of the Aryans, but doubtlessly retained some of their original customs, perhaps in a modified form.'[194] Federalism thus provided a structural framework for enabling regional forces that could undermine the pan-Indian religious categories envisaged by legislature, and this was not exclusive to Hindu law alone.

Capacious Majority and Uniform Minority

The consolidation of regional identities, however, did not always result in the preservation of local customs. While the Christian law, owing to local resistance, could not be universalized in Kerala, as discussed earlier, for Muslims the state legislature abolished local customary laws and extended the Shariat Application Act of 1937 uniformly to all Muslims in 1962.[195] As Fyzee had pointed out in his correspondence with Nehru, there were a number of hybrid communities that inhabited Kerala. Most of these communities followed the Aliyasanthana and Marumakkathayam systems of inheritance and succession even while they professed Islam. These customary laws were permitted under the Mappilla Succession Act, 1918,[196] applicable in Malabar, the Travancore Muslim Succession Act (XI of 1108) applicable in Travancore, and the Cochin Muslim Succession Act[197] applicable in Cochin.[198] But once the regions (*taluks*) were merged, the government again invoked 'Entry 5' of the concurrent list, which stated that '[m]arriage and divorce; infants and minors; adoption; wills, intestacy and succession; joint family and partition; all matters in respect of which parties in judicial proceedings were, immediately before the commencement of this Constitution subject to their personal law'.[199] Thus, the Shariat Application Kerala (Amendment) Act, 1963, stated:

> Notwithstanding any custom or usage to the contrary, in all questions regarding intestate succession, special property of females, including personal property inherited or obtained under contract gift or any other provisions of personal law, marriage, dissolution of marriage, including *talaq, ila, zihar, lian, kzhula* [sic], and *mubarat*;[200] maintenance, dower, guardianship, gifts, trusts, and trust properties

---

[194] File No. 17/61/67, Judicial I, Ministry of Home Affairs, NAI, New Delhi.
[195] File No. 17/171/62, Judicial, Ministry of Home Affairs, NAI, New Delhi.
[196] Madras Act 1 of 1918 in ibid.
[197] File No. 17/171/62, Judicial, Ministry of Home Affairs, NAI, New Delhi.
[198] Ibid.
[199] Ibid.
[200] Different procedures of dissolution of Muslim marriages.

and *waqfs*[201], the rule of decision in cases where the parties are Muslims, shall be the Muslim Personal Law (Shariat).[202]

However, it is also worth noting that the relationship between the Government of India and the Communist Government of Kerala had been turbulent since the state was carved out in 1957; therefore, party politics, once again, cannot be ruled out from the way in which personal law was negotiated in the region. In 1959, Nehru, allegedly on the advice of his daughter Indira Gandhi, had dismissed the Communist government led by E. M. S. Namboodiripad, the first non-Congress government in the Union of India.[203] The dismissal was on the ground that the introduction of the Land Reform Ordinance was too radical and prompted the breakdown of law and order in the state.[204] The church in Kerala as well as the Muslim League also postured against the Communist government in the state owing to their advocacy against religious education. In 1963, the Congress came to power in Kerala with the support of the Muslim League, an alliance which was the first of its kind since India's partition, which kept the Left parties out of power.[205] While the entering of the Muslim League in the ruling alliance and the extension of the Muslim Personal Law (Kerala) Amendment Act in 1963 may be coincidental, a connection between the two is also plausible.

While the receding and extending of personal laws took place at the dawn of federalism, Krishnaswamy's work differentiates between genuine federal conflicts and others that have a purely partisan political character.[206] In both instances of Madras and Kerala, the partisan character of the conflict cannot be overlooked. Thus, while a thorough engagement with the working of federalism is outside the scope of this chapter, it is important to acknowledge that some of the new regional parties that formed the state governments in the 1960s were organized along

---

[201] Land for an Islamic religious charity.

[202] The bill further intended to make the central Act applicable in the respect to agricultural lands 'for the purpose of unification', which had been specifically left out in the previous amendments.

[203] Robin Jeffrey, 'Jawaharlal Nehru and the Smoking Gun: Who Pulled the Trigger on Kerala's Communist Government in 1959?', *Journal of Commonwealth and Comparative Politics* 29, no. 1 (1991): 72–85.

[204] 'Skulls and Bones Displayed: Clash Reported in Trivandrum', *Times of India*, 2 September 1959. President's rule or Emergency was imposed on the state six times, which is one of the highest number of times any state has been subjected to the Emergency between 1957 and 1980.

[205] Jeffrey, 'Jawaharlal Nehru and the Smoking Gun'.

[206] Sudhir Krishnaswamy, 'Constitutional Federalism in the Indian Supreme Court', in *Unstable Constitutionalism: Law and Politics in South Asia*, 355–80.

caste lines and therefore challenged the universality of Hinduism.[207] Regional movements added to the durability of federalism and ensured (especially after the 44th Amendment discussed in the next chapter) that arbitrary interventions of the central government became untenable over the years.[208]

The primary regional party in the state of Tamil Nadu had been born out of an anti-caste movement which was focussed on popularizing norms of equal status of partners in a marriage and was postured against ritualism in marriage ceremonies. These new political parties were also ones that first challenged the Congress Party out of power in their state's elections, even when the Congress had a stronghold over the centre and most of the other Indian states. Thus, federalism, by allowing for the flourishing of regional parties, also aided in the recognition of difference that these parties insisted upon. This recognition of 'difference' in many ways was the recognition of customary and cultural practices and therefore contributed directly to expanding the category of 'personal law'.

The homogenization of Hindu, Muslim, and Christian law curtailed some aspects of regional diversity either in the name of reform or in the hope of unification. While the Madras government had, under the Hindu Marriage (Madras Amendment) Act, sought the acceptance and recognition of certain customary practices, the Kerala government sought uniformity within Muslim law. Whether the law was widened or unified was contingent on the group affected. While the central government grudgingly accommodated regional and caste differences within Hindus, it sought to nationalize Muslim personal law and Christian law was amended in states before a national law amendment came about. This also suggests that Hindu personal law could be expanded to incorporate caste differences that made the Hindu religion capacious, while the consolidation of the Muslim personal law only added to the rhetoric of the inviolability of the Shariat Application Act, 1937, a trend that was strengthened over the decades, discussed later in the book.

---

[207] The Bahujan Samaj Party, which consolidated the Dalit vote bank in UP, was founded in 1984; the Shiv Sena (the Army of Shivaji) in Maharashtra was organized to consolidate the Marathi vote in 1966. On federalism, see chapter 2, 'Federalism' in Madhav Khosla, *The Indian Constitution: Oxford India Short Introductions* (New Delhi: Oxford University Press, 2012), 44–86; Louise Tillin, 'United in Diversity? Asymmetry in Indian Federalism', *Publius: The Journal of Federalism* 37, no. 1 (2007): 45–67; and James Manor, 'Center–State Relations', in *The Success of India's Democracy*, ed. A. Kohli, J. Breman, and G. P. Hawthorn (New Delhi: Cambridge University Press, 2001), 78–102.

[208] Austin, *Working a Democratic Constitution*. See also Jyotirindra Dasgupta, 'India's Federal Design and Multicultural National Construction', in *The Success of India's Democracy*, 49–77.

In fact, Hindu law was given wide and flexible interpretations even in judicial decisions. For instance, when a group asserted its identity as separate from Hinduism, as in the case of *Satsang Sabha* and *Ramkrishna Mission cases*, the Court concluded that these were sects within Hinduism - which is a plural religion. Separate contractual or inheritance laws or difference in custom did not qualify them to opt out of Hindu identity nor give up their distinctiveness, so long as they remained even tenuously within the Hindu fold.[209] In the Muslim cases, the *Bai Tahira*[210] and *Fazlunbi Biwi*[211] cases discussed in greater detail in the next chapter produced decisions favourable to women but with an emphasis on 'authentic' and linear reading of Islamic law.

The insistence on the resilience of 'colonial codes' in the writing of Indian legal history appears to be an overstated assumption in the light of the endeavours of the 1950s and 1960s, which inherently transformed the politics of personal law if not the personal law itself. Denault and Newbigin have shown, importantly, that attributing law making to the colonial state has marginalized if not negated the contributions of 'users' and 'implementers' of law. They advocate for studying the mechanisms of law itself rather than reducing law to mere evidence for theorizing other 'larger concerns' of colonialism or neo-colonialism.[212] To a degree, there are evidences of both continuity and change from colonial law but the postcolonial preoccupation with personal law shows that a range of rationales guided the repeated meddling with personal status laws.

The state, in fact, chose to involve itself in matters of religion and of the private domain more fiercely than before, as visible from the numerous committees and commissions set up to amend religious law. Therefore, it was in the interest of the state to recognize difference, so that citizens accepted its regulatory authority especially where it was difficult to reach a consensus on the recognition of common or shared practices. The central and state governments competed for greater legitimacy and greater jurisdiction by extending legal protection to a diversity of customs and the organization of their family structure.

---

[209] *Shanti Sarup v. Radhaswami Satsang Sabha* AIR 1969 All 248; *Sri Ram Krishna Mission and Anr. v. Paramanand and Ors.* AIR 1977 All 421. See R. Sen, *Articles of Faith: Religion, Secularism, and the Indian Supreme Court* (Oxford: Oxford University Press, 2010) for a discussion on definitions of Hinduism in court rulings.

[210] *Bai Tahira v. Ali Hussain Fidali Chothia*, 1979 SCR (2) 75.

[211] *Fazlunbi v. Khader Vali*, 1980 SCR (3)1127.

[212] Eleanor Newbigin, Leigh Denault, and Rohit De, 'Introduction: Personal Law, Identity Politics and Civil Society in Colonial South Asia', *Indian Economic and Social History Review* 46, no. 1 (2009): 1–4.

The central government responded to these contestations by commissioning reports on the subject of personal law. Thus, the preoccupation with family law continued in the decades that followed the codification of Hindu law.

In a context where exceptions had already been granted to all personal laws to circumvent the fundamental right to equality (Article 14),[213] regional amendments can be seen as attempts to democratize the category of personal law itself. These amendments seek to recognize regional or caste differences, even as they ultimately broaden the prefix of 'Hindu' *through* the law. These encounters with personal law sometimes reinforced old hierarchies or generated new ones. Thus, greater recognition of plurality aided the democratic process and wherever the plurality was denied became fertile ground for democratic movements and protests, discussed in the following chapters.

Conclusion

In the 1960s, the state expressed its concern with personal law in the form of successive Law Commission reports on Christian marriage law and Muslim personal law. This was the state's attempt to legitimize its own authority by writing religion in a statutory form, and regulating the intimate lives of citizens, while also reaffirming the space of religion in law and legislation. The commissions attempted, with very limited success, to bridge the gap between the state and society which may have been motivated by an urge to enhance state control but entailed, instead, a surrender of power. Such regulatory objectives were inevitably undermined by the decentralized and diffused authority of the state itself, where parliament attempted to wrest out personal law from the judiciary; within parliament, committees were instituted and defeated in brief conversations between key individuals, and state and central governments also locked horns on matters of marriage.

The efforts made towards codifying religious difference in the 1960s were top-down attempts often initiated and monitored directly by the Prime Minister's Office.[214] Law reform commissions and committees acted as buffer zones for accommodating civil society activists, religious leaders, and the federalist urge for diversity, but did not immediately succeed in precipitating new laws. In the case of Christian law, the discussion resulted in an amendment bill which was not prioritized in parliament with the same enthusiasm as Hindu family law, but prompted provincial amendments and was eventually implemented five decades later in 2001.

---

[213] *The State of Bombay v. Narasu Appa Mali* AIR 1952 Bom 84.

[214] The public response to codifying Muslim personal law followed in the 1970s after the top-down attempts such as the Muslim Law Committee were aborted; this is analysed in the next chapter.

For Muslim law, the formation of a quasi-government-judicial committee that prepared a draft bill was sabotaged internally at the executive level itself. Regardless of the legislative impact of these reports, the discussions they provoked proved to be significant and instructive for some of the judgments and amendments in later decades. For instance, the Sarla Mudgal case in 1995[215] shed light on the problem of bigamy enabled by conversion of religion and resulted in an intense public debate and the formation of yet another Law Commission on the subject of the convert's marriage in 2009.[216]

The 1960s were characterized by piecemeal but consistent changes to the law. The consensus on practices that appeared to form the core of 'religious law' were embodiments of the norms of the upper-caste elite's version of 'good laws' as was the case in Hindu law. However, the process was hardly a permanent one. Codification provided a skeletal structure for the state for codifying tradition and 'statutorizing' more local ways of life. The amendments to Hindu marriage laws, thus, demonstrate the fluidity of the category of personal law and its dynamic nature.

Exceptions, exemptions, and regional variation in laws came to characterize the afterlife of Hindu law codification. This made the legislative process dynamic and responsive, a characteristic that is often attributed to the Indian constitution.[217] This was possible in Hindu law because most related aspects of Hindu family law had been codified and, therefore, could be contested through the instrument of the law, and were open to amendments. However, in the case of minorities, particularly Muslim law, which was contained in a few brief Acts, personal law was rigidified and nationalized in order to mark off a jurisdictional territory based on religious difference rather than expanded to accommodate differences within religion as 'hybrid' communities were formally brought under the Shariat Application Act, 1937, even on matters of inheritance.[218] Thus, while Hindu law became increasingly more capacious, Muslim law, even in the contemplation of its reform, was sought to be aligned with textual sources with an emphasis on relinquishing regional diversity.

---

[215] *Sarla Mudgal v. Union of India*, 1995 SCC (3) 635. See discussion in Chapter 5, section II.

[216] 227th Report, Law Commission of India, 'Preventing Bigamy via Conversion to Islam: A Proposal for Giving Statutory Effect to Supreme Court Rulings', 2009.

[217] Zoya Hasan, Eswaran Sridharan, and R. Sudarshan, *India's Living Constitution: Ideas, Practices, Controversies* (Delhi: Permanent Black, 2005); ch. 1, 'Settling into the Harness', in Austin, *Working a Democratic Constitution*. See also Khosla, *The Indian Constitution*.

[218] The Bombay High Court bench attempted to curtail the right of men to affect arbitrary and unilateral *talaq*. Parsi law also saw very few piecemeal amendments to narrow the gap between rights of men and women in family law.

Marriage, divorce, succession, and conversion remained matters of contention for the government. Thus, as Basu suggests, it was only through encounters with legal authorities that the state and the citizen enter into intimate conversations.[219] Within such a mechanism, citizens increasingly surrendered aspects of their way of life to be mediated by the state. Gupta further suggests that while the state is not necessarily centralized, it is through disaggregated authorities that the state enables regulation and protection.[220] Ever increasing regulation, however, in turn produces more arenas for contest. This also explains somewhat the litigious nature of the Indian state. Thus, the urgency to codify law can be seen as a reaction typical of a postcolonial state which was seeking greater legitimacy through the instrument of the law.

By consolidating the category of 'religion' in statutory form, the state enabled itself to mediate the extent of the religiosity of an individual. This was not merely a categorization of civil or criminal aspects of religion but was fundamentally about the monopolization of the authority to determine these distinctions. Committees became a channel for conversation between the civil society–endorsed 'law reform' and the provincial legislatures that prompted minor amendments; and often provided modular bills for national legislations. Therefore, while the postcolonial state continued to utilize local groups in order to extend and expand its own sovereignty, at the same time, it postured itself against granting legitimacy to local practices or customs in *perpetuity*. Yet with time, the authority on personal law became so diffused that it was increasingly harder to establish when the state and its institutions may be regulating and when they are indeed a party, and not the adjudicator of the regulatory process. The next chapters trace this changing relationship of personal law with state actors that could provide a window into a unique trajectory of democracy in India.

---

[219] Basu, *The Trouble with Marriage*, 6.

[220] Akhil Gupta, *Red Tape: Bureaucracy, Structural Violence, and Poverty in India* (Durham, NC: Duke University Press, 2012). See also Thomas Blom Hansen, 'Sovereigns beyond the State: On Legality and Authority in Urban India', in *Sovereign Bodies: Citizens, Migrants, and States in the Postcolonial World*, ed. T. B. Hansen and Finn Stepputat (Princeton, NJ: Princeton University Press, 2005), 169–91.

3

Social Movements, National Emergency, and the Custody of the Constitution, 1967–79

> Marriage is essentially a social affair and therefore succeeds in indoctrinating coming generations in the ideology implicit in it.
>
> — *Towards Equality* Report, 1974[1]

In the 1970s, India witnessed the rise of diverse social movements, many of which focussed on women's rights, and some specifically on women's rights in relation to marriage.[2] Autonomous women's movements were gaining momentum[3] and the decade was also characterized by several influential reports and further amendments to address gender discrimination. The decade also saw tremendous political turmoil during the years of the Emergency which, among other things, brought with it the addition of the word 'secularism' to the preamble of the Indian constitution. The national Emergency of 1975 was also followed by a certain reverence for the constitution, and a veneration for the courts. These simultaneous events and processes had very specific effects on the personal law story. This chapter will explore a series of negotiations between and among activists, state actors, and stakeholders, many of which were directed towards precipitating legal change. Emphasis on legal change in turn advanced the idea that the law could be an end goal rather than a means to an end.

The enhanced focus of the social movements on the law yielded outcomes that included protective legislation and progressive judgments for women as well as populist

---

[1] Government of India (GoI), *Towards Equality: Report of the Committee on the Status of Women in India* (New Delhi: Department of Social Welfare, Ministry of Education and Social Welfare, Government of India, 1974), 63.

[2] For a history of women's movements in India, see Radha Kumar, *The History of Doing: An Illustrated Account of Movements for Women's Rights and Feminism in India 1800–1990* (New Delhi: Zubaan, 1997); Radha Kumar and Amrita Basu, *From Chipko to Sati: The Contemporary Indian Women's Movement* (Boulder, Colorado: Westview Press, 1995); Gail Omvedt, *Reinventing Revolution: New Social Movements and the Socialist Tradition in India* (London: ME Sharpe, 1993).

[3] Nandita Gandhi and Nandita Shah, *The Issues at Stake: Theory and Practice in the Contemporary Women's Movement in India* (New Delhi: Kali for Women, 1992).

measures that pleased religious orthodoxy. These negotiations with the law are demonstrated through three cases of conflict. First, the disagreement between Muslim orthodoxy and the women's rights movement over intervention in Muslim personal law which provoked a confrontation also between parliament and the court. Second, the women's movement in the decade focussed significantly on legal reform and the influential *Towards Equality* Report of 1974 added further impetus to the reformative potential of the law. However, the national Emergency subsequently stalled social movements across the country and also accelerated the confrontation between the legislature and the judiciary. The decade concluded with the introduction of the public interest litigation (PIL) that enhanced the citizen's access to judicial remedies. The rise in the judicial element of the state, therefore, had direct consequences for Muslim personal law, and women's rights activism in the decades that followed. Lastly, the Emergency also entailed a substantial debate on secularism in parliament. These largely non-overlapping conversations and unconnected debates produced outcomes that were deeply connected and contingent, as discussed in the three sections of the chapter.

The first section explores the public concern on the subject of Muslim personal law, which had been building steadily since the sixties, and reached its zenith in the seventies. The 'pro' and 'anti' reform agitations on the subject of Muslim personal law competed for relevance and influence within the Muslim community in this decade. The framing of the movement for reform of Muslim personal law as merely a response to the *Shah Bano* judgment (1985) or a reaction to the rise of Hindu nationalism which has dominated scholarship[4] does not acknowledge the history of internal wrestling between groups over the question of women's rights within Muslim personal law. Such an assessment of the subject brushes under the carpet the thriving debate within and beyond the Muslim community as to what religious reform meant. These contestations predated the formation of the BJP (1980) and the Hindu nationalist commitment to the Uniform Civil Code. The first battle over Muslim personal law was fought in the 1970s rather than the 1980s, and it was not between Hindu nationalists and the Muslim orthodoxy, but within the Muslim community itself.

---

[4] Zoya Hasan, 'Gender Politics, Legal Reform, and the Muslim Community', in *Appropriating Gender: Women's Activism and Politicized Religion in South Asia*, ed. Patricia Jeffery and Amritu Basu (Cambridge: Routledge, 1998), 71–88; Archana Parashar and Amita Dhanda, *Redefining Family Law in India: Essays in Honour of B. Sivaramayya* (New Delhi: Routledge, 2008); Ashutosh Varshney, 'Contested Meanings: India's National Identity, Hindu Nationalism, and the Politics of Anxiety', *Daedalus* 122, no. 3 (1993): 227–61; Siobhan Mullally, 'Feminism and Multicultural Dilemmas in India: Revisiting the Shah Bano Case', *Oxford Journal of Legal Studies* 24, no. 4 (2004): 671–92.

The hard-line position of the newly consolidated All India Muslim Personal Law Board (AIMPLB) in 1973 was a response to the growing movement for personal law reform in Maharashtra. The immediate trigger that hastened AIMPLB's formation was the Adoption Bill, 1972, under discussion in parliament from which AIMPLB desired an exemption for Muslims. One witnesses a new narrative of conflicts and contestations within the Muslim community with women's movements emerging in Bombay, while the Muslim 'old-guard' consolidated itself anew in Lucknow and Delhi. Processes of claim making that stemmed from movements for reform of personal law led to bitter battles over the custody of the constitution. The binary of 'rights' and 'religion', as ideas in conflict with one another, preoccupied the public.[5] The law was central to the conversation as a demand for it and resistance to it became the chief strategies behind which groups mobilized.

If the movement on the streets seeking changes in Muslim personal law found an ally in the Indian courts, the orthodox votaries against reform found sympathizers in parliament. Parliament repeatedly offered concessions to the latter which were overruled by the judiciary in piecemeal judgments.[6] This disagreement within the wings of the state was characteristic of the 1970s and Indira Gandhi's regime more generally.[7] During this period, audacious amendments were passed by the legislature, and these were subsequently struck down by the judiciary on the grounds of their inconsistency with the constitution, or to protect its 'basic structure'.[8] Thus, yet another struggle for the custody of the constitution marked the relationship between the courts and parliament. The 1970s made manifest the dual pressures on the constitution: first, the increasing power of the legislative

---

[5] Partha Chatterjee distinguishes between civil society and political society. For Chatterjee, civil society represented modern associations composed of 'citizens' whereas a political society was a larger associational form which could mediate institutions between a civil society and the state and was composed of a larger category of the 'population'. In this chapter, the term indicates that 'population', or rather more than just civil society organizations, were involved in the discussion of the Muslim personal law. Partha Chatterjee, *The Politics of the Governed: Reflections on Popular Politics in Most of the World* (New York, Chichester: Columbia University Press, 2004).

[6] See cases *Bai Tahira v. Ali Hussain Fidali Chothia*, 1979 SCR (2) 75 and *Fazlunbi v. Khader Vali*, 1980 SCR (3)1127.

[7] R. C. Rao, 'Mrs. Indira Gandhi and India's Constitutional Structures: An Era of Erosion', *Journal of Asian and African Studies* 22, nos. 3–4 (1987): 156–75.

[8] For judicial activism, see Pratap Bhanu Mehta, 'The Rise of Judicial Sovereignty', *Journal of Democracy* 18, no. 2 (2007): 70–83. For 'basic structure', see Sudhir Krishnaswamy, *Democracy and Constitutionalism in India: A Study of the Basic Structure Doctrine* (New Delhi: Oxford University Press, 2011).

element of the state which accumulated greater authority through amendments;[9] and second, the rise of social movements which located the constitution as the protector of their rights against competing groups as well as against the state.

The second section of the chapter analyses women's rights initiatives which were beginning to reject the idea of women being cast as mere beneficiaries of the state's benevolent paternalism. Women instead sought to become stakeholders in state policy. The women's movement's challenge to the centrality of religion in defining the family through the instrument of the law is exceptionally well documented in this period.[10]

Indira Gandhi's own commitment to women's rights, however, became embroiled in a grander political narrative of challenges to the dominance of the Congress Party that resulted in the imposition of the national Emergency in 1975. Social movements, thus, became the collateral damage of the national Emergency.[11] The legislative prowess of the fifth Lok Sabha, under Indira Gandhi's regime, subjected the constitution to the most amount of amendments in India's postcolonial history until then. The next section, therefore, analyses the formidable 42nd Amendment, through which the Indian democracy suffered a near-constitutional review, as the amendment fundamentally altered the relationship between the state and the federal governments, as well as the legislature and the judiciary. The amendment centralized the power of the state machinery in the office of the prime minister.[12]

The 42nd Amendment also constitutionally committed India to secularism—an issue that lay at the heart of any debate on personal law. The rise of Muslim politics in that decade, the emergence of a women's movement which explicitly discarded the framework of religion, and the rise of regional parties that was accompanied by communal conflict collectively informed the secularism of the 1970s. Thus, ironically, secularism as an instrument of democracy was installed in the constitution amidst the crisis of democracy—the Emergency.

Subsequently, in the post-Emergency era, when the new government sought to repeal the 42nd Amendment, the addition of the term 'secularism' to the

---

[9] Granville Austin, *Working a Democratic Constitution: A History of the Indian Experience* (New Delhi: Oxford University Press, 2003).

[10] For a critical reading of women's relationship with the law, see Flavia Agnes, 'Protecting Women against Violence? Review of a Decade of Legislation, 1980–89', *Economic and Political Weekly* 27, no. 17 (1992): WS19–WS33, and Ratna Kapur and Brenda Cossman, *Subversive Sites: Feminist Engagements with Law in India* (New Delhi: Sage Publications, 1996).

[11] Omvedt, *Reinventing Revolution*, on the impact of the Emergency on social movements.

[12] Sumantra Bose, 'From Independence to 1989', in *Transforming India*, ed. S. Bose (Cambridge, MA: Harvard University Press, 2013), ch. 1, 9–56.

preamble proved to be one of the few resilient clauses that survived the reversal. The final section demonstrates that post-emergency, the state of political flux engendered by the unstable coalition of the Janata Party served to strengthen the position of the courts, as both parliament and the judiciary claimed to be united in their endeavour to temper the absolute powers of the legislature.[13] This shift towards the judiciary was strengthened through newly mobilized legal instruments, such as the PIL, demonstrated a realignment of the relationship between the law and the democratic movements.[14] Eventually, this led the judiciary to assume positions that were noticeably confrontational towards the legislature.[15] The court's judgments, particularly after the PIL, responded much faster to demands for social change, than parliament's bills or commission reports. This permitted the stakeholders to circumvent the legislative debate and process when seeking change and the jurisdiction of the courts expanded to a hitherto unforeseen extent. The courts, however, proved to be uncertain allies of the women's movement.

Interestingly, the period of the 1970s sees the language of constitutional rights become the vocabulary of social movements at the same time as extraordinary powers are invoked in the name of the constitution through which those very movements were subdued. The Emergency, therefore, had different effects on all three stories the chapter considers—the Muslim dialogue on personal law, the women's movement, and the relationship between the legislature and the judiciary. This story of the 1970s challenges the writing of Muslim personal law's history in India around critical events or bombastic judgments and instead shows that events occasionally prompted changes in strategies of resistance, but were part of a longer dialogue within and between the community, family, and the institutions of the state.

---

[13] See Baxi on rise of the social action litigation in the 1970s where he argues that judicial activism of the early 1980s was a cathartic response to the excesses of the Emergency. Upendra Baxi, 'Taking Suffering Seriously: Social Action Litigation in the Supreme Court of India', *Third World Legal Studies* 4, no. 1 (1985): 107–32.

[14] Danial Latifi's petition against the Muslim Women's Act in 1987, Vishwa Lochan Madan's petition against Islamic courts, and Sarla Mudgal's case on conversion and bigamy are cases that evidence of how in the decades to come personal law began to be challenged in courts through writ petitions rather than through amendments. This is discussed in detail in Chapter 5 of the book.

[15] For judicial activism, see S. P. Sathe, *Judicial Activism in India* (New Delhi: Oxford University Press, 2002); and Mehta, 'The Rise of Judicial Sovereignty'. Judicial activism with respect to personal law is discussed in greater detail in Chapter 5.

I

Personal Law and Muslim Politics

The Urdu-speaking elite of north India had historically monopolized claims to the representation of the extremely heterogeneous Muslim community.[16] Bayly[17] and Robinson's[18] work on the late nineteenth century also illustrates that Muslim politics was dominated by north Indian Muslims in the United Provinces in late colonial India. Post-partition and independence, the representation of Muslims in all-India services and in municipalities and legislative assemblies had remained low. Issues of cow slaughter and religious conversion also remained politically charged and frequently triggered instances of violence, particularly in UP.[19] Hasan has argued that Muslim politics was gradually absorbed within Congress politics.[20] However, the elections of 1962 and 1967 witnessed a minor but consistent reduction of the Muslim vote for the Congress.[21] To Nehru's dismay, UP Congress leaders such as Purushottam Das Tandon, Thakur Das Bhargava, and Acharya Kriplani were selectively sympathetic to the ideology of the Hindu Mahasabha, particularly on the issues such as the Hindu Code Bill and cow slaughter.[22] The sporadic acts of violence against Muslims following the partition created a sense of disenchantment among Muslims with the Congress Party.[23] Thus, the Congress was, in fact, unable to absorb Muslim politics which after independence had evolved in regionally specific conditions and decidedly broke away from the pre-partition

---

[16]   Ayesha Jalal, *The Sole Spokesman: Jinnah, the Muslim League and the Demand for Pakistan*, vol. 31 (Cambridge: Cambridge University Press, 1994).

[17]   C. A. Bayly, *The Local Roots of Indian Politics: Allahabad, 1880–1920* (Oxford: Clarendon Press, 1975).

[18]   Francis Robinson, *Separatism among Indian Muslims: The Politics of the United Provinces' Muslims, 1860–1923* (Cambridge: Cambridge University Press, 2007).

[19]   Letters to Nehru from the minister of scientific research and cultural affairs and the law minister from 1958–63 in Humanyu Kabir Papers, Sr. No. 368, Sub File no. 161–273, 1957–65, Nehru Memorial Museum and Library (hereafter NMML), New Delhi.

[20]   Mushirul Hasan, *Legacy of a Divided Nation: India's Muslims since Independence* (London: Hurst & Co., 1997).

[21]   Election Commission Reports 1962 and 1967.

[22]   All India Congress Committee Papers (hereafter AICC), I instalment, File No. CL-10 /1946–7, NMML, New Delhi. Incidentally, this was also the lobby that was rallying for making Hindi a national language.

[23]   Steve I. Wilkinson, *Votes and Violence: Electoral Competition and Ethnic Riots in India* (Cambridge: Cambridge University Press, 2006).

politics of the Muslim League.[24] Muslims, for instance in Bihar, voted along caste lines,[25] while in UP they moved beyond the Congress dominance,[26] and had a significantly different representation in Maharashtra with flourishing civil society movements. Muslim politics also evolved in response to events, rather than led simply by any pan-Indian party or identity. Personal law, with the expansion of the Shariat Application Act in the 1960s, had the potential to somewhat become a pan-Indian issue. Even concerns about communal violence eventually merged with the demand for the protection of personal law—a demand more easily yielded to by the state than protection against violence.

For instance, in 1969, communal hostilities in Ahmednagar, Maharashtra, instigated retaliatory violence in the neighbouring districts of Bhiwandi in 1970.[27] Amidst tensions, in 1970, the celebrations of 'Shiv Jayanti', a Hindu festival in Maharashtra which had historically included Muslims as musicians, was marked by its exclusive 'Hindu' character.[28] In preparation of the Shiv Jayanti in 1970, the Rashtriya Utsav Dal, a Hindu hard-line outfit, campaigned to trail the processions through a Muslim-majority area in Nizampura, Maharashtra, deviating from the route the processions had historically taken. This sparked off tensions as 3,000 to 4,000 Hindus from the adjoining villages joined the procession armed with *lathis*,[29] and Muslims retaliated by pelting stones at the procession. The triggers for violence were small and spontaneous but the incident had repercussions as riots followed in the neighbouring districts such as Poona in 1972–73, and several hundred people, mostly Muslims, were killed.[30]

The reports of these incidents provoked responses from various organizations including the Muslim Personal Law Convention in Bombay, Aligarh Muslim University in UP in 1972, and Jamia Milia Islamia, Delhi, in March 1973. These congregations expressed concerns over heightened communalism but,

---

[24] Meher Fatima Hussain, 'The Freedom Movement and the Muslims of Bihar: Delineations on Minority Identity and National Independence', in *Islam in a Globalized World: Negotiating Fault Lines*, ed. Mushirul Hasan (Gurgaon: imprintOne, 2010), 311–29.

[25] AICC, II instalment, File No.1222.OD- 41(A), Bihar, NMML, New Delhi.

[26] AICC, II instalment, File No. 3811, Parliamentary Board Papers, NMML, New Delhi.

[27] 'P.M. Urges Concerted Bid by All: Parties to End Communalism', *Times of India*, 15 May 1970.

[28] Justice D. P. Madon Commission of Inquiry into the Communal Disturbances at Bhiwandi, Jalgaon, and Mahad in 1970, Part III, Government Central Press, 1975.

[29] A long (generally, bamboo) stick.

[30] In all, according to the Justice D. P. Madon Commission of Inquiry Report, the violence resulted in 164 deaths, of whom 142 were Muslims and 20 were Hindus. In Bhiwandi alone, and in the adjacent villages of Khoni and Nagaon, the report said that 78 persons died: 17 were Hindus and 50 were Muslims. Report (Part III), 46–52.

interestingly, they warned in particular against any encroachment on Muslim personal law by the state.[31] During this period, organizations such as the Muslim Majlis-e-Mushawarat (AIMM),[32] in an alliance with the Jamat-e-Ulema-e-Hind, Jamaat-e-Islami Hind (JIH), and the IUML provided a united coalition against any interference in Muslim law—or rather against further legislation or amendments to Anglo–Mohammedan statutes that were codified to constitute the Muslim personal law in the 1930s.[33] Although the AIMMM explicitly stated that it did not function like a political party, its influence among Muslims became noticeable as the organization's structure penetrated various levels from provinces to districts to towns. By 1973, the AIMPLB was also established, and although it was not a statutory body, it began to gain the approval of the orthodox quarters of Muslim society. While the former was an organization with a broad base and diverse agenda, the latter started with a particular focus on Muslim personal law and its interpretation.

The period witnessed a growing public concern with Muslim personal law and, equally, a public engagement on the question of secularism. Several significant public figures, politicians, and activists expressed concern over potential threats to secularism. This was evident in the impetus that the reform of Muslim personal law had received. In this period, Muslim politics faced controversies on a number of issues including granting of minority status to institutions, notably, the Aligarh Muslim University;[34] and the fatwa (non-binding legal opinion issued by a recognized religious head)[35] issued against the recital of the national song 'Vande Mataram' by Muslims alleging that the song had Hindu connotations.[36] Dr Moin Shakir, a well-known activist, noted that the 1970s was a turning point in Muslim politics.[37]

[31] 'Change in Muslim Personal Law Resented', *Times of India*, 28 April 1973.
[32] The All India Muslim Majlis-e-Mushawarat (AIMMM) was formed in August 1964 to serve as a forum for promoting religious, cultural, educational, linguistic, and economic interests of the Muslim community and, consequently, the interests of the nation. Although headquartered in Delhi, it had working committees across the country. One of its foremost listed aims and objects was the promotion of unity among various communities in India, Hindus, Muslims, Harijans, Christians, Sikhs, Parsees, Buddhists, Jains, and so on. http://www.mushawarat.com/.
[33] Cyclostyled copy of pamphlet issued on 22 August 1973, accessed in June 2013, AIMPLB Office, Okhla, New Delhi.
[34] 'Aligarh Not to Be Declared Minority University', *Times of India*, 7 April 1973.
[35] A fatwa is a non-binding legal opinion in Islamic law, generally an answer to a question posed, but it does not have a legal sanction.
[36] 'Councillor Grilled on "Vande Mataram" Issue', *Times of India*, 18 January 1975.
[37] Shakir stated: 'The Muslim leadership had failed to comprehend the danger in the two-nation theory. The community had been led to believe that any change in status-quo must be resisted lest they would be assimilated in the Hindu-mass.' In 'Indian Muslims', *Times of India*, 3 September 1970.

Muslim Personal Law and Civil Society Movements[38]

The Muslim Satyashodhak Samaj and the Indian Secular Society in Maharashtra were two of the major organizations that kept the agenda for personal law reform in the public eye. A. B. Shah, the founder of the Indian Secular Society (1970) in Poona, became a significant voice advocating the reform of personal law.[39] Born in Gujarat, Shah was a self-proclaimed atheist, and also signed the Humanist Manifesto.[40] His interest in Muslim law grew particularly out of his friendship with Hamid Dalwai, who was a co-founder of the Muslim Satyashodhak Samaj. Shah argued against an unqualified support for Muslim personal law on issues of marriage and divorce in his publications *Religion and Society in India* and *What Ails Our Muslims?* both published in 1981.[41] While the initiatives of the 1970s brought personal law to the centre stage, these were in no way confined to the questions of personal law alone, but attempted to frame the Muslim community's concerns, marginalization, and neglect in state policies.

The pro-reform agitations appeared to be ideologically consistent with the writings of D. E. Smith, an English academic and lawyer, who suggested a tripartite arrangement of state–religion–individual relationship that treated the state and religion as separate spheres that do not overlap—a popular argument on secularism that generally dominated the writings of the 1960s and the 1970s.[42] The movement for reform was a step away from the proximity between state and religion that the legislative initiatives in the 1960s had envisaged through committees that viewed personal law as positive freedoms. It was also distinct from the debates on the Hindu Code Bill in the 1950s where parliament had relentlessly tried to anchor the new code into religious doctrines to present a modern and 'secular' face of Hinduism *through* the law rather than create a distance between law and religion. The Hindu Law Acts had barely resembled religious scriptures but the parliamentary debates on the Hindu Code Bill discussed in Chapter 1 reveal the insistence on trying to tenuously link the law to religion by framing the reform measures as the 'original' or 'true' intent of religion itself. Those discussions were also marked by a repeated framing of Hinduism as a modern and secular religion

---

[38] A version of this section has been published in Saumya Saxena, 'Commissions, Committees, and the Custodians of Muslim Personal Law in Post-Independence India', *Comparative Studies of South Asia Africa and Middle East* 38, no. 3 (2018): 423–38.

[39] 'Indian Secularism: Changing Public Attitude', *Times of India*, 22 October 1976.

[40] The Humanist Manifesto laid out a humanist world view in three parts that followed in 1933, 1973, and 2003. While they vary considerably, the central theme remained the lack of belief in a deity or a high power. The manifestos were signed by prominent academics.

[41] A. B. Shah, *What Ails Our Muslims?* (Bombay: Books LLC, 1980).

[42] D. E. Smith, *India as a Secular State* (Princeton, NJ: Princeton University Press, 1963).

rather than viewing religion and secularism as oppositional. However, the new movements of the 1970s, particularly in Maharashtra, sought a negative liberty of freedom *from* religious practices that violated the fundamental rights granted by the constitution.[43]

The period was characterized by a number of conferences organized by NGOs and women's rights groups on the subject of Muslim personal laws. The participants of these conferences travelled from many parts of Maharashtra including Poona, Sangli, Kolhapur, Ichalkaranji, Ahmednagar, and Bhiwandi. A major conference was held in December 1971, which was planned for up to 200 delegates from Maharashtra, as well as Delhi, Calcutta, and Aligarh, where the prominent speakers were all women.[44] In 1971, Begum Sharifa Tyabjee, another social activist based in Maharashtra, spoke openly against the 'tyrannical and unilateral provisions of Muslim personal law with respect to marriage'.[45] Besides arguing for the rights of Muslim women within family law and a Uniform Civil Code, it is interesting to note that the conference also cast light on the partition of Pakistan and extended support to the newly formed Bangladesh, calling for a celebration of the end of the 'brutal regime of Pakistan'.[46] The conference was more than just an attempt to offer issue-based resistance to certain provisions of Muslim personal law; it also placed Muslim women as a politically relevant group.[47] Unlike the Hindu Code Bill that sought to purge Hinduism from 'mortifying principles' inconsistent with modernity,[48] these articulations by Muslim civil society activists recognized 'women' as a primary identity, with a limited rhetoric of curing Islam.

In 1972, the All India Muslim Women's Conference was co-organized by the Muslim Satyashodhak Samaj and the Indian Secular Society in

---

[43] For the relationship between fundamental rights and directive principles of State Policy, see G. Bhatia, 'Directive Principles of State Policy: Theory and Practice', in *Oxford Handbook of the Indian Constitution*, ed. S. Choudhry, P. B. Mehta, and M. Khosla (Oxford: Oxford University Press, 2016), 645–61. See also C. A. Bayly, *Recovering Liberties: Indian Thought in the Age of Liberalism and Empire*, vol. 100 (Cambridge: Cambridge University Press, 2011) on negative liberties.

[44] Sharifa Tyabjee, Nazma Sheikh, Talimunnisa Saidani, Mumtaz Momin, Nadir Bano, and Shamim Attar were the notable names among others. 'All-India Muslim Women's Talks Planned', *Times of India*, 29 December 1971.

[45] 'Muslim Personal Law', *The Hindu*, 28 December 1971.

[46] 'Muslim Conference Condemns Pak Brutality', *Times of India*, 6 December 1971.

[47] The period of the 1970s was also very significant for legal reforms in Pakistan, although the movements in India do not reference the changes across the border. The amendments in Pakistan included the Family Courts Act, 1964 (West Pakistan), the Dowry and Bridal Gifts (Restriction) Act, 1976, and the Offence of Zina (Enforcement of Hudood) Ordinance, 1979.

[48] *Lok Sabha Debates*, 2 May 1955, Hindu Marriage Act, Gadgil's speech, col. 7291.

Poona, Maharashtra.[49] This was a coming together of civil society activists on the issue of personal law positing it primarily as a women's issue and not a religious question. The conference claimed to represent the new Muslim leadership, which consistently pleaded for a revision of their personal law. The conference, the fourth of its kind, was widely hailed as a 'Call to Muslim Women'.[50]

The conference paved the way for concrete proposals on issues such as laws concerning inheritance and divorce clauses, and included examples of other Islamic countries such as Tunisia[51] and Turkey,[52] where the *sharia* had been interpreted differently.[53] The delegates accused the Muslim orthodoxy of perpetuating obscurantism, and called for educational reforms and the encouragement of sciences in the madrasa (school for Islamic education) curriculum. The conference demanded the right to monogamy for Muslim women and the extension of the right to legal redress in cases of bigamy and sought the right to property (transfer of one-third of the property to the wife upon divorce or separation). Their demands were not restricted to rights for Muslim women alone. They sought changes to the Citizenship Act to provide a special rule for Indian women marrying foreigners, and the inclusion of cruelty and desertion as grounds for divorce in the Hindu Marriage Act.[54] Recommendations of free education and the introduction of sex education in middle school also suggested that the agendas were expanding. They deployed the language of fundamental rights to demand changes in personal law rather than settling for welfare provisions for women.

Hamid Dalwai, the vice president of the Muslim Satyashodhak Mandal and the Indian Secular Society, said that he considered the conference a fight of poor rural Muslims against the indifference of the rich urban Muslims.[55]

---

[49] 'Reforms Overdue', *Times of India*, 2 January 1972.

[50] Ibid.

[51] Article 21 CSP, 1956 (Personal Status Law in Tunisia), polygamy is punishable in case the husband practices it and can be nullified through legal procedures; for the wife to have more than one husband is considered illegal.

[52] Turkish Civil Code bans polygamy and has fixed property regimes for spouses which will govern all the distribution of property upon divorce.

[53] For comparative Islamic law, see N. Subramanian, 'Legal Change and Gender Inequality', *Law and Social Inquiry* 33, no. 3 (2008): 631–72. For a comparison of divorce grounds available to women in Islamic countries, see *Talaq-i-Tafwid: The Muslim Woman's Contractual Access to Divorce: An Information Kit*, ed. Lucy Carroll and Harsh Kapoor (1996). In March 1990, Women Living Under Muslim Laws (WLUML) published a document in French, titled, *Le kit d'information sur le droit de délégation du droit au divorce par contrat ou Talaq ba Tafouiz*, available at http://www.wluml.org/, accessed on July 2014.

[54] 'Reforms Overdue', *Times of India*, 2 January 1972.

[55] Syed Bhai and Anwar Rajan, 'For the Human Rights of Women—The Work of Muslim Satyashodhak Samaj', *Manushi* (1986), available at http://www.manushi-india.org/.

Sayed Mehboob Shah Qadri, a close associate of Dalwai, was also a vocal opponent of triple *talaq*. Having seen his sister suffer as a consequence of unilateral divorce, he became an influential voice within the Mandal and the movement.[56] A. B. Shah argued that the conference was fighting the obscurantism that tended to keep Muslims in their 'own self-imposed' ghetto.[57] The conference delegates passed a series of resolutions ranging from national integration, education, to the Uniform Civil Code.[58] Many of the issues raised in the conference evidenced Muslim engagement with national issues rather than cultural rights alone.

The Backlash

This public lament against Muslim personal law, however, also witnessed a severe backlash. The Maharashtra government was forced to make heavy police arrangements for the conference's venue, Maratha Mandir, given the rumours of a threat to blow up the building.[59] Such a backlash by orthodox groups indicated that the pro-reform collectives had shaken up their intended audience, the Muslim old guard of the JIH, to take note of the deficiencies in Muslim personal law.[60] There were also a number of counter-conferences organized in the following year in response to the Muslim Women's Conference in Maharashtra. One such conference was the Muslim Personal Law Convention which was held under the auspices of the JIH in Bombay, where the need for an apex body for the protection of personal law was first expressed. At a follow-up meeting in Hyderabad in early 1973, the AIMPLB came into existence. The pro-reform movement hailed this as an achievement that signified their arrival on the political scene.

The AIMPLB, however, chose not to communicate with the growing movement for amendments to Muslim personal law, but instead consolidated its opposition against parliament's introduction of the 'Adoption Bill' in 1972, as part of their commitment to preserve Muslim personal law. The Adoption Bill was introduced to simplify procedures for the adoption of children. This was in addition to the Guardians and Wards Act of 1890, which laid down the procedures for the adoption of children as wards and taking them into foster care. Apart from Hindus, who had the right to adopt a child under the Hindu Adoption and Maintenance Act, 1956, Muslims, Parsis, and Christians

---

[56] Sayed Mehboob Shah Qadri, *Jihad-e-teen talaq* (Pune: Samkaleen Prakashan, 2014).
[57] 'Muslim Progressives Urge Sweeping Reforms', *Times of India*, 26 March 1973.
[58] Ibid.
[59] Ibid.
[60] 'Muslim Personal Law', *The Hindu*, 9 January 1973.

in India did not have express provisions for adoption, and the new Adoption Bill was aimed at creating a universal provision for adoption for parents of any religion. The AIMPLB insisted that under the Islamic law, adoption of children was not permitted and used this as a springboard for initiating a movement to prevent any meddling with personal laws.[61] Even though such a reading of Islamic law remains disputed, AIMPLB refused to revise its stance. Later in the decade, even Parsi opposition to the Adoption Bill consolidated under the Bombay Zoroastrian Jashan Committee, seeking exemption on the adoption law.[62] Thus, much before the *Shah Bano* judgment of 1985, it was, in fact, the Adoption Bill that set off the first wave of protest against any perceived interference with Muslim personal law after independence. An intra-Muslim discord was central to the politicization of Muslim law. Hamid Dalwai's brother Husain Dalwai, another leading pro-reform activist who later joined the Congress Party,[63] commented:

> Muslims who protest loudly about the noble Islamic principles of non-violence and tolerance, publicly and unabashedly threw the same to the winds when they pelted with stones a small procession of their fellow religionists who were protesting against obscurantist views of the organisers of the convention [Muslim Personal Law Convention].[64]

The counter-convention of the JIH, however, claimed to have included more women than the Muslim Women's Conference could gather,[65] and declared that reform activists were 'anti-*sharia*'. Press reports highlighted a quote from another 'no change' activist Qaiser Begum Niazi, who univocally claimed that any changes in personal law would make women the 'losers'.[66] She further claimed that 7,000[67] women delegates from all the states attended the conference (most of whom she described as 'burqa-clad') pledging their support to preserve and protect Muslim

---

[61] AIMPLB, http://aimplboard.in/objectives.php. Whether adoption is forbidden or discouraged or even supported in Islamic law has been subject to debate.

[62] John R. Hinnells, 'Parsis in Post-Independence Bombay', in *The Zoroastrian Diaspora: Religion and Migration*, ed. John Hinnells (Oxford: Oxford University Press, 2005), ch. 2, 33–137.

[63] Dalwai was elected to the Maharashtra state legislature in 1998 and is currently a member of parliament.

[64] *Times of India*, 9 January 1973.

[65] This was disputed by Husain Dalwai of the Muslim Satyashodhak Samaj.

[66] 'Muslim Women Seek Guarantee on Personal Law', *Times of India*, 2 May 1973.

[67] This figure was also disputed, other newspapers reported differently. The Muslim Satyashodhak Samaj refused to accept this as an authentic estimate of the numbers.

personal law as it was.[68] The presence of women in the anti-reform movement also evidenced women's growing political agency within religious bodies. Often such participation within religious bodies was accessible to women who sought rights while remaining within the acceptable boundaries of a 'good Muslim' with her prime symbol of modesty, the burqa.

The pro-reform movement saw religion as something to overcome. Both Shah and Dalwai were not only atheists but also openly critical of religion and sought the containment of religion in the private realm. According to Dalwai, justifying social reform with religious reasoning would only strengthen those with monopoly over religious knowledge. He was more comfortable vesting that authority to reform in constitutional law instead, which here is seen to be not monopolized by the state but produced through democratic procedures and universal fundamental rights. This wariness with religious knowledge somewhat weakened the pro-reform movement as it presented women with an unfair choice between religion and constitutional rights. Thus, a Uniform Civil Code desired by the reform movements and an inviolability of the Muslim personal law demanded by the AIMPLB left very limited avenues for the expression of dissent for a 'religious' Muslim woman. The movement suffered from limitations arising out of its focus on the reformative potential of the law where only the realm of institutional politics was capable of bestowing political agency.[69] The new reform movement offered an inadequate rhetoric of 'saving Islam' from degenerate customary practices such as bigamy and spontaneous unilateral *talaq* in comparison to the debates on the codification of Hindu law, where Hinduism itself was invoked to argue for women's rights by calling out practices such as sati, bigamy, and the denial of rights to divorce as customary and degenerate. For Muslims, the debate was framed in a way that developed a binary between the subjugated-victim (the burqa-clad Muslim woman) and the resisting-agent (the woman who sought a Uniform Civil Code).[70]

The press reports alternated in an interesting pattern echoing the binary 'Overdue Reforms'[71] followed by '[a]ny change in custom would lead to immorality'.

---

[68] 'Muslim Women Seek Guarantee on Personal Law', *Times of India*, 2 May 1973.

[69] Saba Mahmood, *Politics of Piety: The Islamic Revival and the Feminist Subject* (Princeton, NJ: Princeton University Press, 2011). Mahmood's work on the piety movement in the mosques of Egypt sheds light on women's participation and problematizes the oversimplified correlation between legal unification through 'secular' institutions and justice.

[70] For a critique of legal and institutional tools for resistance and deriving political agency, see Mahmood, *Politics of Piety*. See also Saba Mahmood, 'Religious Reason and Secular Affect: An Incommensurable Divide?', *Critical Inquiry* 35, no. 4 (2009): 836–62, for an analysis of the different ways in which individuals imagine their relationship with the divine.

[71] *Times of India*, 2 January 1972.

Another article reported, 'Muslim Progressives Urge Sweeping Reforms',[72] which was followed by 'Muslim Women Oppose Changes in Personal Law'.[73] Interestingly, the Urdu newspapers in circulation in northern India, such as *Siasat* and *Musalman*, focussed only on stories of JIH's and AIMPLB's formation, with limited or no mention of the groups that opposed them. In 1975, the Muslim Satyashodhak Samaj declared a 'talaq jihad'—a war against the inhuman system of divorce.[74] A number of related organizations joined the cause with varied but broadly similar concerns rooted in the language of constitutional rights. They framed personal law as obscurantist practices that were violative of fundamental rights to equality (between sexes) and liberty (of women). There was little acknowledgment of the disapproval of the husband's use of the *biddat* (customary, casual or wavered) form of unilateral, instantaneous divorce within Islamic jurisprudence. Regardless of its interpretation as a custom or even a misinterpretation, it remained, in effect, a standard albeit problematic in interpretation of Hanafi law. The pro-reform movement invoked comparative Islamic jurisprudence but only to illustrate alternate legal models of the *sharia* rather than making any claim about the intrinsic goodness of Islam or a reading of the Quran that favoured equal rights for women.[75] Thus, the 'reform from within' argument that finds more currency in the 1990s and continues until the 2000s did not find vocal presence in the 1970s. Social movements of the 1970s focussed predominantly on the abolition of personal laws rather than their reinterpretation or revision.

Reform remained a legal pursuit rather than a social one. The Muslim women's movement however did succeed in making the personal overtly public if not immediately political. The protests and meetings became frequent and proliferated during the decade. In many such meetings, women gathered and exchanged stories about their experience of arbitrary divorce or dowry threats. In one event, a group of 350 women narrated their experiences of being denied jobs because of their divorce caused often due to infidelities of their husbands. Bombay University Professor

---

[72] *Times of India*, 26 March 1973.

[73] *Times of India*, 1 May 1973.

[74] 'Talaq Jihad', *Times of India*, 4 December 1975.

[75] For Muslim movements that encouraged and emphasized the 'correct' and 'devoted' religious practice based on religious texts, see B. D. Metcalf, 'Living Hadīth in the Tablīghī Jamā'āt', *The Journal of Asian Studies* 52, no. 3 (1993): 584–608. Metcalf suggests that Muslim social movements such as the Tablighi Jamaat focussed on assimilating women which they saw as normative Islamic standards. However, these movements were expressly withdrawn from the public arena of elections and political parties encouraged 'quietism' even as they acknowledged the suffering of others (11).

Kulsum Parikh narrated the story of a 60-year-old man who divorced his wife on grounds that he had a fancy for 'sari-wearing women' and not 'salwar-wearing women' and then married another woman of the age of 16.[76] Although many of the grievances and consequent recommendations went unheard at this point, they resurfaced in later decades and contributed to producing powerful new insights on feminism, secularism, and citizenship that informed feminist writing and Muslim women's organizations, discussed in the final chapter.[77]

The initiatives for reform were further fuelled when Abdul Rehman Antulay, the minister of law and judiciary in the Legislative Assembly of Maharashtra,[78] also a Muslim, recommended that parliament impose a ban on the practice of polygamy.[79] A. A. A. Fyzee remained a prominent voice on the subject since his involvement with the Muslim Law Committee in 1961, discussed earlier in Chapter 2. He remarked that the state was pandering to the pressures of Muslim orthodoxy for what he dubbed were reasons of 'political convenience'.[80] Their statements were widely reported in the English press. The celebration of pro-reform movements in the press, however, conveyed only a partial story.[81] The movement for reform in Maharashtra was symptomatic of the general rise of women's rights movements in the decade and made itself heard on the streets and in the press. However, simultaneously, the state machinery lent an ear to the orthodox counter-mobilizations of the AIMPLB. This was, therefore, by no means a fight between equals.

Muslim Personal Law and the State Machinery

Who constitutes the abstract category of 'Muslim leadership' was ultimately determined by whoever had proximity to the political elite. Bilgrami argues that often the most 'shrill and communal' voices within communities assume the role of representation of the community.[82] The very category of 'moderate Muslim' or 'Muslim women' was rendered incoherent when the choice and agency to dispute any religious commitments was denied to them. The institutions of the state and of religion were significantly monopolized by men who determined what the

---

[76] 'Divorced Muslim Women Narrate Their Plight', *Times of India*, 24 November 1975.
[77] Chapter 6 focusses on global debates of Islamic feminism, feminist relationship with the law, and the disagreements within the women's movement.
[78] He later became the minister of minority affairs, Government of India.
[79] State legislative assembly speech, reported in the *Times of India*, 30 December 1976.
[80] 'Muslim Progressives Urge Sweeping Reforms', *Times of India*, 26 March 1973.
[81] Srikanta Ghosh, *Muslim Politics in India* (Harvard: APH Publishing, 1987).
[82] Akeel Bilgrami, 'What is a Muslim? Fundamental Commitment and Cultural Identity', *Critical Inquiry* 18, no. 4 (1992): 821–42.

'essential' religious commitments ought to be. The resistance against the Adoption Bill was one such 'religious commitment' and non-maintenance of divorced wives after a three-month *iddat* period was another, over which there was no real consensus. This section analyses the communication between the institutions of the state and the pro- and anti-reform movement through delegations, meetings, and petitions before courts, which ultimately also had the state divided into pro- and anti-intervention camps.

On the question of adoption, AIMPLB raised a number of objections and they were joined by Parsi and Christian organizations, which insisted that a provision of foster care provided under the Guardians and Wards Act, 1890, was sufficient. These objections were rooted in the fear that the availability of the option of voluntary adoption could encourage couples to opt for it, and this would violate religion. The Adoption Bill was dissolved in 1977 and reintroduced by the Janata Party in 1979, and again by the Congress in 1980, when the demands of AIMPLB's delegation were ceded to. Indira Gandhi took note of their objections and AIMPLB successfully stalled the inclusion of Muslims from the adoption legislation. The 1980 Bill explicitly excluded Muslim parents and children from its purview.[83]

In 1973, the government brought in a revised version of the Code of Criminal Procedure (CrPC). The code's Section 125[84] contained the provisions regarding the maintenance of wives, children, and parents. Consensus emerged among the prominent north-Indian Muslim men[85] that Muslims ought to be excluded from the application of the Section 125 of the CrPC because the provision on maintenance violated Muslim personal law, particularly, on the question of the maintenance of a 'divorced wife'. On the question of the maintenance of wives, overlaps between the general law and personal law is also noteworthy as maintenance was a matter of criminal procedure. A few members of the judiciary, such as the former chief justice of Orissa and the retired judge of the Madras High Court, who had shared sympathies with AIMPLB and the JIH, collectively approached Indira Gandhi on 18 August 1973 to discuss the effect of the CrPC on Muslim personal law.[86] The delegation of men argued that under Muslim personal law, the obligation

---

[83] *Lakshmi Kant Pandey v. Union of India*, 1984 AIR 469.

[84] Section 125: Order for maintenance of wives, children, and parents. Definition of 'wife'; 'wife' includes a woman who has been divorced by, or has obtained a divorce from, her husband and has not remarried.

[85] Represented by the AIMPLB, Majlis-e-Mushawarat, and the Jamiat-e-Islami Hind.

[86] Abdul Ghafoor Noorani, ed., *The Muslims of India: A Documentary Record* (New Delhi: Oxford University Press, 2004).

to maintain a divorced wife was limited to a period of three months (*iddat*)[87] whereas if the definition of 'wife' was to include the 'divorced wife', then the provision for maintenance under Section 125 would apply beyond the *iddat* period, and thus be in violation of Muslim personal law. The government ultimately conceded to inserting a clause that 'the order for maintenance to a divorced wife [under section 127] would be liable to be cancelled if the former husband had discharged his obligations under any personal or customary law'.[88]

Despite the Bombay groups' agitations to extend legal protections, Indira Gandhi, in fact, reduced statutory entitlements to Muslims on two crucial issues of the adoption of children and the maintenance of wives. While scholarship has concertedly blamed Rajiv Gandhi for bending before the conservative Muslim groups in the aftermath of the *Shah Bano* case for consolidating the Muslim 'vote-bank',[89] Indira Gandhi had accommodated the demands of the AIMPLB more than a decade earlier. Men like A. A. A. Fyzee, who had found favour in Nehru's regime, now found themselves on the losing end of the battle, with the doors of the Prime Minister's Office opened to conservative quarters. In a sense, there were two opposing processes taking place where, on the one hand, the state encountered pressures to step back and grant exception to personal law and, on the other hand, the reformist strand sought intervention in personal law, but determined the 'content' of reform not through commission reports or consultation with the government, but through public agitations instead. In both scenarios of opposing and seeking legal intervention, the state's capacity to understand religion and generate just statutes is challenged. The legislation, judiciary, and commissions collectively appeared to absorb demands that were fundamentally different and, therefore, the 'state' response itself was never coherent or consistent towards questions of personal law.

Prominent activist and writer A. G. Noorani's collection of letters and resolutions of the All India Muslim Personal Law Convention and its exchanges with the government suggest that the government took a placatory approach on the subject of the modification of Muslim personal law. In return, certain political parties such as the Muslim League also pledged their support to the Emergency.[90] Significantly, however, the Supreme Court decided against the

---

[87] This is a period of three months (or three menstrual cycles) after the divorce after which the husband is no longer obliged to maintain his wife.

[88] Clause 'b' in subsection 3 of Section 127 of the Criminal Procedures Code. Pamphlet distributed by All-India Muslim Consultative Convention, AIMPLB office, New Delhi.

[89] A. A. Engineer, *The Shah Bano Controversy* (Bombay: Orient Longman, 1987), 11–25; Zakia Pathak and Rajeshwari Sunderrajan, 'Shah-Bano', *Signs* 14, no. 3 (1989): 558–82.

[90] Noorani, ed., *The Muslims of India*. See also Partha S. Ghosh, *The Politics of Personal Law in South Asia: Identity, Nationalism and the Uniform Civil Code* (New Delhi: Routledge India, 2007).

exceptions granted to Muslims on the question of maintenance. In the decisions of *Bai Tahira v. Ali Hussain Fidali Chothia*[91] and *Fazlunbi Bibi v. Khader Vali*[92] cases, the court chose to grant maintenance to divorced women by subjecting Muslim law to a 'broader' interpretation. In 1978, Justice Krishna Iyer, in the *Bai Tahira*[93] case overlooked (and not for the first time) the shariatic provision for the maintenance of wives which was limited to the three months *iddat* period and the payment of *mahr* (dower).[94] He, in fact, read the provisions of Section 125 of the CrPC on the maintenance of wives as not contradictory to Islamic law.

> The payment of illusory amounts by way of customary or personal law requirement will be considered in the reduction of maintenance rate but cannot annihilate the rate unless it is a reasonable substitute. The legal sanctity of the payment is certified by the fulfilment of the social obligation, not by a ritual exercise rooted in custom....[95]

The same judge then delivered a similar judgment in the *Fazlunbi* case in 1980, where he recalls Lord Denning's reference in his *The Discipline of the Law* to Portia's plea in the *The Merchant of Venice* for 'the pound of flesh but not a drop of blood ...' to emphasize a 'humane obligation' of the provisions of the Indian Penal Code (IPC) Sections 125 and 127 concerning the maintenance of wives. By seeking to reconcile Muslim law with protections to women under the IPC, a pound of flesh would indeed not draw blood.[96] Therefore, when the women's movement could not find a ready ally in parliament, it found relief in sporadic court judgments. Iyer wrote:

> Before we bid farewell to Fazlunbi it is necessary to mention that Chief Justice Baharul Islam, in an elaborate judgement replete with quotes from the Holy Quran, has exposed the error of early English authors and judges who dealt with talaq in Muslim Law as good even if pronounced at whim or in tantrum, and argued against the diehard view of Batchelor, that this view *'is good in law, though bad in theology'*.[97]

Iyer interpreted the law by considering what would be 'good in theology' and concluded that the payment of maintenance to a divorced wife was consistent with Muslim law. Judicial opinion on personal law was beginning to consolidate, as a number

---

[91] *Bai Tahira v. Ali Hussain Fidali Chothia*, 1979 SCR (2) 75.

[92] *Fazlunbi v. Khader Vali*, 1980 SCR (3) 1127.

[93] *Bai Tahira v. Ali Hussain Fidali Chothia*, 1979 SCR (2) 75.

[94] *Mahr* is not the exchange or consideration given by the man to the woman for entering into the contract of marriage, as it may be generally implied, but an effect of the contract imposed by the law on the husband as a token of respect for his wife in case of a divorce.

[95] *Bai Tahira v. Ali Hussain Fidali Chothia*, 1979 SCR (2) 75, para 15.

[96] *Fazlunbi v. Khader Vali*, 1980 SCR (3) 1127.

[97] Ibid., para 1142 (emphasis mine).

of judges and jurists voiced their concerns audibly against the continuation of personal law regimes.[98] P. B. Gajendragadkar, former chief justice of India, delivered a speech at Aligarh critiquing the 'conservative attitudes' that injured Indian democracy and argued for the abolition of polygamy.[99] In a similar vein, former chief justice of India K. Subba Rao suggested evolving a Uniform Civil Code by integrating the 'personal law of all religions'. Justice Khalid of the Kerala High Court called for the codification of Muslim personal law and expressed fear about the *ulemas* monopolizing the debate.[100]

The pro-reform civil society movements viewed the Uniform Civil Code as an individualist argument wherein women's relationship with democracy was not mediated through membership of religion but through 'law'. The framing of women's rights in personal law debates had been more a parliamentary or *legislative* prerogative since the Hindu code debates increasingly became a *judicial* one, that is, a matter of judicial discretion or interpretation by the court rather than parliamentary law. Prominent court decisions in the absence of any clear statutory provision, and the limited potential of committee reports on Muslim law reform aided the narrative that the courts were allies of the weak. This alliance between the court and the civil society, however, was neither consistent nor always compatible.

In *Yousuf Rawthar v. Sowramma*[101] in 1970, Justice Krishna Iyer also allowed a lenient reading of the Dissolution of Muslim Marriages Act, 1939, arguing that *khula* (woman's right to initiate divorce) for women was equivalent to the option of *talaq* available to men, that is, they could both be unilateral. The lower court had granted the wife's plea for divorce, and accepted her second marriage as valid. But this was subsequently challenged by the husband who argued that his wife's claim did not find basis in the Dissolution of Muslim Marriage Act and that it was a prerogative of the husband to, in fact, 'accept' the *khula* initiated by his wife. Iyer upheld the divorce and the second marriage of the wife and in his dismissal of the first husband's appeal, he observed:

> ... Now that both parties were married to others, it was urged that the decree for divorce may be upheld. Precedents are legion that a court must have due regard to subsequent developments which fundamentally alter the jural relations or make the relief originally sought altogether unworkable or unjust.... Certainly, the wife cannot jettison her husband through court by hurriedly marrying another when the case is

---

[98] 'Codify Muslim Law, Says Kerala Judge', *Times of India*, 20 March 1973.
[99] 'Put Secularism First, Says Gajendragadkar at Aligarh', *Times of India*, 29 January 1969. P. B. Gajendragadkar was the chief justice of India in 1964.
[100] 'Codify Muslim Law, Says Kerala Judge', *Times of India*, 20 March 1973.
[101] *Yousuf Rawthar v. Sowramma* AIR 1971 Ker 261.

pending and force the court to grant what is the subject of dispute; for, 'if the law supposes that', borrowing the words of Mr. Bumble, in Oliver Twist, 'the law is an ass–an idiot'.[102]

In his writing, he rooted his reasoning in long citations of the Quran, and texts on Islamic law while also insisting upon its consistence with secular law in India and further comparing it to 'no fault' divorce enacted in Germany: 'I may also point out with satisfaction that this secular and pragmatic approach of the Muslim law of divorce happily harmonises with contemporary concepts in advanced countries.'[103] Iyer's zeal towards aligning personal law with constitutional law should also evoke scepticism about arguments that favour judicial reform as an alternative to parliamentary law—given that a single judge had authored most of the influential judgments on Muslim personal law.

Moreover, when the UP Zamindari Abolition and Land Reforms Act was challenged in the Supreme Court in 1980 in *Ambika Prasad Misra v. the State of UP*[104] for excluding women as tenure holders, the court, with Iyer, again, as its presiding judge, had infamously prioritized class interests by protecting the size of the landholding even as it came at the cost of women being denied their share.[105] Iyer decided against women's claim to land on the ground that it may lead to the fragmentation of landholdings.

> Such a scheme may marginally affect gender justice but does not abridge, wee-bit, the rights of women. If land-holding and ceiling thereon are organised with the paramount purpose of maximizing surpluses without maiming women's ownership, any plea of sex discrimination as a means to sabotage what is socially desirable measure cannot be permitted.[106]

Thus, judicial rulings could be contingent on the willingness of the bench, or a response to political context,[107] and its 'progressive' interventions also raise questions about judicial overreach on law making and its hesitation can often privilege existing hierarchies. The judicial commitment to women's rights was

---

[102] Ibid., para 20.

[103] Ibid., para 17.

[104] *Ambika Prasad Misra v. the State of UP*, 1980 AIR 1762.

[105] Bina Agarwal, *A Field of One's Own: Gender and Land Rights in South Asia* (Cambridge: Cambridge University Press, 1994).

[106] *Ambika Prasad Misra v. the State of UP*, 1980 AIR 1762. Ibid., 1173 D-F.

[107] Baxi, in 'Taking Suffering Seriously', suggests that Emergency remained the backdrop of many of Iyer's 'activist' decisions. Iyer was the judge who granted Indira Gandhi a 'stay' order that permitted her to remain in the seat of power for an interim period, but Gandhi declared an Emergency the very next day. This is discussed later in the chapter.

particularly suspect in the light of the history of orthodox rulings and biased court judgments which often reproduced cultural stereotypes of women's role within the family. This was visible in a range of decisions, for instance, in the case of *Dawn Henderson v. D. Henderson*[108] in 1970, where a husband forced his wife into prostitution; the court admitted the evidence of 'cruelty' as a ground for divorce but rejected the divorce petition on the basis of insufficient evidence of adultery by the husband. Judgments favourable to women were often contingent on them having been a 'good wife', and the rights within family laws remained accessible primarily to whoever the court understood to be 'honourable' women subjects. Works of Agnes, Kapur, and Cossman provide a thorough record of the ways in which women have historically remained at the receiving end of orthodox rulings, regardless of religious codes.[109]

Even in criminal cases where 'uniform' laws did apply, such prejudice was apparent. The infamous *Mathura* case of 1972 was a glaring example of prejudiced reading of the law, where a teenager was failed by multiple levels of the judiciary after being subject to sexual violence in police custody. The sessions court ruled that because Mathura was 'habituated to sexual intercourse', her consent was voluntary; under the circumstances only sexual intercourse could be proved and not rape. On appeal the accused were sentenced to one year and five years' imprisonment, respectively, by the high court. However, in September 1979 the Supreme Court reversed the high court ruling and again acquitted the accused policemen. The Supreme Court held that Mathura had raised no alarm and also that there were no visible marks of injury on her person, thereby suggesting no struggle and therefore no rape.[110] The story was further complicated by the fact that Mathura, a tribal girl, was in love with an upper-caste boy. The court's sympathy towards the accused policemen was also informed by the fact that Mathura's own family considered her to be promiscuous and the arrest of the couple was made upon the complaint of Mathura's brother.

These cases highlighted deeply embedded assumptions about women's roles and identities in the family and in the reading of the law, including those laws that had been ostensibly designed for women's well-being.[111] They represented the norm rather than an exception.[112] Similarly, the judgments in family law

---

[108] *Dawn Henderson v. D. Henderson* AIR 1970 Mad 104.

[109] Agnes, 'Protecting Women against Violence?'; Kapur and Cossman, *Subversive Sites*.

[110] *Tukaram v. State of Maharashtra*, 1979 AIR 185.

[111] Kapur and Cossman, *Subversive Sites*, 63–65. Even in criminal cases where 'uniform' laws applied, such prejudice was apparent.

[112] The reading of the law as offered in the *Mathura case* can be traced back to colonial courts as well. Elizabeth Kolsky, '"The Body Evidencing the Crime": Rape on Trial in Colonial India, 1860–1947', *Gender and History* 22, no. 1 (2010): 109–30.

cases repeatedly reiterated the significance of the virtues of chastity and showed indifference or even sympathy towards adulterous or violent husbands indicating that the judiciary's commitment to uniformity could also universalize male domination and patriarchal family structures. Therefore, the judiciary's insistence on 'personal law reform' for the religious minorities was not necessarily motivated by the agenda of women's rights alone but rather by their 'moral' reservations about practices such as bigamy, easy divorce, and so on. Thus, the commitment to a secular code was certainly not a guarantee against oppression.

Institutions innovated as much in the name of providing 'true' interpretations of religion as they did in the name of a commitment to secularism, because innovation was invariably contingent on the users and the interpreters of law. Thus, 'secular' in these contexts is only a language to resist any custom, tradition, idea, or ritual which could be deemed orthodox. But in practice, religion, tradition, and orthodoxy could thrive in even the most recognizably secular prototypes. The protest against the *Mathura* judgment was an outcry against traditional and orthodox stereotypes being routed through secular or neutral statutes. The protests eventually led to a Law Commission report and an amendment to the law against rape in India. The amendment to criminal law in 1983 did not labour over the definition of consent but it did recognize custodial rape, and prescribed minimum mandatory sentences.

Thus, in bargaining with the law, women's groups as well as religious organizations did substantially aid in aggregating the authority of the state in the 1970s. The growing umbrella of the state and its attempt to absorb oppositional claims through different institutions (legislature and judiciary), however, was a fragile arrangement. The next section explores the parallel stories of the high point of the women's movement—the *Towards Equality* Report, and the highest point of state centralization, the Emergency.

II

Towards Equality and Emergency

The state's unpredictability in interventions in the family was exemplified in everyday citizen–state interaction. Government officials or police personnel commonly refused to register cases of domestic violence which were dismissed as 'family' matters (*ghar ka masla*) where the court (*kachehri*) should be avoided to the greatest extent possible. Even by abstaining from intervention, these government institutions contributed to generating acceptable and unacceptable sexual behaviour or notions of marital harmony, and so on. This has historically allowed for 'secular' or 'general' laws also to be aligned with orthodox opinions. For instance, if the court decided in favour of granting maintenance to 'hapless' Muslim women, it could just as easily attribute haplessness to the policemen against a 'promiscuous' Mathura. Moreover, the law itself was produced by and given effect to by, predominantly, the men manning state institutions; it had the potential to remain an instrument of control. The law could never, therefore, deliver the 'change' or even the 'revolution' it promised. For matters of the family, the law simply became a means to challenge the privacy afforded to the family, and was successfully deployed by women's organizations to this end.

While the state and its institutions hid intimate violence (or tacitly condoned it) behind the argument of curtailing excessive litigiousness in an intimate relationship such as marriage, religion, by contrast, displayed fewer qualms about explicitly dictating sexual behaviour. In South Asia, the consummation of marriage or girls reaching puberty have been matters that entailed ceremonies,[113] as well as exclusion from religious rituals and entry into temples. These were issues that the women of the house discussed openly among themselves, and even in women's withdrawal from household activities and public places during menstruation made their exclusion conspicuous and counteracted any individual-based notions of privacy.[114]

For instance, there was a visible consensus across all influential religious groups, organizations, and popular religious leaders against homosexual partnerships. Similarly, a consensus was found in issues ranging from banning women from entering temples during menstruation, to making the validity of the pronouncement of *talaq* contingent on *tuhr* (period between menstrual cycles), to the Sinhalese rituals around female puberty, or the stigma attached to pre-marital sex; each illustrating the role of religion and custom in mediating sexuality and sexual relationships. Symbols such as the *sindoor* (vermillion), the *mangalsutra* (sacred beads worn by Hindu married women), or headscarves worn by women have historically remained means of identifying status, caste, or religion. These symbols evidenced that culture was created on women's bodies and these cultural beliefs were endorsed or opposed through the legal machinery. The influence was

---

[113] Nur Yalman, 'On the Purity of Women in the Castes of Ceylon and Malabar', *The Journal of the Royal Anthropological Institute of Great Britain and Ireland* 93, no. 1 (1963): 25–58.

[114] For an ethnographic study of songs, specific festivals, customs, seasons, and how these invoked kinship ties and cultural practices and rituals, see G. G. Raheja and A. G. Gold, *Listen to the Heron's Words: Reimagining Gender and Kinship in North India* (Berkeley: University of California Press, 1994). See also Patricia Jeffery, *Frogs in a Well: Indian Women in Purdah* (London: Zed Press, 1979).

visible in court judgments which raised questions about the chastity of the victim, or legislative enactments which hesitated in granting maintenance to women if the ground for divorce was adultery, or if the wife was insufficiently 'homely'.

Basu suggests that the theorization of the family as an 'intimate space' conveys that the family needs protection from the law, rather than by it.[115] Subramanian has shown how the law was instrumental in popularizing new models of family, in particular the 'nuclear' family.[116] Agarwal's research, on the other hand, shows that there is incredible diversity in what is recognized as 'family' across different states and the law has incentivized certain forms of family on the pretext of addressing gender inequalities, but gave way to other forms of discrimination while also leaving many familial structures and everyday lives untouched.[117] The 1970s, however, is a period when the growing umbrella of women's movement had achieved considerable success in establishing women as a separate 'constituency'. This is not to suggest that the 1970s can be located as the 'emergence' of the women's movement, but that this marked the next wave of feminism, where women's initiatives rejected the language of the state's paternalism which cast them as beneficiaries or recipients of state policy, and rather demanded to be stakeholders. A change in the law was a visible objective for a number of women's organizations.

Groups rallied around the rights of women in various positions; as widows, or as workers, taking up issues of forced motherhood, prostitution, dowry, and violence against women and demanded state action.[118] Women also participated in protests against price rise or alcoholism-related domestic violence where they were at the forefront as home-runners. The issue-based mobilizations ensured that the participant base was not limited to the middle classes. The decade was marked by the emergence of a number of women's organizations, some of which were particularly active in western India in the period, such as the Self-Employed Women's Association (1972), the Annapurna Mahila Mandal (1975), the Stree Shakti Jagruti Samiti (1975), the Forum against Oppression of Women (1980), among many others.[119] Moreover, these initiatives were emboldened by the

---

[115] Srimati Basu, *The Trouble with Marriage: Feminists Confront Law and Violence in India*, vol. 1 (New Delhi: University of California Press, 2015), 51.

[116] Narendra Subramanian, *Nation and Family: Personal Law, Cultural Pluralism, and Gendered Citizenship in India* (Stanford: Stanford University Press, 2014).

[117] Agarwal, *A Field of One's Own*.

[118] Progressive Organisation of Women in Hyderabad (leaflet 1974), campaigned against harassment, followed by demonstrations in Delhi, 1979. See also Gandhi and Shah, *The Issues at Stake*.

[119] For social movements and women's rights initiatives in the 1970s, see Kumar, *The History of Doing*; and chapter 4, 'The Women's Movement', in Omvedt, *Reinventing Revolution*, 76–99.

declaration of the year 1975 as the international women's year by the United Nations.

The initiatives of the 1970s allowed for the recording of women's history rather than a history of women, as it witnessed the break from theorizing 'women's role' in the dominant narrative, to treating women's narratives as alternate histories, complete in themselves.[120] This was different from the earlier decades when only a few influential organizations such as the All India Women's Conference (AIWC) bore the onus of introducing women's issues into the public discourse. The 1970s witnessed a proliferation of multiple autonomous organizations which focussed on wide-ranging issues but remained under the recognizable and overarching banner and umbrella of the Indian women's movement.[121]

In the long-standing debate between equality and difference feminism,[122] the Indian women's movement in the 1970s was firmly on the side of equality. While both positions on equality and difference contribute valuably towards the discourse on feminism, universal theories can rarely capture the complexities of women's experiences. Equality feminism sought to treat women same as men, arguing commonly for equal wages, equal access to public spaces, but may insufficiently acknowledge how the default norm commonly privileged men. Difference feminism has alternatively been accused of overstating notions of femininity which not only essentializes women but may even promote 'group essentialisms'.[123]

Activists and academics have argued that the feminist movements of the 1970s and 1980s in India were often neither sufficiently democratic towards minority women nor immune from the pressures of majoritarianism, as these prioritized

---

[120] Gisella Bock, 'Women's History and Gender History: Aspects of an International Debate', *Gender and History* 1, no. 1 (1989): 7–30.

[121] See also Geetanjali Gangoli, *Indian Feminisms: Law, Patriarchies and Violence in India* (Hampshire, England: Ashgate Publishing Ltd, 2012). Gangoli attributes the emergence of feminism in the 1970s to the increased employment and educational opportunities in the period among other factors. See also Mary E. John, 'Gender, Development, and the Women's Movement', in *Signposts: Gender Issues in Post-Independence India*, ed. Rajeshwari Sunder Rajan (New Delhi: Kali for Women, 2000), 101–23.

[122] See debates on multiculturalism and equality versus difference feminism in Seyla Benhabib, *The Claims of Culture: Equality and Diversity in the Global Era* (Princeton, NJ: Princeton University Press, 2002). See also Susan Molar Okin, *Is Multiculturalism Bad for Women?* (Princeton, NJ: Princeton University Press, 1999). These themes are explored in greater detail in the following chapters in discussions on the Muslim Women's Act in 1986 and the Muslim women's movement in the late 1990s to the 2000s.

[123] Carol Gould, 'Diversity and Democracy: Representing Differences', in *Democracy and Difference: Contesting the Boundaries of the Political*, ed. S. Benhabib (Princeton, NJ: Princeton University Press, 1996), 171–86. See also Nancy Fraser, 'Equality, Difference, Public Representation', in *Democracy and Difference*, 218–37.

'mainstream' or Hindu women's problems and also overemphasized the reformative potential of the law.[124] On the contrary, this chapter suggests that just as in the case of personal law, the recognition of a distinct internally homogenous community gave an opportunity for internal differences to emerge, be they regional, caste, or class. Even in the case of the women's movement, the emergence of a strong and influential 'equality-driven' movement eventually gave way to the acknowledgement of the diversity of women's experiences. This period witnessed the consolidation of the category of 'women' which could then be challenged and diversified.

The exceptionality of the 1970s does not suggest a 'pure origin' of women as a category but the successful establishment of a new, political, powerful, albeit mildly majoritarian or academia-led discourse on feminism.[125] While the exploitation suffered by women was decidedly both 'specific and simultaneous'[126]—that accrued to them both by virtue of them being women and/or Dalit, tribal, religious minorities, peasants, or workers—at the same time, it was during this period that the demand for up to 30 per cent reservation for 'women' in parliament was first articulated.[127]

It was in the absence of a consensus on who constituted the women's movement and whose issues were prioritized that led the movement to develop a dependence on constitutional rights as the only 'neutral' tool that could be deployed universally. The emphasis of such an articulation of rights valorized the Benthamite promise that a good law would make a good society or, in this case, that legal changes would precipitate social change.

A cardinal step in this direction was the *Towards Equality* Report. In 1971, Indira Gandhi directed the Ministry of Social and Economic Welfare to set up a committee on the Status of Women in India, chaired by Phulrenu Guha, as part of the celebration of the International Year of Women in 1975. This became an authoritative text for assessing the position of women in subsequent decades and

---

[124] Nida Kirmani, 'Beyond the Impasse Muslim Feminism(s) and the Indian Women's Movement', *Contributions to Indian Sociology* 45, no. 1 (2011): 1–26; Sylvia Vatuk, 'Islamic Feminism in India: Indian Muslim Women Activists and the Reform of Muslim Personal Law', *Modern Asian Studies* 42, nos. 2–3 (2008): 489–518; Flavia Agnes, 'Redefining the Agenda of the Women's Movement within a Secular Framework', in *Women and Right-Wing Movement: Indian Experiences*, ed. Tanika Sarkar and Urvashi Butalia (New Delhi: Kali for Women, 1995), 136–57.

[125] John, 'Gender, Development, and the Women's Movement', 102.

[126] Gail Omvedt, Chetna Gala, and Govind Kelkar, 'Unity and Struggle: A Report on Nari Mukti Sangharsh Sammelan', *Economic and Political Weekly* 23, no. 18 (1988): 883–86.

[127] GoI, *Towards Equality*. Committee on Status of Women, Ministry of Education and Social Welfare, Department of Social Welfare, Government of India.

its authors included influential scholars such as Vina Majumdar and Lotika Sarkar, among others. The three-volume report noted:

> Religion provides ideological and moral bases for the accorded status and institutionalised roles of women in a society. The social restrictions on women, and also the people's notions about their proper roles in the domestic and extra-domestic spheres, are largely derived from religious conceptions of a woman's basic characteristics, her assumed 'virtues' and vices, her proverbial strengths and weaknesses, and the stereotypes regarding her nature and capacities. Each religion has a treasure of myths and legends which through descriptions of events and activities emphasize certain values.[128]

The report confronted religion, complete with references to religious figures, such as Sita, Savitri, and Draupadi, in religious texts including the *Mahabharata*, the *Ramayana*, and the *Manusmriti*, and the faulty stereotypes these generated on the sexual division of labour that compromised women's agency and glorified their suffering.[129] The *Towards Equality* Report placed the burden of the empowerment of women decidedly on the law and offered a deep criticism of ambiguous areas of religious family law in India.[130] It acknowledged colonial legislations of widow remarriage, the banning of child marriage and sati with a critical lens, but viewed legal interventions largely as positive measures. In one sense this critique of religion also emphasized the relevance of secularism to the women's movement in this period.[131]

Significantly, the report also revealed the diversity of opinion within the Muslim community on the subject of Muslim personal law. The educated middle classes of UP were most hostile towards any changes in Muslim personal law, perhaps owing to the influence of organizations such as the JIH and the AIMPLB, which were active in the region and exercised significant political influence. However, the poorer classes of the same region, for example, *chikan* (embroidery) workers and weavers from Benares, appeared to be more positively disposed towards the idea of reform and expressed a desire to make

---

[128] GoI, *Towards Equality*, 38, para 3.9.

[129] GoI, *Towards Equality*, Chapter IV, 'Women and Law'. The report aimed to uncover gender-based inequalities in processes that were traditionally associated with progress and the promotion of democracy. These ranged from the importance attached to the institution of marriage, the unqualified support for women's work in the absence of the acknowledgment of the sexual division of labour in the household, among others. See also Jitka Malečková, 'Gender, History and "Small Europe"', *European History Quarterly* 40, no. 4 (2010): 685–700, for a similar critique of democracy in the European context.

[130] GoI, *Towards Equality*.

[131] Ibid., para 4.8.

monogamy a norm.[132] In Kashmir, there was a vehement reaction against polygamy and a strong demand for its ban among Muslims, indicating that the desire for reform could also be a function of where Muslims were a majority.[133]

Towards Equality was a bold critique of gender inequality and did not hesitate from placing religion at the centre of gender politics. The report supported causes that had historically remained contentious such as dignified divorce based on mutual consent and offered a strong critique of the cultural sacredness extended to the joint family. It was presented before parliament in 1975, and received substantial support, at least overtly. There was a motion for initiating administrative and legislative measures to address the injustices, disabilities, and discrimination that women encountered.[134]

'Women's rights' remained the entry point of reform of religious laws and the report treated women as a separate constituency. Many aspects of this report were incorporated in policy and legislation over the years. However, most initiatives focussed on expanding criminal provisions on violence against women and setting up new forums such as the National Human Rights Commission, other women's commissions in the states, and the creation of women's self-help groups and family courts. In the months and years following the report, the Hindu Marriage Act and the Special Marriage Act were also taken up for revision in 1974 and 1976 and the 66th Law Commission report on the Married Women's Right to Property Act was released in 1976.[135] The recommendations of the *Towards Equality* Report that involved the family, and also religious minority laws more directly such as the Anti-Dowry Law (1983), the Family Courts Act (1984), the Christian Marriage Law Amendments (2001), among others, took relatively longer to provoke state action, and many of the suggestions on Muslim personal law did not resurface.

Emergency and Family

The resistance against state interventions in the family by religious organizations also extended far beyond personal law. Governmentalizing families has historically remained contentious. Indira Gandhi's family planning policies, for instance, were another significant example where state interventions in the realm of the 'family' faced resistance by religious groups. These policies offered monetary incentives

---

[132] Ibid., para 4.15.

[133] Ibid., para 4.15–4.16.

[134] S. Gopalan, *Towards Equality: The Unfinished Agenda: Status of Women in India 2001* (New Delhi: National Commission for Women (India), 2001).

[135] See chapter 3, 'Feminism and the State: Citizenship, Legislative Debates and Women's Issues', in Gangoli, *Indian Feminisms*, where she discusses the problems that the Marriage Amendment of 1976 inadvertently generated.

for vasectomies and came to symbolize, quite literally, the emasculation of men, and that too by coercive and controversial means. If the contraceptive pill was a revolutionary moment for feminism globally, then Indira Gandhi's policy was shifting the onus back to the male involvement in reproduction. Arguably, she was freeing female sexuality from the burden of reproduction by introducing and incentivizing vasectomy for the male population.

The failure of the initiatives of family planning introduced in 1952 was revisited only in Indira Gandhi's tenure when slogans such as *Hum do, hamare do* (us two, our two) were aggressively popularized focussing particularly on families with two children and this was incentivized by cash and land grants.[136] Small families directly contradicted the notion of a Hindu undivided family (HUF) which had enjoyed tax benefits even after the passage of the Hindu Succession Act, 1956. In another instance, the AIWC in 1969 issued a memorandum to Indira Gandhi protesting the amendment of the Hindu Succession Act in Punjab.[137] This amendment disinherited daughters from receiving agricultural land on the ground that daughters already received dowries and then further claiming their share in land led to fragmentation. Indira Gandhi reportedly supported the AIWC's move against the proposed amendment, and it was stalled.[138] Therefore, her decision to exempt Muslim women from statutory protections as done in the case of the Adoption Bill and the CrPC's provision of the maintenance of wives was yet another instance of minority communities witnessing more hesitant interventions than the majority. Here, religious politics resisted the state's access to the family and, as a corollary, the family became accessible to the state predominantly through religion. Indira Gandhi's direct intervention into the family in her family-planning policies, in many ways, circumvented this mediation through religion.

Predictably, the most vehement opposition to the family-planning policies also came from religious organizations. The popular slogan launched by the Hindu ascetic Shambhoo Maharaj of Gujarat stated, '[T]he boys of today are the soldiers of tomorrow, and the girls of today are mothers of tomorrow.'[139] Archbishop

---

[136] For an account of the implementation of family planning policies in Indira Gandhi's regime, see Emma Tarlo, *Unsettling Memories: Narratives of the Emergency in Delhi* (Berkeley: University of California Press, 2003). The idea of offering land in exchange for vasectomy opens up interesting questions for gender history, and the links between ownership of land and masculinity; however, this is beyond the scope of this book.

[137] All India Women's Conference Papers, File No. 1048, 12 September 1969, NMML, New Delhi.

[138] 'Move to Curtail Daughter's Rights', *The Statesman*, 17 September 1969.

[139] 'Holy War on the Red Triangle', *Times of India*, 5 November 1972.

Arulappa launched an anti-family-planning drive among Christians and the policy also remained unpopular amongst the Muslims.[140]

The 'family' which had been viewed as the woman's domain or the private domain was accessed publicly by a woman prime minister in a way that no former government had managed. Under Indira Gandhi's regime, the law against domestic violence (Section 498A) was introduced, reform of Christian marriage law was taken up again, and the Dowry Prohibition Act, 1961, was also strengthened. Responding to the high instance of dowry in the country, the revised dowry prohibition law introduced a compulsory investigation in case of the death of a married woman within the first seven years of marriage.

Katherine Frank in her biography of Indira Gandhi attributed Indira Gandhi's authoritarian aggression to the initial exclusion she faced in an all-male political coterie. However, she went from being the 'Goongi Gudiya'[141] (dumb doll) to the 'Iron Lady' within her first tenure in the Lok Sabha as prime minister. Her biographies reveal a steady transformation from being reticent to someone who was attributed strong Machiavellian traits. US President Richard Nixon expressed his discomfort with Indira Gandhi, when he referred to her as a 'witch' and a 'clever fox' in his private communication with Henry Kissinger, the secretary of state.[142] The sexism that she grappled with had a bearing on making Indira the tyrant that history would later deem her to be.

It is against this background that the tough policy decisions of the 1970s, such as the abolition of privy purses and the removal of the right to property as a fundamental right, that the Emergency can be evaluated.[143] Kaviraj discusses Indira Gandhi's tenure as a 'sequence of crises' but also concluded that her death did not mark the end of her period but only demonstrated its continuity.[144] One such crisis was the nationalist shift in the political climate with the

---

[140] It is also worth noting that in the recent years the campaign against family planning or population controls has been critiqued by senior members of the RSS and Hindu Mahasabha who made statements encouraging Hindu women to have four children each to keep the Hindu population in majority, which was later echoed by other Hindu orthodox leaders with a revised recommendation of 10 children. 'Now, Saffron Leaders Ask Hindus to Have 10 Kids to Ensure Survival of Religion', *Indian Express*, 19 January 2015.

[141] Ram Manohar Lohiya had remarked that the prime minister is a 'goongi gudiya' in 1966 when Indira Gandhi first became the prime minister. See also Ramachandra Guha, 'Degradation of Discourse, *Times of India*, 6 January 2014.

[142] 'Nixon's Dislike Of "Witch" Indira', BBC, 29 June 2005, available at http://news.bbc.co.uk/1/hi/world/south_asia/4633263.stm

[143] See also Austin, *Working a Democratic Constitution*.

[144] Sudipta Kaviraj, 'Indira Gandhi and Indian Politics', *Economic and Political Weekly* 21, no. 38/39 (1986): 1697–708, 1708.

Jana Sangh's communal posture, and also the Shiv Sena's[145] aggressive and polarizing mobilization in Maharashtra which provoked violence against non-Marathis and Muslims as Section I of the chapter discussed.[146] In one of her speeches, Indira Gandhi contended:[147]

> The main question raised by the mover of the motion was with regard to the Senas. When I just spoke about the Jan Sangh, and in all the speeches I made a point not only to speak against the communal point of view. In an anti-communal stance, but also against any kind of attitude that promoted casteism, regionalism or parochialism which could make anyone who was an Indian citizen feel that he did not enjoy equal rights with any other citizen, regardless of where he was living.... Jan Sangh has a point of view about the minorities which I do not think is in the interest of the unity of this country.... I have not said that the Congress party is perfect.... But we have made a constant effort to try and fight these divisive tendencies from the beginning.

The Jana Sangh consolidated itself politically and some of the Congress members who were sympathizers of the Mahasabha had also begun to shift alliances. Ranging from the instances of communal violence across India (in Maharashtra) to the growing intolerance of state governments towards the work of Christian missionaries, discussed in the previous chapter, J. P. Narayan's movement is also often seen to be fraught with anti-secular rhetoric. The involvement of the RSS in mobilization against the Emergency, and their own account of such involvement preserved in their extensive writings on the subject,[148] was an opportunity for the organization's political mainstreaming.[149] The Emergency, however, was the

---

[145] A far-right political party in the state of Maharashtra. Shiv Sena literally translates to 'the Army of Shivaji'; the party is known for its pro-Marathi and anti-minority and anti-migration agenda. For Shiv Sena's politics in Maharashtra, see Thomas Blom Hansen, *Wages of Violence: Naming and Identity in Postcolonial Bombay* (Princeton, NJ: Princeton University Press, 2001).

[146] In 1969, Shiv Sena's founding leader Bal Thackeray was arrested for inciting a border dispute between Maharashtra and Karnataka. This led to Shiv Sena's call for 'Mumbai Bandh' in protest of the arrest when the party allegedly incited violence for three days.

[147] *Lok Sabha Debates*, replying to the 'No confidence' motion in the council of ministers, 20 February 1969, col. 206–23. Surendra Mishra, ed., *Indira Gandhi: Speeches in Parliament 1917–1984* (New Delhi: Jainco Art India for Lok Sabha Secretariat, 1996).

[148] See 'Apatkaleen Mein Sangharsh Gatha' (1978), translated in #SecondFreedomStruggle, 'RSS Stood Between the Dictatorship and Democracy', *The Organiser*, 26 June 2018.

[149] Arvind Rajagopal, 'The Emergency and the Sangh', *The Hindu*, 13 June 2003. Rajagopal writes, 'The Emergency, in fact, rendered the Jana Sangh, the BJP's predecessor, respectable, and paved the way for it to enter the mainstream of Indian politics.'

most anti-democratic antidote to these perceived threats to democracy.[150] The focus on personal law, among other social movements, was therefore eclipsed in this reworking of parliament's relationship with social movements as well as the judiciary.

Indira Gandhi's government introduced a number of socialist policy decisions such as the abolition of privy purses, the nationalization of banks, and the imposition of land ceiling in property holdings. The amendments to the right to property that these changes entailed came to be challenged in three significant cases: the *Golaknath* case in 1967,[151] the *Minerva Mills* case in 1970,[152] and the *Keshavananda Bharti* case in 1973.[153] The court decision in the third case was aimed at disciplining parliament's unhindered amending authority which unleashed a confrontation between the legislature and the judiciary.

In the *Golaknath v. State of Punjab* case of 1967, the court had ruled against the state, observing that the state could not abrogate the fundamental rights (right to property) of an individual.[154] In response to such a judgment, Indira Gandhi's government enacted the constitutional amendments (24th and 25th) through which parliament assumed the power to amend all parts of the constitution, including the fundamental rights, and dismissed the right to property as a fundamental right, reducing it to a legal right.[155] However, in the *Keshavananda Bharti* case in 1973, the court recognized that parliament could amend any part of the constitution, but the 'basic structure' of the constitution could be amended only by a new constituent assembly.[156] While abstaining from defining what the 'basic' or rather 'inviolable' structure of the constitution was, the court attempted to stall the overturning of judgments by hasty amendments.[157] Indira Gandhi responded by interfering directly with the

---

[150] The role of Sanjay Gandhi in Indira Gandhi's political failures and the corruption scandals that blotted her tenure have been explored academically as well as journalistically and have a strong bearing on the way Emergency must be understood, but is beyond the scope of this chapter. Vinod Mehta, *The Sanjay Story* (New Delhi: Harper Collins, 2013).

[151] *Golaknath v. State of Punjab*, 1967 AIR 1643.

[152] *Minerva Mills v. Union of India*, 1980 AIR 1789.

[153] *Keshavananda Bharti v. State of Kerala*, 1973, 4 SCC 225.

[154] For a discussion on amendments and cases on the right to property, see chapters 1 and 2 in Austin, *Working a Democratic Constitution*.

[155] This amended Article 368 of the Indian constitution (power to amend the constitution) to enable parliament to amend fundamental rights.

[156] A part of the 25th and 39th Amendments were declared void as a consequence of this judgment.

[157] See also Krishnaswamy, *Democracy and Constitutionalism in India*; and Upendra Baxi, *The Indian Supreme Court and Politics* (Lucknow: Eastern Book Co., 1980). Krishnaswamy treats the basic structure review as distinct from constitutional judicial review. He argues that a basic structure review stems from Article 13 ('Laws inconsistent with or in derogation of the fundamental rights'), Article 32 ('Remedies for enforcement of rights conferred by fundamental rights'), and Article 226 ('Power of High Courts to issue certain writs') while judicial review could have a wider scope.

appointment of judges and promoted the dissenting judge in the *Keshavananda Bharti* judgment, Justice Ajit Nath Ray, to the position of the chief justice of India. This action annihilated the separation and balance of power between the judiciary and the legislature, compromising the independence of the judiciary. Thus, personal law (among many other social movements) became a forgotten agenda, as the two institutions became embroiled in a larger battle for the custody of the constitution.

The years 1974 to 1977 were also marked by frequent and numerous *bandh*s (closures), strikes, and sloganeering. Although localized when they began, agitations grew in number, size, and influence. Jai Prakash Narayan's anti-corruption movement and his call for a 'total revolution' gained ground beyond Bihar.[158] In 1974, Atal Bihari Vajpayee of the Jana Sangh addressed a conference in Hyderabad echoing Narayan's call.[159] The J. P. Narayan's movement had its support base in the petty bourgeoisie but also had support from the RSS cadres, signalling a coalescence between the anti-corruption movement and religious nationalism.[160]

On 12 June 1975, in a historic judgment, Justice Jagmohan Sinha of the Allahabad High Court invalidated Indira Gandhi's claim to the Prime Minister's Office on the grounds of 'unfair election practices', upholding the victory of the opposition candidate Raj Narain.[161] The judgment became the immediate trigger for the declaration of the Emergency. On 24 June, the Supreme Court granted Indira Gandhi a 'stay of execution' which withheld the court order, and on 25 June 1975, the Emergency was imposed throughout India. The speed of the execution of these measures betrayed the formidable power that Indira Gandhi wielded over her cabinet and the then president of India, Fakhruddin Ali Ahmed, who signed the ordinance for the promulgation of the Emergency overnight (Figure 3.1). The 42nd Amendment that brought in the Emergency stalled a number of social movements and agitations. But among other changes, it also

---

[158] Jai Prakash Narayan was a veteran Gandhian who was agitating against misrule in the state of Bihar and eventually in 1974 directly targeted the national government on account of corruption in high offices. He advocated a social transformation by the means of a 'total revolution' or *Sampoorna kranti*.

[159] For an entirely positive account of the emergency, see V. P. Dutt, 'The Emergency in India: Background and Rationale', *Asian Survey* 16, no. 12 (1976): 1124–38. See also Bipin Chandra, *In the Name of Democracy: JP Movement and the Emergency* (New Delhi: Penguin Books, 2003).

[160] Christophe Jaffrelot, *The Hindu Nationalist Movement and Indian Politics: 1925 to the 1990s: Strategies of Identity-Building, Implantation and Mobilisation (With Special Reference to Central India)* (London: C. Hurst and Co. Publishers, 1996). See also Paul R. Brass, *The Politics of India since Independence*, vol. 1 (Cambridge: Cambridge University Press, 1994).

[161] *State of Uttar Pradesh v. Raj Narain*, 1975 AIR 865.

Figure 3.1 Indira Gandhi surrounded by Congressmen, Parliament House, New Delhi (1967)

Source: Raghu Rai Foundation (photo credit: Raghu Rai Photography).

installed the word 'secularism' to the preamble of the Indian constitution. This addition was significant to the story of personal law, as opposition as well as support for differential personal laws now had to account for the constitutional commitment to secularism.

III

42nd Amendment and Secularism in Letter

> These [secular and socialist] are not empty words or pious wishes ... the time has come that we have to set it right.... Then some people who are very legalistically minded [*sic*] have not been able to appreciate the importance to the amendment of the preamble.... [If] we do not have a correct approach we do not understand what is the significance of the words 'secularism' and 'socialism.' ... let anyone say that socialism and secularism are incapable of definition. Well if that argument were to be accepted, even democracy in that sense is incapable of definition, because is it not understood in different ways in different countries.... But we understand what kind of a democracy we stand for. In the same way we understand what socialism stands for and what secularism stands for.[162]

The members of the Indian Parliament were conscious of the extent of the import of political ideas, and that ideas acquired different meanings and interpretation

---

[162] H. R. Gokhale, law minister, 1976, *Lok Sabha Debates*, vol. 65, nos. 1–6, 5th Series, 18th session, 42nd Amendment Act, 1976. col. 56.

in the Indian experience. This enabled the state to establish a relationship with religion that was shaped temporally, and contingent on circumstance rather than fixed in letter or spirit, which has perhaps given way to the scholarly theorizing of Indian secularism as distinct.[163] This was unlike the uncertainty that characterized the debates in the Constituent Assembly. In the late 1940s, the framing of the debate whether on secularism or the directive principles was framed in the language of 'national integration', whereas in the 1970s, secularism had come closer to being understood as multiculturalism or tolerance.[164]

The defenders of the 42nd Amendment termed the addition of the term secularism as something that was historically amiss, and the correcting of this fallacy addressed the unintended neglect of a crucial concept.[165] Further, the women's movement had successfully highlighted throughout the decade how religious ideologies compromised women's rights. Thus, the two processes collectively ensured that the benevolent paternalism of the soft Hindu state, which characterized the earlier years of independence, receded to give way to a refashioned definition of secularism. The passage of the 42nd Amendment also saw repeated references to the RSS and instances of communal violence which suggests that the immediate context of the addition of secularism to the constitution was informed by the rise of the political element of Hindu nationalism.[166]

The Congress party member Swaran Singh[167] elaborated that the political content of the two new words added to the preamble were vital for the country to remain a 'united and a strong nation'.[168] However, the emphasis remained on multiculturalism.

> So far as secularism is concerned I would at the very outset clarify that our secularism is not synonymous with the dictionary meaning of the word secular and that word flows from a historical background that was faced by several European countries.... But 'secular' now I think is a word that has become a part of Indian language. You go from Punjab to Gujrat even to South; when they make speeches in their own languages they always use the word secular because it has assumed

---

[163] Rajeev Bhargava, 'The Distinctiveness of Indian Secularism', in *The Future of Secularism*, ed. T. N. Srinivasan (Delhi: Oxford University Press, 2006), 20–53.

[164] Akeel Bilgrami, *Secularism, Identity, and Enchantment*, vol. 33 (Cambridge, MA: Harvard University Press, 2014).

[165] *Lok Sabha Debates*, 25–30 October 1976, 5th series, 18th session, vol. 65.

[166] In 1980, the political wing of the Jana Sangh was reconfigured under the banner of the Bharatiya Janata Party.

[167] Swaran Singh was a senior member of the Congress who headed the committee on study of the constitution, instituted by Indira Gandhi, for introducing the 42nd Amendment Act.

[168] *Lok Sabha Debates*, vol. 65, nos. 7–11, col. 22.

a definite meaning ... that there will be equality before the eye of the law in our Constitution with regard to people professing different religions ... more than that there is no connotational [sic] element of anti-religious feeling but there is respect for all religions. It is a concept that is broadly accepted by our country as a whole and therefore we thought it was necessary that it should find a place of pride in the preamble of our country.[169]

Parliament's discomfort with the protestant underpinnings of the term secularism was palpable. The addition of the term 'secular' to the preamble of the constitution sought to 'Indianise' its understanding. Jambhuwantrao Dhote[170] from the Forward Bloc argued: 'The word "secular" has no exact Hindi translation, the translation used (*dharm-nirpeksh*) suggests "religion-lessness" which is unfair to the term secular.'[171] Indian secularism, therefore, had everything to do with religion. Another intervention by Raghunath Keshav Khadilkar[172] further strengthened this position:

In a caste society secularism has a different meaning. Dr. Ambedkar has also discussed this and said that in a caste society, secularism is a very limited concept. It was propounded yesterday that secularism means freedom for all religions. Accepted. But does this mean freedom from caste? At the village levels, you will find that the operative bank, the cng [sic] committee and the *zila parishad*[173] are dominated by caste ... secularism must include caste otherwise it has no meaning.[174]

In other words, the state's commitment to multiculturalism somewhat undergirded its secularism. It was the vocabulary deployed to counter communal polarization but was less passive than religious tolerance. Its addition to the constitution 25 years after the creation of the republic also indicated that secularism did not arrive as an inheritance of the West immediately upon independence, but was introduced as an afterthought and had a managerial import, prompted by concerns over law and order, and public clashes.

---

[169] Ibid., col. 22.
[170] Politician from the Forward Bloc, later joined the Congress in 1979.
[171] Jambhuwantrao Dhote (original):

> Secular shabd ka anuvad Hindi mein 'dharm nirpeksha' kiya gaya hai. Ye secular shabd ke saath insaaf nahi karta.... Iska arth hai iss desh ke sare dharmon bhavnao aur bunyadi baton ka aadar karne wala, sab dharmon ka rajya. Dharm nirpeksha ya nidharmi ka matlab hai jiska koi dharma nahi. (Col. 70, translation mine).

[172] Congress member from Pune, Maharashtra.
[173] District Council.
[174] *Lok Sabha Debates*, col. 46.

Even amidst the clamour of the Emergency, not only did Article 44 surface in the debates, but some members of parliament such as Ebrahim Suleiman Sait recommended removing the Article altogether from the text of the constitution.[175] On the one hand, the preamble was embellished with an obligation of a modified relationship between religion and state through the installation of 'secularism' in the preamble. On the other hand, however, the fundamental rights which included the freedom of religion were made non-absolute, and the directive principles, which included the Uniform Civil Code, were elevated to a higher status.[176] However, the 42nd Amendment emphasized the directive principles in reference to legal aid, education, among others rather than a specific commitment to a Uniform Civil Code. The addition of 'secularism' to the preamble, therefore, did not suggest a rollback of personal law codes. 'Socialism' was the pretext on which directive principles were pushed above the fundamental rights,[177] as another member added: 'We are promising the people that we will provide them food clothing and shelter.'[178]

On 18 December 1976, the 42nd Amendment Bill came into force, and with this India *officially* included the word secularism in its constitution. Rajeev Bhargava has argued that the problem of Indian secularism only began with the insertion of the term in the Indian constitution because this opened it for appropriation by all sides, leading to the distortion of the label of secularism. He writes that the cultural evolution of the term 'secularism' is not just the work of a single political regime, but rather a collective work of meanings formulated by courts, groups, and governments.[179] Secularism had repeatedly been invoked in debates over caste, particularly in context of temple entry movements, inter- as well as intra-religious disputes. But once placed in the preamble of the constitution, secularism had a policy import, which also came to be contested in the decades to come.

The Emergency was followed by the precarious coalition of the Janata Party from 1977 to 1979 that also accommodated the Jana Sangh. Since the inclusion of secularism in the preamble had entailed substantial references to the activities

---

[175] Ibid., col. 152–57. Ebrahim Suleiman Sait:

> If directive principles are to be above fundamental rights then give minorities special protections.... Right from the day when Article 44 was included in the draft constitution presented to Constituent Assembly till this day Muslims have been voicing and expressing their grave concern.... I would therefore feel that the time has come when we are drastically amending our constitution and asking substantive changes to the constitution to remove Article 44 from part VI of the Directive Principles.

[176] *Lok Sabha Debates*, Gauri Shankar Rai, col. 19 (translation mine).
[177] Ibid., col. 56.
[178] Ibid., col. 175–78 (Hindi, translation mine).
[179] Bhargava, 'The Distinctiveness of Indian Secularism'.

of the Sangh, and the RSS itself had been banned in the years of the Emergency, the inclusion of the Jana Sangh in the government produced new tensions for the terminology of secularism. In one sense, the new government was bound by it, but it could now also determine what the policy import of secularism indeed was.

This became apparent as the new government initiated a national 'Freedom of Religion' Bill in 1979 to restrict the activities of Christian missionaries, which was a subject mired in controversy since the late 1960s as discussed in the previous chapter. The Freedom of Religion Bill was introduced by the Janata Party as a 'secular move' that ironically restricted the individual's, specifically Christians', right to propagate religion. Moreover, the volatile Janata coalition[180] engendered also an atypical alliance between the new government and the re-empowered courts, which was cemented by the 44th Amendment to undo the Emergency.

Courts and Curative Constitutionalism of the Janata Government

The authoritarian trends that had unfolded themselves over the past few years were embodied in the 42nd amendment which was bulldozed through parliament. To call it an amendment is a misnomer. It is a betrayal of testament of faith that the founding fathers bequeathed to the people and it subverts the basic structure of the 1950 Constitution. It vitiates the federal principles and upsets the nice balance between the people and parliament, parliament and the judiciary, and the executive, the states and the centre, the citizen and the government ... it is the culmination of the conspiracy to devalue democracy and started with the erosion of the cabinet system, the deliberate and consummate scuttling of democratic processes in the ruling party and the concentration of all power in the hands of a leader who has been sought to be identified with the nation or even placed above it.[181]

It was during the Janata Party's regime that the legislature and the judiciary began to make common cause on various key questions. The Janata-led government was an embodiment of the social movement that preceded it, and therefore, as an anti-establishment agitation, its first attempts were aimed at undoing the structure they had historically opposed and now embodied. Srirupa Roy coined the term 'curative democracy' in her description of the J. P. Movement, suggesting that the

---

[180] For the Janata Party and coalition politics, see P. K. Chhibber and J. R. Petrocik, 'The Puzzle of Indian Politics: Social Cleavages and the Indian Party System', *British Journal of Political Science* 19, no. 2 (1989): 191–210.

[181] Janata Party Manifesto, 1977, NMML, New Delhi.

post-Emergency state assumed a more 'retrospective' posture on policy, aiming at revision, or rollback of schemes rather than introducing new ones.[182]

With the 44th Amendment, the Janata Party (People's Party) sought to restore democracy to the nation in procedural terms. Although the J. P. Movement at first began with an articulation of 'substantive democracy', when the Janata Party finally was voted in as the government, their policies were focussed also on curative *constitutionalism*. This reverence for the constitution built steadily throughout the decade. After the fall of the Janata government in 1980, the courts embraced their position as the guardian of the constitution by devising alternative routes to access the law, such as PIL to enable greater access of citizens to the constitution that explicitly linked the law with democracy.

The Lok Sabha debates illustrate that the Janata Party government managed to hold office on the very premise that they would repeal the 42nd Amendment 'lock stock and barrel'.[183] Shanti Bhushan,[184] who had been the prosecution lawyer for Raj Narain in the case that nullified Indira Gandhi's claim to her office as the prime minister, introduced the 44th Amendment in December 1977 as the law minister of the new government. The shadow of the Emergency loomed so large that the first day of the discussion was concluded without even an agreement on the modalities of undoing the 42nd Amendment, whether it should be repealed in one simple line, or clause by clause, or by a wholesale removal followed by re-addition of the 'good' clauses such as article 39A (free legal aid) and secularism from the repealed Act.[185] P. G. Mavlankar alleged that the 'good parts' of the amendment such as secularism were a smokescreen for the 'wicked' clauses which gave parliament the unbridled power to amend the constitution.[186] Bhushan categorized these clauses as 'innocuous'[187] or dangerous.[188]

---

[182] Srirupa Roy, *Beyond Belief: India and the Politics of Nationalism* (London: Duke University Press, 2007).

[183] *Lok Sabha Debates*, Constitution (44th Amendment) Bill, published in a *Gazette of India Extraordinary*, Part II, Agrahayana 25, 1899 (Saka), 16 December 1977, 3. The motion to amend the constitution passed with the majority of 327 and nil.

[184] The Minister of Law, Justice and Company Affairs, Shanti Bhushan, clarified during the debates on the 44th Amendment that various amendments contained in the 42nd Amendment were not even recommended by the Swaran Singh Committee. *Lok Sabha Debates*, col. 59.

[185] Sections 18, 19, 21, 22, 31, 32, 34, 35, 58, and 59 were deleted. The amendment was passed with the majority of 317 to one.

[186] *Lok Sabha Debates*, P. G. Malvankar, col. 118.

[187] Such as the emphasis on directive principles.

[188] Such as one reducing the powers of the president, *Lok Sabha Debates*, col. 128.

Quoting Ambedkar, Bhushan commented on Indira Gandhi's regime as one characterized by 'Bhakti', or hero-worship, which he argued in politics almost certainly led to degradation and eventual dictatorship.[189] The underlying emphasis of the amendment throughout was the empowerment of the institutions of democracy which led the party increasingly to bestow its faith in the judicial element of the state betraying a 'eulogising' tendency towards the court.[190] This was, therefore, not merely a restoration of the balance of power but, given that the legislature under the Janata government itself was in such a state of flux, the balance of power was tipped decidedly towards the courts instead. Somnath Chatterjee[191] of the Community Party declared the courts to be the sole upholders of constitutional principles during the Emergency:

> I must pay my tribute to the judiciary that by and large, during the last Emergency the judiciary has served the people with great courage and devotion, it has followed the Constitution of India and the oath which was taken. There might have been some unfortunate exceptions. Barring a few judgements, by and large, the learned judges have stood by the side of the people.[192]

The Janata Party's only enduring legacy was the empowerment of the institution of the judiciary and the Supreme Court. The court, for its part, rose to the role of the guardian against tyranny, even though it was judicial delays and the stay order against the high court judgment that aided the orchestration of the Emergency.[193] Over the years, the court emerged as a temperamental ally of social groups—women, minorities, provincial governments, and new political parties.

For instance, in the famous case of *Reverend Stanislaus v. Madhya Pradesh*,[194] the constitutional validity of the Freedom of Religion Act that limited the work of Christian missionaries[195] in Madhya Pradesh (1967) was challenged.

---

[189] *Lok Sabha Debates*, Shanti Bhushan. When questioned by Vayalar Ravi about this unquestioned faith in the judiciary, Somnath Chatterjee responded, 'You have poor understanding, Emergency had perverted you. Have a dialogue with me if you want to learn ... (interruptions) For 19 months you raised not only your hands but your two feet also to support her', col. 102.

[190] Baxi, 'Taking Suffering Seriously', 107–18.

[191] Member of parliament from the Communist Party of India (Marxist).

[192] *Lok Sabha Debates*, col. 26.

[193] Upendra Baxi, *Courage, Craft, and Contention: The Indian Supreme Court in the Eighties* (Bombay: NM Tripathi, 1985) for an analysis of contradictory stances of the court in response to the emergency.

[194] *Rev Stanislaus v. Madhya Pradesh*, 1977 SCR (2) 611.

[195] Discussed in Chapter 2 under 'Conversion Controversy'.

The petitioner, Reverend Stanislaus, argued that the law violated the Christian people's right to propagate their religion and the state legislatures lacked the necessary legislative competence to enact such provisions. The Madhya Pradesh High Court dismissed the appeal stating that provincial government was entitled to do so since the matter was raised as a concern for 'public order'.[196] In 1977, the Supreme Court confirmed the high court decision and again dismissed the appeal.

In the case of *Yulitha Hyde v. State of Orissa* in 1973, which challenged the Freedom of Religion Act of the Orissa government, the Orissa High Court struck down the Act as unconstitutional. The high court held that the fundamental right to freedom of religion, which included the freedom to propagate one's religion, already contained the limitation that conversion as a result of coercion was not recognized.[197] The Supreme Court, however, concluded that the definition of propagation implied 'dissemination' and this did not include conversion, proselytising, allurement, fraud, and a threat to public order.[198] It reversed the Orissa High Court verdict observing that the new Act was valid since it explicitly covered these activities.[199] The judgment came under severe criticism in academic scholarship as well as from within the judiciary.[200] H. M. Seervai, an eminent jurist, offered a substantive definition of the word 'propagate': 'To propagate religion is not to impart knowledge and to spread it more widely, but to produce intellectual and moral conviction leading to action, namely adoption of religion.'[201] This definition clarified that the propagation of religion was guaranteed as a fundamental right and had a broader implication than 'dissemination'.

Once the legislation was redeemed by the Supreme Court in 1978, the Janata government tabled the national 'Freedom of Religion' Bill[202] to regulate conversion, but before it could be enacted, parliament was dissolved in 1979. The Janata Party suffered a catastrophic electoral loss in 1980, paving the way for Indira Gandhi's return with her largest electoral victory. Indira Gandhi, when she returned to power in 1980, closed the conversation on a national 'Freedom of Religion' Act,

---

[196] As 'public order' falls under the 'residuary' category of Entry List 97, subjects on which the states (provinces) can legislate.

[197] *Yulitha Hyde v. State of Orissa* (1977) I SCC 677.

[198] Ibid.

[199] See also Ronojoy Sen, *Articles of Faith: Religion, Secularism, and the Indian Supreme Court* (Oxford: Oxford University Press, 2010) on the *Reverend Stanislaus* case.

[200] Ibid.

[201] H. M. Seervai, *Constitutional Law of India: A Critical Commentary*, vol. 3 (Bombay: NM Tripathi, 1996), 1287.

[202] This was first introduced in 1954 but the bill was rejected by parliament.

citing its incompatibility with secularism and objections raised by the Minorities Commission. Secularism, therefore, in letter may have had little success ideologically, but had substantive use for organizing and routing resistance against threats of majoritarianism in the 1970s and 1980s. It came to stand *for* freedom of religion but against communal politics. Both the bill and objections against it were routed in arguments pro-secularism, but both arguments hinged on secularism being an enabling condition for the 'freedom of religion'. How such a freedom was understood by the political parties and courts differed significantly.

Returning to the question of the courts, however, the decisions on upholding the 'freedom of religion' Acts also protected the emergence of regional parties.[203] The judgment supported regional autonomy and federalism at the cost of the freedom of religion, favouring a very narrow definition of 'propagation of religion' as 'dissemination'. The same court had encouraged a 'broader' interpretation of Muslim personal law with respect to maintenance of divorced wives in the *Bai Tahira* and *Fazlunbi* cases, discussed earlier.

Linear histories of the court decisions to forward an argument on 'effectiveness' (or the ineffectiveness) of the law has been challenged successfully by anthropologists[204] and historians who show that judgments alone say little about the nature of the dispute. In matters of personal law, women's rights or religion and secularism the courts have offered wide ranging and unpredictable rulings. There was an enhanced focus as well as a certain reverence for the courts post the Emergency. Litigating in 'public interest' was seen as a step towards amplifying access to justice, almost giving it a philanthropic feel. The framing of disputes in writs, particularly ones in 'public interest', allowed for idealistic pursuits of 'public spirited' individuals to represent or articulate claims which were otherwise unrepresented. This allowed the courts to emerge as the vanguard of liberalism, a reputation it did not sustain for long.

Social Action in Public Interest: A Footnote on Curative Litigation

One of the most significant measures that connected the courts more firmly to popular social movements was the introduction of PIL. This became an enabler of justice by means of which a third party could present evidence before the court

---

[203] President's rule was imposed in Gujarat and Bihar. Chapter 2, section III also discussed the case of the dismissal of the communist government in Kerala.

[204] Gopika Solanki, *Adjudication in Religious Family Laws: Cultural Accommodation, Legal Pluralism, and Gender Equality in India* (Cambridge: Cambridge University Press, 2011); and Mengia Hong Tschalaer, *Muslim Women's Quest for Justice* (Cambridge: Cambridge University Press, 2017).

on behalf of another, thus fortifying the foundation for judicial activism in India premised on offering democracy through the law.

Justice Krishna Iyer and Justice P. N. Bhagwati were two of the influential jurists who endorsed the cause of the PIL in principle and believed it to be a part of the process of 'participative justice'.[205] Many of the first few writs were constituted out of letters written to Justice Bhagwati during his tenure as the justice of the Supreme Court and the chairperson of the National Committee for the Implementation of the Legal Aid Scheme (1973). Newspapers picked up these letters and reported widely, and the court later treated these letters as writ petitions.[206] The PIL was an attempt to encourage civil society organizations and also individuals to seek redress for injustice on behalf of another, a measure that had long-term repercussions in shaping the relationship between not just parliament and the judiciary but also the political party in power and the judiciary.[207]

The PIL was not necessarily a new concept, but it gained momentum after the Emergency as a form of litigation that offered cures for tyrannical laws.[208] S. P. Sathe in his influential work on judicial activism rationalizes the judiciary's post-Emergency activism as an atonement of self-legitimization to refurbish the power of the courts *vis-à-vis* other organs of the state. He theorizes judicial populism as an aberration which occurs when the court is swayed by euphoria.[209] Baxi chooses to rename it Social Action Legislation (SAL) and again suggests that such litigation was 'catharsis' after the Emergency: 'The court became a third chamber of parliament ... acquiring the characteristics of the House of People, posing alternate modes of lawyering for Indian people or combating repression and governmental lawlessness.'[210]

---

[205] V. K. Iyer, *Of Law and Life* (Columbia, Missouri: South Asia Books, 1979).

[206] *Hussainara Khatoon and Ors v. Home Secretary, State of Bihar*, 1979 AIR 1369. In 1979, Kapila Hingorani had filed a petition on behalf of many prisoners in the Bihar Jail, challenging the treatment meted out to them while awaiting trial. In what came to be known as the *Hussainara Khatoon* case, the court had said that if any accused complained that they had been denied a speedy trial, it could direct the state to set up more courts, or appoint more judges in order to actualize such a trial.

[207] Saumya Saxena, 'Courting Hindu Nationalism: Law and the Rise of Modern Hindutva', *Contemporary South Asia* 38, no. 3 (2018): 423–38.

[208] Raju Ramachandran, 'Supreme Court and the Basic Structure Doctrine', and Gopal Subramanium, 'Emergency Provisions under the Indian Constitution', in *Supreme but Not Infallible: Essays in Honour of the Supreme Court of India*, ed. Ashok H. Desai, Gopal Subramanian, Rajeev Dhavan, and Raju Ramachandran, 107–33 and 134–58. (New Delhi: Oxford University Press, 2000).

[209] Sathe, *Judicial Activism in India*, 108–13.

[210] Baxi, 'Taking Suffering Seriously', 129.

Such petitions encouraged the court's judgments to become more imaginative,[211] as it allowed the courts to gain a moral high ground as it became an ally of the weak. Petitions on occasions also precipitated populist judgments which were aided or preceded by media trials. Nonetheless, this was a significant development in the history of Indian democracy, as it became an important means of challenging various aspects of personal law, such as bigamy, triple *talaq*,[212] or homosexuality[213] in the subsequent decades, as analysed in later chapters. Petitions were filed under Article 32 of the constitution which guaranteed the right to constitutional remedies. PIL, however, went a step further to relax the condition of proving locus standi[214] or the direct stake of the petitioner in a cause that was in public interest.[215] This served to make the constitution more accessible to citizens and inaugurated the rise of the judicial element of state as the courts seized this opportunity to affirm their position as the custodians of the constitution.

The newer scholarship on PILs, however, reads these measures with considerable scepticism. Such an acknowledgement is crucial for furthering our understanding of how court-led activism cannot contain the conversation around complex demands of the society from the state.[216] Iyer's rulings on Muslim personal law evidence how the will of a judge can be central in determining outcomes, particularly wherever there is ambiguity in statutes—common in personal law disputes. Judicial activism and intervention in matters of family law is a consistent and recurring theme in the book and illustrates that moments of such activism were triggered by events, movements, and individuals.

---

[211] Sujit Choudhry, 'How to Do Constitutional Law and Politics in South Asia', in *Unstable Constitutionalism: Law and Politics in South Asia*, ed. Mark Tushnet and Madhav Khosla (Cambridge: Cambridge University Press, 2015), 18–43.

[212] *Ahmedabad Women's Action Group v. Union of India* (1997) 3 SCC 573.

[213] *Naz Foundation v. Government of National Capital Territory of Delhi*, WP(C) No.7455/2001.

[214] The ability of a party to demonstrate before the court, a connection to 'harm' from a law or an action, to justify participation in the case.

[215] PILs can be filed before the Supreme Court (if a fundamental right is violated) under Article 32 which guarantees the right to constitutional remedies. Or they can be filed before the high court which under Article 226 provides an even wider scope for the petition.

[216] Judicial activism in Muslim personal law is discussed in Chapter 5 of this book. See also Anuj Bhuwania, *Courting the People: Public Interest Litigation in Post-Emergency India* (New Delhi: Cambridge University Press, 2017). For a critical discussion on the judiciary, see Baxi, *The Indian Supreme Court and Politics*; Gary Jacobsohn, *The Wheel of Law: India's Secularism in Comparative Constitutional Context* (Princeton, NJ: Princeton University Press, 2004), chs. 5–6; and Mehta, 'The Indian Supreme Court and the Art of Democratic Positioning', in *Unstable Constitutionalism: Law and Politics in South Asia*.

Conclusion

This chapter has demonstrated that the debate on personal law reached a critical juncture in the 1970s. While studies have largely focussed on the Emergency, women's rights activism, or India's foreign policy in this decade, this chapter argued that these themes were in fact brought into a conversation through debates on personal law. The chapter illustrated that women's agency and mobilizations for reform in Muslim personal law in the 1970s were obfuscated as historiography continued to privilege party political narratives of the Emergency and overemphasized the *Shah Bano* judgment and the politics of 'vote banks' as the high point of Muslim politics. This chapter accounts for women's movement's engagement with Muslim personal law and the emergence of opposition from religious movements which produced competing languages of constitutional rights.

Thus, the framing of the debate in a binary of 'women versus community' which haunted the public discourse for decades to come was an inheritance of the 1970s. The social or religious movements of the 1970s demanded changes to the law or sought exemption from it as the ultimate goal of a movement. This provided a greater opportunity for an alliance between social movements and the judiciary which positioned itself as the saviour of individual rights. Women's mobilizations in the decade allow us to recognize that the languages of resistance borrowed from the constitution and also responded to regime change and party politics, and the vocabulary of secularism was a crucial part of the democratic dialogue.

Legislative response to protest was rare, and rarely in consonance with the original demand of the movement. This was visible in the hesitant revision of the laws for women's empowerment after the *Towards Equality* Report, while exceptions requested by orthodox members of religious minorities were easily conceded by parliament during the revision of the CrPC. Despite their claims of being a guardian against tyranny and a messiah of social reform, Indian courts were sporadic in their support to women's rights as seen in the *Mathura* case, and towards minorities as in the *Reverend Stanislaus* case of missionary activities and religious conversion. The reading of the statutory law by courts indicated the implicit biases of the presiding judge, regardless of the label of the statute (Hindu, Muslim, or Christian) in matters of family law. The reliance on the law was nonetheless significant and meaningful to the women's movement in the 1970s.

The law was invoked in various battles waged in the decade, for rights, empowerment, freedom, and democracy. Crucially, the Emergency added secularism firmly in the constitutional vocabulary. This terminology became relevant to Muslim personal law, women's battles against religious patriarchy, and also political promises made to the public. The chapter thus showed that the Emergency directly and indirectly affected the conversation on personal law. Directly, by negotiating support for the Emergency with orthodox Muslim groups, and by breaking the momentum of social movements and protest. Indirectly, the Emergency affected personal laws by first undermining the court's authority that eventually provoked a backlash. Post-Emergency, the regime of the Janata Party was marked by a co-operation between the judiciary and the legislature. The end of the 1970s and the beginning of the 1980s also signified the rise of judicial activism. The battle for the custody of the constitution between the judiciary and parliament was, for the moment, concluded in favour of the judiciary. This induced a productive triangulation between the citizen, the court, and parliament, where a citizen could induce competition between the latter two. This had a bearing on not just personal law debates but also on Indian democracy more generally.

4

Muslim Law, Hindu Nationalism, and Indian Secularisms, 1980–92

> I want to raise a question: Why do they talk of national integration through maintenance law? How is national integration directly concerned with maintenance to a divorcee, I want to ask.
> —Saifuddin Soz, *Lok Sabha Debates*, 22 November 1985, col. 370

The decade, it turns out, was dedicated to debating precisely this connection between divorce, nationalism, national integration, and democracy. The 1980s brought with it significant shifts in the nature of Indian politics. Colour televisions were making their way into India, and the license and regulation raj was gradually giving way to economic liberalization. With the introduction of the New Economic Policy aimed at opening up the markets in 1991 by the Narasimha Rao government, even the public–private divide within households underwent a substantial change. The liberalization of the economy entailed a problematic but definite feminization of labour.[1] Further, the intensified struggle for limited resources produced anxiety and violence, some of which was absorbed by the rising Hindu nationalist movement by offering a common ethno-religious enemy in the Muslims.[2] The idea of secularism became particularly potent with the consolidation of Sangh politics in the 1980s, which informs the broad context of the debates on personal law in the decade.

Formerly known as the Bharatiya Jana Sangh, which had had the support of the Hindu Mahasabha, the Vishwa Hindu Parishad, the Bajrang Dal, and

---

[1] For participation of women in the informal economy post-liberalization, see Kalpana Bardhan, 'Women: Work, Welfare and Status Forces of Tradition and Change in India', *Comparative Studies of South Asia, Africa and the Middle East* 6, no. 1 (1986): 3–16; Rohini Hensman, 'Globalisation: A Perspective for Labour', *Economic and Political Weekly* 38, no. 43 (2003): 4583–85; Barbara Harriss-White, *India Working: Essays on Society and Economy* (Cambridge: Cambridge University Press, 2003); and Amrita Chhachhi, 'Gender, Flexibility, Skill, and Industrial Restructuring: The Electronics Industry in India', *Gender, Technology and Development* 3, no. 3 (1999): 329–60; Stuart Corbridge and John Harriss, *Reinventing India: Liberalization, Hindu Nationalism and Popular Democracy* (New Delhi: Oxford University Press, 2000).

[2] Arjun Appadurai, *Fear of Small Numbers: An Essay on the Geography of Anger* (Durham, NC: Duke University Press, 2006).

the RSS cadres, the party was reorganized under the banner of the BJP in 1980 after a split from the Janata Party. The political party and the social movement collectively represented the Hindu nationalist front.[3] Summoning the writings of V. D. Savakar and M. S. Golwalkar, who had been leading figures of the Hindu Mahasabha in the national movement in the mid-twentieth century, the Hindu nationalist movement in the 1980s invoked the shared heritage and history among Hindus for the ultimate end of establishing a Hindu *rashtra* (nation).[4] One of the party's primary promises was the construction of a Ram Temple in the place of the sixteenth-century mosque, the Babri Masjid, which they claimed was built on the original site of the Ramajanmabhumi—the birthplace of the Hindu god Ram.[5]

Identity politics that gained salience in the 1980s and the 1990s was also closely linked to the emergence of new regional parties. These parties were aided by the extension of caste-based reservation policies introduced by the Mandal Commission report (or the Socially and Educationally Backward Classes Commission [SEBC]) released in 1989.[6] The Hindu nationalist movement attempted to assuage the upper-caste anxieties over the challenge to their historical domination posed by the Mandal policies and the consolidation of new regional formations. A temple at the birth place of God Ram was then projected by the Hindu nationalist movement as the common and collective cause of Hindus. Quite unlike 'religious' movements that historically remained focussed on homogenization, reform, or devotion, Hindu nationalism made itself available as a cultural and political representation of the national majority; a movement born out of democracy rather than religion.[7]

---

[3] For an analysis of the history of the Sangh Parivar, see T. B. Hansen, *The Saffron Wave: Democracy and Hindu Nationalism in Modern India* (Princeton, NJ: Princeton University Press, 1999); and Christophe Jaffrelot, ed., *Hindu Nationalism: A Reader* (Princeton, NJ: Princeton University Press, 2009).

[4] Jaffrelot, *Hindu Nationalism*, 208.

[5] The dispute had been raised in courts since 1949, but was given a fresh lease in the 1980s with the Hindu nationalist campaign for the reconstruction of the Ram Temple.

[6] The Mandal Commission was created by the Janata government in 1979, and its report was implemented by the V. P. Singh government in 1989. The commission extended reservations in public sector and government jobs for Other Backward Classes (OBCs). This included reservations in PSUs, banks, private sector undertakings receiving government grants, colleges and universities. The commission also suggested an age relaxation to OBC candidates, among other recommendation.

[7] P. B. Mehta, 'In Post-Mortem of Secularism, We Are Hand Wringing over Religion, Missing the Real Crisis', *Indian Express*, 11 August 2020.

The rise of Hindu nationalism in India has, therefore, been theorized as a democratic upsurge,[8] a conservative revolution,[9] and an elite revolt,[10] or an elite conspiracy[11]—effected and analysed as a problem of democracy rather than as solely a threat to 'secularism'. The movement has largely been studied as one that hoped to consolidate the vote of the upper-caste Hindus for the BJP. This chapter shows that it also encouraged, as a corollary, a superficial consolidation of Muslim politics on personal law, suppressing the intra-community debates within Muslims that characterized the 1970s. It was this unfair consolidation of Hindu and Muslim monoliths in political parlance that made secularism particularly relevant in the decade. Not merely to manage the religious conflict staged by the BJP over the Ram Temple but also to preserve meaningful difference and diversity. Secularism became the language in which majoritarianism was resisted rather than for installing any boundaries between the state and religion. Unlike the 1950s and the 1960s where the state still hoped to steer conversations on religion and relied on religion to access the family, in the 1980s, the legal realm struggles to absorb assertions of religious difference, religious spectacle, and religious conflict.

It is in this context that the chapter analyses the iconic cases of Shah Bano's divorce and Roop Kanwar's sati. The cases demonstrate women's movement's growing disillusionment with state politics and disappointment with legal reform which further gave way to the emergence of NGOs and collectives later in the decade. The case of Shah Bano's divorce, in the first section of the chapter, illustrates that there were multiple operative relationships between religion and the state. Shah Bano's case not only posited religion and the state as players competing for authority as personal law debates often do.[12] It also showed that the difference between the parliamentary and judicial narrative on religion and secularism is precisely what challenged and diminished the state's authority on adjudicating personal law. The law produced on Muslim women's maintenance, therefore, did not necessarily abridge the rights of Muslim

---

[8] Yogendra Yadav, 'Electoral Politics in the Time of Change: India's Third Electoral System, 1989–99', *Economic and Political Weekly* 34, no. 34/35 (1999): 2393–99.

[9] Hansen, *The Saffron Wave*.

[10] Corbridge and Harriss, *Reinventing India*.

[11] D. L. Sheth, 'Changing Terms of Elite Discourse: The Case of Reservation for "Other Backward Classes"', in *Region, Religion, Caste, Gender and Culture in Contemporary India*, ed. T. V. Sathyamurthy (New Delhi: Oxford University Press, 1996), 314–33.

[12] Tanja Herklotz, 'Law, Religion and Gender Equality: Literature on the Indian Personal Law System from a Women's Rights Perspective', *Indian Law Review* 1, no. 3 (2017): 250–68.

women but instead instituted more judicial discretion in the adjudication of maintenance claims.[13]

The first section of the chapter challenges the notion that rigid religious ideologies produced patriarchal notions of gender and family. Further, it also challenges the idea that patriarchal notions of gender and family were simply preserved and reproduced through statutory law. This chapter will show that religious reinterpretation and secular law both help destabilize power centres within families as well as authorities that adjudicate over them.

The compounding of the vulnerability of women by their dual disadvantage of gender and the membership of a minority community or caste group has been researched extensively.[14] Theoretical writing on family law has also expressed concerns that codification or any legal intervention in personal law is necessarily predicated upon greater coercion, abuse, and centralization of coercive power with the state.[15] Such arguments note that state interventions are rarely prompted by concerns about women's rights, and the promise of criminalizing practices ostensibly rooted in religion instead establishes a relationship between the state and the citizen that is solely carceral. This Foucauldian emphasis on governmentality, however, presumed a far more organized interest in regulation and what must be regulated than is visible in conversations within the institutions of the state. Such a framing has the potential to overestimate the coherence of the 'state's will' and undermine the confusions that characterize the making of the law.

---

[13] Flavia Agnes, 'From Shahbano to Kausar Bano: Contextualizing the "Muslim Women" within a Communalized Polity', in *South Asian Feminisms*, ed. Ania Loomba and Ritty A. Lukose (Durham, NC: Duke University Press, 2012), 33–53; W. F. Menski, 'The Uniform Civil Code Debate in Indian Law: New Developments and Changing Agenda', *German Law Journal* 9, no. 3 (2008): 211–50; both Agnes and Menski show that there are merits in progressive interpretations of law by the courts, that often make legislative interventions unnecessary. This chapter, instead of focussing on the 'use' of this law, analyses the process of its making.

[14] Gail Omvedt, *Reinventing Revolution: New Social Movements and the Socialist Tradition in India* (London: ME Sharpe, 1993). Radha Kumar, *The History of Doing: An Illustrated Account of Movements for Women's Rights and Feminism in India 1800–1990* (New Delhi: Zubaan, 1993). For a framework for cross-cultural analysis of women's movements, see also Jeanne Boydston, 'Gender as a Question of Historical Analysis', *Gender and History* 20, no. 3 (2008): 558–83.

[15] Ratna Kapur, *Gender, Alterity and Human Rights: Freedom in a Fishbowl* (Cheltenham and Northampton: Edward Elgar Publishing, 2018); Talal Asad, *Formations of the Secular: Christianity, Islam, Modernity* (Stanford: Stanford University Press, 2003); Judith Butler, *Antigone's Claim: Kinship between Life and Death* (New York: Columbia University Press, 2002).

While some scholarship acknowledges that state power is 'disaggregated' rather than 'aggregated',[16] theorists continue to accord far too much centrality to the state as a determinant of all political discourses constitutive of democracy, such as secularism, regulation of privacy, and religion. The anthropological counter narrative too, in its zeal to demonstrate the decentralization of personal law adjudication in non-state forums, ends up reproducing the idea that the state's law produced centralization, and decentralization necessarily occurred outside state forums.[17] The negotiations and confusions that this chapter demonstrates over key constitutional concepts such as secularism, freedom of religion, and right to equality, in the eighties, betray the impermanence and uncertainty in the way these meanings are constructed and the law is produced, which in effect decentralizes the authority of the state on personal law.

The second section of the chapter discusses the controversial case of Roop Kanwar's sati, which has largely been analysed in comparison with Shah Bano.[18] The chapter, however, analyses the spectacle of Roop Kanwar's immolation in connection with the dramatic mobilization for a Ram Temple in Ayodhya. The sati case indicated that scriptural sanction was not necessary for validating customary practices, but rather public spectacles could be used to demand the validation of religious practices. Both mobilizations for sati and the Ramajanmabhumi also shared a will to find legal protections for their theatrics and ritualism. Significantly, both also attempted physical constructions, of a sati shrine and a Ram Temple, to act as a foundation for disseminating new ideologies or repackaging old ones. The valorization of the act of sati and the involvement of women in the Hindu nationalist movement for the construction of a Ram Temple in Ayodhya shared a common perception about the peripheral, inferior, and conditional role of women in the public realm.[19] The problematic articulation of strong, self-sacrificing, yet hapless and victimized characterization of women produced a peculiar template

---

[16] Srimati Basu, *The Trouble with Marriage: Feminists Confront Law and Violence in India*, vol. 1 (New Delhi: University of California Press, 2015).

[17] Farrah Ahmed, *Religious Freedom under Personal Law System* (New Delhi: Oxford University Press, 2017).

[18] Veena Das, *Critical Events: An Anthropological Perspective on Contemporary India* (New Delhi: Oxford University Press, 1996).

[19] For women's representation in the Hindu nationalist campaign, see Paula Bacchetta, 'All Our Goddesses Are Armed: Religion, Resistance, and Revenge in the Life of a Militant Hindu Nationalist Woman', *Bulletin of Concerned Asian Scholars* 25, no. 4 (1993): 38–51. Amrita Basu, 'Feminism Inverted: The Real Women and Gendered Imagery of Hindu Nationalism', *Bulletin of Concerned Asian Scholars* 25, no. 4 (1993): 25–36; Tanika Sarkar, 'The Woman as Communal Subject: Rashtrasevika Samiti and Ram Janmabhumi Movement', *Economic and Political Weekly* 26, no. 35 (1991): 2057–62.

for the introduction of any legislation for women's rights within a family, which the BJP emphatically demanded in the form of a Uniform Civil Code.

The 1980s saw the emergence of a politics of permanent performance,[20] as sati and the Ramajanmabhumi were both spectacles that showed a potential to convert public symbols of religion into political moments. It was precisely such a deployment of religion for mobilizing women that relinquished feminist engagement with the reinterpretation of Hinduism. The involvement of women in the Hindu nationalist movement urged the feminist counter-narrative to lean on the law for opposing the discrimination within the Hindu familial ideology. However, the BJP's simultaneous posturing against the Muslims prompted feminist writing that became protective of Muslim women's right to religion and religious difference.

Both the Muslim Women (Protection of Rights on Divorce) Act and the Hindu nationalist campaign produced their own standards of acceptable family life leading to feminist scepticism over uniformity within and between communities. Both also weakened the state's ability to steer or adjudicate conversations on religion. This chapter demonstrates how the strategies of secularism and the defence of religious difference are deployed by different actors in the politics of the codification of personal laws in India. However hollow the vocabulary of secularism, it was formative of public and political discourse in India, and therefore relevant, even if not essential, for democracy.

I

Shah Bano's Divorce: Case and Context

Shah Bano and Mohammad Ahmad Khan had five children—two daughters and three sons. Khan later entered into a second marriage with a cousin of Shah Bano's with whom he fathered seven more children. His two wives quarrelled, and a large family also meant that there were many mouths to feed. Shah Bano was 63 years old when Khan divorced her in 1978. He asked her to move to a shanty near their house, with her three sons. The problem arose when he asked her to vacate even those premises and refused to pay her any maintenance beyond a period of three months (*iddat*).[21] She filed a maintenance claim, which Khan declined. Khan, a lawyer himself, argued that according to Muslim personal law, his obligation to provide maintenance extended no further than three menstrual cycles of his wife, beyond this point, her adult sons were obliged to maintain her.

---

[20] Hansen, *The Saffron Wave*.

[21] Period of three months or three menstrual cycles of a woman (or the entire duration of pregnancy if that is the case) after which a Muslim divorce that has been pronounced becomes final, and parties are free to remarry.

The case travelled from court to court, but the agreed sum of maintenance granted to Shah Bano was reduced each time her husband appealed the judgment in a higher court. In 1985, the Supreme Court confirmed the decisions of the lower courts even as it lowered the maintenance amount granted to Shah Bano, it directed her husband to pay maintenance beyond *iddat* and further recommended the introduction of a Uniform Civil Code for all citizens of the country. Court rulings favoured the granting of maintenance to the wife under Section 125—'order for maintenance of wives, children and parents'—but these were challenged by Khan as violative of his 'right to freedom of religion', which included his right to follow his own personal law protected under Articles 25–28.[22] Khan represented himself in court, and claimed that he was well versed with constitutional as well as Muslim personal law. An honourable Muslim, he argued, will maintain his wife, but while the Quran encourages this, it does not make it obligatory. His legal defence against maintenance was that it was 'dishonourable' but acceptable. Khan argued that he never claimed the moral high ground of being an honourable Muslim man, but was an ordinary one. This was the last case Khan ever fought.[23]

The interpretation of Muslim law in the *Shah Bano* judgment was not drastically different from many preceding judgments such as Justice Krishna Iyer's rulings on *Bai Tahira v. Ali Hussain Fiddali Chothia* or *Fazlunbi v. Kader Vali* discussed previously.[24] Iyer's decisions in the above-mentioned cases did not challenge Muslim personal law but concluded that religious law could be reconciled with other statutory provisions, in this case Section 125, without posing any conflict with constitutional law. Such an interpretation in the 'spirit of justice'[25] did not threaten the existence of religious law. As far as the limited obligation of husbands towards maintaining their wives was concerned, the court once again simply treated the denial of maintenance as *good in law but bad in theology*.[26] The 'bad in theology' argument permitted some scope for judicial discretion. The *Shah Bano* judgment concluded:

---

[22] Article 25: Freedom of conscience and free profession, practice and propagation of religion.
Article 26: Freedom to manage religious affairs.
Article 27: Freedom as to payment of taxes for promotion of any particular religion.
Article 28: Freedom as to attendance at religious instruction or religious worship in certain educational institutions.
See *Narasu Appa Mali* judgment of 1952, discussed in Chapter 1, which had confirmed that personal law was included under the fundamental right to freedom of religion.

[23] 'Revisiting Shah Bano's Family, 31 Years Later: "My Mother Got Threats After SC Order, But Stuck to Stand"', *Indian Express*, 24 April 2016.

[24] *Bai Tahira v. Ali Hussain Fidali Chothia*, 1979 SCR (2) 75; *Fazlunbi v. Khader Vali*, 1980 SCR (3) 1127.

[25] *Fazlunbi Biwi v. Khader Vali*, 1980 SCR (3) 1127.

[26] Ibid. See the discussion in Chapter 3.

The true position is that, if the divorced wife is able to maintain herself, the husband's liability to provide maintenance for her ceases with the expiration of the period of *iddat*. If she is unable to maintain herself, she is entitled to take recourse to section 125 of the Code. *Thus there is no conflict between the provisions of section 125 and those of the Muslim Personal Law on the question of the Muslim husband's obligation to provide maintenance for a divorced wife who is unable to maintain herself.* Aiyat No. 241 and 242 of 'the Holy Quran' fortify that the Holy Quran imposed an obligation on the Muslim husband to make provision for or to provide maintenance to the divorced wife. The contrary argument does less than justice to the teachings of Quran.[27]

The court interpreted Muslim personal law as one that provides maintenance for divorced wives for up to three months, after which the husband's obligation ends, unless, the wife is unable to maintain herself thereafter and is driven to destitution—and that is when Section 125 of the CrPC was meant to come in. The *Shah Bano* judgment upheld what the judges felt was 'good in theology', but the ruling's additional recommendation of a Uniform Civil Code became a point of contestation. The bench recommended that a Uniform Civil Code would alleviate the burden of the courts which repeatedly encountered cases of unpaid maintenance and consequent destitution resulting from Muslim divorces:

A beginning [towards a Uniform Civil Code] has to be made if the Constitution is to have any meaning. Inevitably, the role of the reformer has to be assumed by the courts because it is beyond the endurance of sensitive minds to allow injustice to be suffered when it is so palpable. But piecemeal attempts of courts to bridge the gap between personal laws cannot take the place of a common Civil Code. Justice to all is a far more satisfactory way of dispensing justice than justice from case to case.[28]

This led to strong protests led predominantly by the AIMPLB and JIH in northern India, and scholars from Aligarh Muslim University expressed dissatisfaction against the judicial interference with Muslim personal law.[29] A delegation of men led by the president of the AIMPLB, Maulana Abul Hasan Ali Nadvi, and another senior member, Maulana Minatula Rahmani, met the then Prime Minister Rajiv Gandhi and requested, once again, for the exclusion of the Muslim community from Sections 125–127 of the CrPC and asked for the removal of the directive principle concerning a Uniform Civil Code.[30]

---

[27] *Mohammad Ahmed Khan v. Shah Bano Begum*, 1985 AIR 945, para [859C–D, 862C–D] (emphasis mine).

[28] Ibid., para. 849.

[29] *The Telegraph*, 24 August 1985.

[30] 'Short-Sighted Move to Appease Communities', *The Statesmen*, 1 May 1986.

Parliament in the face of this protest against the judgment, announced its decision to reverse the Supreme Court decision and enact a Muslim Women (Protection of Rights on Divorce) Act, based on what members considered to be 'true interpretations' of the sources of Muslim personal law. This led to a large-scale counter protest against the government's decision by women's groups which echoed across the country. Activists and academics such as Upendra Baxi, Danial Latifi, Seema Mustafa, Zoya Hasan, Reshma Arif, and Tara Ali Beg, among others, were at the forefront of the movement.[31] The protests led by women in India resonated in Pakistan and Bangladesh as well, and large numbers of Muslim women began to rally against this exclusion of Muslims from a 'secular' legal provision that was available to all other citizens.[32]

The government's decision to reverse the judgment (even as it did not quite do so in the final version of the bill) also faced significant opposition from within the members of the Congress Party, which formed the then government led by Rajiv Gandhi. Arif Mohammad Khan, a senior member of parliament of the Congress Party and a lawyer, also the husband of activist Reshma Arif, supported the Supreme Court's judgment and also offered detailed references to the Quran and Hadees in defence of women's rights to maintenance.[33] Khan has remained a relevant figure in the debate and has repeatedly used religious references to argue for constitutional rights. Reshma Arif also led large protests against any bill that excluded Muslim women from the purview of Section 125 and had significant support among Muslim women in her husband's then constituency, Kanpur (and later Bahraich), as well as in Delhi.

Z. R. Ansari, another parliamentarian from the Congress, agreed with Arif Khan on the issue of conceiving lifelong maintenance for the divorcee; however, the two politicians differed widely in their stance on the judgment.[34] While Khan appreciated the spirit of the reading of law in the *Shah Bano* case, Ansari launched a polemical attack on the authors of the judgment, which he considered an audacious attempt to reinterpret Islam.[35] Echoing the sentiment of the Constituent Assembly debates, Ibrahim Suleiman Sait,[36] another member of parliament and

---

[31] Documentary on Muslim women's right on divorce, *In Secular India*, 1988, Riverbank Studios, New Delhi.

[32] Reshma Arif's speech in a documentary, *In Secular India*, 1988, Riverbank Studios, New Delhi.

[33] Arif Mohammad Khan, *Text and Context: Quran and Contemporary Challenges* (New Delhi: Rupa and Co, 2010).

[34] *Indian Express*, 23 November 1985.

[35] *Indian Express*, 21 December 1985.

[36] He was also a co-founder of the AIMPLB and a senior member of the All India Muslim Majlis-e-Mushwarat.

the president of the Indian Union Muslim League, declared that a Uniform Civil Code would only result in the country 'breaking up'.[37]

In the Hindu nationalist narrative, Hindu law stood reformed and Muslim law obscurantist and backward—now evidenced by the fate of Shah Bano. If the nineteenth-century colonial interventions attempted to save Indian women, from Indian men,[38] then arguably in the 1980s, the newly emerging Hindu nationalist political formations also promised to save *Muslim women from Muslim men*, through a Uniform Civil Code. In 1986, the BJP launched its campaign for a Uniform Civil Code to replace personal laws.[39] L. K. Advani, a senior leader of the BJP, declared: 'The government should tackle civil matters by evolving a code drawing from the best of all religions and their provisions on adoption, marriage, divorce inheritance, maintenance.'[40] Other Hindu nationalist outfits such as the Sena Morcha in Bombay also declared that they were going to chalk out a plan of action for the implementation of a Uniform Civil Code.[41] This demand was premised on a high-handed assumption that an 'enlightened majority' could pull forward a 'struggling and shackled' minority.[42]

The BJP, which until 1985 had small numbers in parliament, had declared the Uniform Civil Code as its prime agenda along with the promise of the construction of a Ram Temple on the site of the Babri Mosque in Ayodhya. The sixteenth-century mosque constructed in the Mughal period by Babar's aide Mir Baqi, in the north-Indian city of Ayodhya, was believed by many to have been constructed on the birth place—Janmabhumi—of the Hindu god Ram. Ramjanmabhumi Mukti Samiti (committee for the freedom of the Ramajanmabhumi), a sub-committee of the Vishwa Hindu Parishad (World Hindu Forum), commenced the *Shriram-Janaki rath yatra*[43] (journey of the chariots of Ram and Sita) throughout the state of UP. These processions were restrained by the local administration in February

---

[37] 'The League Warns against Uniform Civil Code', *Times of India*, 25 October 1985.

[38] Lata Mani, *Contentious Traditions: The Debate on Sati in Colonial India* (Berkeley: University of California Press, 1998).

[39] 'CrPC Amendment Will Be Opposed by the BJP', *Times of India*, 8 January 1986.

[40] Ibid. BJP Minister Jaywantiben Mehta reportedly stated that 15,000 cases of divorce of Muslim couples were pending in courts suggesting that Muslim law needed reform.

[41] 'Sena Morcha on Civil Code Planned', Bombay, *Times of India*, 6 December 1985.

[42] Nivedita Menon, 'Uniform Civil Code: The Women's Movement Perspective', *Kafila.org*, 1 October 2014, https://kafila.online/2014/10/01/uniform-civil-code-state-of-the-debate-in-2014/. See also Nivedita Menon, 'State/Gender/Community: Citizenship in Contemporary India', *Economic and Political Weekly* 33, no. 5 (1998): PE3–PE10.

[43] Ram and Sita's journey on chariots. In the campaign, the BJP used Toyota vehicle dressed as *raths* (or horse-drawn chariots) for the *yatra* or the pilgrimage/journey.

1986 to prevent communal violence in the localities that the *raths* traversed.[44]
Political strategies were aimed towards constructing the figure of the Muslim
man as the illegal occupier of the holy land of Ayodhya, who was simultaneously a
threat to Hindu women and also cruel towards Muslim wives.

Perturbed by the pledges of the BJP and its allied organizations for the
reconstruction of a Ram Temple in the place of the Babri Mosque, the AIMPLB
with the support of the Samajwadi Party's political leadership[45] instituted a Babri
Mazjid Action Committee (BMAC) for protecting the Babri Mosque in 1986.[46]
The UP government headed by Mulayam Singh Yadav, chief of the Janata Dal
(People's Party), continued to express concerns over the growing agitation in
Ayodhya.[47] The protection of the Muslim personal law and the Babri Mosque
became twin counter agendas for the BMAC as there was a substantial overlap
between the membership of the board and that of the committee. The convenor of
the committee, Zafaryab Jilani, was an influential member of the AIMPLB.

The public debate ushered in a polarization on the lines of the freedom of
religion *or* the equality between sexes. Feminist writing in the period exposed the
problematic choice that Muslim women confronted. On the one hand, they could
opt to retain access to the existing statutory provision of Section 125 of the CrPC,
which was now endorsed by the political party that openly pledged for a Hindu
rashtra (nation). On the other hand, they could stand by the influential men of
their community who resisted Hindu nationalism but also protested against the
maintenance of wives. In a strange sense, the BJP was now attempting to occupy
the position that the Indian Satyashodhak Samaj and the Indian Secular Society
had occupied in the 1970s. This position also helped stretch a 'secular' veneer on
Hindu nationalist politics, as they worded any deviation from this position of
claimed 'neutrality' of a uniform code as 'pseudo secularism'. This rhetoric was
further aided by the AIMPLB's leadership branding Shah Bano the *na-pak aurat*
or the impure woman who made her community vulnerable to surveillance or
regulation.[48] Shah Bano ultimately withdrew her case.

---

[44] Release of Ram-Janaki Rathas of UP, initiated by Shriram Janmabhumi Mukti Andolan
(Movement for the liberation of Lord Ram's birth place), Vishva Hindu Parishad web archives,
http://vhp.org/shriram-janmabhumi-mukti-andolan/mov1-shriram-janmabhumi-
mukti-andolan-2/, accessed in January 2013.

[45] Samajwadi Party later formed government in Uttar Pradesh (1993–1995).

[46] See the discussion in the Liberhan Commission Report, 2007, Ministry of Home Affairs
website, mha.nic.in/LAC, accessed in July 2013.

[47] Later, in 1992, Mulayam Singh Yadav launched his own political party, the Samajwadi Party
(Socialist Party).

[48] Upendra Baxi, 'Siting Secularism in the Uniform Civil Code', in *The Crisis of Secularism
in India*, ed. Anuradha Dingwaney Needham and Rajeswari Sunder Rajan (Durham, NC:
Duke University Press, 2007), 267–93.

The Ambiguous Act

Na samjha umr guzri but-e-khudsar ko samjhaate,
Pighal kar mom ho jaate agar pattar ko samjhaate.
(a lifetime has gone by in explaining to an idol in vain, even stones would have melted
like wax with the effort.)

Sir, another problem has now cropped up. I spoke for one and a half hours that day
and for two hours today but even after that the hon. Member has not been able to
understand. The narration of the whole Ramayan has now been complete and still
one has not been able to know as to who Sita and who was Ram.[49]

Ansari's sentiment best summarizes the ambiguity surrounding the Muslim
Women (Protection of Rights on Divorce) Act that followed the *Shah Bano*
judgment. Did it resolve the question of maintenance? did it reverse the judgment?
How did it reconcile with the constitution and what did it mean for Section 125 of
the CrPC? Much of the research on the subject has circled around this problematic
choice or the constitution's 'contradictory embrace' of the fundamental right to
freedom of religion, on the one hand, and the directive principle of a Uniform
Civil Code, on the other.[50] This has also prompted a lively debate on individual
and group rights, as well as political secularism. Writings on personal law leaned
on a defence of the 'Uniform Civil Code' as a positive step for women,[51] and
also on its critique highlighting the inadequacies of the one-size-fits-all legal
interventions, which is custom-blind and anti-religion.[52] Other scholars pondered
over the optionality of uniformity and of diversity[53] and yet others challenged
what indeed was the original intent behind a Uniform Civil Code.[54] This literature
acknowledges that the propositions for a Uniform Civil Code are undergirded

---

[49] *Lok Sabha Debates*, Vaisakha 15, 1908 (Saka), *Muslims Women Protection of Rights on Divorce Bill*, Z. R. Ansari, 20 December 1985, col. 440 (translation mine).

[50] Vrinda Narain, *Reclaiming the Nation: Muslim Women and the Law in India* (Toronto: University of Toronto Press, 2008).

[51] Vasudha Dhagamwar, *Towards the Uniform Civil Code* (New Delhi: Indian Law Institute, 1989). Archana Parashar, *Women and Family Law Reform in India: Uniform Civil Code and Gender Equality* (New Delhi: Sage Publications, 1992).

[52] Flavia Agnes, 'The Supreme Court, the Media, and the Uniform Civil Code Debate in India', in *The Crisis of Secularism in India*, 294–315. See also Seyla Benhabib, ed., *Democracy and Difference: Contesting the Boundaries of the Political* (Princeton, NJ: Princeton University Press, 1996).

[53] Nivedita Menon, 'A Uniform Civil Code in India: The State of the Debate in 2014', *Feminist Studies* 40, no. 2 (2014b): 480–6.

[54] Peter Ronald D'Souza, 'Politics of the Uniform Civil Code in India', *Economic and Political Weekly* 50, no. 48 (2015): 50–57.

by hopes for Hindu supremacy.[55] This also informed the women's movement's position on the Uniform Civil Code as well as the Muslim Women (Protection of Rights on Divorce) Act.[56]

The parliamentary debate on the Muslim Women (Protection of Rights on Divorce) Act evidences the confusions, uncertainties, and incoherencies within the state over what secularism meant. In aligning statutory law with religious, customary, or even popular morality of the time, the legislature ceded rather than strengthened its authority as the adjudicator of disputes over personal law. Its authority dwindled first by building in judicial discretion into the bill, and eventually was surrendered to groups and collectives that could contest the interpretations of religious texts in courts. Groups such as the AIMPLB had begun to wield influence over the Muslim personal law in the 1970s, but they had also pushed open the door for influences other than themselves to reach out to state institutions as better possessors of 'religious knowledge'. The Muslim Women (Protection of Rights on Divorce) Act in early 1986 was introduced to create an alternative to Section 125 of the CrPC, that is, the maintenance of wives, children, and parents for the Muslim community. Parliament's enactment and the judiciary's interpretation of the new law itself produced two versions of the new statute, and even more interpretations of the existing provision of Section 125 of the CrPC, as this section will illustrate.

The passage of the bill also saw divisions on party lines and a shuffle of party alliances by some of the influential voices in the debate. Inside parliament, public debate exhibited itself through different factions. The debate was no longer limited to committees and reports as it was in the 1960s, nor to granting of exemptions and exceptions to the Muslim community from state laws without any alternative statutory provisions that characterized the 1970s. Muslim personal law had finally entered parliamentary debates, not in relation or comparison with another religion, not as an affected party in a land reform, but with its 'reform' or 'codification' as an end in itself.[57] The move has been attributed to political

---

[55] Parashar, *Women and Family Law Reform in India*; Dhagamwar, *Towards the Uniform Civil Code*; and Zoya Hasan, 'Gender Politics, Legal Reform, and the Muslim Community in India', in *Appropriating Gender: Women's Activism and Politicized Religion in South Asia*, ed. Patricia Jeffery and Amrita Basu (New York: Routledge, 1998), 71–88.

[56] Flavia Agnes, 'Redefining the Agenda of the Women's Movement within a Secular Framework', *South Asia: Journal of South Asian Studies* 17, no. s1 (1994a): 63–78; Siobhan Mullally, 'Feminism and Multicultural Dilemmas in India: Revisiting the Shah Bano Case', *Oxford Journal of Legal Studies* 24, no. 4 (2004): 671–92; and others.

[57] The discussions on Islamic law in the course of the discussion on the Zamindari Act and the Wakf Act had hardly entailed debates as spectacular or polarizing as the ones on marriage and divorce.

motives, to vote-bank politics,[58] a bargain for failure to protect the Babri Masjid,[59] as well as a commitment to women's rights.[60] However, what the parliamentary debates tell us is a story of a lost opportunity and lack of consensus.

Same but Different

A. K. Sen, the law minister, suggested in his speech (with much interruption from the members of the house) that the desirability of the Uniform Civil Code was still in question and had never been universally endorsed: 'For Muslims this [personal law] is an article of faith ordained by law.'[61] Sen insisted that with the exception of a few countries such as Egypt and Tunisia, the vast global Muslim population still accepted the law as stated in the proposed bill. The bill did not address controversial practices of triple *talaq*—unilateral oral divorce which only a husband could give effect to—or bigamy or nikah halala[62] that generally led women to destitution, but instead concerned itself with the limited question of the three-month limitation on maintenance of the divorced wife.

---

[58] Zoya Hasan, 'Minority Identity, Muslim Women Bill Campaign and the Political Process', *Economic and Political Weekly* 24, no. 1 (1989): 44–50.

[59] In chapter 5, 'Shah Bano Case', Noorani termed the Muslim Women Bill as a 'quid pro quo' for opening the gates of the Babri Masjid. A. G. A. M. Noorani, ed., *The Muslims of India: A Documentary Record* (New Delhi: Oxford University Press, 2003).

[60] 'Women Look Forward to Property Rights', *Times of India*, 26 October 1985.

[61] *Lok Sabha Debates*, Vaisakha 15, 1908 (Saka) *Muslims Women Protection of Rights on Divorce Bill*, 23 April 1986–5 May 1986, col. 310–14.

[62] *Halala*, which implied 'being made eligible to reunite with former husband', was a practice observed among a small minority of Sunni Muslims. This customary practice was allegedly introduced to make the reconciliation between divorced couples more difficult in order to discourage frivolous divorce. It implied that upon divorce, the wife could only reconcile with her husband if she was lawfully married to another man and the second husband freely consented to divorce her. If granted divorce, she could return to her former husband. In practice, this came to mean that if couples desired reconciliation, the wife had to marry again and also consummate that marriage before seeking divorce to reunite with her former husband. *Maulvis* dissolving the marriage were often approached to act as intervening husbands in cases where reconciliation was sought. For more on *nikah halala* and *talaq-e-biddat* (triple *talaq*), see Lucy Carroll and Harsh Kapoor, eds., *Talaq-i-Tafwid: The Muslim Woman's Contractual Access to Divorce: An Information Kit* (1996), based on the 1990 publication by an international network called 'Women Living Under Muslim Laws', www.wluml.org/sites/wluml.org/files/import/english/pubs/.../talaq-i-tawfid-eng.pdf. See also Saumya Saxena, '*Nikah Halala:* The Petition, the Promise, and the Politics of Personal Law', in *Mutinies for Equality: Contemporary Developments in Law and Gender in India*, ed. Tanja Herklotz and Siddharth Peter De Souza (Cambridge: Cambridge University Press, 2021), 133–54. S. S. Ali, 'Cyberspace as Emerging Muslim Discursive Space? Online Fatawa on Women and Gender Relations and Its Impact on Muslim Family Law Norms', *International Journal of Law, Policy and the Family* 24, no. 3 (2010): 338–60. The the popular bollywood film *Nikaah* released in 1982 depicted the harsh reality of arbitrary divorce and the idea of *halala*.

Sen also clarified that Section 125 would remain intact even after the enactment of the Muslim Women's Protection of Rights on Divorce Bill. The law minister assured that very little would change for anyone after the enactment of the bill.

Eduardo Faleiro, a Christian member of parliament from Goa, termed the bill a 'bold statement'[63] and immediately contradicted himself, arguing that the bill essentially rephrased the existing precedent without creating a new one, only with greater concessions to the divorced woman.[64] This betrayed precisely how the rhetoric of maintaining fixity had to be repeatedly reinforced, and that concessions to Muslim women were only palatable so long as they could find a tenuous link to the prevailing custom. Faleiro announced, 'Article 44 [The state shall endeavour to enact a Uniform Civil Code throughout the territory of India] cannot be read in isolation, but together with Article 25 [freedom of conscience and free profession, practice and propagation of religion].'[65] This argument is significant because it entirely endorsed the court's ruling on *Khader Vali v. Fazlunbi*,[66] which had emphasized that reconciliation between the religious and civil statutes was possible.[67] The decision on the *Shah Bano* case had also, albeit grudgingly, upheld this principle, and even after the enactment of the Muslim Women (Protection of Rights on Divorce) Act, 1986, the courts continued to follow the same precedent illustrating that parliament had hoped to alter very little and without ruffling too many feathers.

The discussions encouraged a wider interpretation of religious law for offering financial protections to women or the secular ideal (or both), without amending the Shariat Application Act, 1937, and with only minor amendments to the Dissolution of Muslim Marriage Act, 1939. Parliament, therefore, proceeded to address practices of Muslim personal law that the court had already classified as *good in law but bad in theology* in the *Bai Tahira* and *Fazlunbi* judgments and others that preceded these, but made no attempt to retrieve the practices that were 'good in theology', even in its attempt to enact 'religious' law.

The emphasis on a lack of change, and the rhetoric preserving customs through the bill by certain members, obfuscated the substantial challenge that these conversations were posing to the imagination of a family. Some of the speeches emphasized that divorce was not stigmatized among the Muslim community, as it was in other religions. A. K. Sen in his speech had argued:

---

[63] *Lok Sabha Debates*, Vaisakha 15, 1908 (Saka) *Muslims Women Protection of Rights on Divorce Bill*, 23 April 1986–5 May 1986, col. 342.

[64] Ibid., col. 343–48.

[65] Ibid., col. 343.

[66] As discussed in the previous section and in Chapter 3.

[67] This had remained a persevering sentiment even in colonial rulings.

'The husband is supposed to ensure that his ex-wife is married well…. This is a revolutionary concept … where as in Christian law, divorce was unthinkable.'[68] Attacking the description of daughters as *paraya dhan* or 'another's wealth', common among Hindus, Abida Ahmed, another member of parliament argued:

> In Islam the daughter is not a burden of her parents but a grace of God. She is not donated at the time of marriage … So, if she comes back her parents would happily embrace her…. Why should a self-respecting woman ask for maintenance from a man who has divorced her?[69]

Importantly, this discussion had the potential to expose the link between legal imaginations of 'financial protection' with tolerating violence in a marriage. The debate demonstrated that women would potentially be willing to opt out of financial aid but sought, instead, an assurance for a fresh start, with no ties to their former husbands or memories of their violent marriages. In principle, though not necessarily in practice, Muslim personal law jurisdictions provided a wider imagination of marriage than the monogamous norm. Concepts that some jurisdictions, such as Norway, already contained or contemplated introducing, such as prenuptial agreements and parentage by more than two people, and three-person families[70] were models that could potentially be compared to *nikahnamas*, if indeed women could exercise agency in effecting these agreements. The concept of *wakf*s as charity institutions was discussed in parliament as an alternate system of 'social security',[71] to support welfare state objectives. This was particularly pertinent at a time of liberalization of the economy when the state was beginning to withdraw from welfare objectives.[72] Parliamentarian Madhu Dandavate even suggested that the provision of the *wakf* be nationalized.[73]

Parliamentary Discontentment and Judicial Discretion

The proposer of the bill, G. M. Banatwala,[74] of the Indian Union Muslim League, repeatedly ridiculed any questions pertaining to 'authentic' or alternate

---

68 *Lok Sabha Debates*, A. K. Sen's speech, col. 414.

69 Ibid., col. 418.

70 A. J. Andersen, 'Sexual Citizenship in Norway', *International Journal of Law, Policy and the Family* 25, no. 1 (2011): 120–34. See the discussion on the policy related to gay couples and cohabitants.

71 *Lok Sabha Debates*, 5 May 1985, 'Matters under Rule 377'.

72 W. F. Menski, *Comparative Law in a Global Context: The Legal Systems of Asia and Africa* (Cambridge: Cambridge University Press, 2006).

73 *Lok Sabha Debates*, 5 May 1985, 'Matters under Rule 377'.

74 G. M. Banatwala later became the president of the Indian Union Muslim League in 1993.

definitions of *talaq* and the meaning of *mata* (maintenance or provision for maintenance).[75] Even as the Muslim Women Act, 1986, repealed sections of the Dissolution of Muslim Marriages Act of 1939, it witnessed a limited rhetoric of reclaiming the 'scriptural sanction' that marked colonial codification but saw a greater focus on accepting prevailing practices. Triple *talaq* and *nikah halala* were preserved simply by silence on the matter in the bill. Members of the Communist Party of India (Marxist), Somnath Chatterjee and C. Madhav Reddi, argued that various provisions of the proposed bill were ultra vires of the constitution since practices such as unilateral *talaq* could not be reconciled with Article 14, the right to equality, and these were not debated.[76] Women members such as Geeta Mukherjee also continued to rally around the issue of equality and opposed the exempting of Muslim women from Section 125 of the CrPC. Others expressed fears that granting of one exception could be a slippery slope that would lead to demands for other exceptions on religious grounds, beyond the scope of family law—such as the question of school education.[77] Madrasa education in some states had also been recognized as a separate school board the same year.[78] However, this argument did not provoke debate.

The bill also showed a complete disregard for an inherent in-built flexibility within Islamic law and Banatwala refused to entertain any amendments or hear alternate interpretations of religious texts, insisting upon the inviolability of personal law.[79] Legal interpretations of Islamic jurisprudence could be evolved or revised through dialogue and consultations between qualified *alim* (scholars). Islamic concepts such *ijma* (process of building consensus through consultations) or *ijtihad* (independent reasoning or debate in Islamic law) meant that there was scope for debate, particularly on issues that were not made explicit in the Quran and the Hadees.[80] The sources of Islamic law, the Quran, Hadees, *qiyas* (Islamic jurisprudence, generally entails comparisons between Quran and the Hadees), and *ijma* (process of building consensus through consultations in Islamic law), in that order, found mention in parliamentary debates to argue that Islam itself relied on multiple sources of jurisprudence and these granted significant agency to the users

---

[75] *Lok Sabha Debates*, Indrajit Gupta's speech, col. 604–07.

[76] *Lok Sabha Debates*, col. 291–98, Somnath Chatterjee, 'This is not a civilised law', col. 298.

[77] *Lok Sabha Debates* , Dinesh Goswami's speech, col. 299–300.

[78] Later in 2004, the National Monitoring Committee for Minorities Education (NMCME) was constituted under which was launched the Scheme for Providing Quality Education in Madrasas in 2009, in an attempt to standardize madrasa education across the states.

[79] *Lok Sabha Debates*, col. 586.

[80] For a detailed study of *ijtihad* in the twentieth century, see M. Q. Zaman, *The Ulama in Contemporary Islam: Custodians of Change* (Princeton, NJ: Princeton University Press, 2010).

of the law. These, however, did not translate to the law ultimately produced.[81] The Shariat Application Act, 1937, in some senses had already extracted family law from the authority of the state and built in the discretion of the *qazi*. Section Two of the Shariat Application Act, 1937, stated:

> Notwithstanding any custom or usage to the contrary, in all questions (save questions relating to agricultural land) regarding intestate succession, special property of females, including personal property inherited or obtained under contract or gift or any other provision of Personal Law, marriage, dissolution of marriage, including talaq, ila, zihar, lian, khula and mubaraat, maintenance, dower guardianship, gifts, trusts and trust properties, and wakfs (other than charities and charitable institutions and charitable and religious endowments) the rule of decision in cases where the parties are Muslims shall be the Muslim Personal law (Shariat).

The Shariat Application Act, 1937, permitted the discretion of the *qazi* on deciding questions relating to marriage and divorce. The Act also stated that rules could be determined partially by state (provincial) governments but it largely implied that these could be determined only by someone with the knowledge of the *sharia*. The new bill, Banatwala claimed, was derived from the *sharia*. The new section in the Muslim Women Act, which was to apply to Muslims in the place of Section 125, placed the foremost responsibility of maintenance of the wife on the husband, but for/within the limited period of *iddat*. Besides the return of the *mahr* and other properties listed in Clause 3 of the Act, the wife could approach the magistrate within a month of filing an application, who could direct the husband to make a provision 'having regard to the needs of the divorced woman, the standard of life enjoyed by her during her marriage and the means of her former husband or, as the case may be, for the payment of such *mahr* or dower or the delivery of such properties'[82]. The magistrate, who already possessed the power to determine maintenance under various personal laws as well as under CrPC 125, also now had vested in them some of the powers that the *qazi* had also enjoyed, through the new 'religious' statute. Reconciling religiosity with the statute, Z. R. Ansari had argued that there were various (four) types of *mahr* corresponding with four types of divorces, 'in the end it has been provided that every woman who has been divorced shall be paid "*mata-umbilmaruf*"'[83]. This he translated as 'small benefit', 'some benefit', or 'temporary benefit'.

---

[81] Saifuddin Soz, 'Our ulema should not think that the doors of *Ijtehad* are closed', 22 November 1985, *Lok Sabha Debates*, col. 371.

[82] Muslim Women (Protection of Rights on Divorce) Act, 4.

[83] *Lok Sabha Debates*, col. 397–98, 22 November 1985.

The move may appear to be benign and consistent with colonial motivations for codification, but it signalled the first direct amendment to Muslim personal law after the 1940s. In claiming a 'derived from the sharia' status, the bill opened up possibilities of the re-imagination of the community which slowly began to challenge laws on the grounds of the violation of the *sharia*. The discrimination hidden in the vagueness of the Shariat Application Act got a clear form in the Muslim Women (Protection of Rights on Divorce) Act, which could be challenged for being unconstitutional and inauthentic Islam. Krishna Sahi, a Congress member who rose in support of the bill, argued:

> People are saying that the bill nullifies section 125 but I think it is an extension of section 125. [A]t first the woman use to knock [from] door to door to get her *mahr* now she can get it all [from] the court under the orders of a single magistrate. There is no mention of the needs of the divorced woman in section 125, but this bill mentions it. If she leads a decent life with her husband she will get a share in the property of her husband.[84]

Further, Section 4, subsection 1, of the new law contained that if the wife was unable to maintain herself beyond the period of *iddat* and had not remarried, the magistrate had the power to direct her parents or relatives to pay such reasonable and fair maintenance which he determined as 'fit and proper'.[85] The relatives would be approached in order of how they were entitled to inherit her property after her death.[86] If the woman had children over the age of 18, they would be ordered to provide for her maintenance.[87]

The determination of what was 'fit and proper' was contingent on the needs of the divorced woman, the standard of life she enjoyed during her marriage, and also the ability of the relatives who would maintain her, and finally the assessment of the magistrate, allowing tremendous scope for judicial discretion. Moreover, Section 3(b) of the Act also stated that '[p]rovided that if the Magistrate finds it impracticable to dispose of the application within the said period, he may, for reasons to be recorded by him, dispose of the application after the said period'. The magistrate could record reasons for delaying the disposal of the application, which meant that cases of non-payment of maintenance under the Act could easily extend beyond three months of *iddat*.

Judicial discretion also permitted religious and constitutional vocabulary to further overlap interpretations of religious laws. The versatility of Indian

---

[84] Ibid., col. 439–42.
[85] Muslim Women (Protection of Rights on Divorce) Act, 1986.
[86] Ibid.
[87] Ibid., Section 3(b).

'secularism' was instrumental in legitimizing the exceptionality bestowed upon religious laws while simultaneously making personal law subject to greater judicial discretion. Thus, legislative secularism was the promise to protect religion by preserving personal laws, but it delegated to the judiciary the everyday interpretation of this religion, and in that process inherently transformed the life of the law as well as everyday religion. Religion and secularism were indeed far more blurred in practice, despite one being frequently used to counter the other in public discourse. What bridged the two precisely was personal law, where the fluidity of boundaries had to be confessed. The very creation of a religious law was seen as an act of secularism.

All-pervading Secularism

The definition of 'Indian secularism' as proposed by A. K. Sen suggested that it is 'one that *allows* the other's philosophy to flower, ... if we start on a fine mosaic and try to draw one single pattern all over the country, then we shall be playing absolutely against the very foundation of our philosophy'.[88] Krishna Sahi added that granting exemptions to the Muslim community was 'consistent with the Hindu philosophy of tolerance' and 'Indian civilisation'.[89] Not only was secularism cast in Hindu terms in parliament, but the Hindu then became the giver and the Muslim the receiver of freedom of religion. In 'allowing' Muslim personal law to prevail, both Hindu openness and Muslim religiosity is deployed towards an adequate provision of maintenance for divorced wives. The meaning of secularism, therefore, was crucial to women's relationship with the law, and their entitlement to maintenance.

Some members argued for protecting the personal laws of minority communities as an act of secularism, and others argued for its preservation because of personal law's link to the divine and the inviolability of the word of God. The extreme ends of the political spectrum on the left and the right both argued for a Uniform Civil Code, again, in defence of secularism. There was a range of 'secularisms' favouring both a Uniform Civil Code as well as diverse personal laws, but no argument for an open endorsement of the theological state. Instead, the version that ultimately informed the bill identified a secular state as one that saw religion as a freedom, even as other voices in the same debate cast religion as the betrayal of secularism and constitutionalism. Secularism certainly had the potential to be cast in civilizational terms, but religious law was equally touted as 'even more liberal' or 'revolutionary' than the general law.[90]

---

[88] *Lok Sabha Debates*, col. 441 (emphasis mine).
[89] *Lok Sabha Debates*, Krishna Sahi, col. 439–42.
[90] *Constituent Assembly Debates*, see ch. 1.

Secularism, for the purposes of the bill, meant bowing to influential religious opinion even if it were somewhat against constitutional liberalism. It was believed that if the constitution granted fundamental rights, it was secularism read alongside the constitution that granted religious freedom in the true sense. Secularism helped actualize the fundamental right to freedom of religion.

Nandy would perhaps dub such an allegiance to secularism as a dubious commitment to a neoliberal ideology.[91] For Nandy, it was religious traditions in Indian society that allowed for 'religious tolerance' and he lamented the tyranny of the secular intelligentsia and the 'loss' of religion.[92] Asad would also be uncomfortable by claims of 'multiple secularisms' here, emanating out of multiple liberalisms which he writes off as an attempt towards declaring secularism as universal, such that every state would have to be able to word its relationship with religion as secular. Thus, the very attempt to make secularism foundational to all actions essentially hollows out the term. Asad writes,

> ... secularism is the modern state's power to reorganise substantive features of religion and it makes a dual claim of privatising religion and yet allowing public interventions making group and individual rights simultaneously meaningful.... The paradox of political secularism is its regulatory impulse and the promise of freedom.... The modern states disavowal of religion from politics and at the same time its reliance on religious categories to structure and regulate social life therefore linking the private and the public that secularism had to keep apart shows an inherent contradiction.[93]

In this imagination, on the one hand, secularism makes religion appear indifferent to the distribution of rights and freedoms, and, on the other hand, it portrays minority rights as a failure to eradicate parochial communal affiliations. They contend that while secularism is not solely producing religious conflict, it is one of the enabling conditions for it. Secularism, for Asad (and later Mahmood), is a state-led scheme rather than a condition imposed upon the state by repeated demands of competitive religious politics and social movements.

However, in the Muslim Women (Protection of Rights on Divorce) Act, 1986, the members of parliament do precisely the opposite in insisting that religion is not, in fact, indifferent to rights, which is how it can be reconciled with the constitution.

---

[91] Ashis Nandy, 'An Anti-secularist Manifesto', *India International Centre Quarterly* 22, no. 1 (1995): 35–64.

[92] See chapter 4 in Ashis Nandy, 'Return of the Sacred: Politics of Religion in Post-Secular Age', in *Regimes of Narcissism, Regimes of Despair*, ed. Ashis Nandy (New Delhi: Oxford University Press, 2013).

[93] Asad, *Formations of the Secular*; Mahmood, *Religious Difference in a Secular Age*.

The 1980s debates show that the binary between secular and religion or simply secular and non-secular alternatives is not necessarily produced by the state. Multiple state schemes and policies, and laws and precedents have leaned on religion for legitimacy and success, but also selectively borrowed from secularism and modernity. The state invokes 'secular religion' rather than modern secularism alone. Saifuddin Chowdhury, for instance, argues that the bill simultaneously violates the Quran and the constitution.

> I had already spoken on how this bill violates the Quran and the Prime Minister will not accept it. This bill is fortification of fundamentalism. What about maintenance of child, and wife after iddat or any fixed period for that matter. How is dependence on a defunct Waqf Board even constitutionally valid? Then these charities should receive money from tax and be properly maintained....[94]

And he later stated,

> Sir, our country is secular, and there is a very good section in CrPC in this regard ... here we see that the state is not interfering with personal law, but personal law is interfering with secular law ... the Supreme Court judgement is totally supported by the Quran.... In the name of secularism a kind of hypocrisy is going on.[95]

This speech led to substantial interruption and protest.[96] Both the Quran and the constitution are collectively invoked to argue against the bill. Z. R. Ansari asked: 'What is secularism?' to which Chowdhary replied, 'Secularism is not mixing of all religious passions; state has to be separate from religions ... what did we see in 1937? The British enacted the 1937 Act.' This led to sarcastic responses 'wonderful!' to angry outbursts that Chowdhary was misleading the house and insulting the community by suggesting that it was the British who enacted the *sharia*.[97]

From the Hindu Marriage Act to the Muslim Women's Protection of Rights on Divorce Act, the legislature desperately attempted to reconcile rights guaranteed in religion with constitutional law. Arif Mohammad Khan further announced, I will maintain that the bill is inhuman an[d] anti-Islamic. It will push the women into a pre-Islamic era where women were treated as chattel.' Justice Krishna Iyer, too, who had authored few of the most significant judgments on Muslim personal law, in his strongly worded opposition to the bill in the form of a letter to the

---

[94] *Lok Sabha Debates*, 5 May 1985 (Matters under Rule 377)

[95] Ibid., 20 December 1985, col. 446–47.

[96] Ibid., col. 448.

[97] Ibid., Ebrahim Sulaiman Sait and Owaisi, col. 448.

prime minister called it 'a sin against the Quran', 'blatantly unconstitutional', and a dangerous mistake.[98]

It is not, therefore, the regulatory impulse of the state that this chapter contests, but it reveals only the chinks in the state's armour. The sheer inability to regulate the family shows that the state may have no urge whatsoever to privatize religion, as it is dependent on it. Secularism, therefore, was simply one of the many tools, and a largely legal instrument used by ordinary citizens as well as movements to organize resistance, challenge the imagination of a community, and also occasionally deployed by the state to manage public demands.

The diversity of Muslim opinion and the spectrum of Muslim religiosity became acutely visible in parliament which is best captured in parliamentarian Saifuddin Soz's[99] exasperated lament in positioning himself between the oppositional views of Arif Mohammad Khan and G. M. Banatwala: *'Zahide tang nazar ne mujhe kafir jana, Aur kafir ye samjha ke musalman hun main'*[100] (The intolerant ascetic deemed me a non-believer and the non-believers thought I was a Muslim.)

Separating the state's regulatory impulse from secularism allows us to stumble upon the dialogic nature of the 'law' (formal, informal, statutory, customary, and so on) that forces a labouring over coherence in definitions of 'secularism' and 'religion' for first staging and then managing the conflict between the two. Family law, therefore, is one arena where coherent definitions of religion and secularism collapse and are reworked in every legislative and judicial encounter with the family.

In the course of the debate on the bill, Dinesh Singh, another parliamentarian from the Congress Party, framed his argument on the bill as: 'We should try and understand the susceptibility of the minorities and not give them the feeling that we are bull-dozing over their rights. It is my hope that the bill creates a greater sense of confidence among the minority as well as a majority.'[101] Zainul Basheer echoed: '[T]oday the minority is thankful to Congress for calming the fears that the opposition had created.'[102] Saifuddin Soz, in his speech, stated: 'This secular state which we are trying to create should not do anything to the way of life and religion of the people.'[103] Codifying a 'religious' law and delegating the task of reconciliation of religion with constitutional law to the courts intrinsically

---

[98] Krishna Iyer's letter to Rajiv Gandhi, 28 February 1986, in *The Judge Orates: Selected Writings of VR Krishna Iyer* 'Letters to political elites' (Universal publication, 2015).

[99] Soz was a member of the Jammu and Kashmir National Conference Party.

[100] *Lok Sabha Debates*, Agrahayana 1 1907 (Saka) (Code of Criminal Procedure, Amendment Bill), 22 November 1985, col. 356.

[101] *Lok Sabha Debates*, 5 May 1985.

[102] Ibid.

[103] *Lok Sabha Debates*, 22 November 1985, col. 364.

transformed religion, and also the law. It also made the religious and the secular inseparable and could be used interchangeably, for both religious law (Muslim Women Act) and the secular provision (Section 125 of the CrPC), and both provisions could produce an identical end.

Separating 'modern secularism' into modernity and secularism allows for tradition and modernity to not be seen as doctrinal positions but rather as 'languages', and as Kaviraj argues, the consequences they provoke could be unintentionally (or deliberately) similar.[104] The language of 'tradition' or religion could be used to arrive at just and liberal outcomes as much as that of secularism could be. For instance, Professor Nirmala Kumari Saktawat of the Congress Party argued in favour of the bill in parliament: 'Muslim law in its essence tries to preserve a marriage. Unlike how it was before the Prophet. This bill is a precursor to a Uniform Civil Code.'[105] She simultaneously leans on traditional notions of marriage but hopes for a secular modern outcome in the form of a Uniform Civil Code. Z. R. Ansari in his response to Saifuddin Chowdhury's speech had retorted that 'secularism is not values established by Marx and Lenin but the values established by leaders and *religious leaders* of this country'.[106]

Secularism is rarely seen as a threat to religion in India. In popular cultural illustrations of secularism, Hinduism and Islam are frequently invoked together to show interlinkages in a glorious age rather than religion-less peace. Hybridization is promoted through secularism which does not limit public life of religion. Thus, the failure of secularism to contain parochial or communal interest[107] happened precisely because even in its defence of rights (of minorities, of freedom of speech, and freedom of religion, and equality), the state relied overwhelmingly on religion (minority and majority religions) as the enabler of peace, of rights and harmony. Stephens has noted that a similar sentiment may have prevailed for Mughal rule, who 'were able to assert the universal moral authority of Islam while accommodating diverse religious practices'.[108] She argued in the colonial context that the very notion that the colonial state is secular and the indigenous populations were not, lies at the basis of theorizing secularism as an exported value.[109]

---

[104] Sudipta Kaviraj, 'Languages of Secularity', *Economic and Political Weekly* 48, no. 50 (2013): 93–102.

[105] *Lok Sabha Debates*, 5 May 1985.

[106] Ibid., 20 December 1985, col. 439.

[107] As was perhaps the expectation from secularism from the works of Jaffrelot, Stuart Corbridge, and John Harris.

[108] Julia Stephens, *Governing Islam: Law, Empire, and Secularism in Modern South Asia* (Cambridge: Cambridge University Press, 2018), 26. See also Ayesha Jalal, *Partisans of Allah: Jihad in South Asia* (Cambridge: Harvard University Press, 2008), 26–35.

[109] Stephens, *Governing Islam*.

In India, secularism has often been theorized as a potential antidote for religious politics but fundamentalists also do not overtly oppose it for undermining the place of religion in public life.[110] Religious conservatives use the vocabulary of secularism to appear before courts and lobby for bills that preserve religion. The Hindu nationalist movement also staked its claim to secularism, calling the Congress's position 'pseudo-secularist'.[111] Therefore, an overt or rather an optical political commitment to secularism was never contested in India.[112] Yet by production of a statute, religion was made amendable and challengeable on grounds other than secularism alone.[113] While secularism and democracy can certainly be pitched as contradictory processes, where one flourishes at the cost of the other, in family law, where the law has to be anchored simultaneously in religion and secular constitutionalism, the result more often is uncertainty and ambiguity rather than the concentration of power.[114] Thus, the debates on Muslim personal law tell us that the state's understanding of secularism was itself so incoherent that its imposition on the democratic electorate would have little value when the meaning of the term is fundamentally disputed, and differently understood within the state.

Secularism, therefore, made religious politics somewhat reliant on the law, even as the law remained vulnerable to manipulation by religious politics. Agrama's writing in context of Egypt remains wary of the politics that the indeterminacies

---

[110] See Mahmood's *Religious Difference in a Secular Age: A Minority Report* (Princeton, NJ: Princeton University Press, 2015), for a critique of secularism where she argues that religious fundamentalists oppose secularism for impeding upon the domain of religion.

[111] 'LK Advani: A Scorching Campaign', *India Today*, 31 May 1991. In this interview, Advani described Congress policies as 'pseudo-secular'; the term was popularized after this interview and also incorporated in the BJP's election manifesto.

[112] Rajeev Bhargava's conceptual distinction between ethical secularism and political secularism suggests that while the former may not have been realized, the latter implied a more institutional commitment to secularism. 'Ethical secularism', on the other hand, for Bhargava entailed more than mere 'tolerance' for other religions but rather demanded equal 'respect'. Rajeev Bhargava, 'Political Secularism', in *The Oxford Handbook of Political Theory*, ed. John S. Dryzek, Bonnie Honig, and Anne Philips (Oxford: Oxford University Press, 2006), 637–53; Rajeev Bhargava, *The Promise of India's Secular Democracy* (Oxford: Oxford University Press, 2010).

[113] Practices of religion could be challenged as 'non-essential' to religion, or contradictory to constitutional provisions, or even as an incorrect understanding of religion itself.

[114] The demolition of the Babri Mosque and the violence in Gujarat collectively informed the scholarship on the failure of secularism as a democratic promise. In Shah Bano's case, and the following bill, however, secularism was deployed in very different ways. ·

of secular power and decision are capable of producing. He writes that these 'indeterminacies continually provoke suspicions and anxieties around the legal resolutions of religious issues, which in turn spill out into a politics aimed at reforming the law'.[115] For him, the law that is subsequently produced from such politics does not allay these suspicions but only the contrary consolidates the state's position as the sole authority on determining what constitutes religion and how much it must regulate social life. The state's vigilance to check the abuse of power, in turn, for Agrama, strengthens the state's own power to regulate intimate lives. Agrama demonstrates this by narrating the fate of Abu Zayd, whose writings led him to being declared an apostate from Islam in Egypt. A group of private citizens relied on the 'uncodified concept' of *hisba* or 'the commanding of the good, when it has become neglected, and the forbidding of the evil, when its practice becomes manifest', to challenge Zayd's scholarship before the court.[116] The court accepted this claim of apostacy and Abu Zayd's marriage was consequently dissolved against the will of both him and his wife, since a Muslim woman's marriage in Egypt is dissolved if her husband ceased to be a Muslim. Agrama analyses how the idea of *hisba* was incrementally but perhaps incorrectly 'secularised' as the protest against the court order by liberal citizen groups prompted a legislation that restricted the use of *hisba* interventions to public officials. This angered both the religious groups for limiting the scope of *hisba* and the liberals for bringing *hisba* on to the statute.

It may appear that the Muslim Women Act, 1986, may have done the same for concepts such as 'iddat' or even 'mata' (maintenance). By bringing religion on to the statute, the legislature maintained its monopoly in determining the scope of religion and the meaning of religious terminologies. The intervention angered civil society groups for pandering to the conservative Muslim opinion, and it also upset Muslim religious groups for bringing state intervention into matters of religion. The difference, however, lies in how little an influence this legislation wielded and how quickly it was undermined—not by citizens protests and the clergy alone, but by the state itself. The next two chapters carry forward the story of the fate of this Act and its systematic as well as unintended reversal, judgment after judgment. The *Danial Latifi*[117] judgment practically reinstated the *Shah Bano* judgment by reinterpreting the Muslim Women Act

---

[115] Hussein Ali Agrama, 'Secularism, Sovereignty, Indeterminacy: Is Egypt a Secular or a Religious State?', *Comparative Studies in Society and History* 52, no. 3 (2010): 504.

[116] Ibid.

[117] *Danial Latifi v. Union of India* (2001) 7 SCC 740.

to endorse the court's stand on Shah Bano in 2001. In the *Shabana Bano*[118] case, the judgment reiterated that Section 125 would continue to apply to Muslim women.

The idea that a demand for 'rights' to access or subvert religion by citizens privileges the state is contingent on the assumption that sovereignty rests very firmly with the state.[119] In the case of family law, it does not. Statutory law looked for religious justifications to establish legitimacy and acceptability.

The discussion in the Lok Sabha on the Muslim Women Act engendered an instrumental and capacious meaning of secularism without any introspection into its ethical foundations. The word 'secular' here simply hid the arbitrariness of the law and its deviations and disagreements with constitutional commitments contained within both fundamental rights and directive principles. By stretching the definition of secularism, the state accommodated a greater spectrum of religiosities, thereby expanding the domain of religion rather than containing it. In fact, it was the centrality accorded to religion by the state that led to Muslim women's groups in later decades to attempt to reclaim Islamic law with state support.

In the case of the Muslim Women Act, the 'secular' act of creating a 'religious statute' did not convince its detractors of its universality or neutrality. Thus, the law sought a sacred veneer, and yet the sacred was amendable. Thus, the difference between civil and religious jurisdictions was not deepened by secularism, but bridged by it. Family life in India remains deeply regulated—by local *panch*s, elders of the family, *qazis*, *jagadgurus*, *mahila adalats*, *dar-ul-qaza*s, *khap* panchayats, family courts, family matriarchs or patriarchs, political parties, higher judiciary, and parliament. The limited legislation on Muslim personal law ensured that it becomes even more decentralized by building in more judicial discretion into legislation, creating one more statute alongside the existing Section 125 of the CrPC. This earned the new law the rejection by the clergy as well as the academy, which kept re-emerging in the form of petitions challenging the statute.

The Act and Its Discontents

On 16 May 1986, the bill was presented for its final reading and did not entertain any amendments. From the Muslim League to the BJP, and the Congress Party

---

[118] *Shabana Bano v. Imran Khan*, 2009 (14) SCALE 331.

[119] Ratna Kapur suggests that secularism reduces religion to politics of rights and recognition and privileges the agency of the State which itself is far from a neutral arbitrator of religious difference. R. Kapur and B. Cossman, 'Secularism's Last Sigh: The Hindu Right, the Courts, and India's Struggle for Democracy', *Harvard International Law Journal* 38, no. 1 (1997): 113.

to the women members of parliament, the Act did not appear to satisfy any group sufficiently. The atmosphere remained tense and younger members such as Saifuddin Chowdhury of the Communist Party of India[120] raised multiple objections confronting the old guard, such as G. M. Banatwala of the Muslim League. The IUML had a mere 14 seats in parliament when the bill was presented. The All India Muslim League and the Union Muslim League had come together in 1985; members had close ties with the AIMPLB, and many had affiliation with the Aligarh Muslim University. Thus, it was not the case of a Hindu majority parliament that was enacting laws for a Muslim minority because the enactment only evidenced that a very small number of influential men could steer the debate successfully. In one sense, the Act privileged the view of a Muslim representative body, such as the AIMPLB, over Muslim elected representatives, such as Arif Mohammad Khan, Saifuddin Chowdhury, among others.

Saifuddin Chowdhury pleaded that issuing a 'party whip' to enact such a discriminatory bill amounted to a 'whip' used against Muslim women,[121] while Somnath Chatterjee of the Communist Party dubbed it a 'lawless law'.[122] Parliamentary debates conveyed a sense of universal discontentment with the bill but, equally, an urgency to pass the new law. Opposition from women members was also not very significant; they constituted only 42 members in a parliament of 514 and did not necessarily form a consolidated bloc.[123] The position of the Congress at this point was secure in parliament but regional parties were beginning to pose a competition.[124] While the move to enact the bill has been largely reported on as a move to consolidate the Muslim vote in the upcoming Assam elections,[125] the results proved that Muslims voted neither collectively nor necessarily for the Congress.[126] While on the one hand, the Congress government found it easy to give force to legislation given that it had a parliamentary majority, on the other hand, the debates reveal that there was a significant resistance to the bill from

---

[120] Saifuddin Chowdhury later formed the Party of Democratic Socialism in 2001.

[121] *Lok Sabha Debates*, col. 360.

[122] Ibid., col. 298.

[123] Election Commission of India Report, 1984 (General Election).

[124] Election Commission of India Report, 1984 (National). Indian National Congress held 404 seats in parliament in 1984, Janata Dal held 10, and a mere two seats were held by the BJP when the Muslim Women's Act was tabled. Among the Left parties, there was CPI with six seats and CPM with 22.

[125] Girilal Jain, 'The Muslim Women Bill: Why Rajiv Has Pushed It', *Times of India*, 14 May 1986.

[126] See Statistical Report on General Election, 1985, To the Legislative Assembly of Assam, Election Commission of India, https://eci.gov.in/files/file/4119-general-election-1985-vol-i-ii/, accessed in July 2013.

within the Congress Party. This internal conflict reached its zenith when, in an Ambedkarite fashion, the senior Congress leader Arif Mohammad Khan resigned from the party in protest over the bill's exclusion of divorced Muslim women from protection offered under the national law CrPC's Section 125.[127]

Law and legislation have, therefore, historically dissatisfied its authors and disappointed the recipients, yet changes to Muslim personal law transformed religion's relationship with the state. The Act was immediately challenged in the Supreme Court of India by Shah Bano's lawyer Danial Latifi, who was joined by a number of academics, women's organizations, and members of parliament, for being in violation of the right to equality granted by the constitution. The Supreme Court merged these petitions and heard them collectively in the case of *Danial Latifi v. Union of India*, the outcome of which, decided in 2001, is discussed in the next chapter.

The Congress did not win the subsequent election in 1989. The discontentment with the Act was also palpable among the Muslim youth for both interference with Muslim personal law as well as the government's failure in countering the growing campaign for the demolition of the Babri Mosque. Salman Khurshid of the Congress Party, the then deputy minister of commerce, was an emerging voice in Muslim politics. Khurshid noted that from the point of view of most Muslims, the legislation, meant to reverse the *Shah Bano* judgment, did not do so. In a personal interview, he described a meeting between Rajiv Gandhi and a delegation of students from the Aligarh Muslim University in 1990. Rajiv Gandhi assuaged the concerns of the students on personal law: '... I understand that you have particular way of looking at life, ... and the mistake that we are making is that we are looking at life our way and imposing it on you.'[128] In this meeting, the prime minister also mooted the idea of a Rapid Action Force, a special branch of the police to respond to riot situations, to address the students' concerns about the Babri Masjid.

The Act and the Impact

There were different narratives on the use of the new law within feminist scholarship. Agnes' writing reveals that the new law was effective in extracting

---

[127] Khan, *Text and Context*. In a personal interview on 16 February 2016, he also mentioned that he and his wife continued to campaign against the Act and addressed many public meetings. He also mentioned that the urgency to pass the new legislation betrayed the Congress leadership's fears about how many of its members were beginning to resist the new law.

[128] Personal interview with Salman Khurshid, 1 August 2013. The Rapid Action Force (RAF) is a specialised wing of the Central Reserve Police Force of India to manage riot and crowd control situations.

maintenance sums from husbands; in cases where the husband was unable to pay, owing to bankruptcy or any other reason, the responsibility was passed on to parents and other relatives. Muslim husbands challenged the constitutionality of the Muslim Women Act multiple times suggesting that the Act has been much more widely applied and progressively interpreted in favour of women than Section 125 may have been. This indicates that the consequences and 'achievements' of the Muslim Women Act may have been underwritten in scholarship.[129] The three-month fixed period for deciding the matter and ordering the provision for maintenance also meant that these cases had the potential to be decided faster. Women frequently hoped for clear and absolute breaks from exploitative marriages rather than pursuing maintenance claims, which entailed repeated interaction with abusive former husbands. Solanki's study also showed that the Muslim Women Act proved to be a beneficial law particularly for women of upper and middle classes in negotiating maintenance, as it was difficult for them to prove a threat of potential 'destitution' as required under Section 125. Under the Muslim Women Act, on the other hand, a 'reasonable and fair' provision could be more widely interpreted.[130]

An NGO based in Lucknow, Advocacy and Legal Initiatives (AALI), in its study of the Lucknow High Court found that women continued to use Section 125 for maintenance. Up to 51 per cent of all women surveyed used Section 125 for seeking maintenance, but only 18 per cent of these petitions were granted, compared to 27 per cent of the divorces that were granted.[131] For instance, after the 1986 Act, if a Muslim man could not maintain his wife, and could prove this inability before the magistrate, the responsibility of maintenance would lie with her paternal family and then further on to relatives in order of their share in the inheritance of her property. If they failed to pay, the magistrate could direct the State Wakf Board established under Section 9 of the Wakf Act, 1954 (29 of 1954), to maintain the woman. But everyone's refusal to pay maintenance was a common consequence.

Muslim women's reliance on non-state forums particularly in matters of divorce evidences the fact that not only was the 'speed' of the resolution of dispute an incentive to opt out of courts but also the outcomes of maintenance requests. *Maulvi*s and *qazi*s commonly made the granting of a *talaqnama*

---

129 Agnes, 'From Shahbano to Kausar Bano'.
130 Solanki, *Adjudication in Religious Family Laws.*
131 IWRAW Asia Pacific, *Baseline Report: Rights of Women in Relation to Marriage in India* (Malaysia: AALI and IWRAW Asia Pacific, 2016), 49, http://aalilegal.org/wp-content/uploads/2016/01/Publications_BaselineReport-RightsofWomen.pdf, accessed in December 2017.

(divorce document) contingent on repayment of the *mahr* amount to women, but husbands often did not provide alimony and other obligations.[132] Further, despite the new Act, it was uncommon for women to move court against their natal families, and rarely did the State Wakf Board ever get involved.[133] Vatuk also showed that the Act had a limited impact on women who were not financially well-off, and in her research in Hyderabad, she found that most women continued to use Section 125. More Muslim women used Section 125 *during* the marriage than after, and far more frequently than Hindu women. While remarriage among Muslims was certainly more common and acceptable than among Hindus, families did hesitate in maintaining divorced daughters.

In many ways, having 'one's own' religious law codified as a statute made it more accessible to Muslim women, even as the Act left much to be desired. The Muslim Women Act focussed on creating a provision for the problem of maintenance rather than engaging with the idea of equal rights in divorce. Legislation in India has frequently hesitated from confronting the gender discrimination that lay at the foundation of various religious practices, but instead chose to address the 'effect' of these practices. This made the law extremely dynamic but also somewhat ineffective in the sense that new laws often merely proliferated weak regulation within society without creating deterrence against the abandonment of wives and the denial of maintenance to them. Such mediocre but hasty law making also conveys intimacy between citizen groups and state institutions.[134]

The state, pandering to religious orthodoxy and maintaining the rhetoric of reform to regulate, exhibited a simultaneous dynamism and redundancy of the law in India. Either religious principles had to be reinterpreted to reconcile with the law, or they were ignored, and in other moments, legislation boasted of having endorsed a 'genuine' interpretation of religion into legislation. By recognizing cultural differences in separate religious laws, sometimes the peculiarities of particularities of groups became visible.[135] Such visibility allowed for the recognition of violation

---

[132] Sylvia Vatuk, *Marriage and Its Discontents: Women, Islam and the Law in India* (New Delhi: Women Unlimited, an associate of Kali for Women, 2017), ch. 8, 246–68. See also Narendra Subramanian, 'Legal Change and Gender Inequality: Changes in Muslim Family Law in India', *Law and Social Inquiry* 33, no. 3 (2008): 631–72.

[133] Vatuk, *Marriage and Its Discontents.*

[134] See also Lucy Carroll, *The Muslim Women (Protection of Rights on Divorce) Act 1986- A Retrogressive Precedent of Dubious Constitutionality* (New Delhi: Indian Law Institute, 2015).

[135] This was the case with the Hindu Marriage Act Madras Amendment discussed in chapter 2. Further, Hindu Succession Act has also been forced to confront regional diversity in inheritance systems over the years.

and violence in very specific contexts. For instance, the case of the Muslim Women Act provoked conversations on triple *talaq* and *nikah halala*.

Moreover, in an attempt to make personal law systems appear more egalitarian and adept at administering justice, the State Wakf[136] Board in Madhya Pradesh also sprang into action and offered a sum of maintenance to Shah Bano which was higher than the amount granted by the Supreme Court.[137] Such actions, however, were contingent and temporary solutions rather than well-planned policy decisions. There were several inconsistencies in the State Wakf Board administration with four distinct schools of thought under Islamic law: Hanafi, Shaifai, Maliki, and Ismaili, between which the functioning of *wakf*s varied significantly.[138] *Wakf*s also varied across states. None of them had equal or even similar provisions for maintenance of destitute women, and there was no consensus on the amount to be paid, or how the sum would be determined. There was also a variation in terms of the timeframe for which maintenance would be provided.[139] But the focus on *wakf*s was revived in public debates and that brought in the central Wakf Act in 1995. Ironically, even the new Wakf Act made no guarantees of maintenance to divorced wives.

The insistence on 'difference' in personal laws can therefore be both enabling and discriminatory. Uniformity could entail a custom-blind law, which puts customs beyond state regulation, transferring its regulation potentially to a *dar-ul-qaza*, a *mahila adalat*, or elsewhere, but the custom would not necessarily disappear. With the decentralization of the state authority on personal law, the legislature and the judiciary could appeal to a wider range of religiosities, as the court room remained a stage for debate within and between interest groups who had an interest in having their version of religion confirmed as an 'essential practice' or 'authentic reading'. The 'family' that remained under surveillance by the clergy, community, or extended family could never quite be regulated by the state in isolation. The Muslim Women Act instead preserved and perpetuated personal law codes as inadequately representative law regimes, but also provided a

---

[136] Land for an Islamic religious charity.
[137] Shah Bano had sought relief from the lower court under Section 125, for maintenance and prevention of destitution of the divorced wife or even older parents or children. The court at the district level upheld Section 125, granting a sum of 25 rupees for maintenance of Shah Bano after her husband had given her the irrevocable (third) pronouncement of *talaq*. The Madhya Pradesh High Court revised this amount to 179 rupees per month against which her husband appealed again. Zakia Pathak and Rajeshwari Sunder Rajan, 'Shah-Bano', *Signs* 14, no. 3 (1989): 558–82.
[138] Khalid Rashid, *Wakf Administration in India: A Socio-Legal Study* (Delhi: Vikas, 1978).
[139] Ibid., 58.

space for women to seek maintenance that the court deemed 'fit and proper' rather than mere subsistence promised in Section 125 of the CrPC.

The debate on the Muslim Women Act favoured the acceptance of a status quo or preservation of the existing condition with respect to the position of women within a Muslim family, that is, the law only institutionalized what was common practice and delegated all potential 'reform' and 'protection' of Muslim women to the judiciary. The courts categorically overturned the status quo and the apparent rigidity of Islamic law that some in the legislature emphasized. Acquiescing to religion, in the nature or the name of reform or even secularism, is precisely what permitted multiple narratives of the Muslim Women Act to emerge, its success or failure, its use, misuse, and redundancy. The sheer incapacity of the state to govern the intimate space assured that politics over secularism and religion would remain continuous and democracy was contingent on precisely these moments of resistance.[140] The variability of secularism and the then government's insistence on overusing secularism became relevant precisely when Hindu nationalism showed potential for embodying the universal.

II

Personal Muslim and the Public Hindu

Excessive legislation on religion, it appears, helps it generate characteristics of neutrality. The words 'personal law' are rarely used to describe Hindu Marriage or Succession Acts; these laws, once codified, could be treated as neutral and universal. The Hindus could, therefore, disregard common problems of the abandonment of wives, denial of maintenance, and violence within marriage as unrelated to religious or cultural morality or as 'fringe' incidents occurring despite the presence of a 'reformed' law. For the Muslim community, however, any violence against women was pinned collectively on the deficiencies of the mostly uncodified Muslim personal law. Despite the internal differences within the Muslim community on personal law, Hindu nationalism wilfully propagated the idea of a consolidated Muslim consensus on discrimination of women and the occupation of land in Ayodhya. Thus, even in public perception, the Muslim community became complicit in Shah Bano's suffering, but the Hindu community did not collectively bare the blame for Roop Kanwar's sati (widow immolation) that followed in the year 1987.

---

[140] Sheldon S. Wolin, 'Fugitive Democracy', in *Democracy and Difference: Contesting the Boundaries of the Political*, ed. Seyla Benhabib (Princeton, NJ: Princeton University Press, 1996), 31–45.

In September 1987, in a small village in Rajasthan, Deorala, a 17- or 19-year-old girl, Roop Kanwar, ascended to the funeral pyre of her dead husband, Maal Singh. Large crowds witnessed the act and 45 people present at the ritual were initially accused of aiding and abetting the sati but were later acquitted, owing to a lack of evidence even as it was revealed that Kanwar was possibly drugged as she was led to the pyre.[141] Delhi and Jaipur saw large-scale protests against the valorization of the practice of sati, in particular, against the local demand for a carnival in Deorala, for celebrating Roop Kanwar's sacrifice and selling sati memorabilia.[142] Significant Hindu religious leaders from the Arya Samaj movement[143] also joined the protest against the practice of sati. However, women activists protesting against the organization of the *mela* (carnival), organized under the banner of the National Federation of Indian Women, were deemed as 'western' and 'elitist' by the local strongmen in the area. Even the Government of Rajasthan showed reluctance in taking action on the matter and hesitated to stall the festivities.[144] A large counter-procession was organized by local groups in Rajasthan, led by the Sati Dharma Raksha Samiti (Sati Protection Committee), seeking the protection of women's right to commit sati and demanded the construction of a shrine at the place of the sati to commemorate Roop Kanwar.[145] It was a re-packing of tradition, through shrines or *mahotsavs* (celebratory events or carnivals) in uniquely modern ways.[146]

The pro-sati protest was admittedly a weaker voice compared to the anti-sati agitations, but is worth taking note of because the defence of sati introduced the argument that a Hindu woman's right to commit sati should be guaranteed as her right to 'freedom of religion', or 'Hindu religious personal law'. This defence of sati made the oblique argument that Shah Bano, a Muslim woman, had been, in effect, granted her religious right to remain in destitution, as she

---

[141] This was followed by the acquittal of 11 accused on a later investigation (2004) for the glorification of the practice of sati. Eventually, investigations concluded that Maal Singh's 15-year-old brother had lit the pyre but being a minor at the time, he was not convicted.

[142] This included *chunaree*s with Roop Kanwar's image and others.

[143] There was also opposition to the practice of sati from some leaders of the Hindu sect of Arya Samajits lead by Swami Agnivesh; see 'Swamiji's March to Deorala', http://www.swamiagnivesh.com/naarisudhar.htm, accessed in March 2018.

[144] 'Deorala Finds Place on Religious Map', *Times of India*, 25 September 1987; 'Deorala Sarpanch Assails Sati', *Times of India*, 21 December 1987.

[145] See chapter 11, 'The Agitation against Sati', in Kumar, *The History of Doing*.

[146] Sudesh Vaid and Kumkum Sangari, 'Institutions, Beliefs, Ideologies: Widow Immolation in Contemporary Rajasthan', *Economic and Political Weekly* 26, no. 17 (1991): WS2–WS18.

withdrew her case; the same should be permitted to a Hindu woman seeking to self-immolate.[147]

The High Court of Rajasthan issued an order to prevent both the *chunari mahotsav* (veil or head scarf carnival) and the construction of a temple/shrine at the site of sati, the *sati sthal*.[148] The Government of Rajasthan also promulgated the Sati (Prevention) Ordinance, 1987, at a time when the Legislative Assembly was not in session, and news reports indicated that such an ordinance may not have been democratically endorsed and it lacked popular consensus.[149] Radha Kumar's work illustrates how a number of members of parliament and local leaders paid tribute at the *sati sthal*, even as parliament debated a law to prohibit glorification of the practice.[150] The Shiv Sena was one of the few political parties that actively supported the pro-sati mobilization.[151]

Several writ petitions were filed challenging the weak Rajasthan state ordinance for its inability to stall the *mahotsav* and the attempts to construct the sati temple which violated both the court order and the ordinance.[152] It was not the lack of the law alone, but the lack of political will, particularly of the Government of Rajasthan, to prosecute Maal Singh's family, which allowed the pro-sati lobby to withstand the pressures of a much larger anti-sati campaign.[153] Subsequently, the government brought in a national legislation to prevent the construction of any sati temple in the future, as well as any felicitation or glorification of the practice.[154]

---

[147] The framing of the right to commit sati as a matter of 'choice' provokes an inquiry into the nature and condition of the 'choice'. The case highlights the inadequacy of liberal feminism which emphasizes liberty or freedom in absolute terms without identifying the context within which the 'choice' is exercised. For a socialist critique of liberal feminism, see A. M. Jaggar, *Feminist Politics and Human Nature* (Totowa, NJ: Rowman & Allanheld, and Brighton, UK: Harvester Press, 1983). For notions of voluntary and involuntary sati in colonial India, see also R. S. Rajan, 'The Subject of Sati: Pain and Death in the Contemporary Discourse on Sati', *The Yale Journal of Criticism* 3, no. 2 (1990): 1. Andrea Major, *Sovereignty and Social Reform in India: British Colonialism and the Campaign against Sati, 1830–1860* (New York: Routledge, 2010).

[148] *Madan Singh s/o Sumer Singh v. State of Rajasthan*, 1988 (1) WLN 551.

[149] 'Furore over Sati Still on', *Times of India*, 23 October 1987.

[150] Kumar, *The History of Doing*.

[151] Although some in the party later distanced themselves from the practice.

[152] *Madan Singh s/o Sumer Singh v. State of Rajasthan*, 1988 (1) WLN 551.

[153] Madhu Kishwar and Ruth Vanita. 'The Burning of Roop Kanwar', *Manushi* 42, (September–December 1987): 15–25.

[154] The Commission of Sati (Prevention) Act, 1987. The Act treated the ritual as 'murder or suicide' and, therefore, held that women committing sati were also liable to be punished.

The Hindu nationalist movement positioned itself against the practice of sati and was quick to distance sati from Hinduism. The BJP popularized the idea of sati and *johar* (collective performance of sati) was historically a form of protest by women to deny the enemy or the Mughal/Muslim invader access to their bodies.[155] Although sati has had a strong connotation with Hindu identity and mythology,[156] it was framed as a response to Muslim violence rather than as an intrinsic part of Hinduism. Women's suicides, rapes, and murders during the partition violence have also frequently been cast in nationalist rhetoric as evidence of Muslim brutality. In a personal interview with Subramanian Swamy, on the subject of sati, soon after he joined the BJP in 2013,[157] he emphatically argued: 'Hindus are thoroughly against [sati]. How can we [condone it] when the three most important subjects in the heaven are held by women: "Durga" for defence, "Lakshmi" for finance, and "Saraswati" for education.'[158] Hindu nationalists also propagated definitions of indigenous 'democracy', 'nationalism',[159] and 'secularism' as an ancient Hindu concept of *sarva dharma sambhava* or 'tolerance for all religions'. This narrative was replete with claims that monarchy in the 'Vedic age' was far from absolute[160] and that democracy had existed in India pre-Islam and pre-colonial India.

Gods and goddesses were readily invoked in Hindu nationalist campaigns, as the women's wings of Hindu nationalist organizations were simultaneously beginning to campaign for the Ram Temple in Ayodhya. Goddesses Sita, Sati, and Savitri found repeated mentions in training campaigns as 'ideal women' and yet the Hindu nationalist movement managed to distance itself from the murder of Roop Kanwar. The Hindu nationalist campaign for Ayodhya shared many commonalities with how the pro-sati mobilizations were organized, both prompting religious

---

[155] Ashis Nandy, 'Sati: A Nineteenth-Century Tale of Women, Violence and Protest', in *Sati, the Blessing and the Curse: The Burning of Wives in India*, ed. J. S. Hawley (Oxford: Oxford University Press, 1994), 131–48.

[156] In the mythological legend, Goddess Sati had immolated herself, unable to bear her father's insults and rejection towards her husband, Lord Shiva.

[157] Personal interview with Subramanian Swamy, 8 July 2013, New Delhi. Swamy is an economist and a politician who was in the Jana Sangh from 1974 to 1978, in the Janata Party from 1979 to 2014, and in 2014 he joined the BJP, and he is currently a member of the Rajya Sabha.

[158] Durga is the goddess of strength (the invincible), Lakshmi is the goddess of wealth, and Saraswati is the goddess of knowledge in Hindu mythology.

[159] Sumantra Bose, 'Hindu Nationalism and the Crisis of the Indian State: A Theoretical Perspective', in *Nationalism, Democracy and Development: State and Politics in India*, ed. Sugata Bose and Ayesha Jalal (Oxford: Oxford University Press, 1997), 104–64.

[160] See the BJP manifesto for the year 1989. www.bjp.org, accessed in December 2014.

spectacles followed by political propaganda. Both were contingent on miraculous occurrences. In Roop Kanwar's case, her pyre 'miraculously' burst into flames on its own and no one got convicted for lighting it, despite multiple witnesses in the case. Vaid and Sangari characterize the violence that surrounds the spectacle of sati as 'spontaneous and popular and therefore uncontrollable',[161] such as 'the pyre lit itself' or 'the *henna* appeared out of nowhere', and served to absolve the onlooker from the sense of responsibility towards the actual event, and to view it as an eventuality. It blurred the memory of the events that preceded the sati that constituted crucial evidence which could have led to conviction.[162]

Similarly, in the case of the Ramajanmabhumi in Ayodhya, an idol of infant Ram had 'miraculously' appeared overnight in the Babri Mosque at Ayodhya in 1949. This 'inexplicable' appearance of the idols had led Gopal Singh Visharad[163] to file a civil suit in the Faizabad District Court for permission for Hindus to worship at the mosque in 1950.[164] In 1986, amidst heavy mobilization by the BJP, the District Court of Faizabad ordered the opening of the lock placed on a grill leading to the sanctum-sanctorum of the shrine. In 1989, Devki Nandan Agarwal filed a suit as the 'friend of the deity' (*sakha*) to represent Lord Ram himself, signalling that gods and goddesses could access legal apparatus.[165]

The construction of a Ram Temple in Ayodhya was to serve a similar purpose of marking off geography by ritual performance which was in this case A. B. Vajpayee's suggestion of a *yagya* (prayer by fire) on the land of the Ramajanmabhumi, much like the demand for a *sati sthal* in Deorala.[166] Once the Babri Mosque was demolished by a mob, no one knew who launched the first stone or struck the first blow to the mosque,[167] just as no one knew who

---

[161] Vaid and Sangari, 'Institutions, Beliefs, Ideologies'.

[162] For an interesting analysis of the transformative potential of fire in the context of communal riot in Bombay in 1992–93, see Thomas Blom Hansen, 'The Political Theology of Violence in Contemporary India', *South Asia Multidisciplinary Academic Journal* 2 (2008): 1–14.

[163] After the death of Gopal Singh Visharad, his son Rajendra Singh took forward the case.

[164] *Gopal Singh Visharad v. Zahoor Ahmad and Others*, regular suit no. 2 of 1950. This was followed by another suit filed by the Nirmohi Akhara seeking possession of the mosque in 1959, *Nirmohi Akhara and Others v. Baboo Priya Datt Ram and Others*, regular suit no. 26 of 1959; and another on 18 December 1961, by the Sunni Central Wakf Board, demanding possession of the site and removal of idols from the mosque premises.

[165] *Bhagwan Sri Ram Lala Virajman and Others v. Rajendra Singh and Others*, regular suit no. 236 of 1989.

[166] Vajpayee's speech, 5 December 1992, https://www.youtube.com/watch?v=-EhMmJEwbTg, accessed in December 2013.

[167] Hansen, 'The Political Theology of Violence in Contemporary India', on the spontaneity of violence in the context of riots that followed the demolition of the Babri Mosque in Bombay in 1993.

lit Roop Kanwar's husband's funeral pyre. While hundreds of men *karsevaks* (workers or volunteers)[168] participated in the demolition, women were also at the forefront of the movement and stepped forward only to wash the feet of *karsevaks* (a ritual they would generally perform for their gods/elders, or perhaps husbands) not only valorizing their act of violence, but simultaneously accepting their subordinate position within the movement. In the case of sati, women participated by dressing up the widow in her bridal finery, but did not participate in her cremation. The iconography of a Ram Temple as well as the *sati sthal* did not exclude women from performance and practices, but they managed to generate a consensus on violence and also on the subordination of women.

Much of the campaigning around the issue of Ayodhya, analogous to the campaign for a sati temple in the *Roop Kanwar* case, was theatrical in nature and replete with legends from mythology. As in the case of sati, where a shrine at the *sati sthal* was the focal point for the origin for disseminative ideologies, the Janmabhumi movement was premised on a similar assumption about Lord Ram's place of birth—*janmasthan*. There were stories and propaganda on the numerous struggles to 'free' the Janmabhumi during the Mughal period, but with little or unconvincing evidence.[169] The Ramajanmabhumi movement, therefore, also transcended the geography of Ayodhya by seeking symbolic support through the blessing of bricks or offering of prayers from ones' home as a gesture of contribution to temple building.[170] The Rani Sati Temple Trust, a Kolkata-based organization, had also immediately challenged the Prevention of Sati law to seek continuation of rights to worship at existing sati temples, even as construction of new temples was banned. The court granted this and thus donations continued to pour in and glorifying 'past' satis through yearly *mohatsavs* did keep the practice in public memory. Pro-sati and the Ramajanmabhumi movements indicated that even scriptural sanction was not necessary for validating customary practices; instead, public spectacles could be used to demand validation of practices in the language of religious rights.[171]

The Sangh applied a series of populist tactics in order to control and co-opt the identity of Ram—the most popular and uniformly (across castes) accessible Hindu god, and the protagonist of Valmiki's epic—the *Ramayana*. The unifying image

---

[168] Voluntary workers for the construction of the Ram Temple.

[169] Romila Thapar, 'Imagined Religious Communities? Ancient History and the Modern Search for a Hindu Identity', *Modern Asian Studies* 23, no. 2 (1989): 209–31. Romila Thapar's seminal work on Ayodhya indicated that the presence of a Hindu shrine was not archaeologically verifiable, thus suggesting that the contemporary search for sacred topography could be a mobilization tactic in the 1980s, where first religious sentiment had to be cultivated and then capitalized on, for political power.

[170] See chapter 5 in Hansen, *The Saffron Wave*.

[171] See chapter 11, 'Sati', in Kumar, *The History of Doing*.

of Ram was deployed to prevent the slipping away of lower-caste votes to newly ascendant regional parties that emerged in the aftermath of the reservation policies of the Mandal Commission.[172] The use of the militant symbolism of *rath yatras* (chariot processions) for the 'liberation of temples' was used to reassert upper-caste Hindu supremacy against the perceived centrality of Muslim (the response to the *Shah Bano* judgment and the banning of Salman Rushdie's *Satanic Verses* by the government) and backward caste issues, as well as Dalit conversions.[173] The BJP further announced that actors of the popular television adaptation of the Ramayana (characters who played Sita and Ravan) were to be BJP candidates in the upcoming election in 1991.

The two cases of Roop Kanwar's sati and the Ramajanmabhumi movement exemplify the salience of customary law and practice in India and the way in which this shaped women's subjectivities. Yet by distancing itself from sati, Hindu nationalist politics continued to cast the Muslim women's veil, and her divorce, as evidences of Muslim barbarism in the private realm while simultaneously threatening public symbols of Muslims such as the Babri Mosque. Bringing to life a falsely unified Muslim collective that was necessarily invested in preserving personal law and the Babri Mosque was Hindu nationalism's greatest success.

Ayodhya and the Crisis of Feminism in India

So far as the law was concerned, the 1980s had been a yielding decade for women-specific legislation, however doubtful be the impact of these enactments.[174] Amendments to the criminal provisions against rape after the *Mathura* case were placed on statute in 1983. The Dowry Prohibition Act, 1961, was amended in 1986, and was followed by the enactment of the Indecent Representation of Women (Prohibition) Act, 1986. The Family Court's Act of 1984 had also come as a part of the implementation of the *Towards Equality* Report. Judgments such as *Reynold Rajmani v. Union of India* in 1982 urged the amendment of the Christian Matrimonial Clauses Act to address discrimination against women and widen the grounds for divorce available to Christians to include 'mutual consent'.[175] The Commission of Sati (Prevention) Act, 1987, despite its criticisms, had also

---

[172] Achin Vanaik, *Communalism Contested: Religion, Modernity and Secularization* (New Delhi: Vistaar Publications, 1997).

[173] C. Jaffrelot, *The Hindu Nationalist Movement and Indian Politics: 1925 to the 1990s: Strategies of Identity-Building, Implantation and Mobilisation (With Special Reference to Central India)* (Princeton, NJ: C. Hurst and Co. Publishers, 1996).

[174] Flavia Agnes, 'Protecting Women against Violence? Review of a Decade of Legislation, 1980–89', *Economic and Political Weekly* 27, no. 17 (1992): WS19–WS33, for the limited impact of legislation on women.

[175] *Reynold Rajmani v. Union of India*, 1982 AIR 1261.

been a quick response to women's rallies.[176] Therefore, the supposed reversal of the *Shah Bano* judgment appeared to specifically pull away legal protections from Muslim women, even though in reality it had not quite altered much. With the Muslim Women Act, the idea of Muslim difference and exceptionality, aided also by the Hindu nationalist propaganda, became further entrenched. The positive use of the law and the yields of the *Latifi* judgment that progressively interpreted the Act became apparent only later in the years that followed and its benefits remained largely contained within academic debates.

The women's movement of the 1980s and early 1990s became increasingly sensitive to the diversity of women's experiences as it confronted the threat of Hindu domination that masqueraded behind a plea for legal uniformity. This encouraged the development of multiple strands of the women's movement which broke away from the all-purpose collectives of the 1970s, breaking also the consensus on a Uniform Civil Code. Many writings in this period emphasized the importance of recognition of the religiosity of the female subject. 'Kali for Women', one of the first and most influential publishing houses established in the 1980s, borrowed the symbol of the Hindu goddess Kali, harnessing her image as a courageous woman and formidable warrior with unbridled sexuality. Incidentally, Kali was also different from Durga and Lakshmi, goddesses invoked in Hindu nationalist campaigns, which distinguished her as a goddess predominantly not worshipped by Hindu upper castes. The NGO Manushi was also example of feminism within the discourse of tradition.[177] But references to Hinduism and Hindu goddesses for inspiration gradually phased out of feminist arguments. Women's collectives began to work outside the framework of religious reforms, particularly for Hindus; Hindu nationalism to an extent had already deployed the

---

[176] The 1980s did see legislative and judicial developments on women's issues such as the additions made to the Dowry Prohibition Act of 1961 in the form of two new sections introduced into the Indian Penal Code in 1983 and 1986. Section 498A promised immediate arrest of the groom's family in case of a dowry complaint and Section 304B enhanced the punishment on dowry deaths substantially. Even in Christian personal law, the 1980s saw a significant judgment in the case of *Mary Roy vs State of Kerala* 1986 AIR 1011, which addressed gender discrimination within the Syrian Malabar Nasrani community in Kerala. Mary Roy was herself a women's rights activist and an educator, and she sued her brothers for disallowing her to inherit ancestral property after her father's death. The Supreme Court confirmed equal rights for inheritance for sons and daughters (after one-third property deducted for the widow). Prior to this ruling, Syrian Christian women inherited less than their brothers, under the provisions of the Travancore Succession Act of 1916 and the Cochin Succession Act, 1921. However, the analysis of these is beyond the scope of this chapter.

[177] Nida Kirmani, 'Beyond the Impasse: "Muslim Feminism(s)" and the Indian Women's Movement', *Contributions to Indian Sociology* 45, no. 1 (2011): 1–26.

vocabulary of the 'pious, yet liberated' Hindu women. Hindu nationalist claims of Hindu universality rather than religious reform distinguished it from religious movements such as the Arya Samaj, and the Bhakti or Shuddhi movements. For instance, unlike the nineteenth-century debates where Rammohun Roy had argued that 'true Hinduism' advocated ascetic widowhood rather than widow immolation, the Hindu nationalist movement by contrast rarely attempted scriptural reinterpretation. Rather than presenting a version of authentic Hinduism, it instead looked for references of 'authentic' democracy, secularism, and liberalism in Hinduism.

This phase witnessed innovation in political campaigns as these were marked by rituals, fiery speeches, and the wide circulation of cassettes, pamphlets, and posters for mobilizing support for the temple construction on the streets and within households.[178] The Hindu nationalist campaign witnessed a very specific nature of women's involvement. Not only were women everywhere in the forefront, they also took on active roles in public protests. The RSS *shakha*s (branches) and the Vishwa Hindu Parishad recruited a number of women in their women's wing called the Durga Vahini (the carrier of the Hindu goddess Durga), which was very active in the Ramajanmabhumi movement.[179] The mobilization could access households as the recorded speeches of the *sanyasins* (female devotees) were distributed, especially for women listeners. These strategies helped make the listener somewhat complicit in the movement.[180]

The most influential women leaders of the Hindu Nationalist movement, Uma Bharti and Sadhvi Rithambara, however, also departed from conventional female roles.[181] Both were celibate and of a 'lower' caste, which made them perfect symbols representing the weaker constituencies in a bid to undermine the emerging caste-based parties gaining traction in the state of UP. This was particularly so, post the Mandal Commission's recommendations, which incentivized political identification with caste identities.[182] The two women in their speeches provoked men to violence

---

[178] David E. Ludden, *Making India Hindu* (London: Oxford University Press, 1996).

[179] Tanika Sarkar, 'The Women of the Hindutva Brigade', *Bulletin of Concerned Asian Scholars* 25, no. 4 (1993b): 16–24.

[180] Sikata Banerjee, 'Armed Masculinity, Hindu Nationalism and Female Political Participation in India: Heroic Mothers, Chaste Wives and Celibate Warriors', *International Feminist Journal of Politics* 8, no. 1 (2006): 62–83.

[181] Paola Bacchetta, 'All Our Goddesses Are Armed'-Religion, Resistance, and Revenge in the Life of a Militant Hindu Nationalist Woman', in *Against All Odds: Essays on Women, Religion, and Development from India and Pakistan,* ed. Kamla Bhasin, Ritu Menon, and Nighat Said Khan, (New Delhi: Kali for Women, 1994), 132–56.

[182] Javeed Alam, 'Is Caste Appeal Casteism? Oppressed Castes in Politics', *Economic and Political Weekly* 34, no. 13 (1999): 757–61.

by denigrating the feminine. Their notions of manhood commanded Hindu men to their masculine duty to protect the Hindu women. They questioned, '[A]re you wearing bangles [like women] in your hands [that you cannot fight]?'[183] The movement employed the specific vocabulary of sacrifice, motherhood, and chastity to gender the process and to justify violence as an outburst of manhood.[184]

Women protestors were often referred to as heroic mothers, chaste wives, and celibate warriors.[185] This glorified the image of a chaste woman within the bounds of kinship and granted her participation in the movement at the cost of her sexuality. The Hindu nationalist leadership frequently deployed the vocabulary of the 'violation of honour' of a woman to suggest a parallel with India's partition, terming it as damage to Mother India (Bharat Mata) and attributing the violation to Muslims.[186] A. B. Vajpayee, in his fiery poetry on Pakistan in the course of the election campaign, questioned, 'Did you [Muslims] not feel ashamed, violating/destroying your mother?'[187] Veena Das has argued that motherhood can be recognized as a 'traditionally available method for women's democratic participation', but the sort of participation it enabled split femininity as *familial but fierce*, or *single but powerful* tropes.[188] There was an obvious divide however between the *participating but conforming women of the households* and the *leading but celibate women* who had forsaken the heterosexual family for their devotion to religion and nationalism. While domesticity was taught and encouraged in training camps alongside military training, it did not find political translations, which was reserved for the *yoginis*, *sadhvis*, and *tapasvis* (women ascetics) for whom religious duty surpassed domestic responsibility. It further split masculinities as Bachetta identified as 'decent and acceptable' masculinity of the Hindu male and 'violent and sexually aggressive' masculinity of the Muslim.[189] Muslim exceptionality was therefore not created only within the realm of family law but outside it as well,

---

[183] Translation mine, original: *Haathon mein choodiyan pehen rakhi hain?* Sarkar, 'The Women of the Hindutva Brigade'.

[184] Gabriel Dietrich, 'Women's Movement and Religion', *Economic and Political Weekly* 12, no. 4 (1986): 157–60.

[185] Banerjee, 'Armed Masculinity, Hindu Nationalism and Female Political Participation in India'.

[186] Ibid.

[187] See http://bjpkarnataka.org/news/-poem-on-pakistan-by-atal-bihari-vajpayee/, accessed on 13 February 2013. (Translation mine.) 'माँ को खंडित करते तुझको लाज न आई' (*Maa ko khandit karte tujhko laaj na aayi*).

[188] Banerjee, 'Armed Masculinity, Hindu Nationalism and Female Political Participation in India', 67.

[189] Bacchetta, 'All Our Goddesses Are Armed', 153.

constructed by what a Muslim ate (meat, beef in particular) and what they wore—burqa-clad supressed women and skullcap-wearing 'predatory man'.

In the Hindu nationalist discourse, 'nari-shakti' or women's power was essentially understood in the language of sacrifice and stoicism within the bounds of which women's empowerment could be imagined.[190] The exhibition of their agency, their access to the public space, was largely contingent on their conformity within the private space and performance of traditional gender roles and responsibilities. There was a repeated emphasis by the Hindu right on women not disturbing the dynamics within families. Sarkar captures this perfectly in a statement by a samiti worker 'hum ghar torne-wali nahin hain' (we are not home-wreckers).[191]

The women's movement rejected this co-option of women into the rhetoric of Hindu nationalism, which offered women a presence in the public space on heavily compromised terms. The women's movement in India confronted not only the appropriation of Hindu culture but also that of the constitutional provision of a Uniform Civil Code by Hindu nationalists. Thus, in one sense, Hindu nationalism as well as the Muslim Women Act also generated a problematic binary for women, between legal equality and protection for minorities.

The unfair political alternatives generated an impasse that characterized feminist scholarship in the early 1990s. The Muslim Women (Protection of Rights on Divorce) Act and the demolition of the Babri Mosque were both moments that compromised women's position in legal and political realms. This encouraged the Indian women's movement to create an altogether different language to counter the religious patriarchy in its statutory and political form. Despite the Muslim Women Act and the *Danial Latifi* judgment collectively providing relief for Muslim women, feminist activism became increasingly suspicious of state interventions in Muslim personal law as Hindu nationalism also became a party to this debate. The Hindu nationalist's projection of a Muslim law as inherently discriminatory and uniformly acceptable by the Muslim community, therefore, encouraged women's fight for new imaginations of community, explored in next the two chapters.

Conclusion

The enactment of the Muslim Women (Protection of Rights on Divorce) Act, 1986, allowed for the acknowledgement of imperfections within codified Muslim law. By producing a legal template which could be challenged as a

---

[190] See also Basu, 'Feminism Inverted'.
[191] Sarkar, 'The Woman as Communal Subject', 2062.

faulty statute, it tempered the critique of religion as inherently obscurantist, attributing this instead to a statute. This chapter illustrated that secularism was deployed by the state in order to extend control over its religious Muslim citizens and to engender intimacy between the state and religion. Therefore, even as the state installed religious laws, the emphasis on religion and religious practices was always couched in the vocabulary of secularism and the state incompetently tried to maintain monopoly over what constituted 'legitimate religion'. The judicial discretion built into the law and the all-encompassing definition of secularism which was used to justify the Muslim Women Act aided the accommodation of a wider spectrum of religiosities. This also allowed litigants to challenge aspects of religion in their codified form for their violation of the Quran and the constitution simultaneously.

The chapter also demonstrated how much was riding on the 'vocabulary' of secularism, as it promised to counter Hindu supremacy, protect minorities, and much else. This created uncertainties over the sort of secularism the women's movement must then chose, leading to significant shifts in women's relationship with the state and with the law. The Hindu nationalist propaganda against the Babri Mosque not only influenced the legislation on Muslim women's divorce but also impacted women's relationship with the law more generally. The Hindu nationalist movement exploited the ambiguities in Muslim personal law to the maximum effect. This period also witnessed religious and customary practices gaining salience not only from the support of the law but also through public spectacles. Cultural nationalism and pride replaced the valorization of constitutional morality that characterized the 1970s. The calls for the construction of a shrine for Roop Kanwar and a temple for Lord Ram were examples of theatrical techniques that expanded the public life of religion. Women who participated in religious spectacles and rituals inhabited 'honourable' but incarcerating stereotypes. The process aided in rendering public symbols of Hinduism as acceptable and those of Muslims as oppressive. The Babri Mosque and the women's burqa could collectively be critiqued as symbols of oppression in the Hindu nationalist rhetoric.

The feminist movement of the time rejected both the BJP's insistence of a Uniform Civil Code and the AIMPLB's insistence on the inviolability of their interpretation of the *sharia*. The women's movement began to focus on larger narratives of violence and discrimination seeking not mere equality but the recognition of their religious difference to address the particularities of women's concerns. Hindu nationalism, by contrast, struggled to find an anchor in the law for its political strategies and cultural claims. This paradoxical relationship between the law and religion is analysed in the next chapter.

5

The Court in Context, 1992–2000s

Let me interpret the decision of the Supreme Court for you.... It does not ask us to stop the Karseva [in Ayodhya]. In fact, Supreme Court has given us the right to perform Karseva. Tomorrow, by performing Karseva we are not violating the order of the Court, we are honouring it. It is true that the court has said do not do any construction work. But the Supreme Court has said that we can sing bhajans,[1] and perform kirtan.[2] Now, one person alone cannot sing bhajans, and kirtan cannot be performed standing upright. Until when will we keep standing? There are sharp stones emerging from the ground. We will have to make the land hospitable, a yagya[3] will need to be organised and the ground will have to be levelled.

—Atal Bihari Vajpayee, 5 December 1992, Lucknow[4]

On the morning following Vajpayee's speech on 6 December 1992, approximately 150,000[5] karsevaks (volunteers) armed with sickles, sticks, and stones attacked the Babri Masjid, a sixteenth-century mosque. Riots between Hindus and Muslims broke out in Ayodhya and spread to neighbouring districts, then to cities across India, and the invocation of Supreme Court's order in public speeches somehow made it complicit in the event of the demolition.

All parties in the Indian Parliament laid claim to the interpretation of 'secularism' in their response to the demolition. Since almost all political action, however religiously tinted, could be couched in the language of secularism. Even in the demolition of the Babri Mosque, the karsevaks saw themselves vindicated by a recourse to secularism—as an ideology deemed consistent with destroying a

---

[1] Hymns and prayers.

[2] Chanting of prayers, generally accompanied by musical instruments *dholak* or *dhol* (percussion rhythm instruments) and *manjeera*, a pair of small hand cymbals.

[3] Prayer ceremony centred around fire.

[4] Vajpayee's speech delivered on 5 December 1992, Lucknow, UP. ABP News coverage (translation mine), available at https://www.youtube.com/watch?v=-EhMmJEwbTg, accessed on January 2012. A. B. Vajpayee was a veteran leader of the BJP. He was later the prime minister of India briefly in 1996, 1998, and later for a full term from 1999 to 2004.

[5] Mark Tully, 'Tearing Down the Babri Masjid: Eyewitness', BBC News, 5 December 2002.

'colonial' or 'Mughal' symbol.[6] While the period indeed witnessed a democratic upsurge with challenges to the Congress Party's domination and the mushrooming of regional political parties,[7] there was a crisis of the legitimacy of state structures as the calls for a Hindu *rashtra* also became plausible with the BJP's ascent to power in the late 1990s.

To make themselves more palatable to citizens who self-identified as secular, the BJP undertook considerable effort to appropriate judicial instruments to legitimize their claims to governance. This was particularly so because organizations such as the RSS, which constituted the BJP's support base, had a long and hostile history with the law. The organization was banned thrice, once in the aftermath of the assassination of Gandhi in 1948, and again during the years of the emergency (1975–77), and then once again after the demolition of the Babri Masjid. Contrary to the stance of Hindu nationalist organizations against the codification of Hindu law and state interference in matters of religion at the time of independence, the movement now relied significantly on judicial instruments for its own legitimacy and for proliferating new definitions of religious nationalism by seeking the patronage of the law. For instance, this was done by framing the 'right to pray' at Ayodhya not only as a 'freedom of religion' under the fundamental rights of the constitution but also as 'Hindu personal law'. Further, in 1989, in the ongoing suit in the Babri Mosque dispute, a suit was filed in the name of the infant Lord Ram himself. God's counsel—a friend of the deity—represented his claim over his place of birth, on the assumption that God Ram was a minor (infant) in perpetuity in his place of birth and unable to represent himself.[8] Thus, in the run up to the demolition of the Babri Mosque, the Ramajanmabhumi issue was not only BJP's political performance playing out in the streets through *rath yatras* and travelling bricks, but it was also being staged in the courtroom.

The expansion of the legal or the regulatory frontier through legislation on religion that was witnessed since independence was somewhat transformed in the 1990s as the expansion of the public and political face of organized religion could no longer be regulated in the vocabulary of secularism. Traditional value

---

[6] Lal Krishna Advani, *My Country, My Life* (New Delhi: Rupa Publications, 2008).

[7] Atul Kohli, Jan Breman, and G. P. Hawthorn, eds., *The Success of India's Democracy*, vol. 6 (Cambridge: Cambridge University Press, 2001); Yogendra Yadav, 'Electoral Politics in the Time of Change: India's Third Electoral System, 1989–99', *Economic and Political Weekly* 34, no. 34/35 (1999): 2393–99; and Lucia Michelutti, *The Vernacularization of Democracy: Politics, Caste and Religion in India* (New Delhi: Routledge, 2008).

[8] *Bhagwan Sri Ram Lala Virajman and Others v. Rajendra Singh and Others*, Other Original Suit No. 5 of 1989 (Regular Suit No. 236 of 1989).

systems and customs have historically informed statutory law in India.[9] In the 1990s, however, India witnessed conversations that were distinct from a Hindu-favouring definition of legal and political concepts, such as secularism, rights, or tolerance that characterized even the Constituent Assembly debates or debates on the Muslim Women Act. In the 1990s, a political party that identified openly as religious leaned on the law for legitimacy of their majoritarian campaign strategies and political promises. This had a profound impact on the ways in which religious minorities, especially women of minority communities, sought to interact with the state.

Determining the place of religion in public campaigns, political mobilization, and personal law was therefore increasingly left to the courts. Delegating secularism to the courts came with its own challenges. This chapter demonstrates that the Supreme Court's relationship with secularism and Hindu nationalism was as inconsistent as the legislature's, and this also had repercussions on the framing of personal law debates. This interface of organized religion and courts can be understood through a series of judgments where the courts tried to respond to the threats to secularism (*S. R. Bommai*),[10] the upsurge of Hindu nationalism (Hindutva judgments),[11] and simultaneously to women's group's petitions challenging Muslim personal laws (*Shamim Ara, Danial Latifi, Parveen Akhtar*, and others)[12] in the 1990s and early 2000s.

By analysing a few of the most significant and controversial judgments in Indian legal history, this chapter traces how political ideologies became reliant on the court's approval. Case law was welded into electoral narratives to appeal to the Indian public. This is key when we want to understand why women movements opted for litigation and moved away from legislative lobbying. With the meaning of secularism under extreme pressure, the demand for any changes in personal law by women's groups had to be re-imagined.

---

[9] W. F. Menski, *Hindu Law: Beyond Tradition and Modernity* (New Delhi: Oxford University Press, 2008); W. F. Menski, 'From Dharma to Law and Back? Postmodern Hindu Law in a Global World', working paper no. 20, Heidelberg papers in South Asian and Comparative Politics, 2004; J. D. M. Derrett, *Hindu Law, Past and Present: Being an Account of the Controversy which Preceded the Enactment of the Hindu Code, the Text of the Code as Enacted, and Some Comments Thereon* (Calcutta: A. Mukherjee, 1957); and Masaji Chiba, 'Legal Pluralism in Sri Lankan Society: Toward a General Theory of Non-Western Law', *The Journal of Legal Pluralism and Unofficial Law* 25, no. 33 (1993): 197–212.

[10] *S. R. Bommai v. Union of India* (1994) 3 SCC 1.

[11] *Dr Ramesh Yashwant Prabhoo v. Shri Prabhakar Kashinath Kunte*, 1996 SCC (1) 130; *Manohar Joshi v. Nitin Bhaurao Patel and Another*, 1996 SCC (1) 169; *Prof. Ramachandra G. Kapse v. Haribansh Ramakbal Singh*, 1996 SCC (1) 206.

[12] *Shamim Ara v. State of U.P. and Anr*, AIR 2002 SC 3551; *Danial Latifi v. Union of India* (2001) 7 SCC 740; *Parveen Akhtar v. Union of India*, 2003-1-LW370.

The effect of the Babri Mosque demolition on personal law has been analysed extensively.[13] Scholars suggest that Muslim vulnerability under the onslaught of the Hindu nationalist propaganda served to obliterate dissent within the community on the subject of personal law, since the demolition made differences within Muslim community appear unwise, if not ill-timed. This chapter, however, reiterates that women's history and, in particular, Muslim women's history was not an apologetic reflex to the rise of Hindu nationalism; rather, Hindu nationalism caused these movements to alter their strategy. Many of these groups were faced with the possibility of a potentially hostile government, as the BJP's electoral success became imminent. They looked to the judiciary for interventions on matters of Muslim women's rights since the Muslim Women (Protection of Rights on Divorce) Act, 1986, enacted by the Congress, had been unsatisfactory and the BJP's claimed commitment to minority issues appeared ironic in the light of the demolition of the Babri Mosque. Moreover, the chapter explores the link between Hindu nationalism and Muslim politics within the judicial discourse, since its relationship, politically and socially, is well documented.

The expectations from the court building steadily post the Emergency reached their zenith at the turn of the century. Both the BJP as well as the Muslim women's movement leaned on the courts, and both these movements brought a greater focus on religion in political discourses, but towards very different ends. The courts dealings with Hindutva in the 1990s did generate controversy but it also meant that if the courts entertained petitions from Hindu gods and admitted mythological texts as evidence, they were also well placed to not only 'progressively interpret' the Quran but indeed admit and record its reinterpretations in judgments. The 2000s saw a more organized attempt to strike down discriminatory provisions in personal laws with non-governmental organizations (NGOs) and women's groups backing individual women in their struggles. The court room witnessed nuanced debates on religious laws and alternate readings of religious sources that the legislature had not captured.

The court's admission of alternate interpretations of Islamic law on marriage and divorce posed a challenge not only to personal law statutes but also to the authority of the AIMPLB that had since the 1970s enjoyed proximity to the legislature. The court had rendered religious law also open to rephrasing and reinterpretation

---

[13] A. G. A. M. Noorani, ed., *The Muslims of India: A Documentary Record* (New Delhi: Oxford University Press, 2003). Zoya Hasan, 'Gender Politics, Legal Reform, and the Muslim Community', in *Appropriating Gender: Women's Activism and Politicized Religion in South Asia*, ed. P. Jeffery and A. Basu (London: Routledge, 1998), 71–88; Siobhan Mullally, 'Feminism and Multicultural Dilemmas in India: Revisiting the Shah Bano Case', *Oxford Journal of Legal Studies* 24, no. 4 (2004): 671–92, and others.

not by legislators and 'experts' alone, but by common citizens who identified as 'religious'. Admitting alternate interpretations in courts in the form of 'observations' rather than 'orders' did betray the court's reluctance in intervening, but this also encouraged a proliferation of women-led alternate dispute resolution forums in the decade which were aimed at direct and faster access to justice. Judicial overreach attracted criticism for undermining the legislature and tipping the balance of power, but in the process, the courts decentralized religion and religious authority. The courts often did not *become* this authority but they could vest this authority in 'alternate' interpretations of terms like Hindutva, *mata*, *talaq*, and so on, proposed by citizen groups.

The chapter is divided into three sections. The first discusses how the Supreme Court dealt with the Babri Mosque's demolition and the popularization of Hindutva in election campaigns. This aided the launch of a new dawn of Hindutva which could then become pluralized and made synonymous with secularism, democracy, or development. The second part analyses the maturing alliance between courts and civil society movements. The growing legitimacy of the judiciary, accompanied by the legislative reluctance to approach the question of Muslim personal law, eventually provoked bold and audacious precedents on the question of maintenance and divorce of Muslim women. The final section recognizes the court as a critical site for the staging of political contestation. It traces the court's unpredictable responses to political and social campaigns in the recent years.

I

Demolition and the Supreme Court[14]

In 1993, the Narasimha Rao–led Congress government invoked the emergency provisions or 'President's rule' (Article 356 of the constitution of India) bringing the four riot-affected states' administration under the central government's authority in the aftermath of the Babri Mosque's demolition. S. R. Bommai, the president of the Janata Party, filed a suit against the use of emergency provisions invoked by the central government. The *S. R. Bommai v. the Union of India*[15] case came to be known as one of the most significant rulings that influenced the

---

[14] Some parts of Part 1 of the chapter were published in an article, Saumya Saxena, '"Court"ing Hindu Nationalism: Law and the Rise of Modern Hindutva', *Contemporary South Asia* 26, no. 4 (2018): 378–99.

[15] *S. R. Bommai v. Union of India* (1994) 3 SCC 1.

relationship between the central and state governments in India. Article 356, which detailed the provisions in the case of the failure of constitutional machinery in a particular state, had historically been subject to controversy for undermining the federal character of the country. Under Indira Gandhi's regime, this Article was invoked 39 times, and often aimed at dismissing state governments ruled by her political opponents.[16] The Article's imposition after the demolition of the mosque was premised on a 'threat to secularism', and the public unrest that followed the demolition. Owing to the overuse of secularism with no consensus over its meaning in public discourse, the courts took it as their own prerogative not only to interpret and reflect on secularism but also to execute it, alongside its pronouncements on federalism. The *S. R. Bommai* judgment opened the issue with a quote from the erstwhile president, Dr Radhakrishnan:

> When India is said to be a secular State, it does not mean that we reject reality of an unseen spirit or the relevance of religion to life or that we exalt irreligion. It does not mean that Secularism itself becomes a positive religion or that the State assumes divine prerogatives. Though faith in the Supreme is the basic principle of the Indian tradition, *the Indian State will not identify itself with or be controlled by any particular religion.*[17]

The *Bommai* judgment stressed that the addition of the word 'secular' in the preamble only made explicit what was already implicitly embedded in constitutional philosophy. 'Articles 25–30 of the Constitution are precisely about protection of the rights of minorities and these do constitute the basic structure of the Constitution.'[18] The term 'secular', the judgment stated, 'has advisedly not been defined presumably because it is a very elastic term not capable of a precise definition and perhaps *best left undefined*'.[19]

---

[16] See chapter VI of the Sarkaria Commission Report, Ministry of Home Affairs, available at www.mha1.nic.in/par2013/, accessed in December 2015. See also James Manor, 'Making Federalism Work', *Journal of Democracy* 9, no. 3 (1998): 21–35.

[17] Cited in *S. R. Bommai v. Union of India*, 1994 3 SCC 1 (emphasis supplied in the case description).

[18] Article 25 of the constitution of India provided, subject to public order, morality and health, that all persons shall be entitled to freedom of conscience and the right to profess, practice and propagate religion. Article 26 grants to every religious denomination or any section thereof, the right to establish and maintain institutions for religious purposes and to manage its own affairs in matters of religion. These two articles clearly confer a right to freedom of religion. Article 27 provides that no person shall be compelled to pay any taxes, the proceeds whereof are specifically appropriated in payment of expenses for the promotion or maintenance of any particular religion or religious denomination. Article 28 relates to attendance at religious instructions or religious worship in certain educational institutions. Articles 29 and 30 refer to cultural and educational rights.

[19] *S. R. Bommai v. Union of India*, 1994 3 SCC 1, para 29 (emphasis added).

The judgment upheld the imposition of President's rule in the states of Himachal Pradesh, Madhya Pradesh, and Rajasthan where the law-and-order situation plummeted out of control. In the wake of communal riots that broke out in many parts of India, the government had imposed a ban on all activities of the RSS enforced under the Unlawful Activities (Prevention) Act, 1967, which was lifted in June 1993. The court took into account the fact that the chief ministers of these states were members or sympathizers of the RSS, which had been instrumental in the demolition of the Babri Mosque. The court stated: '... It is neither possible nor realistic to dissociate the Governments of Madhya Pradesh, Rajasthan, and Himachal Pradesh from the acts and deeds of their party.'[20]

The verdict was not the first engagement of the Indian courts with secularism, but it has since become the yardstick against which religious tolerance is measured. The judgment reiterated the 'constitutional status' of the term secular as a legal and philosophical principle—secularism was not an ideology but a constitutional commitment. Therefore, the court not only laboured over the definition of secularism but also its 'implementation'—under the constitution's preambular commitments to equal citizenship, national integrity, and fraternity that secularism enabled. Secularism needed to be performed and not just interpreted. Once embedded in the constitution, secularism had an instrumental value as law. Thus, while attempting to *implement* secularism, the Supreme Court concluded, 'In matters of State, religion has no place. No political party can simultaneously be a religious party.'[21]

India was one among many examples that illustrate that separation between the state and religion is not a precondition for democracy but with the BJP's promotion of a 'Hindu nation', the court had deemed democracy to be contingent on secularism. Democracy had yielded an outcome so majoritarian that it had put its own existence in peril.[22] Secularism, therefore, was also the language in

---

[20] Ibid., para 141.

[21] Ibid. (conclusion), para 291.

[22] On the Ramajanmabhumi movement, Hindu nationalism, and democracy, see also T. B. Hansen, *The Saffron Wave: Democracy and Hindu Nationalism in Modern India* (Princeton, NJ: Princeton University Press, 1999); C. Jaffrelot, *The Hindu Nationalist Movement and Indian Politics: 1925 to the 1990s: Strategies of Identity-Building, Implantation and Mobilisation (With Special Reference to Central India)* (Princeton, NJ: C. Hurst and Co. Publishers, 1996); Neeladri Bhattacharya, 'Myth, History and the Politics of Ramjanmabhumi' in *Anatomy of a Confrontation: Ayodhya and the Rise of Communal Politics in India*, ed. Sarvepalli Gopal, 122–40 (New Delhi: Penguin Books, 1991); S. Bose, 'Hindu Nationalism and the Crisis of the Indian State: A Theoretical Perspective', *Nationalism, Democracy and Development State and Politics in India*, vol. 32, ed. Sugata Bose and Ayesha Jalal (Oxford: Oxford University Press, 1997), 104–64; D. E. Ludden, Making India Hindu (New Delhi: Oxford University Press, 1996); and Saumya Saxena, 'Reinvention of Communal Identities and Implications for Democracy', *Economic and Political Weekly* 48, no. 34 (2013): 47–53.

which the courts articulated the threats to Indian democracy. Secularism became synonymous with democracy in the *Bommai* judgment to the extent that the judgment's upholding of the dismissal of state governments was seen by many as a compromise on federalism to accommodate secularism.[23] This, however, appears to be a misplaced assumption as the judgment also emphasized an obligation on the government to seek the consent of both houses of parliament within two months of the imposition of President's rule.[24] This caveat made it extremely difficult for the central government to impose Article 356. It is precisely this feature of putting a leash on the central legislative authority of the government, on the one hand, and reprimanding Hindutva propagandists, on the other, that rendered the courts very powerful in the 1990s.

The Supreme Court clarified in this judgment that the demolition was the culmination of a sustained campaign and not a sudden event. The BJP and its allied organizations had consistently expressed a desire to construct a Ram Temple in the place of the mosque. The judgment quoted from the BJP's manifesto released in 1993 that had condoned the demolition of the mosque and contained the following statement in the manifesto under the heading 'Ayodhya':

> On December 6, 1992 kar-sevaks from all over India assembled in Ayodhya to begin the reconstruction of the Rama Temple.... Matters took an unexpected turn when, angered by the obstructive tactics of the Narasimha Rao government, inordinate judicial delays and pseudo-secularist taunts, the kar-sevaks took matters into their own hands, demolished the disputed structure and constructed a makeshift temple for Lord Rama at the garbha griha (sanctum sanctorum). This BJP [*sic*] is the only party which is categorical in its assurance to facilitate the construction of the Rama Temple at the site of the erstwhile Babri structure. *This is what the people desire.*[25]

Thus, the court's decision was a response to what it felt was a genuine threat to law and order by the common public who were provoked to constitute riotous communities through a sustained campaign.

Ismail Faruqui *and the Legality of Demolition*

The central government's response to the threat to law and order post the demolition was to hurriedly issue an ordinance which was later turned into the

---

[23] See also Arun Shourie's interview in Gary Jacobsohn, *The Wheel of Law: Indian Secularism in Comparative Constitutional Context* (Princeton, NJ: Princeton University Press, 2004).

[24] Though the power of dissolving of the Legislative Assembly can be said to be implicit in Clause (1) of Article 356, it must be held, having regard to the overall constitutional scheme that the President shall exercise it only after the proclamation is approved by both Houses of Parliament under Clause (3) and not before. (*S. R. Bommai v. Union of India*, 1994 3 SCC 1, para 365)

[25] Ibid., para 85–86 (emphasis added).

Acquisition of Certain Area at Ayodhya Act, 1993 (Ayodhya Act), to acquire 67.7 acres of land within Ayodhya, of which 2.77 acres comprised the site of the Babri Mosque. Further, on 7 January 1993, the then president Shankar Dayal Sharma made a 'presidential reference' to the court to inquire into whether indeed a Hindu temple had existed at the disputed site before the construction of Babri Mosque. The Ayodhya Act was subsequently challenged in court in the *Ismail Faruqui* case;[26] its validity was upheld barring one section,[27] and the bench 'respectfully' declined to respond to the presidential reference, citing that determining whether a structure or indeed a Hindu structure or Ram Temple existed prior to the mosque had to be established by archaeologists and not the courts.[28]

However, the court's decision to uphold the validity of the Ayodhya Act meant that the demolished mosque would not simply be rebuilt. The Act's objects and reasons made it clear that on the disputed land, now, a mosque, a temple, and much else would be accommodated:

> ... As it is necessary to maintain communal harmony and the spirit of common brotherhood amongst the people of India, it was considered necessary to acquire the site of the disputed structure and suitable adjacent land for setting up a complex which could be developed in a planned manner wherein a Ram temple, a mosque, amenities for pilgrims, a library, museum and other suitable facilities can be set up.[29]

The judgment of *Ismail Faruqui v. Union of India* had started giving way to the argument that the demolition was the work of a few 'miscreants', overlooking the BJP's manifesto that claimed that 'this is what the people desire'. The process of absolving the organized political campaign that directly precipitated the demolition had begun. For instance, the minority judgment in the *Faruqui* case by Justice Bharucha (and Justice Ahmadi concurred) contained the paragraph:

[26] *Ismail Faruqui v. Union of India*, 1994 6 SCC 360.
[27] Ibid., para 96. (l)(a) Sub-section (3) of Section 4 of the Act abates all pending suits and legal proceedings without providing for an alternative dispute resolution mechanism for resolution of the dispute between the parties thereto. This is an extinction of the judicial remedy for resolution of the dispute amounting to negation of rule of law. Sub-section (3) of Section 4 of the Act is, therefore, unconstitutional and invalid.
[28] Ibid., para 154. 'The Court being ill equipped to examine and evaluate such material, it would have to appoint experts in the field to do so, and their evaluation would go unchallenged.'
[29] Statement of Objects and Reasons, The Acquisition of Certain Area at Ayodhya Ordinance, 1993.

We have no doubt that the moderate Hindu has little taste for the tearing down of the place of worship of another to replace it with a temple. It is our fervent hope that that moderate opinion shall find general expression and that communal brotherhood shall bring to the dispute at Ayodhya an amicable solution long before the Courts resolve it.... The miscreants who demolished the mosque had no religion, caste or creed except the character of a criminal and the mere incident of birth of such a person in any particular community cannot attach the stigma of his crime to the community in which he was born... The Hindu community must, therefore, bear the cross on its chest, for the misdeed of the miscreants reasonably suspected to belong to their religious fold.[30]

And further that:

... the word 'Hindutva' is used and understood as a synonym of 'Indianisation', i.e., development of uniform culture by obliterating the differences between all the cultures co-existing in the country.[31]

The judgment also cited the existence of religions other than Hinduism in India as an example of the 'tolerance' enshrined in Hinduism, which essentially is responsible for 'enabling' Islam, Christianity, Zoroastrianism, Judaism, Buddhism, Jainism, and Sikhism to exist in the country.[32] The use of words like 'shelter' and 'support' to describe the accommodation of non-Hindu religions in India betrayed the refugee status accorded to other religions in the perception of the court. The *Faruqui* judgment held that given the mosque had also not been in use since the 1950s, it could be acquired now by the state as any other religious place could be. However, it infamously observed:

A mosque is not an essential part of the practice of the religion of Islam and Namaz (prayer) by Muslims can be offered anywhere, even in open. Accordingly, its acquisition is not prohibited by the provisions in the Constitution of India.[33]

The *Faruqui* judgment steered clear of presidential reference, but once again confirmed that the mosque would not be easily restored, and passed the responsibility of managing the disputed area to the government. Simultaneously, the court read down a section of the Ayodhya Act that prevented further litigation

---

[30] *Ismail Faruqui v. Union of India*, 1994 6 SCC 360, para 55–56.
[31] Maulana Wahiddudin Khan's 'Indian Muslims – Need for a Positive Outlook' (1994) in *Ismail Faruqui v. Union of India*, 1994 6 SCC 360.
[32] *Ismail Faruqui v. Union of India*, 1994 6 SCC 360, para 156.
[33] Ibid., para 82.

on the matter, thus reviving all pending litigation since the 1950s.[34] The court thus continued to remain central to the dispute, even as political parties promised to build a temple or rebuild a mosque or protect the minorities in their respective manifestos.

The Hindutva Judgments: Recasting Secularism

In the run-up to the Maharashtra state assembly elections scheduled in 1990, some of the speeches made by local candidates of two Hindu nationalist political parties, the BJP and the Shiv Sena, stoked communal tensions. While Article 19(1) (a) of the Indian constitution guaranteed the fundamental right to freedom of speech and expression, Article 19(2) provided a few exceptions on grounds of decency, morality, or public order. The speeches in the Maharashtra election were ·acerbic enough to qualify for this exception. Moreover, under the Representation of People Act, 1951, Section 123 (subsection 3 and 3A) defined the use of religion in election campaigns as a 'corrupt practice'.[35] This led the opposing candidates who lost the election to file three petitions against candidates of the BJP and Shiv Sena for using religion to garner votes in elections. These petitions were collectively referred to as the Hindutva cases decided in 1996.

In the *Yashwant Prabhu*[36] case, the Bombay High Court declared the election of Prabhu as invalid under Section 123 of the Representation of People Act, on the basis that the use of religion was a corrupt practice. Prabhu's subsequent appeal to the Supreme Court was also dismissed. The Supreme Court expressed 'distress' at

---

[34] Ibid., para 96. Preserved section (1)(a) Sub-section (3) of Section 4 of the Act abates all pending suits and legal proceedings without providing for an alternative dispute resolution mechanism for resolution of the dispute between the parties thereto. This is an extinction of the judicial remedy for resolution of the dispute amounting to negation of rule of law. Sub-section (3) of Section 4 of the Act is, therefore, unconstitutional and invalid.

[35] Corrupt practice in Section 123 of Representation of People Act is defined as:

> The appeal by a candidate or his agent ... to vote or refrain from voting for any person on the ground of his religion, race, caste, community or language or the use of, or appeal to religious symbols ... for the furtherance of the prospects of the election of that candidate or for prejudicially affecting the election of any candidate. (3A) The promotion of, or attempt to promote, feelings of enmity or hatred between different classes of the citizens of India on grounds of religion, race, caste, community, or language, by a candidate or his agent or any other person with the consent of a candidate or his election agent for the furtherance of the prospects of the election of that candidate or for prejudicially affecting the election of any candidate.

[36] *Dr Ramesh Yashwant Prabhoo v. Shri Prabhakar Kashinath Kunte*, 1996 SCC (1) 130. Kunte was the Congress Party candidate who lost the election to Prabhu from the constituency Vile Parle, Bombay.

the nature of the speeches given, and 'condemned' the derogatory terms attributed to religious minorities.[37] However, so far as the term 'Hindutva' was concerned, the court observed that it did not necessarily refer to a religion, but to a 'way of life'.[38] The court, even as it dismissed Prabhu's appeal, concluded that the use of the term alone did not amount to invocation of religious identity for votes.

> Considering the terms 'Hinduism' or 'Hindutva' per se as depicting hostility, enmity or intolerance towards other religious faiths or professing communalism, proceeds form an improper appreciation and perception of the true meaning of these expressions emerging from the detailed discussion in earlier authorities of this Court.... The *mischief* resulting from the misuse of the terms by anyone in his speech has to be checked and not its permissible use. It is indeed very unfortunate, if in spite of the liberal and tolerant features of 'Hinduism' recognised in judicial decisions, these terms are misused by anyone during the elections to gain any unfair political advantage.
>
> ... It may well be, that these words are used in a speech to promote secularism or to emphasise the way of life of the Indian people and the Indian culture or ethos, or to criticise the policy of any political party as discriminatory or intolerant....[39]

Bound by secular commitments that had been painstakingly established in the *Bommai* judgment, Hinduism had to be separated from Hindutva in order for Hindutva to remain a legitimate campaign slogan without its use attracting penalties under Section 123 of the Representation of People Act. The courts entered into the definition of Hindutva/Hinduism when the requirement was only that of ascertaining the 'corrupt' practice of using religion in a campaign. The decisions for the other candidates followed a similar line of argument. In the *Manohar Joshi* case in 1990,[40] Joshi in his speeches had repeatedly expressed a desire for a nation constituted by and for Hindus. However, the Supreme Court took a rather sympathetic tone towards Joshi's use of the term 'Hindu state'.

> In our opinion, a mere statement that the first Hindu State will be established in Maharashtra is by itself not an appeal for votes on the ground of his religion but the expression, at best, of such a hope. However despicable be such a statement, it cannot be said to amount to an appeal for votes on the ground of his religion.[41]

---

[37] Ibid., para 62.
[38] Ibid., para 37, 39–42.
[39] Ibid., para 42–43 (emphasis mine).
[40] *Manohar Joshi v. Nitin Bhaurao Patel and Another*, 1996 SCC (1) 169, 'Concluding remarks'.
[41] Ibid., para 62.

The court concluded that his election was valid. In the third case,[42] the speeches of two prominent leaders of the Hindu nationalist movement, Sadhvi Rithambara[43] and Pramod Mahajan,[44] had called for Hindu votes to be cast in favour of the BJP candidate, Ramchandra Kapse, who responded to these speeches by standing and acknowledging the crowds. The Bombay High Court concluded that the two public speeches were aimed at specifically seeking the votes of the Hindu community for Kapse. The Supreme Court reversed this ruling and concluded that the candidate was, in fact, 'not liable' for Rithambara's or Mahajan's speeches and concluded that the election was valid.

The courts aided the universalizing of Hinduism and, as a corollary, aided the shrinking of other religions as specific, reducing politics around these as parochial. This also meant that the judiciary would debate Hinduism but discussions of other religions were largely permitted within the limited space of 'personal laws'. The court has historically pursued progressive interpretations of religion,[45] but not attempted to separate Islam from *Islamiyat* (Islamism) or the Christian 'sentiment' of charity from the proselytizing agendas of missionaries (*Reverend Stanislaus v. State of Madhya Pradesh* discussed in Chapters 2 and 3), as it did for Hindutva from Hinduism in these cases.

Earlier precedents also reveal an underlying will of the courts to accept the universality, secularity, or the flexibility of Hinduism.[46] In the *Satsang* case of 1966, the 'Satsangis' petitioned to be treated as a separate community outside of Hinduism, and expressed a desire to be governed by separate contractual and inheritance laws.[47] Similarly, the Ramakrishna Mission, another sect, claimed to be distinct from Hinduism with respect to their 'way of life'.[48] However, in both cases, the court concluded that these sects were mere branches of Hinduism and

---

[42] *Prof. Ramachandra G. Kapse v. Haribansh Ramakbal Singh*, 1996 SCC (1) 206.
[43] The founding chairperson of the Durga Vahini (Durga's army), the women's wing of the Vishwa Hindu Parishad.
[44] A veteran leader of the BJP in the 1980s and 1990s; also, a member of the RSS.
[45] Mitra Sharafi, 'The Semi-Autonomous Judge in Colonial India: Chivalric Imperialism Meets Anglo-Islamic Dower and Divorce Law', *Indian Economic and Social History Review* 46, no. 1 (2009): 57–81. W. F. Menski, 'Asking for the Moon: Legal Uniformity in India from a Kerala Perspective', *Kerala Law Times, Journal Section* 2006 (2): 52–78.
[46] Ronojoy Sen, *Articles of Faith: Religion, Secularism, and the Indian Supreme Court* (Oxford University Press, 2010). See also *Kultar Singh v. Mukhtiar Singh*, 1965 AIR 141. In this case, there was a similar disagreement on the use of the term 'panth' and whether it referred to religion itself or the political party (Akali Dal in Punjab), the court had held that 'Panth' in this case did not refer to religion.
[47] *Shanti Sarup v. Radhaswami Satsang Sabha*, AIR 1969 All 248.
[48] *Sri Ram Krishna Mission and Anr. v. Paramanand and Ors*, AIR 1977 All 421.

favoured a wider interpretation of Hinduism. The *Hindutva* cases, on the contrary, had narrowed the definition of Hinduism in order to yield that characteristic to Hindutva instead. The capacious definitions that were attributed to secularism in the *Bommai* judgment came to be attributed to Hindutva in the 1990s. The umbrella of Hindutva could then become so big that it would practically become the new 'secular', if not the new 'national'. The observation of the court in effect embraced Savarkar's theorization of 'Hindu' as a subset of Hindutva.[49] V. D. Savarkar described the concept of Hindutva as not a mere 'word' but 'history', of which Hinduism is merely a derivative form.[50] The BJP's publication on the 'party's philosophy' contains that Hindutva or 'cultural nationalism' represents the party's conception of Indian nationhood and notes that Hindutva was a nationalist, and not a religious or theocratic, concept.[51]

Once the courts dissociated Hindutva from religion, it could be treated as a secular idea or critiqued as any other political ploy without the guilt of blasphemy. The real win for the Hindutva ideologues was not merely that their philosophy was deemed by the courts as synonymous with Indianization or Indian culture, but rather that it was deemed a 'secular' ideology. A major obstacle that lay in the path of Hindu nationalism transitioning from movement to government was its questionable relationship with the constitutional commitment to secularism. The judgments made that commitment irrelevant by equating Hindutva with secularism. And since secularism was argued to be a defence of democracy in the Bommai judgment, the Hindu nationalist movement became that self-styled 'democratic voice' which was committed ironically to 'liberal' constitutional values of equality, freedom of speech, and so on. The Hindu nationalist claim over 'equality' was established by dismissing affirmative action or special provisions as a compromise on the constitutional commitment to equality by casting itself as suppressed and vulnerable—vocabulary thus far attributed to marginalized minorities.[52]

These judgments received substantial scholarly attention and severe criticism for lending legal currency to the term 'Hindutva', which signalled the collapse of secularism in India.[53] Sitapati argues that the Hindutva judgments put clauses

---

[49] Vinayak Damodar Savarkar, *Hindutva: Who Is a Hindu?* (New Delhi: Hindi Sahitya Sadan, 1923, republished 2003).

[50] For a critical analysis of the historical evolution of the term, see Hansen. *The Saffron Wave*, ch. 2.

[51] See www.bjp.org, sub-head 'Our Philosophy', accessed on 31 July 2013.

[52] Jacobsohn, *The Wheel of Law*.

[53] P. Kapur and B. Cossman, 'Secularism's Last Sigh: The Hindu Right, the Courts, and India's Struggle for Democracy', *Harvard International Law Journal* 38, no. 1 (1997): 113; Rajiv Dhavan, 'The Ayodhya Judgement: Encoding Secularism in the Law', *Economic and Political Weekly* 29, no. 48 (1994): 3034–40.

of free speech and freedom of expression and the constitutional commitment to secularism in a hierarchy.[54] He argues if a 'justification' of the judgments lay in a 'liberal' narrative, that is, defence of freedom of speech and expression,[55] its flaw can be discovered in the 'secular' narrative which took a strict view of 'religion' under the Representation of People Act[56] that characterized the 'use of religion' as a corrupt election practice. The 'secular' considerations were, therefore, made subservient to a 'liberal' reading of the law.

For Jacobsohn too, India's restrictions on religious speech in the Hindutva judgments were derived from 'content-neutral principles' that are in conformity with the contemporary conceptualizations of the 'liberal State'. This meant that the court could defend freedom of speech while criticizing the 'content' of the speech but also simultaneously hold the content and intent of the speeches off limits for being tested under constitutional provisions. The bench employed strict 'statutory standards' in assessing the speeches on the limited point of whether the speeches used religion in a way that such use could be characterized as a 'corrupt practice' under the Representation of People Act.[57] However, in its bid to prevent censorship of controversial ideas, the court offered a sympathetic reading of a speech that openly called for Muslim isolation and targeting. Jacobsohn illustrates this with remarkable precision when he states that if it were '*Chief Minister* Joshi, rather than *Candidate* Joshi, who had expressed the aspiration for a Hindu state of Maharashtra, a dismissal of his government under President's rule could, following *Bommai*, plausibly be upheld by the Supreme Court'.[58]

The Hindutva judgments not only salvaged the term Hindutva from its anti-Muslim usage in election campaigns, it helped construct a fresh benign meaning of the term.[59] While scholarship has focused on arguments of 'free speech' and 'secularism' (ameliorative,[60] equidistance,[61] or contextual[62]), the Hindutva judgments became a powerful intervention that separated Hinduism from religious fundamentalism. In one sense, the bench drew two opposing conclusions.

---

[54] Vinay Sitapati, 'Doing a Rashomon on the Hindutva Cases', *Economic and Political Weekly* 43, no. 10 (2008): 72–77.
[55] Article 19 of the fundamental rights.
[56] Section 123(3A) of Representation of People Act.
[57] Jacobsohn, *The Wheel of Law*.
[58] Ibid., 195.
[59] Noorani in Jacobsohn, *The Wheel of Law*, 209.
[60] Jacobsohn, *The Wheel of Law*.
[61] Ashutosh Varshney, 'Contested Meanings: India's National Identity, Hindu Nationalism, and the Politics of Anxiety', *Daedalus* 122, no. 3 (1993): 227–61.
[62] Rajeev Bhargava, 'The Distinctiveness of Indian Secularism', in *The Future of Secularism*, ed. T. N. Srinivasan (New York: Oxford University Press, 2007), 20–53.

One, that the invocation of Hindutva was not the same as Hinduism and, therefore, there were no 'corrupt' practices deployed in election campaigns that sought votes on the grounds of religion. Two, that Hindutva could stand for 'Indianness', and since Hinduism shared many a principle with Hindutva, the Hindu religion itself was rather secular, or as had been previously stated in Constituent Assembly debates[63] and in parliament, that it 'allows other religions to flower'.[64]

In principle, Hindutva, much like Hinduism, was difficult to define, with no central canonical text or single deity, but in practice it could be the creation of a 'Hindu state'. Attributing religious fundamentalism to miscreants obfuscated the breadth of support for Hindu nationalism, blinding the bench to the possibility that the emerging movement could become the government, and if it did, a Hindu state would be a policy goal rather than a humble 'hope'.[65] Similarly, the bench also drew a distinction between benign and violent Hindutva without labouring over the difference between the two. The court 'condemned'[66] the vitriol, the potential of violence and racial supremacy, but permitted the benign philosophical values of Hindutva as valid invocations to a cultural idea which can be deployed in elections. To the common public, this distinction may well have been irrelevant. Not all people, if presented with an opportunity, may have participated in demolishing the mosque, but many did rejoice at the act of demolition as spectators. The 'way of life' that Hindutva espoused may have had completely different meanings for the subscribers or sympathizers of Hindutva which could range from hatred towards minorities to shared cultural heritage, to national pride, to secular coexistence and simultaneously a Hindu state. The presumption that it was the benign meaning of the term that appealed for most of the population was a fallacious one, especially given that the speeches extolled the idea of a Hindu *rashtra* cautioning against the idea of a 'green' Hindustan.[67] Thus, neither the conflation of Hindutva and secularism nor the appropriation of secularism by Hindu nationalism was exclusive to the 1990s. But the Hindutva judgments' explicit acceptance of Hindutva as

---

[63] See Chapter 1 in this book.

[64] See chapter 4, *Lok Sabha Debates*, Vaisakha 15, 1908 (Saka), *Muslims Women Protection of Rights on Divorce Bill*, 23 April 1986–5 May 1986.

[65] *Manohar Joshi v. Nitin Bhaurao Patel and Another*, 1996 SCC (1) 169, 'Concluding remarks', para 62.

[66] *Dr Ramesh Yashwant Prabhoo v. Shri Prabhakar Kashinath Kunte*, 1996 SCC (1) 130, 21:

> We cannot help recording our distress at this kind of speeches given by a top leader of a political party. The lack of restraint in the language used and the derogatory terms used therein to refer to a group of people in an election speech in indeed to be condemned.

[67] Ibid., para 57.

secularism now meant that the Hindu nationalist ideology could no longer as easily be called out for perpetuating religious intolerance towards minorities or women as it had historically been. In the debates on the Hindu Code Bill, on the 42nd Amendment, or on the mobilization around Ramajanmabhumi, legal or constitutional definitions of secularism had repeatedly challenged religious norms or forms. If the secular status for India at the time of independence was the negation of theocracy, then with the court's acceptance of a 'hope' for a Hindu state as legitimate, it became increasingly difficult for the vocabulary of secularism to remain a negation of theocracy.

Hindutva as 'Indianness' is an idea that has crystallized over time to the extent that rather than provoking scepticism amongst media commentators and general public in statements such as 'a Hindu Rashtra is not possible without minorities',[68] a claim made by RSS Chief Mohan Bhagwat at a recent conference, the statement was treated largely as evidence of how secular the organization is. To the counter question on why the RSS refuses to admit Muslims and Christians, Bhagwat responded: '[C]an boys be admitted to girls' schools?' Thus, the idea of a Hindu state that is benevolent to minorities but sees them as inadequately assimilated with the majority now defines the new secular. Bhagwat further stated, 'Everyone who lives in India is Hindu by identity, nationality.' Thus, the very language in which Hindutva was opposed for decades (that is, secularism) now became synonymous with it.

The courts were sensitive to regime changes and to political shifts; however, the rise of judicial activism cannot be read merely as post-PIL populism.[69] It was also a response to repeated invocations by political parties, civil society movements, and federal governments to the Supreme Court to address what they alleged was the 'betrayal' of core constitutional values. The government accused the BJP and its affiliates of violating the court order that permitted peaceful prayer. The members of opposition lamented the violation of secularism in the government's inability to prevent the Babri's demolition, on the one hand, and the BJP, on the other hand, saw the arrest of L. K. Advani and the dismissal of the federal government as a curtailment of the freedom of expression and a compromise on federalism. All parties looked to the court.

It is, therefore, in this context of Hindutva's universal acceptability across state institutions that the scepticism about a Uniform Civil Code emerged.

---

[68] 'No Hindu Rashtra without Muslims, Hindutva Based on Unity in Diversity: Mohan Bhagwat', *Indian Express*, 30 September 2018.

[69] Upendra Baxi, 'Taking Suffering Seriously: Social Action Litigation in the Supreme Court of India', *Third World Legal Studies* 4, no. 6 (1985): 107.

While the impact of Hindu nationalism on personal law has been studied extensively, this chapter illustrates that the courts were crucial to the relationship between the two. Personal law had historically defined religion through bills, acts, and judgments but the court's ruling on Hindutva was all about circumventing religion, emphasizing its indefinability. The critique of the judicial understanding of secularism is relevant only to emphasize the backdrop in which questions of family law also had to be debated. Such definitions of secularism meant that if Hinduism was so easily reconciled with secularism, secularism could hardly claim 'neutrality'. This raised legitimate suspicion that if Hindutva was secular, what would 'universal' family laws look like?

In the early 2000s, leading jurists began to call for a Uniform Civil Code primarily to cure the deficiencies created by Muslim personal law or Christian personal law. Chief Justice V. K. Khare stated that matters of marriage or succession were 'secular matters' which must not be brought under the guarantees of freedom of religion.[70] Justice A. R. Lakshmanan publicly concurred with Khare and was joined by Justice S. B. Sinha in advocating the quashing of certain provisions of the Indian Succession Act, 1925, which was applicable to Christians.[71] Lending currency to Hindu universality, the court also produced judgments that emphasized Muslim exceptionality as the prime reason behind the failure of a universal, 'neutral' civil code. When it came to Muslim personal law, the courts delved deeper into what was 'true Islam'—whether it permitted triple *talaq*, bigamy, or *nikah halala*. Hindutva, on the other hand, had a certain immunity. If used for votes it was not quite 'religion', and if it were indeed Hinduism, Hinduism was a secular religion.

The next section analyses the court's intervention in Muslim personal law at the high point of Hindu nationalism, that is, when the BJP formed coalition governments in 1996, 1998, and, finally, for a full term in 1999. The courts had historically been entitled to substantial discretion in handling family disputes under personal law codes. Innovation in courts on religious issues in determining meanings, limits, and essential practices of religion had led to the expansion of the sphere of religion in the public space rather than its containment and inadvertently generated public interest and inquiry into religious tenets.

---

[70] Enshrined in Article 25: Freedom of conscience and free profession, practice and propagation of religion. Article 26: Freedom to manage religious affairs. Article 27: Freedom as to payment of taxes for promotion of any particular religion. Article 28: Freedom as to attendance at religious instruction or religious worship in certain education institutions.

[71] *John Vallamattom and Anr. v. Respondent: Union of India*, AIR 2003 SC 2902. This was a case concerning the inheritance and succession and death-bed donations under Christian personal law.

Interestingly, however, the court's references to the religious texts also encouraged Muslim women to seek a reinterpretation of religious law wording their claims as their 'right to religious freedom', 'right to practice Islam uncorrupted by custom', rather than to tirelessly prove popular practices' incompatibility with the constitution. This generated a different type of negotiation between state structures and the society.

Judicial engagement with Muslim personal law, despite its track record of aiding Hindu universality, yielded some substantial benefits for women. The courts began to attempt not only uniform and reconciliatory interpretations of different statutes but also made bolder assertions about the 'true' understanding of religious texts, and what constituted authentic religion. This provoked the immediate discomfort in scholarship on secularism and religion, about the state's increased regulatory capacity and monopoly over determining the scale and scope of religion. However, in India, it led to the opposite. Judicial enthusiasm in the 1990s and the 2000s over religious personal law through the reinterpretation of religious texts was critical in rendering the idea of a Uniform Civil Code and a parliamentary intervention unnecessary; particularly within feminist politics. In its dealings with religion, the court significantly empowered the petitioners, be they political parties or civil society organizations, who could determine the 'true' interpretations of religion and have these interpretations popularized through the courts. Religious social movements borrowed from progressive judicial precedents to argue for religious reinterpretation and, in turn, negotiate authority within community to interpret religion. The lack of legislative intervention, and tentative judicial support for religious reform, led to the further decentralization of religious authority rather than its concentration with the state.

II

The Quran and the Court

This section shows the case-by-case evolution of jurisprudence on Muslim personal law where the courts were an arena for contest and not sites for the production of rigid law. Judicial responses on Muslim personal law did not follow a pattern. However, the 1990s and the 2000s did witness a steady change in Muslim women's relationship with the courts. The chapter illustrates that while the universality of Hinduism was commonly invoked in parliament, political campaigns, and confirmed by the courts,[72] yet through the 1990s and the 2000s, the courts remained a fertile ground for contestations between women and patriarchy, religious and statutory law, liberalism and orthodoxy, and so on. Though these decisions did not always yield memorable outcomes, they nonetheless demonstrate that the law enabled conversations and the vocabulary of secularity and religion could be utilized towards similar ends. While the chapter focuses on the Muslim movements, the period is generally marked by the emergence of social collectives that focussed on service delivery rather than relying solely on law and legislation.[73]

The lead up to a legislative intervention was preceded by piecemeal efforts of women's organizations and was also deeply informed by party politics. The section considers a series of cases where women challenge personal laws as being violative of secularism, of fundamental rights, and of religious tenets. The court on its part responded by reconciling different statutes, reconciling religion and statutes, and applying 'progressive interpretations' of religion and, in the process, aided the narrative that Muslim personal law is misunderstood rather than misogynistic. This opened up Muslim personal law to further public and political scrutiny.

Decentralizing Muslim Divorce

In 1990, an international network known as Women Living under Muslim Laws (WLUML) published a document on the subject of women's right to

---

[72] In a number of judgments, the Supreme Court has squarely pinned the lack of a Uniform Civil Code on the presence of Muslim personal law. A significant example is the case of *Sarla Mudgal v. Union of India* (1995) 3 SCC 635, where the court observed:

> Those who preferred to remain in India after the partition fully knew that the Indian leaders did not believe in two-nation or three-nation theory and that in the Indian Republic there was to be only one Nation—Indian nation—and no community could claim to remain a separate entity on the basis of religion.... It appears that even 41 years thereafter [since Nehru's speech in 1954, quoted in the judgment], the Rulers of the day are not in a mood to retrieve Article 44 [Uniform Civil Code] from the cold storage where it is lying since 1949. The Governments—which have come and gone—have so far failed to make any effort towards 'unified personal law for all Indians'. (para 10)

[73] The first public LGBTQI protests can also be traced to the 1990s. In 1992, the Durbar Mahila Samanvay Samiti was formed which later extended support to transgender sex workers. In 1994, the Naz Foundation was set up, which later petitioned for the repeal of the law criminalizing homosexuality. These were some among the many collectives that came to life in the 1990s, dedicated predominantly to extending social support to vulnerable groups.

delegated divorce, or *talaq-i-tawfid*, detailing women's absolute right to divorce.[74] In 1996, *Talaq-i-Tawfid: The Muslim Woman's Contractual Access to Divorce— An Information Kit* was published with a particular focus on South Asia and this compiled several model *nikahnama*s that could be used in Muslim marriages for negotiating better terms of contract for wives.[75] This was followed by a proliferation and popularization of a number of model *nikahnama*s that restricted in particular the husband's right to pronounce oral unilateral divorce or triple *talaq*. A *nikahnama* drafted in 1987 by a scholar of Islam, Zeenat Shaukat Ali, resurfaced in the 2000s and Danial Latifi, Shah Bano's former lawyer, also drafted a new *nikahnama* and had it stamped by the chief *qazi* of Aligarh in 2003. These provided for improved terms of agreement for the wife with regard to divorce, and provided restrictive conditions for polygamy.[76]

The idea that innovative models of *nikahnama*s were somehow largely replaced by universal statutory codes in the 1930s can be misleading. The Shariat Application Act, 1937, did not put forth any model *nikahnama* or *talaqnama*, nor did the Act explicitly permit or ban bigamy. After independence, women continued to rely on legal instruments to negotiate better rights within marriage and within and outside statutory law—by popularizing model *nikahnama*s, on the one hand, and petitioning before courts, on the other. Secular strategies were initiated for religious reasons, and religious rationale deployed for reaching secular ends. Thus, characterizing the resistance by women as secular modern *or* religious[77] may not capture the overlapping spectrums of religious belief and secular action.

The newly enacted Muslim Women (Protection of Rights on Divorce) Act, 1986, had also opened up further debates since codified statutes of Muslim law could now be amended or challenged through the instrument of law for violating both religion and the constitution. One of the greatest troubles with potential amendments to the Shariat Application Act, 1937, had been that it was simply an 'application' Act and not in itself a codified version of the *sharia*. So, the practices under challenge had no statutory backing but instead it had to be determined whether these were

---

[74] Lucy Carroll and Harsh Kapoor, eds., '*Le kit d'information sur le droit de délégation du droit au divorce par contrat ou Talaq ba Tafouiz*', produced by Women Living Under Muslim Laws, available at www.wluml.org.

[75] Lucy Carroll and Harsh Kapoor, eds. '*Talaq-i-Tafwid: The Muslim Woman's Contractual Access to Divorce—An Information Kit*', 1996, www.wluml.org/sites/wluml.org/files/import/english/pubs/.../talaq-i-tawfid-eng.pdf.

[76] Sylvia Vatuk, 'Islamic Feminism in India: Indian Muslim Women Activists and the Reform of Muslim Personal Law', *Modern Asian Studies* 42, nos 2–3 (2008): 489–518.

[77] Saba Mahmood. *Religious Difference in a Secular Age: A Minority Report* (Princeton, NJ: Princeton University Press, 2015).

essential to religion, or came under fundamental right to freedom or religion or were against the fundamental right to equality.[78] The Dissolution of Muslim Marriages Act, 1939, and the Muslim Women (Protection of Rights on Divorce) Act, 1986, laid down statutory rules and procedures that could potentially be challenged and amended.

Feminist organizations such as the Awaaz-e-Niswaan (1998),[79] and later the Muslim Women's Rights Network[80] (MWRN) (1999), which grew out of a conference held by the Awaaz-e-Niswaan in 1999, were also debating model *nikahnama*s which could be in accordance with the *sharia*. The MWRN also worked in collaboration with international networks such as the WLUML. The organization suffered a setback with respect to resources in the aftermath of the demolition of the Babri Mosque, but their volunteers continued to work in relief camps during the riots and established a resource centre in 2003. Other women's organizations such as the Forum Against Oppression of Women (1980), Jagori (1984), Majlis (1991), Association for Advocacy and Legal Initiatives (AALI) (1998), among many others, were active during this period. Many of these were directly engaged in legal advocacy and others also had substantial interface with the state in seeking support for shelter homes, counselling for rape survivors, assisting in filing complaints with the police, and so forth. Though not focussed exclusively on Muslim personal law, these organizations distanced themselves from the idea of the enactment of a Uniform Civil Code that the BJP promised, particularly after the demolition of the Babri Mosque. Muslim women, often aided by NGOs, therefore, challenged personal laws as violating the Quran as well as the constitution in a series of cases.

---

[78] Ronojoy Sen, 'Secularism and Religious Freedom', in *Oxford Handbook of the Indian Constitution*, ed. Sujit Choudhry, Madhav Khosla, and Pratap Bhanu Mehta (Oxford: Oxford University Press, 2016), section on religion and its 'essential practices', 885–903. Sen in his study shows how the Supreme Court determined whether a practice was essential to religion, complied with public interest, and was also consonant with the reformist requirements of the constitution.

[79] Awaaz-e-Niswaan is a feminist collective of students, academicians, and activists committed to women's rights. In 1985, a woman named Shehnaz awaited her court hearing in a case of unilateral divorce and met other women who suffered a similar fate; these chance meetings resulted in women filing a petition against unilateral *talaq* and continued to hold weekly meetings and discussion. The organization eventually flourished. http://www.niswaan.org/node.

[80] For Muslim women's movements in contemporary India, see A. E. Varghese, 'Personal Laws in India: The Activisms of Muslim Women's Organizations published' (doctoral dissertation, Trinity College, 2015).

Constitutional Challenges

In 1997, the Ahmedabad Women Action Group (AWAG), another NGO, challenged various aspects of all personal laws, alleging that these laws violated the fundamental rights of individuals.[81] The petition argued that Muslim personal law permitted the right of unilateral and oral *talaq* only to men, and polygamy was also the exclusive right of husbands and this offended various articles of the constitution that guaranteed the right to equality between sexes (Article 14) and right to live with dignity (Article 21).[82]

The court acknowledged the problem in no uncertain terms but in effect forwarded the petition to parliament: 'They are issues of state policy with which the Court will not ordinarily have any concern and that the remedy lies somewhere else and not by knocking at the doors of the Courts.'[83] The case nonetheless ensured that family law remained in focus. The petition provided an exhaustive list of multiple provisions of all personal laws that are discriminatory towards women and challenged them simply as violations of fundamental rights. These included sections of the Muslim Women (Protection of Rights on Divorce) Act, 1986, the Hindu Marriage Act, 1955, the Hindu Succession Act, 1956, the Hindu Minority and Guardianship Act, 1956, sections of the Indian Divorce Act, 1869, provisions relating to Indian Christians, among others.

Danial Latifi also filed a writ petition immediately after the enactment of the Muslim Women (Protection of Rights on Divorce) Act, 1986, challenging the constitutional validity of the Act. And his petition was clubbed together with various other petitions by academics and activists. While the constitutional validity of the Muslim Women (Protection of Rights on Divorce) Act had remained precarious since its enactment, for potentially violating the fundamental right to equality, it was the decision on the *Danial Latifi* case that provided a reinterpretation of the Act, with some finality. The bench concluded that the 'intention' of parliament was conveyed by

---

[81] *Ahmedabad Women Action Group v. Union of India* (1997) 3 SCC 573. See also *Reynold Rajmani v. Union of India*, 1982 AIR 1261: 'whether a provision for divorce by mutual consent should be included in the Indian Divorce Act is a matter of legislative policy. The courts cannot extend or enlarge legislative policy by adding a provision to the statute which was never enacted there [in parliament].'

[82] Article 13, that is, laws inconsistent with or in derogation of the fundamental rights, and Article 14, right to equality, and also Article 15, prohibition of discrimination (in this case) on grounds of gender/religion.

[83] *Ahmedabad Women's Action Group v. Union of India* (1997) 3 SCC 573.

the very title of the Act, that is, Muslim Women (Protection of Rights on Divorce) Act and, therefore, all interpretations by the courts must centre on the protection of women.[84]

The ambiguity in the 1986 Act, on issues of the maintenance of wives, among others, gave unbridled power to the courts to interpret the clause of maintenance. The definitions of religious terminology, 'mata' or 'talaq', debated and accepted by parliament, were at best contested and, at worst, incorrect. The court in the *Danial Latifi* case, one of its most creative rulings concluded that the word *mata* implied not merely 'maintenance' that expired at the end of the three-month *iddat* period, but a 'provision for maintenance' *within* the *iddat* period which extended for life. The bench of five judges[85] declared that 'this very court in Shah Bano's case may have dismissed this aspect by holding that it is a distinction without a difference'.[86] The judge concluded that the Muslim husband is expected to make 'preparatory arrangements' that were 'reasonable and fair' to include a provision for her residence, her food, her clothes, and the like.[87] The court stated:

> The expression 'within' should be read as 'during' or 'for' and this cannot be done because words cannot be construed contrary to their meaning as the word 'within' would mean 'on or before, 'not beyond' and, therefore, it was held that the Act would mean that on or before the expiration of the *iddat* period, the husband is bound to make and pay a maintenance to the wife and if he fails to do so then the wife is entitled to recover it by filling an application before the Magistrate as provided in Section 3(3) *but nowhere parliament has provided that reasonable and fair provision and maintenance is limited only for the iddat period and not beyond it.* It would extend to the whole life of the divorced wife unless she gets married for a second time.[88]
> Though it may look ironical that the enactment (Muslim Women Act, 1986) intended to reverse the decision in Shah Bano's case, actually codifies the very rationale contained therein.[89]

---

[84] Flavia Agnes, 'From Shahbano to Kausar Bano: Contextualizing the "Muslim Women" within a Communalized Polity', in *South Asian Feminisms*, ed. Ania Loomba and Ritty A. Lukose (Durham, NC: Duke University Press, 2012), 33–53.

[85] Constituted by G. B. Pattanaik, S. Rajendra Babu, D. P. Mahapatra, Doraiswamy Raju, and Shivraj V. Patil.

[86] *Danial Latifi* and *Another v. Union of India* (2001) 7 SCC 740, para 30.

[87] Ibid., para 29.

[88] Ibid. (emphasis mine).

[89] Ibid.

Shah Bano had ultimately withdrawn her case but her divorce left a persevering legacy. Even as the court dismissed Latifi's petition, it reinterpreted the 1986 Act to concur with the *Shah Bano* judgment, paving the way for maintenance offered to the divorced Muslim women to be extended for life.[90] This judgment reiterated the very essence of the argument in the *Shah Bano* case, that is, that the husband, despite having paid *mahr*, followed by the maintenance for the *iddat* period, had not made a 'reasonable and fair provision' for his divorced wife. Moreover, Section (4) of the Muslim Women (Protection of Rights on Divorce) Act, which mentioned an order of maintenance for the divorced woman by her relatives, did not mention the word 'provision'. This led the bench to conclude that the right to a 'fair and reasonable provision' for the divorced wife was enforceable *only* against her former husband, failing which the relatives of the woman were required to step in. If any of the relatives were unable to pay maintenance, the magistrate would direct the State Wakf Board to pay the maintenance.[91] The *Latifi* judgment interpreted the Muslim Women (Protection of Rights on Divorce) Act to appear as an equally beneficial scheme as the Section 125 of the CrPC, with an added emphasis on disposing off of the cases within three months. This ruling, in one stroke, settled a contested question of maintenance of divorced women.[92] The *Danial Latifi* judgment addressed the ambiguity surrounding the Act, and confirmed that all statutes and all procedures could yield a similar end.

---

[90] See Chapter 4, the reinterpretation of the word *mata* as 'provision for maintenance' and not 'maintenance'.

[91] Danial Latifi, Private Paper S. No. 476, 1930–84, NMML, New Delhi. Latifi, along with Reshma Arif Mohammad Khan (wife of Arif Mohammad Khan), was agitating against the Act since its commencement. Latifi's private collection of papers has a number of published and unpublished articles and letters under the title, 'Repartee by Danial Latifi', 7 August 1994; 'The Issue of Shah Bano and Taslima Nasreen Should Not Be Confused', 2 November 1994.

[92] The following cases—*Arab Ahemadhia Abdulla and etc v. Arab Bail Mohmuna Saiyadbhai and Ors*; *Ali v. Safaira*; *K. Kunhashed Hazi v. Amena*; *K. Zunaideen v. Ameena Begum*; *Karim Abdul Shaik v. Shenaz Karim Shaik*; *and Jaitunbi Mubarak Shaikh v. Mubarak Fakruddin Shaikh and Anr*—presented in the judgment where the interpretation of Sections 3(1)(a) and 4 of the Muslim Women Act is fairly consistent and reiterates the Muslim women's right to maintenance *beyond* the *iddat* period. Contrary readings of the Act in *Umar Khan Bahamami v. Fathimnurisa*; *Abdul Rashid v. Sultana Begum*; *Abdul Haq v. Yasima Talat*; and *Md. Marahim v. Raiza Begum* were also cited where it has been held that the liability of the husband is limited for the period of *iddat* and thereafter if the wife is unable to maintain herself, she has to approach her relatives or the Wakf Board. Thus, the *Latifi* judgment favoured the former position of the high court rulings and concluded, 'preponderance of judicial opinion is in favour of what we have concluded in the interpretation of Section 3 of the Act. The decisions of the High Courts referred to herein that are contrary to our decision stand overruled.'

The *Shabana Bano* case in 2009[93] further demonstrated that Muslim women also continued to file their maintenance claims under Section 125 of the CrPC and the family courts routinely upheld their claims. Shabana Bano was married to Imran Khan. Things quickly soured between the couple as Imran's parents began to harass Shabana for dowry. Shabana was pregnant when she returned to her parent's house and after the delivery of the child, Imran refused to let her back into his house. The family court decided in favour of the wife's plea for maintenance but the Gwalior High Court later reversed the order. When the case reached the Supreme Court on appeal, the court made two significant interventions. One, it reconciled Section 125 of the CrPC with the Muslim Women (Protection of Rights on Divorce) Act, 1986, and secondly, it confirmed the jurisdiction of the family courts in deciding matters under Section 125.[94] The court concluded:

> Learned Single [High Court] Judge appeared to be little confused with regard to different provisions of Muslim Act, Family Act and Cr.P.C. and thus was wholly unjustified in rejecting the appellant's Revision.

> Cumulative reading of the relevant portions of judgements ... would make it crystal clear that even a divorced Muslim woman would be entitled to claim maintenance from her divorced husband, as long as she does not remarry. This being a beneficial piece of legislation, the benefit thereof must accrue to the divorced Muslim women.

> ... It is held that even if a Muslim woman has been divorced, she would be entitled to claim maintenance from her husband under Section 125 of the Cr.P.C. after the expiry of period of *iddat* also, as long as she does not remarry.[95]

Innovations in court, therefore, were eventually making up for the lack of clear legislation, which for legal practitioners made it possible to negotiate favourable orders for women. The intervention in the *Shabana Bano* judgment, however, was far less publicized compared to the *Shah Bano* judgment. Political context informed the publicity that personal law interventions received. The judgment clarified (yet again) that Section 125 continued to remain accessible to Muslim women, which was the very source of controversy in the *Shah Bano* case. Some of the most beneficial judicial interventions on the subject of maintenance in the cases of *Danial Latifi* and *Shabana Bano* continue to be underwritten outside of academic discourse.

---

[93] *Shabana Bano v. Imran Khan*, 2009 (14) SCALE 331.

[94] Ibid. 'Thus, from the abovementioned provisions it is quite discernible that a Family Court established under the Family Act shall exclusively have jurisdiction to adjudicate upon the applications filed under Section 125 of Cr.P.C.'

[95] Ibid., concluding paragraph.

256 Divorce and Democracy

Customary Divorce

In the *Shamim Ara*[96] case in 2002, the Supreme Court also decided to grant maintenance to Shamim Ara who was divorced by her husband Abrar Ahmad through oral unilateral divorce or triple *talaq*. Shamim Ara had married Abrar Ahmad and the couple had had four sons. There was uncertainty over whether or not the divorce had taken place on the said date, owing to the nature of divorce—triple *talaq*, unilateral oral divorce, for which no proof was made available to the court. The Supreme Court in upholding the maintenance claim deemed triple *talaq* 'unacceptable' owing to the lack of proof of such a divorce:

> The particulars of the alleged talaq are not pleaded nor the circumstances under which and the persons, if any, in whose presence talaq was pronounced have been stated. Such deficiency continued to prevail even during the trial and the respondent ... adduced no evidence in proof of talaq said to have been given by him.... There are no reasons substantiated in justification of talaq and no plea or proof that any effort at reconciliation preceded the talaq.[97]

The judge quoted Justice Khalid of the Kerala High Court in *Mohd. Haneefa v. Pathummal Beevi*, 'Should Muslim wives suffer this tyranny for all times? Should their personal law remain so cruel towards these unfortunate wives? Can it not be amended suitably to alleviate their sufferings? My judicial conscience is disturbed at this monstrosity.'[98] These, however, were observations (*obita dicta*) of the court and formed the non-binding part of the court order. The petition had been filed for maintenance and the effective part of the order related only to the matter for which the court was moved, that is, maintenance. Although not enforceable, this observation became an oft-quoted part of the judgment.

Ex-parte divorces and abandonment of wives was common among Hindu families[99] but the presence of codified modular 'law', however flexible, shielded Hinduism from being demonized as regressive in popular perception whereas Islam became an embodiment of women's oppression. Hindu law also continued to see developments as discussed in Chapters 2 and 3, and limited codification of Muslim law contributed significantly in producing the rhetoric of Muslim exceptionality in family law, even as women of both communities encountered nearly identical scenarios.

---

[96] *Shamim Ara v. State of U.P. and Anr* AIR 2002 SC 3551.
[97] Ibid., para 15.
[98] *Mohd. Haneefa v. Pathummal Beevi*, 1972 KLT 512, para 7.
[99] *Shailesh Kumari v. Amod Kumar Sachan*, C.M. Application No. 107245 of 2015 in First Appeal No. 91 of 2006, Allahabad High Court.

The court's dealings with Hindu customary divorce in recent years make for an interesting comparison with triple *talaq*. For instance, in a very similar case of *Rameshchandra Rampratapji Daga v. Rameshwari Rameshchandra Daga*,[100] the husband had refused to maintain his wife claiming that her previous marriage was not dissolved. The couple's previous marriage had been dissolved through a local custom in accordance with the prevalent custom in the Maheshwari community, a *chhor chithhi* or a letter of dissolution of marriage, which had been executed between the wife and her previous husband. This was later registered. The Supreme Court ultimately also upheld the wife's claim to maintenance. Significantly, the court had observed, 'The facts of this case tell the tragic tale of an Indian woman, who having gone through two marriages with a child born to her apprehends destitution as both marriages have broken down.'[101]

Despite wives getting maintenance in both cases, Muslim personal law in public perception remains demonized whereas for Hindu law, once codified, could absorb all discrimination within a Hindu society, without bringing Hinduism in conversation, even as Section 29 of the Hindu Marriage Act explicitly recognizes custom under Section 29(2).[102] Practices such as *karewa*, that is, marriage of a widow with the brother of her husband, was common in Haryana and Punjab and that of *maitri karar* or friendship deed (informal, temporary marriage) remained prevalent in Gujarat and Rajasthan, even after the Hindu Marriage Act, 1955. The high courts in these states routinely decided on the validity of such marriages, as they did on customary divorces such as triple *talaq*, but Hindu law on the whole was never indicted in these judgments. In both Hindu and Muslim cases, there remained evidence of customary divorce yielding outcomes favourable to women or not, much like how sporadic it was under official law.[103] Thus, there were worlds of law in which the state was not absent, but also not in control. In one sense, it can be said that official law evolved through amendments routed through commissions for Hindu law but Muslim law was reconfigured mainly in the courts. Muslim women challenged personal laws and practices on

---

[100] *Rameshchandra Rampratapji Daga v. Rameshwari Rameshchandra Daga*, AIR 2005 SC 422.

[101] Ibid., para 1.

[102] For Hindu customary divorce, see Livia Holden, 'Official Policies For (Un)official Customs: The Hegemonic Treatment of Hindu Divorce Customs by Dominant Legal Discourses', *The Journal of Legal Pluralism and Unofficial Law* 36, no. 49 (2004): 47–74. Holden's research shows a series of cases where consensual customary divorce under Hindu law can be manipulated and denied by the state to the detriment of women.

[103] Livia Holden, *Hindu Divorce: A Legal Anthropology* (London: Ashgate, 2016); Katherine Lemons, *Divorcing Traditions: Islamic Marriage Law and the Making of Indian Secularism* (Ithaca, NY: Cornell University Press, 2019).

multiple occasions. When constitutional arguments against customs failed, women challenged these practices as being incompatible with religion. Such an argument was made legible before the courts by showing that a practice that violates the central text of Islam then could not constitute an 'essential practice' of Islam.

Religious Challenges

In 2002, Parveen Akhtar in her petition argued that the Quran advocated for reconciliation before a divorce was made irrevocable, but this obligation was not incorporated in any statute, and further that *talaq-ul-biddat*, or triple *talaq*, was not a recognized form of divorce in the Quran but continued to be commonly practiced in India.[104] The petition challenged the arbitrariness with which divorce was effected, but argued that it violated not only the constitution but also the Quran. The petitioner sought redress in the language of 'women's right to freedom of religion' rather than seeking the containment of religion by constitutional remedies. The petition termed triple *talaq* a 'spiritual offence' rather than a constitutional one, and that the recognition of such a form of divorce interfered with the Muslim women's right to freedom of conscience and free profession, practice and propagation of religion as guaranteed by the constitution.

The petitioner, Parveen Akhtar, was a 27-year-old woman whose husband unilaterally divorced her through oral divorce or *talaq-ul-biddat*. In her strained marriage, Parveen had faced violence that included a forced abortion and she was humiliated for not bringing an adequate dowry. She further stated that she was compelled to leave her matrimonial home upon the inability of her parents to provide a 'scooter'[105] demanded by her in-laws. The husband refused to 'take-back' his wife arguing that an irrevocable unilateral *talaq* had been given.[106] The petitioner, Parveen, contended that the Shariat Application Act of 1937 incorrectly sanctioned a mode of *talaq* which was considered 'sinful' in Islam. Such a practice was not only injurious to human rights but also offended fundamental rights to equality,[107] against discrimination,[108] and to live with dignity[109] guaranteed by the constitution. In essence, the petition leaned on constitutional remedies to assist in the establishment and recognition of the true principles of Islam.

---

[104] *Parveen Akhtar v. Union of India*, 2003-1-LW370.
[105] A light, two-wheeled open motor vehicle.
[106] *Parveen Akhtar v. Union of India*, 2003-1-LW370.
[107] Constitution of India, Article 14, 'Equality before Law'.
[108] Article 15 of the constitution states that 'no person shall be discriminated against on the basis of religion, race, caste, sex or place of birth'.
[109] Constitution of India, Article 21. Protection of Life and Personal Liberty: No person shall be deprived of his life or personal liberty except according to procedure established by law.

The added respondents in the case were two NGOs, the Association for Women's Assistance and Security (AWAS) and Tamil Nadu Advocates Meelad Forum, both of which reiterated in their submissions that the triple *talaq* form of divorce not only rendered women destitute but was un-Islamic and anti-Quranic. The *Parveen Akhtar* judgment provided comprehensive citations for the condemnation of *talaq-ul-biddat*—a heretical or irregular form of divorce, from within Islam. The counsel for Parveen further introduced a report before the judges, authored by Sayeda Hamid, a member of the National Commission for Women (1997–2000),[110] which highlighted the particularly disempowered position of Indian Muslim women and that unilateral right of husbands to divorce often in practice did not even require the presence of the wife.[111] Parveen's counsel drew attention to a quote by Syed Ameer Ali,[112] who was a member of the judicial committee of the Privy Council, whose works on Islamic law had remained of great significance. In his book *Mohammadan Law*, 1914, he wrote:

> He [the Prophet] pronounced, 'talaq to be the most detestable before the Almighty God of all permitted things, for it prevented conjugal happiness and interfered with the proper bringing up of children.' ... *When it is borne in mind how intimately law and religion are connected in the Islamic system, it will be easy to understand the bearing of the words on the institution of divorce.*[113]

The plurality within Islam, apparent in the existence of different schools of Islamic jurisprudence and practice, the Hanafis, the Malikis, the Shafais, and the Shias, which had gone unacknowledged in the passage of the Muslim Women (Protection of Rights on Divorce) Act of 1986, was reasserted by civil society networks in the citations for the *Parveen Akhtar* petition.[114] The Shia and the Maliki did not recognize the validity of the *talaq-ul-biddat* while the Hanafi and the Shafai schools recognized a divorce in the *biddat* (wrongful innovation) form as valid,

---

[110] 'Voice of the Voiceless: Status of Muslim Women in India' by Syeda Saiyidain Hameed, March 2000, cited in *Parveen Akhtar v. Union of India*.

[111] The report highlighted how women were left stranded with children, while the husbands could utter the three words and abandon their families with impunity. In cases considered by the commission, they discovered that *talaq* was given over the telephone or communicated through a postcard.

[112] Syed Ameer Ali was a known jurist and scholar of Islam. For more on Ameer Ali, see C. A. Bayly, *Recovering Liberties: Indian Thought in the Age of Liberalism and Empire*, vol. 100 (Cambridge: Cambridge University Press, 2011), 243.

[113] Syed Ameer Ali, *Mohammedan Law*, 5th ed. (1914), 572, in *Parveen Akhtar v. Union of India*, 2003-1-LW370 (emphasis mine).

[114] *Parveen Akhtar v. Union of India*, 2003-1-LW370, para 14.

but they warned that 'in its commission, the man incurs a sin'.[115] A notably large section of Sunni Muslims, following the Ahl-e-Hadis or Salafi, also abstained from recognizing such a divorce as legitimate.[116]

The *Parveen Akhtar* judgment quoted from the book *Muhammadan Law*, authored by Faiz Badruddin Tyabji, the former vice chancellor of Aligarh Muslim University,[117] which suggested that the benchmark set by the Prophet was 'too novel', and people resorted to *talaq-ul-biddat* which eventually became acceptable in law but continued to be sinful.[118] The text claimed that in the second century, the Omeyyada monarchs interfered with the practice in order to circumvent the checks that the Prophet had imposed.[119] Parveen Akhtar's petition absolved Islam from the root of the problem and questioned the state's version of the law (as the Hindutva judgments had for Hinduism). It emphasized that inconsistencies in the reading of Islam occurred not just through misinterpretation but were also borne out of custom or practice. Importantly, the case also challenged the assumption of uniformity within Muslim personal laws. Thus, the cases invoked both religion and secular law to argue against the disadvantaged position of women.

While this discussion offered clarity on the disapproval of the idea of instantaneous divorce, the court concluded that there was a lack of evidence for an absolute ban on the practice of unilateral *talaq* within sources of Islamic law. This, the court observed, left scope for ambiguity since religious scriptures clarified the procedure of divorce for 'good' or a 'believing' Muslim, but a 'bad' Muslim could still, in practice, divorce his wife through triple *talaq*. This did not threaten a Muslim man's membership to the community, albeit earned its reprimand at the most. The statute did not embody the practice of a 'good' Muslim but indicated merely what was *permissible*. A 'bad Muslim' in the *Shah Bano* judgment was not allowed to deny maintenance to his wife; he could, however, the *Parveen Akhtar* judgment concluded, give triple *talaq*.

---

[115] Faiz Badruddin Tyabji, *Muhammadan Law*, 3rd ed. (1940), in the judgment *Parveen Akhtar v. Union of India*, 2003-1-LW370.

[116] Ibid.

[117] An Indian Civil Service officer who also later served as the vice chancellor of Aligarh Muslim University.

[118] Tyabji, *Muhammadan Law*, in the judgment *Parveen Akhtar v. Union of India*, 2003-1-LW370.

[119] The verse clearly indicates that divorce is to take place only when there is proven immorality committed. The wife is not to be driven from the home or to be allowed to go away unless 'they commit immorality'. See also Tahir Mahmood, *The Muslim Law of India* (Princeton: Law Book Co., 1980); and Tahir Mahmood, *Statutes of Personal Law in Islamic Countries: History, Texts and Analysis* (New Delhi: India and Islam Research Council, under an arrangement with [the] Centre for Advanced Socio-Legal Studies, 1995).

The *Parveen Akhtar* judgment also referred to a decision of the Jammu and Kashmir High Court in the case of *Ahmed Giri v. Mst. Begha*,[120] in which it was observed that *talaq-ul-biddat* was the most common form of divorce among Muslims in India.

The judgment also acknowledged and applauded the precedents set by the *Danial Latifi* and the *Shamim Ara* cases.[121] However, citing the *AWAG* judgment, the judgment conceded that creating a new legislation to ban triple *talaq* or amending the Shariat Application Act, 1937, to explicitly ban the practice, remained the prerogative of parliament. Therefore, on this occasion, the judge stopped short at an expression of 'regret' avoiding a confrontation with parliament, and the case was dismissed in 2003. Triple *talaq* repeatedly appeared before courts owing to genuine ambiguity that surrounded the oral divorce. And also because women's organizations continued to demand a ban on this form of divorce. These precedents generated significant public interest and to a large extent compensated for the lack of statutes on the subjects of family law, by plugging many loopholes. The BJP's repeated calls for a Uniform Civil Code as the 2004 general election loomed also contributed to popularizing these judgments which were then used by Hindu nationalists to seek uniformity and by many women's groups to show precisely the opposite—the lack of a need for parliamentary intervention.

Ruffling Feathers, Reclaiming Spaces

The AIMPLB faced considerable pressure from the chief opposition party as well as an increasing number of women, and women's rights organizations, that demanded reform. Although not a statutory body, the AIMPLB, by the 1990s and the early 2000s, boasted of being a representative body of almost 400 leaders of the community who claimed to enjoy significant legitimacy in the eyes of the community. Influential members of the AIMPLB such as Mirwaiz Maoulvi Farooq continued to insist that the *sharia* had divine sanction which 'no power on earth could change'.[122] Another senior member of the AIMPLB, Yusuf Muchhala, declared that the state needed to create an atmosphere of trust and dialogue

---

[120] *Ahmed Giri v. Mst. Begha* AIR 1955 J and K 1.

[121] See also *Yousuf Rawther v. Sowramma* AIR 1971 Ker 261, where the court held that

> since infallibility is not an attribute of the judiciary, the view has been ventured by Muslim jurists that the Indo-Anglian judicial exposition of the Islamic law of divorce has not exactly been just to the Holy Prophet or the Holy Book.... The view that the Muslim husband enjoys an arbitrary, unilateral power to inflict instant divorce does not accord with Islamic injunctions.

[122] 'Don't Change Laws on Talaq: Ulema Council', *Times of India*, 1 July 2004. See also 'Greater Empowerment of Muslim Women Is Our Goal', *Times of India*, 4 July 2004.

especially after the Gujarat riots of 2002.[123] He further suggested that religious autonomy was the only basis for potential reform. By 2003, the AIMPLB's delay in ratifying a model *nikahnama* resulted in several activists questioning the motives of the AIMPLB as well as its authority.[124] Activists such as Hasina Khan, who was then the coordinator of the NGO Awaaz-e-Niswaan, publicly condemned the AIMPLB, stating: 'If the clauses are alright from the religious point of view why hasn't the Nikahnama come into being ... that is because it never will. AIMPLB is a body that is patriarchal and conservative and does not believe in women's rights.'[125]

Sensing the pressure from these agitations, and the repeated mention of a Uniform Civil Code by the government, later the same year, the AIMPLB announced a nationwide agitation if triple *talaq* in a single sitting were to be made invalid through the law. Yusuf Muchhala reportedly said:

> The board was set up on the 70s ... primarily to protect Muslim Personal Law within the framework of Shariat at the same time usher in social reforms. It took initiative in the practice of doing away with dowry.... Now working towards greater empowerment of women.... We will not be discussing the 'talaqnama' at tomorrow's meeting, but Nikahnama.[126]

Thus, over time, it is noticeable that the AIMPLB was also not impervious to the sustained efforts of women's organizations and also began to accept minor reform or changes as an alternative to a Uniform Civil Code.[127] The AIMPLB repeatedly

[123] For a history of the Gujarat riots, see Asghar Ali Engineer, 'Gujarat Riots in the Light of the History of Communal Violence', *Economic and Political Weekly* 37, no. 50 (2002): 5047–54; and S. I. Wilkinson, 'Putting Gujarat in Perspective', *Economic and Political Weekly* 37, no. 17 (2002): 1579–83. For a journalistic account, see Siddharth Varadarajan, *Gujarat, the Making of a Tragedy* (New Delhi: Penguin Books, 2002).

[124] Shabnam Minwalla and Vaishnavi C. Sekhar, 'Feminists Now Split over Uniform Code: *Sunday Special*', *Times of India*, 27 July 2003.

[125] Radha Rajadhyaksha, 'Instant Triple Talaq Only Practiced in India', TNN Mumbai, 25 July 2003.

[126] 'Model Nikahnama', *Times of India*, 26 December 2004.

[127] 'Triple Talaq to Go Out Softly: Muslim Personal Law Board to Launch Campaign Against "Social Evil"', *Times of India*, 5 July 2004. See also 'Introspection Uniformly Needed: Legally Speaking, Armin Wandrewala', *Times of India*, 12 August 2003. Although the Uniform Civil Code featured regularly in print debates, the discussion in parliament on the subject was never formally attempted. As scholarship of the early 2000s suggests, feminist writing in the period remained divided over a Uniform Civil Code and the code continued to be viewed by some as a secular idea and not wholly a Hindu nationalist ploy.

argued that *talaq* in one sitting ought to be discouraged, but maintained that the third pronouncement was final and binding. The AIMPLB and local women's activists particularly in Maharashtra and UP wrote, sanctioned, and debated *nikahnama*s and the *talaqnama*s in the period. English dailies and select Urdu newspapers reported regularly on the exchanges between them.

Bombay, now Mumbai, remained the hot-bed for social movements since the 1970s. Popular figures of the film industry, theatre, and media also aided in keeping the agenda in the public eye by offering vocal support for codifying or reforming Muslim personal law. The organization Secular Muslim Democracy[128] hosted influential Muslim figures from the film industry such as Javed Akhtar, Shabana Azmi,[129] Ishaq Jhamkanwala,[130] and Javed Anand, who positioned themselves against the Sangh Parivar as well as the Muslim extremists. Their statements were carried in news dailies particularly towards the latter half of 2003 and conveyed a confrontational stance against the BJP.[131] In public gatherings, the activists also announced that '[w]e are here to call the bluff of imams and mullahs',[132] adding to the internal challenge against the clergy. Thus, a pro-intervention but anti-BJP stance was gaining ground. These public articulations separating personal law reform from Hindu nationalism's commitment to a Uniform Civil Code were particularly relevant in light of the impending election of 2004, where in the BJP's election manifesto, a Uniform Civil Code and Ram Temple at Ayodhya came jointly.

By 2004, the BJP suffered an electoral loss and the newly elected government, the United Progressive Alliance, with the Congress Party at its helm, made a significant

---

[128] This included many members of the erstwhile Muslim Satyashodhak Samaj and the Indian Secular Society introduced in Chapter 3.

[129] At the end of her tenure as a member of parliament, former actress Shabana Azmi went on record to support the Uniform Civil Code pointing to personal laws such as triple *talaq*, polygamy, and unfair property distribution created the recognition of the 'Hindu undivided family' as discriminatory. Karishma Upadhyay, '"Misfit" Who Turned a Firebrand MP: At the End of Her Tenure, Shabana Azmi Goes Down Memory Lane', *Times of India*, 23 August 2003.

[130] 'Revolution behind the Veil', *The Hindu*, 27 May 2001. Dr Ishaq Jamkhanwala, an educationist and member of the Maharashtra Legislative Assembly from the Janata Party, recommended that a draft of the code may be circulated to 'all religious heads and intellectuals'. Jamkhanawala assumed the presidency of the organization Anjuman-i-Islam in 1983. He introduced reforms in the institution which included the introduction of job-oriented courses which helped in gaining employment in vocational, medical, and engineering spheres.

[131] 'Ghetto to Mainstream: Emergence of the Modern Muslim', *Times of India*, 22 September 2003.

[132] 'We Are Here to Call the Bluff of the Imams and Mullahs', *Times of India*, 3 October 2003.

intervention by instituting the Sachar Committee for reviewing the status of Muslims in India.[133] This proved to be one of the most meaningful inquiries into the status of Muslims in India and until date remains an oft-cited report. It was the first to link economic deprivation and lack of education to sustained political marginalization and wilful neglect of minorities by the state authorities.

With the fear of the imposition of a Uniform Civil Code allayed with the change in regime, the unified opposition against the code, which was encashed by the AIMPLB, also began to crumble. This was visible in the breaking of the AIMPLB which lost political mileage and relevance after their core opponent's— the BJP's—electoral loss. In 2005, the AIMPLB split into Shia and Sunni groups and the All India Muslim Women's Personal Law Board (AIMWPLB) was also founded in the same year.[134] In 2007, the BMMA was co-founded by Zakia Soman and Noorjehan Safia Niaz.[135] Both women had begun work in relief camps following the Gujarat riots in 2002.

The BMMA and AIMWPLB emerged as organizations that worked on the reinterpretation of Muslim personal law, in 'light of the Quran'. The BMMA, which has been identified by Tschalaer in her incisive analysis[136] as a 'secular' women's organization, was indeed secular when it came to the strategies for empowerment and the relationship with the law. But the organization was also unapologetic in its commitment to reclaiming religion from orthodoxy, and did not view religion as an oppressive force but as essential for the self-realization of an individual.[137] The new religious-women's movements seized this opportunity to wrest out religious texts from the orthodoxy as well as the government, in an attempt to recover 'true' religion for protecting women's rights. This decentralization of religious authority itself occasionally borrowed 'constitutional' language to argue for religious rights. The BMMA, in fact, began its women's *sharia adalat*s in response to the multiple such all-male non-state forums, *adalat*s or *dar-ul-qaza*, which were already in place for adjudicating disputes in Muslim personal law. Organizations such as the MWRN (1998) and the BMMA (2007) differed

---

[133] Sachar Committee Report, 2006, Nehru Memorial Museum and Library, New Delhi. The report was announced in 2004 and formally commissioned in 2005.

[134] For splits in the AIMPLB, see Justin Jones, '"Signs of Churning": Muslim Personal Law and Public Contestation in Twenty-first Century India', *Modern Asian Studies* 44, no. 1 (2010): 175–200.

[135] BMMA is an Indian Muslim women's organization in India. The organization is based in Mumbai. It released a draft bill on 23 June 2014, 'Muslim Marriage and Divorce Act' recommending that polygamy be made illegal in Muslim personal law of India.

[136] Mengia Hong Tschalaer, *Muslim Women's Quest for Justice: Gender, Law and Activism in India* (New Delhi: Cambridge University Press, 2017).

[137] 'Why Should Women Have to Leave the Fold to Get Rights?', *Indian Express*, 27 June 2016.

in their approach towards addressing discrimination against women. The MWRN (and later the Bebaak Collective) maintained that by routing rights through religion and religious texts, it was impossible to challenge some of the assumptions and stereotypes that were prevalent in religious or cultural myths and legends. On the other hand, the BMMA illustrated that to address the cause of Muslim women—a minority within a minority—distance from religion, or abandonment of religion in favour of abstract rights could be an unreasonable expectation.[138]

The idea of the representation of the members of a community through personal law, therefore, became more complex in the 2000s when the state could no longer steer these conversations effectively through legislations produced after closed-door consultations. *Sharia adalats, dar-ul-qazas, mahila adalats,* or family courts continued to grant divorces, determine maintenance, assist with maintenance claims or return of the *mahr,* and so on, which is discussed in the final chapter. The courts too were slowly becoming more decisive in judgments rather than containing their distress over discriminatory practices as 'observations' or pushing law reform towards parliament.

With the BJP's return to power in the 2014 election, the emphasis on a Uniform Civil Code was renewed. This time the BJP held substantial strength in parliament and again repeated its promises of a Uniform Civil Code and a Ram Temple at Ayodhya. The Uniform Civil Code became a part of household vocabulary and the debate entered school classrooms and dominated social media and television prime-time debates. Civil society movements which worked from the peripheries in the 1980s and 1990s now found themselves hounded for interviews by TV channels, and the AIMPLB found itself cornered in this trial by the media. The work of multiple non-state forums had also allowed for the emergence of multiple versions of Islamic law, and while it was possible to locate the textual sources, the non-textual interpretations of the Hadees came from diverse sources. National dailies carried a series of opinion pieces on the various meanings and interpretations of the Quran and the constitution on the question of Muslim divorce.

In 2015, the Narendra Modi–led BJP government mandated the 21st Law Commission of India to produce a report on a Uniform Civil Code. Although initially favouring a Uniform Civil Code, the Law Commission began to lean towards the codification of personal laws soon after it began consultations with religious organizations, women's groups, lawyers, and select Muslim politicians. A number of women's rights organizations, such as the Forum Against Oppression

---

[138] Women's organizations and religious feminism is discussed in the next chapter.

of Women, the Association for Advocacy and Legal Initiatives, Majlis, the BMMA, the Bebaak Collective, the People for Law and Development, Labia, Saheli, Jagori, among many others, corresponded with the commission. Despite their varying positions on intervention in Muslim personal law, these organizations collectively voiced their rejection of a Uniform Civil Code. However, before the Law Commission of India formally rejected a Uniform Civil Code in favour of personal law reform, in 2018, the issue of triple *talaq* and *nikah halala* had once again reached the Supreme Court.

Triple *talaq* was finally set aside in 2017, in the *Shayara Bano v. Union of India*.[139] Shayara Bano, a 35-year-old woman from the northern state of Uttarakhand and a mother of two, was divorced by her husband Rizwan Ahmed through triple *talaq*. After enduring more than a decade of violence and torture in her marriage, it was the separation from her two children that led Shayara Bano to challenge the arbitrary pronouncement of divorce by her husband. Shayara Bano's petition was joined by both the BMMA and the Bebaak Collective. These organizations were simultaneously responding to the Law Commission's call for suggestions on the amendment to Muslim personal law. The BMMA had sent in extensive survey material to the commission to evidence how common Shayara Bano's story was. In the course of the consultation process with the Law Commission, the BMMA and the Bebaak Collective expressed a desire for the codification of Muslim family law, but they also distanced themselves categorically from the ruling party. In court, however, with the central government, and members of the BJP joining Shayara Bano's petition, both these organizations reluctantly occupied the same position on legal intervention as the BJP. Thus, the activism routed through courts comes with limitations. The courts in their very structuring of any dispute in legal form require two recognizable sides—the petitioner and the respondent. When political agendas and social causes were both routed through the judiciary, the appropriation of social issues by the state was enabled in the binary framing of the dispute.

In court, on the opposing side, the AIMPLB, the Jamat-e-Ulema-e-Hind, and Jamaat-e-Islami Hind (JIH) also joined Shayara Bano's husband and they were represented by a leading lawyer from the Congress Party, Kapil Sibal. Thus, even while the Congress distanced itself from the practice of triple *talaq*, in public perception they occupied the side of the AIMPLB and the JIH. Prominent academics and politicians, Indira Jaising, Anand Grover, Arif Mohammad Khan, Salman Khurshid, Flavia Agnes, Kapil Sibal, and in various capacities of joint petitioners, *amicus curae* (friends of the court) or directly as lawyers for the parties

---

[139] *Shayara Bano v. Union of India* (2017) 9 SCC 1.

or the state all argued before the court. Every minute of the six-day hearing was reported live on all media channels.

The 298 page-long judgment ended with a one-line order: 'In view of the different opinions recorded, by a majority of 3:2 the practice of "talaq-e-biddat"— triple talaq is set aside.'[140] The judgment was largely hailed as a 'historic' one, but earned criticism for not engaging with feminist jurisprudence in settling a question of women's rights, nor did it, from the point of view of the law, resolve the core contradictions between religious personal law regimes and fundamental rights guaranteed under the constitution.[141] Unsurprisingly, the court delivered the 'safest' possible order on the limited question of triple *talaq* without entering into the intricacies of the constitutional stand-off between the 'right to equality' and the 'right to freedom of religion'. The court, quoting extensively from the *Shamim Ara* and *Parveen Akhtar* judgments, ruled that the practice was 'arbitrary' and 'bad in theology' and, therefore, bad in (personal) law, that is, drawn from such theological considerations.

It appeared as though the court agreed on an outcome and found reasons rooted in religion to support it. The minority judgment was even more perplexing as Justice Khehar and Justice Nasser first established the inviolability of personal law citing its protection from interference guaranteed under fundamental rights and then sought its amendment through legislation.[142] The judgment, however, led to a celebration within and outside court. The AIMPLB went on record to say that the judgment was 'not against' Muslims and they would not oppose it so long as there was no further interference in the matter. This was in sharp contrast with their 2004 stance when the AIMPLB had promised an all-India agitation if triple *talaq* was tampered with. The AIMPLB also, after their initial boycott of the Law Commission, initiated correspondence with it in 2018. They sent detailed references to the Law Commission on how the practice of triple *talaq* is discouraged in the Quran, but insisted on accepting the finality and irreversibility of the third oral pronouncement.[143]

Within months of the judgment, a BJP leader, Ashwini Kumar Upadhyay, filed a petition against the Muslim practices of polygamy and *nikah halala*, which

---

140 Order of the court in ibid.
141 Saptarshi Mandal, 'Out of Shah Bano's Shadow: Muslim Women's Rights and the Supreme Court's Triple Talaq Verdict', *Indian Law Review* 2, no. 1 (2018): 89–107.
142 For a critique of the judgment, see 'Triple Talaq Verdict: Wherein Lies the Much Hailed Victory?', *The Wire*, 28 August 2017.
143 The AIMPLB's submission to the Law Commission of India during a consultation held on 13 February 2017.

was clubbed with two other petitions of Muslim women challenging the same.[144] Thus, the connectedness of party politics to sustained campaigns by the women's groups in these petitions only demonstrates that the courts were instrumental to multiple campaigns. The court room remained a meaningful space for debates on Muslim personal law and was accessed readily and repeatedly by Muslim women. While Hindu law could evolve from precedent to legislation, Muslim personal law moved only from precedent to precedent. This did not, however, mean that Muslim jurisprudence in India was more passive but simply conveyed that substantive conversations on Muslim personal law had to take place largely in arenas other than the legislature. Court rooms, covertly and overtly, made religion contestable. They generated unintended consequences such as encouraging campaigns for religious reforms among the clergy, or taking the wind out of potential legislative interventions by settling controversial matters in courts. The court's potential to generate bombastic observations but benign orders ensured that not only could social movements pin their hopes on the judiciary but even governments began to push election promises through courts, provoking scholarly scepticism over the court's populist interventions.

III

'Court'ing Politics

The Indian Supreme Court has attracted substantial scholarship and pronounced criticism in recent years.[145] Sathe's work on judicial activism provides an account

---

[144] Writ Petition (Civil) No. 202 of 2018. See *Sameena Begum v. Union of India* Writ Petition(s) (Civil) No(s). 222/2018, para 57 of the petition, which stated:

> The Constitution makers wanted to establish a 'Secular State' and with that purpose they codified the Article 25(1) which guaranteed freedom of religion, freedom of conscience and freedom to profess, practice and propagate religion, to all persons. But at the same time they sought to distinguish between the essence of a religion and other secular activities, which might be associated with religious practice but yet did not form a part of the core of the religion, and with this end in view they inserted Clause 2(a) as thus: 'Nothing in this Article shall affect the operation of any existing law or prevent the State from making any law regulating or restricting any economic, financial, political or other secular activities, which may be associated with religious practices.'

[145] Anuj Bhuwania, *Courting the People: Public Interest Litigation in Post-Emergency India*, vol. 2 (New Delhi: Cambridge University Press, 2017); Tarunabh Khaitan, '*Koushal v. Naz:* Judges Vote to Recriminalise Homosexuality', *The Modern Law Review* 78, no. 4 (2015): 672–80; Pratap Bhanu Mehta, 'India's Unlikely Democracy: The Rise of Judicial Sovereignty', *Journal of Democracy* 18, no. 2 (2007): 70–83; and Baxi, 'Taking Suffering Seriously'.

of how the Supreme Court has historically also helped maintain the separation of political parties in the majority, and the governments they constitute, to the extent that it has found itself accused of judicial overreach.[146] For instance, in the *Aruna Roy v. Union of India*[147] case in 2002, the court stalled the BJP government's attempt to introduce changes to the secondary school syllabus in order to include a more Hindu-inflected interpretation of history. The court held that such recommendations would offend Article 28(3)[148] of the constitution, which provided that educational institutions recognized or aided by the state could not subject their students to any religious instruction or worship without the consent of their guardians. However, the idea that the judiciary in recent years assumed the role of the watchdog over an uncertain or insincere executive is no longer unchallenged. Mehta takes the view that often the principles on which the judiciary asserts its authority and independence such as 'basic structure', or 'separation of powers', and 'public interest' are far too abstract and therefore have been inconsistently applied: 'Many of the high principles that the Supreme Court invokes are more like dice throws in a judicial roulette.'[149]

The Indian Supreme Court while vacillating between absorbing the populist and liberal sentiment shows it picks its vulnerable minorities worthy of protection selectively. In the *Naz v. Koushal*[150] case, the court recriminalized homosexuality arguing that repealing the law is a legislative prerogative and the criminalization of homosexuality under Article 377 affects a 'miniscule minority'.[151] The same court, however, intervened to set aside the practice of triple *talaq*—even though this is indeed a relatively rare procedure for divorce. Finally, when the Supreme Court did decriminalize homosexuality in a much celebrated judgment in 2018,[152] it emphasized the acceptance of sexual diversity within Hinduism, complete

---

[146] Satyaranjan Purushottam Sathe, *Judicial Activism in India*, vol. 2 (New Delhi: Oxford University Press, 2002).

[147] *Aruna Roy v. Union of India* (2002) 7 SCC 368.

[148] Article 28(3) provides that: No person attending any educational institution recognised by the State or receiving aid out of State funds shall be required to take part in any religious instruction that may be imparted in such institution or to attend any religious worship that may be conducted in such institution or in any premises attached thereto unless such person or, if such person is a minor, his guardian has given his consent thereto.

[149] P. B. Mehta, 'The Indian Supreme Court and the Art of Democratic Positioning', in *Unstable Constitutionalism: Law and Politics in South Asia*, ed. M. Khosla (Cambridge: Cambridge University Press, 2015), 260.

[150] *Suresh Kumar Koushal v. Naz Foundation* (2014) 1 SCC 1.

[151] See also Khaitan 'Koushal v. Naz'. The ruling was reversed on 6 September 2018, and consensual sex between same-sex individuals was decriminalized in the judgment *Navtej Singh Johar v. Union of India*, 2018 (1) SCC 791, Writ Petition (Criminal) No. 76 of 2016.

[152] *Navtej Singh Johar v. Union of India*, 2018 (1) SCC 791.

with references to the figure of 'Shikhandi' from the Hindu epic Mahabharata; squarely pinning the criminalization of homosexuality on colonial-Christian morality.[153] Therefore, in its attempt to reach just outcomes through progressive interpretations, the courts have often reiterated that the ideas of justice are anchored in religious morality or at least find some translation in religion. Further, bowing to what Bhuwania recognizes as 'neoliberal sensibilities', the court has also embodied the numerically weak urban elite's urge to inhabit a clean, smart city through recent PILs filed in relation to issues such as the removal of hawkers and vendors, cleaning the streets, and saving heritage buildings.[154] The court's ability to absorb contestation and yield faster outcomes than legislation also undercut the party politics surrounding personal law.

The inability to confirm judicial leanings in any predictable way also indicates that judicial rulings may be an embodiment of the will of the judge.[155] The court encouraged a 'broader' interpretation of Muslim personal law for granting maintenance to divorced wives in the *Bai Tahira*[156] and *Fazlunbi*[157] cases. But in the *triple talaq*[158] case, the court again took a 'narrower' view of Islam to conclude that triple *talaq* was a customary-arbitrary practice that is not an essential part of Islam. In fact, triple *talaq* was held to be violating the fundamental right to equality not because of the content of the law but because the practice was 'arbitrary'. In both cases, it ultimately made progressive interventions to mitigate if not eliminate discrimination. Thus, the courts also absorbed demands for reform that the legislature was unlikely or unwilling to act on.

Mullaly's insightful piece on women's rights in Pakistan provides a story that makes interesting parallels with the Indian case.[159] The Supreme Court of Pakistan has also routinely overturned high court judgments that struck down many of the provisions of the Muslim Personal Law Ordinance for their incompatibility with Islam as the Indian court did in the case of triple

---

[153] Jason Keith Fernandez, 'Cassandra at the Feast: Interrogating the Freedoms of Gay Liberation in India' ('Shaping Law, Shaping Gender: Experiences from India' workshop, Humboldt University, Berlin, October 2018), 11–13.

[154] Bhuwania, *Courting the People*.

[155] See Upendra Baxi, *The Indian Supreme Court and Politics* (Lucknow: Eastern Book Co., 1980); Jacobsohn, *The Wheel of Law*, chs. 5–7; and Mehta, 'The Indian Supreme Court and the Art of Democratic Positioning'. Chapter 3 of this book notes that in Muslim personal law, in particular, Justice Krishna Iyer's judgments offered some decisive interpretations of religious law.

[156] *Bai Tahira A v. Ali Hussain Fissali Chothia*, 1979 AIR 362.

[157] *Fazlunbi Biwi v. K. Khader Vali*, AIR 1980 SC 173.

[158] *Shayara Bano v. Union of India* (2017) 9 SCC 1.

[159] Siobhan Mullally, '"As Nearly as May Be": Debating Women's Human Rights in Pakistan', *Social and Legal Studies* 14, no. 3 (2005): 341–58.

talaq and maintenance cases. Pakistan's Supreme Court warned against the 'euphoria of instant Islamisation'.[160] In 1999, in *Humaira Mehmood v. State*,[161] the Lahore High Court decided in favour of a woman who married a spouse of her own choosing, whose parents had moved court against her under the Zina (illicit sexual relations) ordinance. The Lahore High Court concluded that Islam protects a woman's right to freely contract her marriage, and a coerced marriage had no legal validity. In another case, the same high court issued a firm sentence against a man who murdered his daughter, her husband, and their child in the name of protecting the honour of his family, and the court once again affirmed that both Islam and the constitution protect women's right to freely contract a marriage and convicted her father of murder. A 'Commission of Inquiry' that followed also emphasized the grave human rights violations against women and in particular of killings in the name of family honour. Yet Pakistan's Senate—the upper house—refused to pass a resolution to condemn the murders of women in the name of honour.

Much like the Indian case, the courts in certain ways have offered quicker solutions to issues that representative legislative bodies hesitate to debate. However, the court's self-proclaimed reformist agendas have also meant that political parties lean on the courts for the fulfilment of political promises as much as social movements do. The BJP, since it came to power in 2014, has systematically taken a judicial route in order to propagate its political and historical narrative, and for the fulfilment of election promises that could not be granted through legislative endeavours. Its first major promise was that of a Uniform Civil Code and yet no debate was initiated on a Uniform Civil Code in parliament. The government instead became a co-petitioner in the *Shayara Bano* case. The government's participation in the hearing became yet another way to delegate to the judiciary the troubling contradictions of religious personal laws and the courts continue to reiterate the need for a Uniform Civil Code.

Thus, the BJP's vocal opposition to polygamy among Muslims is not presented before parliament, where it may need to confront the fact that polygamy among Hindus remains higher in absolute numbers;[162] instead, party members now tie themselves (often as a joint petitioner) to Muslim women's existing petitions before the court. The court's intervention on a religious practice is then usurped by the party members involved in the case. Cherry-picking the ambiguities and disparities in family law, with a targeted focus on minority law, the BJP camouflages the Hindutva agenda as a secular response to religious dogma.

---

[160] Ibid., 350.

[161] *Humaira Mehmood v. State PLD* (1999) Lahore 494.

[162] 'Muslim Women and the Surprising Facts about Polygamy in India', *Scroll.in*, 24 June 2018.

In 2014, the BJP politician Subramaniam Swamy wrote a letter to Prime Minister Narendra Modi seeking a day-to-day urgent hearing on the matter of the Ram Temple.[163] The hearing was a dramatic one, where the counsels for the Babri Masjid Action Committee demanded that the case be heard by a larger bench of five to seven judges and that the court must explain why it is yielding to the demand of an 'urgent hearing' timed conveniently before the Indian states of Gujarat and Himachal Pradesh went into election in 2017. The BJP's insistence on judicial pronouncement on the matter betrays the legislative inability to resolve the dispute. On 9 November 2019, the Supreme Court allowed for the reconstruction of a Ram Temple in Ayodhya, allocating a separate piece of land for the reconstruction of a mosque. The decision hugely benefitted the ruling party (the BJP) as one of its primary election promises was yielded by the court.

The court's overt engagement with religion, however, in translating the Quran, assessing Lord Ram's claim over his birthplace, temple entry, among others,[164] also wrested out religion from the monopoly of the clergy. In lending currency to Hindutva and admitting alternate interpretations of the Quran, the courts did not merely respond to regime change or social activism, but also decentralized religious authority. The authority to determine the constitutional basis for religious demands rather than becoming vested within the state apparatus was transferred to political actors or even mobs.

Hadiya and the Love-Wars of Contemporary India

The court's dealing of the *Hadiya* case is a particularly significant example of political battles played out in courts. The case illustrated that even small victories and ostensibly favourable orders for women are a result of disproportionately hard-fought battles. In Hadiya's case, the conversion of a Hindu girl to Islam and her subsequent marriage to a Muslim man became reworded as a threat not only to Hinduism but also to national security in the national press, as the State government suspected that conversion was part of a recruitment mission by the Islamic State.[165] Hadiya (formerly Akhila Ashokan), a 23-year-old girl, married Shefin Jahan, a Muslim. In 2017, the Kerala High Court asked Hadiya to return to her parents who petitioned that she had been forcibly converted to Islam through

---

[163] 'Subramanian Swamy Writes to PM Modi, Seeks Early Hearing in Ayodhya Case', NDTV, 13 January 2016.

[164] Sabrimala temple entry case, *Indian Young Lawyers Association v. the State of Kerala*, Writ Petition (Civil) No. 373 of 2006 on 28 September 2018.

[165] 'Now, NIA to Probe Hadiya's Husband Shefin Jahan for Terror Links', *India Today*, 6 January 2018.

her marriage to Shefin Jahan. The petition originally filed by Hadiya's father stated that her conversion was part of a 'well orchestrated and well oiled scheme'. The petition stated:

> It is submitted that the Applicant has also been following media reports of similar cases from India and various other countries where young and vulnerable girls are identified and trapped by coercion or fraud marriages, indoctrinated and used for the purpose of propagating terrorist and anti-national activities of Jihad.[166]

Hadiya, however, pleaded that she had converted to Islam years before her marriage, and she and Jahan had married by their own free will. The Supreme Court initially responded to Jahan's desperate appeal to reunite with his wife by ordering a probe by the National Investigation Agency (NIA) to look into forced conversions to investigate the suspected links of these conversions to the Islamic state.[167] Although the court ultimately decided in favour of the couple's right to freely contract a marriage and upheld Hadiya's wilful conversion to Islam, the case was used by a number of Hindu nationalist organizations to demonstrate the threat of Islamization through 'love-jihad', and she was counselled by Hindu leaders about the dangers of conversion.[168] Outside court, the question of forced conversion of Hindu women to Islam began to dominate the media. Hadiya's family found themselves surrounded by the media and a Hindu activist controversially also released footage of Hadiya arguing with her parents in her house, and popularized his recordings as the 'love-jihad' tapes. Hadiya was eventually allowed by the court to cohabit with her husband against her parents will, when the NIA probe found no links between her conversion to Islam and sympathy for the Islamic State of Iraq and Syria (ISIS). In its oddly worded defence for personal liberty, the Supreme Court observed:

> Rainbow is described by some as the autograph of the Almighty and lightning, albeit metaphorically, to be the expression of cruelty of otherwise equanimous 'Nature'. Elaborating the comparison in conceptual essentiality, it can be said that when the liberty of a person is illegally smothered and strangulated and his/her choice is throttled by the State or a private person, the signature of life melts and living becomes a bare subsistence.[169]

---

[166] *Shafin Jahan v. KM Ashokan and Ors* AIR 2018 SC 1933.
[167] 'Now, NIA to Probe Hadiya's Husband Shefin Jahan for Terror Links', *India Today*, 6 January 2018.
[168] 'No One Forced Me to Convert, Want to Go with My Husband: Hadiya', *India Today*, 25 November 2017.
[169] *Shafin Jahan v. KM Ashokan and Ors* AIR 2018 SC 1933.

The judgment was celebrated as the court's support for 'love' over hate. Here, even though the secular provision of the Special Marriage Act was never used, the couple's marriage became a symbol of freedom and secularism. Senior lawyer Kapil Sibal, a prominent face of the chief opposition party, the Indian National Congress, represented Shefin Jahan. The ruling party, the BJP, on the other hand, continues to have close ties with the organizations such as the Hindu Mahasabha as well as the RSS, which campaign against love-jihad, and the party benefits directly from the panic over forced conversions to Islam. The following year, in 2019, two BJP-led governments in the states of UP and Madhya Pradesh introduced laws criminalizing religious conversion for the purpose of marriage.

Interestingly, Hadiya's husband filed for 'restitution of conjugal rights', a provision that was not codified under Muslim personal law, but under Section 22 in the Special Marriage Act, 1954, to seek the return of his wife who was being held captive by her parents.[170] Restitution of conjugal rights has long been opposed by women's groups and there are petitions seeking for the section to be struck down for its frequent and deliberate misuse to force wives to cohabit with their husbands.[171] This is a particularly potent tool deployed by men against wives who leave their abusive marital homes and seek maintenance from their husbands. Demanding the return of wives through restitution of conjugal rights is often aimed precisely at denying maintenance claims. Yet, in this case, the provision is put to innovative use to recognize the validity of marriage and subsequently the right to cohabit arising out of that. Hadiya's reunion with her husband became the face of the triumph of love over religious hate and, more importantly, of the court upholding women's right to choose their own partner (Figure 5.1). The case also showed that the court remained a space for staging religious, gender, and political conflict.

---

[170] Restitution of conjugal rights—When either the husband or the wife has, without reasonable excuse, withdrawn from the society of the other, the aggrieved party may apply by petition to the district court for restitution of conjugal rights, and the court, on being satisfied of the truth of the statements made in such petition, and that there is no legal ground why the application should not be granted, may decree restitution of conjugal rights accordingly. [Explanation—Where a question arises whether there has been reasonable excuse for withdrawal from the society, the burden of proving reasonable excuse shall be on the person who has withdrawn from the society.] Restitution of conjugal rights is contained in Section 9 of the Hindu Marriage Act of 1955, Section 22 of the Special Marriage Act of 1954, and Order 21, Rules 32 and 33 of the Code of Civil Procedure, 1908.

[171] A PIL petition was filed by two law students again in 2019, challenging the restitution of conjugal rights. The petition stated that the provision forced women to cohabit with their estranged husbands.

Figure 5.1 Hadiya demands state relief (15 May 2018)

Source: *Deccan Chronicle*, 15 May 2018.

Conclusion

Court decisions were significant as they aided the consolidation of women's demands towards the codification of personal law and against uniformity; this became steadily more pronounced towards the second decade of the 2000s. It can be argued that the courts learnt to thrive on the ambiguity produced by the personal law regime in order to consolidate their position as a 'liberal' institution within the structure of the state. The courts found ingenious ways to move towards a more liberal interpretation of personal law which began to obliterate the need to unify family law as the interpretations of different personal laws became increasingly uniform. Such judgments had the potential to transform litigants and the law, and produce modern interpretations of religion. Civil society initiatives, in particular women's rights groups, gradually took to popularizing alternate interpretations of religious texts because the court had begun admitting these interpretations into lengthy judgments.[172] This contributed towards the decentralization of the divorce law as the court conceded to changes desired by the litigants (who were often supported by activists and academics).

---

[172] For a study of the law's influence on litigants in colonial India, see also the discussion on Dirk's study, 'From Little King to Landlord: Property, Law, and the Gift under the Madras Permanent Settlement', *Comparative Studies in Society and History* 28, no. 2 (1986): 307–33; Brimnes, 'Beyond Colonial Law'; in Eleanor Newbigin, Leigh Denault, and Rohit De, 'Personal Law, Identity Politics and Civil Society in Colonial South Asia', *Indian Economic and Social History Review* 46, no. 1 (2009): 3.

Non-binding observations by the court can promise much more than they can deliver. The reformist role occupied by the courts has often meant that the court reserves its distaste and condemnation for violence, communalism, and sexism in 'observations' but hesitates from pronouncing direct orders on controversial matters—as in the case of Hindutva judgments, the *Parveen Akhtar* case, and the Ayodhya decision. In its dealings with religion, whether towards a liberal or a fundamentalist end, the court has allowed the sabotage of constitutional secularism. In the Hindutva judgments, it accepted Hinduism as an inherently 'secular' religion.

The growing currency of Hindu nationalism and the lack of statutes covering Muslim personal law collectively contributed to compromising Muslim women's access to legislative reform of Muslim personal law and they looked instead to the judiciary. Limited legislative intervention and later a majoritarian government engendered new engagement between people and the state over religion through the courts. The courts, on their part, did occasionally enter nuanced debates on Islam and entertained a greater diversity of sources than parliament had ventured into. While some judgments aligned existing personal law statutes with women's demands (*Danial Latifi*), others aligned religion with constitutional law (*Shayara Bano*). The petitions the court entertained offered arguments in defence of religion, of secularism, of supremacy of religious texts, and of constitutional rights.

This lack of a pattern has to be understood with reference to the various influencers and users of the law that participate in the court room. The individual will of the judge, the popularity of the lawyer, the media coverage of the case, and the organizations behind the petitioners go into the making of a judgment. Many of these cases were supported by NGOs, symbolizing a collective push for reform by civil society initiatives and the court's endorsement of that position only served to supplement that plea. In many cases, the government became a party, and in others, lawyer-members of political parties took up controversial matters to debate in court against political opponents. With the increased expectation of reconciling religiosity with women's rights, self-proclaimed upholders of religious law (consolidated under the JIH and the AIMPLB) were under pressure to revise their position in order to be able to continue to wield their influence over the community. Acknowledging this chaos allows also for a critique of legal scholarship which delves into judgments as though they dramatically altered situations, attempting to find patterns where none may exist. This chapter, while acknowledging the vibrant spectacles of a court room, remains sceptical of focussing exclusively on petitions and judgments so as to not overemphasize the finality of the judgment or the potentiality of the petition.

The centrality that personal law acquired in the political domain forced stakeholders to engage in public dialogue on the role of religion and the state in determining women's rights within family law. The state in its attempt to regulate the private life of citizens through the law generated greater flexibility than fixity.[173] Bina Agarwal, Rina Verma Williams, and Scott Alan Kugle have argued in colonial and post-colonial contexts that customs when granted the status of a 'law' through legislation or court precedent could thwart innovation and promote standardization, which could universalize rather than undermine patriarchy. But this argument presumes standardization in the state's behaviour, which does not account for the deviations in state law caused by regime change, institutional disagreements, social movements, events, will of presiding judges, and so forth. The fast turnover between demand and decision, and public protest and law, should allow us to open up the debate on the frailty of state law and innovations in its use. This innovation is exhibited in evolving precedents, and translating laws to non-state forums, where categories of the law, such as religious, scriptural, customary, and statutory, overlap.

Judicial interventions were deeply embedded in the social and political context of the time. Precedents provided more than 'case by case' solutions, but enabled conversations between unlikely parties and produced co-petitioners that made strange bedfellows. The next chapter discusses how many of the invested actors in the personal law debate remained deeply divided on the very idea of legal intervention in family law.

---

[173] Menski, *Hindu Law*; Werner Menski, *Modern Indian Family Law* (Richmond: Curzon Press, 2001); Jeffery Redding, 'Secularism, the Rule of Law, and Sharia Courts: An Ethnographic Examination of a Constitutional Controversy', *Louis ULJ* 57 (2012): 339.

6

From the Courtroom to the Courtyard
The Public Life of Personal Law, 2000–Present

Social movements have historically demanded a change in law, in the hope that social change will eventually follow. In India, however, in many ways the nature of social activism, gender and party politics has overturned the Benthamite notion that 'better laws make better societies', particularly towards the turn of the twenty-first century. Innovations outside the law preceded the law and were slowly absorbed by legal institutions in the form of encouraging judgments, commission and committee reports, or hasty legislative interventions. This became especially palpable with activism around Muslim personal law where non-state institutions had already begun to successfully challenge and counter certain forms of discrimination against Muslim women which was only confirmed by the court later.[1] Similarly, the idea that a Uniform Civil Code would be a solution to familial patriarchy had largely been rejected by many strands of the Indian women's movement after considerable debate in the early 2000s. This scepticism over a Uniform Civil Code was established years before the 21st Law Commission of India finally acknowledged that a uniform code may not yield just outcomes for women, in a consultation paper in 2018.[2]

In the 1980s, there was a strong voice in favour of a 'secular' intervention in personal law within the women's movement. Overtime, however, increased scholarly focus on non-state adjudication of family law demonstrated that often religious reasoning could also underlie outcomes that are favourable to women. Through the study of divorce disputes across multiple forums, the chapter makes

---

[1] Women's access to delegated divorce, *talaq-e-tawfid*, predated the Dissolution of Muslim Marriages Act, 1939. *Khula*, or a woman's right to initiate divorce, continues to be granted in *sharia adalat*s and *dar-ul-qaza*s alongside judicial divorce. Recently, the Kerala High Court clarified that women also have the right to initiate *khula* as part of judicial divorce. 'Landmark Kerala HC Judgement Clarifies Muslim Women's Right to Initiate Divorce', *Indian Express*, 26 April 2021.

[2] 21st Law Commission of India, 'Consultation Paper on Reform of Family Law', August 2018.

two central claims. First, the incoherence of legal communications, the uncertain implications of legislative and judicial interventions on personal law, and the misunderstandings that surround the interpretations of religious law and practice invariably decentralizes authority over authentic religious knowledge. Second, the legal archive produced through petitions, judgments, legislative debates, police records, and so on, is not representative of the spectrum of legal experience.[3] Yet the unrecorded and unwritten experience of engaging the law provides meaningful insights on women's relationship with the state, religious community, and contemporary politics. Often this shared adjudication[4] and inter-legality[5] in personal law allows women to alter the terms of engagement and deploy new strategies of engagement or resistance against religious, communitarian, and state patriarchy.

The debate on family law during 1990–2000 was punctuated by the Hindu nationalist outfits' vociferous demand for a Uniform Civil Code. The demand for 'saving their Muslim sisters', however, could no longer be separated from the sexual violence that Muslim women, and Muslims in general, were subjected to at the hands of the same groups. The instances of riots in Ayodhya, Bombay, in 1992–93, and in Gujarat in 2002, and a series of incidents of lynching and violence against Muslims cast a shadow on the religious 'neutrality' that their code promised.[6] For many, it was not the idea of a Uniform Civil Code itself but a potentially majoritarian template of such a code that was problematic. In the recent focus on Muslim personal law in the current decade, the liberal position on the Uniform Civil Code has been uncertain, and feminists have come to view it with legitimate suspicion.[7] The women's movement remained divided on the question of state intervention on Muslim personal law which is explored in the first section of the chapter.

---

[3] Dipesh Chakrabarty, 'The Subject of Law and the Subject of Narrative', in *Habitations of Modernity: Essays in the Wake of Subaltern Studies*, ed. D. Chakrabarty (Chicago: University of Chicago Press, 2002), ch. 7, 101–14.

[4] Gopika Solanki, *Adjudication in Religious Family Laws: Cultural Accommodation, Legal Pluralism, and Gender Equality in India* (Cambridge: Cambridge University Press, 2011).

[5] Mengia Hong Tschalaer, *Muslim Women's Quest for Justice: Gender, Law and Activism in India* (New Delhi: Cambridge University Press, 2017). See also Deniz Kandiyoti, 'Bargaining with Patriarchy', *Gender and Society* 2, no. 3 (1988): 274–90.

[6] The 9/11 attack, the Afghan war, the disturbances in Kashmir, and the global focus on 'Islamic' terrorism also had an undeniable influence on the Muslim relationship with the state.

[7] 'Is It Time for a Uniform Civil Code? 50,000 Muslim Women Sign Up against Triple *Talaq*', *India Today*, 1 June 2016.

The Muslim clergy not only shared women's discomfort with a potential uniform code but also found their own influence under challenge by women. The AIMPLB, therefore, inched towards accommodating women's demands by discouraging unilateral instant divorce, and considering new model marriage contracts, *nikahnamas*, to avoid any governmental intervention. Further, women's groups responded by directly questioning the clergy's monopoly over religious texts by clergymen. This was also concurrent with the global focus, more generally, on religious feminism. The insufficient legal protection of women shifted the gaze of feminist movements from chasing purely 'constitutional' solutions, as was the case in the early 1970s, to instead straightening out oblique interpretations of Islamic religious texts in state and non-state forums. The 'private' realm of the family and religion found dedicated 'public' spaces in the form of *mahila adalats* (women's courts) and religious courts where versions of personal law were duelled. The discussion on forums, and the conflicts or cooperation between these, shows that decentralization of authority on family law generates a hospitable arena for new forms of Muslim politics to emerge that challenged the imagination of a community.[8]

The women's movement's insistence on reading the context of Hindu nationalism alongside Muslim women's demands from the state, tempered or at least delayed the state's promise of a Uniform Civil Code. Simultaneously, another strand within the movement insisted on fighting the 'legal' battle, allowing Muslim women to successfully challenge religious patriarchy, which was consolidated under the umbrella of an all-male clergy, out of its self-appointed position as the custodians of the *sharia*. Read together, the two divergent positions on non-intervention and intervention within the women's movement have allowed, ultimately, for the conversation on reform of Muslim personal law to remain firmly with its stakeholders. In a chaotic balancing act, the former prevented the appropriation of Muslim women's causes by the Hindu nationalist state; the latter by influential men of the Muslim community.

The second section of the chapter demonstrates that women's demand as well as opposition to state intervention on Muslim personal law, Muslim divorce procedures in particular, had an impact on institutions beyond the realm of government. Conversations in *dar-ul-qazas, sharia adalat,* family courts,

---

[8] Muslim women have also remained at the helm of the protest against the 2020 Amendment to the Citizenship Act that specifically denied Muslim refugees from India's three Muslim-majority neighbouring countries the right to claim Indian citizenship. The protests culminated in almost a year long peaceful assembly at Shaheen Bagh, a neighbourhood in the south-eastern edge of Delhi and was cleared only due to the Covid-19 pandemic in March 2020.

the higher courts, and parliament were interspersed with references of the Quran as well as the constitution. These institutions witnessed translations of resistance as well as biases from one forum to the other. A dialogue on law produced interesting exchanges between institutions that are best captured in a recent example of the AIMPLB announcing that all its appointed *qazi*s be trained in constitutional law.[9] Women's *sharia adalat*s, on the other hand, simultaneously trained women in Islamic law alongside knowledge of the constitution.[10]

The conversations on personal law, in this chapter, have been pieced together through interviews with key actors from this period, who were or are currently engaged in adjudication of personal law disputes across various forums.[11] The study is limited to interviews with actors who were also parties in the case of *Shayara Bano v. Union of India*. All forums provide spaces for challenging as well as reinforcing authorities of various kinds—religious scripture, customs or *dastoor*, statutory law, judge, husband, the mother-in-law, the police, men, and so on. Innovation in alternate dispute resolution is one of the major findings that emerged in the late twentieth and early twenty-first century, which highlighted interesting ways in which rights are negotiated in non-state forums and in the lower judiciary.[12] This chapter builds on these works to demonstrate how the consumers of the law also transform the state and its constituents. This transformation was visible in confrontational judgments where courts usurp religious authority, government schemes and policies that imitate non-state forums, indicting reports that question the government's motives and, consequently, quick-fix bills by the government to make up for untenable political promises.

The negotiations between the law and religion, and religious and secular feminisms in India contribute a new dimension to the global debates on Islamic

---

9 'Qazis in Darul Qaza to Now Get Lessons in Indian Constitution', News18, 2 March 2019.

10 '"Here, No Man Decides": Meet India's First Female Sharia Court Judges', *VICE*, 13 April 2018.

11 The study focussed on three organizations, the AIMPLB, the BMMA, and the Bebaak Collective. While the latter two organizations joined Shayara Bano's petition against triple *talaq*, the former was the respondent in the case (discussed in Chapter 5). Women's organizations differed widely in their stance on the intervention in Muslim personal law; this study limits its focus on the two petitioners, and three members of AIMPLB. Interviews conducted before and after the judgment, many of these were informal conversations over multiple meetings over the years. Only recorded interviews are cited.

12 Tschalaer, *Muslim Women's Quest for Justice*; Solanki, *Adjudication in Religious Family Laws*; Srimati Basu, *The Trouble with Marriage: Feminists Confront Law and Violence in India*, vol. 1 (New Delhi: University of California Press, 2015); Sylvia Vatuk, *Marriage and Its Discontents: Women, Islam and the Law in India* (New Delhi: Women Unlimited, an associate of Kali for Women, 2017).

feminism, which is discussed in the final section of the chapter. The analysis breaks away from the usual trope of casting women as victims being manipulated by the state, political parties, and the influential men in their own communities, and instead sees women as agents, with distinct political agendas and strategies. These voices do not inhabit neat categories of Muslims, women, or minority, nor do they identify clearly as a group or as individuals, religious or secular.

I

The Feminist Divide in Framing Resistance

When women frame their battles through the law, they are confronted with two obvious challenges. First, their experiences of violence and violation have to be made legible to the law or the adjudicator. Second, a courtroom or even an alternative forum requires parties to occupy a binary—the violator and the violated, the culprit and the victim. This means that parties may find themselves clubbed with co-petitioners who they strongly oppose ideologically, so long as the end goal, 'the prayer', is for a similar end. Opposition to any aspect of Muslim personal law by Muslim women's movements, organizations, or individual women remains vulnerable to appropriation by the Hindu nationalist political establishment. This put women's demands in a precarious paradox of simultaneously opposing Hindu nationalism and also bargaining with them. On the other hand, any argument to protect minority practices found 'legal' endorsement before a court by organizations such as the AIMPLB, and, therefore, the feminist stance on the protection of minorities shared an uncomfortable space with the orthodox clergy. To recover the particularity of Muslim women's articulations, focussing our analysis on the means of resistance and the strategy preceding the law—judgment or bill—becomes crucial.

The founding members of the two Muslim women's organizations that had joined Shayara Bano's petition in court against the practice of triple *talaq*, the Bebaak Collective and the BMMA, expressed disappointment with the lack of support by feminist organizations that identified as secular.[13] They also expressed their disappointment over their co-petitioners—Ishrat Jahan and Shayara Bano's direct or tenuous association with the BJP, as Jahan later joined the BJP and Bano was also offered a position in the party in Uttarakhand. Moreover, they suggested that this co-option into the BJP might be a consequence of the inability of secular feminist mobilization to accommodate Muslim women's

---

[13] Personal interviews with Hasina Khan, 13 August 2018 and 19 March 2019, and Zakia Soman, 14 Match 2019.

demand for legal remedies in family law.[14] The strategies of the Bebaak Collective and the BMMA differed substantially. Hasina Khan of the Bebaak Collective self-identified as secular; she stated that the objective of the collective was to take 'the voice of women from the street to Parliament' (*auroton ki awaaz sadak se sansad tak*).[15] The BMMA, on the other hand, also identified as a secular women's organization, but with a focus on Muslim women and placed significant emphasis on routing their activism through provisions within Islamic religious texts. The two organizations disagreed particularly on the Muslim Women's Protection of Marriages Act, 2019 (discussed in the next sub-section), which criminalized the pronouncement of triple *talaq*. While the Bebaak Collective opposed it, the BMMA supported it with some reservations.

The BMMA was consolidated in 2007 as part of the relief efforts for Muslims in the aftermath of the Gujarat riots. The organization emerged from movements and networks active from the late 1990s that were dedicated to recovery of women's rights within Islam, such as Awaaz-e-Niswaan (1987), All India Muslim Women's Rights Network (1999), among others. The BMMA drew inspiration from writings on Islamic feminism and global movements like the Musawah[16] and argued that the reading of the Quran by women would allow them to access their religiously guaranteed rights that are repeatedly denied to them in practice. For the BMMA, rights were sourced from the Quran as their *haq* (right) but in enabling women to access these rights, they did not foreclose the use of legal strategies. In 2016, the Bebaak Collective was born out of a convention of many women's organizations. Hasina Khan who formerly worked with Awaaz-e-Niswaan (until 2013) became one of the leading voices of the collective. In a personal interview, she said that she found the framework of religion very restrictive. She contended that while she was well acquainted with the rights granted to women under the Quran, she also believed that book could be questioned: 'What if one is an atheist-Muslim? ... someone who culturally identifies as a Muslim but is not religious.' She regretted that the women's movement has been divided on the issue of legal intervention and framed it as a betrayal for Muslim women: 'Shayara Bano was not the first woman I met who had suffered the fate that she did. We had worked with many women who had suffered triple *talaq* and we had tried a lot to convince these women to file a case in court.'[17] She argued that the realities and issues of each minority are very different.

---

[14] Personal interview with Hasina Khan, 19 March 2019.

[15] Ibid.

[16] Musawah translates to 'equality' in Arabic. Launched in February 2009, it is a global movement for equality and justice in the Muslim family.

[17] Personal interviews with Hasina Khan, 13 August 2018 and 19 March 2019 (translation mine).

Has she ever [named an activist] ever gone to the Jama Masjid and tried discussing why women have to wear burqa? The way Christian women are able to talk about homosexuality, or Hindu women on temple entry?[18] Why do we hesitate in talking about Muslim women's sexuality- we only talk about Muslim women's 'rights' why is only *roti*, *kapda*, *makaan* [food, clothing, shelter] important for Muslim women. Why do groups say Muslim women community is not ready? Sometimes its 1992 [demolition of the Babri mosque], or 2002 [Gujarat riots] will there ever be a good time to talk about Muslim women? Why do they want to prepare us to survive and suffer [*rehne*, *pisne*] within the community, have our own mosques, own schools, are we not citizens?[19]

Khan highlighted that specific causes can occasionally become collateral damage in larger battles to oppose Hindu nationalism. It poses a critical question: Should Muslim women have to forsake any conversation on legal remedies until the general problem of Islamophobia and Muslim marginalization by the state and the public is addressed? And further, can a conversation with the state on reform of Muslim personal law really be of consequence when Islamophobia characterizes almost all contemporary state interventions? Muslim conservatives and secular intelligentsia shared their opposition to Hindu nationalism and consequently to legislative intervention in Muslim personal law. Not only did this reproduce the privatization of personal law, but not separating the law from its makers undermined the dialogue that the law had the potential to generate.

Yet despite the disagreement between the BMMA and Bebaak's leadership on religion as a source of rights, in the triple *talaq* case, the petitions of both organizations were clubbed together (along with the prayer of the government). These parties ultimately desired state intervention in matters of Muslim family law, and more specifically an end to instant, unilateral divorce. After the Supreme Court verdict on triple *talaq*, the BMMA expressed its intentions of filing fresh petitions against practices of bigamy and *nikah halala* as well, which were issues that had been expressly omitted from consideration by the court in the hearing on triple *talaq*. A number of petitions were subsequently filed by Muslim women as well as BJP members against the practices of *nikah halala* and bigamy, which remain pending before court. The BMMA is yet to file its own.[20]

---

[18] Women between the ages 12–50 were permitted entry into the Sabrimala Temple, in February 2019, after the India Lawyer's Association filed a writ challenging the temple's rule of excluding women of a 'menstruating' age from entering the temple.

[19] Personal interviews with Hasina Khan, 13 August 2018 and 19 March 2019.

[20] Saumya Saxena, 'Nikah Halala: The Petition, the Promise, and the Politics of Personal Law', in *Mutinies for Equality: Contemporary Developments in Law and Gender in India*, ed. Tanja Herklotz and Siddharth Peter De Souza (Cambridge: Cambridge University Press, 2021), 133–54.

The women's movement became particularly divided on the question of bigamy.[21] Scholar and activist Flavia Agnes argued that a ban on polygamy may deprive Muslim second wives of their existing rights and reducing their status of a 'mistress' or 'keeps', terms that the Supreme Court frequently used to describe second wives, which would never be attributed to women under Muslim law. While the idea of bigamy pushed the conversation towards new imaginations of a family, in most cases in India, women had no agency in declining a bigamous arrangement, and contracting a second marriage was also an exclusive right for men. This argument created an odd-line position whereby citing the failure of the bigamy prevention law among other communities and the plight of second wives among Hindus, bigamy could be defended as a 'protection' for Muslim women.[22]

This echoed the debates on the Hindu Marriage Act that suggested that women's discomfort with bigamy should somehow be overlooked in the face of potential destitution that stares at them outside or without the status of marriage.[23] Financial protection then gets worded as a better 'choice' rather than living with an adulterous spouse. Such an argument created a strange binary between secular law in favour of the first wife and religious (here, Islamic) law potentially in favour of the second. In BMMA's Soman's experience, women sought more from a marriage than just financial support. Women often preferred to exit a difficult or an adulterous marriage rather than continuing in one solely to retain the rights of maintenance.

Women's organizations that focussed predominantly on legal aid and assistance[24] had encountered the detrimental consequences of excessive regulation. Many of these organizations used existing legislation in the Indian Penal Code (IPC) against cruelty and bigamy to get relief for their clients rather than demanding new laws. Section 494 of the IPC prohibits bigamy, and can also be invoked by Muslim women, but in most cases, the courts accept bigamy as legal within Muslim personal law. General laws such as Section 498A of the IPC on cruelty or the Domestic Violence Act have been used efficiently by many women's organizations to challenge triple *talaq* as well as bigamy as a form of cruelty. Yet women in their letters to the Law Commission sought explicit legislation to invalidate triple *talaq*. Women looked to the law with hope. For instance, several women in their responses to the Law Commission's questionnaire were postured

---

[21] Audrey D'Mello, 'Uniform Civil Code: "Gender Just" Laws Can Work against Women', *Hindustan Times*, 18 August 2016.

[22] 'Muslim Polygamy and the Bigamous Hindu', *National Herald*, 13 April 2018.

[23] See Chapter 1, the section 'Divorce as Destitution and Bigamy as Protection'.

[24] Partners for Law and Development, Majlis, Advocacy and Legal Initiatives, and others.

even more strongly against bigamy than unilateral divorce. One sent a personalized note to the Law Commission expressing fear about a potential second marriage that her husband may contract and demanded that the commission recommend a ban on the practice of bigamy immediately.[25] Such a demand could also imply a meaningful transformation in Muslim women's relationship with the state and claims on its resources.

Within NGOs committed to women's welfare, often it was the leaders of organizations who invoked reports (in particular the Sachar Commission report) or commented on policy—the women they worked with narrated stories and demanded immediate readdresses than long term goals. Correspondingly, the former offered a critique of government interventions but the latter demanded state action. Activists frequently emphasized that triple *talaq* was not an immediate priority—education and poverty were—and that Muslim women are not being allowed to set their own agenda and triple *talaq* was an agenda dictated by the government.[26] However, others even as self-identified as pious, religious Muslim women were not averse to a limited state intervention such as the enforcement of compulsory registration of marriages.[27]

Both positions for and against intervention were significant but it increasingly became clear that the movement would not speak in one voice. Women did not always want to choose between legal change in family law *or* the general welfare of Muslims (health, education, and employment). Such a binary reinforced the idea that women's rights within family law are not an end in itself, but a peripheral part of a larger agenda of Muslim well-being. It imposed a hierarchy within the demands of the Muslim populations from the state, in which family law and household affairs occupied a significantly low position. Muslim women's relationship with the law has a longer history than the BJP's recent appropriation of their demands as Chapters 3 and 4 demonstrated. Statutory interventions and religious arguments in support of women's rights, therefore, coexist across various forums, and are not always contradictory. The next section discusses how the period of the 2000s witnessed a number of legislative interventions in family law, but demands for an intervention in Muslim personal law faced particular and peculiar difficulties.

---

[25] Letter dated 23 December 2016, 21st Law Commission of India, Law Commission of India Archives, 4th Floor Lok Nayak Bhawan.

[26] Farah Naqvi, 'Muslim Women Rights and Reality, Charting out an Action Programme', India Habitat Centre, 4 July 2018.

[27] Uzma Naheed runs an NGO Iqra International Women's Alliance (IIWA). She popularized a *nikahnama* which carried a clause stating triple *talaq* is wrongful divorce and worked closely with the members of the AIMPLB in Mumbai. She supported the idea of compulsory registration of Muslim marriages. Roundtable, 'Muslim Women Rights and Reality, Charting out an Action Programme', India Habitat Centre, 4 July 2018.

A comparative picture of statutory interventions in Hindu and Christian personal law reiterates the claim that Muslim personal law was chiefly debated in courts than in parliament, as Chapter 5 demonstrated.

Who Can Amend and Who Must Contend

In 2001, the government tabled the Indian Divorce (Amendment) Act, which finally wiped the dust off 1960 and 1961 Law Commission of India's reports on amendments to Christian marriages (Chapter 2). The tone of discussion in the 2001 Christian Marriage Amendment was not dismissive of religion but was an attempt to accommodate religious sentiments, albeit rather superficially. For instance, even though the law in question dealt with the subject of 'divorce', the then Law Minister Arun Jaitley of the BJP insisted on the substitution of the word 'divorce' with 'dissolution of marriage'. This was in consideration towards the Christian community which 'does not appreciate the term "divorce"'.[28] Similarly, while introducing the controversial 'mutual consent' argument as a ground for divorce, an olive branch was extended in the form of a two-year period of separation preceding divorce, as opposed to the one-year period under the Special Marriage Act and the Hindu Marriage Act. This was despite protests against such an exception by several women members of parliament. Beatrix D'Souza protested, 'Are only Christian women expected to have so much fortitude to wait for four years to get a divorce?'[29] (A sentiment later echoed by Hasina Khan in her disappointment over lack of intervention in Muslim personal law.)

Margaret Alva,[30] a senior parliamentarian and lawyer from the Indian National Congress, however, hailed this amendment as a significant step forward for Christian women.

> ... I pay tribute to the Christian women groups and organisations which have been lobbying since 1980s to get these amendments passed. When I was the minister for women and child development in the Rajiv Gandhi government, we made this demand and Shri Rajiv Gandhi, having faced the repercussions of the *Shah Bano* case and judgement said to me, 'go and get 10,000 signatures of Christians asking for the change and I will respond.' I said we got 10 lakh [one million] signatures from around the country of men, women supporting the amendments of Christian laws.[31]

---

[28] *Lok Sabha Debates*, The Indian Divorce (Amendment) Bill, 2001, Act No. 51 of 2001, 30 August 2001 to 24 September 2001, col. 389–90. Law Minister Arun Jaitley: 'I am correcting myself and I am preferring to use the words "dissolution of marriage" because of the factors, particularly in a large section of Christians says that the marriages are not really intended to be divorced.'

[29] *Lok Sabha Debates*, col. 419.

[30] Alva later served as the governor of the state of Uttarakhand and Rajasthan.

[31] *Lok Sabha Debates*, col. 394.

She further pointed out that women often hesitated in filing a criminal case fearing that they will be thrown out of their matrimonial home; therefore, criminalizing bigamy only on the complaint of the aggrieved served a limited purpose.[32] Some members of parliament such as Francis George,[33] in his speech, recommended that the courts and the church should work in collaboration in handling the proceedings of the dissolution of marriages.[34] Others argued for the recognition of Catholic Churches for arranging more speedy annulments of Christian marriages than the courts would. Beatrix D'Souza, who represented the Anglo-Indian community from Tamil Nadu, argued:

> Even if a Catholic gets divorced under this Act, the Catholic will still have to go to a Catholic Church to get an annulment (interruptions). If Catholics do not get an annulment and marry under the Special Divorce Act [sic], they will be living in sin. Therefore, this Act is really not very helpful. But I am sure, the Catholic Church will give us more speedy annulments.[35]

The law minister, however, ruled out the proposal for officially recognizing multiple jurisdictions despite their obvious presence and influence, as he feared that this would lead to similar demands by other communities: 'This will not be in consonance with the rule of law as it is accepted in India.'[36] He quoted the 15th Law Commission report, in 1960,[37] which granted that the 'Court constituted under the law of the country will have exclusive authority to determine disputes relating to civil rights, and there can be no surrender or abdication of that authority'.[38]

---

[32] Ibid., col. 397: At this point on the mere mention of 'bigamy', that there was an uproar in parliament, the content of the speech is lost in the interruptions but snippets of the recorded phrases suggested that she clarifies that she is not talking about just Muslim law. This indicates that the objections to banning of bigamy were probably over Muslim personal law.

[33] K. Francis George, chairman of the Janadhipathya Kerala Congress Party.

[34] *Lok Sabha Debates*, col. 424–25.

[35] Ibid., col. 424.

[36] Ibid., col. 430.

[37] The 15th, 19th, 22nd, and 164th reports of the Law Commission of India dealt with provisions of marriage laws of Christians in India. It is worth noting, however, that different provincial high courts had already quashed provisions such as the confirmation of divorce by a full bench of the high court.

[38] *Lok Sabha Debates*, col. 430. The government's stance denying exceptions to legal authority, however, was not absolute. This exception is visible in the case of Nagaland. With 90 per cent of the population of Nagaland being Christian, the member of parliament from Nagaland, Sangtam, argued that according to the 16-point agreement of the Naga People's Convention guaranteed in the 13th Constitutional Amendment of 1962, Article 371A, the agreement guaranteed a 'total recognition of the genuine aspirations of the Naga people' in return for territorial integrity. Law Minister Jaitley confirmed that the new law will not affect Nagaland's special status in any way. The regional differences qualified for exceptionality with greater ease than religious categories, as discussed in Chapter 2.

The 2001 Amendment to the Indian Divorce Act offered substantial gains for women. It introduced more grounds for divorce including mutual consent divorce, and also simplified the procedure for divorce for Christian couples. It clarified and limited the procedure for the appeal of nullity of marriages so as to allow people to remarry without conflict. The first woman chief justice of India Leela Seth noted in her biography that the 2001 Act had given the Indian women's movement much hope that their efforts were being rewarded.[39]

The Hindu Code Bill had also inched towards diversity in the years following its enactment and slowly shed its Brahminical bearings by the incorporation of the Madras Amendment (1967) to simplify marriage procedures as seen in Chapter 2. It incorporated changes in property and inheritance laws, and acknowledging regional difference with respect to recognition of women as coparceners, or marriages within prohibited degrees of relationships (*sapinda*). The 174th report of the Law Commission of India on 'Property Rights of Women: Proposed Reforms Under the Hindu Law' preceded the 2005 amendment to the Hindu Succession Act that recognized women as coparceners. The journey from the bill in 2004 to the Act in 2005 was routed through yet another commission, the 'Standing Committee on Law and Justice', which entertained further consultations and depositions. This was a significant achievement and again driven chiefly by efforts of women's groups and academics. Bina Agarwal, who was involved in the discussions of the potential bill with the Law Commission, wrote: 'There is a popular misconception that gender-equal inheritance laws can only benefit a few women. In fact, millions of women—as widows and daughters—stand to gain.'[40] The Act was hailed as an achievement both symbolically and economically for women.[41] It did receive some criticism particularly from states that had already abolished coparceners such as Kerala. In other state such as Tamil Nadu, the new Act meant that an increase in the daughter's share came at the cost of the of widow's share in property, which now fell even lower than the share of her children.

---

[39] Leela Seth, *On Balance: An Autobiography* (New Delhi: Penguin Books, 2008).

[40] 'Landmark Step to Gender Equality', *The Hindu*, 25 September 2005.

[41] Ibid. Agarwal also criticized the Act observing:

> In States where the wife takes a share on partition, as in Maharashtra, the widow's potential share will now equal the son's and daughter's. But where the wife takes no share on partition, as in Tamil Nadu or Andhra Pradesh, the widow's potential share will fall below the daughter's. Abolishing the Mitakshara system altogether would have been more egalitarian, as some of us had suggested.

See also Geetanjali Gangoli, *Indian Feminisms: Law, Patriarchies and Violence in India* (Aldershot, Hampshire: Routledge, 2016).

State-specific conflicts in law did emerge, and Hindu women's right to property saw further consideration.[42]

After this, there were many more Law Commission reports on Hindu women's rights within marriage. The 18th Law Commission's three reports on 'Proposal to Amend the Hindu Succession Act, 1956 as Amended by Act 39 of 2005' (204th), 'Laws on Registration of Marriage and Divorce—A Proposal for Consolidation and Reform' (211th), followed by the 252nd report on 'Right of the Hindu Wife to Maintenance: A Relook at Section 18 of the Hindu Adoptions and Maintenance Act, 1956' continued to absorb demands for change. Finally, in August 2020, the Supreme Court confirmed that the 2005 Act can be applied retrospectively, which meant that daughters born before 2005 could also claim their share as coparceners. In a judgment recorded over 121 pages, the guiding sentiment was summarized in the awkward opening that stereotypically pits the daughter against the daughter-in-law: 'A daughter always remains a loving daughter. A son is a son until he gets a wife. A daughter is a daughter throughout her life.'[43]

In 2010, and then again in 2013, a bill to recognize 'irretrievable breakdown of marriage' as a ground for divorce,[44] in the Hindu Marriage Act and the Special Marriage Act, was introduced in parliament but was met with much opposition and eventually it lapsed. The National Commission for Women and the Law Commission (report 217 in 2012) of India both submitted their reports addressing the drawbacks of the bill, but more than 70 organizations (mostly men's rights activists and senior citizen groups) sent in their delegations labelling the bill as the 'collapse of marriage' and it could not be enacted.[45] The Law Commission also contemplated making registration of marriages compulsory (211, 212, and 270).

The Law Commission's report on bigamy by conversion to Islam (report 227) did not prompt a bill. Muslim women's demands for changes to family law were also not even making it to the commissions, which generally responded to movements, however superficially. Thus, state intervention was becoming exclusive to non-Muslims, and Hindu law received substantially more attention.[46] When a legislation on Muslim law finally did arrive, in 2019, it confirmed many fears about the law's potential to target religious minorities.

---

[42] Werner Menski, *Hindu Law: Beyond Tradition and Modernity* (New Delhi: Oxford University Press, 2008).

[43] *Vineeta Sharma v. Rakesh Sharma*, Civil Appeal No. 32601/2018.

[44] Marriage Laws Amendment Bill, 2013.

[45] 'Bill to Make Divorce Easier May Be Dropped', *The Hindu*, 19 February 2015.

[46] Parsi law has also encountered relatively less legislative attention after independence but is beyond the scope of the book. For a study of Parsi personal law which was largely codified before independence, see Mitra Sharafi, *Law and Identity in Colonial South Asia: Parsi Legal Culture, 1772–1947* (Cambridge: Cambridge University Press, 2014).

The Triple Talaq Bill: A Missed Opportunity

On 4 August 2016, leading activist turned politician of the Congress Party, Husain Dalwai, introduced a private member's bill in parliament titled the 'Dissolution of Muslim Marriages Bill, 2016' that codified procedures of divorce for Muslim men and women and expressly excluded triple *talaq*. Parliament, however, did not take this up for debate. Instead, in 2017, the BJP government tabled the Muslim Women's Protection of Rights on Marriage Bill, that sought to criminalize the pronouncement of triple *talaq*.[47] This was shortly after the Supreme Court judgment on triple *talaq* which declared the practice invalid in August 2017.[48] M. J. Akbar, the member of parliament who presented the bill, announced at the very outset that the underlying sentiment about the bill was 'never destroy the good in search of the ideal', admitting that the bill may have been far from ideal.[49]

Arif Mohamad Khan, who had resigned from the Congress over the introduction of the Muslim Women (Protection of Rights on Divorce) Act, 1986, was also central to the debate on the Muslim Women's Protection of Rights on Marriage Bill, 2018. The ghost of Shah Bano, therefore, loomed large in parliamentary debates, and the bill was posited as an opportunity to correct a historical wrong despite evidence to the contrary of the 1986 Act having been progressively interpreted. The insistence on enacting the triple *talaq* bill within a day and without entertaining any discussion on amendments and the severe criminal law provisions it attached to the pronouncement of triple *talaq* raised concerns about its potential misuse. The bill potentially enabled any person to report an incident of triple *talaq* without the involvement of the wife or her family, who was the chief sufferer of the unilateral *talaq*. Some of these provisions were watered down in a subsequent draft but there remained glaring uncertainties in the bill.

For instance, on many occasions when a petitioner approached the court, it was to seek that the triple *talaq* or instant divorce given at whim, or in a moment

---

[47] For a detailed analysis and critique of the Muslim Women's Protection of Rights on Marriage Act, see Jyoti Punwani, 'Triple Talaq Judgement and After', *Economic and Political Weekly* 53, no. 17 (2018): 12–16, who captures the various responses to criminalization of the practice of triple *talaq*. See also Jyoti Punwani, 'Muslim Women: Historic Demand for Change', *Economic and Political Weekly* 51, no. 42 (2016): 12–15; Saptarshi Mandal, 'Instant Triple Talaq Bill: Tabling Legislation in Parliament Is Political Move, BJP's Attempt to Play Protector of Muslims', *Firstpost.com*, 22 December 2017.

[48] *Shayara Bano v. Union of India* (2017) 9 SCC 1. See the discussion in Chapter 2.

[49] M. J. Akbar's speech in parliament, 28 December 2019, reported live, ANI. Akbar remains a controversial figure in the BJP who presented the triple *talaq* bill in the name of 'gender justice'. but, ironically, he was accused by 11 women of sexual harassment. 'MeToo: Here's What 11 Women Journalists Have Accused MJ Akbar of', *India Today*, 14 October 2018.

of anger, can be disregarded and invalidated so that the marriage can subsist. With a jail and severe criminal consequences attached with the pronouncement of triple *talaq*, the bill presumed a *de facto* separation even as the marriage technically continued to subsist. This was particularly problematic because the Supreme Court judgment in setting aside the practice of triple *talaq* had essentially declared that the pronouncement of instant oral unilateral divorce by a man would no longer remain a 'legal moment'. The new bill, therefore, in one sense, reinstated the validity of triple *talaq* in the law as a 'crime' which would entail punishment. Focussing entirely on 'pronouncement', it overlooked that it was the resultant 'abandonment' or 'economic abuse', which could justifiably attract penalties. The bill held the husband responsible for the maintenance of his wife, but there was ambiguity on how maintenance could be guaranteed if the husband faces a jail term. There were further sections and clauses on the custody of children, which for all practical purposes presumed the dissolution of the marriage rather than its subsistence.

The bill overemphasized discontent over the 'speed' of such a divorce, overlooking that it was to the arbitrary and unilateral decision that women had objections. Unilateral *talaq*, therefore, would continue to remain an exclusive privilege of men, even after making triple *talaq* (*talaq-ul-biddat*) a criminal offence. Even the remaining methods of *talaq-e-ahsan* and *talaq-e-hasan*—where divorce proceedings took three months to complete and were conditional upon attempts to reconcile—were unilateral. Men did not need to cite any reasons for initiating such a divorce. The Dissolution of Muslim Marriages Act of 1939, also did not recognize adultery or bigamy by the husband, or conversion of religion by the wife, as grounds for seeking divorce. For non-judicial divorce, women instead approached non-state institutions or *qazi*s for seeking *khula* or exercising their right to delegated divorce (*talaq-e-tawfid*), but unlike for men, they often needed external intervention to confirm the divorce. On occasions, women also had to forgo their *mahr* and maintenance to exit a marriage. To address the unevenness of judicial divorce, the 21st Law Commission in its consultation paper on family law, in 2018, had observed:

> Section 2 of the (Dissolution of Muslim Marriages) Act, 1939 provides for a number of grounds based on which women can seek divorce. Men on the other hand are not required to qualify their decision under any of these grounds. Therefore, uniformly applying the grounds available under the Act, 1939 to both men and women will have greater implications of ensuring equality within the community rather than equality between different communities.[50]

---

[50] 21st Law Commission of India's 'Consultation Paper on Family Law Reform', August 2018.

The BMMA in its draft bill circulated in the public and presented to the Law Commission of India also suggested that women must also be allowed to divorce using the method of *talaq-e-ahsan*, ensuring parity between men and women with respect to the procedure for divorce.[51] Dalwai's bill had also suggested that men and women have equal rights in divorce and bigamy be a ground for divorce for both spouses. The 2018 Bill, however, did not consider many amendments, nor did it amend the 1939 Act. It twice failed the test on the floor of the house and eventually the government attempted to bring it in as an 'ordinance'. Ordinances, under Article 123 of the constitution of India, could be brought in under special circumstances to address an immediate need or an emergency situation, in case where consensus could not be built on a law and parliament was not in session when the need for a law arose. But since the issue did not qualify as 'urgent', the government could not promulgate an ordinance and the bill found itself in yet another parliamentary 'committee' for further review.

In July 2019, after the BJP's landslide victory and increased strength in parliament after the national election, the bill was enacted as the Muslim Women's Protection of Rights on Marriage Act, 2019. Despite its criticisms, the bill also had support from some Muslim women's organizations, who had hoped that the legislation would bring relief to multiple women who live under the constant fear of being thrown out of their homes by their husbands without reason or warning. The opposition to the bill in the Lok Sabha largely focussed on the BJP's historical anti-Muslim propaganda rather than on the legal deficiencies of the bill. For many members, the trouble with the bill was the rhetoric of 'saving Muslim women' when Muslim women had been subjected to unparalleled violence and injustices in the state of Gujarat in 2002 under the watch of the BJP government in the state. Sanjay Singh of the Aam Aadmi Party notes, 'Those people are concerned about Muslim women who have never, from 1952 until today, given a ticket to a Muslim woman or made her an MLA, MP or a minister.'[52] Digvijaya Singh of the Congress was even more direct: 'In 2002, during the Gujarat riots, pregnant women's stomachs were cut open and the child killed, did you talk about (giving them) justice? Where was your love for Muslim women then?'[53] The conversation on *talaq* thus raised concerns about the strength of democracy itself. Importantly, it provoked confrontation within parliament about secularism and the vulnerability of minorities.

---

[51] 'Talat Talaq Talaq, No More!', BMMA, https://bmmaindia.wordpress.com/2015/11/21/bmma-publications-no-more-talaq-talaq-talaq-muslim-women-call-for-a-ban-on-an-unislamic-practice/.

[52] *Lok Sabha Debates*, Live Lok Sabha TV, 30 July 2019.

[53] Ibid.

Other critiques emerged from the disproportionate punishment for Muslim men for a crime that was common across communities. Manoj Jha of the Rashtriya Janata Dal echoed, 'For rioting, two years, for negligent driving, two years, and for even bribery there is perhaps just one year. And in this [triple *talaq*], three years! What do you want? To demonise Muslim men.'[54] A member of the Congress Party, Amee Yagnik, objected, 'Now, the same woman will seek bail from the [magistrate] court for her husband, seek custody of children and maintenance[55],' indicating that the bill only embroiled women into more legal hassles and procedures.

A jail term and strict criminal action for divorce also embodied society's existing anxiety over the breaking of families. The criminalization of the pronouncement of *talaq* generated substantial opposition from other political parties and even women's groups. The three-year jail term meant that while Hindu and Christian husbands faced up to a year's jail term for the crime of abandonment under the existing Domestic Violence Act, Muslim husbands faced a harsher punishment, and also easier conviction. This provision, however, was amended in 2018, bringing the jail term down to 'up to three years', with minimum being one year. Abandonment of wives by their husbands was common across communities but abandonment through triple *talaq* is specific to Muslim women. The recognition of this particularity was an acknowledgement of the need for separate codification of personal law, in a situation where the Domestic Violence Act had hitherto failed to create deterrence for the abandonment of wives through oral divorce.

Scholars have expressed concerns over how the state's bid to defend human and women's rights often encouraged policing and surveillance that augments state authority and threatens minorities.[56] But these writings hesitate to acknowledge that their general opposition to the carceral authority of the state often plays out on the body of the Muslim woman. In one sense, such a framing pits the vulnerability of Muslim men against the suffering of Muslim women. Further, a history of the disaggregated management of family law by the state assures that the realm of the personal law remains challengeable and dialogic. One day after the new law received presidential assent, the Jamat-e-Ulema-e-Hind and a Kerala-based organization, the Samastha Kerala Jiamthul Ulema, challenged the Act in the Supreme Court. The petition was followed by another one by a Delhi-based advocate, Shahid Ali.[57] There are currently up to 10 petitions before

---

[54] Ibid.

[55] Ibid.

[56] Ratna Kapur, '"Belief" in Law and Hindu Majoritarianism: The Rise of the Hindu Nation', in *Majoritarian State: How Hindu Nationalism Is Changing India*, ed. Angana P. Chatterji, Thomas Blom Hansen, and Christophe Jaffrelot (London: Hurst & Company, 2020), 354–70.

[57] 'Kerala Based Muslim out Challenges Triple Talaq Law in Supreme Court', *Economic Times*, 2 August 2019.

the court that challenge the triple *talaq* bill, the most recent one being by a Kerala-based woman Noorbeena Rasheed who is the general secretary of Indian Union Women's League, an affiliate of the political party, the IUML on 6 July 2020.[58] Subsequent to this in 2021 the AIMPLB released an 11-point *nikahnama* banning dowry and wasteful expenditure that also discouraged triple *talaq* alongside dancing and other 'non-Islamic activities'. The battle in court continued too with BJP's Ashwini Kumar Upadhyay incessantly filing petitions for uniform ground of divorce, succession, and so on, and these were countered by Muslim women petitioning against the introduction of uniformity.[59] Whether this law succeeds eventually in creating deterrence for triple *talaq* is yet to be determined but Soman reiterated that it can become a tool that significantly increases the bargaining power of women within a household. Even as no one quite knows what the law may entail, it shadows household disagreements.

Even while the bill was in flux, it generated dialogue. The AIMPLB saw some high-profile resignations. Ruksana Lari, a senior member of AIMPLB, resigned over her disagreement with the board over its rigid stand on triple *talaq*.[60] AIMPLB announced its campaign against triple *talaq* and that the *dar-ul-qazas* be treated as mediation centres rather than alternative to courts.[61] AIMPLB further announced that it would train its *qazis* in constitutional law. Women volunteers associated with *mahila adalats* and family courts also warned litigants that the pronouncement of triple *talaq* could land men in trouble, even if one did not know what kind of trouble. The general perception that Muslim women's agendas are not being determined by themselves[62] was transforming in the 2000s. Kirmani writes that 'despite the symbolic import that "Muslim women" have come to hold, until recently, it has been rare that the actual voices of Muslim women themselves are heard in debates about their own supposed oppression'.[63]

---

[58] 'First Woman Moves Supreme Court over Triple Talaq Law', *Hindustan Times*, 8 July 2020.

[59] 'AIMPLB's New Nikahnama Bans Dowry, Extravaganza', *Daily Pioneer*, 1 April 2021; 'Muslim Woman Opposes PIL for Uniform Law for Divorce, Maintenance and Alimony before Supreme Court', *Livelaw.in*, 24 March 2021.

[60] 'Muslim Law Board Shows the Door to Woman Member Who Opposed Triple Talaq', *Hindustan Times*, 11 May 2017.

[61] 'There Was No Conflict between Civil Courts and Darul-Qaza: AIMPLB Secretary', *The Pioneer*, 10 July 2018.

[62] Farah Naqvi in the Roundtable, 'Muslim Women—Rights and Reality—Charting Out an Action Programme', 4 July 2018. 'Darul Qazas Aren't Courts but Counselling Centres', *Tehelka*, 17 September 2018, http://tehelka.com/darul-qazas-arent-courts-but-counselling-centres/#:~:text=The%20All%2DIndia%20Muslim%20Personal,up%20a%20parallel%20judicial%20system.

[63] Nida Kirmani, 'Claiming Their Space: Muslim Women-Led Networks and the Women's Movement in India', *Journal of International Women's Studies* 11, no. 1 (2009): 73.

The mainstreaming of Muslim women's concerns through a dialogue on the law and their demands from the state deserves a fair analysis without an overt attempt to present Muslim women's movement as either self-sufficient, anti-intervention activism, or as co-opted into or unaware of Hindu nationalism.[64] The heterogeneity within the Muslim community, and intra-community conflict, whether in the form of different interpretations of religious texts or supporting different political parties, deserves due acknowledgement.

The sustained efforts of Muslim women to reimagine what represents Islam and Islamic law have achieved significant success in disrupting men's historical monopoly over religion. The collective force of legislation along with forums dedicated to reclaiming religious scriptures by women transformed the relationship between citizens and religion. It is in this context of polarizing political debates that alternate forums for adjudication of family disputes become spaces for producing a new kind of politics. The next section analyses interviews conducted with some of the key actors involved in adjudicating conflicts within family. These interviews were conducted from 2012 to 2019 and focussed primarily on the question of codification efforts of the government(s).

II

Forums and the Family

This section compares the working of different forums—*dar-ul-qaza*s, family courts, *sharia adalat*s, police helplines, and so on—as articulated by the actors who help run these forums. Each forum produces its own performances, generates its own disciplinary regime, creates its own virtuous subjects, and defines its own delinquents.[65] Thus, if actors themselves inhabit categories of victim, wife, daughter-in-law, and so on, as some sort of a conformist resistance in the courts,[66] versions of these roles are also reproduced in other forums. These inhabited roles yield different outcomes in forums depending on whether religious rationalities or customary law or feminist consciousness is informing the imagination of

---

[64] Ahmed, *Religious Freedom under the Personal Law System.*

[65] For adjudication forums for marital disputes, see Shalini Grover, *Marriage, Love, Caste and Kinship Support: Lived Experiences of the Urban Poor in India* (London: Routledge, 2017); Julia Kowalski, 'Between Gender and Kinship: Mediating Rights and Relations in North Indian NGOs', *American Anthropologist* 123, no. 2 (2021): 330–42. See also Ravinder Kaur and Rajni Palriwala, eds., *Marrying in South Asia: Shifting Concepts, Changing Practices in a Globalising World* (New Delhi: Orient Blackswan, 2014).

[66] See Basu, *The Trouble with Marriage.*

retribution and justice. While detailed studies of forums for adjudication tell us about the peculiarities of these spaces,[67] this section focuses on their interrelationship and possible influences on one another. The interviews were largely focussed on dissolution of marriage but meandered into conversations about politics and personal lives. This study zooms in on specific cases in Lucknow and tries to place them in a wider context of writings on alternate dispute resolution forums.

The Dar-ul-Qaza

The Firangi Mahal *dar-ul-qaza* inhabited a grand, ageing building in the old centre of Lucknow. It also housed a madrasa for young children, a library, meeting rooms, and a court, among other buildings. The three members of the AIMPLB interviewed were active participants in the Firangi Mahal *dar-ul-qaza*. All of them emphasized the 'speed' at which the cases were concluded as well as the privacy the forum afforded to women as the primary arguments in favour of the *dar-ul-qaza* over family courts. However, it became apparent that even while women managed speedy divorces, and quicker orders, these did not always translate to meaningful settlements with respect to desired maintenance, *hazanat* or guardianship of their child, and so on. Many of the decisions were geared towards generating what *qazis* recognized as 'workable solutions' based in Islamic law, without a long discussion on the law itself. On many occasions, their readings of the situation were particularly practical and liberal. Positive *fatwas* could be extracted out of *dar-ul-qazas*, even as the terms of engagement, with all-male judges, often remained unfavourable to women. At the same time, it was also common for *qazis* to accept the lack of a male child as justification for bigamy, and to reduce the *mahr* amounts to women considered disobedient wives. As Vatuk noted in her study that the secretary of the AIMPLB had once suggested that 'women are too emotional to be given the privilege of divorcing on demand'.[68] The fear that granting women an equal right to divorce would increase divorce rates and result in social chaos was palpable. The forum, nonetheless, remained busy and its facilitators often shared personal relationships with the litigants.

---

[67] Jeffrey A. Redding, *A Secular Need: Islamic Law and State Governance in Contemporary India* (Seattle: University of Washington Press, 2020); Gopika Solanki, 'Beyond the Limitations of the Impasse: Feminism, Multiculturalism, and Legal Reforms in Religious Family Laws in India', *Politikon* 40, no. 1 (2013): 83–111; Tschalaer, *Muslim Women's Quest for Justice*; Justin Jones, '"Signs of Churning": Muslim Personal Law and Public Contestation in Twenty-First Century India', *Modern Asian Studies* 44, no. 1 (2010): 175–200. Sagnik Dutta, 'Bounds of Righteous Agency: The Gendered Subject of Minority Rights in Contemporary India' (PhD dissertation, University of Cambridge, 2020).

[68] Sylvia Vatuk, 'Islamic Feminism in India: Indian Muslim Women Activists and the Reform of Muslim Personal Law', *Modern Asian Studies* 42, nos. 2–3 (2008): 489–518, 503.

Aside from his legal practice, the prominent advocate Zafaryab Jilani also informally advised his clients on the provisions of the *sharia*, particularly on matters of family law that were likely to reach the *dar-ul-qaza* for resolution. Jilani was also a former chairman of the Babri Masjid Action Committee, and a prominent member of the AIMPLB. Frequently, he encouraged clients to avoid a tedious legal process by settling family disputes outside the courts and opt for remedies in the *dar-ul-qaza*s. He narrated a case where a man had come to him for legal advice whose wife had an affair with his older brother and the two had started to live together.[69] Jilani inquired if there was any possibility of reconciliation between the man and his wife, but the husband conveyed that it was unlikely that she would return to him. Jilani advised the husband to give his wife *talaq* in one sitting so that she could 'lawfully' marry his brother and live a 'moral' life. He concluded, 'What is the point of her living an immoral life with another man?'[70] In this case, neither the advising authority nor the prevailing of customary law for divorce chastised the woman for immorality or adultery but instead enabled her to cohabit with a partner of her own choosing. Jilani argued that triple *talaq* is frequently misused but unlike many other Muslim countries, Indian legislation has not made this a punishable crime. In spite of his advice to the young client, he recognized that triple *talaq* was a problem, but a rare occurrence. He also emphasized a potentially 'correct use' of instant *talaq*, which had the potential to benefit both men and women. Jilani understood Muslim personal law as essentially 'scientific' and 'practical' but largely misunderstood owing to the popularity of incorrect interpretations and wrongful practices. *Dar-ul-qaza*s rather than the Indian courts, for him, were therefore spaces where fair readings of the Islamic law on family matters were possible.

In the same breath he emphasized that bigamy, although rare, was permitted in Islam with restrictions, and on many occasions, he continued, 'Women (first wives) allow it, if they are unable to procreate or something.' He explained further that this was better than live-in relationship which amounted to living in sin. He remained strongly postured against state intervention: 'Codification is man-made, but Islamic law is God-made.' Even as he interpreted Islamic law in relatively flexible ways, he maintained that these interpretations were always consonant with the Quran.

***

---

[69] Interview with Zafaryab Jilani, additional advocate general, UP (2012) and convener of the BMAC and a senior member of the AIMPLB. Interviewed on 4 December 2012.
[70] Ibid.

Ruksana Lari was the first woman in her family to receive formal education. She came from a religious family in Lucknow and she later joined the AIMPLB, and was an influential member of the Board.[71] When asked about where she stood on the status of Muslim personal law in the country, she responded, 'Look, we do want codification to happen, for whatever laws of Muslims that exist ... and because India is a secular nation we all have the permission to follow our own culture and customs and solve our problems according to whatever solutions exist within our own religious systems.'[72] For Lari, codification consonant with Islam was a good idea. She described an instance where recently, a few people known to her family had informally approached her with a dispute: 'They faced some problem ... with regard to *khula* [divorce initiated by the wife] or divorce when it is not being given easily from the boy's side of the family ... it was being resisted, there was some trouble.' She advised the family to file an application before a *dar-ul-qaza* describing the problem. There were no monetary charges. 'The procedure is entirely free, besides the amount you spend on the paper or for transportation and unlike the courts, there is no harassment, or mockery of the women, no asking inappropriate questions....'[73] Both parties are called thrice and the couple's close relatives are also given an opportunity to intervene, before the *qazi* recommends any solutions, or makes his decision. More importantly, for her, by approaching a *dar-ul-qaza*, the parties could avoid undue public attention and are spared the exposure to the media.

The woman petitioner was eventually granted *khula* but Lari was unsure of how alimony and other arrangements were concluded. Further, *khula* is generally a process where the wife can initiate divorce but requires consent of the husband. It was unclear whether he eventually formally consented or whether the *qazi* accepted the *khula* on his own discretion. In both Jilani and Lari's examples, much was riding on the individual interpretation of the *qazi* or the judge. While they lauded 'correct' interpretations and lamented unfair ones, they did not view the decisions of the *dar-ul-qaza* as ones that should be challenged. They saw the *dar-ul*-qazas as better, safer, even fairer, alternatives to state courts. Lari confessed that she was uncomfortable with women pushing boundaries when they already have rights within Islam which are sufficient. She, however, felt strongly about women's rights within Islam and maintained that triple *talaq* as a form of divorce was against Islam. In 2017, Lari quit the AIMPLB because of an internal

---

[71] Lari, however, later quit the AIMPLB in 2017 over its rigid stance on the issue of triple *talaq*.

[72] Interview with Ruksana Lari, former member of the AIMPLB women's wing, Lucknow, 4 December 2012 (translation mine).

[73] Ibid.

confrontation over the Board's official stance on triple *talaq*, which was that such a form of divorce is disgraceful but a third pronouncement is final, and dissolves a marriage nonetheless.

***

Maulana Rasheed, the Shahi Imam-e-Eidgah of the Firangi Mahal, Lucknow, also a member of the AIMPLB, often presided over cases such as the ones discussed above. He reiterated a process similar to Lari's narration for seeking *khula* initiated by women. He added that *talaq* given by the husband is also preceded by attempts to reconcile at the *dar-ul-qaza*.[74] He believed that unilateral *talaq* was not as arbitrary as it may appear in public perception. Maulana expressed a desire for the Board's version of Muslim law to be recognized and accepted by the state. This version was derived from the Quran and Hadees, and on matters where there was ambiguity, through *qiyas* (scholarly opinion) and *ijma* (consultation among qualified *alim* [scholar of Islamic law]).

> ... codification of course is crucial and the AIMPLB has taken many steps to codify it and a book has already been prepared on that matter. It is in Urdu, however, it has not received legal sanctity yet from a government. But efforts are being made to translate it to English so that it can be given to some retired judges who can translate this in legal language. So that we can take it to the government and seek its approval.[75]

He had impressively well-ordered record books; the compound also contained meeting rooms and housed many members of the staff for the upkeep and management of the premises. Maulana Rasheed accepted some statutes such as the Shariat Application Act, 1937, and the Dissolution of Muslim Marriages Act, 1939, as 'authentic', but expressed reservations about the Muslim Women (Protection of Rights on Divorce) Act, 1986. He was also strongly postured against the BJP-led triple *talaq* bill (later the Muslim Women [Protection of Rights on Marriage] Act, 2019) that was under discussion in parliament, from 2017 to 2018.

In Jilani, Lari, and Maulana Rasheed's saw the *dar-ul-qaza*s as more practical and convenient forums. It is noteworthy that it was mostly women who approached these forums for confirming their divorce, or for seeking the return

---

[74] There are also other procedures through which a marriage could be annulled like *faksh* where a *qazi* could annul a marriage if the husband has absconded for more than a period of three years. *Faksh* can also be granted if the *qazi* concludes that the husband has failed in his marital duties in other ways. In my fieldwork experience, cases of *faksh* being granted easily were very uncommon.

[75] Interviews with Maulana Rasheed, 3 December 2012 and 7 March 2018 (translation mine).

of their *mahr* upon divorce.[76] But this also had to do with the fact that men could divorce unilaterally, whereas *khula* given by women had to be confirmed by a *qazi* or accepted by the husband. In their bid to emphasize convenience, they also lent support to traditional gender roles and the sexual division of labour. For instance, Maulana Rasheed mentioned that for women, their prayers are 'nine times more effective' if they pray from inside the house and for men, it is that much more effective if they prayed at a mosque. This belief, he continued, was introduced only for the convenience of women, so that they need not tire, or worry about leaving young children behind at home for offering prayers five times a day at a mosque. Thus, women could have a private relationship with the divine, but for men it was public. On another instance, as the discussion moved to government schemes and interventions, Maulana Rasheed, lending support to a scheme of the UP government in 2013 of providing cycles to college-going women, said, '[T]here was a lot of opposition from the Muslim community to such a scheme, but I assuaged their concerns and said, is it not safer for women to travel by cycle on their own than in public buses with other men?'[77]

The relationship between Islamic and statutory law in the Firangi Mahal *dar-ul qaza* was uncertain. The Dissolution of Muslim Marriages Act, 1939, and the Shariat Application Act, 1937, on rare occasions even found mention in the proceedings. The grounds for divorce for women listed in the Dissolution of Muslim Marriages Act, 1939, were often the basis on which *khula* was granted, its translation in Urdu was also available, but the Act was not referenced in written orders. Tschalaer, in her recent book *Muslim Women's Quest for Justice*, discusses the figure of Maulana Athar who also used provisions of statutory law on the maintenance of wives to appeal to the husband's sense of responsibility invoked in purely religious terms—essentially trying to find a justification for statutory law in Islam. She writes that the essence of Section 125 of the CrPC, on the maintenance of wives and children, was embraced by informal mediators who depended on inclusion rather than exclusion of secular or modern law in local understandings of Muslim law.[78] As a matter of policy, Maulana Rasheed had stated that *dar-ul-qazas* tried not to take up cases that were sub judice. Often the presiding *qazis* were aware of the laws against domestic violence and dowry that could potentially be deployed by women and these had a minor potential to influence their orders. The forum also confronted state law in other indirect ways such as a presence of women lawyers during some of the proceedings.

---

[76] Vatuk makes a similar observation on more women than men approaching *qazis* and *maulvis*, in *Marriage and Its Discontents*.

[77] Interviews with Maulana Rasheed, 3 December 2012 and 7 March 2018 (translation mine).

[78] Tschalaer, *Muslim Women's Quest for Justice*, 119, 131.

Advocacy and Legal Initiatives (AALI) is a Lucknow-based women's legal aid NGO, which had had relative success in negotiating favourable *fatwas* for women in the *dar-ul-qaza*s. AALI identifies as a secular, women's-rights NGO with a focus on women of marginalized communities. Intercaste, interreligious couples who are facing social backlash as well as domestic violence cases form the bulk of their matters which are argued primarily in family courts and sessions courts, before the magistrate. Their work also entailed visits to the Police *thana*s (small police station), and the *dar-ul-qaza*s in Lucknow.

Shubhangi Singh, the resource centre coordinator for AALI and a lawyer, noted that the organization shared almost 20 years of goodwill in religious forums in Lucknow.[79] It predominantly provided support to women in these forums rather than arguing on the merits of Islamic law. The mere presence of their volunteers in the room encouraged caution in *fatwas*—the option of an alternate legal intervention became visible in the presence of the volunteer. AALI negotiated multiple *khula*s from the *dar-ul-qaza* where women wanted to exit a marriage because of violence, or desired maintenance, and so on, and the local *qazi* offered what Singh recognized as reasonable decisions: 'If they say something too wayward, they know we will object, and tell them that this will not stand in court.'[80] On obtaining these *khula*s, the lawyers from AALI go to court to get it declared. Thereafter, if the husbands held back maintenance, AALI took them to court; the case did not return to the *dar-ul-qaza* for further negotiation. Sometimes women also approached AALI after having obtained a *khula* through the *qazi* to have it confirmed further by the court in order to ensure better guarantees for maintenance. Maintenance claims by divorced wives, in AALI's experience, were almost always filed under Section 125 of the CrPC. Legal strategies, however, also differed between NGOs. As Chapter 4 discussed, the Mumbai-based Majlis could deploy the Muslim Women (Protection of Rights on Divorce) Act, 1986, to negotiate better outcomes for women. For AALI, Section 125 of the CrPC remained far more pervasive because of the better penetration of the statute, down to the local *thana*, the magistrate's court, and so on.

The Family Court

The establishment of family courts in 1984, on the recommendation of the *Towards Equality* Report of 1974, had hoped to introduce an informal and efficient lawyer-less space for settling marital disputes. These family courts enabled parties to interact without the presence of lawyers, where litigants could argue

[79] Personal interview with Shubhangi Singh, 19 March 2019.
[80] Ibid.

their cases in plain language.[81] Often, however, these courts were more resistant to the dissolution of marriages than religious forums and had a greater emphasis on reconciliation and settlement remaining 'vigilant allies of the family'.[82] AALI assisted in many disputes in Lucknow's Family Court and confirmed that the family court remained inhospitable to women in their structure, function, and outcome. Singh noted that the courts did not even have proper toilets for women.

AALI's reports showed that despite there being laws and precedents in place, the family court in Lucknow was routinely providing maintenance only to children and not wives in cases of divorce.[83] Further, some casual procedures had emerged around the registration of civil marriages under the Special Marriage Act. One such procedure was the new requirement of couples filing an affidavit stating that no first information report (FIR) is lodged against any of them if they wished to marry under the Special Marriage Act. FIRs were common in cases when couples were attempting to elope. Women's families often filed kidnapping and abduction cases against their daughter or sister's lover. Such FIRs accused men of luring 'innocent daughters' or taking them by force, to bring disrepute to the family. Accusations of rape along with kidnapping were common. This also contributed to the existing police apathy towards women and engendered a common perception among the police that most rape cases are false. Thus, couples could almost never guarantee on an affidavit that there were no FIRs against either of them. Undue police enquiries preceded the confirmation of marriage under the Special Marriage Act which defeated its very purpose as a law that enabled inter-caste and inter-religious marriages. Clever women who 'roped in' unsuspecting men and men who ran away with or kidnapped hapless women also formed a common part of stories, particularly when parents disapproved of their children's choice in partners. Parental disapproval found legal translation as cases of kidnapping and rape often filed against the woman's partner. Outside the legal realm also couples were vulnerable to abandonment, isolation, and even honour killings.

Couples marrying without the consent of their parents frequently opted for temple weddings, Arya Samaji weddings, or weddings after conversion to Islam. Quick marriages in religious forums also demanded a degree of conformity by mandating conversion of the woman in a *nikah* or rituals of *sindoor* (vermillion), and so on, in temple weddings. A number of women's groups also, therefore, began to

---

[81] For an interesting discussion on the working of the family courts in Kolkata, see Basu, *The Trouble with Marriage*.

[82] Ibid., 103.

[83] Personal interview with Shubhangi Singh, 19 March 2019. See also IWRAW Asia Pacific, *Baseline Report: Rights of Women in Relation to Marriage in India* (Malaysia: AALI and IWRAW Asia Pacific, 2016), http://aalilegal.org/wp-content/uploads/2016/01/Publications_BaselineReport-RightsofWomen.pdf, accessed in January 2019.

resist compulsory registration of marriages[84] because visibility before the state made eloping couples vulnerable. 'People convert and go to a different state to marry,' Singh continued, 'at one point, Arya Samaji weddings became so common that Lucknow bench [of the Allahabad High Court] said Arya Samaji certificates were considered unacceptable as proof of marriage.'[85] Two-hour wedding ceremonies complete with a registration certificate are also promised by online websites. Court Marriage Lucknow is a website that offers an Arya Samaji wedding, with basic wedding rituals and then offers a 'professional' who can accompany the couple for registration.[86]

Couples leaning on religion for quick ceremonies and then on the law for protection, on religious forums for a speedy divorce, and then on statutory law for maintenance in case of divorce shows a tremendous degree of movement across institutions. Berti's work is particularly pertinent here as she shows how court and out-of-court narratives flow into one another. She shows, in the context of criminal proceedings, how a party's choice of approaching a court may only be an 'initial' one, which is frequently deserted for other forms of compromises.[87] This made exclusively state-led regulation difficult, and also made *fatwa*s and so on vulnerable to legal challenge, such that power was, in fact, unable to adapt to forms of resistance.[88] This is particularly well illustrated in the case of the BMMA's women's *sharia adalat*s, where authority is sourced from the Quran, but the organization uses religious vocabulary to prompt state action.

The Sharia Adalat

To counter the idea that men alone could become *qazi*s, BMMA launched *sharia adalat*s headed by women *qazi*s. Zakia Soman, one of the founding members of the BMMA, described a case where a woman had been given triple *talaq* and turned away from her matrimonial home. She approached the BMMA for support.[89] The BMMA summoned the husband at their counselling centre and the couple

---

[84] Partners for Law and Development (PLD) in their submission to the Law Commission of India recommended that compulsory registration of marriages was detrimental to women, particularly when the lack of proof could be used to invalidate a marriage, and it also made consenting couples vulnerable to the State's and the family's surveillance. In 2020, the rule of the publishing of details 30 days prior to marriage was challenged as violative of the right to privacy in the Supreme Court by a law student from the state of Kerala. 'Plea in Supreme Court over Special Marriage Act Provisions', *Hindustan Times*, 4 September 2020.
[85] Personal interview with Shubhangi Singh, 19 March 2019.
[86] See http://www.courtmarriagelucknow.com/.
[87] Daniela Berti, 'Hostile Witnesses, Judicial Interactions and Out-Of-Court Narratives in a North Indian District Court', *Contributions to Indian Sociology* 44, no. 3 (2010): 235–63.
[88] Michel Foucault, *The History of Sexuality*, vol. 1 (New York: Random House, 1978).
[89] Personal interview with Zakia Soman, 14 March 2019.

were informed that whatever outcome is arrived at will be in 'light of the Quran' (*Quran ki roshni mein*). The couple was summoned to BMMA's *adalat* where a female *qazi* heard the dispute and explained to the husband that the pronouncement of triple *talaq* was the most shameful way to divorce one's wife. 'Will Allah forgive you for abandoning your wife like this?' the *qazi* asked. On a subsequent hearing of the case, Soman explained, the husband admitted that he did not know that his actions violated the Quran, he wished to reconsider his *talaq* and take his wife back. The *qazi* confirmed that the couple could reconcile and the question of *halala* never arose. *Nikah halala* translates as a type of marriage (*nikah*) through which a wife is made eligible or lawful (*halala*) to reunite with her husband, after the couple has been divorced.[90] In practice this meant that upon divorce from her husband, a woman could only remarry that same man after marrying another man, consummating her second marriage, and then divorcing the second husband, to reconcile with the first. This customary practice was allegedly introduced to make reconciliation between divorced couples more difficult in order to discourage frivolous divorce.[91] Whether at all *nikah halala* was even deemed necessary before a couple's reconciliation also varied from case to case and even forum to forum.

On another instance, a woman sought divorce and her husband was unwilling to grant it, 'in such cases we summon the husband three times, and if he does not respond, we grant the *khula* to women. We are training our own *qazis* and have trained 17 so far'.[92] If men do not turn up upon their summons, the BMMA also involved male *qazis* whose summons were more promptly responded to. BMMA also involved the police as and when needed in domestic violence cases, and simultaneously they conducted surveys with Muslim women and prepared draft bills for circulation and draft petitions against practices such as triple *talaq*, polygamy, and *nikah halala* to be filed in court. As part of a two-pronged strategy, the organization ran its *sharia adalats* but continued to bargain with the state for expanding legal remedies for Muslim women. BMMA's support for Shayara Bano's petition against triple *talaq* led many to accuse Soman of cooperating with the Hindu nationalists. Soman also encountered tremendous backlash for her efforts to train women *qazis* from within the Muslim community.

---

[90] Lucy Carroll and Harsh Kapoor, eds., *Talaq-i-Tafwid: The Muslim Woman's Contractual Access to Divorce: An Information Kit* (1996). This kit was published in 1996, based on the 1990 publication by an international network called 'Women Living Under Muslim Laws', www.wluml.org/sites/wluml.org/files/import/english/pubs/.../talaq-i-tawfid-eng.pdf.

[91] Saxena, 'Nikah Halala', 133–54.

[92] Personal interview with Zakia Soman, 14 March 2019.

She added, 'You see we can choose to view everything (agitations against triple *talaq*) from the prism of BJP being in power, or one can just view the BJP being in power as one of the incidents of politics.'[93]

In another case in Lucknow, a woman gave unilateral *khula* to her husband.[94] Having been subjected to years of torture and failed attempts at reconciliation, she signed a *khulanama* (document of divorce initiated by women) on a ten-rupee stamp paper and posted it to her husband. Naish Hasan, a BMMA activist in Lucknow, supported the declaration and stated that *khula* is indeed the equivalent of triple *talaq*. Maulana Rasheed in his statement also did not dispute this, but stated that for *khula* to be valid, it has to be approved by a *dar-ul-qaza*, where the woman's husband has the right to be heard.[95] Soman noted that if men do not respond to repeated summons, the organization helps women get unilateral *khula* which they get approved by their *qazi*, 'after all, the Quran grants this right to women'. Strikingly, the BMMA supported women's absolute and unilateral right to divorce, even as it petitioned against the practice of unilateral divorce by men.[96]

Translating activism into law and policy therefore took various different forms. For Maulana Rasheed and Ruksana Lari, codification of Muslim law as per the *sharia* was important—they desired state protection for their version of personal law. For the BMMA, religion was inherently meaningful and leaning on state support was only a means to enable the free practice of religion. For organizations such as AALI, which encounter the limitations of the law in everyday advocacy, further legal interventions only complicated dispute resolution and strengthened state authority. Thus, while statutes were penetrating *dar-ul-qaza*s and *sharia adalat*s, the family courts were themselves not entirely committed to statutes. There were multiple processes of the translation of state law to local context, and often it was not for enforcement of 'rights' but instead for the 'reconciliation' or 'management' of disputes. Family law, therefore, remains a fertile ground for democratic negotiation and contest.

Translations of Strategies and of Biases into State Policy

Throughout history, ideas travelled across forums, sometimes bad laws produced good outcomes and good laws remained completely redundant in practice.

---

[93] Personal interview with Zakia Soman, 14 March 2019.

[94] 'UP: Woman Delivers "Khula" On Mail, Clerics Say Follow Rule', *Times of India*, 8 September 2019.

[95] Ibid.

[96] See also Sagnik Dutta, 'Divorce, Kinship, and Errant Wives: Islamic Feminism in India, and the Everyday Life of Divorce and Maintenance', *Ethnicities* 21, no. 3 (2021): 454–76.

The personality of the judge, or *qazi*, the political party in the power or even the support of an influential local NGO frequently influenced the nature of outcomes. Sometimes every problem was given a legal translation,[97] and on others, the law was aligned with local sensibilities.[98] Women did not always have opportunities to pick and choose, or compare the options available to them.

State and non-state forums also contradicted one another and decisions of non-state forums could be challenged in the courts.[99] Even outside of the court, the decisions of non-state forums provoked strong reactions. For instance, the growing number of Islamic *sharia* courts were also cited by members of the Hindu Mahasabha to launch a new counter-initiative of 'Hindu courts', which promised to deliver fast justice as per Hindu dharma in 2018. The Hindu court, in Meerut, UP, announced that it had its own prisons and was entitled to order the 'death penalty'.[100] Such courts were postured specifically against inter-religious marriages between Hindu women and Muslim men and love marriages more generally. They also took up non-adjudicative roles such as framing demands from the government for the construction of Ram Setu (Ram's bridge) in the Indian Ocean or collection of money for temple construction activities. Despite Hindu law being 'codified', Hindu forums and caste *panchayat*s are not uncommon across India. Kokal's study of *panchayat*s in Maharashtra illustrates how state law trickles into disputes, even without the presence of state institutions such as a local police *thana* or court, through social networks of individuals.[101] Equally, state- and non-state institutions not only overlap in jurisdiction but contradict with one another on 'postulational values', where state law is read as a 'foreign' element.[102]

DAKSH, a Bengaluru-based organization in 2018 completed their eight-part documentary on alternate dispute resolution forums in India.[103] Their findings on non-judicial bodies echoed many writings on these forums in the past decade that these non-judicial bodies were not only seen to be resolving disputes

---

[97] Julia Eckert, 'From Subjects to Citizens: Legalism from Below and the Homogenisation of the Legal Sphere', *The Journal of Legal Pluralism and Unofficial Law* 38, nos. 53–54 (2006): 45–75.

[98] Tschalaer, *Muslim Women's Quest for Justice*.

[99] *Vishwa Lochan Madan v. Union of India* (2014) 7 SCC 707. See also Jeffrey A. Redding, 'Secularism, the Rule of Law, and Sharia Courts: An Ethnographic Examination of a Constitutional Controversy', *Louis ULJ* 57 (2012): 339.

[100] 'Hindu Mahasabha Sets up "First Hindu Court"', *The Wire*, 17 August 2018.

[101] Kalindi Kokal, *State Law, Dispute Processing and Legal Pluralism: Unspoken Dialogues from Rural India* (London: Routledge, 2019).

[102] Masaji Chiba, ed., *Asian Indigenous Law: In Interaction with Received Law* (London and New York: KPI, 1986).

[103] DAKSH, 'Justice Access and the Nations Approaches (JANA)', video series, 21 January 2019, available at https://www.youtube.com/playlist?list=PLPsk7i7tKdZlZ1jFMKh_7TEvJFnuTLZ7l, accessed on 22 January 2019.

faster and cheaper than their judicial counterparts but also producing some problematic outcomes. The documentary contained interviews with individuals heading *gram panchayat*s, local goons with political patronage, local police, and leaders of religious forums—the *nyayapeeth*s (Hindu forums for justice). Customary or religious authority was socially, customarily, and even morally valid and, therefore, also localized.[104] Some forums privileged caste identities, others promised speedy resolution, and yet others appeared to be led solely by vigilante groups. The documentary highlighted some interesting statements by local political volunteers of the Hindu nationalist political party, the Shiv Sena, which hinted that they 'have their own methods' (*hamare apne tareeke hain*) for ensuring that justice is done, hinting at the use of threats and petty violence for getting things done.[105] Eckert's work describes the political nexus between local goons and the state where *dada*s (local strongmen), dons (leaders of organized crime groups), and *dalal*s (brokers between state offices and the population) act as middlemen, and political parties rely significantly on these networks.[106] Eckert concludes that legal norms inform local notions of justice and 'good order'. DAKSH's documentary showed that alternate forums imitate the court and have technology to digitize petitions, but painstakingly distinguish themselves from the law and legal thinking. Some of these institutions required only a written petition, which was followed by issuing notice to the concerned parties to appear before the forum headed by village elders, *jagadguru*s (teacher of the world), *mahapanch*s (heads of *panchayat*s), and so on. Some forums had infrastructure that trumps the facilities (or the lack thereof) in courts. Petitions before Jagadguru Dr Shivamurthy Shivacharya Mahaswamiji (21st of their lineage of the Tarabalu Math) were summarized and digitized before the parties are allowed to speak. He noted, 'I don't pronounce a formal judgment like in the court. In court one party loses other wins, in my Saddharma Nyaypeetha, both parties win and both the parties lose. I try to bring about an understanding ... I don't look at law books, I look at human suffering.'[107]

---

[104] Bernard S. Cohn, 'Anthropological Notes on Disputes and Law in India', *American Anthropologist* 67, no. 6 (1965): 82–122.

[105] DAKSH, 'Justice Access and the Nations Approaches (JANA)' video series, 21 January 2019, available at https://www.youtube.com/playlist?list=PLPsk7i7tKdZlZ1jFMKh_7TEvJFnuTLZ7l, accessed on 22 January 2019.

[106] Eckert, 'From Subjects to Citizens', 45–75. Eckert, in her study in Mumbai, shows multiple instances where the law is deployed successfully against the state itself. A court order against police action, or police action against municipal corporations, and so on.

[107] DAKSH, 'Justice Access and the Nations Approaches (JANA)' video series, 21 January 2019, https://www.youtube.com/playlist?list=PLPsk7i7tKdZlZ1jFMKh_7TEvJFnuTLZ7l, accessed on 22 January 2019.

These forums' responses and insistence on mediation and settlement—*suleh karwana*—in particular, the *panchayats*, and 'management' in situations raises concerns about how these forums can encourage a sustained erasure of violence that many of the narrated experiences may have entailed.[108]

Negotiations within the ambit of statutory law meant that one's desire or grief within a marriage had to be accommodated within legal categories in courts or police stations. However, it also meant that negotiations with religious rationales, religious scripture, cultural practices, or familial norms, which found currency in a *dar-ul-qaza*, a *sharia adalat*, a *khap panchayat*, *nyayapeeth*, or a joint family, also demanded a folding of behaviours into different acceptable notions of piety or morality. The easier, faster settlements in non-state forums not only show the state's dependence on these but also provoke government action to imitate these. This is visible in the form of bills on 'irretrievable breakdown of marriage' (2013) to simplify divorce procedures and court decisions to waive the mandatory period of six months before confirming a mutual consent divorce.[109] At a more localized level, policy initiatives also tell us the story of how resistance strategies of women's rights groups as well as biases of local communities translate into government initiatives.

Dave in her detailed research on the police's special cells in Mumbai has similarly shown how these cells slowly evolved in their response to violence against women.[110] She demonstrates that many women preferred a limited intervention by state authorities. They wanted violence against them acknowledged and moderated rather than petitioning before courts for divorce and so on. Her study also shows that women's ease of access to provisions of the Domestic Violence Act evolved slowly and local state presence—in the form of police special cells—was effective in enabling the law. Thus, the state did not exist as a unitary entity but in multiple forms and some of these could yield to very specific needs of the women who accessed them. Zooming in on the police powerline in Lucknow also demonstrates the extent of state collaboration with non-state agencies.

---

[108] Basu in her analysis of family courts in *The Trouble with Marriage* (2015) shows that settlements and mediations cause a systematic erasure of violence, as the court's emphasis on reconciliation essentially blurs out instances of cruelty that partners, particularly women, may have endured in a marriage.

[109] *Dr Amit Kumar v. Dr Sonila and Ors*, Civil Appeal No. 10771 of 2018 (Arising out of SLP(C) No. 21786/2018). See also 'SC Allows Couple to Separate without Waiting for Six-month Mandatory "Cooling-Off" Period', *The Hindu*, 16 October 2018.

[110] Anjali Dave, 'Strategic Alliance, a Way Forward for Violence against Women: A Case for the Special Cells, India', *Violence against Women* 19, no. 10 (2013): 1203–23.

The Police Powerline

The state's outreach to women citizens through formal law and prompt legislation only evidences the state's inability to counter crimes against women in India. Its informal attempts, however, which are largely in the form of police outreach programmes, have yielded widely different outcomes, in different states. One interesting example is that of the Women's Powerline 1090 of the UP government initiated by the Samajwadi Party in 2012. This initiative established a 'pre-FIR' intervention, through an interactive voice response system. In minor but meaningful ways, this initiative reflected a significant change in the citizen–state relationship. For instance, the initiative was popularized as a 'powerline' rather than a 'helpline' to underline the idea that women should not be classified as victims in need of protection.[111] Navneit Sikera, the inspector general of police, who led the charge of the Women's Powerline, acknowledged,

> [O]ur biggest problem was that either women were complaining to the police and the police were not responsive, or alternatively women did not want to complain at all due to fear or family and relatives and suffered in silence but were unwilling to start the daunting process of filing an FIR and following up on the case.[112]

The powerline assured women callers that their identity would be protected, and they would not be called to a police *thana* or *chowki* (small police station) as far as possible. Their calls would always be answered by women police officers, who remained in touch with the caller until the reported problem is 'completely resolved'. There was a follow-up mechanism in place where callers and women police remained in contact for the first three months of the complaint and then again after six months from the initial complaint to confirm if the harasser has attempted to contact the women again. Male officers responded to the harassers and warned them over the phone about the potential laws that they could be booked under. The culprit's responses ranged from immediate apology and promise of restrain or complete denial of having called, stalked, or harassed anyone. In case of repeat offenders, FIRs were lodged, and men were taken into custody.[113]

---

[111] The 2017 summary of the UP Powerline reveals that 87 per cent of the complaints they received were related to harassment over the phone or text, 9 per cent in public places, and only 1.9 per cent for domestic violence. The data suggests multiple possibilities, including that serious complaints of violence and dowry harassment may not be getting rooted through the powerline. That may also explain the high 'resolution rate' given that situations where women find themselves in immediate danger and still reported to the police line dialled on 100, rather 1090.

[112] Interview of Navneit Sikera, 2 February 2017, at the 1090 Centre, Lucknow.

[113] Women's powerline tapes, accessed on 2 and 9 February 2017 at the 1090 Centre, Lucknow.

This initiative could easily have metamorphosed into police surveillance but there was repeated reiteration of 'consent' in the language of interaction and the structure of the initiative. The compound of 1090 was situated beside a major road intersection in Lucknow and contained its own seminar room for workshops and training and also crèche facilities for young mothers. The circular building of the 1090 assured that there were no hierarchies of coveted 'corner offices' and all employees inhabited one large workspace with multiple work stations. Infrastructurally, this was drastically different from the family court.

The powerline's emphasis on 'shielding women' from being forced to confront aggressors is also comparable to the assurances of privacy that the dar-ul-qazas offer. The powerline also had a relationship with local schools in Lucknow where girls were encouraged to join the police force, or train with the powerline and also engage in counselling and outreach activities. Such training was often conducted with the help of NGOs. The powerline had a very direct reliance on non-state organizations. While social movements were critical of various state interventions, they also exerted pressure on the state to maintain these resources.[114]

State schemes and policies, however, also had the potential to embody, imitate, and reproduce biases rather than reflect resistance alone. In 2017, the newly elected BJP-led government in UP launched anti-Romeo squads across the state for the 'protection of women'.[115] As part of this scheme, policemen in plain clothes lurked in public places, particularly around schools and colleges on a lookout for women who could be 'under threat'. The squads earned flak for rounding up and demanding identification of men for 'loitering' or being seen with women, or celebrating Valentine's Day. In some cases, men were made to do sit-ups for merely being in the presence of their lovers in a public park.[116] These squads could let off aggressors with a warning, inform their parents, or even initiate criminal action. They were later renamed 'Nari Suraksha Bal' (women's protection squad), which not only reinforced the rhetoric of 'protection' over 'empowerment' but also generated new regimes of surveillance and control.[117] In an unfortunate move, the women's powerline and the 'Nari Suraksha Bal'

---

[114] Masaji Chiba, 'Legal Pluralism in Sri Lankan Society: Toward a General Theory of Non-western Law', *Journal of Legal Pluralism and Unofficial Law* 25, no. 33 (1993): 197–212.

[115] 'What Are Anti-Romeo Squads? How Do They Operate?', News18, 22 March 2017.

[116] 'The UP CM and His Anti-Romeo Squad Seem to Have Very Conflicting Ideas about "Romeos"', *Huffington Post*, 7 April 2017.

[117] In 2018, the UP government declared its intention to merge 1090 and the Nari Suraksha Bal. The interviews and fieldwork on 1090, in this book, were conducted before this merger.

were merged by the government in 2018. Such ever-increasing potential for surveillance is precisely what makes disagreements within feminist strategy and methodology on state intervention extremely relevant and valuable.[118] Privileging any one kind of framework as most yielding or best suited overlooks the effect of the collective entanglement of strategies.[119]

Actors leading or constituting a movement bring together not only transnational, legal, or 'secular' strategy with local, home-grown resistance strategies but both mutually transform the articulation of violation, of violence, or of discrimination.[120] Moreover, what actors and agents bring to the table is not just global human rights frameworks but commonly an indigenous legal rights framework, a new political consciousness, different levels of education, local experience, and so on. Not all such transformations can be understood as a 'secularizing' effect, nor can all local resistance be assumed to embedded religiosity. The police powerline chief had expressed an interest in recruiting more women from minority communities as one of their major goals. The Suraksha Bal, however, perceived Muslim men as predators. This transformation had the potential to change Muslim women's relationship with the local police.

In these already incoherent legal spaces, therefore, women are unwilling to be co-opted into any meta-narrative of Muslim identity, minority rights, or even feminism, which would restrict their access to tools and strategies for negotiation. Their 'strategic essentialism' allows for the alignment with groups, individuals, and the state, but these alliances are neither permanent nor always ideological. Challenging the idea that there ever was a Muslim consensus against state

---

[118] See also Menaka Guruswamy and Aditya Singh, 'Accessing Injustice: The Gram Nyayalayas Act, 2008', *The Economic and Political Weekly* 45, no. 43 (2010): 16–19. Similarly, much like the initiative of the family court, in 2008, the government enacted a Gram Nyayalaya Act, aimed at establishing a 'speedy' and 'accessible' justice system tailored particularly to rural India. It came with limited procedural guarantees, to adjudicate small matters of whether minimum wages were being given, or if bonded labour continued to prevail. In essence, the policy was meant to follow up on constitutional guarantees provided under other laws. However, despite its claimed objectives, the Act perpetuated the idea that rural India accessed a separate legal system with limited procedures of appeal.

[119] Menski's emphasis on the progressive interpretation of religion in courts, therefore, undermines the transformation of religious law and politics outside the court through demands on the legislature as well as pressure on and from alternative forums. Similarly, Ahmed's emphasis on all family law negotiations exclusively through ADR also blurs out Muslim women's relationship with state institutions. Werner F. Menski, 'Asking for the Moon: Legal Uniformity in India from a Kerala Perspective', *Kerala Law Times, Journal Section* 2 (2006): 52–78.

[120] Sally Engle Merry, 'Transnational Human Rights and Local Activism: Mapping the Middle', *American Anthropologist* 108, no. 1 (2006): 38–51.

intervention in personal law in the last decade has given way to a new relationship between Muslim women and the state, where they negotiate with the Hindu nationalist government but do not necessarily vote for it. Many of these women's initiatives challenge notions of community and use legal spaces to produce a dialogue on religion rather than distance from it. In doing so, in the limited realm of family law, they undermine the law's potential to create permanent categories of minorities and majorities, and the oppressor and the oppressed. Thus, Hasina Khan's impatience with the Muslim 'readiness' for reform and Soman's desire for a statutory intervention for a religious and humanitarian end offer a window into how Muslim women in India are articulating the fine distinctions that Valentine Moghadam recognizes between Muslim and Islamic feminisms.[121] It opens up the conversation of the spectrum of Muslim religiosities challenging the theorization of a coherent Muslim monolith as well as that of the category of 'minority'.

III

Making a Community: Against a Resolution

The debate on group versus individual rights, or secular and religious feminism is an old and ongoing one. This section is not an attempt to necessarily pick a side, but to illustrate that the articulation of demands by individual women or women collectives frequently utilize arguments of individual and group rights simultaneously. Post the *Shah Bano* case, Muslim women were caught in a bind where influential organizations of Muslims, in particular the AIMPLB and the Jamaat-e-Islam-e-Hind, demanded non-interference in religion, and women's legal rights came at the cost of making their community vulnerable to an onslaught by Hindu nationalism. Privileging communities in the name of the appreciation of 'difference' in a democracy generated various forms of politics around identities— and these identities could both subsume or embolden women's voices. The search for identity, therefore, as Benhabib argues, was essentially a pursuit to create difference.[122] The generation of group versus individual rights polarization then has to be seen as cyclical or repetitive. And cannot simply be seen as a state's conspiracy to keep these categories relevant, but rather as people's active strategy.

---

[121] Valentine M. Moghadam, 'Islamic Feminism and Its Discontents: Toward a Resolution of the Debate', *Signs: Journal of Women in Culture and Society* 27, no. 4 (2002): 1135–71. See also Haideh Moghissi, 'Islamic Feminism Revisited', *Comparative Studies of South Asia, Africa and the Middle East* 31, no. 1 (2011): 76–84.

[122] Seyla Benhabib, ed., *Democracy and Difference: Contesting the Boundaries of the Political* (Princeton, NJ: Princeton University Press, 1996).

For Parashar, recognizing 'differences' in religious communities runs the risk of being lost in political rhetoric as family-related matters are subsumed within debates about religious identity.[123] Often state-enacted and state-enforced rules which are deemed 'essential to religion' not only shared a tenuous connection to the divine but also gave statutory force to discrimination.[124] This is precisely what Ayelet Shachar termed the 'paradox of multicultural vulnerability'.[125] Even well-intentioned policies of the state for addressing inequalities between the minority community and the wider society unintentionally permitted the 'systematic maltreatment of individuals within that accommodated minority group. This impact, in certain cases, was so severe that it nullified individuals' rights as citizens'[126], as was the case in numerous legislative interventions enacted ostensibly to preserve the essential practices of religion. Communities may not necessarily be 'enabling spaces' that resist the homogenizing efforts of the state, or of a majoritarian politics. A 'community' could also colonize an individual's life by binding individuals with an idea of a shared past, which was utilized to perpetuate customs and to generate a consensus on 'moral solidarity'.[127] Overplaying the notion of 'difference' between communities also led to an assumption, as Sarkar notes, that 'tradition, community and inherited condition constitute the sole source of authentic meaning and value, outside of which there can only be a loss of identity'.[128]

Religious feminism further disrupts the individual versus community debate in India. Religious feminisms have popularized other modes of religious knowledge where religion is not 'a problematic tool of oppression used against women, rather than as a viable form of feminist agency'.[129]

---

[123] A. Parashar, *Women and Family Law Reform in India*: *Uniform Civil Code and Gender Equality* (New Delhi: Sage Publications, 1992).

[124] See also Rohini Hensmen, 'A Response to "Uniform Civil Code": The Women's Movement Perspective', *Kafila.org*, 8 October 2014.

[125] Ayelet Shachar, 'On Citizenship and Multicultural Vulnerability', *Political Theory* 28, no. 1 (2000): 64–89.

[126] Ayelet Shachar, 'Puzzle of Interlocking Power Hierarchies: Sharing the Pieces of Jurisdictional Authority', *The Harv. CR-CLL Rev.* 35, no. 2 (2000): 385–426. See also Shachar, 'On Citizenship and Multicultural Vulnerability'.

[127] Veena Das, *Critical Events* (Delhi: Oxford University Press, 1995).

[128] Tanika Sarkar, *Hindu Wife, Hindu Nation, Community, Religion, and Cultural Nationalism* (New Delhi: Permanent Black, 2001), 235, for a discussion on the Age of Consent Bill.

[129] Therese Saliba, Carolyn Allen, and Judith A. Howard, eds., *Gender, Politics, and Islam* (Chicago: Orient Blackswan, 2005), 3. Contributions of Lila Abu-Lughod and Mir-Hosseini to this debate are particularly valuable. Lila Abu-Lughod, *Do Muslim Women Need Saving?* (Cambridge, MA: Harvard University Press, 2013); Z. Mir-Hosseini, 'The Challenges of Islamic Feminism', *Gender and Research* 20, no. 2 (2019): 108–22.

This opens up questions of what circumscribes ideas of agency, and the capacity and confidence that constitute it.[130] It is precisely the battle over ownership of religion that distinguishes women's articulations in the 2000s. While post–*Shah Bano* writings had begun to point out that women were being subjected to the unfair choice between constitutional rights *or* religious identity, women's rejection of this binary became visible when religious women demanded 'secular' or rather 'legal' interventions for accessing rights guaranteed to them in authentic religion. Ethnographic studies have also shown that women often negotiate religious rights in religious forums and yet produce a secularizing effect, by challenging the definition of religion and religious community.[131] Different forums yield very different kinds of expectations that women have from any adjudication process.

Religious feminists rooted their arguments in the inherent 'misunderstanding' of religion in state laws that compromised not just women's rights but also their relationship with the community.[132] The reinterpretation of Islamic texts from a feminist perspective has become a common practice across many parts of the world. Global movements such as the Musawah have inspired new initiatives in India. Such attempts have also attracted substantial scholarship acknowledging the influence of these movements as well as the conversations this has prompted for 'secular' feminism. Secular feminists, on the other hand, challenge religious feminism's ability to limit the tools for resisting power structures by closing the possibility of critique of religion itself.[133] They contend that this limits not only the vocabulary of resistance but also reinforces religious authority as the only permanent and valid source of the law/truth.

Religious feminism could demand not just conformity but could be exclusionary, where it views women's demands for a secular law or state intervention as compromising their politics and position within a community.[134] Religious

---

[130] For a discussion on agency, see Sumi Madhok, 'Action, Agency, Coercion: Reformatting Agency for Oppressive Contexts', in *Gender, Agency, and Coercion*, ed. Sumi Madhok, Anne Phillips, and Kalpana Wilson (Basingstoke: Palgrave Macmillan, 2013), 102–21.

[131] Katherine Lemons, *Divorcing Traditions: Islamic Marriage Law and the Making of Indian Secularism* (Ithaca, NY: Cornell University Press, 2019).

[132] For women and Islam and Islamic feminism, see Fatima Mernissi, *Women and Islam* (Oxford: Basil Blackwell, 1991); and Saliba, Allen, and Howard, *Gender, Politics, and Islam*.

[133] Moghadam, 'Islamic Feminism and Its Discontents'; Moghissi, 'Islamic Feminism Revisited'; Deniz Kandiyoti, ed., *Women, Islam and the State*, vol. 105 (Philadelphia: Temple University Press, 1991).

[134] Rajeswari Sunder Rajan, ed., *Signposts: Gender Issues in Post-Independence India* (New Brunswick, NJ: Rutgers University Press, 2001).

feminism could burden participants with proving allegiance to the community, and making their agency within a community contingent on proving religiosity or piety. Women's membership to the community could then become contingent on obedience or observance. Vatuk points out that this may create new standards of virtuous behaviour.[135]

The Indian women's movement in India, however, does not inhabit a neat distinction of reifying Islam, on the one hand, and the extermination of religion through law, on the other.[136] On the contrary, Muslim women's organizations disagree with secular organizations precisely over the latter's overt and clear opposition to state intervention for Muslim women's rights. Nor does secular feminism in India share substantial similarities with global movements. When it comes to legal strategies, secular feminist resistance to legislative intervention in Muslim law inadvertently reproduces the rhetoric of Muslim vulnerability and the consequent need for recognition of Muslim exceptionality in personal law. This makes certain secular feminist articulations vulnerable to critiques that would normally be valid for global 'Islamic' feminists, whose activism is also premised on Muslim exclusivity and rights bestowed on women within religion.

For instance, Moghissi writes in context of Iran that celebrating 'Islamic feminism' on occasions has undermined the struggles of Muslim women against the legal and moral authority of Islamic clerics.[137] In India, on the contrary, Muslim women's struggles against Islamic clerics have been critiqued by certain secular feminist groups who viewed these struggles as 'blinkered' for targeting the clergy when indeed secularism was under threat by Hindu nationalist politics that could institutionalize discrimination against religious minorities.[138] Such a reading casts Muslim women's engagement with the state as though it has somehow missed the hostile political context. This severely undermines how well Muslim women have managed to bargain with a hostile state and an influential clergy. Secular feminism on the Muslim question, in the Indian context, ends up responding far more authoritatively to the genuine threat to secularism than rendering support to Muslim women's politics. The uncertain and malleable definition of secularism significantly influences the strategies and the vocabularies of resistance, traced throughout the text of the book.

[135] Vatuk, 'Islamic Feminism in India', 489–518.
[136] See also Dipesh Chakrabarty, *Habitations of Modernity: Essays in the Wake of Subaltern Studies* (Chicago: University of Chicago Press, 2002), 140, where he argues that the opposite mode of fixed identity is proximity where 'difference is neither reified nor erased but negotiated'.
[137] Moghissi, 'Islamic Feminism Revisited', 81.
[138] 'This Muslim Organisation's Campaign for a Ban on Triple Talaq Is Commendable but Blinkered', *Scroll.in*, 20 June 2016.

Moreover, boundaries between religious and secular figures in India remain fluid. For instance, religious scholars such as Fyzee and Syed Qadri (Chapter 3), and politicians such as Arif Mohammad Khan (Chapter 4) are frequently referred to as 'secular icons'. Muslim women, on the other hand, who supported the banning of triple *talaq*, such as Zakia Soman and Ruksana Lari, who also identify as religious or practising Muslim women were accused of being insufficiently Muslim by influential men of the Muslim community. While Soman received personal threats, Lari was made to resign from the AIMPLB. A member of the AIMPLB accused Soman, in particular, of having secretly converted to Hinduism and she was targeted on social media for months on end. Tschalaer's writing on the figure of Shaista Amber, the president of the All India Muslim Women's Personal Law Board (AIMWPLB) is very revealing of how women have an additional burden of keeping their community identity and legal demands repeatedly reconciled.[139] Men, on the other hand, swing between the liberal and conservative axis. Their membership to community or innate Muslimness is never in question.

For instance, Asaduddin Owaisi, a Hyderabad-based politician,president of the All India Majlis-e-Ittehadul Muslimeen (AIMIM) and a parliamentarian, in his defence of triple *talaq* simultaneously occupied secular and obscurantist positions.[140] His speeches reported in national dailies called out the BJP's hypocrisy in their commitment to Muslim women's welfare—a secular stance—but equally he argued strongly against state intervention in a Muslim family where triple *talaq* was an acceptable mode of divorce for men.

Muslim women's initiatives for codification of Muslim personal law provide a counter narrative to the general anxieties that characterize writings on Muslim personal law at the high point of Hindu nationalism.[141] It was precisely the incapacity of the state to centralize the authority on family law, which produced a new vocabulary of protest. The breaking of the Muslim consensus against state intervention in Muslim personal law that characterized the 1980s has given way to new understandings of the relationship between the state and the Muslim citizen. This has allowed for the voice on Muslim personal law reform to become one that can be identified solely with Muslim women, unlike the case of Hindu reform which was spearheaded by national figures such as Ambedkar and Nehru. The deep entrenchment of the Hindu caste system in law and politics in India demonstrates the fractured category of the 'Hindu' and scholarship has recognized

---

[139] Tschalaer, *Muslim Women's Quest for Justice.*
[140] '"Triple Talaq Bill Is Unconstitutional", Says Asaduddin Owaisi', NDTV, 18 June 2019.
[141] Kapur, '"Belief" in Law and Hindu Majoritarianism'; Flavia Agnes, *Family Law*, vol. I: *Family Laws and Constitutional Claims* (New Delhi: Oxford University Press, 2011).

the specificities of caste discrimination that women encounter.[142] Similarly, Islamic feminism in India has also not been homogenizing. The disagreements within the Muslim women's movement have emerged more on lines of strategy than Islamic identity.

While the myth of the Hindu monolith, or 'bahumat', projected by the BJP has attracted tremendous scholarship,[143] acknowledging the diversity of Muslim voices has largely remained limited to the cultural or sectarian differences rather than the diverging trends within Muslim politics. The terms of engagement between Muslim women and the Hindu nationalist government may appear to disproportionately favour the government but, crucially, it highlights the government's most apparent failures. The BJP tried to yield to Muslim women's demands, and yet did not necessarily gather their vote. The women's movement's diverse strategies but a largely unified resistance to a Uniform Civil Code, succeeded in provoking the 21st Law Commission to recommend against government policy of a Uniform Civil Code. The commission's consultation paper on the reform of family law, however, did recommend substantial amendments relating to no-fault divorce, common age for marriage, common provisions for adoption, banning bigamy in Islam, equal inheritance rights between men and women, among Muslims and Parsis, and so on. The government did not incorporate these recommendations into bills.

Through an analysis of law-related processes rather than the law itself, we encounter multiple negotiations between the state and the citizen, and a constitution and reconstitutions of religious communities and gender politics. State interventions as well as decisions of alternate forums could both be to the detriment of women and also provide avenues for competition and challenge. Diversity in strategy, therefore, is an achievement of feminism rather than a challenge. The minor disagreements on strategy within the feminist movement are perhaps best left unresolved, particularly when both secularism and religious feminism in India have widely variable understandings. It is what Harding describes as the

---

[142] Sharmila Rege, *Writing Caste, Writing Gender: Reading Dalit Women's Testimonios* (New Delhi: Zubaan, 2006); Nivedita Menon, 'Sexuality, Caste, Governmentality: Contests over "Gender" in India', *Feminist Review* 91, no. 1 (2009): 94–112.

[143] T. B. Hansen, *The Saffron Wave: Democracy and Hindu Nationalism in Modern India* (Princeton, NJ: Princeton University Press, 1999); Christophe Jaffrelot, *The Hindu Nationalist Movement and Indian Politics: 1925 to the 1990s: Strategies of Identity-Building, Implantation and Mobilisation (With Special Reference to Central India)* (New Delhi: Penguin Books, 1999); Yogendra Yadav, 'Electoral Politics in the Time of Change: India's Third Electoral System, 1989–99', *Economic and Political Weekly* 34, no. 34/35 (1999): 2393–99.

lack of a specific feminist methodology[144] that disallows a resolution precisely because it hesitates in imposing categories and labels in the face of the diversity of women's experiences. As Menon puts it, feminist solidarities as well as disjunctures in solidarity must be viewed as 'conjunctural, fluid and radically negotiable'.[145]

Conclusion

The discussion on forums evidences the impossibility of state regulation of family law. It shows the disaggregated nature of state authority as well as the decentralized interpretation and application of religious/Muslim personal law. It demonstrates how challenges to the legal authority of the state have yielded room to manoeuvre for women with respect to negotiating remedies against familial violence. This dialogue demonstrates that the regulatory authority of the state is repeatedly challenged in courts, commissions, *thana*s, petitions, the state's own schemes, alternate dispute resolution forums, and so on. Legal strategies may enhance the state's regulatory capacity, as much as a *dar-ul-qaza* does for that of a *qazi*. There is a dual decentralization, where state institutions not only contradict each other but also attempt to absorb versions of religious knowledge into statutes, judgments, or reports.

State forums often imitated and reinforced familial hierarchies and alternate forums imitated the state structure to the extent that they could pronounce decisions, mediate, and enforce religious orders. Muslim women's groups in India did not seek legal unification but they did lean on secular institutions for enabling women's political agency. Without a discussion on women's strategies, it may appear that secularism has the potential to essentialize religious communities, encourage identity politics around religion, and generate permanent minorities. The idea of a minority as a permanent category, however, has been challenged repeatedly by religious feminist interventions persuading us to read a critique of secularism together with feminist politics.

While secularism has largely been criticized for being comfortably reconcilable with Christianity, in the Indian context it was reconciled with Hinduism, and in

---

[144] Sandra G. Harding, ed., *Feminism and Methodology: Social Science Issues* (Bloomington: Indiana University Press, 1987).

[145] Nivedita Menon, 'Is Feminism about "Women"? A Critical View on Intersectionality from India', *Economic and Political Weekly* 50, no. 17 (2015): 37–44.

Egypt somewhat with Muslim reforms—leading one to wonder whether secularism reconciles with any dominant religion? Or does legislation create a public Hindu and a public Muslim around which politics can be generated. And eventually the publicness of religion aligns religious law with notions of justice rather than an abstract commitment to secularism? With the law as that crucial tool bridging the public and the private, religion when sufficiently embroiled in legislative debate acquires characteristics of neutrality by sheer publicity. The law was, therefore, neither merely an instrument of control nor solely a tool for resistance. The law was, in fact, a dialogue.

Conclusion

We must not make a scarecrow of the law, setting it up to fear the birds of prey, And let it keep one shape, till custom make it their perch and not their terror.
— William Shakespeare, *Measure for Measure*

The question of personal laws in India follows this Shakespearean logic as the state routed its engagement with family law through religion to exercise more significant and intimate control over citizens. But as it proceeded to write customs and religion into statutes, alternate authorities/movements emerged to usurp or to challenge the statutes of religious personal laws in India. Furthermore, the statute itself remained a scarecrow with little uniformity in its understanding and inefficient implementation. If one were to extend this Shakespearean metaphor, however, the ineffectual scarecrow provided a perch for the birds of prey (as patriarchy got written into statutes) but was more visible to the watchful farmer (the stakeholders) than before when her adversaries were camouflaged amidst the thickets. Women could rally against an unjust or an ill-interpreted religious statute, than build a critique of religion alone. The codification of personal laws thus achieved the unique feat of making the personal public. It politicized the domestic sphere and rendered religion amendable rather than purging it from public life. Not only did religion acquire characteristics of neutrality but the law also acquired the characteristics of religion.

The interconnectedness and, indeed, reliance of state power on religion, religious forums, and disagreements within the institutions of state rendered impossible the imputation of any will to the state itself. Thus, while the state's complicity in patriarchy and the stifling language of the law it generates has been well established in scholarship, the book traces the historical trajectory of negotiations with the law, offering a glimpse into India's democracy through a conversation over divorce.

Legislation did not tighten the grip of the state on personal law. Complex law-related processes, however, produced an awareness of differences, religious, caste, regional, or customary, which were in a constant state of calibration. This book aimed to capture the shifting meanings and interrelationship between law, religion, family, minority rights, and gender by tracing key developments in personal law in postcolonial Indian politics. Taking a longue durée approach, it argued that regulating personal law has been a key instrument through which the Indian state managed religion, shaped religious identities, infiltrated the family, and engaged with citizens. When religion was transformed to act as a 'law', it was strengthened with the backing of a statute, but this also made religion subject to surveillance by the state, scrutiny by civil society, and open to challenge by the clergy and the ordinary citizen. By including religion in statutes, the state could hope to become the 'supra-authority'[1] that could be appealed to for conflict resolution, arbitration, and protection. However, it increasingly became apparent that the state was not always the sole arbiter but often a party in family law conversations. State inaction was capable of triggering social change, and state action encountered resistance such that legislating on family law remained a slow, controversial, but also a relatively ineffectual process.

After independence, much of the debate on personal law, secularism, and fundamental rights, regardless of which side of the argument one found oneself on, used the vocabulary of constitutional rights. All arguments found some basis in the constitution. The argument for the preservation of personal law was framed around the 'constitutional' right to retain such laws. The codification of separate but reformed personal law was also anchored in the idea that the constitutional right to the freedom of religion allowed for the propagation of the 'true' meaning or form of religion over heretical customs. Conversely, the opposition to any personal laws was also built around the 'constitutionally' guaranteed rights, that religion, tradition, or custom potentially denied to the citizens. Negotiations for cultural, individual, and constitutional rights brought family law to the centre of democratic politics, and the very placeholder of the 'personal' became embroiled in polarizing political debate.

The battle over 'constitutional guarantees' manifested itself in various forums. There were contestations between civil society movements, individuals, and the religious orthodoxy; the state and the civil society; the state and the religious orthodoxy; and the judiciary and the legislature. It was through the constitution that interest politics was facilitated and fuelled. Social movements also contributed significantly to the expansion of the legal horizon through their excessive reliance on the reformative potential of the law.

---

[1] See Bardhan cited in R. S. Sunder Rajan's essay, 'Outlaw Woman', in *Crime through Time*, ed. Saurabh Dube and Anupama Rao (New Delhi: Oxford University Press, 2013), 209–34. Authors argue in reference to dacoit-turned-politician Phoolan Devi's career that the 'supra-authority' of the postcolonial state challenges the local overlord's traditional patronage.

Simultaneously, however, social and religious movements also suggested that religious moralities and sensibilities could become the basis for legal reform. It was only through a dynamic accommodation of plurality that the law could govern. This plurality opening up spaces for disagreements and specific perspectives was a constructive, transformative force which added to the strength of Indian democracy and its unique way of handling secularism through most part of the late twentieth and early twenty-first century.

The very process of writing religion as statutory 'law' contained certain in-built mechanisms of both surveillance and of democratization. First, by establishing the public acceptance of religion in the law (Chapter 1, codification of Hindu law), the state made religious law amendable, and the domestic sphere accessible. Challenges to the modular Hindu law now emerged on account of it being insufficiently diverse, neither sufficiently liberal nor religious. The codification of personal law led the Indian state governments to seek recognition of regional customs prevalent in different Indian provinces into central family law statutes (Chapter 2). Attempts to revise Christian, Muslim, and Hindu law were made primarily through quasi-legal bodies such as committees, commissions with relative success. It was through its ability to mediate and moderate religious claims or demands of social movements that the Indian state mitigated the threats to its authority posed by religious or regional movements. In a sense, the state aided religion in acquiring characteristics of neutrality. These committees served the purpose of converting social protest into the legal language of bills and, therefore, even in the process of absorbing demands for social change, they aided in enlarging the legal sphere. Committees could critique the government, absorb protest, and yet not yield tangible outcomes. This also resulted in the directing of all social movements protesting patriarchy to price rise to demand changes in the law, which was to remain the monopoly of the state (Chapter 3). State responded in many voices through legislation, judgments, and commissions. Each producing distinct readings of religion state relationship, secularism, and even constitutional rights.

Having historically shied away from defining secularism, India instituted a flexible, opportunistic, and revisable relationship between religion and the many institutions of the state. Parliament did not labour over the minutiae of what was the suitable or 'principled'[2] distance between state and religious affairs, or whether the fundamental right to freedom of religion was really in contradiction with the directive principle of a Uniform Civil Code. This resulted in the appropriation of the word 'secular' to a varying extent by majoritarian

---

[2] Rajeev Bhargava, 'What Is Secularism for?', in *Secularism and Its Critics*, ed. Rajeev Bhargava (New Delhi: Oxford University Press, 1998), 487–550.

political parties (particularly during the 1990s) which attempted to universalize the demographically dominant morality as 'national'. 'Nationalism' then, in turn, began to appear as secularized religion. This trend decidedly uncoupled liberal democracy from classical secularism which demands a stricter separation between religion and the state, thereby allowing for political parties to indulge in both secularism and religion.

The Hindu nationalist campaign for a Ram Temple in place of the Babri Mosque alongside their emphasis on a Uniform Civil Code forced religious minorities to momentarily reconcile any internal differences and align their political interests with conservative religious leadership.[3] The Muslim Women Act of 1986 became an important moment for Muslim politics in India, and despite the ambiguous nature of the legislation, the responses to the *Shah Bano* judgment and the subsequent Act had an ideological import (Chapter 4). The articulations of Muslim political identity continued to be internally challenged in subsequent years. With greater pressure to unify a legal system (here, divorce law and maintenance under Muslim personal law), the state was forced to confront greater plurality.[4] This was not, however, antithetical to the Indian state's legislative impulse as greater plurality meant that there would be a corresponding demand for codification of difference and this consequently enlarged the sphere of the law. The court played catch-up and intervened in settling religious questions from a self-styled pedestal of liberalism to counteract parliamentary populism and religious favouritism (Chapter 5). If the 1950s legislation aimed at the writing of religion in legal form as an exercise in secularizing religion, the 1990s and 2000s witnessed powerful public and political campaigns on religious lines such that the court in the Hindutva judgments concluded that the religious was the new secular. As for Muslim personal law, the court continued sporadically to align religious law with liberal or constitutional ideas, an exercise that pre-dated independence, but its interventions in early 2000s gained particular popularity.

Realizing that the state's secularism was flexible at best and opportunistic at worst, many contemporary women's movements in the twenty-first century confronted religious orthodoxy by reclaiming religion from the monopoly of the male clergy rather than reclaiming secularism from Hindu nationalism (Chapter 6). Some of these movements tugged at religious feminism and claimed to represent 'true' religion that challenged the prejudiced or chauvinist representation of their religious identity in parliament and in the public sphere

---

[3] The Muslim vote began to consolidate with the Samajwadi Party in UP, under the leadership of Mulayam Singh Yadav. For the Samajwadi Party, see Lucia Michelutti, *The Vernacularisation of Democracy: Politics, Caste and Religion in India* (New Delhi: Routledge, 2008).

[4] Werner Menski, 'From Dharma to Law and Back? Postmodern Hindu Law in a Global World', working paper no. 20, Heidelberg papers in South Asian and Comparative Politics, 2004.

more generally. Muslim women's claims from the Hindu nationalist state in the 2000s, therefore, also allows for a lively rethink of whether regulatory impulses of the state were turned on its head as enabling strategies in the limited arena of family law. Personal law's link with the constitution is established through the instrument of secularism. The state used the rhetoric of the reformative potential of the law to encourage the codification of religious practices to access and govern the family and legitimize its authority by co-opting religion into the law. This triumph of the law, however, remained deeply contingent on having accommodated religious sentiment.

This book contends that the relationship between religion and the state is a dynamic, competitive, and a sustained negotiation. It aims to fill the gap in the extant literature on meanings of secularism, mostly conducted at a fairly abstract level,[5] by fleshing out the legislative and judicial response to decades of public debates and activism on the question of family law and personal law in independent India. The acknowledgement of faith in the public space and public culture was how the inviolability or immutability of religious commandments (or personal laws) could be subjected to questions and contestations through the instrument of the law. It was also a means through which citizens could question the legitimacy of the state. At different points in history, the idea of uniformity and individual rights was appropriated by Hindu nationalists, the defence of personal law and group rights was heralded by Muslim conservatives. The monopolization of these positions by predominantly male-dominated socially conservative organizations is precisely why the binary opposition between individual and group rights became insufficient tools for analysis of personal law regimes. Both state and citizens deployed group, community, and individual identities and both showed commitment for towards religion and secularism in their politics. These negotiations were impossible to absorb into a coherent 'law'. It begs the question then, does decentralization necessarily diminish governmentalization? To what degree does state power adapt to forms of resistance?

State institutions hesitated in deploying the law in the realm of the family and marriage and leaned on religion and religious personal laws to justify, regulate, invalidate, or preserve customs and traditions. In a sense, therefore, personal law was decentralized such that it could acquire new meanings that varied across forums and between adjudicators. The content of 'rights' and 'essential practices of

---

[5] An empirical study of secularism through the prism of the maintenance of 'public order' can be found in the work of Thomas Blom Hansen, and Tariq Modood, 2016. 'Secularism, Popular Passion and Public Order in India', in *Contesting Secularism: Comparative Perspectives*, ed. Anders Berg-Sørensen (Farnham, Surrey: Ashgate, 2013), 207–31.

religion' was constantly infused with fresh meanings in encounters between the state and the citizen. The multiplicity of legal spaces allowed for the reimagination of constitutional and religious values, notions of rights, and the vocabularies of protests.

The Afterlife of Cases, Codes, and Committees: *A Postscript*

The history of democracy witnessed competition, negotiation as well as collapse of institutions and movements. Tracing this history also allows for the recognition of phases where and when democratic dialogue in the realm of law stalled. Postcolonial scholarship has overwhelmingly centred on Emergency in emphasizing state centralization, which needs to be reassessed in light of current politics, where law is increasingly becoming a tertiary or even an irrelevant tool for centralization of authority. The status of commissions, committees, the fate of petitions and protests featured in the course of the book is particularly relevant to remember in the current phase of Indian politics, which future historians may recall as the unmitigated crisis of Indian democracy. The renewed issue of a Uniform Civil Code after the BJP-led National Democratic Alliance formed the government in 2014 has evoked sharp reactions from the AIMPLB[6] but had vocal support from the Hindu Mahasabha, the RSS, and the Vishwa Hindu Parishad.[7] Concern about the template of such a code has been pronounced[8] within civil society movements and academic institutions.[9]

---

[6] 'Exclusive: Muslim Law Board's Meet with Narendra Modi in Offing', *India Today*, 5 March 2015.

[7] 'Implement Uniform Civil Code, Demands VHP's Singhal', *The Hindu*, 1 October 2015.

[8] 'Uniform Civil Code or Unilateral Civil Code', *Live Law*, 15 July 2016; 'The Modi Government's Hindutva Ideology Could Stall Any Progress on the Uniform Civil Code', *The Wire*, 7 July 2016; 'Pranab Mukherjee: "One Form or Uniformity Disastrous for Development"', *Indian Express*, 14 July 2016; 'Catholic Leaders in India Want Cross-faith Talks to Repeal Religious Law', *Premier*, 14 July 2016; 'When It Comes to Uniform Civil Code, One Size Won't Fit All', *New Indian Express*, 9 July 2016; and 'Silent Reform in Courtrooms Is Already Ending the Patriarchal Stranglehold on Islam', *Scroll.in*, 8 July 2016.

[9] In February 2016, controversy arose in the Jawaharlal Nehru University when leaders from the student wing of the Communist Party of India were arrested for speeches that were allegedly 'anti-national'. The arrest caused a national stir where students from different political wings protested, and resulted in many violent clashes. Signature campaigns expressing solidarity with JNU, #standwithJNU, commenced across universities in many parts of the world. The controversy dominated national media and, in fact, resulted in media becoming completely divided on the issue. The mishandled controversy is believed to have had a role in the eventual replacement of the Minister of Human Resource Development Smriti Irani with Prakash Javdekar, in the cabinet reshuffle of July 2016.

The Law Commission of India, however, after a series of consultations with select women's groups, recommended many amendments to specific personal laws but decided strongly against a Uniform Civil Code. Owing perhaps to their strong stance against a government's electoral promise, the commission's report emerged as a 'consultation paper' rather than a report, one day before the 21st Law Commission completed its term. Since August 2018, the next commission (22nd) has not been constituted and for the first time in the history of independent India, there has been no Law Commission for over a period of three years.

Personal law continues to emerge before the courts in multiple petitions. BJP members repeatedly filed or joined pleas of Muslim women against the practices of *nikah halala* and bigamy, on implementation of Article 44, and on 'uniform grounds of divorce for all religions'. In July 2021, the Delhi High Court pressed for a universal code mainly to address the complications and confusions owing to application of personal laws and customs.[10] The BJP has reiterated its promise to bring in a uniform code for family law before the end of its government's term in 2024. Virtually all electoral promises that were meant to be borne out of the tenor of legislative debate from the Ram Temple to the Uniform Civil Code are being routed through the courts. Both the Allahabad and Delhi High Courts observed the urgent need for a Uniform Civil Code pointing to customary exceptions that create confusion in family law and declared further that inter-religious couples would benefit from it. The Central government has taken an ambivalent stand on these petitions and promised to mandate with next Law Commission (22nd) with the task of framing this code.[11] In response, the AIMPLB annouced that the code could be unacceptable and urged further that a law be enacted to criminalize blasphemy.

The controversial Hindutva judgments were reopened in February 2014 with the appointment of a seven-judge bench to revisit the case. However, the report left the effect of the judgments unaltered.[12] The Supreme Court decided the title suit on the Ram Temple–Babri Mosque dispute in favour of the Hindus, and the temple

---

[10] 'Delhi HC Calls for Uniform Civil Code, Asks Centre to Take Action', *Indian Express*, 10 July 2021. 'Allahabad High Court Urges Centre to Speed Up Uniform Civil Code', *The Hindu*, 19 November 2021, https://www.thehindu.com/news/national/allahabad-high-court-urges-centre-to-speed-up-uniform-civil-code/article37582213.ece.

[11] 'Centre's denial of the rich debate on Uniform Civil Code exposes its hypocrisy, as revealed by its latest affidavit before Delhi HC' The Leaflet 25 January 2022. https://www.theleaflet.in/centres-denial-of-the-rich-debate-on-uniform-civil-code-exposes-its-hypocrisy-as-revealed-by-its-latest-affidavit-before-delhi-hc/.

[12] 'Supreme Court's Seven Judge Bench to Revisit Hindutva Judgement', *New Indian Express*, 2 February 2014.

construction commenced on 5 August 2020 amidst the global pandemic. Sustained violence against the Muslim community in incidents of mob lynching and cases of false prosecution remain at their zenith.[13] The court on the Babri Mosque–Ram Temple verdict had also held that the act of the demolition was a 'crime' but the accused BJP leadership of the 1990s has not yet been convicted by the Supreme Court. The courts remained in the eye of the storm as four prominent judges came together in a press conference in January 2018 to raise serious concerns about the compromise of the judiciary's independence. The court's passive stance on the arrests of academics and activists[14] and further on the prolonged lockdown in the state of Kashmir pushed it into further controversy.

In a sense, law became irrelevant to majoritarian politics as no constitutional safeguards for minorities could prevent the attacks on Muslims or Dalits, and violence and power are evermore inseparable. A law banning cow-slaughter is again being contemplated only after numerous incidents of mob lynching for suspected beef-eating have occurred with no consequences for the accused. Laws banning conversion of religion for marriage, for instance, which BJP government in the states of Uttar Pradesh and Madhya Pradesh in 2020 enacted, came only after attacks on couples and their forced separation was already quite routine. The narrative of 'love-jihad' had already provoked communal riots in Uttar Pradesh. Writing this violence into an anti-conversion law, however, has allowed it to be challenged in courts through multiple petitions, albeit with little hope of its repeal.[15] The dialogic history of law that characterised divorce debates in democratic India is diminishing as aggregation of power in the political establishment is fast making contestations between state institutions impossible, with committee critiques becoming irrelevant and judiciary reiterating political promises of the government.

Civil society, on infrequent occasions, found its way around the finality of even the Supreme Court rulings by once again tapping the constitution. 'Curative petitions' emerged as a means to challenge the judgments delivered by the highest court of appeal. The basis for such a petition is that the judgment does not satisfy

---

[13] 'Indian Student Activist Umar Khalid Arrested over Delhi Riots', *The Guardian*, 14 September 2020; 'Feminists from Across the World Express Solidarity with Arrested Pinjra Tod Activists', *The Wire* , 4 June 2020; and 'Inside Delhi: Beaten, Lynched and Burnt Alive', *The Guardian*, 1 March 2020.

[14] 'Delhi Police Spreads Riots "Conspiracy" Net, Drags in Eminent Academics and Activists', *The Wire*, 12 September 2020.

[15] 'SC to Hear Case against Love Jihad Laws of 4 States, Himachal, Madhya Pradesh Added as Parties', *India Today*, 17 February 2021.

the 'public conscience',[16] or common sense. The very idea of a 'curative' petition is precisely what renders the law impermanent.[17] Whether these petitions necessarily translated to 'justice' remains unanswered, but a negotiation with the law certainly became a democratic dialogue enabled by the law to challenge the law. One of the few achievements of such petitions included the reading down of Section 377 of the Indian Penal Code that criminalized homosexuality. Thus, a constant pressure for the incorporation of plurality into the legal discourse on relationships and marriage emerges as the sole force against the majoritarian demands for uniformity.[18]

At many points in history, the robustness of India's democracy was not anchored in or contingent on constitutional law. On the contrary, popular sanction pushed the limits of constitutional liberalism. Yet the 'constitution' remained central even to protests against the law, or demands for instituting religious orders. This is particularly pertinent in the context of the government's amendment of the Citizenship Act in 2019 to extend citizenship status selectively to refugees who were Hindu, Sikh, or Christian from its three Muslim-majority neighbouring countries. This conspicuously anti-Muslim law saw substantial public protest across the country. The protestors saw the Citizenship Amendment Act as an assault on religious minorities as well as on the constitution of India. This separation of legislative law with the constitution in public sentiment is precisely what has allowed the constitution of India to remain an uncontested symbol of

---

16 The court dismissed the plea against the death penalty of a convicted terrorist Afzal Guru, held to be responsible for the attack on the Indian parliament in 2001. Death penalty was awarded to him by the supreme court on grounds that 'public conscience' would only be satisfied if Afzal Guru was executed. This earned Supreme Court the title 'Supreme Court of Indians' rather than the 'Supreme Court of India'. See also Upendra Baxi, 'Demosprudence versus Jurisprudence: The Indian Judicial Experience in the Context of Comparative Constitutional Studies', *Macquarie LJ* 14 (2014): 3–23.

17 Article 141 (also Article 142) of the Indian constitution reads: 'The law declared by the Supreme Court shall be binding on all courts within the territory of India.' This Article implies that the Supreme Court decision would serve as the law unless it is specifically replaced by an alternate legislation through a new law or an ordinance. Thus, if a favourable judgment could be precipitated through petitioning the court, it would be a quick and immediate relief rather than awaiting legislative change.

18 Homosexuality came to be decriminalized (2010) and recriminalized (2013) by the Delhi High Court and the Supreme Court, respectively. The Supreme Court's decision on the criminalizing of homosexuality, however, was challenged by a 'curative petition' and it was decriminalized in 2018 with some finality as it read down parts of Section 377 that criminalized homosexual intercourse. See *Navtej Singh Johar v. Union of India*, writ petition (criminal) no. 76 of 2016.

freedom and democracy,[19] even as Indian democracy finds itself imperilled in the face of authoritarianism.[20] Personal law demands that specific religious statutes and the constitution be read separately, and yet not be 'unconstitutional', thus producing litigiousness and an infinite loop of entanglement between religion and the state.

Thus, the paradox is that uniformity, in fact, is being generated through plurality. The proliferation of plurality has engendered a 'universal' discourse across religions and groups that acknowledges various forms of gender discrimination far more effectively than any commitment to uniformity as a constitutional directive. One the one hand, the courts had historically attained some universality through their judgments in clandestine or overt ways. Strands of the women's movements, on the other hand, inched towards establishing gender-just or gender-sensitive principles within religion or religious sources through the instrument of law. This has led to a shift in the terms of debate away from the constitution and instead over religion—recovering pure forms of Islam, or even nostalgia over tolerant Hinduism.[21] In the realm of family law, this has meant that the official law produced weak legal interventions that shared an uncertain relationship with the constitution that remained vulnerable to challenges. This may make a potential Uniform Civil Code a bit of a scarecrow that may alter little in reality, and only re-emphasize the institution of marriage, as preceding laws have done. Divorce, however, would remain a potent question, which could challenge more than one discriminatory regime—patriarchy, family, community, or state.

---

[19] Madhav Khosla, *India's Founding Moment: The Constitution of a Most Surprising Democracy* (Cambridge, MA: Harvard University Press, 2020); Rohit De, *A People's Constitution: The Everyday Life of Law in the Indian Republic*, vol. 18 (Princeton, NJ: Princeton University Press, 2018).

[20] 'Modi Accused of Treason by Opposition over India Spyware Disclosures', *The Guardian*, 19 July 2021; 'Pegasus: Why Unchecked Snooping Threatens India's Democracy', BBC, 21 July 2021.

[21] For this debate, see the exchange in English dailies: 'Secularism Gave Up Language of Religion. Ayodhya Bhoomi Pujan Is a Result of That', *theprint.in*, 5 August 2020; 'In Post-Mortem of Secularism, We Are Hand Wringing over Religion, Missing the Real Crisis', *Indian Express*, 11 August 2020; and 'The Indian Liberal Nostalgia for a Tolerant Hinduism Is Misplaced', *The Wire*, 31 August 2020.

Glossary

adalat	court
akhada	arena
alim	scholar of Islamic law
Aliyasanthana	matrilineal system of inheritance practiced by the Billava, Bunts, and certain other communities in the coastal districts of Karnataka
Brahmin	priestly caste in the Hindu caste order
biddat	customary, casual or wavered
chaturvarna	fourfold categorization of Hindu castes
chowki	small police station
chunari	scarf
chuniri mahotsav	veil or head scarf carnival
dar-ul-qaza	Islamic (*sharia*) courts
dastoor	tradition
Dalit	oppressed people outside the Hindu caste order
dalal	broker
Dayabhaga	system of inheritance in Hindu law prevalent in Bengal (before Hindu code)
faksh	the dissolution of a marriage by an Islamic Court on application of the wife
fatwa	non-binding legal opinion in Islamic law
Hadees	commandments in Islamic law based on spoken words or observed actions of the prophet
hawan	ritual of purifying by fire
haq	right
haram	forbidden
hazanat	custody
Hindutva	ideology of Hindu nationalism
iddat	period of three months of abstinence from sexual intercourse or three menstrual cycles of a woman after divorce in Muslim law, after which the couple is free to remarry

ijma	process of building consensus through consultations in Islamic law
ijtihad	legal reasoning in Islamic law based on debate and consultation
imam	the leader of Islamic prayers
jagadguru	adjudicator in a court of justice
johar	collective performance of sati
kabin-nama	interim contract
karewa	the practice of a widow being married to her late husband's (generally younger) brother
karsevak	worker or volunteer
khula	divorce initiated by the wife in Islamic law
khulanama	document of divorce initiated by women
Lok Sabha	the lower house of the Indian parliament
madrasa	an educational institution primarily for the study of Islam, theology
mahapanch	head of the *panchayat*
mahila adalat	women's court
mahr	dower, settled at the time of a Muslim marriage
mahotsav	celebratory event or carnival
mangalsutra	bead necklace worn by married Hindu women in India
Manusmriti	laws of Manu, ancient Hindu legal text
mandir	temple
masjid	mosque
mata	maintenance or provision for maintenance in Islamic law
maulvi	Muslim priest
mela	carnival
Mitakshara	one of the systems of inheritance in Hindu law prevalent predominantly in northern India before the Hindu Succession Act, 1956, where sons become owners or joint owners of ancestral property at birth
mut'a	temporary marriages contracted in certain sects under Shia law; children born to this marriage are legitimate, but there is no right of inheritance between the couple
Marumakkathayam	a system of matrilineal inheritance prevalent in Kerala among the Nairs
na-pak	dishonourable or impure
nikah	performance of the ceremony of a Muslim marriage

nikah halala	the practice prevalent among a minority of Sunni Muslims by which women could be made eligible to reunite with their divorced husbands by marrying another man and consummating the second marriage and then acquiring wilful divorce from the second marriage to reunite with the first husband
Hanafi	one of the four schools of Islamic jurisprudence among Sunni Muslims in India (named after Abu Hanifa)
nikahnama	Islamic marriage contract
nyayapeeth	Hindu forums for justice
pandit	Hindu priest
purdah	curtain/screening of women from men/strangers
qazi	a Muslim judge in a *dar-ul-qaza* or a *sharia* court/ adjudicator of Islamic religious law
qiyas	Islamic jurisprudence, generally entails comparisons between Quran and the Hadees
Ramajanmabhumi	birth place of the Hindu god Ram
Rajya Sabha	upper house of the Indian parliament
rath yatra	chariot processions
rashtra	nation
sanatanist	someone who believes in (Hindu) *sanatan dharma*, that is, eternal dharma, where practices have evolved through centuries
sanyasin	female devotee
saptpadi	ritual of taking seven steps or seven circumambulations around the sacred fire in a Hindu marriage
sati	widow immolation
sati sthal	site of the sati ritual
Shaifai	one of the four schools of Islamic jurisprudence among Sunni Muslims (named after Imam Shafi)
shakha	branch
sharia	Islamic law
shastra	treatise or commandments, generally used as a prefix for different categories of rules
sindoor	vermillion worn by married Hindu women on their foreheads
stridhan	property that a woman obtains at the time of her marriage
Suyamariathai or Seereemariathai	priest-less marriages
talaq	divorce

talaq ahasan	a single pronouncement of divorce, followed by a period of sexual abstinence for *iddat*, three menstrual cycles of the wife
talaq-e-tawfid	delegated divorce
talaq-e-hasan	three pronunciations of *talaq* during three consecutive menstrual cycles
talaqnama	document of divorce
talaq-ul-biddat	three pronouncements of divorce made in succession in a single *tuhr* to irrevocably dissolve a Muslim marriage, a heretical form of divorce
thana	small police station
tuhr	the period between menstrual cycles
ulema	Islamic scholars
varna sanskar	Hindu caste order
wakf	land for an Islamic religious charity
zamindari	a system of land ownership

Bibliography

Government Archives

National Archives of India, New Delhi, 1949–84

Ministry of Home Affairs, Judicial Branch Files.
Ministry of Home Affairs, Public Branch Files.
Ministry of Home Affairs, Political Branch Files.
Ministry of External Affairs Files.

Police Record Room, Lucknow, Uttar Pradesh, 1948–49

Weekly Record of Political Activity, 1948 and 1949, Subject 'Political'. Criminal Investigation Department, United Provinces, Intelligence Bureau.

Reports

Law Commission Reports, 1958–2015, Ministry of Law, Government of India

Compulsory Registration of Marriages, 270th Report, 2017.
Converts' Marriage Dissolution Act, 1866, 18th Report, 1961.
Christian Marriage and Matrimonial Causes Bill, 22nd Report, 1961.
Hindu Marriage Act, 1955, and Special Marriage Act, 1954, 59th Report, 1974.
Indian Divorce Act, 164th Report, 1998.
Review of Rape Law, 172nd Report, 2000.
Laws of Civil Marriages in India: A Proposal to Resolve Certain Conflicts, 212th Report, 2008.
Law Relating to Marriage and Divorce Amongst Christians in India, 15th Report, 1960.
Preventing Bigamy via Conversion to Islam—A Proposal for giving Statutory Effect to Supreme Court Rulings, 227th Report, 2009.
Prevention of Interference with the Freedom of Matrimonial Alliances (in the Name of Honour and Tradition): A Suggested Legal Framework, 242nd Report, 2012.

Right of the Hindu Wife to Maintenance: A Relook at Section 18 of the Hindu
    Adoptions and Maintenance Act, 1956, 252nd Report, 2015.
Reform of Family Law, consultation paper, 2018.

Other Reports, Ministry of Home Affairs and Ministry of Human Resource Development

D. P. Madon Commission on the Bhiwandi, Jalgaon and Mahad Riots, 1975.
Election Commission of India Report of State Legislative Assembly, Assam, 1985.
Election Commission of India Report, General Elections 1984, Volume I.
Election Commission of India, Report, General Elections, 1967, Volume I and II.
Liberhan Commission Report, 2009.
Nanavati Commission Report, 2014.
Niyogi Commission Report, 1956.
Sachar Commission Report, 2006
Sarkaria Commission Report, 1988.
Towards Equality: Report of the Committee on the Status of Women in India, 1974.
Verma Commission Report, 2013.

Private Papers

Nehru Memorial Museum and Library, New Delhi
Danial Latifi Papers.
Hansa Mehta Papers.
Humanyu Kabir Papers.

Papers of Organizations

Nehru Memorial Museum and Library, New Delhi
All India Women's Conference Papers.
All India Congress Committee Papers.
All India Hindu Mahasabha Publication: The Hindu Outlook.

All India Muslim Personal Law Board, Okhla, New Delhi
Publications and Pamphlets of All India Muslim Personal Law Board.

Women Living under Muslims Laws
Talaq-i-Tafwid: The Muslim Woman's Contractual Access to Divorce: An Information
    Kit, 1996.

Parliamentary Debates

Nehru Memorial Museum and Library, New Delhi, 1946–92
Constituent Assembly Debates.
Lok Sabha Debates.

Uttar Pradesh Legislature Library, Vidhan Sabha, Uttar Pradesh, 1985–2008
Lok Sabha Debates.

Hansard Archive (digitized debates of the House of Commons)
United Kingdom Parliamentary Debates, 1968–70.

Political Party Manifestos

Janata Party Manifesto, 1977, 1979.
Bharatiya Janata Party Manifesto, 1989, 1996, 1999, 2004, 2014.

Consultations Held by the 21st Law Commission of India

December 2016–July 2018.

Collected Works

Munshi, K. M., ed. *Indian Constitutional Documents*, vol. I. Cambridge: Centre for South Asian Studies, 1967.
Sarvepalli, Gopal, and Madhavan K. Palat. *Selected Works of Jawaharlal Nehru*, Second Series. Cambridge: Centre for South Asian Studies, 1984.
Vasant, Moon, ed. *Babasaheb Ambedkar Writings and Speeches*. New Delhi: Dr Ambedkar Foundation, 1979.

Journals and Newspapers

Newspapers and Magazines in English, 1951–2020
Business Insider
Daily Mail
Deccan Herald
Economic Times
Financial Times

Hindustan Times
India Today
Indian Express
National Herald
Patriot
Premier
The Frontline
The Herald
The Hindu
The Pioneer
The Statesman
The Wire
Times of India

Newspapers in Hindi and Urdu
Dainik Jagran (Hindi)
Siasat (Urdu/English)
Musalman (Urdu)

Statutes

Statutes in India
Citizenship Amendment Act, 2019.
Commission of Sati (Prevention) Act, 1987.
Constitution of India, 1950.
Criminal Code of Procedure, 1973.
Dissolution of Muslim Marriages Act, 1939.
Family Courts Act, 1984.
Freedom of Religion Act, 1967 (Madhya Pradesh).
Freedom of Religion Act, 1968 (Orissa).
Hindu Marriage Act, 1955.
Indian Divorce (Amendment) Act, 2001.
Indian Penal Code, 1860.
Muslim Women's Protection of Rights of Marriage Act, 2019.
Muslim Women (Protection of Rights on Divorce) Act, 1986.
Representation of People Act, 1951.
Shariat Application Act, 1937.
Special Marriage Act, 1954.
The Madhya Pradesh Freedom of Religion Act, 2021.
Uttar Pradesh Prohibition of Unlawful Religious Conversion Ordinance, 2020.

Statutes in Rest of the World

Article 21 CSP, 1956, Tunisia.
Code of Protection of the Family and Prevention of Violence against Women, Turkey.
Divorce Act, R.S.C. 1970, c. D-8, Canada.
Divorce Reform Act, 1969, United Kingdom.
Dowry and Bridal Gifts (Restriction) Act 1976, Pakistan.
Family Courts Act 1964 (West Pakistan), Pakistan.
Matrimonial Clauses Act, 1973, United Kingdom.
Offence of Zina (Enforcement of Hudood) Ordinance 1979, Pakistan.
Sindh Hindu Marriage Act, 2016, Pakistan.

List of Cases

Abdul Haq v. Yasima Talat, 1998 CriLJ 3433.
Abdul Rashid v. Sultana Begum, 1992 CriLJ 76.
Ahmed Giri v. Mst. Begha, AIR 1955 J and K 1.
Ahmedabad Women's Action Group v. Union of India, 1997 3 SCC 573.
Ali v. Safaira, 1988 3 Crimes 147.
Ambika Prasad Misra v. the State of UP, 1980 AIR 1762.
Arab Ahemadhia Abdulla and Ors v. Arab Bail Mohmuna Saiyadbhai and Ors, AIR 1988 Guj 141.
Aruna Roy and Ors. v. Union of India and Ors, AIR 2002 SC 3176.
Bai Tahira A v. Ali Hussain Fidaalli Chothia, 1979 AIR 362.
Bhagwan Sri Ram Lala Virajman and Others v. Rajendra Singh and Others, Regular Suit No. 236 of 1989.
Bhagwan v. Warubai (1908) 32 Bom 300.
Budansa Rowther And Anr. v. Fatma Bi and Ors (1914) 26 MLJ 260.
Bhaurao Lokhande v. State of Maharashtra, AIR 1965 SC 1564.
Burden and another v. UK (Application No 13378/05) [2008] 2 FLR 787.
D.Velusamy v. D.Patchaiammal (2010) 10 SCC 469.
Danial Latifi and Anr. v. Union of India, AIR 2001 SC 3958.
Dattaray v. Gangabhai (1922) 46 Bom 541.
Dawn Henderson v. D Henderson AIR 1970 Mad 104.
Deivanai Achi v. Chidamberam Chettiar AIR 1954 Madras 657.
Dr Ramesh Yashwant Prabhoo v. Shri Prabhakar Kashinath Kunte, 1996 SCC (1) 130.
Dr Amit Kumar v. Dr Sonila and Ors., Civil Appeal No. 10771 of 2018 [Arising out of SLP(C) No.21786/2018].
Fazlunbi Biwi v. K. Khader Vali AIR 1980 SC 173.
Githa Hariharan and Anr v. Reserve Bank of India and Anr (1999) 2 SCC 228.
Golaknath v. State of Punjab, 1967 AIR 1643.

Gopal Singh Visharad v. Zahoor Ahmad and Others, Regular Suit No. 2 of 1950.

Hussainara Khatoon and Ors v. Home Secretary, State of Bihar, 1979 AIR 1369.

Indian Young Lawyers Association vs The State of Kerala, 2018 SCC OnLine.

Ismail Faruqui v. Union of India AIR 1995 SC 605.

Itwari vs Smt. Asghari and Ors, AIR 1960 All 684.

Jaitunbi Mubarak Shaikh v. Mubarak Fakruddin Shaikh and Anr, 1999 (3) Mh.L.J. 694.

John Vallamattom and Anr. v. Respondent: Union of India AIR 2003 SC 2902.

K. Kunhashed Hazi v. Amena, 95 Cri.L.J. 3371.

K. Zunaideen v. Ameena Begum (1998) II DMC 468.

Karim Abdul Shaik v. Shenaz Karim Shaik, 2000 Cr.L.J. 3560.

Keshavananda Bharti v. State of Kerala (1973) 4 SCC 225.

Kultar Singh v. Mukhtiar Singh, 1965 AIR 141.

Kurian August v. Devassy Aley AIR 1957 Travancore Cochin (1).

Lakshmi Kant Pandey v. Union of India, 1984 AIR 469.

Madan Singh S/O Sumer Singh and Anr. v. State of Rajasthan, 1988 (1) WLN 551.

Manohar Joshi v. Nitin Bhaurao Patel and Another, 1996 SCC (1) 169.

Mary Roy vs State Of Kerala and Ors on 24 February 1986, AIR 1011.

Md. Marahim v. Raiza Begum, 1993 (1) DMC 60.

Minerva Mills v. Union of India, 1980 AIR 1789.

Mohd. Ahmed Khan v. Shah Bano Begum, 1985 AIR 945.

Navtej Singh Johar v. Union of India, Writ Petition (Criminal) No. 76 of 2016.

Naz Foundation v. Government of National Capital Territory of Delhi, WP(C) No. 7455/2001.

Nirmohi Akhara and Others v. Baboo Priya Datt Ram and Others, Suit No. 26 of 1959.

Parveen Akthar v. The Union of India, 2003-1-LW370.

Prof. Ramachandra G. Kapse v. Haribansh Ramakbal Singh, 1996 SCC (1) 206.

Rahmat Ullah And Khatoon Nisa v. State of U.P. II (1994) DMC 64.

Rajathi v. Selliah (1966) II M.L.J. 40.

Rameshchandra Rampratapji Daga vs Rameshwari Rameshchandra Daga, AIR 2005 SC 422.

Rev Stanislaus v. Madhya Pradesh, 1977 SCR (2) 611.

Reynold Rajmani v. Union of India, 1982 AIR 1261.

Robasa Khanum v. Khodadad Bomanji Irani (1946) 48 BOMLR 864.

S. Nagalingam v. Sivagami, 2001 (2) SCR 454.

Sainuddin v. Latifannessa Bibi (1919) ILR 46 Calcutta 141.

Sarla Mudgal v. Union of India, 1995, AIR 1531.

Shafin Jahan v. KM Ashokan and Ors AIR 2018 SC 1933.

Shakti Vahini v. Union of India, Writ Petition (Civil) No. 231 of 2010.

Shamim Ara v. State of U.P. AIR 2002 SCW 4162.

Shanti Sarup v. Radhaswami Satsang Sabha AIR 1969 All 248.

Shayara Bano v. Union of India (2017) 9 SCC 1.

Smt. Usha Devi. v. State of U.P., Surendra Nath Singh, Criminal case no. 1746 of 2001.

SR Bommai v. Union of India (1994) 3 SCC 1.

Sri Ram Krishna Mission and Anr. v. Paramanand And Ors AIR 1977 All 421.

State of Uttar Pradesh v. Raj Narain, 1975 AIR 865.

The State of Bombay vs Narasu Appa Mali AIR 1952 Bom 84.

The Sunni Central Board of Waqfs, U.P. and Others v. Gopal Singh Visharad (Since Deceased), Regular Suit No.12 of 1961.

Tuka Ram and Anr v. State of Maharashtra, 1979 AIR 185.

Umar Khan Bahamami v. Fathimnurisa, 1990 Cr.L.J. 1364.

Vilayat Raj v. Sunila, AIR 1983 Delhi 351.

Vishwa Lochan Madan v. Union of India, 2014 SCCOnline SC 542.

Yousuf Rawther v. Sowramma, MANU/KE/0059/1971.

Yulitha Hyde v. State of Orissa (1977) I SCC 677.

Personal Interviews

Jeelani, Zafaryab. Additional Advocate General, Uttar Pradesh, and convenor of the Babri Masjid Action Committee. Interviewed on 4 December 2012.

Khan, Arif Mohammad. Indian politician, former minister for Civil Aviation and Energy, current governor of the state of Kerala, 2019–present. Interviewed on 16 February 2015.

Khan, Hasina. Member, Bebaak Collective, former member of Awaaz-e-Niswaan, New Delhi. Interviewed on 13 August 2018 and 19 March 2019.

Khurshid, Salman. Member of the Indian National Congress Party, former Minister of Law, Minority Affairs and External Affairs. Interviewed on 1 August 2013.

Mahmood, Tahir. Distinguished jurist chair, professor of eminence, and chairman, Institute of Advanced Legal Studies. Interviewed on 3 August 2013.

Rasheed, Khalid. Maulana of Firangi Mahal, Lucknow. Interviewed on 4 December 2012 and 7 March 2018.

Singh, Shubhangi. Research coordinator, Association for Advocacy and Legal Aid (AALI), Lucknow. Interviewed on 19 March 2019.

Sikera, Navniet. Indian Police Service, Lucknow. Interviewed on 2 February 2017.

Soman, Zakia. Founder, Bharatiya Muslim Mahila Andolan. Interviewed on 14 March 2019.

Swamy, Subramanian. Indian politician, economist, and member of parliament, former cabinet minister. Interviewed on 8 July 2013.

Autobiographies and Personal Memoirs and Publications by Politicians

Advani, L. K. *My Country, My Life*. New Delhi: Rupa Publications, 2008.

Khan, A. M. *Text and Context: Quran and Contemporary Challenges*. New Delhi: Rupa and Co., 2010.

Seth, L. *On Balance: An Autobiography*. New Delhi: Penguin Books, 2008.

Secondary Sources

Abu-Lughod, L. 'The Romance of Resistance: Tracing Transformations of Power through Bedouin Women'. *American Ethnologist* 17, no. 1 (1990): 41–55.

———. *Do Muslim Women Need Saving?* Cambridge: Harvard University Press, 2013.

Agarwal, B. *A Field of One's Own: Gender and Land Rights in South Asia*, vol. 58. Cambridge: Cambridge University Press, 1994.

———. 'Gender and Command over Property: A Critical Gap in Economic Analysis and Policy in South Asia'. *World Development* 22, no. 10 (1994): 1455–78.

Agnes, F. 'Protecting Women against Violence? Review of a Decade of Legislation, 1980–89'. *Economic and Political Weekly* 27, no. 17 (1992): WS19–WS33.

———. 'Redefining the Agenda of the Women's Movement within a Secular Framework'. *South Asia: Journal of South Asian Studies* 17, no. s1 (1994): 63–78.

———. 'Hindu Men, Monogamy and Uniform Civil Code'. *Economic and Political Weekly* 30, no. 50 (1995): 3238–44.

———. 'Law and Gender Inequality.' In *Writing the Women's Movement: A Reader*, edited by M. Khullar, 113–30. New Delhi: Zubaan, 2005.

———. 'Patriarchy, Sexuality and Property: The Impact of Colonial State Policies on Gender Relations in India'. In *Family, Gender, and Law in a Globalizing Middle East and South Asia*, edited by K. M. Cuno and M. Desai, 19–42. Syracuse: Syracuse University Press, 2009.

———. 'The Supreme Court, the Media, and the Uniform Civil Code Debate in India.' In *The Crisis of Secularism in India*, edited by Anuradha D. Needham and Rajeswari S. Rajan, 294–315. Ranikhet: Permanent Black, 2009.

———. *Family Law: Marriage, Divorce, and Matrimonial Litigation*, vols. I and II. New Delhi: Oxford University Press, 2011.

———. 'From Shahbano to Kausar Bano: Contextualizing the "Muslim Women" within a Communalized Polity'. In *South Asian Feminisms*, edited by Ania Loomba and Ritty A. Lukose, 33–53. Durham, NC: Duke University Press, 2012.

Agrama, H. A. 'Secularism, Sovereignty, Indeterminacy: Is Egypt a Secular or a Religious State?'. *Comparative Studies in Society and History* 52, no. 3 (2010): 495–523.

———. *Questioning Secularism: Islam, Sovereignty, and the Rule of Law in Modern Egypt*. Chicago: University of Chicago Press, 2012.

Ahmed, F. *Religious Freedom under the Personal Law System*. New Delhi: Oxford University Press, 2016.

Alam, J. 'Is Caste Appeal Casteism? Oppressed Castes in Politics'. *Economic and Political Weekly* 34, no. 13 (1999): 757–61.

Ali, S. S. 'Cyberspace as Emerging Muslim Discursive Space? Online Fatawa on Women and Gender Relations and Its Impact on Muslim Family Law Norms'. *International Journal of Law, Policy and the Family* 24, no. 3 (2010): 338–60.

Ambedkar, B. R. *What Congress and Gandhi Have Done to the Untouchables*. New Delhi: Gautam Book Centre, 1946.

———. *Annihilation of Caste: An Undelivered Speech*. New Delhi: Arnold Publishers, 1990.

Anagol, P. 'The Emergence of the Female Criminal in India: Infanticide and Survival Under the Raj'. *History Workshop Journal* 53, no. 1 (2002): 73–93.

Anandhi, S. 'Women's Question in the Dravidian Movement c. 1925–1948'. *Social Scientist* 19, no. 5/6 (1991): 24–41.

Andersen, A. J. 'Sexual Citizenship in Norway', *International Journal of Law, Policy and the Family* 25, no. 1 (2011): 120–34.

Appadurai, A. *Fear of Small Numbers: An Essay on the Geography of Anger*. Durham, NC: Duke University Press, 2006.

Asad, T. *Formations of the Secular: Christianity, Islam, Modernity*. Stanford, California: Stanford University Press, 2003.

Austin, Granville. *Working a Democratic Constitution: A History of the Indian Experience*. New Delhi: Oxford University Press, 2003.

Bacchetta, P. 'All Our Goddesses Are Armed: Religion, Resistance and Revenge in the Life of a Militant Hindu Nationalist Woman'. In *Against All Odds: Essays on Women, Religion, and Development from India and Pakistan*, edited by Kamla Bhasin, Ritu Menon, and Nighat Said Khan, 132–56. New Delhi: Kali for Women, 1994.

Baird, R. D., ed. *Religion and Law in Independent India*. New Delhi: Manohar Publishers and Distributors, 2005.

Bajpai, R. *Debating Difference: Group Rights and Liberal Democracy in India*. New Delhi: Oxford University Press, 2011.

Banerjee, N. 'Whatever Happened to the Dreams of Modernity? The Nehruvian Era and Woman's Position'. *Economic and Political Weekly* 33, no. 17 (1998): WS2–WS7.

Banerjee, S. 'Armed Masculinity, Hindu Nationalism and Female Political Participation in India: Heroic Mothers, Chaste Wives and Celibate Warriors'. *International Feminist Journal of Politics* 8, no. 1 (2006): 62–83.

Bardhan, K. 'Women: Work, Welfare and Status: Forces of Tradition and Change in India'. *Comparative Studies of South Asia, Africa and the Middle East* 6, no. 1 (1986): 3–16.

Basu, A. 'Feminism Inverted-The Real Women and Gendered Imagery of Hindu Nationalism'. *Bulletin of Concerned Asian Scholars* 25, no. 4 (1993): 25–36.

Basu, S. *She Comes to Take Her Rights: Indian Women, Property, and Propriety*. New Delhi: SUNY Press, 1999.

———. 'Playing Off Courts: The Negotiation of Divorce and Violence in Plural Legal Settings in Kolkata'. *The Journal of Legal Pluralism and Unofficial Law* 38, no. 52 (2006): 41–75.

———. *The Trouble with Marriage: Feminists Confront Law and Violence in India*, vol. 1. New Delhi: University of California Press, 2015.

Baxi, U. *The Indian Supreme Court and Politics*. Lucknow: Eastern Book Co, 1980.

———. *The Crisis of the Indian Legal System: Alternatives in Development: Law*. New Delhi: Vikas, 1982.

———. 'Taking Suffering Seriously: Social Action Litigation in the Supreme Court of India'. *Third World Legal Studies* 4, no. 1 (1985): 107–32.

———. *Courage, Craft, and Contention: The Indian Supreme Court in the Eighties*. Bombay: NM Tripathi, 1985.

———. 'Siting Secularism in the Uniform Civil Code: A "Riddle Wrapped Inside an Enigma"?'. In *The Crisis of Secularism in India*, edited by Anuradha Dingwaney Needham and Rajeswari Sunder Rajan, 267–93. Ranikhet: Permanent Black, 2009.

———. 'Demosprudence versus Jurisprudence: The Indian Judicial Experience in the Context of Comparative Constitutional Studies'. *Macquarie LJ* 14 (2014): 3–23.

Bayly, C. A. *The Local Roots of Indian Politics: Allahabad, 1880–1920*. Oxford: Clarendon Press, 1975.

———. *Recovering Liberties: Indian Thought in the Age of Liberalism and Empire*, vol. 100. Cambridge: Cambridge University Press, 2011.

Benda-Beckmann, F. von, 'Who's Afraid of Legal Pluralism?'. *The Journal of Legal Pluralism and Unofficial Law* 34, no. 47 (2002): 37–82.

Benhabib, S., ed. *Democracy and Difference: Contesting the Boundaries of the Political*, vol. 31. Princeton, NJ: Princeton University Press, 1996.

———. *The Claims of Culture: Equality and Diversity in the Global Era*. Princeton, NJ: Princeton University Press, 2002.

Benton, L. *Law and Colonial Cultures: Legal Regimes in World History, 1400–1900*. Cambridge: Cambridge University Press, 2002.

Berti, D. 'Hostile Witnesses, Judicial Interactions and Out-of-Court Narratives in a North Indian District Court'. *Contributions to Indian Sociology* 44, no. 3 (2010): 235–63.

Bhagavan, M. 'The Hindutva Underground: Hindu Nationalism and the Indian National Congress in Late Colonial and Early Post-Colonial India'. *Economic and Political Weekly* 43, no. 37 (2008): 39–48.

Bhai, Syed, and Anwar Rajan. 'For the Human Rights of Women—The Work of Muslim Satyashodhak Samaj'. *Manushi* (1986). Available at http://www. manushi-india.org/.

Bhargava, R. *Secularism and Its Critics*. Oxford: Oxford University Press, 1998.

———. 'India's Secular Constitution'. In *India's Living Constitution: Ideas, Practices, Controversies*, edited by Z. Hasan, E. Sridharan, and R. Sudarshan, 105–33. Delhi: Permanent Black, 2005.

———. 'The Distinctiveness of Indian Secularism'. In *The Future of Secularism*, edited by T. N. Srinivasan, 20–53. New Delhi: Oxford University Press, 2007.

———. 'Political Secularism'. In *The Oxford Handbook of Political Theory*, edited by John S. Dryzek, Honig Bonnie, and Anne Phillips, 636–55. Oxford: Oxford University Press, 2008.

———. *The Promise of India's Secular Democracy*. New Delhi: Oxford University Press, 2010.

Bhatia, G. *The Transformative Constitution: A Radical Biography in Nine Acts*. New Delhi: Harper Collins, 2019.

———. 2015. 'Directive Principles of State Policy: Theory and Practice'. 2016. In *Oxford Handbook of the Indian Constitution*, edited by S. Choudhry, P. B. Mehta, and M. Khosla, 645–61. Oxford: Oxford University Press.

Bhattacharya, N. 'Myth, History and the Politics of Ramjanmabhumi'. In *Anatomy of a Confrontation: Ayodhya and the Rise of Communal Politics in India*, edited by Sarvepalli Gopal, 122–40. New Delhi: Penguin Books, 1991.

Bhuwania, A. *Courting the People: Public Interest Litigation in Post-Emergency India*. New Delhi: Cambridge University Press, 2017.

Bilgrami, A. 'What Is a Muslim? Fundamental Commitment and Cultural Identity'. *Critical Inquiry* 18, no. 4 (1992): 821–42.

———. *Secularism, Identity, and Enchantment*, vol. 33. Cambridge, MA: Harvard University Press, 2014.

Birla, R. *Stages of Capital: Law, Culture, and Market Governance in Late Colonial India*. Durham, NC: Duke University Press, 2008.

Bock, G. 'Women's History and Gender History: Aspects of an International Debate'. *Gender and History* 1, no. 1 (1989): 7–30.

Bose, S. 'Hindu Nationalism and The Crisis of the Indian State: A Theoretical Perspective'. In *Nationalism, Democracy and Development State and Politics in India*, vol. 32, edited by Sugata Bose and Ayesha Jalal, 104–64. Oxford: Oxford University Press, 1997.

———. *Transforming India*. Cambridge, MA: Harvard University Press, 2013.

Boydston, J. 'Gender as a Question of Historical Analysis'. *Gender and History* 20, no. 3 (2008): 558–83.

Brass, Paul R. *Factional Politics in an Indian State: The Congress Party in Uttar Pradesh*. Berkeley: University of California Press, 1965.

———. 'The Politics of Ayurvedic Education: A Case Study of Revivalism and Modernisation in India'. In *Education and Politics in India: Studies in Organisation Society, and Policy*, edited by Susanne Hoeber Rudolph and Lloyd I. Rudolph. Cambridge, MA: Harvard University Press, 1972.

———. *The Politics of India since Independence*, vol. 1. Cambridge: Cambridge University Press, 1994.

———. *Language, Religion and Politics in North India*. Cambridge: Cambridge University Press, 1974.

Buch, N. 'State Welfare Policy and Women, 1950–1975'. *Economic and Political Weekly* 33, no. 17 (1998): WS18–WS20.

Butalia, U. *The Other Side of Silence: Voices from the Partition of India*. Durham, NC: Duke University Press, 2000.

Butalia, U., and T. Sarkar, eds. *Women and Right-Wing Movements: Indian Experiences*. London: Zed Books, 1995.

Chakrabarty, D. *Provincialising Europe: Post-Colonial Thought and Colonial Difference*. Princeton, NJ: Princeton University Press, 2000.

———. 'The Subject of Law and the Subject of Narrative'. In *Habitations of Modernity: Essays in the Wake of Subaltern Studies*, edited by D. Chakrabarty, 101–14. Chicago: University of Chicago Press, 2002.

Chakravarti, U. 'Beyond the Altekarian Paradigm: Towards a New Understanding of Gender Relations in Early Indian History'. *Social Scientist* 16, no. 8 (1988): 44–52.

———. 'Whatever Happened to the Vedic Dasi? Orientalism, Nationalism and a Script for the Past'. In *Recasting Women: Essays in Indian Colonial History*, edited by Kumkum Sangari and Sudesh Vaid, 27–87. New Delhi: Kali for Women, 1989.

———. 'Conceptualising Brahmanical Patriarchy in Early India: Gender, Caste, Class and State'. *Economic and Political Weekly* 28, no. 14 (1993): 579–85.

Chandra, B. *In the Name of Democracy: JP Movement and the Emergency*. New Delhi: Penguin Books, 2003.

Chandra, S. 'Rukhmabai: Debate over Woman's Right to Her Person'. *Economic and Political Weekly* 31, no. 44 (1996): 2937–47.

Chatterji, A. P., T. B. Hansen, and C. Jaffrelot, eds. *Majoritarian State: How Hindu Nationalism Is Changing India*. London: Hurst & Co., 2020.

Chatterjee, P. *The Nation and Its Fragments: Colonial and Postcolonial Histories*, vol. 11. Princeton, NJ: Princeton University Press, 1993.

———. 'Secularism and Toleration'. *Economic and Political Weekly* 29, no. 28 (1994): 1768–77.

———. 'Our Modernity', no. 1. SEPHIS and CODESRIA, Rotterdam, 1997.

———. *The Politics of the Governed: Reflections on Popular Politics in Most of the World*. New York: Columbia University Press, 2004.

Chatterjee, N. *The Making of Indian Secularism: Empire, Law and Christianity, 1830–1960*. New York: Springer, 2011.

Chhachhi, A. 'Gender, Flexibility, Skill, and Industrial Restructuring: The Electronics Industry in India'. *Gender, Technology and Development* 3, no. 3 (1999): 329–60.

Chhibber, P. K., and J. R. Petrocik. 'The Puzzle of Indian Politics: Social Cleavages and the Indian Party System'. *British Journal of Political Science* 19, no. 2 (1989): 191–210.

Chiba, M. 'Legal Pluralism in Sri Lankan Society: Toward a General Theory of Non-Western Law'. *The Journal of Legal Pluralism and Unofficial Law* 25, no. 33 (1993): 197–212.

———, ed. *Asian Indigenous Law: In Interaction with Received Law*. London and New York: KPI, 1986.

Choudhry, S. 'How to Do Constitutional Law and Politics in South Asia'. In *Unstable Constitutionalism: Law and Politics in South Asia*, edited by M. Tushnet and M. Khosla, 18–43. Cambridge: Cambridge University Press, 2015.

Cohn, Bernard S. 'Anthropological Notes on Disputes and Law in India'. *American Anthropologist* 67, no. 6 (1965): 82–122.

Collins, P. H. 'What's in a Name? Womanism, Black Feminism, and beyond'. *The Black Scholar* 26, no. 1 (1996): 9–17.

Condos, M. 'Licence to Kill: The Murderous Outrages Act and the Rule of Law in Colonial India 1867–1925'. *Modern Asian Studies* 50, no. 2 (2016): 479–517.

Corbridge, S., and J. Harriss. *Reinventing India: Liberalization, Hindu Nationalism and Popular Democracy*. New Delhi: Oxford University Press, 2000.

Cossman, B., and R. Kapur. 'Communalising Gender/Engendering Community: Women, Legal Discourse and Saffron Agenda'. *Economic and Political Weekly* 28, no. 17 (1993): WS35–WS44.

———. *Subversive Sites: Feminist Engagements with Law in India*. New Delhi: Sage Publications, 1996.

———. 'Secularism's Last Sigh: The Hindu Right, the Courts, and India's Struggle for Democracy'. *Harvard International Law Journal* 38, no. 1 (1997): 113.

Courtright, P. B., and N. Goswami. 'Sati, Law, Religion, and Postcolonial Feminism'. In *Religion and Personal Law in Secular India: A Call to Judgment*, edited by G. J. Larson, 220–25. Bloomington: Indiana University Press, 2001.

Cretney, S. M. *Family Law in the Twentieth Century: A History*. Oxford: Oxford University Press, 2003.

D'Souza, P. R. 'Politics of the Uniform Civil Code in India'. *Economic and Political Weekly* 50, no. 48 (2015): 50–7.

Das, V. *Critical Events: An Anthropological Perspective on Contemporary India*. New Delhi: Oxford University Press, 1995.

Dasgupta, J. 'India's Federal Design and Multicultural National Construction'. In *The Success of India's Democracy*, edited by A. Kohli, J. Breman, and G. P. Hawthorn, 49–77. Cambridge: Cambridge University Press, 2001.

Dave, A. 'Strategic Alliance, A Way Forward for Violence against Women: A Case for the Special Cells, India'. *Violence against Women* 19, no. 10 (2013): 1203–23.

De, R. 'Mumtaz Bibi's Broken Heart: The Many Lives of the Dissolution of Muslim Marriages Act'. *Indian Economic and Social History Review* 46, no. 1 (2009): 105–30.

———. 'The Two Husbands of Vera Tiscenko: Apostasy, Conversion, and Divorce in Late Colonial India'. *Law and History Review* 28, no. 4 (2010): 1011–41.

———. *A People's Constitution: The Everyday Life of Law in the Indian Republic*. Princeton, NJ: Princeton University Press, 2018.

Derrett, J. D. M. *Hindu Law, Past and Present: Being an Account of the Controversy Which Preceded the Enactment of the Hindu Code, the Text of the Code as Enacted, and Some Comments Thereon*. Calcutta: A. Mukherjee, 1957.

———. *Introduction to Modern Hindu Law*. New Delhi: Oxford University Press, 1963.

Devji, F. *Muslim Zion: Pakistan as a Political Idea*. London: Hurst & Co., 2013.

Dhagamwar, V. *Towards the Uniform Civil Code*. New Delhi: Indian Law Institute, 1989.

———. *Law, Power and Justice: Protection of Personal Rights under the Indian Penal Code*. New Delhi: Sage Publications, 1992.

Dhavan, R. 'The Ayodhya Judgment: Encoding Secularism in the Law'. *Economic and Political Weekly* 29, no. 48 (1994): 3034–40.

Dirks, N. B. 'From Little King to Landlord: Property, Law, and the Gift under the Madras Permanent Settlement', *Comparative Studies in Society and History* 28, no. 2 (1986): 307–33.

Dewey, J. 'Force and Coercion'. *The International Journal of Ethics* 26, no. 3 (1916): 359–67.

Dietrich, G. 'Women's Movement and Religion'. *Economic and Political Weekly* 4 (1986): 157–60.

Donald, N. 'Gazing from a Distance: Spatial Reading of a Law Commission Report'. *J. Indian L. and Soc'y* 6, no. 2 (2014): 91.

Doniger, W. *The Hindus: An Alternative History*. Oxford: Penguin Press, 2009.

Dube, S., and A. Rao. *Crime through Time*. New Delhi: Oxford University Press, 2013.

Dutt, V. P. 'The Emergency in India: Background and Rationale'. *Asian Survey* 16, no. 12 (1976): 1124–38.

Dutta, S. 'Divorce, Kinship, and Errant Wives: Islamic Feminism in India, and the Everyday Life of Divorce and Maintenance'. *Ethnicities* 21, no. 3 (2021): 454–76.

Eckert, J. 'From Subjects to Citizens: Legalism from below and the Homogenisation of the Legal Sphere'. *The Journal of Legal Pluralism and Unofficial Law* 38, nos 53–54 (2006): 45–75.

Edrisinha, R. 'Debating Federalism in Sri Lanka and Nepal'. In *Unstable Constitutionalism: Law and Politics in South Asia*, edited by M. Tushnet and M. Khosla, 291–319. Cambridge: Cambridge University Press, 2015.

Engineer, A. A. *The Shah Bano Controversy*. Bombay: Orient Longman, 1987.

———. 'Gujarat Riots in the Light of the History of Communal Violence'. *Economic and Political Weekly* 37, no. 50 (2002): 5047–54.

Faruqi, Z. H. *Dr. Zakir Hussain: Quest for Truth*. New Delhi: APH Publishing Corporation, 1999.

Fernandez, J. K. 'Cassandra at the Feast: Interrogating the Freedoms of Gay Liberation in India', at 'Shaping Law, Shaping Gender: Experiences from India', Workshop, Humboldt University, Berlin, 11–13 October 2018.

Forbes, G. 'The Indian Women's Movement: A Struggle for Women's Rights or National Liberation?'. In *The Extended Family: Women and Political Participation in India and Pakistan*, vols. 49–82, 49–82. New Delhi: Chanakya Publications, 1981.

———. 'The Politics of Respectability: Indian Women and the Indian National Congress'. In *The Indian National Congress: Centenary Hindsights*, edited by D. A. Low, 54–97. New Delhi: Oxford University Press, 1988.

Foucault, M. *The History of Sexuality*, vol. 1. New York: Random House, 1978.

Fraser, N. 'Equality, Difference, Public Representation'. In *Democracy and Difference: Contesting the Boundaries of the Political*, edited by S. Benhabib, 218–37. Princeton, NJ: Princeton University Press, 1996.

Fyzee, A. A. A. *Outlines of Muhammadan Law*. New Delhi: Oxford University Press, 1974.

Galanter, M. 'Secularism, East and West'. *Comparative Studies in Society and History* 7, no. 2 (1965): 133–59.

———. 'The Displacement of Traditional Law in Modern India'. *Journal of Social Issues* 24, no. 4 (1968): 65–90.

———. 'The Aborted Restoration of "Indigenous" Law in India'. *Comparative Studies in Society and History* 14, no. 1 (1972): 53–70.

Gandhi, N., and N. Shah. *The Issues at Stake: Theory and Practice in the Contemporary Women's Movement in India*. New Delhi: Kali for Women, 1992.

Gangoli, G. 'Anti-Bigamy Bill in Maharashtra: Wider Debate Needed'. *Economic and Political Weekly* 31, no. 29 (1996): 1919–21.

———. *Indian Feminisms: Law, Patriarchies and Violence in India*. Aldershot, Hampshire, England: Routledge, 2016.

Ganguly, S. 'The Crisis of Indian Secularism'. *Journal of Democracy* 14, no. 4 (2003): 11–25.

Ghosh, P. S. *BJP and the Evolution of Hindu Nationalism: From Periphery to Centre*. New Delhi: Manohar Publishers, 1999.

———. *The Politics of Personal Law in South Asia: Identity, Nationalism and the Uniform Civil Code*. New Delhi: Routledge, 2012.

Ghosh, S. *Muslim Politics in India*. Harvard: APH Publishing, 1987.

Gopalan, S. *Towards Equality: The Unfinished Agenda: Status of Women in India 2001*. New Delhi: National Commission for Women (India), 2001.

Gould, C. 'Diversity and Democracy: Representing Differences'. In *Democracy and Difference: Contesting the Boundaries of the Political*, vol. 31, edited by S. Benhabib, 171–86. Princeton, NJ: Princeton University Press, 1996.

Gould, W. *Hindu Nationalism and the Language of Politics in Late Colonial India*. Cambridge: Cambridge University Press, 2004.

Granville, A. *Working a Democratic Constitution: The Indian Experience*. New Delhi: Oxford University Press, 1999.

Graycar, R., and Jenny Morgan. 'Law Reform: What's in It for Women?'. *Windsor Yearbook on Access to Justice* 23, no. 2 (2005): 393–422.

Griffiths, J. 'What Is Legal Pluralism?'. *The Journal of Legal Pluralism and Unofficial Law* 18, no. 24 (1986): 1–55.

Grover, S. *Marriage, Love, Caste and Kinship Support: Lived Experiences of the Urban Poor in India*. London: Routledge, 2017.

Gupta, A. *Red Tape: Bureaucracy, Structural Violence, and Poverty in India*. Durham, NC: Duke University Press, 2012.

Gupta, D. 'Communalism and Fundamentalism: Some Notes on the Nature of Ethnic Politics in India'. *Economic and Political Weekly* 26, no. 11/12 (1991): 573–82.

Guru, G. 'Understanding Communal Riots in Maharashtra'. *Economic and Political Weekly* 28, no. 19 (1993): 903–07.

Guruswamy M., and A. Singh. 'Accessing Injustice: The Gram Nyayalayas Act, 2008'. *The Economic and Political Weekly* 45, no. 43 (2010): 16–19.

Gutmann, A., ed. *Multiculturalism: Examining the Politics of Recognition*. Princeton, NJ: Princeton University Press, 1994.

Habermas, J. 'Religious Tolerance—The Pacemaker for Cultural Rights'. *Philosophy* 79, no. 1 (2004): 5–18.

———. 'Religion in the Public Sphere'. *European Journal of Philosophy* 14, no. 1 (2006): 1–25.

Hansen, T. B. 'Globalisation and Nationalist Imaginations: Hindutva's Promise of Equality through Difference'. *Economic and Political Weekly* 31, no. 10 (1996): 603–16.

———. *The Saffron Wave: Democracy and Hindu Nationalism in Modern India*. Princeton, NJ: Princeton University Press, 1999.

———. *Wages of Violence: Naming and Identity in Postcolonial Bombay*. Princeton, NJ: Princeton University Press, 2001.

———. 'Sovereigns Beyond the State: On Legality and Authority in Urban India'. In *Sovereign Bodies: Citizens, Migrants, and States in the Postcolonial World*, edited by T. B. Hansen and Finn Stepputat, 169–91. Princeton, NJ: Princeton University Press, 2005.

———. 'The Political Theology of Violence in Contemporary India'. *South Asia Multidisciplinary Academic Journal* 2 (2008): 1–14.

Hansen, T. B., and F. Stepputat. *States of Imagination: Ethnographic Explorations of The Postcolonial State*. Durham, NC: Duke University Press, 2001.

———. 'Sovereignty Revisited'. *Annual Review of Anthropology* 35 (2006): 295–315.

Hansen, T. B., and T. Modood. 'Secularism, Popular Passion and Public Order in India'. In *Contesting Secularism: Comparative Perspectives*, edited by Anders Berg-Sørensen, 207–31. Farnham, Surrey: Ashgate, 2013.

Hardgrave, R. L. 'The DMK and the Politics of Tamil Nationalism'. *Pacific Affairs* 37, no. 4 (1964): 396–411.

Harding, S. G., ed. *Feminism and Methodology: Social Science Issues*. Bloomington: Indiana University Press, 1987.

Harriss-White, B. *India Working: Essays on Society and Economy*. Cambridge: Cambridge University Press, 2003.

Hasan, M. *Legacy of a Divided Nation: India's Muslims since Independence*. London: Hurst & Co., 1997.

———. *Islam in a Globalized World: Negotiating Fault Lines*. Gurgaon: imprintOne, 2010.

Hasan, Z. 'Minority Identity, Muslim Women Bill Campaign and the Political Process'. *Economic and Political Weekly* 24, no. 1 (1989): 44–50.

———. 'Communalism, State Policy, and the Question of Women's Rights in Contemporary India'. *Bulletin of Concerned Asian Scholars* 25, no. 4 (1993): 5–15.

———. *Forging Identities: Gender, Communities and the State in India*. Boulder: Westview, 1994.

———. 'Gender Politics, Legal Reform, and the Muslim Community'. In *Appropriating Gender: Women's Activism and Politicized Religion in South Asia*, edited by P. Jeffery and A. Basu, 71–88. New York: Routledge, 1998.

———. 'Gender, Religion and Democratic Politics in India'. *Third World Quarterly* 31, no. 6 (2010): 939–54.

Hasan, Z., E. Sridharan, and R. Sudarshan. *India's Living Constitution: Ideas, Practices, Controversies*. Delhi: Permanent Black, 2005.

Hasan, Z., and R. Menon. *Unequal Citizens*. New Delhi: Oxford University Press, 2006.

Hensmen, R. 'Globalisation: A Perspective for Labour'. *Economic and Political Weekly* 38, no. 43 (2003): 4583–85.

Herklotz, T. 'Law, Religion and Gender Equality: Literature on the Indian Personal Law System from a Women's Rights Perspective'. *Indian Law Review* 1, no. 3 (2017): 250–68.

Hinnells, J. R. 'Parsis in Post-Independence Bombay'. In *The Zoroastrian Diaspora: Religion and Migration*, edited by J. R. Hinnells, 33–137. Oxford: Oxford University Press, 2005.

Hodges, S. 'Revolutionary Family Life and the Self Respect Movement in Tamil South India 1926–49'. *Contributions to Indian Sociology* 39, no. 2 (2005): 251–77.

Holden, L. 'Official Policies for (Un)official Customs: The Hegemonic Treatment of Hindu Divorce Customs by Dominant Legal Discourses'. *The Journal of Legal Pluralism and Unofficial Law* 36, no. 49 (2004): 47–74.

———. *Hindu Divorce: A Legal Anthropology*. London: Ashgate, 2016.

Hussain, M. F. 'The Freedom Movement and the Muslims of Bihar: Delineations on Minority Identity and National Independence'. In *Islam in a Globalized World: Negotiating Fault Lines*, edited by Mushirul Hasan, 311–29. Gurgaon: imprintOne, 2010.

Hussin, I. R. *The Politics of Islamic Law: Local Elites, Colonial Authority and the Making of the Muslim State*. University of Washington, 2008.

Iqtidar, H. *Secularizing Islamists?* Chicago: University of Chicago Press, 2011.

Iyer, V. K. *Of Law and Life*. Columbia, Missouri: South Asia Books, 1979.

Jacobsohn, G. J. *The Wheel of Law: India's Secularism in Comparative Constitutional Context*. Princeton, NJ: Princeton University Press, 2004.

Jaffrelot, C. *The Hindu Nationalist Movement and Indian Politics: 1925 to the 1990s: Strategies of Identity-Building, Implantation and Mobilisation (With Special Reference to Central India)*. London: C. Hurst & Co., 1996.

———, ed. *Hindu Nationalism: A Reader*. Princeton, NJ: Princeton University Press, 2009.

Jaffrelot, C., and S. Kumar, eds. *Rise of the Plebeians?* New Delhi: Routledge, 2012.

Jaggar, A. M. *Feminist Politics and Human Nature*. Rowman and Allanheld: Harvester, 1983.

Jalal, A. 'The Convenience of Subservience: Women and the State of Pakistan'. In *Women, Islam and the State*, edited by Deniz Kandiyoti, 77–114. London: Palgrave Macmillan, 1991.

———. *The Sole Spokesman: Jinnah, the Muslim League and the Demand for Pakistan*, vol. 31. Cambridge: Cambridge University Press, 1994.

Jeffery, P. *Frogs in a Well: Indian Women in Purdah*. London: Zed Press, 1979.

Jeffery, P., and A. Basu. *Appropriating Gender: Women's Activism and Politicized Religion in South Asia*. New Delhi: Routledge, 1998.

Jeffrey, R. 'Jawaharlal Nehru and the Smoking Gun: Who Pulled the Trigger on Kerala's Communist Government in 1959?'. *Journal of Commonwealth and Comparative Politics* 29, no. 1 (1991): 72–85.

Jha, S. 'Secularism in the Constituent Assembly Debates, 1946–1950'. *Economic and Political Weekly* 37, no. 30 (2002): 3175–80.

John, M. E. *Discrepant Dislocations: Feminism, Theory, and Postcolonial Histories*. Berkeley: University of California Press, 1996.

———. 'Gender, Development, and the Women's Movement'. In *Signposts: Gender Issues in Post-Independence India*, edited by Rajeshwari Sunder Rajan, 101–23. New Delhi: Kali for Women, 2000.

Jones, J. '"Signs of Churning": Muslim Personal Law and Public Contestation in Twenty-first Century India'. *Modern Asian Studies* 44, no. 1 (2010): 175–200.

Kandiyoti, D. 'Bargaining with Patriarchy'. *Gender and Society* 2, no. 3 (1988): 274–90.

———, ed. *Women, Islam and the State*, vol. 105. Philadelphia: Temple University Press, 1991.

Kapila, S. 'Ambedkar's Agonism: Sovereign Violence and Pakistan as Peace'. *Comparative Studies of South Asia, Africa and the Middle East* 39, no. 1 (2019): 184–95.

Kapur, R., ed. *Feminist Terrains in Legal Domains: Interdisciplinary Essays on Women and Law in India*. New Delhi: Kali for Women, 1996.

———. 'Fundamentalist Face of Secularism and Its Impact on Women's Rights in India'. *Cleveland State Law Review* 47 (1999): 323.

———. *Gender, Alterity and Human Rights: Freedom in a Fishbowl*. Cheltenham, UK: Edward Elgar Publishing, 2018.

———. '"Belief" in Law and Hindu Majoritarianism: The Rise of the Hindu Nation'. In *Majoritarian State: How Hindu Nationalism is Changing India*, edited by A. P. Chatterji, T. B. Hansen, and C. Jaffrelot. London: Hurst & Co., 2020.

Kaur, R., and R. Palriwala, eds. *Marrying in South Asia: Shifting Concepts, Changing Practices in a Globalising World*. New Delhi: Orient Blackswan, 2014.

Kaviraj, S. 'Indira Gandhi and Indian Politics'. *Economic and Political Weekly* 21, no. 38/39 (1986): 1697–1708.

———. 'Crisis of the Nation-state in India.' *Political Studies* 42, no. s1 (1994): 115–29.

———. 'Languages of Secularity'. *Economic and Political Weekly* 48, no. 50 (2013): 93–102.

Keer, D. *Dr. Ambedkar: Life and Mission*. Bombay: Popular Prakashan, 1995.

Khaitan, T. *'Koushal v, Naz:* Judges Vote to Recriminalise Homosexuality'. *The Modern Law Review* 78, no. 4 (2015): 672–80.

Khilnani, S., V. Raghavan, and A. K. Thiruvengadam, eds. *Comparative Constitutionalism in South Asia*. New Delhi: Oxford University Press, 2013.

Khosla, M. *The Indian Constitution: Oxford India Short Introductions*. Oxford: Oxford University Press India, 2012.

———. *India's Founding Moment: The Constitution of a Most Surprising Democracy*. Cambridge, MA: Harvard University Press, 2020.

Kirmani, N. 'Claiming Their Space: Muslim Women-led Networks and the Women's Movement in India'. *Journal of International Women's Studies* 11, no. 1 (2009): 72.

———. 'Beyond the Impasse "Muslim Feminism(s)" and the Indian Women's Movement'. *Contributions to Indian Sociology* 45, no. 1 (2011): 1–26.

Kirpal, B. N., A. H. Desai, G. Subramanium, R. Dhavan, and R. Ramachandran. *Supreme but Not Infallible: Essays in Honour of the Supreme Court of India*. New Delhi: Oxford University Press, 2004.

Kishwar, M. 'Gandhi on Women'. *Economic and Political Weekly* 20, no. 40 (1985): 1691–702.

———. 'Codified Hindu Law: Myth and Reality'. *Economic and Political Weekly* 29, no. 33 (2004): 2145–61.

Kishwar, M., and V. Ruth. 'The Burning of Roop Kanwar'. *Manushi* 42, no. 42/43 (1987): 15–25.

Kohli, A., J. Breman, and G. P. Hawthorn, eds. *The Success of India's Democracy*, vol. 6. Cambridge: Cambridge University Press, 2001.

Kokal, K. *State Law, Dispute Processing and Legal Pluralism: Unspoken Dialogues from Rural India*. London: Routledge, 2019.

Kolsky, E. 'Codification and the Rule of Colonial Difference: Criminal Procedure in British India'. *Law and History Review* 23, no. 3 (2005): 631–83.

———. '"The Body Evidencing the Crime": Rape on Trial in Colonial India, 1860–1947'. *Gender and History* 22, no. 1 (2010): 109–30.

Kothari, R. 'The "Congress System" in India'. *Asian Survey* 4, no. 12 (1964): 1161–73.

Kowalski, J. 'Between Gender and Kinship: Mediating Rights and Relations in North Indian NGOs.' *American Anthropologist* 123, no. 2 (2021): 330–42.

Kniss, F., and G. Burns. 'Religious Movements'. In *The Blackwell Companion to Social Movements*, edited by David A. Snow and Sarah A. Soule, 694–715. Blackwell Publishing Ltd, 2004.

Krishnaswamy, S. *Democracy and Constitutionalism in India: A Study of the Basic Structure Doctrine*. New Delhi: Oxford University Press, 2009.

———. 'Constitutional Federalism in the Indian Supreme Court'. *Unstable Constitutionalism: Law and Politics in South Asia*, edited by M. Tushnet and M. Khosla, 355–80. Cambridge: Cambridge University Press, 2015.

Kugle, S.A. 'Framed, Blamed and Renamed: The Recasting of Islamic Jurisprudence in Colonial South Asia'. *Modern Asian Studies* 35, no. 2 (2001): 257–313.

Kumar, R. *The History of Doing: An Illustrated Account of Movements for Women's Rights and Feminism in India 1800–1990*. New Delhi: Zubaan, 1997.

Kumar, R., and A. Basu. *From Chipko to Sati: The Contemporary Indian Women's Movement*. Boulder, Colorado: Westview Press, 1995.

Laborde, C. 'Minimal Secularism: Lessons for, and from, India'. *American Political Science Review* 115, no. 1 (2020): 1–13.

Lazarus-Black, M., and Susan F. Hirsch, eds. *Contested States: Law, Hegemony and Resistance*. London: Routledge, 2012.

Lemons, K. *Divorcing Traditions: Islamic Marriage Law and the Making of Indian Secularism*. Ithaca: Cornell University Press, 2019.

Liddle, J., and R. Joshi. 'Gender and Imperialism in British India'. *Economic and Political Weekly* 5, no. 2 (1985): WS72–WS78.

Ludden, D. E. *Making India Hindu*. New Delhi: Oxford University Press, 1996.

Lyle, Mary F., and Jeffrey L. Levy. 'From Riches to Rags: Does Rehabilitative Alimony Need to be Rehabilitated?'. *Family Law* Quarterly 38, no. 1 (2005): 3–27.

Madan, T. N. 'Secularism in Its Place'. In *Secularism and Its Critics*, edited by Rajeev Bhargava. New Delhi: Oxford University Press, 1998.

Madhok, S. 'Action, Agency, Coercion: Reformatting Agency for Oppressive Contexts'. In *Gender, Agency, and Coercion*, edited by S. Madhok, A. Phillips, and K. Wilson, 102–21. Basingstoke: Palgrave Macmillan, 2013.

Mahmood, S. *The Politics of Piety: The Islamic Revival and the Feminist Subject*. Princeton: Princeton University Press, 2005.

———. 'Religious Reason and Secular Affect: An Incommensurable Divide?'. *Critical Inquiry* 35, no. 4 (2009): 836–62.

———. *Religious Difference in a Secular Age: A Minority Report*. Princeton, NJ: Princeton University Press, 2015.

Mahmood, T. *The Muslim Law of India*. Princeton: Law Book Co, 1980.

———. *Statutes of Personal Law in Islamic Countries: History, Texts and Analysis*. New Delhi: India and Islam Research Council, 1995.

Major, A. *Sovereignty and Social Reform in India: British Colonialism and the Campaign against Sati, 1830–1860*. New York: Routledge, 2010.

Majumdar, R. 'History of Women's Rights: A Non-Historicist Reading'. *Economic and Political Weekly* 38, no. 22 (2003): 2130–34.

Malečková, J. 'Gender, History and "Small Europe"'. *European History Quarterly* 40, no. 4 (2010): 685–700.

Mandal, S. 'Out of Shah Bano's Shadow: Muslim Women's Rights and the Supreme Court's Triple Talaq Verdict'. *Indian Law Review* 2, no. 1 (2018): 89–107.

Mani, L. *Contentious Traditions: The Debate on Sati in Colonial India*. Berkeley: University of California Press, 1998.

Manor, J. 'Center-State Relations'. In *The Success of India's Democracy*, edited by A. Kohli, J. Breman, and G. P. Hawthorn, 78–102. Cambridge: Cambridge University Press, 2001.

McGuire, J. 'The BJP and Governance in India: An Overview'. *South Asia: Journal of South Asian Studies* 25, no. 3 (2002): 1–15.

Mehta, P. B. 'The Rise of Judicial Sovereignty'. *Journal of Democracy* 18, no. 2 (2007): 70–83.

———. 'What Is Constitutional Morality?'. *Seminar* 615 (2010): 17–22.

———. 'The Indian Supreme Court and the Art of Democratic Positioning'. In *Unstable Constitutionalism: Law and Politics in South Asia*, edited by M. Tushnet and M. Khosla, 233–60. Cambridge: Cambridge University Press, 2015.

Mehta, V. *The Sanjay Story*. New Delhi: Harper Collins, 2013.

Menon, N. 'State/Gender/Community: Citizenship in Contemporary India'. *Economic and Political Weekly* 33, no. 5 (1998): PE3–PE10.

———. 'Sexuality, Caste, Governmentality: Contests over "Gender" in India'. *Feminist Review* 91, no. 1 (2009): 94–112.

———. 'Uniform Civil Code: The Women's Movement Perspective', *Kafila.org*, 1 October 2014. https://kafila.online/2014/10/01/uniform-civil-code-state-of-the-debate-in-2014/.

———. 'A Uniform Civil Code in India: The State of the Debate in 2014', *Feminist Studies* 40, no. 2 (2014): 480–6.

———. 'Is Feminism about "Women"? A Critical View on Intersectionality from India'. *Economic and Political Weekly* 50, no. 17 (2015): 37–44.

Menski, W. F. *Hindu Law: Beyond Tradition and Modernity*. New Delhi: Oxford University Press, 2003.

———. 'From Dharma to Law and Back? Postmodern Hindu Law in a Global World'. Working paper no. 20. Heidelberg papers in South Asian and Comparative Politics, 2004.

———. 'Asking for the Moon: Legal Uniformity in India from a Kerala Perspective'. *Kerala Law Times, Journal Section* 2 (2006): 52–78.

———. 'The Uniform Civil Code Debate in Indian Law: New Developments and Changing Agenda'. *German Law Journal* 9, no. 3 (2008): 211–50.

———. *Modern Indian Family Law*. Richmond: Curzon Press, 2001.

Mernissi, F. *Women and Islam*. Oxford: Basil Blackwell, 1991.

Merry, S. E. 'Transnational Human Rights and Local Activism: Mapping the Middle'. *American Anthropologist* 108, no. 1 (2006): 38–51.

Metcalf, B. D. 'Living Hadīth in the Tablīghī Jama'āt'. *The Journal of Asian Studies* 52, no. 3 (1993): 584–608.

Metcalf, T. R. *Ideologies of the Raj*. Cambridge: Cambridge University Press, 1994.

Michelutti, L. *The Vernacularisation of Democracy: Politics, Caste and Religion in India*. New Delhi: Routledge, 2008.

Minault, Gail. 'Sisterhood or Separatism: The All India Muslim Ladies' Conference and the Nationalist Movement'. In The *Extended Family: Women and Political Participation in India and Pakistan*, 83–108. New Delhi: Chanakya Publications, 1981.

Mir-Hosseini, Z. 'The Challenges of Islamic Feminism'. *Gender and Research* 20, no. 2 (2019): 108–22.

Mitra, S. K. 'Desecularising the State: Religion and Politics in India after Independence'. *Comparative Studies in Society and History* 33, no. 4 (1991): 755–77.

Mitra, Subrata K., and Alexander Fischer. 'Sacred Laws and the Secular State: An Analytical Narrative of the Controversy over Personal Laws in India'. *India Review* 1, no. 3 (2002): 99–130.

Moghadam, V. M. 'Islamic Feminism and Its Discontents: Toward a Resolution of the Debate'. *Signs: Journal of Women in Culture and Society* 27, no. 4 (2002): 1135–71.

Moghissi, H. 'Islamic Feminism Revisited'. *Comparative Studies of South Asia, Africa and the Middle East* 31, no. 1 (2011): 76–84.

Mookerjea-Leonard, D. 'Quarantined: Women and the Partition'. *Comparative Studies of South Asia, Africa and the Middle East* 24, no. 1 (2005): 33–46.

Mullally, S. 'Feminism and Multicultural Dilemmas in India: Revisiting the Shah Bano Case'. *Oxford Journal of Legal Studies* 24, no. 4 (2004): 671–92.

Nandy, A. 'The Politics of Secularism and the Recovery of Religious Tolerance'. *Alternatives* 13, no. 2 (1988): 177–94.

———. 'An Anti-Secularist Manifesto'. *India International Centre Quarterly* 22, no. 1 (1995): 35–64.

———. *Regimes of Narcissism, Regimes of Despair*. New Delhi: Oxford University Press, 2013.

———. 'Sati: A Nineteenth-Century Tale of Women, Violence and Protest.' In *Sati, the Blessing and the Curse: The Burning of Wives in India*, edited by J. S. Hawley, 131–48. Oxford: Oxford University Press, 1994.

Narain, V. *Reclaiming the Nation: Muslim Women and the Law in India*. Toronto: University of Toronto Press, 2008.

Newbigin, E. 'The Codification of Personal Law and Secular Citizenship Revisiting the History of Law Reform in Late Colonial India'. *Indian Economic and Social History Review* 46, no. 1 (2009): 83–104.

———. *The Hindu Family and the Emergence of Modern India: Law, Citizenship and Community*. Cambridge: Cambridge University Press, 2013.

Newbigin, E., L. Denault, and R. De. 'Personal Law, Identity Politics and Civil Society in Colonial South Asia'. *Indian Economic and Social History Review* 46, no. 1 (2009): 1–4.

Noorani, A. G. A. M., ed. *The Muslims of India: A Documentary Record*. New Delhi: Oxford University Press, 2003.

Nussbaum, M. C. 'Sex Equality, Liberty, and Privacy: A Comparative Approach to the Feminist Critique'. In *India's Living Constitution: Ideas, Practices, Controversies*, edited by Z. Hasan, E. Sridharan, and R. Sudarshan, 242–83. Delhi: Permanent Black, 2005.

———. *The Clash within: Democracy, Religious Violence, and India's Future.* Cambridge, MA: Harvard University Press, 2009.

Okin, S. M. *Is Multiculturalism Bad for Women?* Princeton, NJ: Princeton University Press, 1999.

Omvedt, G. *Reinventing Revolution: New Social Movements and the Socialist Tradition in India.* London: ME Sharpe, 1993.

Omvedt, G., C. Gala, and G. Kelkar. 'Unity and Struggle: A Report on Nari Mukti Sangharsh Sammelan'. *Economic and Political Weekly* 23, no. 18 (1988): 883–86.

Pandey, G. 'Can a Muslim Be an Indian?'. *Comparative Studies in Society and History* 41, no. 4 (1999): 608–29.

———. *A History of Prejudice: Race, Caste, and Difference in India and the United States.* Cambridge: Cambridge University Press, 2013.

Parashar, A. *Women and Family Law Reform in India: Uniform Civil Code and Gender Equality.* New Delhi: Sage Publications, 1992.

Parashar, A., and A. Dhanda. *Redefining Family Law in India: Essays in Honour of B. Sivaramayya.* New Delhi: Routledge, 2008.

Pathak, Z., and R. S. Rajan. 'Shah-Bano'. *Signs* 14, no. 3 (1989): 558–82.

Punwani, Jyoti. 'Muslim Women: Historic Demand for Change'. *Economic and Political Weekly* 51, no. 42 (2016): 12–15.

———. 'Triple Talaq Judgement and After'. *Economic and Political Weekly* 53, no. 17 (2018): 12–16.

Qadri, S. M. S. *Jihad-e-teen talaq.* Pune: Samkaleen Prakashan, 2014.

Raheja, G. G., and A. G. Gold. *Listen to the Heron's Words: Reimagining Gender and Kinship in North India.* Berkeley: University of California Press, 1994.

Rajagopal, A. *Politics after Television: Hindu Nationalism and the Reshaping of the Public in India.* Cambridge: Cambridge University Press, 2001.

Rajan, R. S. 'The Subject of Sati: Pain and Death in the Contemporary Discourse on Sati'. *The Yale Journal of Criticism* 3, no. 2 (1990): 1.

———. *The Scandal of the State: Women, Law, and Citizenship in Postcolonial India.* Durham, NC: Duke University Press, 2003.

Randeria, S. 'The State of Globalization: Legal Plurality, Overlapping Sovereignties and Ambiguous Alliances between Civil Society and the Cunning State in India'. *Theory, Culture and Society* 24, no. 1 (2007): 1–33.

Ranger, T. O., and E. J. Hobsbawm, eds. *The Invention of Tradition.* Cambridge: Cambridge University Press, 2012.

Rao, R. C. 'Mrs. Indira Gandhi and India's Constitutional Structures: An Era of Erosion'. *Journal of Asian and African Studies* 22, nos 3–4 (1987): 156–75.

Rashid, K. *Wakf Administration in India: A Socio-Legal Study*. New Delhi: Vikas, 1978.

Rawls, J. *Political Liberalism*. New York: Columbia University Press, 2005.

Redding, J. A. 'Secularism, the Rule of Law, and Sharia Courts: An Ethnographic Examination of a Constitutional Controversy'. *Louis ULJ* 57 (2012): 339.

———. *A Secular Need: Islamic Law and State Governance in Contemporary India*. Seattle: University of Washington Press, 2020.

Rege, S. 'Dalit Women Talk Differently: A Critique of Difference and Towards a Dalit Feminist Standpoint Position'. *Economic and Political Weekly* 33, no. 44 (1998): WS39–WS46.

———. *Writing Caste, Writing Gender: Reading Dalit Women's Testimonios*. New Delhi: Zubaan, 2006.

Robinson, F. *Separatism among Indian Muslims: The Politics of the United Provinces' Muslims, 1860–1923*. Cambridge: Cambridge University Press, 2007.

Rocher, R. 'The Creation of Anglo-Hindu Law'. In *Hinduism and Law: An Introduction*, edited by T. Lubin, D. R. Davis Jr, and J. K. Krishnan, 78–88. Cambridge: Cambridge University Press, 2010.

Roy, S. 'Angry Citizens: Civic Anger and the Politics of Curative Democracy in India'. *Identities* 23, no. 3 (2015): 362–77.

———. *Beyond Belief: India and the Politics of Nationalism*. London: Duke University Press, 2007.

Rudolph, S. H., and L. I. Rudolph. 'Living with Difference in India'. *The Political Quarterly* 71, no. s1 (2000): 20–38.

Saliba, T., C. Allen, and J. A. Howard, eds. *Gender, Politics, and Islam*. Hyderabad: Orient Blackswan, 2005.

Sangari, K. 'Politics of Diversity: Religious Communities and Multiple Patriarchies'. *Economic and Political Weekly* 30, no. 51 (1995): 3287–310.

Sangari, K., and S. Vaid. 'Sati in Modern India: A Report'. *Economic and Political Weekly* 16, no. 31 (1981): 1284–88.

———, eds. *Recasting Women: Essays in Indian Colonial History*. New Delhi: Kali for Women, 1989.

Sarkar, L. *National Specialised Agencies and Women's Equality: Law Commission of India*. New Delhi: Centre for Women's Development Studies, 1988.

Sarkar, S. 'Christian Conversions, Hindutva and Secularism'. In *The Crisis of Secularism in India*, edited by A. D. Needham and R. S. Rajan, 356–67. Ranikhet: Permanent Black, 2009.

Sarkar, T. 'The Woman as Communal Subject: Rashtrasevika Samiti and Ram Janmabhoomi Movement'. *Economic and Political Weekly* 26, no. 35 (1991): 2057–62.

———. 'Rhetoric Against Age of Consent: Resisting Colonial Reason and Death of a Child-Wife'. *Economic and Political Weekly* 28, no. 36 (1993a): 1869–78.

———. 'The Women of the Hindutva Brigade'. *Bulletin of Concerned Asian Scholars* 25, no. 4 (1993b): 16–24.

———. *Hindu Wife, Hindu Nation, Community, Religion, and Cultural Nationalism.* Bloomington: Indiana University Press, 2001.

Sathe, S. P. *Judicial Activism in India.* New Delhi: Oxford University Press, 2002.

Savarkar, V. D. *Hindutva: Who Is a Hindu?* New Delhi: Hindi Sahitya Sadan, 2003.

Saxena, S. 'Reinvention of Communal Identities and Implications for Democracy'. *Economic and Political Weekly* 48, no. 34 (2013): 47–53.

———. 'Commissions, Committees, and the Custodians of Muslim Personal Law in Post-Independence India'. *Comparative Studies of South Asia Africa and Middle East* 38, no. 3 (2018a): 423–38.

———. '"Court"ing Hindu Nationalism: Law and the Rise of Modern Hindutva'. *Contemporary South Asia* 26, no. 4 (2018b): 378–99.

———. '*Nikah Halala:* The Petition, the Promise, and the Politics of Personal Law'. In *Mutinies for Equality: Contemporary Developments in Law and Gender in India*, edited by Tanja Herklotz and Siddharth Peter De Souza, 133–54. Cambridge: Cambridge University Press, 2021.

Scott, J. W. 'Gender: A Useful Category of Historical Analysis'. *American Historical Review* 91, no. 5 (1986): 1053–75.

Seervai, H. M. *Constitutional Law of India: A Critical Commentary*, vol. 3. Bombay: NM Tripathi, 1996.

Sen, R. *Articles of Faith: Religion, Secularism, and the Indian Supreme Court.* Oxford: Oxford University Press, 2010.

———. 'Secularism and Religious Freedom'. In *Oxford Handbook of the Indian Constitution*, edited by Sujit Choudhry, Madhav Khosla, and Pratap Bhanu Mehta, 885–903. Oxford: Oxford University Press, 2016.

Sen, R., and S. Mandal. 'Indian Feminisms, Law Reform and the Law Commission of India: Special Issue on Honour of Lotika Sarkar'. *J. Indian L. and Soc'y* 6, no. 2 (2014): XI.

Sen, S., R. Biswas, and N. Dhawan, eds. *Intimate Others: Marriage and Sexualities in India.* Kolkata: Stree, 2011.

Sezgin, Y. *Human Rights under State-Enforced Religious Family Laws in Israel, Egypt and India.* Cambridge: Cambridge University Press, 2013.

Shachar, A. 'Puzzle of Interlocking Power Hierarchies: Sharing the Pieces of Jurisdictional Authority'. The. *Harv. CR-CLL Rev.* 35, no. 2 (2000): 385–426.

————. 'On Citizenship and Multicultural Vulnerability'. *Political Theory* 28, no. 1 (2000): 64–89.

Shah, A. B. *What Ails Our Muslims?* Bombay: Books LLC, 1980.

Sharafi, M. 'The Semi-Autonomous Judge in Colonial India Chivalric Imperialism Meets Anglo-Islamic Dower and Divorce Law'. *Indian Economic and Social History Review* 46, no. 1 (2009): 57–81.

————. *Law and Identity in Colonial South Asia: Parsi Legal Culture, 1772–1947*. Cambridge: Cambridge University Press, 2014.

Sheth, D. L. 'Changing Terms of Elite Discourse: The Case of Reservation for "Other Backward Classes"'. In *Region, Religion, Caste, Gender and Culture in Contemporary India*, 314–33. Oxford: Oxford University Press, 1996.

Sheth, D. L., and Harsh Sethi. 'The NGO Sector in India: Historical Context and Current Discourse'. *International Journal of Voluntary and Nonprofit Organizations* 2, no. 2 (1991): 49–68.

Siddiqui, N. A. *Hasrat Mohani aur Inqilab-i-Azadi*. Karachi: Oxford University Press, 2004.

Singha, R. *A Despotism of Law*. Oxford: Oxford University Press, 1998.

Sinha, C. *Debating Patriarchy: The Hindu Code Bill Controversy in India (1941–1956)*. New Delhi: Oxford University Press, 2012.

Sitapati, V. 'Doing a Rashomon on the Hindutva Cases'. *Economic and Political Weekly* 43, no. 10 (2008): 72–77.

Smith, D. E. *India as a Secular State*. Princeton, NJ: Princeton University Press, 1963.

Solanki, G. *Adjudication in Religious Family Laws: Cultural Accommodation, Legal Pluralism, and Gender Equality in India*. Cambridge: Cambridge University Press, 2011.

————. 'Beyond the Limitations of the Impasse: Feminism, Multiculturalism, and Legal Reforms in Religious Family Laws in India'. *Politikon* 40, no. 1 (2013): 83–111.

Som, R. 'Jawaharlal Nehru and the Hindu Code: A Victory of Symbol over Substance?'. *Modern Asian Studies* 28, no. 1 (1994): 165–94.

Sreenivas, M. 'Conjugality and Capital: Gender, Families, and Property under Colonial Law in India'. *The Journal of Asian Studies* 63, no. 4 (2004): 937–60.

Stark, Rodney, and William Sims Bainbridge. 'Of Churches, Sects, and Cults: Preliminary Concepts for a Theory of Religious Movements'. *Journal for the Scientific Study of Religion* 18, no. 2 (1979): 117–33.

Stephens, J. 'The Politics of Muslim Rage: Secular Law and Religious Sentiment in Late Colonial India.' *History Workshop Journal* 77, no. 1 (2014): 45–64.

————. *Governing Islam: Law, Empire, and Secularism in Modern South Asia*. Cambridge: Cambridge University Press, 2018.

Stoler, A. L. 'Colonial Archives and the Arts of Governance'. *Archival Science* 2, nos 1–2 (2002): 87–109.

Sturman, R. 'Marriage and Family in Colonial Hindu Law'. In *Hinduism and Law: An Introduction*, edited by T. Lubin, D. R. Davis Jr, and J. K. Krishnan, 89–104. Cambridge: Cambridge University Press, 2010.

Subramanian, A. *Shorelines: Space and Rights in South India*. Stanford, California: Stanford University Press, 2009.

Subramanian, N. 'Legal Change and Gender Inequality'. *Law and Social Inquiry* 33, no. 3 (2008): 631–72.

———. 'Making Family and Nation: Hindu Marriage Law in Early Postcolonial India'. *The Journal of Asian Studies* 69, no. 3 (2010): 771–98.

———. *Nation and Family: Personal Law, Cultural Pluralism, and Gendered Citizenship in India*. Stanford, California: Stanford University Press, 2014.

Suroor, H., ed. *Making Sense of Modi's India*. New Delhi: Harper Collins, 2016.

Swidler, A. 'Culture in Action: Symbols and Strategies'. *American Sociological Review* 51, no. 2 (1986): 273–86.

Tarlo, E. *Unsettling Memories: Narratives of the Emergency in Delhi*. Berkeley: University of California Press, 2003.

Taylor, C. *Multiculturalism*. Princeton, NJ: Princeton University Press, 1994.

Thapar, R. 'Imagined Religious Communities? Ancient History and the Modern Search for a Hindu Identity'. *Modern Asian Studies* 23, no. 2 (1989): 209–31.

Tillin, L. 'United in Diversity? Asymmetry in Indian Federalism'. *Publius: The Journal of Federalism* 37, no. 1 (2007): 45–67.

Tschalaer, M. H. *Muslim Women's Quest for Justice*. New Delhi: Cambridge University Press, 2017.

Tushnet, M., and M. Khosla, eds. *Unstable Constitutionalism: Law and Politics in South Asia*. Cambridge: Cambridge University Press, 2015.

Vaid, S., and K. Sangari. 'Institutions, Beliefs, Ideologies: Widow Immolation in Contemporary Rajasthan'. *Economic and Political Weekly* 26, no. 17 (1991): WS2–WS18.

van der Veer, Peter. 'Ayodhya and Somnath: Eternal Shrines, Contested Histories'. *Social Research* 59, no. 1 (1992): 85–109.

Vanaik, A. *Communalism Contested: Religion, Modernity and Secularization*. New Delhi: Vistaar Publications, 1997.

Varadarajan, S. *Gujarat, the Making of a Tragedy*. New Delhi: Penguin Books, 2002.

Varshney, A. 'Contested Meanings: India's National Identity, Hindu Nationalism, and the Politics of Anxiety'. *Daedalus* 122, no. 3 (1993): 227–61.

Vatuk, S., 2017. *Marriage and Its Discontents: Women, Islam and the Law in India*. Women Unlimited, an associate of Kali for Women, New Delhi, 2008.

———. 'Islamic Feminism in India: Indian Muslim Women Activists and the Reform of Muslim Personal Law'. *Modern Asian Studies* 42, no. 2/3 (2008): 489–518.

Viswanathan, G. 'Literacy and Conversion in the Discourse of Hindu Nationalism'. In *The Crisis of Secularism in India*, edited by A. D. Needham and R. S. Rajan, 333–55. Ranikhet: Permanent Black, 2009.

Washbrook, D. A. 'Law, State and Agrarian Society in Colonial India'. *Modern Asian Studies* 15, no. 3 (1981): 649–721.

Weber, M. 'The Three Types of Legitimate Rule'. *Berkeley Publications in Society and Institutions* 4, no. 1 (1958): 1–11

Weber, M., and Stephen Kalberg. *The Protestant Ethic and the Spirit of Capitalism; with Other Writings on the Rise of the West*, 4th edition. Oxford: Oxford University Press, 2009.

Wilkinson, S. I. 'Putting Gujarat in Perspective'. *Economic and Political Weekly* 37, no. 17 (2002): 1579–83.

———. *Votes and Violence: Electoral Competition and Ethnic Riots in India*. Cambridge: Cambridge University Press, 2006.

Williams, R. V. *Postcolonial Politics and Personal Laws: Colonial Legal Legacies and the Indian State*. Oxford: Oxford University Press, 2006.

———. 'Hindu Law as Personal Law: State and Identity in the Hindu Code Bill Debates, 1952–1956'. In *Hinduism and Law: An Introduction*, edited by T. Lubin, D. R. Davis Jr and J. K. Krishnan, 105–20. Cambridge: Cambridge University Press, 2010.

Wolin, S. 'Fugitive Democracy'. In *Democracy and Difference: Contesting the Boundaries of the Political*, edited by Seyla Benhabib, 31–45. Princeton, NJ: Princeton University Press, 1996.

Yadav, Y. 'Electoral Politics in the Time of Change: India's Third Electoral System, 1989-99'. *Economic and Political Weekly* 34, no. 34/35 (1999): 2393–9.

Yalman, N. 'On the Purity of Women in the Castes of Ceylon and Malabar.' *The Journal of the Royal Anthropological Institute of Great Britain and Ireland* 93, no. 1 (1963): 25–58.

Zaman, M. Q. *The Ulama in Contemporary Islam: Custodians of Change*. Princeton, NJ: Princeton University Press, 2010.

Lectures, Seminars, and Workshops

Hansen, T. B. 'The Sacrificial Self: Recasting Renunciation in South Asia'. The Kingsley Martin Memorial Lecture, University of Cambridge, Cambridge, 17 April 2014.

Kapila, K. 'Unpopular Justice: Law and the Inexpediency of Culture in North India'. Centre for South Asian Studies Seminar, University of Cambridge, Cambridge, 2 June 2014.

Ramnath, K. 'What Is a Legal Archive'. American Society for Legal History Conference Panel, Boston, 20 November 2019.

Roy, S. 'Being the Change: The Aam Aadmi Party and the Politics of Curative Democracy'. Centre of South Asian Studies Seminar, University of Cambridge, Cambridge, 26 November 2014.

Saxena, S. 'Sati, Sacrifice and Sacred Space, Deorala 1987'. Workshop with Thomas Blom Hansen, University of Cambridge, Cambridge, 27 May 2014.

Unpublished PhD Thesis

A.E. Varghese, 'Personal Laws in India: The Activisms of Muslim Women's Organizations'. Doctoral dissertation, Trinity College, 2015.

De, R. 'The Republic of Writs: Litigious Citizens, Constitutional Law and Everyday Life in India (1947–1964)'. Doctoral dissertation, Princeton University, 2013.

Dutta, S. Bounds of Righteous Agency: The Gendered Subject of Minority Rights in Contemporary India'. Doctoral dissertation, University of Cambridge, 2020.

Newbigin, E. 'The Hindu Code Bill and the Making of the Modern Indian State'. Doctoral dissertation, University of Cambridge, 2008.

Films and Documentaries

Chopra, Baldev Raj, dir. *Nikaah*. Bombay: United Producers Production, 1982.

DAKSH. *Justice Access and the Nations Approaches (JANA)*. Video series, 21 January 2019, available at https://www.youtube.com/playlist?list= PLPsk7i7tKdZlZ1jFMKh_7TEvJFnuTLZ7l, accessed on 22 January 2019.

Dutt Guru, dir. *Mr. and Mrs. 55*. Bombay: Mehbub Studio, 1955.

In Secular India. Documentary on Muslim Women Rights on Divorce. New Delhi: Riverbank Studios, 1988.

Web Sources

www.aimplboard.in/index.php
www.aljazeera.com
www.bjp.org
www.hansard-archive.parliament.uk
www.huffingtonpost.com
www.kafila.org
www.lawcommissionofindia.nic.in
www.livelaw.com
www.loksabhalive.in

www.manushi-india.org
www.mha.nic.in
www.mhrd.gov.in
www.mushawarat.com
www.ndtv.com
www.newindianexpress.com
www.parliamentofindia.nic.in/ls/debates/debates.htm
www.rss.org
www.scroll.in
www.thevice.com
www.wluml.org

Index